ND
849
.C3
C55
2008

Constructing Vernacular Culture in the Trans-Caribbean

Caribbean Studies

Series Editors
Shona Jackson, Texas A&M University and Anton Allahar, University of Western Ontario

Editorial Board
Edna Acosta-Belen, SUNY–Albany; Holger Henke, Metropolitan College of New York; Brian Meeks, University of the West Indies; Velma Pollard, University of the West Indies; John Rickford, Stanford University; Sylvia Wynter, Stanford University

Lexington Books' Caribbean Studies Series is committed to publishing scholarship that either rethinks or imagines anew all aspects of Caribbean history, culture, politics, literature, and social organization. The Series will be interested in publishing studies and monographs that deal either with the Caribbean as a discrete geographical region or that treat the Caribbean and its diaspora collectively. Ever since it was brought into the European orbit, the Caribbean has been defined by overlapping cultures of difference and similarity that are always in contest and conversation. This idea of creolization and syncretism defines the Caribbean and its people, and cannot be ignored in any attempt to understand the region and its diasporas. The Series' editors recognize the great insular and regional diversity that characterize the Caribbean and its diasporas and are most keen to highlight the multiplicity of theoretical and intellectual approaches needed to capture this most complex region, both historically and in contemporary times. To this extent they welcome manuscripts written from structuralist, poststructuralist, modernist, postmodernist and even micro-interactionist perspectives. In all of this one thing must remain clear: the Caribbean cannot be subsumed beneath the banner of any one school or perspective. Nor can it be studied (a) independently of each state's own cultural and political situation and contemporary relationship to international capital, or (b) without taking into account the interrelationships among other Caribbean states. In other words, the Series seeks to promote a cross-disciplinary appreciation of the Caribbean that is just as intellectually robust as the Caribbean itself.

Titles in the series

"Colón Man a Come": Mythographies of Panamá Canal Migration
    by Rhonda D. Frederick
Negotiating Caribbean Freedom: Peasants and the State in Development
    by Michaeline A. Crichlow
Ethnicity, Class, and Nationalism: Caribbean and Extra-Caribbean Dimensions
    edited by Anton L. Allahar
Race, Culture, and Identity: Francophone West African and Caribbean Literature and Theory from Négritude to Créolité
    by Shireen K. Lewis
Labour and the Multiracial Project in the Caribbean: Its History and Its Promise
    by Sara Abraham
Alienation and Repatriation: Translating Identity in Caribbean Literature
    by Patricia Joan Saunders
Constructing Vernacular Culture in the Trans-Caribbean
    edited by Holger Henke and Karl-Heinz Magister

Constructing Vernacular Culture in the Trans-Caribbean

Edited by
Holger Henke and
Karl-Heinz Magister

LEXINGTON BOOKS

A division of
ROWMAN & LITTLEFIELD PUBLISHERS, INC.
Lanham • Boulder • New York • Toronto • Plymouth, UK

LEXINGTON BOOKS

A division of Rowman & Littlefield Publishers, Inc.
A wholly owned subsidiary of The Rowman & Littlefield Publishing Group, Inc.
4501 Forbes Boulevard, Suite 200
Lanham, MD 20706

Estover Road
Plymouth PL6 7PY
United Kingdom

Copyright © 2008 by Lexington Books

All rights reserved. No part of this publication may be reproduced, stored in a retrieval system, or transmitted in any form or by any means, electronic, mechanical, photocopying, recording, or otherwise, without the prior permission of the publisher.

British Library Cataloguing in Publication Information Available

Library of Congress Cataloging-in-Publication Data

Constructing vernacular culture in the trans-Caribbean / edited by Holger Henke and Karl-Heinz Magister.
    p. cm. — (Caribbean studies)
  ISBN-13: 978-0-7391-2160-3 (cloth : alk. paper)
  ISBN-10: 0-7391-2160-X (cloth : alk. paper)
  ISBN-13: 978-0-7391-2161-0 (pbk. : alk. paper)
  ISBN-10: 0-7391-2161-8 (pbk. : alk. paper)
  1. Caribbean literature—20th century—History and criticism. 2. Caribbean area—Social life and customs. I. Henke, Holger. II. Magister, Karl-Heinz.
  PN849.C3C55 2008
  306.09729—dc22
                                                2007032713

Printed in the United States of America

♾™ The paper used in this publication meets the minimum requirements of American National Standard for Information Sciences—Permanence of Paper for Printed Library Materials, ANSI/NISO Z39.48–1992.

Contents

Foreword   ix
Anton Allahar

Acknowledgments   xiii

Introduction: Constructing Vernacular Culture in the Trans-Caribbean   xv
Holger Henke and Karl-Heinz Magister

PART I   (RE-)CREATING HOMES IN THE VERNACULAR

1. Premigration Legacies and Transnational Identities: Afro-Surinamese and Indo-Surinamese in the Netherlands   3
   Mies van Niekerk

2. The Many Voices of Caribbean Culture in New York City   23
   Bettina E. Schmidt

3. Family Reunion Rituals of African-Caribbean Transnational Families: Instilling a Historical and Diasporic Consciousness   43
   Constance R. Sutton

PART II   PERFORMING IDENTITIES

4. Dancing around Dancehall: Popular Music and Pentecostal Identity in Transnational Jamaica and Haiti   63
   Melvin L. Butler

5. Rituals, Journeys, and Modernity: Caribbean Spiritual Baptists in New York   101
   Maarit Forde

6 Performing "Difference": Gossip in Olive Senior's
   Short Stories
   Carol Bailey 123

7 "This Is My Vibes": Legitimizing Vernacular Expressions
   in Caribana
   Lyndon Phillip 139

PART III WRITING SELF, OTHER, AND (TRANS-)NATION IN THE TRANS-CARIBBEAN

8 Patrick Chamoiseau's Seascapes and the Trans-Caribbean
   Imaginary
   Wendy Knepper 155

9 "A Local Habitation and a Name": Travelers, Migrants,
   Nomads of "Caribbean New York" in Colin Channer's
   Waiting in Vain
   Karl-Heinz Magister 177

10 Playing Both Home and Away: National and
   Transnational Identities in the Work of Bruce St. John
   Elaine Savory 219

11 The Amerindian Transnational Experience in Pauline
   Melville's *The Ventriloquist's Tale*
   Tanya Shields 267

12 Readings from Aquí y Allá: Music, Commercialism,
   and the Latino-Caribbean Transnational Imaginary
   Raphael Dalleo 299

PART IV THE (TRANS-)NATION (DIS-)EMBODIED

13 Like Sugar in Coffee: Third Wave Feminism and the
   Caribbean
   Patricia Mohammed 321

14 Work That Body: Sexual Citizenship and Embodied
   Freedom
   Mimi Sheller 345

15 Caribbean Cyberculture: Towards an Understanding of Gender, Sexuality, and Identity within the Digital Culture Matrix
     Curwen Best 377

Index 399

Contributors 403

Foreword

Anton Allahar

In a global world where almost everything impacts almost every other thing, it is not easy to identify or pin down that which is original or unique. The notions of *vernacular languages* and *vernacular cultures* are cases in point. With respect to "vernacular language," for example, how far does one go back to find the original, the indigenous or the native use of it that is untouched by outside forces? Add to this the related notion of "vernacular culture" and the proposition becomes even more daunting. For to the extent that language and culture are living things produced by living beings, they are not static. In a dialectical sense both language and culture are changed by their creators just as they in turn serve to change the latter. The search, then, for authenticity in language, culture, ethnicity and even identity, is one that must of necessity take change as constant; but what is more is the concern with power, for no consideration of culture can ignore its power dimension.

This is the task that the contributing editors and authors of *Constructing Vernacular Culture in the Trans-Caribbean* have assumed in the following pages. The editors, Holger Henke and Karl-Heinz Magister, have managed to get their authors to problematize the compound issue of "the power of culture" and "the culture of power" and have produced an intellectually engaging analysis of the Caribbean diasporas in such places as New York, London and Toronto. Reflecting the complex nature of their subject, it is a study that is equally comfortable in the languages and methodologies of the humanities, social sciences and post-modernism. To this extent a major strength is its scope and its audience is broader than a single discipline.

When considerations of identity, authenticity, and belonging are factored into a discussion of a complex entity such as "the Caribbean," the task of analysis becomes that much more difficult. For the Caribbean is many things to many people: a geographic space, a language space (e.g., Dutch-, English-, Spanish-, French-speaking Caribbean), a diasporic space (e.g., Africa and India), or a creole space that transcends geography, language, or original ancestry to produce a common Caribbean *Zeitgeist* that is more than the sum of its parts. But that is not the end, for when we add the prefix *trans* to "Caribbean," we invite a whole host of other social, political and intellectual entanglements that speak to diasporas within diasporas.

In other words, what makes the so-called Caribbean diaspora in New York, London and Toronto a Caribbean diaspora and not a group or set of Caribbean diasporas? And why are these not more properly viewed as African and Indian diasporas twice removed? If the notion of creolization in the Caribbean is sufficient to remove the "African" and "Indian" yearnings for "home," we still need to explain the continuing politics of ethnic identity, race and tribe in the English speaking Caribbean today (Afrocentrism and Hindutva). And herein lies the above-mentioned concern with the political dimension of "culture." In the Trans-Caribbean space of New York, for example, we know that Queens is home to Indians from Guyana and Trinidad, maybe even Suriname, while Brooklyn is home to peoples of African-Caribbean descent from different parts of the region. Paraphrasing M.G. Smith, they may meet and mix, but do they combine?

In the diaspora the vernacular culture can be seen as transported from the Caribbean, or it can be seen to be created in the specific context of the host country. If we were to examine the Toronto Caribana celebration, for example, it is immediately apparent that we are not dealing with a Trinidadian festival or spectacle. For cultures are not easily transplanted in-tact, and as we know, transplanted things do not grow quite as well as they do in their native soil. Caribana is a Toronto festival, complete with the rules, laws, police surveillance and public decorum associated with the city of Toronto. There is a regimentation of the parade and the masqueraders that reviles Trinidadians, who baulk at the claim that it is a "Trini ting." And the same may be said for the Nottinghill Carnival. So Caribana may well be an example of a vernacular Toronto culture that is authentic, original and native to the new generations of a Caribbean-descended population, although there are many who participate and have no Caribbean roots, or who may have one parent with Caribbean beginnings.

What this suggests, then, and what is most noteworthy, is the appearance of second and third generations of Caribbean-parented children in Toronto, New York, London and other major diasporic spaces. These subsequent generations are understandably less "Caribbean" than their Caribbean-born parents in matters of popular culture appreciation (food, music, dress, religion), and very importantly, less "Caribbean" in matters of memory and history. So Trinidad's calypso and Jamaica's reggae give way to a new globalized Caribbean musical culture of soca, dub and ragga, and soon become mixed in with New York rap and hip hop to produce a hybridized Caribbean cultural echo, but one that is fast losing its Caribbeanness. But to the extent that we are living in a globalized world where the diaspora feeds the homeland culturally, financially and so on, popular culture, and particularly youth popular culture in today's Caribbean, is very globalized (and Americanized) as are other aspects of culture: family type (nuclear), political preferences (liberal democracy), economic behavior (consumerism and materialism), and a declining emphasis on personal discipline and self-sacrifice that eventuates in the well-publicized drug culture and the associated problems of crime and violence, high teen pregnancies, increasing school drop out rates, and a general mirroring of the life of inner-city youth in large metropolitan settings.

These are the issues that confront the Trans-Caribbean diasporas as they "invent traditions" and celebrate kin ties in places like "Caribbean New York," as the older generation tries to get the younger ones to "imagine community" and to remember their fictive kin, and as their own memories of "home" fade into the fabrics of their new metropolitan existences. Of course this all begs the idea of "long-distance nationalism" for the Caribbean is not a nation; it is at best a region. And while those first generation migrants in the diaspora age and begin a nostalgic longing for "home," their second generation children and third generation grand-children have very different attitudes and orientations, and have no "memory" of their parents' or grand-parents' "home."

The comfort is in knowing that globalization has made the world smaller, and whether physically or virtually, it is now possible to be in cheap and instant contact with "home." The Trans-Caribbean vernacular language and culture are now to be found both in the Caribbean and in the Caribbean diasporas abroad, and they are seriously infused with sensibilities that were once entirely out of place anywhere in the Caribbean. Thus, political correctness has arrived, and whereas Caribbean people (men and women) used unconsciously to celebrate a macho, patriarchal, homophobic and sexist manner-of-being, today the macho men and women are on the run. For the Trans-Caribbean vernacular culture is also intimately involved in a Trans-Caribbean economics at the level of multinational corporations and a Trans-Caribbean politics in such world bodies as the United Nations where (Trans-) Caribbean peoples daily represent themselves and are represented.

Acknowledgments

The editors would like to acknowledge their immense gratitude to Professor Alissa Trotz (University of Toronto) for her invaluable help with this book, as well as her critical and constructive suggestions regarding a number of conceptual aspects, which occurred at the beginning and in the process of editing this volume. Dr. Trotz took it upon herself to dedicate considerable time when, at the same time, she was also charged with a teaching appointment in two departments at her university, as well as being appointed as the Director of her university's Caribbean Studies Program. In addition to numerous other obligations, her dedication to provide us with detail-oriented comments and a critical focus enhanced the contents—in particular the transnational, gender, and indigenous population aspects—of this book significantly. There is no doubt in our mind that without her scholarly contribution the book would have been less than what it is now.

Introduction

Holger Henke and Karl-Heinz Magister

Constructing Vernacular Culture in the Trans-Caribbean

Transnationalization, one of the main topics of this volume, is a global phenomenon; the increasing mobility of people and high tech communication have facilitated an intensified border crossing and traveling beyond national and cultural boundaries. Globalization and global migration have constructed a specific transnationalism in the Caribbean and its Diasporas. Indeed, one wonders if the "residues of an absentee mentality [that] still linger" in Caribbean societies, as Comitas and Lowenthal observed in the early 1970s, have eventually become the springboard for the overseas communities which Caribbean migrants established in North America and Europe during the twentieth century.[1] This book features a variety of trans-Caribbean concepts that—as a result of the Caribbean peoples' national emancipation in the early sixties—appear as a new type of emergent nationalism. The Caribbean "transnational nationalism" constructs new expressions of familial, communal, and national belonging, and—similar to the trends towards de-materialization in the productive sphere—a de-territorialized understanding of nation. Caribbean transnationalism has varied widely by the diverse flows of Caribbean migrants to North America and to Europe, and by their African and Indian descent, and, last but not least, by Amerindian nativity.

What is this thing, however, that we call the "vernacular"? Originally, the term derives from a distinction being made between the native language of a territory and *linguae francae* or official languages. In a wider sense, such as we attempt to employ in this book, the vernacular refers to cultural expressions that are rooted within the sphere of the indigenous and popular, rather than the sphere of officially anointed "high" culture. Thus, it refers to everyday habits of the mind, secular and spiritual rituals, the production and reproduction of markers of class and ethnicity within a given cultural context, and the sphere from which mass culture often draws its inspiration or refers to in and through its representations. While, in the sense that Dick Hebdige or Michel de Certeau discuss it, vernacular culture may often be critical or counter-hegemonic, it may equally participate in established power relationships without necessarily being critical of them.[2] As Garcia Canclini reminds us, however, one has to keep in mind that Caribbean cultures are hybrid products of a long historical encounter with colonialism and its various transnational implications, and that we have to widen this dichotomy to include "ambiguous processes of interpenetration and mixing in which the symbolic movements of different classes engender other processes that cannot be ordered under the classifications of hegemonic and subaltern, modern and traditional."[3]

This is particularly true when we consider the contemporary acceleration of transnationalism, which has led us to actually speak of a *trans*-Caribbean space. Thus, while many peoples of Caribbean background may reside in diasporic communities in Miami, Flatbush, or Crown Heights (New York), Islington (London), or Toronto, their physical and intellectual movements and negotiations of everyday encounters with other cultures, are increasingly leading to vernacular cultural expressions that can no longer simply be regarded as a Caribbean *Diaspora* (thus, connoting relative cultural conservation and tradition), but must rightfully be seen as the formation of new hybrids that are equally uneasy when relating to their point of (Caribbean) origin, as they are when relating to their new "home" spaces. Thus, trans-Caribbean spaces and the vernacular cultural expressions emanating from them are increasingly becoming translocal, which by no means implies that they are rootless. Rather, we would argue that an expression like "T-Dot" (Toronto) and the sense of location and relation it attempts to transmit, are—to invoke Deleuze and Guattari, as well as Edouard Glissant—rhizomatic signifiers attempting to carve meaning into vernacular transnational space. Such translocal Caribbean populations may be mired between—as Fouron and Glick-Schiller have argued—various forms of long-distance nationalism and transborder citizenship, on the one hand, and the kind of nomadism described by Deleuze and Guattari and—using Colin Channer's novel *Waiting in Vain*—elaborated in this volume by Karl-Heinz Magister, on the other.[4]

To capture some important dimensions of this new, transnational, rhizomatic, vernacular Caribbean culture, we have ordered the chapters of this book in four distinct groupings: 1) (Re-)Creating Homes in the Vernacular, 2) Performing Identities, 3) Writing Self, Other and (Trans-)Nation in the Trans-Caribbean, and 4) The (Trans-)Nation (Dis-)Embodied.

Transnational Caribbeans, in Pauline Melville's *The Ventriloquist's Tale*, are defined as "transnationals before transnationalism"—the Amerindian citizenship in Guyana mixed with European and "Coastlander" cultures and characterized as divided into five areas: local, national, regional, diasporic, and transnational. The migratory groups of the Amerindians in Guyana, who are free to move between South-American ex-colonies and easily cross the borders of Venezuela, Guyana, and Brazil, are those of deterritorialized citizens that reflect the lasting transnational rites of indigenous border communities. As Tanya

Shields elaborates in her chapter, Amerindian practices of nation-building, of creating a Caribbean national identity and of transnationalism undermine colonial concepts of nation based on the sovereignty of the state and advocate a rather pre-colonial Amerindian (Wapisiana) nation and the right of nationhood across hegemonic European-drawn borders and Western administrations. Melville's notion of Amerindian transnationalism embraces Wapisiana and Guyanese citizenships.

Ever since the fundamental research about transnational family networks by Basch, Glick Schiller and Blanc-Szanton we know about the important role of the family as a basic group identity and how much the family facilitates the survival and the mobility of the transmigrants and their socialization into their new transnational way of life.[5] As Constance Sutton argues, "family reunions of Caribbean transnational families" and the re-creation of kin ties more and more develop significant practices as rituals and publicly enacted performances centering on the family. The celebration of family reunions across national and continental boundaries and throughout the Caribbean diaspora are part and parcel of the new concept of "knowing your family."

The transnational negotiation of different cultures and ethnic identities, especially in the North American and European metropolises, may feature as the trans-Caribbean counter-practice to the family reunions. "Caribbean New York" is the result of a transcultural process of West Indian, Latin American, Afro-American, etc. migrations. The "many voices of Caribbean culture in New York City" are negotiated by different cultural processes like mestizaje, creolization, or hybridization (bearing on García Canclini), and—as argued by Bettina Schmidt—by the concept of "polyphonic bricolage," which takes account of the heterogeneity of migrating nations and cultures, and of the diversity of trans-Caribbean models in different metropolitan places, say, of "Caribbean New York," "Caribbean London," "Caribbean Berlin," or "Caribbean Toronto." During carnival the West Indian American Day Parade in Brooklyn serves as a central location for the performance of "Caribbeanness."

The differences of trans-Caribbean urban models on both sides of the Atlantic shed a light on the extent to which transnationalism accelerates the adaptation of Creole cultures to host societies. Thus, as argued by Mies van Niekerk, the migration of the Surinamese population to the Netherlands shows how premigration cultural legacies (of slavery and indentured labor) affect socioeconomic mobility and the assimilation process, how the Surinamese as a typical Creole culture has been spawned by the intermingling of Western and African traditions. Today, in Surinamese Dutch transnationalism, "race" and color are much less pervasive social dividing lines than religion; Afro-Surinamese transnationalism created an ethnic infrastructure that served the preservation of popular religious-cultural traditions.

Caribbean transnationalism is the result of global migration and frequent traveling as well as the impact of the digital revolution on popular culture, religion, vernacular performances, and the feminist movement. In his chapter, Magister argues that the traveler as a nomad, today, is a subject of global ubiquity and velocity. In Colin Channer's novel *Waiting in Vain* (1998) Jamaican travelers' fantasies of migration are proliferating in real time dimensions. Channer's transnational traveling activities are male-centered; they are constantly transgressing national, geographical, cultural, temporal, moral, sexual boundaries, or spanning Caribbeanness and cosmopolitanism. The turn of the twentieth century registers a radical reconceptualization and division of migratory subjects into travelers and economic migrants, tourists and exiled, refugees and explorers, pilgrims and nomads. The postcolonial global traveler is frequently living in "in-between" spaces or in a state of nomadology (after theories by Deleuze and Guattari), or in global spaces of transnational cultures. In cities like New York, Toronto or London, the urban subject's traveling is transformed into walking. Walking in the city becomes—as Michel de Certeau specified—a "practice of everyday life." The pedestrian practice generates a "peripatetic mode of signification," an enunciative function to signify traveling and walking spaces.

Popular culture and religion are the main-stays of Caribbean transnationalism. Melvin Butler argues that the contribution of Pentecostalism in Jamaica and Haiti demonstrates the interdependence of religious and ethno-musicological fieldwork: popular musical styles like reggae, ska, dancehall and hip hop converge with religious traditions like African-inspired, non-Christian belief systems such as Voudou, Myal, and Obeah, and an indigenized Euro-Christianity (Methodism, Baptism). Today's Caribbean Pentecostalism was released by a Pentecostal movement in the nineteenth century and the impact of the Evangelical revival in Britain and the United States on the region. Transnational theology went together with the local congregational musical practices of a long colonial and postcolonial African Caribbean history. The hybridization of popular styles like hip hop, ska and konpa and Jamaican gospel music, which meant a conflation between worldliness and holiness, has unleashed a heavy controversy among Pentecostal congregations and ministers.

West Indian religious transnationalism is of course deeply rooted in African heritage and colonial history, drawing on mythological African and European Christian traditions. From the point of view of North American metropolitan fieldwork, the postcolonial religious group of the Spiritual Baptists in New York City spans colonial cosmology and African ritualism with transnational modernity. Ritual pilgrimages—as Maarit Forde attempts to demonstrate—are crossing national and continental borders and linking the Caribbean to the United States, to Canada and to the United Kingdom, and to various regions of Asia and Africa. Journeys seem to be part and parcel of Spiritual Baptist religion. Spiritual families in Tobagonian church are exemplified as typical transnationals. Traveling in the Spirit from its spiritual West Indian basis to the metropolitan diasporas equals spiritual journeys to modernity: here, religion is signified as emblematic of Caribbean modernity.[6] Their existence resembles in a way some sort of *marronage* that Simon Gikandi—besides *creolization*—conceived of "as a gesture of discursive Caribbean modernism."[7]

As Lyndon Phillip shows in his chapter, global hip-hop practices in Toronto beget a peculiar enunciation of the Trinidadian transnation within the Canadian

INTRODUCTION

carnival of "Caribana." This Canadian version is alleged to be a hegemonic multicultural Canadian policy, which hip hop styles are expected to disrupt and displace, in order to restore an original creolized black Afro-Trinidadian discourse. The vernacular (popular) version of hip hop serves as a cultural site that deals with the ruptures of blackness within postcolonial carnival practices. (Multiculturalism, here, seems be the inadequate matrix for a vernacular enunciation of the Caribbean transnation).

Caribbean transnationalism is also defined as the shifting space/territory between the United States and the island, or between north and south—in the case of Puerto Rican culture: as this "in-between and in-motion positioning" of the "Latino-Caribbean Transnational Imaginary." By setting two texts: that of the popular song *Plástico* by the Nuyorican bandleader San Juan and that of the novel *La guaracha*, written by Aquí y Allá in New York, in a dialogue against each other, Raphael Dalleo traces the cultural exchange between Puerto Rico and its United States diaspora and interrogates the transnational notion of cultural identity. Popular music is posited against fiction as an imaginary form through which the contemporary transnation can be imagined; it is contrasted—by some critics—with the novel as experimental and too pretentious, whereas popular music features as an art form created for the "pueblo." Music, through its wide dissemination by popular media, is presented as more effective in producing transnational and "translinguistic" communities. This far-reaching conclusion sheds a light on the present book's main topics: literary themes are in the minority compared to the larger section of popular medial ones. Here we may conclude a greater preference for popular oral and musical forms instead of for written literature, which may reverse the marginalization of popular cultures. In this sense Carolyn Cooper marks a distinctive turn from the "western literary form, the novel" to "vernacular literacy" and "Jamaican popular culture" as "transgressive" and "oppositional" to literary high culture values.[8] This essay draws its interest in Latino-Caribbean fiction from the novel's poetically inscribed approach to dance, speech and music, which resembles the popular style of the song *Plástico*; the novel is expected to function as a basis for the study of Latino popular culture, for example, to celebrate salsa as the culture of transnational Puerto Rican working classes.

Caribbean popular *vernacular*/indigenous culture always lived by its tension between the local, the regional and the transnational, between the oral and the scribal. The Barbadian poet Bruce St John, through his cosmopolitan education in Barbados, in Canada and the United Kingdom, was extremely concerned about these issues. As Elaine Savory demonstrates, St John considered Bajan language as an English Patois, going back to Africa, using the drum to make up a coded sound of resistance on the West Indian plantation. Drawing on Curwen Best, who relates St John's rhythms to the indigenous music of the Barbadian "tuk" band, with its penny whistle, triangle, and the drums, the essay refers to the history of the slaves times and the colonial repression of drumming, to the Bajan local Creole proverbial language and its use of the popular call and response as the key to St John's rhythm and as an important aspect of the African cultural heritage. His poems are deeply embedded in the history of the Barbadian oral and performance poetry and the ritualized "Bajan litany," but with a strong political impact, expressed in local, regional and transnational contexts.[9]

Wendy Knepper's chapter on Patrick Chamoiseau's writings and critique of the "trans-Caribbean imaginary" follows Stuart Hall's theory of "vernacular modernity" as a re-encounter with Africa, as the memory of enslavement and colonization and the modernity of hybrid black music, from which a "new kind of localism" (Hall) can emerge. Emphasizing a modern commitment to local cultural practices and identities as against current hegemonic discourses of globalization, the essay puts forward a theory of "sea-scapes"—drawing on Arjun Appadurai's theory connected with the suffix "-scapes"—as a way of articulating alternative trans-Caribbean global flows and mobility.[10] Popular cultures of music, religion, and language are evidence of the deterritorialization of the Caribbean and have the potential to influence and transform the global imaginary and to articulate enduring affiliations with local cultures of resistance.

Olive Senior uses "gossip" as a central aesthetic *female* vernacular form to reverse male marginalization and repression of female subjectivity. Focusing on "gossip" as a female oral-performance genre, Carol Bailey argues that it has become a subversive domestic everyday narrative strategy and an important part of a female Caribbean vernacular modernity as well as an alternative way of knowledge to transgress national and regional boundaries.

A black *female sexual* citizenship emerges out of recent discourses of Caribbean feminist emancipation. Transnational sexual politics engender a heterogeneous genealogy of sexual relationships across the trans-Caribbean agency; it connects—as Mimi Sheller's chapter argues—the histories of Caribbean sexuality from the era of slavery up to postcolonial global economy with new challenging issues like national citizenship, transnationalism, political emancipation, agency, and autonomy in a context of transnational migration, tourism, and mobility, as lived through the sexual-racial embodiment. The text's delineation of the female memory of slavery and emancipation, of colonialism and independence echoes Hortense Spillers' epitome of the female being in slavery and post-slavery societies as "stolen bodies," "tortured flesh" and "captured sexualities."[11] A feminist and queer approach to body and politics is here conceived of as a racialized and sexualized understanding of citizenship within embodied performances and as a call for a unity between a politics of sexuality and citizenship. Erotic power in sexual performances (in dancehall, carnival, dance etc.) opens spaces for manifestations of African diasporic female subjectivity, fertility, and reproduction. The struggle for sexual empowerment and citizenship becomes a matter of female agency and embodied freedom. Images of female sexual citizenship and agency are represented by African Caribbean diasporic popular cultural forms such as the Blues, Dancehall, the Reggae or Ragga music and lyrics, in song and dance as the celebration of the female black body and as parody of male patriarchal ideology.

The enhanced trans-Caribbean female agency of the 1990s may be related to—what Patricia Mohammed calls—the "third wave feminism" in the Caribbean of today, when a comprehensive gender consciousness by women *and* men advocated equal rights for women and men. If Mary Wollstonecraft is cited to be the mother of the first wave of feminism, then Jean Rhys, Claude McKay with *Banana Bottom!* (1933), Zee Edgehill, Merle Hodge, Jamaica Kincaid, and Olive Senior are categorized as second wave writers. Edwidge Danticat with her novel *Breath, Eyes and Memory* (1994) is to be representative of a third wave voice of feminist literature, as she discovered different female sexualities and feminist gender positions. Third wave women are thought to have more publicity and openness, more social freedoms and privileges then the second wave, expanding gender possibilities to express their femininity today. This notion of trans-Caribbean third-wave feminism, based mainly on readings of literary samples and subjective political experiences and theoretical gender or women's studies, respectively, sets "gender consciousness versus feminist consciousness," and deplores that "gender studies, like much of feminist activism, have become ghettoized." The concept of a third wave feminism recognizes new challenges for society, among which are enlisted the paradox of inconsistent choices for the modern woman, the deconstruction of masculinity in favor of the rise of a new matriarchy, and the institutionalization as well as the geo-political challenge of feminism.

These radical processes of "third wave feminism" may also have been accelerated by the digital revolution. As Curwen Best argues, "Caribbean cyberculture" and the arrival of the World Wide Web have helped to reconfigure sexual and gender relations in the trans-Caribbean. Today feminist scholars place these aspects in a more global arena and consider the role of women in local *and* transnational contexts. The chapter examines aspects of women's involvement within the early twenty-first century matrix, the possibility of cyberspace to define 'woman' and the role of the technology to shape, encode and digitize gendered responses to Caribbean and trans-Caribbean culture, and to signify and assert women's identities. Female vernacular authors may present themselves on websites in "blogs" ("The Caribbean Writer" etc. online), or may use cyber domains to carry out trans-Caribbean projects on gender and sexuality at home and in the diaspora. The prefix "trans-" in "trans-Caribbean" here indicates significations of cross-gender and cross-sexual activities in the transnational diaspora—contrary to rigid gender roles in Caribbean local communities. The author also draws our attention to the disparity in access to technology use between the sexes known as digital divide, as well as to the public's increasing critical approach to gender—sexuality—cyberspace representations of women as objects of sexual desire via digital media, with trans-Caribbean bodies digitized in videos and big budget films of the entertainment industry.

The editors would like to thank the authors for their contributions to this book and Lexington Books' editor MacDuff Stewart for her assistance in getting the manuscript ready for publication.

Nutley (New Jersey) and Berlin
April 2007

Notes

1. Lambros Comitas and David Lowenthal, *Slaves, Free Men, Citizens. West Indian Perspectives* (Garden City, N.Y.: Anchor Books, 1973).
2. Dick Hebdige, *Subculture. The Meaning of Style* (New York: Routledge, 2002); Michel de Certeau, *The Practice of Everyday Life* (Berkeley: University of California Press, 1988).
3. Néstor García Canclini, *Hybrid Cultures. Strategies for Entering and Leaving Modernity* (Minneapolis: University of Minnesota Press, 2001), 199.
4. Nina Glick Schiller, and Georges Eugene Fouron, *Georges Woke Up Laughing. Long-Distance nationalism and the Search for Home* (Durham, N.C.: Duke University Press, 2001), 20-24; Gilles Deleuze and Félix Guattari, *Nomadology the War Machine* (New York: Semiotext(e), 1986).
5. Linda Basch, Nina Glick Schiller, and Cristina Szanton Blanc, eds., *Nations Unbound: Transnational Projects, Postcolonial Predicaments, and Deterritorialized Nation States* (Langhorne, PA: Gordon and Breach, 1994).
6. Holger Henke, "Mapping the 'Inner Plantation.' A Cultural Exploration of the Origins of Caribbean Local Discourse," *Social and Economic Studies* 45, no. 4 (December 1996): 51-75.
7. Cf. Simon Gikandi, *Writing in Limbo. Modernism and Caribbean Literature* (Ithaca, N.Y. and London: Cornell University Press 1992), 21.
8. Cf. Carolyn Cooper, *Noises in the Blood. Orality, Gender and the 'Vulgar' Body of Jamaican Popular Culture* (London and Basingstoke: Macmillan Caribbean), 3 and 13.
9. Curwen Best, *Roots to Popular Culture: Barbadian Aesthetics* (London: Macmillan, 2001).
10. Cf. Arjun Appadurai, *Modernity at Large* (Minneapolis: University of Minnesota), 33.
11. Hortense Spillers. "Mama's Baby, Papa's Maybe," *Diacritics* 17, no. 2 (1987): 33.

Bibliography

Appadurai, Arjun. *Modernity at Large*. Minneapolis: University of Minnesota, 1996.
Basch, Linda, Nina Glick Schiller, and Cristina Szanton Blanc, eds. *Nations Unbound: Transnational Projects, Postcolonial Predicaments, and Deterritorialized Nation States*. Langhorne, PA: Gordon and Breach, 1994.
Best, Curwen. *Roots to Popular Culture: Barbadian Aesthetics*. London: Macmillan, 2001.
Certeau, Michel de. *The Practice of Everyday Life*. Berkeley: University of California Press, 1988.
Comitas, Lambros, and David Lowenthal. *Slaves, Free Men, Citizens. West Indian Perspectives*. Garden City, N.Y.: Anchor Books, 1973.
Cooper, Carolyn. *Noises in the Blood. Orality, Gender and the 'Vulgar' Body of Jamaican Popular Culture*. London and Basingstoke: Macmillan Caribbean, 1993.

Deleuze, Gilles, and Félix Guattari. *Nomadology the War Machine.* New York: Semiotext(e), 1986.
García Canclini, Néstor. *Hybrid Cultures. Strategies for Entering and Leaving Modernity.* Minneapolis: University of Minnesota Press, 2001.
Gikandi, Simon. *Writing in Limbo. Modernism and Caribbean Literature.* Ithaca, N.Y. and London: Cornell University Press, 1992.
Glick Schiller, Nina, and Georges Eugene Fouron. *Georges Woke Up Laughing. Long-Distance Nationalism and the Search for Home.* Durham, N.C.: Duke University Press 2001.
Hebdige, Dick. *Subculture. The Meaning of Style.* New York: Routledge, 2002.
Henke, Holger. "Mapping the 'Inner Plantation.' A Cultural Exploration of the Origins of Caribbean Local Discourse," in: *Social and Economic Studies* 45, no.4 (December 1996), 51-75.
Spillers, Hortense. "Mama's Baby, Papa's Maybe: An American Grammar Book," in: *Diacritics: A Review of Contemporary Criticism* 17, no. 2 (1987): 65-81.

I

(RE-)CREATING HOMES IN THE VERNACULAR

1

Mies van Niekerk

Premigration Legacies and Transnational Identities: Afro-Surinamese and Indo-Surinamese in the Netherlands

The historical legacies of slavery and indentured labor not only make themselves felt in Surinam, the former Dutch Guiana, but also in the Netherlands. On both sides of the Atlantic, relatively large Surinamese populations are to be found. Whereas the population of Surinam amounts to some 430,000 people, nearly 330,000 people of Surinamese origin live in the Netherlands, including the native-born children of first generation immigrants.[1] As in Surinam, the two largest ethnic groups among the Surinamese in the Netherlands are the Afro-Surinamese or Creoles and the Indo-Surinamese or East Indians (or "Hindustanis"). They make up an estimated forty and fifty percent respectively of the Surinamese immigrant population in the Netherlands.[2]

Migration from Surinam to the Netherlands is as old as the bonds between the two countries. From colonial times onwards a tradition of migration to the Netherlands has existed, but migration only reached its peak around the time of Surinam's independence in 1975. Although the Creoles have a longer tradition of migration to the Netherlands than the East Indians, the large majority of both groups migrated to the Netherlands in the 1970s. They form part of Dutch society for some thirty years now. This chapter considers the integration of Surinamese immigrants and their children into Dutch society and explores the ways in which premigration legacies affect the socioeconomic mobility after migration.[3] At the same time, it will be shown that in the process of socioeconomic integration, the historical legacies and cultural repertoires that immigrants bring along inevitably change, as will their ethnic affiliations and transnational bonds.

In recent academic debates, especially in the United States, one of the controversies is about the extent to which transnationalism affects the incorporation of immigrants into the host society.[4] Some social scientists argue that the ongoing relations of contemporary immigrants with their home countries—made possible by new means of transport and communications hitherto unknown—will result in a radical change of the assimilation process as witnessed among the earlier immigrants who arrived around 1900 in the United States. Contemporary transnational relations are supposed to be totally different in character than the relations of these earlier immigrants, and this is one of the most important factors that help explain why the assimilation process will have distinct characteristics today.[5] According to this point of view, assimilation into the American mainstream is only one of the possible outcomes.[6] Today, assimilation has become a multipath process, which results in an increasingly multicultural society.

Others have cast doubt on the radically different character of the contemporary process of integration of immigrants by pointing to the many similarities between the two large migration flows into the United States. History has shown that the assimilation of immigrants take at least three or four generations, they argue, and the so-called post-1965 immigration is simply too recent to be able to know the end result. The contemporary immigrants mainly belong to the first or 1.5 generation, while the second generation is still largely of school-going age. Therefore, we do not know as yet whether the assimilation process today will differ fundamentally from the earlier assimilation.[7]

Without going further into this debate, I will argue here that the seemingly contradictory notions of ethnocultural retention and transnationalism on the one hand and assimilation or integration[8] on the other, are less incompatible than is often assumed. Ethnic and transnational identifications may become even more pronounced as immigrants and their offspring become more integrated into the receiving society. To show this, I will draw on my study on the Afro-Surinamese and Indo-Surinamese in the Netherlands.[9] The core of this research project consisted of anthropological fieldwork in the cities of Amsterdam and The Hague. It studied first-generation immigrants and their offspring aged eighteen or older, born in either Surinam or the Netherlands. The focus was on immigrants of lower-class origins, who made up the majority of those arriving in the period of mass migration.[10]

Migration and social mobility

As for many other postcolonial immigrants, the pathway to social advancement used to run from the former colony to the metropolis—in this case from Surinam across the ocean to the Netherlands.[11] Coming to the former mother country, however, many Surinamese immigrants became disappointed. The mass migration to the Netherlands took place in a period of economic reconstruction and growing unemployment, and by this fact alone the economic opportunities for newly arrived immigrants were severely limited. Unemployment among the Surinamese rose to unprecedented heights in the 1980s. Racial stereotyping and discrimination further contributed to the disadvantaged position of many of the lower-class Surinamese in the Dutch labor market and in society at large. Although they arrived as Dutch citizens and, thus, right from the beginning had a strong legal status, many felt treated as second-class citizens. Thus, the historical timing of the mass exodus in the 1970s meant a very unlucky start for the Surinamese in Dutch society.

This situation improved considerably in the 1990s, due among other things to economic recovery and increased employment opportunities. From then onwards, the labor market position of the Surinamese improved strongly, and gradually, the educational position of the younger generation also improved considerably.[12] The socioeconomic position of the Surinamese as a group is situated between the ethnic Dutch on the one hand, and the other large immigrant groups, the Turks and Moroccans, on the other. The Surinamese did not arrive as a homogeneously poorly-schooled immigrant population like the recruited laborers from Turkey and Morocco. The Surinamese came from varied social-class backgrounds and, upon arrival, were more or less familiar with the Dutch language and culture. This facilitated their integration into Dutch society. The social mobility the Surinamese experienced since the period of mass migration contributed to the weakening of negative stereotypes about them. Nowadays, the focus of public attention is on Islam and specifically on Muslim immigrants from Turkey and Morocco. In this regard, "race" or "color" appear to be a much less pervasive social dividing line than religion.[13]

What holds for the Surinamese as a group concerning their improved socioeconomic position, also applies to the two major ethnic populations among them, the Afro-Surinamese and Indo-Surinamese. Both groups managed to advance socially, albeit in different ways and at different rates. Contrary to the public images of the two groups, the socioeconomic position of the Indo-Surinamese as a whole is not any better than the position of the Afro-Surinamese. The Indo-Surinamese are often viewed as the more successful of the two groups. This positive image seems to be due to the rapid socioeconomic progress of these former indentured laborers in Surinam and their tradition of self-employment. In the Netherlands, their visible presence in small businesses like, for example, tropical food stores, jewelry shops and take-out restaurants may have contributed to their image as a self-reliant, entrepreneurial group. The public image of the Afro-Surinamese, by contrast, has often been more negative and has been associated with urban unemployment, both in Surinam and the Netherlands. Especially in the 1970s and 1980s, young unemployed and poorly educated black males were highly visible in the Dutch large cities, and were in the spotlight of public attention. Their involvement in drugs concerned only a minority of the lower-class Afro-Surinamese young males, but this perception seems to have dominated the image of the Afro-Surinamese as a group during these initial years.

The public perceptions of the two groups in terms of "success" and "failure" are not, however, sustained by empirical evidence on their respective socioeconomic positions. Quantitative data[14] show that differences in the overall socioeconomic positions of the two groups are not very great. Unlike the popular image of the Afro-Surinamese, unemployment among them is not any higher than among the Indo-Surinamese, and the Afro-Surinamese exhibit higher labor market participation rates, especially women. In addition, the Afro-Surinamese do have higher overall educational levels and, as a result, they have a better labor market position in terms of job levels and income.[15]

These differences in socioeconomic positions between the Afro-Surinamese and Indo-Surinamese refer to the two groups as a whole, and it might well be that subgroups among them suffered more from unemployment and discrimination than others. Although no systematic data on discrimination for the two Surinamese groups exist, qualitative studies do suggest that young, poorly educated Afro-Surinamese males suffered from racial stereotyping and discrimination in the labor market.[16] We do not know, though, whether differential treatment in the labor market occurred and the extent to which this may have led to diverging labor market positions. On the whole, however, differences in socioeconomic position of the Afro- and Indo-Surinamese as a group do seem to be more related to their premigration structural positions in the country of origin than to the structure of opportunities in the host society. After all, both groups arrived virtually at the same time and settled in the same urban areas where they faced similar opportunities in terms of economic climate, labor market, education, housing and government policy. As will be shown in the next section, explanations for their divergent socioeconomic attainments are, therefore, rather to be sought in the historical background of both ethnic groups prior to migration.

Diverging historical legacies

When the Surinamese arrived in the Netherlands in the 1970s, both the Afro- and Indo-Surinamese had a hard time adapting to the labor market and the educational system, and both groups suffered high rates of unemployment and welfare dependency. In this sense, migration to the Netherlands tended to level out some of the differences between the two groups. Nevertheless, the Afro-Surinamese were better able to adapt to the Dutch labor market and the school system, due to their premigration background. The Afro-Surinamese mainly came from the urban centers of Surinam, especially its capital Paramaribo and its surroundings, where better educational provisions were available and where they had been employed in urban occupations that stood them in better stead in the Dutch labor market. In addition, they were generally more familiar with the Dutch culture and language, although this varied considerably according to social class. As a consequence, the Afro-Surinamese enjoyed more occupational continuity after their move to the Netherlands, and were better able to take up jobs and occupations similar to those they had practiced in Surinam. These were mainly in three economic sectors, namely manufacturing industry, clerical work and health care.

The Indo-Surinamese had more difficulty in adapting to the Dutch labor market than the Afro-Surinamese, and their children had more trouble in adjusting to the Dutch schools.[17] This was mainly due to their rural background and relatively recent migration to the city, and—as a result—their lower educational levels and poor mastery of the Dutch language. In contrast to the Afro-Surinamese, many of the lower-class Indo-Surinamese suffered a severe loss of status after their move to the Netherlands. First, many of them lacked the right educational qualifications to enter the same line of work after migration, especially the self-employed among them. Secondly, many suffered from the transition of self-employment or small-scale entrepreneurship to wage labor or benefit dependency.

Notwithstanding this initial disadvantage, the Indo-Surinamese are catching up rapidly—a process that had already begun in Surinam and continued after migration to the Netherlands. Although they generally had a harder time in the initial post-immigration period, the Indo-Surinamese seem to have improved their position rather faster than the Afro-Surinamese of the same lower-class background. This is most evident in education.[18] The educational progress of the younger generation Indo-Surinamese is remarkable in the light of the generally low parental educational levels.

Among the factors that I examined in search of an explanation of this differential social mobility were family-background and the notions that parents convey to their children about life—in particular with respect to their educational and occupational careers. I then traced how members of the next generation reshape such "messages" in accordance with their own experiences. Indo-Surinamese young people are still very conscious indeed of how earlier generations settled in Surinam around 1900. Coming from the Indian subcontinent, the East Indians started as indentured laborers on the plantations, but within a few generations they managed to greatly improve their position in Surinamese society—first in agriculture, later in transport, and more generally in small entrepreneurship. For them, education became a route for advancement only as a second step. This collective history firmly implanted in the East Indian community a belief in "making it," even in the face of severe adversity and social deprivation. This historically rooted optimism still inspires the younger generation of Indo-Surinamese people in the Netherlands. The youth is keenly aware of the chances it has in the Netherlands—chances the parents' generation generally did not have in Surinam. This has instilled a strong educational motivation. The Indo-Surinamese perceive discrimination as less of an obstacle than the Afro-Surinamese tend to do—or rather, they see it as a barrier to be overcome.[19]

The notion of progress is more complicated among the Afro-Surinamese. The characteristic Creole tradition of upward mobility through educational advancement is strongly evident among the Afro-Surinamese immigrants, parents and children alike. The idea that a diploma holds the key to social mobility is typical of the Afro-Surinamese, who have long been a predominantly urban population. Historically, they participated in the school system earlier than the East Indian population, who remained in agriculture for an extended period. Contrary to this educational motivation, however, unemployment and poverty have periodically struck the lower-class Afro-Surinamese, forcing them to devise alternative ways of urban survival. For some segments of the poorer Afro-Surinamese population in Surinam, unemployment and poverty persisted for generations. It fostered in them a certain ambivalence about the mainstream routes of societal advancement. Afro-Surinamese immigrants to the Netherlands arrived amidst a wave of unemployment, which was affecting the cities in particular. Their experience with discrimination in the new country, combined with the serious lack of job opportunities, simply reinforced the doubts that some of the lower-class younger generation already harbored about the value of diplomas.[20] One general perception among Afro-Surinamese immigrants is that the major obstacle to progress lies not so much in cultural difference, but in discrimination.

In short, what I have observed in both groups is the continuing salience of their respective premigration histories in how they perceive their opportunities in the Netherlands. The cultural repertoire that immigrants bring along with them upon migration, and that parents transmit to their children, has a profound influence on the life chances of the younger generation. Although the younger generation obviously moulds its parents' cultural messages to fit its own experiences and life conditions, the older generation's ways of thinking and acting still remain an enduring force.[21]

Changing ways of life

The notion of premigration legacies does not mean, however, that immigrant cultures remain unchanged. If one understands culture, as I do, to be the result of adaptation to a contemporary social context on the basis of a heritage from the past, then it is not surprising that migration sparks rapid sociocultural change. Immigrant cultures undergo change as a consequence of new living conditions and whatever socioeconomic mobility the immigrants have gone through. This is evident, for instance, when immigrant families experience an influx of new immigrants into their neighborhood, or when they leave their neighborhood and move to another. Geographical and social mobility often go hand in hand. People who are socially mobile often leave the district where they initially settled and where they lived amidst former compatriots. They may turn their back on the ethnic community, or more specifically on their lower-class co-ethnics whom they see as poorly integrated, because they opt for better life chances for their children.

One of my informants, for example, an Indo-Surinamese woman aged forty nine, had been living in an old working-class district of The Hague since she first arrived. Despite the serious unemployment conditions prevailing in the initial period, she found a job and built up a successful career as a secretary. As soon as possible she bought a flat on the outskirts of the city, where her children grew up and attended predominantly white schools. She now says she literally feels sick when she walks through her old neighborhood, where many Indo-Surinamese people still live. She summarizes her objections as follows:

> These are people who don't work and who just live on the dole. They drink. They have too many kids and live in small three- or four-room flats. These are people who visit each other the whole time and who hang out in the Indo-Surinamese social clubs.

As this example shows, the process of social mobility implies that people's ways of life change, willingly or unwillingly. The same process is evident in the daily crossing of neighborhood boundaries by immigrant youth who live in lower-class districts and attend schools elsewhere. To illustrate this I quote extensively from the narrative of a young Afro-Surinamese woman.

Denise (24) was born in the Netherlands and now lives in an old working-class district in Amsterdam. After primary school, she completed a five-year secondary school diploma at a combined school in another neighborhood, where most of the pupils were ethnic Dutch. In choosing this type of school she was not an exception in her parents' circle of friends and relatives, but she was unusual compared to her friends from the neighborhood, most of whom went to lower-level schools like the one focusing on home economics. After finishing school, Denise went on to a vocational college where there were many Surinamese students. More than at secondary school, she now spent her leisure time with Surinamese young people, most of whom she knew from the neighborhood or from school. But when she finished that course and went on to business college, she entered a new world altogether. Up to then, she had largely moved in Surinamese circles,

> also because of the neighborhood I lived in. Somehow you always hang out together. That's very different nowadays. I don't think there's a single Surinamese student in any of my classes, so what can I do. [. . .] But I did grow up surrounded by Surinamese people.

With her Surinamese friends she would always go to Surinamese dance parties or clubs. With her Dutch friends, her fellow students now, that changed. Going out meant going to a pub or a film. She went to student parties with music she would never have listened to herself, but that was exactly what she liked about it. "It was suddenly just a totally different world." Denise can move comfortably in both worlds, and she finds the two styles of leisure time activities different but fun. She still enjoys spending time with her Surinamese girlfriends from the neighborhood, but is well aware that she now lives in a different world. Her girlfriends are not as well educated, they have much less contact with Dutch peers, and they already have children. "They don't do anything for themselves, they don't even finish the schools they start, they just quit everything half-way." Like her mother, Denise doesn't want to be dependent on a man later.

> I really got that idea from my mother, the idea that first and foremost you have to be able to fend for yourself, so you need good diplomas. A lot of women I know, they have such a dependent attitude when it comes to guys, their boyfriend or, well, men in general.

All these things make her realize she is different now, and that in a way she has outgrown the neighborhood. "I think if I'd only been associating with my friends from the neighborhood, maybe things would've been very different for me." Not that it bothers her, "but I do think I've become more like a Dutch woman, even when I'm with my Surinamese friends. But what can you expect?"

This story exemplifies the present situation of many other Afro-Surinamese young people who experienced upward mobility in the school system. Her circle of friends is varied, ranging from Surinamese women to Dutch students. She has become slightly estranged from her Surinamese peers from the neighborhood and now feels more at ease with her Dutch peers at college. But that doesn't mean she no longer feels Surinamese. Once, for example, she was deeply offended when a man on the telephone started putting down Surinamese people and immigrants in general. Because of her fluent Dutch with no accent, he did not realize he was talking to someone with a Surinamese background. She then made a firm stand in defense of immigrants.

This phenomenon of "becoming Dutch" and still "feeling Surinamese" is a frequent experience.[22] If culture is the result of adaptation to the social context, then it is inevitable that settlement into a new society will ultimately lead to an erosion of ethnic culture. This does not necessarily mean that people will also lose their *sense* of being different. Far from that, it is often the "most assimilated" who are apt to highlight their ethnic background and work to preserve cultural traditions. In cases where little remains of their former ethnic culture, people may even resort to adopting ethnic symbols, as Gans (1979) noted some decades ago for third- and fourth-generation immigrants in the United States. I only want to stress here that migration and upward mobility lead to sociocultural change—a process that often develops unintended. It does not, however, necessarily result in a decrease of ethnic consciousness.

Ethnic identity and creating community

The fading of ethnocultural differences does not automatically mean that people also lose their sense of being "ethnic." The second and subsequent generations may cling to traditions, or even resort to using ethnic symbols in the event that little is left of the former "ethnic" way of life. The twenty-year-old daughter of the Indo-Surinamese secretary quoted above, for example, was born in the

Netherlands, and in her mother's eyes she is now very "Dutchified." Until recently she attended a predominantly white school. "There I didn't even notice I was different," she recalls. "It wasn't till I went to this college now [with more immigrant students] that I discovered I was Indo-Surinamese." Now she regularly visits the relatives of her Indo-Surinamese boyfriend who live in the old working-class district her mother so disdains. She feels very much at home with his family, and she can always drop in and eat typical Indo-Surinamese dishes. They watch videos from India, and although she doesn't understand the language, she loves the Indian soundtracks. She became acquainted with Hinduism, and the walls of her room now display various pictures of Hindu gods. Thus, even though this second-generation woman from an upwardly mobile family is very "Dutchified," she is now discovering things she didn't find in her mother's home—things that her mother had so much wanted to leave behind. Despite all this, however, her life has not changed very much. Her recently budding interest in her ethnic background, including learning about Hinduism, liking Indian music and Indo-Surinamese food, and interacting and identifying with Indo-Surinamese people, all seem to be rather optional in her life.[23]

Whereas the second generation's search for ethnic roots might be viewed as a "discovery" of one's own ethnic background, the preservation of cultural traditions by the older generation and by ethnic leaders is not a discovery, but a conscious attempt to keep these traditions alive. The Indo-Surinamese community makes determined efforts to preserve its religious, cultural, and linguistic traditions, for example by founding schools and a broadcasting organization. Various forms of classical and popular culture from India are now widespread, some of them influenced by the Indian community in nearby Britain. Indian classical dance and music are practiced and taught to a younger generation. Modern Indian movies and soundtracks are immensely popular, as reflected in the many Indo-Surinamese video shops in the Dutch cities. This emergence of an Indo-Surinamese popular culture has bolstered the already strong ethnic cohesion in the Indo-Surinamese community in the Netherlands. The physically shorter distance to India may also have reinforced the ethnic consciousness of this twice-migrant community. Many older Indo-Surinamese people desire to travel to the Indian subcontinent at least once in their lifetime, often in search of family roots.[24] Among my informants were even parents who went to India to look for a marriageable partner for their children, and young people who went there to learn skills like embroidery or to improve their techniques on their favorite Indian musical instrument.

The Afro-Surinamese community has created far less of an ethnic infrastructure that serves the preservation of religious or cultural traditions. Nonetheless, Afro-Surinamese traditions are being continued, and a wide range of cultural organizations does exist. In many cases, what is being consciously kept alive is not a revived tradition, but a "living" culture, as evidenced by the lower-class religious-cultural tradition of *winti*.[25] Moreover, the Afro-

Surinamese culture is a typical Creole culture, spawned by an intermingling of Western and African traditions. Such influences can be recognized in youth culture and music styles. Afro-Surinamese young people are keenly aware of their African roots, as seen in the popularity of African dance groups in which they actively participate. At the same time, many are active in the international youth and music culture, and in many respects they are trendsetters in the metropolitan leisure scene. Alongside the preservation of black traditions, a cultural influence that appears equally important to the Afro-Surinamese is the collective memory of the historical past of slavery. This heritage is expressed in a variety of ways, from the *anansi tories* (stories passed down across the generations since the times of slavery[26]) to the recent successful campaign to erect a monument in Amsterdam to commemorate slavery. Some Afro-Surinamese people travel to Africa to visit places from where their forebears were once deported as slaves. Their interest in Ghana has been reinforced by the current presence of a large Ghanaian community in Amsterdam. Remembrance of this historical past is as much a part of the cultural heritage of the Afro-Surinamese community as their traditional cultural practices.

Transnational ties and symbolic meanings

The ethnic identifications of the Afro- and Indo-Surinamese and the ways they "create community" seem to be strongly influenced by transnational bonds. Does this mean that transnational ties become more important, even to the extent that an enduring transnational community emerges that might hamper the integration into Dutch society? First of all, this depends on what exactly is meant by transnationalism. Since its invention, the term has become an umbrella concept that covers a wide range of very different phenomena. To be meaningful, the term needs precision. According to Kasinitz (et al.) a broad consensus seems to be emerging that the term transnationalism should be reserved for economic, political and cultural fields that involve individuals and institutions located in more than one nation state, and the activities in these fields must be engaged in regularly by a substantial number of people and form an integral part of the habitual life of at least substantial segments of the migrant community.[27]

If we look at the transnational ties of Surinamese immigrants with the home country from this perspective, it seems to be predominantly the foreign-born generation (the 1st or 1.5 generation) that maintains any enduring relations with Surinam.[28] First generation immigrants not only visit their country of origin more regularly than their Dutch-born children, but they also maintain multifarious material relations with their home country, for example by buying plots of land there or building houses; by supporting economically their relatives who have stayed behind; and by commercial relations and entrepreneurial activities—be it formal or informal.[29] These practices refer, thus, mainly to social and material relations, and they are largely a first generation phenomenon. It is mostly the parents who maintain relations with relatives back home and who send them money or packets with goods, and who invest in their home country as a way of investment or provision for old age. In addition, it is this Surinam-born generation that has the language and cultural skills to operate in both countries. Frequently, the Dutch-born children know Surinam only as a vacation spot, and some prefer other holiday destinations to Surinam. Of course, the second generation is still relatively young and we do not know as yet whether the transnational relations of these young people will change as they get older. For the time being, however, it does not seem likely that the social and material relations of this Dutch-born generation with Surinam will increase. A second-generation study in the United States, for example, concludes that only a small minority of the American-born children of several immigrant groups exhibited the kind of sustained commitment to maintaining meaningful ties to the parental home societies that would seem to be necessary for transnationalism to flourish in the second generation.[30]

Whereas the scope and durability of the actual transnational practices seem to be limited to the first generation and a small minority of the second generation, and are likely to become even less significant over time, some argue that transnationalism remains an enduring impact on the lives of the children of immigrants because they are embedded in transnational social fields.[31] The concept of "transnational social fields" refers to "the domain created by the social relationships of persons who visit back and forth in their country of origin and persons who remain connected even if they themselves do not move."[32] In other words, even if children of immigrants have no direct contact with the sending society, they stay involved in transnational social fields via their parents. This might also be the case for the children of Surinamese immigrants to the Netherlands, but there are at least two reasons why we may doubt the future importance of these so-called transnational fields. First, as geographical distance is among the principal factors that affect transnationalism, the fairly large distance between Surinam and the Netherlands seems to underscore the conclusion that transnational relations will diminish in importance over time.[33] Second, unlike several immigrant groups in the United States and unlike the Turks and Moroccans in the Netherlands, there is no continuing large immigration flow from Surinam to the Netherlands anymore. Marriage partners, for example, are not sought for in the home country as frequently as among the Turks and Moroccans living in the Netherlands.[34] In the case of the Surinamese, there are no large numbers of newly arriving immigrants from the home country that contribute to the renewal of transnational ties and the re-creation of transnational social fields.

What will probably remain, therefore, when transnational practices diminish in importance is a transnational consciousness. As we have seen, though, this is as much directed towards Surinam as to India and "Africa." The interest of the Indo-Surinamese second generation in *Bollywood*—the popular culture of Indian movies and music, and of the Afro-Surinamese youngsters in the African-

American or international pop-culture is growing. Modern means of communication influence the ethnic identifications of immigrant youngsters from a distance and provide them with behavioral models different from the ones in their immediate social environment, varying from American rappers to Indian movie stars. Cultural influences are less than ever bound by geographical location. Present-day means of communication facilitate transnational ties, which may affect immigrants' identities over long distances.[35]

In this sense, then, transnational consciousness and identities of second-generation immigrants are very much akin to ethnicity or ethnic identity because both are essentially "Dutch-made."[36] That is, these ethnic or transnational identifications are expressions of their rediscovery and revaluation of their social and cultural roots that only make sense in the Dutch context. The current celebration of ethnic diversity and multiculturalism offers a receptive ground for adhering to the cultural aspects and symbolic meanings of transnationalism. Whereas for the first generation the ties with the homeland seem to be a natural or logical continuation of their former way of life, for their children the ethnic and transnational identifications are more a matter of choice.[37] In this sense, transnational identifications may go hand in hand with an increasing integration into the society where one lives.

Conclusion

In this chapter I have tried to show that premigration legacies are crucial in understanding the process of structural and sociocultural integration of immigrants and their children into the receiving society. The cultural repertoire that immigrants bring along with them embodies the historical experiences of previous generations. The cultural messages that parents convey to their children influence how they perceive and respond to the structure of opportunities they encounter in the receiving society. In this way the historical background and cultural repertoire of immigrants affect their socioeconomic incorporation. This is not to suggest that culture is handed down unvaryingly from generation to generation. On the contrary, in the process of socioeconomic integration, immigrant ways of life inevitably change. When people move up the socioeconomic ladder, when they leave the immigrant neighborhood and get into close contact with people outside the ethnic community, the old ways of acting and thinking will change accordingly. Structural integration and acculturation often go together, though it is difficult to establish cause and effect. Does upward social mobility result in acculturation or is it acculturation that leads to mobility? This is hard to decide. But if culture as a way of life is the product of the experiences of individuals under specific circumstances, while still informed by a legacy from the past, then cultural change is a process that largely develops unintentionally. It cannot be deliberately manipulated as one pleases. Although individuals are certainly actors in the construction of culture, they are not entirely free to construct culture as they see fit—constrained as they are by conditions in the time and society they live in.[38]

Sociocultural integration does not, however, necessarily oppose ethnic retention or transnational identifications. Here, we may distinguish between the first and the second generation. For first generation immigrants, the desire to preserve ethnocultural traditions and languages can be characterized as "old ethnicity," that is: people are evidently so different that they hardly feel the need to emphasize their being different.[39] The children of immigrants, however, often do feel the need to distinguish themselves from others, just because cultural differences have faded. The presentation of "otherness" may become more important, but is more a matter of choice than for their parents. In either case, though, a distinction should be made between sociocultural integration on the one hand, and ethnic or transnational identifications on the other. A growing awareness of historical and transnational roots is perhaps the other side of the often unwanted but seemingly inevitable erosion of the "ethnic" way of life.

Recent discussions of transnationalism focus on the question whether transnational ties and identities hinder the integration of immigrants and their children. The empirical evidence is still inconclusive, most of all because the second generation is still relatively young—both in the Netherlands and in the United States, where much of this debate takes place.[40] Nevertheless, it seems plausible that integration and transnationalism need not be studied in opposition to each other, because both often coexist in the lives of immigrants and their offspring.[41] I agree with Kasinitz (et al.) who suggest that the contemporary celebration of cultural diversity and transnationalism probably overestimates the importance of conscious volition in the process of assimilation.[42] People may aspire to preserve the cultural traditions they value; they may opt for certain ethnic markers or symbolic expressions of transnational identities, but this does not necessarily alter their way of life. Similarly, although a process of growing ethnic and transnational consciousness may help to reinforce social cohesion in an ethnic community, or even create community, it does not appear to reverse the inevitable process of integration in which immigrants are also involved.

Notes

1. On January 1, 2005, 329,000 persons of Surinamese origin lived in the Netherlands. The first generation numbered 188,000 persons, the second-generation 141,000 persons. The second generation is defined as persons who are born in the Netherlands and have at least one parent who has been born in Surinam (Statistics Netherlands, http://www.CBS.nl).

2. Edwin P. Martens and Arjen O. Verweij, *Surinamers in Nederland. Kerncijfers 1996* (Rotterdam: Institute for Sociological and Economic Research, Erasmus University, 1997), 11.

3. An earlier version of this chapter has been presented at the Conference *Globalization, Diaspora and Identity Formation: The Legacy of Slavery and Indentured Labor in the Caribbean*, 26-29 February 2004, University of Suriname.

4. See for an overview of this debate, for example, Richard D. Alba and Victor Nee, *Remaking the American Mainstream. Assimilation and Contemporary Immigration* (Cambridge: Harvard University Press, 2003); Josh DeWind, Charles Hirschman, and Philip Kasinitz, eds., "Immigrant adaptation and native-born responses in the making of Americans," Special Issue *International Migration Review* 31, no. 4 (1997); Nancy Foner, *From Ellis Island to JFK: New York's Two Great Waves of Immigration.* (New Haven and New York: Yale University Press and Russell Sage Foundation, 2000).

5. It is important to stress that the "new" transnationalism is only one of the key elements in this debate. Among the important factors that make for the radical change in the assimilation of immigrants are also the post-industrial, knowledge-based nature of the economy; continuing immigration; and the non-European descent of contemporary immigrants.

6. Whereas earlier immigrants have assimilated into the American middle class, according to these proponents, current immigrants may also adapt to the native "underclass" in the American inner cities and, thus, experience downward assimilation. Other immigrants, especially those from entrepreneurial groups, become incorporated in an ethnic economy and profit from their relations with coethnics in both the host and sending society—Alejandro Portes, "Children of immigrants. Segmented assimilation and its determinants," in *The Economic Sociology of Immigration. Essays on Networks, Ethnicity, and Entrepreneurship*, ed. Alejandro Portes (New York: Russell Sage Foundation, 1995), 248-80; Min Zhou, "Segmented Assimilation. Issues, Controversies and Recent Research on the New Second Generation," *International Migration Review* 31, no. 4 (Winter 1997).

7. See for example, Alba and Victor Nee, *Remaking*; Herbert Gans, "Symbolic Ethnicity: The Future of Ethnic Groups and Cultures in America," *Ethnic and Racial Studies* 2, (1979); Joel Perlmann and Roger Waldinger, "Second Generation Decline? Children of Immigrants, Past and Present," *International Migration Review* 31, no. 4 (1997).

8. The terms "integration" and "assimilation" are usually used in a somewhat different sense. The term "assimilation" generally denotes the final stage of the integration process.

9. The Netherlands Organization for Scientific Research (NWO) has made this research possible—see Mies van Niekerk, *Premigration Legacies and Immigrant Social Mobility. The Afro-Surinamese and Indo-Surinamese in the Netherlands* (Lanham, Md.: Lexington Books, 2002); see also Mies van Niekerk, "Afro-Caribbeans and Indo-Caribbeans in the Netherlands. Premigration Legacies and Social Mobility," *International Migration Review* 38, no. 2 (2004).

10. Since the focus of the fieldwork was on intragenerational and intergenerational social mobility, I collected individual and family histories, by way of single or repeated interviews and participant observation. By interviewing 102 family members, I collected information on 288 persons belonging to 64 families, 25 of which I regard as "key cases." All were roughly distributed between the two groups. I gathered additional information by interviewing key informants and doing participant observation in the ethnic communities. Most of the fieldwork took place in 1995-1996. The research project additionally included a review of the literature on the premigration histories of the two groups and an

analysis of survey data on the socioeconomic conditions of Afro-Surinamese and Indo-Surinamese in the Netherlands.

11. Cf. Hans van Amersfoort and Mies van Niekerk, "Immigration as a Colonial Inheritance: Post-Colonial Immigrants in the Netherlands, 1945-2002," *Journal of Ethnic and Migration Studies* 32, no. 3 (April 2006): 323-46.

12. For a short overview of the social position and integration of the Surinamese in the Netherlands—see Mies van Niekerk, "Paradoxes in Paradise. Integration and social mobility of the Surinamese in the Netherlands," in *Immigrant Integration. The Dutch Case*, ed. Hans Vermeulen and Rinus Penninx (Amsterdam: Het Spinhuis, 2000), 64-92.

13. Anti-immigrant and anti-Islam feelings have become especially strong after the Van Gogh murder in 2004.

14. For reasons of space, it is impossible to present all the empirical evidence here. See for survey-data on the socioeconomic positions of the Afro-Surinamese and Indo-Surinamese in the Netherlands: Van Niekerk, *Premigration*, 263-67.

15. Van Niekerk, *Premigration*, 30-32; cf. Chan E. S. Choenni, "Maatschappelijke positie van Hindostanen," in: *Hindostanen. Van Brits-Indische emigranten via Suriname tot burgers van Nederland*, ed. Chan E. S. Choenni and Kanta Sh. Adhin (The Hague: Sampreshan, 2003), 70-89.

16. Willem Biervliet, "The hustler culture of young unemployed Surinamers," in *Adaptation of Migrants from the Caribbean in the European and American Metropolis*, ed. Humphrey E. Lamur and John D. Speckmann (Leiden and Amsterdam: Royal Institute of Linguistics and Department of Anthropology and Non-Western Sociology, 1975), 191-201; Peter E. J. Buiks, *Surinaamse jongeren op de Kruiskade. Overleven in een etnische randgroep* (Deventer: Van Loghum Slaterus, 1983); Livio Sansone, *Schitteren in de schaduw. Overlevingsstrategieën, subcultuur en etniciteit van Creoolse jongeren uit de lagere klasse in Amsterdam 1981-1990* (Amsterdam: Het Spinhuis, 1992).

17. Cf. Varina Tjon-A-Ten, "Creoolse en Hindoestaanse kinderen in het Nederlandse lager onderwijs." (PhD diss., University of Utrecht, 1987).

18. For the empirical data on the educational position—see Van Niekerk, *Premigration*, 133-36.

19. Cf. John U. Ogbu, "Variability in Minority School Performance. A Problem in Search of an Explanation," *Anthropology and Education Quarterly* 18, no. 3 (1987).

20. Sansone, *Schitteren*.

21. Parental values and educational motivations are socially embedded, and the social networks inside or outside the ethnic community may either reinforce or challenge these values and aspirations. For a full account of this—see Van Niekerk, *Premigration* (especially Chapters 6 and 7 on "Family Background" and "Social Environment and networks").

22. Cf. Mies van Niekerk, "Becoming Dutch and staying Surinamese: culture as a *way of life* and as a *lifestyle*," in *Dedication & Detachment. Essays in Honour of Hans Vermeulen*, ed. Flip Lindo and Mies van Niekerk (Amsterdam: Het Spinhuis, 2001), 179-92.

23. Cf. Mary C. Waters, *Ethnic Options: Choosing Identities in America* (Berkeley: University of California Press, 1990).

24. Cf. Sandew Hira, *Terug naar Uttar Pradesh: Op zoek naar de wortels van de Surnaamse Hindoestanen* (The Hague: Amrit, 2000).

25. *Winti* is an Afro-Surinamese religion or Surinam vodouism.

26. *Anansi tories* refer to a long oral tradition of stories about the spider Anansi who is always too clever for others. These stories have been brought along by the slaves from Africa to Surinam.

27. Philip Kasinitz, Mary C. Waters, John Mollenkopf, Merih Anil, "Transnationalism and the children of immigrants in contemporary New York," in *The Changing Face of Home. The Transnational Lives of the Second Generation*, ed. Peggy Levitt and Mary C. Waters (New York: Russell Sage Foundation, 2002), 100; see also Alejandro Portes, Luis E. Guarnizo, and Patricia Landholt, "The study of transnationalism: pitfalls and promise of an emergent research field," *Ethnic and Racial Studies* 22, no. 2 (1999).

28. Here, I refer only to the economic and cultural relations, not the political relations. The reason for excluding political relations here is not that they would be less important, but simply because this theme has not been included in my research.

29. Mies van Niekerk, *Surinam Country Report. A Part of the Report on Informal Remittance Systems in Africa, Caribbean and Pacific (ACP) Countries*. Oxford: Centre on Migration, Policy and Society (COMPAS), University of Oxford, 2005. http://www.compas.ox.ac.uk/publications/papers/ Surinam%20050115.pdf; cf. Ruben S. Gowricharn and John Schuster, "Diaspora and Transnationalism: The case of the Surinamese in the Netherlands," in *20th Century Surinam. Continuities and Discontinuities in a New World Society*, ed. Rosemarijn Hoefte and Peter Meel (Kingston and Leiden: Ian Randle Publishers and KITLV Press, 2001), 155-73.

30. Kasinitz et al., "Transnationalism."

31. P. Levitt and Mary Waters, eds., *The Changing Face of Home. The Transnational Lives of the Second Generation* (New York: Russell Sage Foundation, 2002).

32. Georges Fouron and Nina Glick-Schiller, "The generation of Identity: Redefining the second generation within a transnational social field," in *The Shanging Face of Home. The Transnational Lives of the Second Generation*, ed. P. Levitt and Mary Waters (New York: Russell Sage Foundation, 2002), 172.

33. Cf. Philip Kasinitz, Mary Waters, John Mollenkopf, "Becoming American/Becoming New Yorkers: Immigrant Incorporation in a Majority Minority City," *International Migration Review* 36, no. 4 (2002); Portes et al., "The study," 224.

34. Erna Hooghiemstra, "Gemengd huwen en transnationaal huwen in Nederland: enkele feiten," *Migrantenstudies* 16, no. 4 (2000).

35. Benedict Anderson, *Long-Distance Nationalism. World capitalism and the rise of identity politics* (Amsterdam: Centre for Asian Studies Amsterdam, 1992); Anthony Alessandrini, "'My Heart's Indian for All That': Bollywood Film between Home and Diaspora," *Diaspora* 10, no. 3 (2001).

36. Cf. Alejandro Portes and Rubén G. Rumbaut, *Legacies. The story of the immigrant second generation* (Berkeley and New York: University of California Press and Russell Sage Foundation, 2001), 147-91.

37. Cf. Hans Vermeulen, *Etnisch-culturele diversiteit als 'feit' en norm* (Amsterdam: Vossiuspers UvA, 2001), 14.

38. Cf. Eric R. Wolf, "Perilous Ideas: Race, Culture, People," *Current Anthropology* 35, no. 1 (1994), 6.

39. Vermeulen, *Etnisch-culturele diversiteit*, 15.

40. See for example, Alba and Nee, *Remaking*; Nancy Foner, *From Ellis Island to JFK: New York's Two Great Waves of Immigration* (New Haven and New York: Yale University Press and Russell Sage Foundation 2000); Kasinitz, Waters, and Mollenkopf, "Becoming American"; Portes, Guarnizo, and Landholt, "The study"; Levitt and Waters, *The changing face*.

41. Cf. Ewa Morawska, "Immigrant transnationalism and assimilation: a variety of combinations and the analytic strategy it suggests," in *Toward Assimilation and Citizenship: Immigrants in Liberal Nation-state*, ed. Christian Joppke and Ewa Morawska (New York: Palgrave Macmillan, 2003), 133-76

42. Kasinitz, Waters, Mollenkopf, and Anil, "Transnationalism," 99.

Bibliography

Amersfoort, Hans van, and Mies van Niekerk. "Immigration as a Colonial Inheritance: Post-Colonial Immigrants in the Netherlands, 1945-2002." *Journal of Ethnic and Migration Studies* 32, no. 3 (April 2006): 323-46.

Alba, Richard D., and Victor Nee. *Remaking the American Mainstream. Assimilation and Contemporary Immigration*. Cambridge, Mass.: Harvard University Press, 2003.

Alessandrini, Anthony C., "'My Heart's Indian for all that': Bollywood Film between Home and Diaspora." *Diaspora* 10, no. 3 (2001): 315-340.

Anderson, Benedict. *Long-Distance Nationalism. World capitalism and the rise of identity politics*. Amsterdam: Centre for Asian Studies Amsterdam, 1992.

Biervliet, Willem. "The hustler culture of young unemployed Surinamers." Pp. 191-201 in *Adaptation of Migrants from the Caribbean in the European and American Metropolis*, edited by Humphrey E. Lamur and John D. Speckmann. Leiden and Amsterdam: Royal Institute of Linguistics and Department of Anthropology and Non-Western Sociology, 1975.

Buiks, Peter E. J. *Surinaamse jongeren op de Kruiskade. Overleven in een etnische randgroep*. Deventer, NL: Van Loghum Slaterus, 1983.

Choenni, Chan E. S. "Maatschappelijke positie van Hindostanen." Pp. 70-89 in: *Hindostanen. Van Brits-Indische emigranten via Suriname tot burgers van Nederland*, edited by Chan E. S. Choenni and Kanta Sh. Adhin. The Hague: Sampreshan, 2003.

DeWind, Josh, Charles Hirschman, and Philip Kasinitz, eds. "Immigrant adaptation and native-born responses in the making of Americans." Special Issue *International Migration Review* 31, no. 4 (1997).

Foner, Nancy. *From Ellis Island to JFK: New York's Two Great Waves of Immigration*. New Haven and New York: Yale University Press and Russell Sage Foundation, 2000.

Fouron, Georges, and Nina Glick-Schiller. "The generation of identity: Redefining the second generation within a transnational social field." Pp. 168-210 in *The Changing Face of Home. The Transnational Lives of the Second Generation*, edited by Peggy Levitt and Mary C. Waters. New York: Russell Sage Foundation, 2002.

Gans, Herbert J. "Symbolic Ethnicity: The Future of Ethnic Groups and Cultures in America." *Ethnic and Racial Studies* 2 (1979): 1-20.

Gowricharn, Ruben S., and John Schuster. "Diaspora and Transnationalism: The case of the Surinamese in the Netherlands." Pp. 155-73 in *20th Century Surinam. Continuities and discontinuities in a new world society*, edited by Rosemarijn Hoefte, and Peter Meel. Kingston and Leiden: Ian Randle Publishers and KITLV Press, 2001.

Hira, Sandew. *Terug naar Uttar Pradesh: Op zoek naar de wortels van de Surinaamse Hindoestanen*. The Hague: Amrit, 2000

Hooghiemstra, Erna. "Gemengd huwen en transnationaal huwen in Nederland: enkele feiten." *Migrantenstudies* 16, no. 4 (2000): 198-208.

Kasinitz, Philip, Mary C. Waters, and John Mollenkopf. "Becoming American/Becoming New Yorkers: Immigrant Incorporation in a Majority Minority City." *International Migration Review* 36, no. 4 (2002), 1020-36.

Kasinitz, Philip, Mary C. Waters, and John Mollenkopf, Merih Anil. "Transnationalism and the children of immigrants in contemporary New York." Pp. 96-122 in *The Changing Face of Home. The Transnational Lives of the Second Generation*, edited by Peggy Levitt and Mary C. Waters. New York: Russell Sage Foundation, 2002.

Levitt, Peggy, and Mary C. Waters, eds. *The changing face of home. The transnational lives of the second generation.* New York: Russell Sage Foundation, 2002.

Martens, Edwin P., and Arjen O. Verweij. *Surinamers in Nederland. Kerncijfers 1996.* Rotterdam: Institute for Sociological and Economic Research, Erasmus University, 1997.

Morawska, Ewa. "Immigrant transnationalism and assimilation: a variety of combinations and the analytic strategy it suggests." Pp. 133-76 in *Toward Assimilation and Citizenship: Immigrants in Liberal Nation-state*, edited by Christian Joppke and Ewa Morawska. New York: Palgrave Macmillan, 2003.

Niekerk, Mies van. "Paradoxes in Paradise. Integration and social mobility of the Surinamese in the Netherlands." Pp. 64-92 in *Immigrant integration. The Dutch case*, edited by Hans Vermeulen and Rinus Penninx. Amsterdam: Het Spinhuis, 2000.

———. "Becoming Dutch and staying Surinamese: culture as a *way of life* and as a *lifestyle*." Pp. 179-92 in *Dedication & Detachment. Essays in Honour of Hans Vermeulen*, edited by Flip Lindo and Mies van Niekerk. Amsterdam: Het Spinhuis, 2001.

———. *Premigration Legacies and Immigrant Social Mobility. The Afro-Surinamese and Indo-Surinamese in the Netherlands.* Lanham, Md.: Lexington Books, 2002.

———. "Afro-Caribbeans and Indo-Caribbeans in the Netherlands. Premigration Legacies and Social Mobility." *International Migration Review* 38, no. 2 (2004): 158-83.

———. *Surinam Country Report. A part of the report on Informal Remittance Systems in Africa, Caribbean and Pacific (ACP) countries.* Oxford: Centre on Migration, Policy and Society (COMPAS), University of Oxford, United Kingdom, 2005. http://www.compas.ox.ac.uk/publications/papers/ Surinam%20050115.pdf.

Ogbu, John U. "Variability in Minority School Performance. A Problem in Search of an Explanation." *Anthropology and Education Quarterly* 18, no. 3 (1987): 312-34.

Perlmann, Joel, and Roger Waldinger. "Second Generation Decline? Children of Immigrants, Past and Present." *International Migration Review* 31, no. 4 (1997): 893-923.

Portes, Alejandro. "Children of immigrants. Segmented assimilation and its determinants." Pp. 248-80 in *The Economic Sociology of Immigration. Essays on Networks, Ethnicity, and Entrepreneurship*, edited by Alejandro Portes. New York: Russell Sage Foundation, 1995.

Portes, Alejandro, Luis E. Guarnizo, and Patricia Landholt. "The study of transnationalism: pitfalls and promise of an emergent research field." *Ethnic and Racial Studies* 22, no. 2 (1999): 217-231.

Portes, Alejandro, and Rubén G. Rumbaut, *Legacies. The story of the immigrant second generation.* Berkeley and New York: University of California Press and Russell Sage Foundation, 2001.

Sansone, Livio. *Schitteren in de schaduw. Overlevingsstrategieën, subcultuur en etniciteit van Creoolse jongeren uit de lagere klasse in Amsterdam 1981-1990.* Amsterdam: Het Spinhuis, 1992.

Tjon-A-Ten, Varina. "Creoolse en Hindoestaanse kinderen in het Nederlandse lager onderwijs." PhD Diss., University of Utrecht, 1987.

Waters, Mary C. *Ethnic Options: Choosing Identities in America.* Berkeley: University of California Press, 1990.

Wolf, Eric R. "Perilous Ideas: Race, Culture, People." *Current Anthropology* 35, no. 1 (1994): 1-12.

Vermeulen, Hans. *Etnisch-culturele diversiteit als "feit" en norm.* Amsterdam: Vossiuspers UvA, 2001.

Zhou, Min. "Segmented assimilation. Issues, controversies and recent research on the new second generation." *International Migration Review* 31, no. 4 (Winter 1997): 975-1008.

2

Bettina E. Schmidt

The Many Voices of Caribbean Culture in New York City[1]

Caribbean voices can be heard in New York City in various places, for instance during the Caribbean Carnival Parade in Brooklyn but also in a Mexican restaurant where the drums were beaten for Cuban orishas, in a theater where a performance include a welcome of Haitian loas, on the streets in Spanish Harlem where a social center is opened by an offering to the Afro-Caribbean deities, and even in the American Museum of Natural History where a exhibition explains the history of Haitian religiosity. I will explore in this chapter what corresponds with the term trans-Caribbean in New York City. One question will be to investigate how Caribbean migrants living in New York City construe their identity and the elements they include and reject. In order to answer this question one should also include the experiences of the next generation of migrants from the Caribbean and the ways in which they construe their identity and a sense of Caribbean culture. Together these will tell us about the construction of Caribbean culture in New York City.

My chapter is based on research among Caribbean religious communities in New York City conducted in Brooklyn and other areas of the city. I started my fieldwork in February 1998 with a short preparation period in which I made initial contact to religious communities of Afro-Cuban Santería, Haitian Vodou, and Shango from Trinidad and Tobago. In September of the same year I returned to the city for my main research period. While I taught at the City University of New York in Brooklyn, I spent most of my time in Caribbean New York. I participated at religious ceremonies during the weekend and spoke with believers and other experts, but I also went to secular places where I could find representations of Caribbean religions, for instance theaters, workshops, museums, dance schools, and pubs where the drums were beaten and the ceremonial dances performed.[2] As I realized, all had a connection to Caribbean culture and served in one way or another to create a (trans-)Caribbean identity. How might we describe these experiences theoretically? In order to find a solution I looked on the debate about cultural mixture and mixing developed in the area of the world that experienced mixing par excellence, the Caribbean and Latin America. Hence, my chapter will start with a short overview about theories developed by scholars in these areas. Though I will refer also to some scholars from the Caribbean diaspora, my main focus is on theories developed from the perspective of the periphery, hence on the work of those based in Mexico, Cuba, Martinique and other marginalized areas in the Caribbean and Latin America.

Based on this discourse I developed my own concept of polyphonic bricolage which will be presented in the second part of this chapter. The term "bricolage" indicates that a culture is never completed, but in an ongoing state of change while the term "polyphonic" illustrates that such a concept has to be described by many voices equally valued instead of creating an idea of a homogenous entity. By applying the concept of polyphony to bricolage I include the perspective of Caribbean migrants in my interpretation. I argue that their perspectives which are often ignored by Western theorists should be used as equivalent to theoretical standpoints. Hence the third part of the chapter will present some of my observations and experiences living in Caribbean New York. I will refer to my research among Caribbean religious communities in New York City and to cultural events such as the Caribbean carnival in Brooklyn in 1999. My perspective will be on the creation of a trans-Caribbean community and the experiences of the next generation of migrants. I will conclude with bringing all levels together—and separating them again.

Mestizaje, hybridization and creolization: Theories about cultural mixture

Caribbean and Latin American cultures were often used as a base for developing theories of cultural mixture. As Magnus Mörner writes, "no part of the world has ever witnessed such a gigantic mixing of races as the one that has been taken place in Latin America and the Caribbean since 1492."[3] And this process continues and develops very diverse mixtures. Not only has the colonial mixture of indigenous, African and European cultures developed differently in each country, contemporary influences such as migration movements and new communication media change every country in its own way.

The starting point of theories about the mixture of cultures was biological: the mixture of races is based on a mixture of cultures: or, the other way around, the mixture of races results in a mixture of cultures. In the colonial period, mestizos were regarded as weak, barbarous, uncivilized, and also terrifying and beastly. They were illegitimate, without the rights of their Spanish parents though on the social ladder higher than indigenous people. Even in the second half of the nineteenth century, mestizos were made culpable for social and political defects of the new republics because of their weak character.[4] This shifted after Word War II with mestizos glorified by intellectuals as national symbols, albeit not as subjects.[5] The ideology of mestizaje was used to confirm similarity while hiding the diversity of different groups in a homogenous national society.[6] Out of the critique of mestizaje, Latin American theorists construed new concepts based on a concept of cultural heterogeneity. In contrast to mestizaje, cultural heterogeneity pointed to the social situation of indigenous people and questioned the traditional theory of mixture. Instead of describing a future assimilation of marginalized groups, theorists began to praise cultural diversity. Néstor García Canclini's concept of the *culturas híbridas* criticizes the dichotomy of tradition and modern or rural and urban, and argues that they cannot describe the cultural diversity of the national culture and its de-centralistic structure.[7] In order to characterize the intercultural mixtures, in particular in urban settings, he uses the term hybridity though without its negative connotation.[8] Drawing on the definition of hybridity developed in literary studies,[9] García Canclini regards hybridity as a creative concept which illustrates the mixture and dynamic interaction between mass culture, popular culture and so-called "high culture." As Raymondo Mier writes, "the idea of hybrid cultures [. . .] permits the imagination of social morphologies, fields of singularized regularity, designations of catastrophe, but a catastrophe that is not a limiting border, a mere point of singularity, the space of a fracture."[10]

Recently, Aisha Khan presented another contribution into this debate of hybridity though she does not engage García Canclini and the Latin American debate, an approach quite common among theorists working in similar areas but divided by language barriers. Though Khan acknowledges at the beginning that "mixing" is "among the most preserving of cultural themes in most Caribbean and Latin American countries,"[11] she refers to national ideologies such as creolite, embranquecimento and mestizaje but not to the cultural concepts developed by scholars from these countries. Her starting point is mixing as metaphor which she then discusses within the Anglo-American debate. Nonetheless, her cultural trope "callaloo" is an interesting contribution to the debate about cultural concepts. Khan distinguishes between mixing and articulation. While the first refers to the empirical manifestation of mixing challenging the national ideologies, the latter is an analytical device, the theoretical framework with which Khan wants to "identify and explain the connections among domains (such as "race" and "religion") that are typically submerged within the mixing metaphors that express them."[12] Hence, mixing can be expressed, felt and lived while articulation adds the meaning and significance. Khan's Trinidadian case study illustrates a process which García Canclini has already described in urban Mexico. While former theorists have referred to colonial time, García Canclini and Khan investigate postmodern MTV- and MacDonald-societies and the influences of globalization and new communication media.

A different approach to the debate about cultural mixtures can be summarized under the term creolization that has enriched the theoretical debate in particular in the Caribbean but also beyond. Despite the similarities there are two different definitions of creolization based on a different colonial attitude. While in the Spanish context *criollo* described someone born in the colonies, in the French context *creole* indicated generally a racial category for persons of mixed racial descent. The different derivation of Creole still leads to confusion within the debate about creolization or *créolité* as a cultural term. While some scholars understand creolization as a linguistic term, others use it in the sense of the Spanish colonial period and again others as a synonym for mixture or hybridity. It often indicates a pejorative connotation with respect to a superior category whether European culture, a biological or a linguistic "purity."[13] Nevertheless, Caribbean scholars support the use of the term creolization but with a specific meaning with Caribbean discourse. Creolization then describes a positive process despite its violent origin because it demonstrates the fundamental experience of the New World.

The Cuban scholar Antonio Benítez Rojo belongs to the branch of scholars using creolization in the Spanish colonial sense. His definition of creolization is based on the original meaning of "people of Spanish descent born in the colonies." Already living with various restrictions, they did not need to follow the strict orders of the motherland and could live much more freely than the *peninsulares*, their Spanish neighbors born in Spain. Hence, he argues that the *cultura criolla* was construed at the periphery of the plantation economy and not inside the slavery system.[14] Benítez Rojo regards the juxtaposition of equal parts and their constantly renewed interweaving as a typical Caribbean practice, which is manifested in Cuban literature as well as in Cuban religion. He opposes the characterization of creolization as a process because a process means development, but creolization is "a discontinuous series of recurrences, of happenings, whose sole law is change."[15] Because he localizes the *cultura criolla* outside of the plantation, a place of violent suppression, he breaks the Caribbean out of the "model of discourse and anti-discourse, of repression and opposition" and argues at the same time against a synthetic, homogeneous cultural concept. Benítez Rojo argues that even in the concept of transculturation developed by his Cuban processor Fernando Ortiz in his book *Contrapunteo del tabaco y el azúcar* (1940) one can find a perfect example of the *cultura criolla*.

Ortiz's concept of transculturation can be regarded as an early contribution to the debate about culture mixture. He described Cuban cultural history as a process of assimilation of European and African influences. Similar to Benítez Rojo Ortiz connected this process to the tobacco industry instead of to the slave plantations. Tobacco becomes the point of reference outside the sugar plantations, hence the place where social practices could be situated which were different from the repressive, capitalistic sugar plantations as Sabine Hofmann writes.[16] Ortiz creates therefore a dichotomy between sugar and tobacco, between suppression by slavery and creativity by acculturation. According to Ortiz only the tobacco was able to create Cuban identity by mixing European and African elements together. Hence cultural freedom of expression was possible only outside the slavery system.[17] For Manuel Moreno Fraginals, who later elaborated Ortiz's concept by describing a complex process of transculturation and deculturation,[18] the sugar-plantations became even a place of deculturation where the African slaves had no opportunity to celebrate their cultural traditions.

A totally different view takes Édouard Glissant, who regards creolization from the plantation perspective, that is, from the perspective of suppression and uprooting. Glissant argues that there is no *discours antillais* outside the plantation. Even Maroons, the runaway slaves, as representatives of an opposite culture stand in relation to the plantation, the place of the creation of Creole culture. Glissant construes his concept of diversity with reference to the experience of the inhabitants of the Caribbean, mainly the "deported" and "imported" persons, that is, Arawaks, Caribs and African slaves. Glissant defines creolization as an experience of diversity as well as a process that was for a long time unnoticed: "Creolization is not an uprooting, a loss of sight, a suspension of being. Transcience is not wandering. Diversity is not dilution."[19] Glissant limits the process of creolization to areas where the plantation was a central element because the problem of the inhabitants of the plantations was "to give legitimacy to this new dimension of human nature they constitute, the dimension of exchange and mutual change, in a world in which apartheid and racism still rule and dominate."[20] Glissant argues within a temporal continuum. He wants to improve the world, while Benítez Rojo does not want to create a new vision of the future, but offers another way of reading Creole cultures. Benítez Rojo localizes his remarks in a place instead of a time. Despite the differing approaches, both concepts regard culture as "anti-centric structures" without a firm order, but based on an interconnection of various orders, which lead to new, unpredictable phenomena.

Based on this discourse one can understand why Jean Bernabé, Patrick Chamoiseau and Raphaël Confiant begin their *Éloge de la Créolité* with the proud statement: "Neither Europeans, nor Africans, nor Asians, we proclaim ourselves Creoles."[21] The three authors see *creole* identity as the cement of Caribbean culture.[22] Though they argue based on Glissant, Glissant always emphasized the un-finished process of creolization, in opposition to a product such as créolité. Following this lead, Kathleen Balutansky and Marie-Agnès Sourieau recognize in their definition a quite static effort to determine the origin or authenticity of creolization. In opposition to Bernabé, Chamoiseau and Confiant the two authors Balutansky and Sourieau stress the endless transformation process when they define creolization as a syncretic process of transverse dynamics that endlessly reworks and transforms the cultural patterns of varied social and historical experiences and identities.[23] Some cultural theorists go even further than Balutansky and Sourieau and transfer creolization to settings outside the Caribbean. For instance, Ulf Hannerz regards the concept of creolization as global processes. He considers Creole cultures—as Creole languages—"intrinsically of mixed origin, the confluence of two or more widely separate historical currents which interact in what is basically a centre/periphery relationship."[24] Creole cultures have grown over a long period of time, during which they have developed a degree of coherence. Creole cultures have an uninterrupted spectrum of forms of interaction that are visible and active together with several historical sources of the culture.

Polyphonic bricolage

As one can see from this short overview about cultural theories developed in the Caribbean and Latin America, the central point in the debate is the mixture of cultures. The theories stress different aspects and present a variety of ideas, some contradictory, others supplementary. Most of them emphasize the often static imagined—result instead of locking on the creation process. Mestizaje for instance implies cultural homogeneity directed to the assimilation of the foreign though this process neglects the particularity of the other. The theory of hybridization—construed as a counter strategy—emphasizes the incorporation of cultural elements in a dominant system that they will enrich. Though hybridization implies a permanent process of new orientation, it still includes a centralistic perspective. However, though cultures need a framework to arrange new elements, they do not need centralistic structures. Creolization, finally, locates the process of mixture in a specific place, the plantation, the place of slavery (Glissant), or at the border of the plantation, the mines (Benítez Rojo) or tobacco (Ortiz).

All theories have in common the critique of bi-polar models, the dialectical confrontation of modern/tradition, urban/rural, and consequently the idea of an original purity of two opposite categories. The scholars developing these theories focus on mixture instead of origins, although some seem to underemphasize or ignore the perspective of the operative subject. Increasingly, theories emphasize the location of the mixture, and begin to detect ethnographic reality.

Nevertheless, despite the differences, these models have a monologic perspective in common that creates the impression that the members of a group speak with one voice. The theories often neglect that a number of individuals construe a culture speaking with different but equivalent voices. Identity has to be continuously negotiated, in a process that never ends. A cultural concept should include a polyphonic[25] perspective as I recently suggested.[26]

The foundation is the concept of bricolage by Claude Lévi-Strauss, though I use the term bricolage in a more elaborate sense.[27] It represents a culture that is composed of elements of different cultural origin. But these original cultures are not considered as authentically homogenous. There are not such closed entities as "the European culture," or "the African culture" or "the indigenous culture."

Richard Werbner defines bricolage as "the formation of fresh cultural forms from the ready-to-hand debris of old forms."[28] However, as many other scholars, he then reduces the schema of Lévi-Strauss to only one aspect, the mixture, and disregards Lévi-Strauss' intention to illustrate with the term bricolage a special form of thinking and doing. The term bricolage draws our attention to the process and in particular to the active part of the cultural brokers. They are the ones who construct the culture in a never-ending process with the elements at hand, local and global influences as well as individual desires and political intentions. Even political power struggle is therefore part of this creation process.

All elements are combined in an anti-central structure as we learned from the creolization debate. Important elements can become decorative ones, or even vanish in another moment. There are only few fixed elements (for instance, the reference to the Caribbean area) surrounded by constantly diverse combined elements. These elements can even change their meaning as I argue in distinction to Roger Bastide.

Bastide, who transplanted the term bricolage into Afro-American studies, understands bricolage as a process that construes out of a disparate ensemble a new meaning without changing the significance of the elements. He illustrates his assumption with reference to Afro-American societies. According to Bastide they sought new images to fill the gaps produced by slavery, not through adaptation of elements but through a specific way of organization, hence by bricolage.[29] Hence, Bastide—though he illustrates the dynamic movement of the creating process so precisely—remains in a static frame when he insists on the unchangeable meaning of the elements. I argue instead that the cultural agencies have the power to use the elements in the way they intend, even by altering the original meaning.

The meaning as well as the composition of the elements changes depending on the situation, location, time and the creators of the culture. Hence, a culture of a group differs for each member. Each person focuses on different elements and in an individual way. Bastide stresses the importance of local influences and declares that this process is not mechanical but depends on situation, time and environment and therefore constantly renews itself. Bricolage arises therefore in a permanent movement; it ends and begins again, without losing its verve. The process of bricolage includes a view of society, which can manipulate the group and has an important influence on the composition of the handicraft, the culture.

Consequently, it is possible to include foreign elements whenever a member of a group comes in contact with foreign influences and considers them as important. Also, it is possible to exclude old elements whenever they are losing importance for the majority of the members. Bricolage does not imply the mixture of two or three cultures but the rearrangement of elements of diverse origin.

The central characteristics of polyphonic bricolage are therefore the following: The central point of reference is the members of a culture, the so-called bricoleurs, who assemble the culture in their one way, according to their wishes and expectation. Hence, they work autonomously. Though the society or part of it can influence the process, the exchange of elements depends on the wishes of the group itself. It is even possible that the composition changes in opposition to the dominant society, not because of the pressure, but in spite of it. Nevertheless, the location influences the bricoleurs. They alter their culture when they move into new surroundings to adjust to the new environment as one can observe with every migration. Each culture has a close relationship to its ethnographic location, to its local environment while universal models tend to reduce a culture. We have therefore to distinguish between Caribbean New York, Caribbean London or Caribbean Berlin and should avoid referring to the Caribbean diaspora in general. Even in the United States there are fundamentally differences between, for instance, Caribbean communities in Miami and New York City.

The different surroundings lead to the creation of different cultures because the "elements at hand" differ from location to location. Members of a group include new elements into their cultural repertoire when they become aware of the significance of these innovations; hence the elements have to become visible for the members who then have to acknowledge the relevance of the elements for them in the specific situation. The location of the creation of new cultures is therefore at the borderline between different groups, the best place for exchange. Polyphonic bricolage implies the existence of multiple solutions, hence multiple mixtures. While in some moments it is important for the members of a group to express the borderline, hence to exclude other people, it can become important to embrace the other in another moment or by another group. The composition of a culture illustrates the perspective of the members on the world and on themselves. Elements that one member stresses in opposition to other members, point toward his or her perspective and are important for the analysis of the culture, not only of individual decorations. In this process the sensual perception of the cultural elements, in particular the music, dance and other aesthetic decorations, can become relevant for the dialogue between member and non-members, observer and participants because it leads to the direct exchange of elements. Both the acceptance and the rejection of elements enable the interaction that in turn creates a new orientation of the culture.

This flexibility leads to the existence of different statements for the same culture. Instead of an abstract, homogenous concept of culture, each situation allows different (and equivalent) solutions. As Bakhtin wrote with regard to Dostoevsky's work, polyphony indicates that the different voices interact on equal terms; hence we have to be aware of the "multivoicedness of all discourse."[30] Consequently, bricolage can be understood only in relationship to the bricoleur, the operating subject. Every innovative process is inseparably combined with the innovative actor as for example Terence Turner writes.[31] While the members of a group should be in the center of a cultural model, their position has to be reflected in relationship to their position to other members.

This list of characteristics only describes the central aspects of cultural systems, the cornerstones. Nevertheless, it challenges the very popular notion to compare a culture with a mosaic of colorful stones. As the do-it-yourselfer is never satisfied with the result and always tries to alter something, the composition of a culture is a never-ending process. The term "bricolage" indicates that a culture is never completed, but in an ongoing state of change while the term "polyphonic" shows that such a concept has to be described by many voices instead of focusing only on formal elements. Hence, the list of characteristics can also never be complete.

Caribbean culture(s) in New York City: Negotiating Caribbean identity

Caribbean culture in New York City illustrates these characteristics. It integrates elements of diverse origins such as Dominican, Haitian, Cuban, and Jamaican and so on; and these elements are combined in the new surroundings of New York City. Caribbean culture in New York City is not, however, a more or less homogenous mixture of elements from these islands. The parameters of the group—if such a group exists—include the migrants and their next generation, but can also be more expansively defined. While I was working, for instance, about Caribbean religious communities in New York City, I became aware of an increasing influence of African-Americans and even European-Americans joining Caribbean migrants in religious ceremonies. These new believers do not only participate in the ceremonies, they sometimes become members of the community and influence the creation of a new bricolage. Nevertheless, one has to acknowledge that all members interpret their culture quite diversely and individually. Each member marks different fixed aspects of their culture, sometimes language, history, political conflicts or sometimes popular religiosity, depending on the place they live, the aims they are fighting for, the situation they have to cope, and the borders they want to construct. Consequently, they sometimes struggle with each other about the dominant feature of the bricolage. African-Americans, for instance, who join the Cuban religion Santería, reject the Catholic elements of the Afro-Cuban religion and try to clean the religion from its Catholic iconography though, at the end, Santería is still a predominantly Cuban religion and Cuban priests decide in which direction the religion should develop.

Africa is, of course, a main point of reference of Caribbean culture all over the world though with an important difference. While Africa is of central significance for all people of African descent, Caribbean migrants always put Africa in relation to the Caribbean area as the real origin of bricolage. For Caribbean migrants the culturally diverse Caribbean islands are the central aspect of Caribbean culture in New York; even the second and third generations consider themselves as Caribbeans with New York City as their home though the significance of Africa increases in the diaspora.[32]

One main attraction of Caribbean religion as well as Caribbean culture is the aesthetic dimension, the music, dance and other aesthetic elements. Because they are important for the interaction with outsiders, they are also important for the redefinition of Caribbean culture. While some groups position themselves in opposition to outsiders, others integrate along with foreign persons new elements into their cultural repertoire, new movements, new music and sometimes even new spirits. The decision about acceptance or rejection is made by the group itself; even when this means that the group divides into two parts because some members are against new elements.

This leads to another aspect, the interaction with society. The Caribbean representatives in New York City demonstrate a great flexibility in handling society or the dominant part of society. Even if they act under pressure, they may achieve short and long term benefits, as another example with regard to Caribbean religions illustrates: When the animal protection group started to harass Cuban santeros in Florida because animal sacrifices are a main part of the rituals, Cuban santeros fought against the ban with legal steps. At the end, they went to the Supreme Court in Washington, D.C., which lifted the ban because the santeros could provide proof of the ritual significance of the sacrifices. This success strengthened the position of the Cuban priests in Florida but also of Caribbean religions in general in the United States.

These aspects represent the structure of Caribbean cultural bricolage in New York City. Now we have to switch to the polyphonic level and include the voices into the concept. While the structure can be transferred to any other cultural context and will present a frame also to include other migrants' experiences, the ethnographic reality will carry Caribbean aspects. As I explained above cultural homogeneity is just an academic construct. Cultures represent multiple spheres, full of breaks, contradictions and in an ongoing dynamic process of change. Caribbean voices can be found in New York City in diverse places and situation. When I started my investigation in New York—still during the period of preparation—I was invited by a Puerto Rican drummer who performed at Santería ceremonies in New York, to come and meet him in a Mexican restaurant in Queens. Together with Cuban and Puerto Rican musicians he played Latin rhythms every first Monday at this place, sometimes even the ritual music of the orishas. Our second meeting—after I returned to New York for a longer period of time—was in a Cuban Chinese restaurant where I learned more about his involvement in New York Santería. Even those places are part of Caribbean New York.

At this point I will move to a different but important public performance of Caribbeanness in New York City: the Caribbean Carnival Parade in Brooklyn celebrated on Labor Day Monday in September. Here we can observe the negotiating of Caribbeanness par excellence. The term Caribbeanness indicates the identification with the Caribbean, hence the positive affirmation of Caribbean identity, expressed by various elements depending on the group and the situation they are in (in the manner described above with regard to the concept bricolage). But what is meant by "Caribbean" in Brooklyn? Is it really a Caribbean carnival with people from all Caribbean islands or only an ethnic parade of people from the West Indies, hence the Anglophone islands, as the official term *West Indian American Day Carnival* indicates? An answer to this question can bring information about who is allowed to perform and who is not. Since 1969 the *West Indian American Day Carnival* is celebrated with a public parade in Brooklyn. Philip Kasinitz writes about the central meaning of the parade that "[t]he dramatic structure of [such] celebrations [...] serves to interweave the interests of the group with the careers of individual politicians. [...] The Parade presents the image of a unified people marching *behind* their leaders."[33] Nowadays, the parade attracts more than three million visitors, mainly people with Caribbean connections living in the surrounding of New York City or in nearby Canadian towns. It is the biggest gathering of Caribbean people outside the Caribbean though it already has developed to become a tourist spectacle. In particular in election years it draws the attention of political parties whose candidates learned that it is political suicide to ignore the powerful number of Caribbean voters.

However, a closer look beyond the public parade shows that it still fails to represent trans-Caribbean identity. In distinction to the Caribbean carnival in London[34] the Brooklyn parade has still managed (more or less) to combine Calypso and Reggae; hence it has still avoided breaking in two sections, one for people from Trinidad/Tobago and one for Jamaicans. Though Jamaica is still underrepresented—in the carnival organization committee as well as during the parade[35]—, both music styles, hence both traditions, are present during the parade, together, of course, with modern music fashions. While the Brooklyn carnival therefore managed to join different traditions together, non-Anglophone styles, in particular Latin rhythms and French Caribbean beats, are still excluded. The West Indian American Day Carnival Association (WIADCA) which controls the organization of the parade still rejects the performance of non-Anglophone music groups. Even the early morning celebration of Jouvert, a traditional part of Carnival which was introduced in Brooklyn in opposition to the commercialized parade, is still a Trinidadian (or better: Trinbagonian) performance. Though Jouvert—the farewell of carnival at dawn—is celebrated, for instance, in Haiti, too, Haitian groups are not welcomed, not because of the quality of their performance but because of their nationality as I was told by the manager of a Haitian band.[36]

On the other hand, the organizers of both the parade and Jouvert recognize of course the development of a Caribbean community in New York above national identities. In 1998 and again in 1999 (though less dominant), the shameful torture of Abner Louima, a Haitian migrant, in a police station in Brooklyn in 1997 was openly represented during the parade. The parade became a way to challenge the police force from an underdog position. This episode reflects the growing political dimension of the Caribbean community in New York. Though cultural barriers between English and French speaking Caribbean migrants still prevent the creation of a real trans-Caribbean community, the representatives of the distinctive groups know of the importance of having allies in political fights. In the 1980s, when Kasinitz looked at the tensions between African-Americans and West Indians represented at the carnival, he illustrated the ways in which political issues enabled them overcome their problems. More recently, political issues also suggest a route to challenging possible barriers between diverse Caribbean communities, extending even to the overcoming of language barriers as the integration of Haitian groups in 2004 already indicates. The question remains what the second and third generations will do.

In contrast to the first generation, second-generation descendants are familiar with the life in New York City; the next generation from the non-Anglophone Caribbean is even bilingual. Their understanding of the Caribbean is based on the imagination of their parents. It is often their parents' image of "home" which is transferred to the next generation, not their own personal experience or otherwise collected knowledge. Sometimes the first visit of the place their parents call "home" results in a break with the family because of disappointment. Some of the younger generation had to realize that "home" never existed but in the imagination of their parents.

Nevertheless, the Caribbean islands remain "home" even for the second and third generation. Despite of their disapproval of the construed images of the parents, the children still feel a strong belonging to the Caribbean as I observe several times and at different places though some are looking for a Caribbean feeling in different places. For instance, young Caribbean students take classes in Caribbean music and dance or go to workshops outside the colleges to learn more—or at least something—about the Caribbean. For them the national division of the Caribbean ceased to exist. Trans-Caribbean represents a new sphere, a kind of counter-culture that offers an alternative or sometimes even an opposition to the American mainstream society. Some even join Caribbean religious communities such as for example Haitian Vodou temples or casa de santos of Cuban/Puerto Rican Santería. The rituals present a different, esthetic link to the Caribbean. They offer a new stage for individual performance to the second and third generation who often grew up relatively unaware of Caribbean religious traditions. While the popular religions are sometimes regarded as being backward or savage, in particular by migrants who have vehemently embraced the offer of modernity of their new destination, this image becomes less important for the second and third generations. The religious traditions receive the quality of "folklore" as a marker of ethnic barriers. Folklore receives in this perspective a positive connotation. While in Latin America, for instance, "folklorization" of marginalized cultures within a national context supported the ongoing discrimination of these people, in North America the self-identification to be member of an ethnic group goes often hand in hand with the self-identification with a distinctive folklore. Some festival events become touchstones for the strength and cohesion of an ethnic group. American society has—as Geneviève Fabre writes—a tradition of public and dramatic, visual and tangible reenactment of its history "which has been a crucial instrument for the reconstruction and reevaluation of its past and its culture."[37] These visual events are not only important for the mainstream society but for ethnic communities too who create "their own cycle of ritualized events."[38]

Consequently, the ability to perform the dances of the Caribbean deities is nothing to be ashamed of (as it is for Haitian upper class); on the contrary, more and more young Haitians join dance groups to perform the dances on stage (outside a ritual context). In New York City it is possible to serve the orishas or loas and still be a member of the modern society because modernity can embrace local traditions. New York City allows the free expression of very different cultures and life styles; being a New Yorker therefore includes the notion of being different. This diversity of cultural forms makes one of the characteristics of the urban culture of New York City. According to Werner Schiffauer, who investigated Berlin and Turkish towns, three elements define urban culture: an internal heterogeneity, openness towards the outside world and the phenomenon of what he calls with reference to Ulf Hannerz "critical masses."[39] New York City represents all three of them. But one can even characterize the New York trans-Caribbean culture with these three elements. The internal heterogeneity indicate the wide range of different Caribbean identities; Jamaicans, Haitians, Cubans, Dominicans, Puerto Ricans, people from Trinidad and Tobago, Martinique and Saint Lucia—all are part of Caribbean New York Caribbean. The common element is the connection to the Caribbean islands however distant this connection is. The voices speak in different languages and stress very different aspects of Caribbean identity. In spite of power relations and political conflicts (e.g., Haitians and Dominicans still disagree about the massacre under Trujillo even in New York City), the voices (sometimes) join in political battle against the U.S. mainstream society. Yet the co-operation in certain situations may not conceal the social and political differences between and within the communities.

New York Caribbean diversity is not a harmonious one, rather a heterogeneous and diverse assemble full of conflict and disagreement. The internal heterogeneity that Schiffauer marks as one characteristic of urban culture is still under construction inside the Caribbean community; I even presume that it will never reach the quality Schiffauer described for the urban cultures he studied (in particular Berlin). Instead by "internal heterogeneity" trans-Caribbean culture can be characterized by bricolage, an ensemble of many voices, many flavors connected by the image of Caribbean islands. However, the openness towards the outside world is indeed a characteristic of the urban Caribbean culture in New York City. Even people without Caribbean background are accepted if they want, and are offered, for instance, ritual lineage as a new link to the Caribbean.

Schiffauer's third element, the "critical masses" is an important aspect of public life in all global cities, in particular in New York City. As the example of the protest against mistreatment of a Haitian migrant illustrated, the Caribbean carnival in Brooklyn offers Caribbean migrants the space to create a social group based on common political interest.

Conclusion

In my chapter I argue against the notion to create a homogenous image of culture. Nonetheless, I frequently used the expression trans-Caribbean culture as if there is such a homogenous entity. It seems that I entrapped myself in the seductive notion of Caribbean culture despite my statement that I want to challenge the notion of many theorists to create standardized concepts of culture. When I speak about trans-Caribbean I am arguing against boundaries. As David Lehmann writes about the Western globalization debate, I argue that we must avoid prejudging boundaries in order to understand them. National boundaries are not suitable starting points of investigations, and even other boundaries (as racial, ethnic and religious) "should not be described as if they were ready made and to be taken for granted."[40] Ready-made categories conceal vast differences between people, also within Caribbean New York. What is a Dominican, Haitian, Puerto Rican, Cuban, and Jamaican and so on? In particular when we realize how many of the second and third generations have parents with mixed ethnic background, this question becomes impossible to answer. What ethnic identity has a girl whose father is Haitian and her mother is African-American or Latina? How does she identify herself? The answer depends on various aspects and contexts. Nevertheless, as soon as she joins a Vodou temple she continues to stress her Haitian heritage as I have observed it in New York City. The decision to join a religious community goes hand in hand with a new self-identification with Caribbean descent. For decades Caribbean religions such as Vodou and Santería spread throughout the world. Vodou ceremonies are performed nowadays not only in New York and Haiti but in Quebec, France and every place with a large Haitian community; Santería ceremonies in Spain, Venezuela, Uruguay, Mexico and so on. However, in every city, at every location the performance has a slightly different meaning for the practitioners. Though the belief system is of course similar—the Vodou practice outside Haiti is based for instance on the urban version of Vodou of Port-au-Prince—the meaning for the individual is different. Santería for African-Americans differs fundamentally from the Cuban/Puerto Rican version; even the term Santería is rejected by many African-Americans because of its Catholic connotation as already mentioned above. People with European or Asian background also have another emphasis. We have to look behind boundaries, but also at how boundaries are created.

I presented in this chapter the concept of polyphonic bricolage as an alternative to the established models of hybridization and creolization and so on because it draws the attention to the process of mixing (bricolage) and to the multivoicedness of equivalent discourses (polyphonic). Bakhtin coined the term polyphony with reference to Dostoevsky though he later also portrayed Rabelais's work in a similar way without using the term again. Dostoevsky and Rabelais lived in ambivalent historical periods, Rabelais during the renaissance, "the only period in the history of European literature which marked the end of a church language and a linguistic transformation,"[41] and Dostoevsky during the "traumatic impact of capitalism upon Russian traditionalism in the early nineteenth century."[42] The same crossing of borderlines and conflicting views can be observed in Caribbean New York. Hence trans-Caribbean culture does not imply the mere co-existence of two or more cultures in New York City, but the self-consciousness of Caribbean New Yorkers, hence their awareness of borderlines within the community and in relation to the outside world. Caribbean New York creates a sphere for active plurality of ideas and cultures connected to the ability "to see one's own media from the outside, that is, through the eyes of other."[43] Hence, the creativity of a polyphonic culture in New York City is based not only on the arrival of the Caribbean migrants in New York City but on their interactions with their surroundings, their struggles with the neighborhoods and the other ethnic communities amongst whom they live and work, the dialog between the different communities as well as inside the Caribbean community itself. Polyphony does not indicate a perfect fixed system but a border zone with many voices which are equally valued.

Notes

1. A short version of this chapter was presented at the annual Conference of the Caribbean Studies Association in Santo Domingo in 2005. I am grateful to the British Academy and the Faculty of Theology of the University of Oxford for sponsoring my participation at this conference. I would also like to thank the participants of the panel as well as the reviewers of this chapter for their helpful comments.

2. Though I have been in the Caribbean several times before and after the research in New York City, this chapter is based on my experiences in the diaspora communities and the way in which they interact with their surroundings. I left New York in the summer of 2001, hence the chapter is based on New York before 9/11.

3. Magnus Mörner, *Race Mixture in the History of Latin America* (Boston: Little, Brown and Comp., 1967), 1.

4. See Peter Mason, *Deconstructing America: Representations of the Other* (London and New York: Routledge, 1990).

5. J. Jorge Klor de Alva, "The postcolonization of the (Latino) American experience: a reconsideration of 'colonialism,' 'postcolonialism,' and 'mestizaje,'" in

After Colonialism: Imperial History and Postcolonial Displacement, ed. Gyan Prakash (Princeton, N.J.: Princeton University Press, 1995), 241-75.

6. Martin Lienhard, "De mestizajes, heterogeneidades, hibridismos y otras quimeras," in *Asedios a la heterogenidad cultural: Libro de homenaje a Antonio Cornejo Polar*, ed. José Antonio Mazzotti and U. Juan Zevallo Aguilar (Philadelphia: Asociación Internacional de Peruanistas, 1996), 66-7.

7. Néstor García Canclini, *Culturas híbridas: estrategias para entrar y salir de la modernidad* (Mexico: Ed. Grijalbo, 1990), 265.

8. Homi K. Bhabha, for instance, introduced the term hybrid in relation to the colonial discourse as replacement for mimicry—Homi K. Bhabha, "Signs taken for wonders: questions of ambivalence and authority under a tree outside Delhi, May 1871," *Critical Inquiry* 12, no. 1 (1985): 154-55; Bhabha uses the term in a different meaning, based on the British tradition—see Robert J. C. Young, *Colonial Desire: Hybridity in Theory, Culture and Race* (London and New York: Routledge, 1995), for information about the British school.

9. García Canclini uses the term in the sense of Tzvetan Todorov who was inspired by Mikhail Bakhtin, the Russian literary studies scholar. Bakhtin deployed the term hybrid to designate the variety of ways of speaking in novels that is the mixture of styles and languages. Todorov elaborates the term in order to describe the bicultural situation of interaction that took place in America during the Spanish conquest, where the coexistence of two different cultural and language systems became possible. Hence, Todorov regards the successful interaction of two cultures as a hybrid result of this contact—see Tzvetan Todorov, "Le croisement des cultures," *Communications* 43, (1986): 20.

10. In Néstor García Canclini, "The hybrid: a conversation with Margarita Zires, Raymundo Mier, and Mabel Piccini," in *The Postmodernism Debate in Latin America*, ed. John Beverly, José Oviedo and Michael Aronna (Durham, N.C., and London: Duke University Press, 1995), 77.

11. Aisha Khan, *Callaloo Nation: Metaphors of Race and Religious Identity among South Asians in Trinidad* (Durham, N.C.: Duke University Press, 2004), 2.

12. Khan, *Callaloo*, 226.

13. André-Marcel d'Ans, "Créoles sans langue créole: les 'criollos' d'Hispano-Amérique," in *Contacts de langues, contacts de cultures, créolisation: mélanges offerts à Robert Chaudenson à l'occasion de son soixantième anniversaire*, ed. Maria-Christine Hazaël-Massieux and Didier de Robillard (Paris: L'Harmattan, 1997), 29-50.

14. Antonio Benítez Rojo, *La isla que se repite: El Caribe y la perspectiva podmoderna* (Hanover: Ed. del Norte, 1989), 18.

15. Antonio Benítez Rojo, "Three words toward creolization," in *Caribbean Creolization: Reflections on the Cultural Dynamics of Language, Literature, and Identity*, ed. Kathleen Balutansky and Marie-Agnés Sourieau. (Gainesville and Barbados: University Press of Florida and The Press University of the West Indies, 1998), 55.

16. Sabine Hofmann, "'La terre rhizomée' und 'La isla que se repite'—Poststrukturalistische Modelle bei Edouard Glissant und Antonio Benítez Rojo," in *Lateinamerika denken*, ed. Birgit Scharlau (Tübingen, Ger.: Narr, 1994), 257.

17. Fernando Ortiz, *Etnia y sociedad* (La Habana, Cuba: Editorial de Ciencias Sociales, 1993), 152-153.

18. Manuel Moreno Fraginals, "Apports culturels et déculturation," in *L'Afrique en Amérique Latine*, ed. Manuel Moreno Fraginals (Paris: UNESCO, 1984), 10.

19. Édouard Glissant, "Creolization in the making of the Americas," in *Race, Discourse, and the Origin of the Americas: A New World View*, ed. Vera Lawrence Hyatt and Rex Nettleford (Washington, D.C., and London: Smithsonian Institution Press, 1995), 269.
20. Glissant, "Creolization," 270.
21. Jean Bernabé, Patrick Chamoiseau and Raphaël Confiant, *Éloge de la créolité: in praise of creoleness* (Paris: Gallimard, 1993), 75.
22. With reference to Édouard Glissant, they demand to turn away from the Caribbean orientation towards France and to remember their own Creole culture, which they define as "the interactional or transactional aggregate of Caribbean, European, African, Asian, and Levantine cultural elements, united on the same oil by the yoke of history"—see Bernabé, Chamoiseau and Confiant, *Éloge*, 87.
23. Bernabé, Chamoiseau and Confiant, *Éloge*, 3
24. Ulf Hannerz, *Cultural Complexity: Studies in the Social Organization of Meaning* (New York: Columbia Univesity Press, 1992), 264.
25. The idea of polyphony is based on Mikhail Bakhtin and his literary studies (in particular his book about Dostoevsky, Mikhail Bakhin, *Problems of Dostoevsky's Poetics* (Manchester: Manchester University Press,1984).
26. See Bettina E. Schmidt, *Karibische Diaspora in New York: Vom "Wilden Denken" zur "polyphonen Kultur"* (Berlin: Reimer Verlag, 2002).
27. Lévi-Strauss introduced the term bricolage as a metaphor for the mythical thinking of traditional societies. In myths and rites he discovered a different way of reflection that is no less scientific than the natural sciences and results in no less real findings. Lévi-Strauss compares this way of thinking with technical handicraft. He writes that a *bricoleur* represents a person, "who works with his hands and uses devious means compared to those of a craftsman"—see Claude Lévi-Strauss, *The Savage Mind (La pensée sauvage)* (London: Weidenfeld and Nicolson, 1968), 16-17. Mythical thinking uses a limited number of means to develop a solution to a problem in a concrete situation. The creation process is limited in a continuously new arrangement of elements that were used in other situations and with a different function.
28. Richard Werbner, "Afterword," in *Syncretism/Anti-Syncretism: The Politics of Religious Synthesis*, ed. Charles Steward and Rosalind Shaw (London and New York: Routledge, 1994), 215.
29. Roger Bastide, "Mémoire collective et sociologie du bricolage," *L'Année Sociologique* 3, Série 21 (1970): 100.
30. Pam Morris, "Introduction," in *The Bakhtin Reader: Selected Writings of Bakhtin, Medvedev and Voloshinov*, ed. Pam Morris (London: Edward Arbold, 1994), 14, referring to Bakhtin.
31. Terence Turner, "'We are parrots,' 'Twins are birds': play of tropes as operational structure," in *Beyond Metapher: The Theory of Tropes in Anthropology*, ed. James W. Fernandez (Stanford, Ca.: Stanford University Press, 1995), 151.
32. See Paul Gilroy, *The Black Atlantic: Modernity and Double Consciousness* (Cambridge, Mass.: Harvard University Press, 1993).
33. Philip Kasinitz, *Caribbean New York: Black Immigrants and the Politics of Race* (Ithaca, N.Y., and London: Cornell University Press, 1995), 147.
34. See Abner Cohen, "Drama and politics in the development of a London carnival," *Man: The Journal of the Royal Anthropological Institute* 15, no. 1 (1980): 65-87,

and Abner Cohen, "A polyethnic London carnival as a contested cultural performance," *Ethnic and Racial Studies* 5 (1982): 23-41.

35. Kasinitz, *Caribbean New York*, 150.

36. As I was informed recently, in 2004 Haitian carnival culture became integrated and a large group of Haitians participated with music performances in the parade. This development reflects the increasing openness of carnival, not only in Brooklyn but also in other places: in 2005 I saw even a group from Mauritius participating at the London Caribbean carnival.

37. Geneviève Fabre, "Feasts and Celebrations. Introduction," in *Feasts and Celebrations in North American Ethnic Communities*, ed. Ramón A. Gutiérez and Geneviève Fabre (Albuquerque: University of New Mexico Press, 1995), 3.

38. Fabre, "Feasts," 2.

39. The term "critical masses" describes the ability of creating social groups based on interest and worldview—see Werner Schiffauer, *Fremde in der Stadt: zehn Essays über Kultur und Differenz* (Frankfurt am Main: Suhrkamp, 1997), 128-29, with reference to *Exploring the City* (1980) by Ulf Hannerz. Only the urban surrounding offers enough space for the creating of subcultures. Schiffauer argues therefore in favor of the investigation of the system of heterogeneity within an urban culture; hence, he wants to investigate the way how groups integrate and exclude elements, as well as the frame in which subcultures are construed.

40. David Lehmann, "Religion and Globalization," in *Religions in the Modern World*, ed. Linda Woodhead (London: Routledge, 2002), 311.

41. Mikhail Bakhtin, *Rabelais and his World* (Cambridge, Mass., and London: MIT Press, 1968), 465.

42. Morris, "Introduction," in *Bakhtin*, 15.

43. Bakhtin, *Rabelais and his World*, 471.

Bibliography

d'Ans, André-Marcel. "Créoles sans langue créole: les 'criollos' d'Hispano-Amérique." Pp. 29-50 in *Contacts de langues, contacts de cultures, créolisation: mélanges offerts à Robert Chaudenson à l'occasion de son soixantième anniversaire*, edited by Maria-Christine Hazaël-Massieux and Didier de Robillard. Paris: L'Harmattan, 1997.

Bakhtin, Mikhail. *Rabelais and his World*. Cambridge, Mass., and London: MIT Press, 1968.

———. *Problems of Dostoevsky's Poetics*. Manchester: Manchester University Press, 1984.

Balutansky, Kathleen, and Marie-Agnés Sourieau, eds. *Caribbean Creolization: Reflections on the Cultural Dynamics of Language, Literature, and Identity*. Gainesville and Barbados: University Press of Florida and The Press University of the West Indies, 1998.

Bastide, Roger. "Mémoire collective et sociologie du bricolage." *L'Année Sociologique*, 3. Série, vol. 21 (1970): 65-108.

Benítez Rojo, Antonio. *La isla que se repite: El Caribe y la perspectiva podmoderna*. Hanover, N.H.: Ed. del Norte, 1989.

———. "Three words toward creolization." Pp. 53-61 in *Caribbean Creolization: Reflections on the Cultural Dynamics of Language, Literature, and Identity*, edited by Kathleen Balutansky and Marie-Agnés Sourieau. Gainesville and Barbados: University Press of Florida and The University of the West Indies Press, 1998.

Bernabé, Jean, Patrick Chamoiseau and Raphaël Confiant. *Éloge de la créolité: in praise of creoleness*. Paris: Gallimard, 1993.

Bhabha, Homi K. "Signs taken for wonders: questions of ambivalence and authority under a tree outside Delhi, May 1871." *Critical Inquiry* 12, no. 1 (1985): 144-65.

Cohen, Abner. "Drama and politics in the development of a London carnival." *Man: The Journal of the Royal Anthropological Institute* 15, no. 1 (1980): 65-87.

———. "A polyethnic London carnival as a contested cultural performance." *Ethnic and Racial Studies* 5 (1982): 23-41.

Fabre, Geneviève. "Feasts and Celebrations. Introduction." Pp. 1-9 in *Feasts and Celebrations in North American Ethnic Communities*, edited by Ramón A. Gutiérez and Geneviève Fabre. Albuquerque: University of New Mexico Press, 1995.

García Canclini, Néstor. *Culturas híbridas: estrategias para entrar y salir de la modernidad*. México D. F., Mexico: Ed. Grijalbo, 1990.

———. "The hybrid: a conversation with Margarita Zires, Raymundo Mier, and Mabel Piccini." Pp. 77-92 in *The Postmodernism Debate in Latin America*, edited by John Beverly, José Oviedo and Michael Aronna. Durham, N.C., and London: Duke University Press, 1995.

Gilroy, Paul. *The Black Atlantic: Modernity and Double Consciousness*. Cambridge, Mass.: Harvard University Press, 1993.

Glissant, Édouard. "Creolization in the making of the Americas." Pp. 268-75 in *Race, Discourse, and the Origin of the Americas: A New World View*, edited by Vera Lawrence Hyatt and Rex Nettleford. Washington, D.C., and London: Smithsonian Institution Press, 1995.

Hannerz, Ulf. *Cultural Complexity: Studies in the Social Organization of Meaning*. New York: Columbia University Press, 1992.

———. *Transnational Connections: Culture, People, Places*. London and New York: Routledge, 1998.

Hofmann, Sabine. "'La terre rhizomée' und 'La isla que se repite'—Poststrukturalistische Modelle bei Edouard Glissant und Antonio Benítez Rojo." Pp. 252-65 in *Lateinamerika denken*, edited by Birgit Scharlau. Tübingen, Ger.: Narr, 1994.

Kasinitz, Philip. *Caribbean New York: Black Immigrants and the Politics of Race*. Ithaca, N.Y., and London: Cornell University Press, 1995.

Khan, Aisha. *Callaloo Nation: Metaphors of Race and Religious Identity among South Asians in Trinidad*. Durham, N.C.: Duke University Press, 2004.

Klor de Alva, J. Jorge. "The postcolonization of the (Latino) American experience: a reconsideration of 'colonialism,' 'postcolonialism,' and 'mestizaje.'" Pp. 241-75 in *After Colonialism: Imperial History and Postcolonial Displacements*, edited by Gyan Prakash. Princeton, N.J.: Princeton University Press, 1995.

Lehmann, David. "Religion and Globalization." Pp. 299-315 in *Religions in the Modern World*, edited by Linda Woodhead. London: Routledge, 2002.

Lévi-Strauss, Claude. *The Savage Mind (La pensée sauvage)*. London: Weidenfeld and Nicolson, 1968.

Lienhard, Martin. "De mestizajes, heterogeneidades, hibridismos y otras quimeras." Pp. 57-80 in *Asedios a la heterogenidad cultural: Libro de homenaje a Antonio Cornejo*

Polar, edited by José Antonio Mazzotti and U. Juan Zevallo Aguilar. Philadelphia: Asociación Internacional de Peruanistas, 1996.

Mason, Peter. *Deconstructing America: Representations of the Other.* London and New York: Routledge, 1990.

Moreno Fraginals, Manuel. "Apports culturels et déculturation." Pp. 9-25 in *L'Afrique en Amérique Latine*, edited by Manuel Moreno Fraginals. Paris: UNESCO, 1984.

Mörner, Magnus. *Race Mixture in the History of Latin America* Boston: Little, Brown and Comp., 1967.

Morris, Pam. "Introduction." Pp. 1-24 in *The Bakhtin Reader: Selected Writings of Bakhtin, Medvedev and Voloshinov*, edited by Pam Morris. London: Edward Arbold, 1994.

Ortiz, Fernando. *Etnia y sociedad*. La Habana, Cuba: Editorial de Ciencias Sociales, 1993.

———. *Contrapuncto cubano del tabaco y el azúcar*. La Habana, Cuba: Editorial de Ciencias Sociales, 1991.

Schiffauer, Werner. *Fremde in der Stadt: zehn Essays über Kultur und Differenz.* Frankfurt am Main: Suhrkamp, 1997.

Schmidt, Bettina E. *Karibische Diaspora in New York: Vom "Wilden Denken" zur "polyphonen Kultur."* Berlin: Reimer Verlag, 2002.

Todorov, Tzvetan. "Le croisement des cultures." *Communications* 43, (1986): 5-26.

Turner, Terence. "'We are parrots,' 'Twins are birds': play of tropes as operational structure." Pp. 121-158 in *Beyond Metapher: The Theory of Tropes in Anthropology*, edited by James W. Fernandez. Stanford, Ca.: Stanford University Press, 1995.

Werbner, Richard. "Afterword." Pp. 212-15 in *Syncretism/Anti-Syncretism: The Politics of Religious Synthesis*, edited by Charles Steward and Rosalind Shaw. London and New York: Routledge, 1994.

Young, Robert J. C. *Colonial Desire: Hybridity in Theory, Culture and Race.* London and New York: Routledge, 1995.

3

Constance R. Sutton

Family Reunion Rituals of African-Caribbean Transnational Families: Instilling a Historical and Diasporic Consciousness*

> "Knowing your family is knowing yourself—bottom line!"
> (Interview TM-5898)

Over the past two decades, family reunions have become an important ritual among African-Caribbean transnational migrants. Dispersed across a large number of North Atlantic countries, they have turned to organizing events specifically designed to reunite kinfolk. Re-creating kin ties among those spread across different nations and ensuring that kin-based connections are transmitted to offspring, these rituals celebrate what family means to African-Caribbeans living in the diaspora.[1] They foreground the role of family as a significant basic group identity for African-Caribbeans, an identity in which, as one interviewee emphatically told me, "Knowing your family is knowing yourself—bottom line!" In this chapter I discuss the meanings associated with the concept of "knowing your family," as expressed in the signifying practices of three transnational family reunions—one held in Barbados, one in Grenada, and one in both Trinidad and Barbados. I report on the role these family reunions play in maintaining Caribbean family connections, not just between "home" and country of residence, but throughout the diaspora. And I call attention to what I found to be the important role of family reunions in instantiating both an historical and diasporic consciousness among participants.

It was in the early 1990s that I first began to hear my New York African-Caribbean friends talk about their going to family reunions "back home" in the Caribbean. Their excitement about attending these events and the enthusiastic reports they brought back piqued my interest. They carefully distinguished these events from the usual visits to the Caribbean to "see family," attend a funeral, participate in Carnival, Crop-Over, or Emancipation Day festivities, making it clear that these "family reunions" were rituals specifically focused on a publicly enacted performance centering on family. Undertaken to reunite kin folk who were widely dispersed across several national boundaries, these rituals represented a way that members of transnational families sought to re-engage in face-to-face interaction that would keep alive both family ties and memories of family, to re-instantiate and celebrate their concept of family.

In recent years, rituals have become an important site for anthropologists to examine how social facts and collective identities are made and remade,[2] how social practices and events are invested with meaning, and how unwritten social memory is constructed, performed, and transmitted.[3] With this in mind, I decided in 1998 to interview some of the individuals I knew who had recently participated in family reunions. My approach was to view their rituals as "signifying practices," that is, as expressive performances that call public attention to customs and values and create a consciousness of valued behavior and beliefs, even when these are disputed.[4] Hence, I wanted to know what participating in these rituals meant. What light did they cast on the meaning of family to them? I wondered about the generational depth and the range of kin that would be represented. What kin-based activities preceded these events and eventuated from them? Why had the family reunion fervor emerged at this particular point in time? What kinds of subjectivities and identities did the events evoke in the participants? Finally, what role did memory, history, and the past play in these ritualized gatherings and with what possible effect on the future?

This article then is about the family reunion rituals which African-Caribbeans were organizing in the 1990s, reunions specifically designed to reunite them in their "homelands" with their kinfolk dispersed among many countries. The continued involvement of those who migrated abroad with their kin who remained behind was something I initially noted in my field research in a sugar plantation village in Barbados in the late 1950s. In the early 1970s I began, with my students and colleagues, to track the increase in the bidirectional exchanges occurring between kin abroad and those "back home." By the 1980s the exchanges were multi-directional and we were able to document the fact that transnational family networks constituted one of the major channels of transmission for important exchanges—economic, political, and cultural. Summarizing this research about transnational family networks, Basch et al. wrote:

> The family is the matrix from which a complexly layered transnational social life is constructed and elaborated. [It] facilitates the survival of its members, their class formation and mobility; and as the repository of cultural practices and ideology shaped in the home society, it mediates identity formation in the new setting as it socializes its members into a transnational way of life.[5]

But what had not been noted in the literature of the time was the emergence during the late 1980s and 1990s of family reunion rituals among transnational families. Hence a close look at these reunion rituals would supplement what we already knew about the meaning of family to African-Caribbean transmigrants [immigrants who maintain multiple social, political, economic and cultural connections across national borders and with their home/ancestral countries].[6]

So what do these family reunion rituals, initiated by the migrants, not by those "back home," tell us? I collected in-depth information about the rituals from eight participants who belonged to three different descent groups that had held family reunions in Barbados, Grenada, and Trinidad/Barbados between 1993 and 1998. These individuals were either adult immigrants or the offspring of immigrants. The account of each of the reunion rituals is filtered through the views and perspectives of the individuals interviewed. The three case studies are not "definitive" accounts of what happened in each reunion, nor do they necessarily reflect the different meanings the rituals had for the wide range of people who attended. They are studies of how the events were perceived, constructed and experienced by those I interviewed.

The dispersed transmigrants who attended the reunion rituals came from places reflecting differing migration trajectories: the United States, Canada, Britain, France, Germany, Ghana, Guyana and various places in the Caribbean. The size of the reunions varied from a total of 46 participants to an estimated 250 participants. In all but one of the reunions, participants who came from overseas outnumbered the participants who lived on the island where the event was held. The reunions of the three descent groups not only differed in scale but in the scope of activities undertaken, the degree of formality in the arrangements, and in what was regarded as the main intent of the reunion. These differences reflected the differing class status of the core kin-groups who organized the reunion rituals: working-class, middle-class, and elite.

However, the rituals all shared a number of common features. A core sibling group and their paternally and/or maternally linked cousins, initially all of them and as many as four generations, were represented at all the reunions. They were inclusive in their definition of the kin who were invited and came: half-siblings, "outside" children,[7] spouses of legal and non-legal unions and their descendants were all present; and this included occasional individuals of different racial and ethnic backgrounds. Furthermore, the concept of family embraced in the reunions was highly elastic and egalitarian; it over-rode the status differences among kin folk which influence their everyday social interactions. Non-kin friends on the islands who were "like family to us" participated in some of the family reunion activities, underscoring the inclusive nature of the concept of family being celebrated. There were other features in common too. An elderly male or female kin or a recently deceased kin was often said to be the reason for having the reunion at the time and place where it was held—a practice related to the importance placed on showing respect to one's elders and receiving their blessing in return. And at all the family reunions, an ancestor's home or grave was visited.

All the reunions were preceded by mini-family reunions at which the idea of bringing *everyone* together was put forth. Following the reunions, there was more frequent visiting with kin living in different western countries, with the kin whom one "came to know" at the reunions. Children were more frequently sent across national boundaries to visit their cousins. Finally, adults stressed the importance of bringing all the children together so that they *"get to know their family."* This was one of the main rationales for holding the family reunion.

The significance of the rituals was captured in the frequent iterations that "we are a very tight-knit family, a very close one," "family is everything," or "knowing your family is knowing yourself." These statements were made to explain why family reunions were important. "Knowing your family" referred not only to learning *who* you are but *whom* you can count on for support—a support that materializes in exchanges of goods, advice, services, "favors," monetary assistance, and the welcoming of kin who may wish to stay with you for shorter or longer periods. And, as I learned, a great deal of time, effort and money goes into the rituals that focus on creating this knowledge, the knowledge that "family" is your most basic (collective) identity.

I turn now to accounts of the reunions of three family groups whom I shall call: the Marshalls, the Bishops, and the Williams.

The Marshalls

Over the Christmas-New Year holiday of 1997-1998 the Marshalls organized their first formal family reunion in Barbados. They were siblings and cousins who had grown up in a sugar plantation village in the middle of Barbados, the island where I had carried out my early doctoral research and remained in touch with many of the people over the years. The brothers and sisters of the core Marshall group were now living in England, Canada, and the United States and had children who were in college or about to go to college, as well as brothers and sisters who had remained in Barbados. A few years before this reunion was organized, some of the family from elsewhere had met in Barbados for the funeral of their father, at which time they decided they wanted to gather together again as a family to maintain face-to-face contact. Forty-seven people were part of their reunion ritual. Smaller in scale and scope than the other family reunions I discuss, there was also a greater informality in the activities in which participants engaged. While Christmas and New Year's dinners brought together the entire kin group to enjoy good *Bajan*[8] food, other joint activities involved smaller segments who visited the deceased father's home (now occupied by one of the brothers), the cemetery where he was buried, the village where the core kin group grew up. The rest of the time was spent relaxing and "liming" ("hanging out" together), taking trips around the island, taking sea-baths in the Caribbean Sea, and going to clubs together. The men, often with the women joining them, engaged in their favorite past-time of sitting around drinking, talking, and arguing about world and local events. There was a considerable exchange of personal memories and "catching up" on what and how everybody was doing. Youngsters exchanged e-mail addresses to ensure continued, rapid communication. The memorabilia of this reunion were limited to photographs and videos.

The several members of this family reunion I spoke with said the event was important and should be repeated. The adults emphasized the desire to reconnect with kin on a face-to-face basis and to refurbish their more distantly-known kin connections. Of equal importance, they wanted to make sure their children (born elsewhere) "get to know their family and their parents' Bajan culture." The Marshalls regard their family culture as superior to that in the different societies where they now reside. They believe that if their children learn the family values of their homeland culture, they will be better able to confront the dangers one faces living in northern metropoles.[9]

Thus, for members of this group their family reunion had the twin purpose of re-creating a kin-based collective identity and transmitting it to the younger generation. Did this happen? I can partly answer this for Andrea, who was born and grew up in New York City. She is my god-child, was twenty years old at the time of the interview, and is the daughter of a black Barbadian father who was a member of the core kin group organizing the reunion, and a mother who is a white American professional. The long interviews I had with her touch mainly on issues of identity in relation to her biological family, her extended kin group, and with respect to race, place, and nation. Andrea had been to Barbados a few years earlier on the occasion of her paternal grandfather's funeral and also when she was very young. However, now that she was older, she claimed this family reunion ritual altered her perceptions of her parents and her conflicts about her own racial identity in the United States:

> I've always had issues about who I am and what that means relative to my father's culture and race and my mother's background.... I needed to know my ancestry... and getting to know the island put my father into a context that I'd never been able to imagine.... [It helped me understand] why there are conflicts [between us] and that there is richness to our relationship [that I did not recognize before]. I didn't understand it until I went [to the reunion], was on that island [and watched him with all the people there]. It was so powerful. It really changed my perspective of him.... I also watched my mother for the first time be more comfortable around people than I had ever seen her before; and it was so nice. It made me feel more at ease also to just watch her walk around and say hello to these people who weren't close family [but] who were family [and] totally incorporated her.

Andrea was impressed by and strongly attracted to the incorporative bonding that occurs during family reunions. She struck up a relationship with a distant cousin and a particularly close and warm relationship with her half-sister, Shawn, who was her father's "outside child" and was attending the University of the West Indies in Barbados:

> You know I didn't know how to address him [their father] to Shawn [her half-sister]; I didn't know whether to say "our father" or "'my' father".... It surprised me how much I looked up to Shawn, how smart I thought she was, and how I wanted to be so much like her ... she had this regalness to her.... She

totally was like . . . this is who I am and you can come into it. And I felt so honored to be part of her.

Andrea explored the many meanings of the phrase "we family," which people in her father's village said to her when she met them. She also noted that this concept may be metaphorically extended to encompass a broad range of people who, because they "grew up together . . . must be family."

The evolution of Andrea's discourse expressed her strong feelings about "belonging to family" and its importance as a newly acquired identity. Her comments also revealed a number of interesting identity conflations. Early in the interview she speaks of feeling like a tourist as she walks around the village where her father grew up. She follows this by saying that she began to realize that the village was "in some sense an extension of the family." This is her initial equation of family identity with place identity. The slippage occurs again later in the interview when she speaks about her pleasure in realizing she "had this family in this place" and follows this comment with a comment about how comforting it is that she has now found "a place in the world I can go *home* to" [. . .] Reflecting on this, she muses, "And here's Andrea who thought she never *really* had family. . . . But then she goes back [to Barbados] and finds she got a whole country."

As Andrea deepens and enlarges her embrace of a family identity, she also expands her concept of the place identity of home to encompass the entire island. But what does this family-like island identity mean to her? Paralleling family/island conflations is her slippage between kin history and island history as she states her desire to learn more about the history of her kin connections and, later in the interview, about Barbadian history, politics, and linguistic practices. Her comments point to the ways kin and nation identities are linked by tropes that draw on notions of a common ancestry. However, in this case it was not the nation-state appropriating family-like tropes but rather of Andrea extending her concept of family and place to include nation. And as the interview drew to an end, her comments trump her kin/home/nation images of identity:

> You know, I do look to the future and think I'd love to have these family reunions and be an organizer of one of them myself when I am older. I want to go down to Barbados and see family. I want to be involved with my family. I want to have that kind of relationship *even though they're spread all over the world. I want to have that sense of coming together.* I want to have that sense of coming together . . . because I didn't grow up with it.

One could ask whether "that sense of coming together" Andrea experiences in the family reunion provides her with the grounding for another identity—that of belonging through one's transnational kin ties to the brothers and sisters of an African-Caribbean or an African diaspora? Here again the slippage from family-specific identities to ethnic, national and diasporic identities is facilitated by images of a common descent. But the question of a diasporic identity, which also hovers in the background of the larger and more formal reunion rituals held in Grenada, Trinidad, and Barbados, cannot be answered directly with the interview material at hand. While it was clear that family reunions created a consciousness of diasporic connections, what this implies with respect to possessing a wider African diasporic identity remains an important question to be researched.

Before turning to the family reunion of another kin group, I want to briefly note how Andrea's brother Gregory, who was some four years younger, responded to the Marshal family reunion event. He was motivated when he returned home to create a Marshall family website that displays a genealogical chart tracing four generations of kin connections, along with pictures of several individual family members. I was also able to document that for the Marshall kin group interaction intensified and expanded after the reunion. There were more frequent visits to family living in Canada, first-time visits to siblings living in England, and more frequent visits to New York City from family in these countries and from Barbados. Andrea carries on a weekly email exchange with her half-sister in Barbados. Andrea's father, who became a wiz in operating hi-tech computer programs, tells me he now has weekly face-to-face conversations with family members in "real time"—using the "instant messenger" computer program to talk directly to family members. And for those who also have a camcorder camera attached to their computers, he is able to see the people he is talking with. "Does this make you feel closer," I asked. "Definitely . . . we have never been so close since we were little in Barbados." And in November 2006, the Marshalls held another large family reunion in Barbados that brought together many of the same people who attended the 1997-1998 family reunion plus a few other family members who had not come to the prior event.

The Bishops

The 1995 Grenada family reunion was also the first of its kind for this core kin group. It brought together approximately 250 people who came from places such as England, Germany, Canada, Aruba, Trinidad, Guyana, Puerto Rico, the United States, "even someone from Africa came." Unlike the Marshall reunion, the number of kin who came outstripped the number living on the island than, and large numbers of those who attended had never met before. Norma, the thirty-nine-year old woman I interviewed who works as a dental assistant in New York City, tells me that "when I was sent to meet some of them [unknown kin] at the airport [in Grenada], I could recognize them because their faces look like family—we feature each other [a frequently used phrase for recognizing family connections based on facial features]." Relatives living on the island who participated in the reunion ritual included Norma's mother, sister, maternal aunt, father's brother and "my father's outside kids and their children, and my mother's brother's children (inside and outside) and their children."

The 250 family members spent a week together in August engaged in a fairly elaborate itinerary of activities that included participating in Carnival, swimming at the famous Grand Anse beach, visiting "family land" and old family houses, holding a special church ceremony, visiting a plantation, partying (dancing, drinking and having a fête), putting on various performances, and examining what Norma considered the central feature of the reunion: *the huge family tree*. It had been drawn on a large canvas and put up on an outside wall for all to see. She explained that it was the idea of drawing up a family tree that gave birth to the idea of having a reunion. She, her sister, and her paternal male cousin had put it together. The idea originally came from the cousin, a gynecologist in Washington, D.C. Neither he nor his children had visited Grenada, unlike Norma, her husband, her daughter, and her sister who frequently visited Grenada. Norma explains that it was her cousin who was motivated to have a family reunion:

> Because he often meet people that have the same last name as we do. And he keep trying to trace his family. He keep trying to trace because every time he would meet someone and they have the same last name, he would ask them, who is their mother, who is their brother, who is their sister? And he keep asking. And sometimes he, they, we, just couldn't get to the bottom of it, with the same last name. Who is your family? And they tell him but he couldn't get the link of it, cannot put it all together. And often that happened to him and he felt very bad. So that's what really happen, because he really wanted to know, how do you call it, his race. That's when he started writing, to make a [genealogical] chart. Well my sister knew him and so they both put their ideas together, and that is when we said, we gonna have a family reunion, to see where everybody comes from. So it took us a lot of years. About four years, we've been planning it. Four years—We had a small one, but it was just our little family. It wasn't even a family reunion. But the one I talking about that took four years to put together. It was, oh, I just can't tell you [how great it was] . . . the family tree. I remember my sister saying it go back to the 18th century. But all I really wanted, really, is to go to Grenada and see how much of us there is, who is who and you know.

Norma goes on to say that:

> The family reunion was very exciting—everyone get to know each other. My daughter also very excited. She learned who to call "uncle" and "auntie." I was excited to see people I hadn't seen for a long time and to meet people I never met. I plan to contact them if I travel to where they live, places like Boston, Aruba, England, Germany, Canada.

Toward the end of my interview with Norma, I asked whether she thought the 1995 Grenada family reunion was the beginning of a new tradition. Her answer differs sharply from the way Andrea experienced the Barbados reunion. Norma felt there was no reason to have another big family reunion because "*we all met; next one, it will have to be up to the children.*" This suggests that the

1995 Grenada reunion, though much larger and more formally organized than the Marshall reunion, is not likely to become a tradition. It had accomplished its purpose, which, according to Norma, was *to find and meet family* in Grenada, a place considered "home." And this is what made it a joyous, empowering experience. One might note that Norma shares with Andrea the concept of a Caribbean place identity—"home"—where the core kin group originated, where kin elders still live, and where some of the migrants at the reunion intend to return to live.

The Bishops' reunion required longer and more complicated preparations than the Marshalls'. It began with a search for relatives identified by "name," entailed contacting them and then arranging to assemble a large number of people who did not formerly know they were kin. It also resulted in a huge depiction of the Bishops' family tree "with its 210 long branches and 110 small branches." This genealogy was displayed at the reunion for all to examine, to be impressed with, and to feel empowered by its size. A compressed representation of the genealogical tree was put on a pin and on a T-shirt, and distributed as memorabilia of the event.[10]

Reflecting on how the reunion affected family relations, Norma stated that it did bring family closer together. Members living in different countries began visiting one another more often. She also commented that the Bishop reunion had inspired a number of other people from the island to hold similar family reunions.

The Williams

In turning to the Williams, we find some new complexities of kin and place identity and a different slant on what the family reunions signify for their participants. I report on three of the Williams' reunions: a small family reunion of twenty-one cousins that preceded and promoted the two large family reunions: the first one in Trinidad in 1993 where an estimated 175 people came, and a second one in Barbados in 1995 where the same number were estimated to have come. Members of the Williams' kin group were of middle to upper middle-class status with university educations. They can be characterized as belonging to transnational professional families with multiply-rooted identities and a cosmopolitan consciousness. I jointly interviewed two cousins who had assisted in organizing the two family reunions. They were offspring of the core kin group of sisters who initiated the family reunions. The husband of one of the cousins was also present and had assisted in the organizing of the reunions. The two cousins spoke of belonging to a group of cousins that saw one another frequently. The Williams' core kin group now reside in northern urban centers where some hold positions that have them traveling widely around the world. The cousins described their kin group as follows: "Everyone is all over the place. Some are extremely well off; others have problems paying their monthly electric bill." Nonetheless, the cousins stated emphatically that the Williams regard themselves "as a very close-knit family [...] family is everything."

The cousins, born in Trinidad, Barbados, and Canada, have all lived part of their early lives with their grandmother in Trinidad. They also lived for shorter or longer periods with aunts located elsewhere. The idea of a "cousins' reunion" came from:

> a general feeling that our grandmother was getting older; and since all of us had lived with her for at least a year or two or four at some time during our lives [...] and it is there we got the basic grounding and the feeling of pride; so we all wanted do something to celebrate her who through her children had given birth to us.

During Christmas 1992, the twenty-one cousins who had never all come together held a reunion in Trinidad. They put on a fashion show, sang, danced, and showcased their talents:

> Honoring our grandmother during the whole thing and then we went to my grandmother's house with tape recorder and pencil to get the stories and the background and the recipes. Our meeting [in Trinidad] proved to be such a love-fest that we decided, let's go for the big one.

While the idea for the 1993 big family reunion began during the cousins' meeting in Trinidad in 1992, the notion was abetted by fact that an uncle of theirs had gone to Barbados in the 1960s "to search the archives for our family roots which he had wanted to trace back to Africa; but when it turned out that the root-work led him back to Ireland, he was upset and threw it away." However, the mother of one of the interviewees "caught it and decided to see what she could do with it." In the early 1990s, she mobilized several people to work on the project, including her daughter and son-in-law [whom I was interviewing]. They phoned, wrote letters, looked at newspapers, and used computer programs to produce a genealogy that went back to 1702. The "founding ancestors" constituted three different intermarrying families in Barbados and began when a white (Irish) Barbadian man divorced his white wife to marry his housekeeper who was of part-African ancestry. The genealogy, produced as a book, was forty-nine pages long, had entries for some 150 people, and was called *Family Cōmmix '93: our family's story* (1st edition). Its preface states that it is written as "an introduction for an extended family where connections and relations can be initiated; and [...] for a better understanding of the past where our children may grow knowing their roots" (1993: i). "*Cōmmix*," I was told, "means to mix together, blend, to mix smoothly and acceptably together." The term was printed on the back of T-shirts that had a computer graphic on the front showing a condensed family tree. Like the Bishop's document, the genealogy was used to invite people to the 1993 reunion meeting in Trinidad, where many of the people who came (from the United States, Canada, England, Barbados) met for the first time. And again, similar to the Bishop reunion, I was told that:

everybody want to come; want to know where they came from, to know their connections and how the names passed down; some like to pull on "blood ties" but we all family [so we must] meet on common ground; and everybody was given a name tag and a copy of the *Family Cōmmix '93* which they carried around.

According to the cousins, a death in the family which occurred just before the Trinidad reunion made the older people want to have another reunion as soon as possible. "They wanted to experience it again and meet all the people they hadn't known or seen for a long time." In July of 1994 a newsletter appeared to which one of the cousins had contributed. It was called *The Drum: One Sound—our family Cōmmix news*. The one-sound drum icon represented, as of old in Africa, a "news conveyor" that "will be our link with the past as we continue to discover more names for our individual family tree ... [it] will make our bonds stronger" (*The Drum*, 1994:2). The newsletter also announced that the second Williams reunion would be held in Barbados in 1995.

Barbados was chosen because a large part of the family had ancestors living in Barbados and because the African Americans who came to the Trinidad reunion wanted to have the next one in Barbados. The 1995 reunion had many "new faces we had not seen before," based on a further tracing of genealogical links and on information obtained at the 1993 reunion. The cousins mentioned that the large contingent of African Americans who came said they had no previous knowledge of their genealogical connections to West Indians. Nor did they feel closely connected to a recently deceased ancestor. The cousins I was interviewing also saw the African Americans as wanting a stronger role in organizing the subsequent reunions. This added to a resentment these younger cousins were already experiencing due to their feeling somewhat brushed aside by their parental generation who took over managing and expanding a range of activities related to expanding the family reunions. It had been decided in 1995 that the reunion was to be an event that occurred annually or bi-annually. When I interviewed the cousins in early 1998 another smaller family reunion organized by African Americans was planned for later in the year. It was to take place in the Poconos in New York State, at an expensive black resort. The cousins did not attend, but their parents' generation did "in order to make sure that the rest of the family's vote is being heard."

Unlike both the Marshalls and the Bishops, the Williams family reunions have become an institutionalized recurrent event. This has involved reaching out to increase the size, breath, generational depth and formality of family reunions. It has also meant that a "homeland" place-centered identity for holding family reunions was abandoned as the connections linking some of the people no longer focused on a place-centered "home" identity in the Caribbean. The cousins I interviewed claimed to feel distanced from the organization that emerged. They saw the older generation engaged in "power plays" and competition between those whose primary self-identity was African American [with distant Caribbean ancestry] and those whose primary self-identity was African-Caribbean. These tensions led to a move to establish a junior branch within *Family Cōmmix* for those who had spent time in the Caribbean as children, even if not born there, and who chose to self-identify as African-Caribbean.

Discussion and conclusion

My three case studies clearly indicate that the rituals of family reunions are about reaffirming known kin connections among folks who are widely dispersed internationally and creating new ties, for the younger generations and among those laterally who have not yet met. Despite the fact that generally African-Caribbean migrants try to maintain transnational kin ties, their continual migrations across countries can cause a weakening, sometimes even a loss, of these connections. Family reunion rituals are designed to offset this. They occur because losing kin contact and regaining it *matters*. It matters because of the precept that *"knowing your family is knowing yourself."* This "knowing," it should be noted, includes knowing about *your ancestors and the kinds of lives they lived*. The family reunion rituals I studied were highly successful in achieving these goals. Moreover, following the reunion rituals, contact with kin was intensified and considerably expanded in all three cases studied. The positing of an indissoluble connection between self-identity and a kin-based collective identity, expressed in these rituals, sets off this African-Caribbean concept of self-identity from that prevalent in the mainstream United States where the individualism of one's identity is stressed. Most importantly, family reunion rituals publicly assert the existence of a distinct kin-based collective identity that supersedes other identities and is diasporic.

Yet "knowing family" had differently nuanced meanings in the three case studies. The size of the kin group that came together, and the meeting of new relatives was significant for Norma in the Grenada reunion. It also played an important role in the Trinidad and Barbados reunions of the Williams family. Norma, who grew up in Grenada, was already immersed in close family ties, visited Grenada annually, was building a house there and had plans to return in a few years. She already had strong family ties which the reunion ritual enlarged. Andrea, on the other hand, was engaged in actively acquiring family ties and constructing a new identity during the Barbados Marshall family reunion. What mattered to Norma was knowing that *she belonged* to a large kin group and that all of them "make it" (have gained *good* jobs).[11] Norma's kin group included a mixture of working-class and middle-class people, with either advanced technical training after high school or with college and post-graduate degrees. This class element was also present in the two large reunions of the Williams. As the cousins commented, the core-kin group of organizers held a cosmopolitan status. In the case of the Williams' reunions, generational and ethnic-based differences appeared to create tensions. What mattered to Andrea in the reunion of the Marshalls was the intense and personalized sense of belonging that incited her desire to return to Barbados, her newly acquired home (which she did three years later). And it was this more personalized sense of belonging to a significant kin group that also characterized the smaller cousins' meeting in Trinidad. Some of these nuanced differences relate to whether one is born or grew up in the Caribbean vs. the northern metropoles, as well as to generational differences. Nonetheless, the individuals interviewed all felt that the reunion ritual was an empowering experience. What was empowering was to collectively experience the knowledge of belonging to a large set of kin-connected people with common ancestors that reach back in time and kin connections stretching into the future.

Another important aspect of these rituals is the element of history-making. People assembled learn not only about their recent and founding ancestors or about the size of their present-day kin network. They also share memories about the cultural histories inscribed in their lives—thus learning about the historical contexts of their "roots." This too was regarded as an essential part of coming to *know* yourself as a person, a person with a collectivized kin-based identity, a member of a distinct genealogical "imagined community."[12] The ritual instills memories of the past—the family past and what times were like then. For the dispersed migrants it re-inscribes former memories of close family ties, creating a sense of continuity by instantiating a traditional notion about the closeness of family ties. This is meaningful to both the migrants and those who have remained "at home."

What then is the African-Caribbean concept of family and family values being projected and celebrated in the reunion rituals? Here one can take note that the concept of family operative in the reunions consisted of bilateral extended kin networks embedded in an ideology of mutual support that links family members within and across households, communities, and nations. It is supported by the strong belief in family as *lifeline*.[13] In both family emphasis and in the residential patterns practiced, the family-centered template is one that is broadly consanguineal rather than conjugally-centered. The relations central to the collective nature of kin units are sibling ties and ties among cousins.[14] This concept of family also builds on the diverse social ties that emerge from different forms of conjugal unions, engaging in child fostering practices, and maintaining strong consanguineal links within and across generations. There is a broad inclusiveness to this notion of family, making its boundaries highly elastic.[15]

Experiencing and celebrating the sentiment of "all o' we is one" during the reunions entailed a certain amount of social leveling—a diminishing of the social distinctions among kin folk that exist in other contexts. It was the perceived absence of this egalitarian sentiment in the Williams' reunions that led the young cousins to point to the fissures they felt existed. Nonetheless, the reunions projected a notion of family attractive to the interviewees. Family came to constitute something akin to a socio-religious group, linking you to a past that shapes who you are, and underwriting a future through family continuity. It was reason enough to want "to keep the family thing going."[16]

In the Caribbean where transnational migrations have been a distinct feature of these island societies since the mid-nineteenth Century, and perhaps earlier, this desire for family connectivity is not new. What is new is enacting this desire in the form of family reunion rituals, cultural practices which appear in the African-Caribbean region to have begun some time in the 1970s.[17] Changing world conditions have facilitated their occurrence: the increased income of many migrants, the increased ease of transnational air flights, and the hi-tech computer-based communications revolution. The latter directly affects kin connectivity by making it easier to access information on genealogical connections, to sustain frequent contact through email, and to engage with kin folk in weekly and even daily "face-to-face conversations in real time." This space-time compression of "new age" technology has opened new ways for African-Caribbeans to sustain, re-establish, and intensify their family relations. In addition, African American concern with "roots," and the growth of "heritage industries" in the Caribbean, underwritten since the 1970s by its principal industry of tourism, has contributed to fostering an interest in holding family reunions.[18] This influence can be seen in both the Bishops and Williams reunions where tracing genealogies to founding ancestors and producing large "family trees" played a central role, along with visiting family land and houses and heritage sites.

It is true that the heritage industries and festivals reify "history" and "culture." Likewise, "family trees," family reunion newsletters, and the memorabilia of T-shirts help objectify the concept of "family." However, these new developments do not obliterate the real personal sentiments individuals have about their family, its history, or its cultural values. Concepts such as heritage and roots are often consequential to people's understanding and sentiments about their history, culture, and in this case, their particular family forms and values. What this study reveals is that for African-Caribbean transnational migrants "living in the diaspora," their distinct "creole" concept of family provides them with a fundamental collective kin-identity they wish to preserve, celebrate, and transmit.

The three case studies raise a number of interesting questions for further research. I mention here only a few. Comparisons with other ethnic groups and time periods would be of interest. Here one might note that African Americans have a longer tradition of holding family reunions whose rituals seem to have a somewhat different focus.[19] Brackette Williams stated (in a telephone conversation) that while African American family reunions began after emancipation, in the 1930s when southern plantations became historic sites, the reunions would take place there. Both white and black folk who "belonged" to the plantation would come together, making the "ole plantation" a symbolic site where they could meet without having to acknowledge the specific inter-racial production of black and white relatives during and after slavery. These reunions also made public a symbolic proprietary claim that African Americans had on the heritage plantation.

A second question is whether the home country will remain the anchoring place of identity and of periodic return over the generations. Related to this is the issue of how a rapidly changing world situation will affect the nature of cross-border, transnational kin ties, as well as the meanings attached to the culturally specific concepts of family. A third concern that requires further exploration and specification is one I stress in this article; namely, the role of family reunion rituals in heightening a consciousness of living in a diaspora and of adding a diasporic identity to the transnational family/kin identity. In all, I see family reunion rituals as an important site to explore how current global processes affect not only peoples' movements but the forms of shared collective identities they construct.

Acknowledgments

To the people I interviewed, I want to express my deeply-felt gratitude for your willingness to spend long hours sharing your experiences, and for your patience in guiding me through the details of kin connections and reunion rituals. My special thanks go to Andrea, Michelle, and Norma, and to my close friend and colleague, Sue Makiesky-Barrow, whose interest and help with this project informs its analyses. Faye Harrison's article (1995) set a model for what I might look for in the family reunion data I collected and I want to also thank her for her quick and helpful responses to my queries. I wish also to give grateful thanks to Karen Olwig for her useful ideas about family reunions and her good suggestions about how to write up my material, to Mary Chamberlain whose writings inspired me to take on this project, and to Antonio Lauria-Perricelli who made many useful comments as he bore the brunt of my distraction while I worked on this project and chapter.

Notes

* This is a revised and updated version of my article "Celebrating Ourselves: the family reunions of African Caribbean transnational families," published in *Global Networks* 4(3): 243-57, 2004.

    1. Mary Chamberlain, *Family Love in the Diaspora: migration and the Anglo-Caribbean experience* (Kingston, Jamaica: Ian Randle Publishers, and London: Transaction Publishers, 2006).
    2. Jean Comaroff and John Comaroff, "Introduction," in *Modernity and its Malcontents: ritual and power in postcolonial Africa*, ed. Jean Comaroff and John Comaroff (Chicago: University of Chicago Press, 1993), xi-xxxviii.
    3. Paul Connerton, *How Societies Remember* (Cambridge: Cambridge University Press, 1989).
    4. David Parkin, "Ritual as Spatial Direction and Bodily Division," in *Understanding Rituals*, ed. Daniel de Cuppet (New York: Routledge, 1992), 11-25.
    5. Linda Basch, Nina Glick Schiller, and Cristina Szanton Blanc, *Nations Un-*

bound: transnational projects, postcolonial predicaments and deterritorialized Nation-States (Langhorne: Gordon & Breach, 1994), 79.

6. See Basch et al., *Nations Unbound*, and Nina Glick Schiller and Georges Fouron, *Georges Woke Up Laughing: long-distance nationalism and the search for home* (Durham, N.C.: Duke University Press, 2001), for discussion of the concepts of "transmigrant," and "transnational nations," and for rich ethno-graphic accounts of transnational family life. See also Mary Chamberlain, *Narratives of Exile and Return* (London: Macmillan, 1997); Mary Chamberlain, "Praise Songs of the family: lineage and kinship in the Caribbean diaspora," *History Workshop Journal* 50, (2000): 114-128; Chamberlain, *Family Love*; and Karen Fog Olwig, "Follow the People: Movement, Lives, Family" (paper presented at conference on Migration and Transnational Theory Re-examined: Place, Generation, Identity, Santo Domingo, Dominican Republic, April 1999), for analyses of transmigrants' oral histories relating to family.

7. In local usage an "outside child" generally refers to a man's child who is born out of wedlock in a relationship which is not subsequently converted into a co-residential consensual union or a state and church sanctioned marriage. Mothers do not use the term, regardless of the legal status of a child of theirs. According to the state-sanctioned definition, however, 75 to 80 percent of children in the West Indies are born out of wedlock, that is, in relationships which have not been state and church sanctioned at the time of the birth of a child. "Wedlock," when it occurs, usually takes place after the birth of a child or two.

8. "Bajan" is the term Barbadians use for their creole language, food, and life style. Since Independence in 1966 Bajan has increasingly become a way of asserting that one is a "true, true" Barbadian. This references what they regard as their culturally distinct non-English life style, which co-exists with their knowing how to speak and act according to the hegemonic British (and now United States) life styles. Barbadians, like other West Indians, engage in practicing a linguistic and cultural duality that entails code-switching.

9. In her study of West Indians living in England, Chamberlain also found that their concept of family, with its values and prescriptions, is what lay at the heart of the political and cultural identity they developed abroad. This was the legacy they most wanted to transmit. Chamberlain, "Praise Songs," 126, and Chamberlain, *Family Love*.

10. The tracing of ancestry that results in constructing a computer-generated family tree has become an important rationale for holding family reunions. Family members share in the discovery and come to feel connected as they identify their lines of descent on the diagram. Such events are not only public but often publicized, as was the case with the 40-foot family tree of the 140 descendants of Thomas Hazlewood of Bridgetown, Barbados, born into slavery in 1804. The event was reported in the U.S.-published *CaribNews* (August 10, 2004), 27.

11. Both size of the kin group and the achievements of individuals were important components in the African American family reunions described by Harrison—see Faye V. Harrison, "Give me that old-time religion: Genealogy and the Cultural Politics of an Afro-Christian Celebration in Halifax County, North Carolina," in *Religion in the Contemporary South: Diversity, Community, and Identity*, ed. O.K. White, Jr. and Daryl Whites (Athens: University of Georgia Press, 1995), 34-45. And an African American graduate student, on learning that I was writing about family reunions, recalled that she went to the first one at the age of ten and found it truly impressive. But, she added, the more recent one meant more to her because it created for her "a certainty about my going on to graduate school."

12. Abbey Lincoln, the U.S. jazz singer, incorporates this notion in her song "You

Got Some People in You," which lists (and praises) all the past people "who make you who you are."

13. See Joyce Aschenbrenner, *Lifelines: Black Families in Chicago* (Prospect Heights, Ill.: Waveland, 1983).

14. This is also reported for African American family reunions in the U.S. South—see Yvonne Jones, "Kinship affiliation through time: black homecomings and family reunions in a North Carolina County," *Ethnohistory* 27, no. 1 (1980): 49-66.

15. These African-Caribbean concepts of family have drawn on and reworked past West African concepts of family as lineage. Family as lineage, though greatly modified today, continues to inform how family is viewed and constructed—see Chamberlain, "Praise Songs"; Chamberlain, *Family Love*; Constance R. Sutton, "Foreword," in *Women and the Ancestors: Black Carib Kinship and Ritual*, Virginia Kerns (Urbana and Chicago: University of Illinois Press, 1997); and Constance R. Sutton, "'Motherhood is Powerful': embodied knowledge from evolving field work," *Anthropology and Humanism* 23 (1998).

16. Chamberlain, "Praise Songs," 126; Chamberlain reports that West Indians in London engage in a discourse about family which echoes in genre well-known West African praise songs. Their discourse, she tells us, are "'Praise Songs' of the Family, Lineage and Kinship in the Caribbean Diaspora"—see Chamberlain, "Praise Songs" and Chamberlain, *Family Love*.

17. For Nevis—see Karen Fog Olwig, *Global Culture, Island Identity: continuity and change in the Afro-Caribbean community of Nevis* (Switzerland and Philadelphia: Harwood Academic Publishers, 1993), 192-196.

18. See Karen Fog Olwig, "The Burden of Heritage: Claiming a Place for a West Indian Culture," *American Ethnologist* 26, no. 2 (1999).

19. Aschenbrenner, *Lifelines*; Harrison, "Give"; Jones, "Kinship."

Bibliography

Aschenbrenner, Joyce. *Lifelines: Black Families in Chicago*. Prospect Heights, Ill.: Waveland, 1983.

Basch, Linda, Nina Glick Schiller, and Cristina Szanton Blanc. *Nations Unbound: transnational projects, postcolonial predicaments and deterritorialized Nation-States*. Langhorne: Gordon & Breach, 1994.

Chamberlain, Mary. *Narratives of Exile and Return*. London: Macmillan, Ltd., 1997.

———. "Praise Songs of the family: lineage and kinship in the Caribbean diaspora." *History Workshop Journal* 50 (2000): 114-128.

———. "Small Worlds: childhood and empire." *Journal of Family History* 27, no. 2 (2002): 186-200.

———. *Family Love in the Diaspora: Migration and the Anglo-Caribbean Experience*. Kingston, Jamaica: Ian Randle Publishers, New Brunswick, N.J., London: Transaction Publishers, 2006.

Comaroff, Jean and John Comaroff. "Introduction." Pp. xi-xxxviii in *Modernity and its Malcontents: ritual and power in postcolonial Africa*, edited by Jean Comaroff and John Comaroff. Chicago: University of Chicago Press, 1993.

Connerton, Paul. *How Societies Remember*. Cambridge: Cambridge University Press, 1989.

Glick Schiller, Nina, and Georges Fouron. *Georges Woke Up Laughing: long-distance nationalism and the search for home.* Durham, N.C.: Duke University Press, 2001.

Harrison, Faye V. "Give me that old-time religion: Genealogy and the Cultural Politics of an Afro-Christian Celebration in Halifax County, North Carolina." Pp: 34-45 in *Religion in the Contemporary South: Diversity, Community, and Identity*, edited by O.K. White, Jr. and Daryl Whites. Athens: University of Georgia Press, 1995.

Jones, Yvonne. "Kinship affiliation through time: black homecomings and family reunions in a North Carolina County." *Ethnohistory* 27, no. 1 (1980): 49-66.

Olwig, Karen Fog. *Global Culture, Island Identity: continuity and change in the Afro-Caribbean community of Nevis.* Switzerland and Philadelphia, PA, 1993.

———. "The Burden of Heritage: Claiming a Place for a West Indian Culture." *American Ethnologist* 26, no. 2 (1999): 370-388.

———. "Follow the People: Movement, Lives, Family." Paper presented at conference on Migration and Transnational Theory Re-examined: Place, Generation, Identity, Santo Domingo, Dominican Republic, April 1999.

Parkin, David. "Ritual as Spatial Direction and Bodily Division." Pp. 11-25 in *Understanding Rituals*, edited by Daniel de Cuppet. New York: Routledge, 1992.

Sutton, Constance R. "Foreword." Pp. ix-xv in *Women and the Ancestors: Black Carib Kinship and Ritual*, Virginia Kerns. Urbana and Chicago: University of Illinois Press, 1997 (2nd ed.).

———. "'Motherhood is Powerful': embodied knowledge from evolving field work." *Anthropology and Humanism* 23 (1998): 139-46.

II

PERFORMING IDENTITIES

4

Melvin L. Butler

Dancing around Dancehall: Popular Music and Pentecostal Identity in Transnational Jamaica and Haiti

In part because of its long history of transnational flows, the Caribbean region presents a dilemma for anthropologists and other researchers of expressive culture. I believe this dilemma stems, in part, from the need to attend adequately to both local and global contexts of practice. When analytical approaches that limit their purview to the level of the community or village are applied to "pre-postmodern" Caribbean societies, which have been described as "inescapably historical," "inherently colonial," and "inescapably heterogeneous," these approaches become most clearly problematic.[1] Michel-Rolph Trouillot laments the fact that "few students of Caribbean culture (especially Caribbean-born or African-American scholars) dare to cross linguistic or colonial borders." He cautions that even regional studies of the Caribbean focusing solely on Anglophone societies overlook the fact that, for example, "a comparison of women in Jamaica and Haiti would be at least as interesting as one between women in Jamaica and Trinidad." The apparent dearth of comprehensive studies of individual Caribbean communities can be read as "a healthy sign that Caribbean ethnographers often realize that the story they were after does not end with their village."[2] These realizations motivate me to consider the global alongside the local and to embrace a multi-sited approach to conducting ethno-musicological fieldwork and writing about Pentecostalism, popular culture, and musical practice in Jamaica and Haiti. Music is an expressive means through which Jamaican and Haitian Pentecostals index both their global cosmology and also the local and transnational contexts in which they traverse. My discussion thus highlights the relationship between the spaces of global theology and those of local congregational musical practice in the African Caribbean.[3]

The African-Caribbean is home to a wide variety of musical styles and belief systems, with which Jamaican and Haitian Pentecostals often have direct involvement prior to Christian conversion. Part of the broader religious context in which African-Caribbean varieties of Pentecostalism are observed, popular musics associated with African-inspired belief systems such as Vodou and Obeah are a common target of mission-affiliated pastors, who preach adamantly against them. In fact, even lay Pentecostals generally deem the stakes of spiritual warfare too high to risk meddling in religious practices outside of mainstream Pentecostal Christianity. Non-Pentecostal ritual musics are believed to evoke supernatural entities, usually characterized as "demonic spirits," which not only oppose the Christian Holy Spirit, but also may bring about physical and emotional torment.[4] Pentecostals thus acknowledge the mystical powers of non-Christian spirits and understand them to pose a serious threat to the lives and souls of those who worship them through song. Unlike incompatible religious musics, however, songs of the dance club are not generally believed to possess the same levels of inherent spiritual potency. Rather, it is the latter's lyrical content and associations with nightclub life that are seen as most problematic. Understanding how commercial popular genres relate to Pentecostal church music requires a grasp of the ways in which boundaries between sacred and secular are socially and musically established.

This essay examines the ways in which Jamaican and Haitian Pentecostals construct and negotiate religious and national identities through musical style. Musical participation facilitates the articulation of overlapping collective identities that are profoundly shaped and negotiated through stylistic and conceptual distinctions between sacred and secular forms of musical practice. Following Catherine Bell, I employ the concept of "ritualization" to discuss the "various culturally specific strategies for setting some activities off from others, for creating and privileging a qualitative distinction between the 'sacred' and the 'profane,' and for ascribing such distinctions to realities thought to transcend the powers of human actors."[5] Ritualization theory also helps to convey the manner in which Pentecostals distinguish sacred and worldly musical styles and promote a religious brand of cultural nationalism that is predicated on Pentecostal identities. My discussion centers on the ways in which believers use music to position themselves in relation to commercial popular culture and counter national identities endorsed by government officials and reinforced by stereotypes cultivated abroad.

To what extent are Pentecostals able to uphold standards of holiness and appropriateness without sacrificing their sense of cultural and national identity? By focusing on the ways in which believers address this challenge, I aim to shed light on the relations among nationalism, Pentecostal identity, popular culture, and musical style. I begin by problematizing some of the stereotypical depictions of Jamaica and Haiti, the propagation of which has historically hindered our grasp of these nations' complex socio-religious landscapes. My discussion then turns to the emergence of Protestantism in these locales, as I chronicle the arrival of early missionaries and examine the impact of evangelical revivals during the nineteenth and early twentieth centuries. My intention here is to highlight both the similarities and differences between Jamaica and Haiti that have, in different ways and at different times, given rise to modern Pentecostal practice. Drawing on ethno-musicological fieldwork I conducted in these two countries from 2000 to 2004, I offer case studies describing Pentecostals' musical attempts to construct religious and national identities in contradistinction to commercial popular genres such as dancehall reggae and *konpa* (Haiti's commercial dance music). I hope also to elucidate the impact of black music from the United States in generational debates over what constitutes "appropriate" forms of Pentecostal musical practice. By "dancing around dancehall," Jamaican and Haitian Pentecostals assert identities that are both local *and* global, national *and* transnational, distinct from, yet dependent upon, the "secular" popular cultures in which they are embedded. Finally, I comment briefly on the politics of positionality that undergirds African-Caribbean Pentecostals' attempts to musically situate themselves in opposition to spiritual and cultural Others. I argue that this strategic positioning also relates to contemporary ethnographic research and writing.

(Re-)Constructing the Caribbean

Zora Neale Hurston's comparative study, *Tell My Horse: Voodoo and Life in Haiti and Jamaica* (1990), explored two socio-religious landscapes that have since undergone tremendous change. Global mass media have spread misconceptions about Haitians and Jamaicans widely among North American and European societies. Jamaicans are too often typecast as dreadlock-wearing Rastafarians, drug dealers, marijuana addicts, or witchdoctors. It is perhaps ironic, although not surprising, that Jamaica remains a hot spot for North American tourists, many of whom seek to bask in an "exotic" island culture imagined to be pleasurably different from their "normal" routines. In *Consuming the Caribbean*, Mimi Sheller highlights this perception of exotic difference, which is fueled by advertising campaigns, tourist brochures, and word-of-mouth. She also critiques the "deep layering and reiteration" of such representations because they reinforce notions of the Caribbean as "a carnivalesque site for hedonistic consumption [. . .] where the normal rules of civility can be suspended." The Caribbean region is portrayed as "a chain of 'unreal' fantasy islands" offering a wild alternative to the "civilized" spaces of North America and Europe. Such depictions "reflect a long history of the inscription of corruption onto the landscapes and inhabitants of these 'Paradise isles.'"[6]

Written during the American occupation of Haiti (1915-1934), William Seabrook's *The Magic Island* did much to perpetuate an image of Haiti as a strange, wild, and horrific land where crazed "Voodoo" devotees run rampant. Seabrook contrasts these devotees with the "literary-traditional white stranger" who witnesses

> all the wildest tales of Voodoo fiction justified: in the red light of torches which

> made the moon turn pale, leaping, screaming, writhing black bodies, blood-maddened, sex-maddened, god-maddened, drunken, whirled and danced their dark saturnalia, heads thrown weirdly back as if their necks were broken, white teeth and eyeballs gleaming, while couples seizing one another from time to time fled from the circle, as if pursued by furies, into the forest to share and slake their ecstasy.[7]

Citing "one of the more thoughtful students of the religion," Mintz and Trouillot note, "'Qui dit Haiti, pense 'Vaudoux,' c'est un fait devant lequel on doit se contenter d'emettre une vaine protestation' [Whoever says Haiti thinks 'voodoo,' a state of affairs over which one can only protest in vain]."[8]

The notion that Vodou is emblematic of the Haitian people is reinforced by the writings of scholars such as Roger Bastide, who contends that Vodou is Haiti's "national creed," serving as a spiritual expression of "the sum of all that is specifically and originally Haitian."[9] Vodou is thus viewed unproblematically as the sine qua non of "authentic" Haitian culture, expressed by Michael Dash in a more recent repetition of a popular characterization of Haiti's religious landscape: "Haiti is 90 percent Catholic and 100 percent vaudou."[10] Despite the perpetuation of this persistent, yet misleading adage, some figures indicate that, by turn of the twenty-first century, as much as one-third of Haiti's population self-identified as Protestant or Pentecostal.[11] Over the course of the twentieth and early twenty-first centuries, Haiti's religious landscape has grown to include numerous mission-affiliated and independent Pentecostal churches.

Likewise, and contrary to popular belief, Pentecostalism is widespread in Jamaica.[12] In fact, Pentecostalism has been developing steadily on the island since the 1920s, thriving along with belief systems such as *Kumina*, Revival (or *Pocomania*), and Rastafarianism.[13] Despite the predominance of Catholicism and Anglicanism throughout the African Caribbean in much of the twentieth century, evangelical revivals in both Jamaica and Haiti have attracted increasing numbers of Protestant and Pentecostal missionaries, sparking the emergence of African Caribbean Pentecostal churches (founded by transnational migrants) in the United States. Multiple forms of charismatic Christianity are currently being practiced in Jamaica, Haiti, and their diasporas, even as other popular religious practices continue to flourish.

Early Protestantism in Jamaica and Haiti

While Protestant missionary activity flourished in Jamaica throughout the nineteenth and early twentieth centuries, it was challenged by the persistence of popular religions such as Myal and the indigenized versions of Christianity practiced by Native Baptists and Revivalists. By the 1930s, Rastafarianism had become yet another threat. In Haiti, the early work of Protestant missionaries was dwarfed by the practices of Catholicism and Vodou. Despite facing obstacles,

Protestant and Pentecostal churches managed to emerge in both locales, albeit at different times and with varying degrees of success.

In Jamaica, the British established the Anglican Church after taking control of the island in 1655, but most white planters refused to share their religion with the slaves, who were generally deemed too unsophisticated for Christian conversion. Furthermore, many whites feared that religious instruction would contribute to feelings of equality and entitlement among the blacks.[14] George Simpson reports that "for nearly a hundred years after Britain acquired Jamaica [...] no missionary work was carried on in the island."[15] But by 1738, an evangelical revival had begun in England, and this religious fervor inspired a movement, led by John Wesley, to reform the Anglican Church. The Wesleyan Methodist movement soon spread to the New World, where missionaries in Jamaica began to make attempts at Christianizing the slave population.[16] In 1754, the Methodist presence in Jamaica was supplemented by the United Brethren, or Moravians, who arrived from Germany.[17] However, the Moravian Church had only limited success, baptizing fewer than one thousand slaves by 1800.[18]

During the closing years of the American War of Independence, one of the more fruitful missionary endeavors was launched in Jamaica, as some American families loyal to England chose to emigrate from the United States and settle in Canada, the Bahamas, and Jamaica. Two former slaves, George Lisle and Moses Baker, accompanied their masters to Jamaica in 1782 or 1783[19] and brought their Baptist religion with them. Lisle and Baker planted the first highly successful missionary enterprise on the island, and their work had an enormous impact on the development of Baptist religion from the latter eighteenth through the nineteenth century. The Wesleyan Methodists and Moravians experienced most of their early successes among the "Free Blacks and Coloureds of Kingston," particularly the black and brown churchgoers who were discriminated against in the capital city's Anglican cathedral.[20] However, Lisle and Baker reached enslaved blacks both in Kingston and on rural plantations. These two preachers exemplify the African American migrants who "contributed decisively to the shaping of an Afro-cultural world that embraced the American South and a number of Caribbean islands."[21] Moreover, the endeavors of these blacks from the United States reveal "both the transatlantic and the inter-American dimensions of the religious transformation" of Anglophone Caribbean nations in the late eighteenth century.[22]

Neither Lisle nor Baker was a novice at ministering to oppressed black slaves. For example, Lisle brought to Jamaica his experience preaching before black congregations in the United States,[23] and both men knew intimately the pains of slavery. This first-hand knowledge allowed them to pass along "a tradition of passionate concern for the enslaved and for the mass of the people," while building a church family in which "African-Jamaicans were at home and participated both in managing its religious affairs and also in maintaining the principles of freedom, equality, [and] brotherhood."[24]

In many ways, Lisle and Baker are pivotal figures in the history of Jamaican religion. They started a tradition of appointing traveling preachers, known as "daddys" or "deacons," who assisted church leaders by exhorting others to convert to Christianity. Both men and women were appointed as "warners" whose duties included telling the unconverted about the urgent need for salvation and warning them of the dangers of sinful living. The practice of appointing unlicensed, itinerant preachers was significant in that it led to a socio-religious hierarchy established and maintained from within the black population. Sherlock and Bennett explain that the hierarchy constituted "a 'ranking' of the slaves by blacks and not by white owners, masters, overseers; an appointment of slaves by the preachers to guide, counsel and convert, not to act as drivers whose symbol of authority was the whip." In this way, Lisle and Baker contributed greatly both to the organizational structure and general mission of the Protestant churches in Jamaica. Furthermore, the Bible and the hymnal "became the treasured library of the African-Jamaican people."[25] Lisle and Baker also helped to prepare the way for white Baptist missionaries from England, who did not launch full-fledged missionary endeavors in Jamaica until some thirty years after black Baptist churches had been established.[26]

In the early 1790s, disputes began to arise between black Baptists, such as Lisle and Baker, and various splinter groups that were embracing more energetic musical and bodily worship practices.[27] These groups attracted increasing numbers of blacks by "blending the Christian message with traditional African modes of worship, including spirit possession, dancing, the clapping of hands and swaying of the body."[28] Most black Baptists eventually became known as "Native Baptists" because of their adoption of an indigenous style of worship, characterized by large-scale black involvement and leadership. Their use of bodily and musical participation as a means of achieving states of ecstasy and transcendence foreshadowed the twentieth-century Pentecostal movement.

By late summer 1791, while neighboring St. Domingue was experiencing the onset of its violent Revolution, Native Baptist churches in Jamaica continued to grow. Even Lisle's church in Kingston had already gained 450 members, most of whom were black slaves. This was a time of great nervousness for many white planters, as news of the St. Domingue rebellion spread quickly and British abolitionists stepped up their campaign to end slavery.[29] Geggus notes that the pro-slavery stance of the white Jamaican planters was likely strengthened by the Haitian Revolution. The plantocracy argued that abolitionists' efforts were largely responsible for stirring the St. Dominguan slaves to revolt. The planters contended, furthermore, that the absence of a similar rebellion in Jamaica proved that the institution of slavery was noble and beneficial to the colony.[30] As French refugees from St. Domingue poured into Kingston, the Jamaican economy was strengthened by the flow of capital and the non-enforcement of French trade laws. Geggus also argues that, in some ways, St. Domingue and Jamaica grew closer, as transnational bonds formed between the planter classes of the two colonies. These bonds "cut across the political divide," even as antagonisms among the white classes in Jamaica were exacerbated.[31] One major source of class tension was the issue of slavery. Wealthy white planters and overseers saw slave labor as a critical means of gaining tremendous economic profit. They perceived the growing abolitionist movement and the Christianization of slaves—ideas embraced by some less wealthy whites—as serious threats to their financial well-being. White Wesleyan Methodists fought for the right to teach Christianity to slaves, while many planters saw such efforts as increasing the probability of slave uprisings.[32]

The success of the St. Domingue revolt thus struck fear in the hearts of white overseers in Jamaica and "strengthened their misgivings about missionary enterprises."[33] In 1802, the Jamaican House of Assembly published an act aimed at persons described as "ill-disposed, illiterate, and ignorant enthusiasts," who addressed "meetings of Negroes and persons of color, chiefly slaves, unlawfully assembled," inciting them to "concoct schemes of much private and public mischief."[34] Although the British king overturned this act in 1804, the Kingston Council passed a similar act in 1807. This new legislation, approved only three years after Haitian Independence, reflected the anxiety of white power holders, many of whom were no doubt still fearful of the capacity for religiously inspired slaves to revolt. The 1807 act forbade slaves to hold religious gatherings at night, which was their only free time. Other prohibited practices included "all preaching, teaching, the offering of public prayer, and the singing of psalms by unauthorized persons of any sect or denomination [. . .] within the boundaries of Kingston."[35] This crackdown on religious practice, which even applied to singing or reciting certain psalms and hymns, was not without precedent in colonial Jamaica. Moses Baker was once arrested for including the words to the following hymn in his sermon:

> Shall we go on in Sin
> Because Thy grace abounds,
> or crucify my Lord again
> And open all His Wounds?
> We will be slaves no more
> Since Christ has made us free,
> Has nailed our tyrants to the cross
> And bought our liberty.[36]

After the Methodists complained to the British Crown that the 1807 act excluded some 400,000 slaves from any form of public worship, the legislation was finally overturned in 1809. As the white planters and clergy jockeyed for control over the degree to which black slaves could receive religious instruction, Native Baptists continued to flourish. However, their indigenous worship style was displeasing to most white missionaries. Despite fierce planter opposition, the Jamaican Assembly therefore resolved in 1816 to "consider the state of the religion among the slaves, and to carefully investigate the means of diffusing the light of *genuine* Christianity among them (my italics)."[37] However, it seems the white missionaries were dependent on the plantocracy for certain economic favors. Consequently, the 1816 resolution had little effect because "the resistance of the Planters to teaching Christianity to slaves was so strong that no clergyman would dare risk his benefits to do so."[38]

It is very important to keep in mind that the growth of Native Baptist religion in late eighteenth- and early nineteenth-century Jamaica coincided with the proliferation of African-inspired popular cults in both Jamaica, which had received an influx of African slaves accompanied by their masters from St. Domingue,[39] and also Haiti, where the power of the Catholic Church had been significantly weakened. The indigenous churches founded by Lisle and Baker grew alongside a multiplicity of African-influenced religious practices flourishing in Jamaica around the turn of the nineteenth century.

Burton posits that by the 1820s, "a religious version of the Creole language continuum" was in place.[40] Drawing on the work of Brathwaite,[41] he claims that this continuum stretched "from the Euro-Christianity—principally Methodist—of the free colored class through the 'Creo-Christianity' of the white-led Baptist churches to the black-led Afro-Christianity of the slave masses."[42] Slave religious practices "remained at least as much 'Afro' as 'Christian,' and in the marriage of Myalism and Christianity, much of the substance of the former had received only the thinnest veneer of the latter."[43] The ongoing interpenetration of Protestant Christianity and popular religion among the slaves widened the gulf between the Native Baptists and the more European-influenced Wesleyan Methodists. Once the first British Baptists arrived in Jamaica in 1813, they tried unsuccessfully to absorb the Native Baptist Church. The latter avoided being taken over by white Baptists by splitting off "to follow their own style of worship, which, giving a Christian form to long-established Myalist practices, emphasized music and dancing, 'spirit possession,' prophecy, and speaking in tongues."[44]

Protestant Christianity had a profound impact on both Obeah and Myal practices. Austin-Broos notes that the belief systems of Myal evolved gradually as a means of undoing the negative effects of Obeah. "The logic of Jamaican obeah," she maintains, "with its various techniques to 'put on spirits' and the myal rites to take them off, therefore is seen more properly as a Jamaican phenomenon shaped by a Christian presence."[45] Although Christian practice certainly impacted Myalism, the latter was viewed by those who practiced it as a distinct and even oppositional form of religious expression. The experiences of trance and speaking in tongues were central to Myal religion, and these phenomena were supported by singing, dancing, and drumming. Women were crucial to the efficacy of the rituals, "but probably not leaders." Authority rested in the hands of "Myal men," also known as "faith men" or "angel men" who presided over the female majority.[46]

There are some striking similarities between Jamaican popular religion of the early nineteenth century and the Pentecostal practices that would emerge a century later. These similarities include the predominant role of women despite mostly male leadership and the use of music to invite manifestations of the Holy

Spirit. Burton also points out that Myal "involved inspiration by 'the Spirit' rather than possession by 'the spirits' as in Afro-Catholic cults such as Vodou, Shango, Santería, and Candomblé."[47] This is one of the important ways in which modern-day Pentecostals in Haiti distinguish their religion from other belief systems in the African Caribbean. J.H. Buchner, a Moravian missionary who witnessed Myal practices in the late 1700s, paints a vivid portrait of a ritual that could have taken place in numerous African Caribbean locales during this era.

> As soon as darkness of evening set in, they assembled in crowds in open pastures, most frequently under large cotton trees, which they worship, and counted holy; after sacrificing some fowls, the leader began an extempore song, in a wild strain, which was answered in chorus, the dance followed, grew wilder and wilder, until they were in a state of excitement bordering on madness. Some would perform incredible revolutions while in this state, until, nearly exhausted, they fell senseless to the ground, when every word they uttered was received as divine revelation. At other times obeah was discovered or a shadow was caught; a little coffin being prepared in which it was enclosed and buried.[48]

In rituals such as this one, drumming and dancing are always vehicles for spirit possession, through which ancestors provide revelations to the community. These revelations are sometimes given through glossolaic utterances (i.e., words spoken in an unknown language) understood only by the possessed, and they may provide a cure for an illness or serve as a warning of impending danger.[49] Although Barrett refers to this late eighteenth-century event as a "kumina" ceremony, Ken Bilby admonishes that kumina did not actually emerge in Jamaica until slave Emancipation in 1838, after which African indentured laborers from the Congo region migrated to the island and began cultivating the practice.[50] Barrett's use of the term probably reflects a certain terminological looseness, which has long characterized written accounts of Jamaican popular religion. Moreover, there appears to be considerable overlap among various Jamaican belief systems and popular religious practices, many of which involve the use of drums, dancing, and singing to evoke spiritual manifestations and invite possession. Bilby discusses a number of religious practices with African origins, of which one of the most notable is the maroon tradition known as "kromanti play." Like the kumina rituals brought to Jamaica in the nineteenth century, kromanti play ceremonies "revolve around the possession of participants by ancestral spirits who use their powers to help the living solve various problems."[51]

Through the first third of the nineteenth century, both white Wesleyan Methodists and black Native Baptists thrived, and the leaders of these two groups trained blacks to preach and proselytize. Although the Christian education of black slaves incurred the wrath of white planters toward both religious groups, this did not prevent serious political differences, in addition to variations in worship style, from surfacing between Methodists and black Baptists. Citing Ba-

Bakan,[52] Burton stresses that while the Methodists wanted slaves to be patient and wait for slavery to be legally abolished, black Baptists leaders exhorted their congregations to pursue freedom immediately.[53] One such leader was Samuel Sharpe, a black Baptist deacon, who led an anti-slavery resistance movement known as "the Baptist War" in 1831.[54] As a deacon, Sharpe enjoyed greater traveling privileges than non-ranked slaves. This relative freedom allowed him to visit various plantations, where, in gatherings disguised as prayer meetings, he enlisted the cooperation of other slaves. The Baptist War did not succeed in overthrowing the institution of slavery overnight, but it was one of many tactics employed by Sharpe and other black leaders in Jamaica to destabilize the existing system of black oppression in Jamaica. Black Baptists continued to oppose white hegemony even after Emancipation in 1838. In fact, "even more than before it was religion, understood in a sense very different from that of white missionaries, that would be the focus of the Jamaican dream of real, rather than merely formal, freedom and equality."[55] By 1838, a great majority of blacks were nominal Christians. In some cases, slaves had done more than simply receive baptism; a considerable number of slaves "had been married according to the church they belonged to." Social and economic tensions between ex-slaves and ex-masters increased over the ensuing three decades, as did the conflicts between white missionaries and black preachers "over the *kind* of Christianity that was to hold sway in Jamaica."[56]

As we have seen, the situation in early to mid-nineteenth-century Haiti was much different from that in Jamaica. Under French colonial rule, evangelical Protestantism had made few inroads because of the dominant influence of the Roman Catholic Church on slaves and free members of society. After overthrowing the whites in 1804, Haiti remained an unlikely destination for most missionary groups. Nevertheless, there were some Protestant endeavors that managed to take root in the newly founded black republic. As early as 1806, Protestant churches may have been started in southern Haiti by black slaves who escaped from the American colonies. Indigenous "Baptist" churches were also started by African Americans in northern Haiti in 1824. Wesleyan Methodists from England started work in Haiti in 1817, as they had done in Jamaica several decades prior.[57] Logan notes that Mark Baker Bird, a Methodist missionary, arrived in Haiti in 1839 and established a number of churches and schools. By 1854, Bird, who spoke both English and French, opened an English-language church catering to the significant numbers of blacks who had migrated to Haiti "after the decline of the British West Indian sugar islands." In 1879, Bird left Haiti because of lack of financial and institutional support.[58]

Despite the successes of these early Protestants in Haiti, their work pales in comparison to the growth of Methodist and Baptist churches in Jamaica. The different degrees of Protestant success in Jamaica and Haiti have much to do with the colonial histories of these two nation-states during the nineteenth century. Haiti's War of Independence resulted in its international non-recognition and a split with the Vatican in Rome. As Vodou practices flourished in Haiti,

Protestantism found a more welcome home in Jamaica, where indigenous versions of Christianity emerged and set the stage for the Pentecostal movement of the twentieth century. Although both Jamaica and St. Domingue thrived on plantation economies maintained by large-scale African slave labor, the religious landscapes of the two colonies took increasingly different shapes in the nineteenth century.[59]

In many ways, the years 1860-1865 marked a watershed moment in the historical development of religion in Haiti and Jamaica. In Haiti, of course, relations were restored with Rome, and this led to the return of Catholic priests, the attempted institutional suppression of Vodou, and only a relatively small role for Protestant missions.[60] Nevertheless, shortly after the signing of the Concordat in 1861, the Episcopal Church was established in Haiti by James Theodore Holly, an African American clergyman from Detroit, Michigan.[61] Reverend Holly arrived in Haiti accompanied by 110 blacks who were fleeing racial oppression in the United States. Although two-thirds of the new arrivals died or returned home, Holly managed to continue his work. In 1874, he was appointed bishop, and he served in that capacity for over thirty-five years.[62] Later in the nineteenth century other Protestant groups such as the Seventh Day Adventists and Baptists arrived.[63] Both of these groups were more concerned with the social uplift of the masses, and, consequently, they experienced growth at a faster rate.

Evangelical revivals and the Pentecostal movement

The latter half of the nineteenth century saw even more dramatic developments in the religious landscapes of the African Caribbean. Evangelical revivals that swept through the United States and Britain in 1858 and 1859 had perhaps the strongest repercussions in Jamaica. Representatives from the Church of Christ arrived in Jamaica as early as 1858. These missionaries planted the seeds of a revival that, although initially sown on the east coast of the United States,[64] would yield fruit in Jamaica throughout the remaining decades of the nineteenth century. Charles Finney, a Presbyterian theologian, Phoebe Palmer, a New York-based Methodist evangelist, and Henry Clay Fish, a Baptist preacher from New Jersey, were leading figures in the U.S. revival. Baptists were also at the forefront of revivalism in England, and in 1859, the Baptist Missionary Society sent two delegates, Edward Bean Underhill and J.T. Brown, to Jamaica, where they began revival meetings soon after arriving. By 1861, a new wave of evangelical preachers had reached the island, finding converts among the Native Baptists, Methodists, and other Protestant groups.[65] Commenting on the impact of the Great Revival in Jamaica, Austin-Broos notes, "The logic of malaise and healing," central to many African-derived popular religions, "was imbued with Christian ideas of sin." In addition, Protestant Christianity became an intractable element within Jamaican ritual practice. The Great Revival "secured in Jamaica the salience of local Christian forms. Thereafter, for many Jamaicans, the Bible would be a textbook of life, and Christian practice, whatever its form, would be the bracketing experience of being."[66] Most scholars agree that the revival atmosphere of the early 1860s led to the formation of religious cults such as Revival Zion and Pocomania, which have continued to thrive in Jamaica through the twentieth and early twenty-first centuries.

The period following the American Civil War (1861-1865) was characterized by an even greater increase in evangelical activity in the United States. As a holiness movement swept the country, numerous camp meetings were held in the southern United States during the latter half of the nineteenth century. Although these meetings were at first run by Methodists, many Methodist church leaders began to express discomfort with the intensity of the religious services, which often featured ecstatic behavior, glossolalia, dancing, and weeping as participants responded emotionally to fiery sermons and the felt presence of the Holy Spirit. By 1894, the Methodist Episcopal Church denounced the holiness movement, labeling it unorthodox and unbiblical. Consequently, many of the movement's supporters left the Methodist church and began to form their own holiness organizations, such as the Church of the Nazarene and the Church of God in Christ.[67]

Meanwhile, in Jamaica, the doctrinal and experiential boundaries between Orthodox and Native Baptists were beginning to solidify, and many of the latter became known as Zion Revivalists after the Great Revival of 1861.[68] These Revivalists continued to engage in spiritual practices such as "trumping," "sounding," and "laboring in the Spirit,"[69] which were condemned by most missionaries. Rather than privileging the missionary ideals of ethical rationalism and strict discipline, Revivalists placed a great emphasis on divine healing, not only from physical ailments, but also from the "sickness" of sin. Another controversial aspect of Zion Revival included the belief that participants could become the expressive vehicles for Old Testament figures such as Moses, Joshua, and Elijah, or angels such as Michael or Gabriel. By becoming "possessed" with one of these spiritualized entities, Revivalists believed they gained the power to bring about healing.[70] Revival pastors often used herbal remedies, which worked along with repentance on the part of the afflicted individual and supernatural intervention from the Holy Spirit. Throughout the second half of the nineteenth century, Revivalists held on to many of the basic tenets of nineteenth-century missionary Christianity. However, they modified these tenets in practice to deploy a broader range of spiritual resources for healing and cleansing from sin. Jesus and the Holy Ghost (or Holy Spirit) were given special emphasis for practical matters pertaining to community spiritual, moral, and physical health, while God became viewed as omnipresent yet largely uninvolved in most mundane matters.[71]

Revivalists' emphasis on the accessibility of Jesus and the healing power of the Holy Spirit would become prominent characteristics of twentieth-century Pentecostal practice. By 1900, Jamaican religious society featured an undeniable split between "respectable" Orthodox Baptists associated with middle-class mores and "uncivilized" possession cults deemed "African" and thus inferior.[72] Many of the Orthodox Baptists "looked askance at the American revivals that were spreading to Jamaica." Middle-class churchgoers began to place an even stronger emphasis on British-influenced values, including a "tempered and law-like" style of worship. They also eschewed healing and possession practices, which they considered both superstitious and immoral. The stigmatization of Revivalism came partly in response to Methodists and Anglicans, who exerted considerable influence on Jamaican Orthodox Baptists, especially those in Kingston.[73]

The latter half of the nineteenth century also saw a tremendous increase in the amount of Protestant missionary work being carried out in Haiti. Not surprisingly, much of this evangelizing was done by British Baptists, who, by 1845, had established a mission in Jacmel. Unlike Mark Bird's earlier Methodist mission, which received criticism because its leaders often spoken no French or Haitian Creole and focused mostly on non-Haitian immigrants, the British Baptists reached out to rural Haitians. The Jacmel mission was, as Conway notes, "supported by funds from London and Jamaica."[74] Jacmel's location on Haiti's southern coast made it a relatively easy stop for ships traveling from London to Kingston. The Great Revival in Jamaica during the 1860s, the holiness movement in the United States, and the convenience of accessible shipping lanes no doubt contributed to the growth of the Baptist presence in southern Haiti. Conway states that "by the 1890s the church [. . .] had 49 baptized members and considerable more 'believers,' both in the town and in 'stations' around the town."[75] By the turn of the twentieth century, the Jacmel church was no longer being run by British missionaries, and Nossirehl Lherisson, a Haitian pastor (whose name is a palindrome), took over the mission. Citing Haitian evangelist Myrthil Bruno, Conway notes that Lherisson "saw that the future of Protestantism [in Haiti] lay more in its potential appeal to the rural population than to the middle and upper class[es]," who embraced the French language and Roman Catholicism.[76] Haitian theologian, Edner Jeanty, remarks, "*Jacmel est l'endroit où le Protestantisme est synonyme de Baptisme plus que toute autre région du pays*" ["More than any other region of the country, Jacmel is the place where Protestantism is synonymous with the Baptist faith"—my translation].[77] Drawing on the formal and informal education he had gained through his travels to France, England, and Jamaica,[78] Lherisson evangelized along Haiti's southern coast to win converts and establish stations. By the time of his death in 1934, the Baptist church had twelve hundred baptized members and over three thousand congregants.[79] Missionaries from the Baptist Missionary Society in Jamaica had a major impact on the Baptist church not only in Jacmel, but also in St. Marc, a town farther north. In reference to the St. Marc church, Jeanty writes, "*Il y avait presque toujours un Jamaican à donner un coup de main*" ["There was almost always a Jamaican to lend a helping hand"—my translation],[80] until a Haitian pastor was eventually appointed.

The 1906 Azusa Street Revival in Los Angeles was a key event precipitating the global resurgence of Pentecostalism and the birth of numerous Pentecostal organizations.[81] As David Martin writes, "What happened following the explosive star-burst of the end of the trail in Los Angeles, and equally following all the other parallel star-bursts worldwide, was a hurling of people in every direction."[82] After the Azusa Street Revival, two basic types of Pentecostal organizations emerged: trinitarian groups, such as the Assemblies of God, the Church of God, and the Church of God in Christ (COGIC); and apostolic or "oneness" organizations, such as the United Pentecostal Church (UPC) and the Pentecostal Assemblies of the World (PAW). All of these organizations established missions in Haiti and Jamaica by the middle of the twentieth century and have remained global in reach.

The 1920s marked the start of large-scale missionary work in Haiti. However, most of these Protestant groups were Baptist missions, fueled by the triumphs of earlier endeavors in Jacmel. The Church of God was the first Pentecostal group to achieve success in Haiti, planting a church there in the mid-1930s.[83] Conway estimates that Protestants did not penetrate very much of Haiti's interior until the 1940s.[84] He argues that although the American occupation (1915-1934) and the consequent media sensationalization of Vodou probably gave foreign missionaries a greater impetus to rescue Haitians from "Voodoo," Protestant and Pentecostal missionary work did not grow significantly during this period. Nevertheless, the occupation "provided a context for the flourish of American Protestantism in Haiti and indirectly was responsible for reducing the prevalent influence of the Catholic Church."[85] The 1950s and 1960s saw a more dramatic increase in Protestant and Pentecostal missionary activity, particularly after the 1957 inauguration of Haiti's notorious president, François "Papa Doc" Duvalier.[86] Although Duvalier is often associated with Vodou, he also earned the title, "Father of Protestantism," because of the remarkable growth Protestant churches experienced during his reign. Duvalier believed Protestants were a valuable resource because they provided the country with moral instruction and public health care without becoming politically active or posing a collective threat to his power. In fact, he saw Protestantism as a way of strengthening his own political power vis-à-vis the Catholic Church. Protestant churches were growing at an even faster rate during the 1970s, but Conway regrets that "more recent statistics are not available."[87] Lain and Louis offer more recent estimates of the percentages of Protestants and Pentecostals among Haiti's churchgoers.[88]

Pentecostals made inroads in Jamaica considerably earlier than in Haiti. The Holiness Church of God, an important predecessor to the Jamaican Pentecostal movement, arrived on the island in 1908 and is mentioned in several articles in the *Jamaica Daily Gleaner* from the 1920s.[89] In 1918, A.J. Tomlinson, founder of the Pentecostal Church of God in Cleveland, Tennessee, sent an evangelist, J.S. Llewellyn, to Jamaica. This trinitarian church changed its name to the New Testament Church of God and is now the largest Pentecostal organization in Jamaica. In the 1920s, there were also notices in the *Gleaner* concerning Pentecostal groups such as the Apostolic Church of God, the Church of God in Christ, and the Pentecostal Assemblies of the World. It was this latter organization that experienced the most rapid growth in Jamaica during this time, largely through the efforts of George and Melvina White. George White began pastoring in St. Elizabeth and Kingston in the mid-1920s. By 1926, he had claimed affiliation with the Pentecostal Assemblies of the World, and a year later, the Whites traveled to the United States to visit the organization's headquarters. During this visit, George White gained accreditation and formal recognition as a minister of the gospel and marriage celebrant. White's success in achieving accreditation and his active role in negotiating the social hierarchy is seen by Austin-Broos as a chief characteristic of Anansi, the cunning trickster-spider character prominent in Jamaican folktales: "White displayed the achievement proudly and with a degree of Jamaican verve that cast him and his contemporaries as serious religionists who also played trickster to the state. They circumvented the government's restrictions by association with American churches."[90] Anansi's ability to gain material advantage by outwitting or "tricking" other characters despite their apparent superiority is thus viewed as analogous to early Jamaican Pentecostals pastors' use of transnational linkages to acquire status and circumvent local state authority. Drawing on the work of Pelton and Turner,[91] Austin-Broos likens Jamaican Anansi tales to the "liminal phase" of ritual transformation, in which "persons elude or slip through the network of classifications that normally locate states and positions in cultural space."[92] This liminality is understood as a "permanent possibility" rather than as a transitional stage of ritual action.[93] For Austin-Broos, Jamaican Pentecostal and Revival pastors exemplify key traits of Anansi the trickster by employing (perhaps unwittingly) a Christian hermeneutic that incorporates the "Afro-Caribbean aesthetic of play." This is primarily done, she claims, "through interpretations of the moral in terms of malaise and embodied rite" and "the interpretation of joy as a this-worldly human and sensuous concern." Austin-Broos further maintains that "as healing rejected a disembodied ethic, Anansi and the world of play opposed the mission's endorsement of work as an essential dimension of moral redemption."[94]

Worldliness, holiness, and musical practice

> I beseech you therefore, brethren, by the mercies of God, that you present your bodies a living sacrifice, holy, acceptable to God, which is your reasonable service. And do not be conformed to this world, but be transformed by the renewing of your mind, that you may prove what is that good and acceptable and perfect will of God. (*Romans* 12:1-2)

Most African Caribbean Pentecostals are taught strict guidelines concerning the kinds of music acceptable for worship services, and they generally strive to adhere to the holy, consecrated standard of living advocated by church leaders.

To embrace a holy lifestyle is to abide by biblical teachings and to reject the ways of "the world," which include drug and alcohol consumption, profanity, extramarital sex, and immodest apparel. This all-encompassing standard of holiness also mandates that believers eschew commercial popular musics such as dancehall reggae in Jamaica and *konpa* in Haiti, which are often seen as emblematic of their respective nation-states. Nevertheless, Pentecostals often express national and cultural pride and enjoy emphasizing their distinctiveness from North Americans. Amidst an onslaught of gospel music from the United States, Jamaican and Haitian Pentecostals celebrate their cultural identities by infusing their religious music with indigenous stylistic characteristics. However, confronted with local secular genres that are equally pervasive, they strive extra carefully to maintain a healthy distance from commercial popular musics, which are more likely than foreign genres to be considered worldly and, therefore, inappropriate.

The distinction between worldliness and holiness is a central component of the biblical doctrine embraced by most Pentecostals. When individuals are "saved" or "born again," they become delivered from the penalty and power of sin and initiated into a global community of believers who have been baptized in water and filled with the Holy Spirit. This body of believers, collectively referred to as "the Church," comprises those who have been "called out" and divinely distinguished from a sinful realm of existence known as "the world." The world thus represents a way of living that is characteristic of pre-conversion status and generally understood to lie outside the boundaries of acceptability that God has established for his chosen people.

In sermons and songs, the transition from the world into the Church is often compared with the Bible's account of the Israelites' exodus from Egypt. This exodus, through which Moses led God's people out of slavery by miraculously crossing the Red Sea, is viewed as symbolic of an individual's rescue from spiritual bondage. The world is thus a type of spiritual Egypt, and the Church represents Canaan, a type of spiritual Promised Land to be enjoyed not only in this life, but also eternally in heaven. The call to "come out from among them" (2 *Corinthians* 6:17-18) rests upon the notion that a spiritual Promised Land awaits those who willingly leave behind a worldly lifestyle and claim their inheritance as one of God's chosen children.

Once born again, an individual is considered a "babe in Christ"—one who has just set out on the path to holiness or sanctification, as described in the lyrics of the following verse to the classic hymn "Holiness unto the Lord."[95] Like numerous hymns from this era, this piece equates worldliness with spiritual bondage.

> Called unto holiness, Church of our God.
> Purchase of Jesus, redeemed by His blood;
> Called from the world and its idols to flee.
> Called from the bondage of sin to be free.

Holiness is understood as an inward state attained through an ongoing process of maturation during which believers constantly strive toward a state of spiritual "perfection." Perfection, in this sense, does not necessarily mean without fault, but, rather, suggests a consecrated Christian walk in which one demonstrates spiritual maturity by maintaining a healthy, growing relationship with God. For Pentecostals, a state of holiness, sanctification, or perfection is attained only through an ascetic lifestyle of submission to God, obedience to divinely selected leadership, and diligence in prayer and fasting. Holiness also requires abandoning worldly pleasures, which include secular musics associated with dancehall cultures. Jamaican Pentecostals sing numerous hymns and choruses that reinforce this belief in the mandates of holiness. For example, the popular hymn, "I Surrender All," which is found in *Redemption* Songs (number 581), expresses complete submission to Jesus by forsaking worldly pleasures. The second verse and chorus of this hymn are as follows:

All to Jesus I surrender,
Humbly at His feet I bow;
Worldly pleasures all forsaken,
Take me, Jesus, take me now.
I surrender all.
I surrender all
All to Thee, my blessed Savior,
I surrender all.

Living a holy lifestyle requires a firm commitment to resist worldly temptations in order to walk the Christian path. The traditional chorus, "Goodbye World," which has been re-popularized in Jamaica through a 2000 recording by African American gospel singer, Donnie McClurkin, expresses this idea of being convinced to leave the world behind.

Goodbye, world. I'll stay no longer with you.
Goodbye, pleasures of sin. I'll stay no longer with you.
I made up my mind to go God's way the rest of my life.
I made up my mind to go God's way the rest of my life.

For many Jamaican Pentecostals, the "reggae-ish" rhythmic accompaniment featured in McClurkin's rendition, with its guitar and keyboard offbeats, is in tension with the song's lyrics, which are understood to celebrate the eschewal of "the dancehall" indexed by the song's rhythmic feel.[96] Therefore, Pentecostals usually sing "Goodbye World" with an underlying groove that is less easily identified with the classic reggae sound of the 1970s or with the contemporary dancehall. In the context of this chorus, saying goodbye to the world does not involve a physical removal from earthly existence or the Jamaican nation-state. On the contrary, congregants are generally encouraged to make the most of life by excelling in education, working hard at one's job, voting in political elections, and taking advantages of opportunities to prosper financially for the benefit of family and church. Pentecostals often describe themselves as being "in the world, but not of the world," meaning that while they are physically located within the larger society, they remain "separate" from it by personally upholding a distinct spiritual and moral framework.

Cheryl Sanders uses the concept of "exile" to describe African American Pentecostals' paradoxical condition of being embedded within a national society whose moral paradigm and norms of respectability often conflict with Pentecostal beliefs and practices. As Sanders explains, the condition of spiritual exile resonates strongly with churchgoers in the United States, who constitute both a racial and religious minority.[97] For African Caribbean Pentecostals in the United States, this spiritual exile is made even more acute, reinforced by marginalization according to both race and ethnicity. In Jamaica, Pentecostals experience a spiritual exile that produces somewhat contradictory attitudes toward popular musics such as mento, ska, reggae, and dancehall, which may constitute expressions of Jamaican cultural nationalism.

Music and morality in a Pentecostal church

During evening services at Mount Olivet,[98] one can usually discern the pounding of a bass drum emanating from some distant sound system—a ubiquitous reminder of the expressive power and influence of secular dancehall culture. For Mount Olivet's pastor, the proximity of these dancehall sounds presents a dangerous temptation, particularly for the church's teens and young adults, who are challenged to adhere to acceptable forms of musical expression in the midst of what is described to them as a hostile sonic environment. Eric, age forty-one, is Mount Olivet's keyboardist and minister of music. He regularly works with the youth, giving them music lessons and encouraging them to stay faithful to God. After one church service, when an instrumentalist began mimicking the bass line to a popular dancehall piece, Eric scolded him, "Never play that in the church!" Policing the boundary between worldliness and holiness is one of the hardest challenges Pentecostal leaders face in trying to keep young people from falling away from the church, a process known as "backsliding." Eric feels that he and other leaders have a crucial responsibility to help prevent youth from yielding to worldly temptations and becoming enmeshed in dancehall culture.[99] During our interview, he spoke about the significance of generational differences within Pentecostal churches as they relate to the need for young people to find an appropriate means of musical self-expression.

    Melvin: Do you think music helps to keep young people in the church?
    Eric: That's one of the thing the church needs to do. Young people—even in the young people's choir, 'cause we have two choirs here—they want to sing

music they can't sing, because you know, they [are] not ready for it.
M: You mean the young people's *choir* isn't ready, or the congregation?
E: The congregation—it's the leadership. You know, the young people waan [want to] sing the Donnie McClurkin, the—
M: Kirk Franklin?
E: Yes! And the church people they not ready for that kind of thing. So what we need to do is try to meet the young people halfway. Not to give up too much, but you know, come halfway. A lot of kids come to church and the music help them express themselves. You know, the beat is fast and they can dance and move. But sometimes they say, well, "In the church me cyan express myself, so me nah stayin' in de church. Me goin' to the dancehall where I can express myself."[100]
M: So right now do you think the church is succeeding? Is music helping to stop young people from backsliding?
E: Sometimes. But we still have to do some more work to meet them halfway. It's goin' take time, because they like to sing—like the choir, they wanna sing this song, "Shake your Booty for Jesus."
M: [laughs] What?
E: Yeah! "Shake your Booty for Jesus," by Beenie Man.

Eric was actually referring to "Gospel Time," the first song on Beenie Man's 1999 recording, *The Doctor*. Among Beenie Man's recordings, "Gospel Time" is unique in that it juxtaposes traditional church choruses against a hip-hop groove and a dancehall vocal style, deliberately creating a striking dissonance between the sacred and the profane, the church and the dance club. The introduction to "Gospel Time" is a slow gospel rendition of "Praise Him" in triadic harmony, after which the rhythmicized chorus is sung, featuring a hip-hop drum loop that accompanies the jarring lyrics, "Shake that booty in the name of the Lord." This provocative chorus is interpolated between well-known gospel songs, such as "Everybody Has to Know," "He's So Real to Me," and "Down by the Riverside." Referring to the chorus, Eric noted, "If you look at the lyrics, they don't really say anything of substance. A lot of the new songs [are] like that. They like to sing them, but they don't really speak of a true experience, like as in 'How Great Thou Art'—where you just look outside at the trees and the grass and say how great God is. The older songs tell of a true experience."

African-American influences and Jamaican youth

Many young Jamaican Pentecostals with whom I spoke are strongly drawn towards African American gospel music styles, which they sometimes experience as "black" though not necessarily "Jamaican."[101] In both New York and Jamaica (especially in Spanish Town and Kingston), African American styles provide a means for some Pentecostals to express a "modern" Pentecostal aesthetic while counter-identifying against the "white" hymnody and "white-sounding" imported gospel music preferred by some churches. "Black" styles are associated mostly with contemporary R&B- and hip-hop-influenced gospel artists from the United States, but also with the traditional choruses and the ska and dancehall rhythms characteristic of contemporary Jamaican gospel music. Whether they emanate from Jamaican or foreign soil, however, the use of "black" gospel styles significantly impacts the experiential framework of Pentecostals' "local" social activity. Moreover, the espousal of African American gospel music by Jamaican and Haitian Pentecostals may even provide a sense of empowerment and facilitate their participation, on some level, in a spiritual warfare whose battlegrounds have become increasingly transnational in scope. In Haiti, by comparison, I found a greater tendency to conflate "blackness" and "Haitianness." In light of Haitian history, this is not at all surprising.

The opposition that some Jamaican preachers express towards African American cultural influence takes the form of a scathing critique of contemporary church practices, which, they contend, have strayed too far from the more "authentic" practices of yesteryear. One of the perceived dangers in moving away from traditional practices is that Jamaican Pentecostal identities are compromised as worldly influences begin to infiltrate congregations. The "modern" musical activities of many Jamaican churches are deemed inauthentic or "artificial" to the extent that they rely on emotionalism and entertainment rather than on the Holy Spirit for their affective impact. One Spanish Town preacher urged his congregation not to "sit down" on God by refusing to offer him praise. The modern-day church, he argued, has also become too lazy to "make a joyful noise" as the Bible commands. A spirit of apathy has become prevalent, he claimed, and many churchgoers lack the spiritual "unction"—that "Holy Ghost anointing"—that would compel them to sing and shout praises to God. He exhorted, "Give me that *old time* Holy Ghost—that Holy Ghost that make[s] me want to sing and dance and preach! I don't want the quiet one! Oh glory! I want the one that make[s] me jump up and shout 'hallelujah!' I just can't keep quiet!"

A similar message was delivered by Bishop Christie, a Jamaican minister visiting from New York, who also expressed a desire for a return to old times characterized less by "emotional" musical practices that "tickle the ear" but more by the transforming power of God's anointing.[102] He began his sermon by lamenting the many changes that have moved the church away from a genuine experience of the Holy Spirit. "What we need today is not more music and emotional singing, but we need the old time anointing. We need not more charismatic preachers, but *Holy Ghost* preachers, *anointed* preachers! The present-day church has changed! The *pastors* have changed! The *bishops* have changed! The *music* has changed! The *preaching* has changed!" Although the present generation relies heavily on musical participation to experience a feeling of ecstasy, the "old time anointing," Bishop Christie preached, does not depend on music. He feels that many of the younger believers today are sacrificing a true relationship with God for the temporary pleasures of musical sound. He continued, "This generation has to make so much music because they have to create an *artificial* joy! In the old times, the people *shouted.* They didn't dance, 'cause it was the *Holy Ghost*! They didn't even have a lot of instruments. But when they sang 'What a Friend We Have in Jesus,' oh my! I don't need no organ to help me preach!"

The significant point here is that worldliness and "African-Americanness" are conflated, at least implicitly, in the discourses of some Jamaican Pentecostals. Indeed, most of the "changes" mentioned by Bishop Christie are experienced by older Jamaican churchgoers not only as more "modern" and "artificial" but also as evidence of African American influence on traditional Jamaican Pentecostal practices. For example, Bishop Christie suggests a fascinating distinction between the terms "dancing" and "shouting,"[103] both of which denote bodily movements that Pentecostals generally assume to be spiritually induced. Although many Pentecostals view these terms as synonymous, "shouting" is sometimes used to describe a type of holy dancing that appears relatively more spontaneous, less stylized, and less controlled.[104] Shouting is a form of bodily praise occurring during intense moments of singing and handclapping that spur an individual to transcendence. The terms "dancing in the Spirit" and "holy dancing" hold different connotations for Bishop Christie, who apparently uses them to refer to a more stylized dance pattern that some Pentecostals argue is more controlled by the dancer than by the Spirit. Moreover, the use of stylized foot patterns and jig-like dance steps is more prevalent among African American Pentecostals than among Jamaican Pentecostals.

Bishop Christie's reference to the hymn, "What a Friend We Have in Jesus" provides evidence of a Jamaican preference for the meaningful lyrics of traditional hymns and "sober songs" over the "one-liners" and simpler choruses whose appeal derives more obviously from rhythmic or melodic elements. Although hymn singing is practiced by many African American Pentecostals, it is noticeably more prevalent among Jamaican churchgoers. Bishop Christie's emphatic statement, "I don't need no organ to help me preach," refers to the organist's practice of interjecting percussive chordal attacks in between a preacher's words during a sermon. This occurs most often when a preacher switches to a singing or "intoned" style of sermonizing, which is more characteristic of African American preachers than Jamaican ones. The use of the organ to complement or "help" the preacher is not commonly found in Jamaica's Pentecostal churches, although I did occasionally notice it in urban areas such as Kingston and Montego Bay, where churches often attract preachers visiting from, or influenced by, the United States. Television and radio play a major role in transmitting African American styles of preaching and singing to the island.

Judith, age twenty, belongs to Lighthouse Assembly, a five hundred-member Pentecostal church in Kingston. She spoke to me about the frustrations of teens and young adults who are attracted to African American gospel music styles but feel that they are denied opportunities to express themselves musically because of the traditional tastes of some church leaders. Judith noted that the church's musicians, most of whom are under age thirty, often attempt to sneak jazz elements into their pieces during services. She also spoke about the differences between the jazz-tinged accompaniment played by the instrumentalists and the traditional style preferred by older church leaders. I began by asking her to describe what she meant by "jazz."

> Judith: Okay, it's not straight jazz, but there's a flavor of jazz in there. Like, for example, when the offering is being taken, they'll maybe put hymns, like "Just a Closer Walk with You," in jazz form. It's generally traditional songs, but with a jazz taste.
> Melvin: And what did the older generation think of that?
> J: At first they were quite resistant, 'cause, you know, anything that is not traditional is worldly.
> M: Well, what does "traditional" mean?
> J: Traditional means four-four beat, four beats to the bar, no variation, no ad-libbing, as is.
> M: So would they just sing a hymn or something?
> J: They would sing a hymn or a regular chorus, but with no twist, no flavor—just as is, verbatim. No style. [laughs] Just straight.

Since Judith's parents were members of Lighthouse before she was born, she has been attending the church for as long as she can remember. Since the age of five, she has also been quite active in the church. Currently, Judith sings in the choir. The choir, she explains, is an outlet for many youth who find congregational hymn singing unfulfilling. Most of the Lighthouse choristers are teens and young adults, many of whom sang in the now defunct Youth Choir, which had to disband because so many congregants have been migrating to the United States and England in recent years. In 2001 alone, the church lost eight families to out-migration. Despite the preponderance of youth in the choir, Judith still feels that the choir is limited by the overly conservative tastes of the choir director. Although the director is only in her late thirties, she happens to be the daughter of the pastor, Bishop Wheaton, and is committed to staying within the boundaries of appropriateness determined by her father's musical preferences. Judith continued, "We have an *assistant* choir director who is a younger person, but there still is sort of like a muzzle on things because *the* director is not very open to contemporary stuff. No, if it's not traditional, if it's gonna cause a ruption, they're not gonna listen to it. And she has the final word."

Judith indicated that even traditional songs can be deemed inappropriate and "cause a ruption" if the rhythmic accompaniment does not correspond to accepted norms. She manages to find humor in the reactions of conservatively minded believers to musical selections that stray from traditional guidelines.

> J: Right now, we have a song that we are in the process of practicing. It's an old song, "Saved by His Power Divine" but I'm not too sure it is going to go over very well because it has a calypso-funky beat. And I'm really nervous about it! [laughs]
> M: So what would it mean for it not to go over well? Have you had experiences

like that before?

J: Oh yes! [laughs] Where the pastor's wife, she won't say anything but she'll start fidgeting—[imitates pastor's wife acting nervously]—and getting really uncomfortable and sitting at the edge of her seat. And that's generally how you know it's a problem. And then, she has this way of just—You see the tension. She may not say it right away. But pastor [Bishop Wheaton] will be like "Ahhh," and you know he wants to say something, but he doesn't quite know how to come out and not offend the choir and not offend [his wife]. And like the next time we choose to do the song the director will be like [shakes her head] no, unh-uh. Do the next one, because we keep getting that response.

Both Bishops Christie and Wheaton express views toward music not unlike other Jamaican Pentecostals of their generation. They strive to maintain a delicate balance between allowing the use of music as a tool of transcendence and avoiding an overdependence on musical sound to experience the anointing of the Holy Spirit. These church leaders recognize the positive potential of inspired musical participation, but they are careful not to mistake the pleasures of sound for the touch of the Spirit. "Emotion is not Spirit!" Bishop Christie proclaimed at one point during his sermon. He expounded, "When the music is played to its highest potential, it has something in it to stir the soul and touch the heart. But you've got to have the Holy Ghost that you can feel [even] when you kneel to pray, so you know it is not [just] the music." He thus recognizes the power of musical sound but deems it worthless apart from the Holy Spirit who channels that power and uses it not merely to rouse emotions but, rather, to transform lives. Keeping a healthy distance from African American influences is often a key mandate in this transformation process.

Negotiating Haitian popular music

"*Se Tabou! Sa se Tabou!*" ("It's Tabou! This is Tabou!") The lead singer belted the lyrics while motioning the crowd of jubilant spectators to wave their hands and sing along. I marveled at the synchrony of the more than six thousand bodies swaying to and fro in rhythm with the konpa beat. It was August 1996, and I was nearing the end of a two-month Caribbean tour with Tabou Combo, one of the premiere dance bands to emerge from Duvalier-era Haiti. Based in and around New York City, Tabou Combo always used young North American horn players to supplement their core membership, which had remained mostly intact since the group's inception in the late 1960s.[105] I had just begun playing saxophone and writing horn arrangements for this renowned group, after having spent the previous two years working with Phantoms, one of many *nouvel jenerasyon* (new generation) konpa bands also based in the Haitian diaspora. By the time I visited Haiti with Tabou Combo, I was accustomed to the music's infectious rhythm and the enthusiastic fans who recognized Tabou Combo as international superstars. As I began thinking seriously about pursuing a deeper study of

Haitian music and culture, I took note of the strong emotional impact that konpa seemed to have on those who attended our concerts and festivals. I would eventually discover that this genre, which "has become a symbol for Haitians in Haiti and the diaspora,"[106] is negotiated in a variety of ways by Haitian Pentecostals.

What struck me most during my travels with Tabou Combo were the experiential similarities I noticed between Pentecostal worship services and the outdoor konpa concerts in which I played. In both contexts, participants place a premium on lively music and bodily expression, collectively producing energy or "heat" that marks the success of the event. At the music's most intense moments, the heat flowing from the performers to the crowd and among all those who danced and sang along was even capable of producing spiritual manifestations. Members of Tabou Combo report that a *lwa* even appeared during a concert in the late 1990s. The lwa allegedly entered into a listener who marched onto the stage and began to chew glass during the band's performance of a piece containing roots rhythms. Tabou Combo stopped performing the piece shortly thereafter because, according to one member of the group, "Some people didn't like it." During other konpa concerts, I have witnessed participants lose control of themselves to the point that they had to be restrained or carried away by other audience members.

As I observed audience behavior while playing in Tabou Combo's horn section, I often reflected on the claim made by some Pentecostals that music and worship are inseparable. Disagreeing with characterizations of secular music as "devil worship," I had chosen rather to view the konpa concerts in which I played simply as entertainment. While blowing saxophone lines, however, I sometimes secretly wondered whether I was supporting the musical and bodily worship of an Evil Force.[107] Given the non-Christian character of most commercial konpa lyrics and the ways in which couples sometimes danced,[108] it hardly seemed as though those gyrating their bodies and waving their arms in the air were trying to "make a joyful noise unto the Lord."[109] But then, who or what was being glorified in the konpa concerts in which I played? Did these musical events really have to be placed on one side or the other of the boundary between holiness and worldliness, as I had often heard preached? Or could secular konpa be spiritually neutral? Already struggling with these types of issues throughout my performing career, I found that they took on a heightened relevance once I began conducting ethno-musicological research among Pentecostals in the Caribbean.

All of the Haitian Pentecostals to whom I talked frown upon konpa featuring the kinds of bawdy lyrics sung by performers such as Michel Martelly (a.k.a. Sweet Mickey). Some, however, object strongly to konpa even when played as an instrumental genre or used to support Christian lyrics during church services. These objections, usually voiced by pastors, are based on the fact that konpa is played in nightclubs where "unholy" behaviors, such as drinking, smoking, social dancing, and fornicating, are believed to find support. During a service I attended at a Church of God in Christ in Port-au-Prince, the pastor condemned the hypocrisy of those who profess to be Christians but surreptitiously listen to dance bands. The sermon was based on *Romans* 12:1-2 and emphasized believers' mandate to avoid conforming to the fads and fashions of the world. The pastor used humor to make his point, bemoaning the fact that he would sometimes walk by a saint's home and hear the popular songs of konpa artists such as Tropicana or Sweet Mickey instead of *mizik evanjelik*. For many leaders, the konpa rhythm thus indexes worldliness and unrighteous living. Some church leaders go so far as to preach that konpa "is not a rhythm of the Body [of Christ]" ("*se pa yon rit ko a*") and chastise church musicians who play in a style that too closely resembles the konpa beat. Most of the Pentecostals I met disagree with such extreme viewpoints and feel that konpa is appropriate provided the rhythm does not overpower the singing or become a distraction. Knowing that the status of konpa is controversial among Pentecostals, I usually avoided discussing my prior involvement with Tabou Combo whenever I found myself among churchgoers. However, I felt much less awkward talking about my experience playing African American musical styles such as blues, jazz, and gospel, which, unlike konpa, did not index worldliness or make Haitian Pentecostals uncomfortable.[110] In fact, in churches where konpa is forbidden, congregational singing was usually accompanied by music obviously influenced by commercial popular musics from the United States. Timothy Rommen discusses a similar phenomenon in his ethno-musicological study of Protestant Christianity in Trinidad. The "negotiation of proximity," as he terms it, involves the processes through which churchgoers develop a preference for musical styles that are farthest from them. Discussing the controversies surrounding "gospelypso," Rommen explains that this genre "is situated much too close to home to remain unfettered and uncomplicated." By contrast, North American gospel songs remain "fundamentally Other" despite their integration into Trinidadian religious culture. Unlike gospelypso, which is "implicated in the messiness of everyday life," gospel choruses from abroad maintain a distanced position that ultimately makes them easier to incorporate into worship services.[111]

A very similar phenomenon occurs among Pentecostals in Haiti, where local styles, such as konpa, are more likely to be viewed as a negative influence. Part and parcel of the "messiness of everyday life," konpa's proximity renders it a greater threat, while musical genres that hail from abroad are less ethically complicated and more easily embraced. It is as though their distance renders them innocuous even if they are deemed problematic in their country of origin.

Conclusion

There are some tremendous difficulties in maintaining one's commitment to a religious tradition that says, "We know by faith and not by sight," while maintaining habits of critical inquiry that rest on relentless interrogation of the warrants, grounds, bases, and assertions of truth put forth in all sorts of intellectual communities, including religious ones. . . . In many ways, I see myself as a rhetorical acrobat, navigating through varied communities of intellectual interest and pivoting around multiple centers of linguistic engagement, since all of these commitments have their own languages, rhetorics, and vocabularies.[112]

The "rhetorical acrobatics" that I perform in ethnographic projects such as this one involve positioning myself in relation to the Jamaican and Haitian Pentecostals with whom I have worshipped and conversed. Just as they dance around dancehall to negotiate their identities, I discursively dance with and around the fields of ethnomusicology and anthropology, attempting to juxtapose religious and academic perspectives, provide descriptions and analyses of Pentecostal music in African Caribbean contexts, and establish my identity as a scholar and a Pentecostal. In so doing, I join Renato Rosaldo in "contest[ing] the equation of analytical distance and scientific objectivity." "Social analysts," he argues, "should explore their subjects from a number of positions, rather than being locked into any particular one."[113] The positioning of Self and Other must be seen as part of the "crisis in representation" discussed at length by Clifford and Marcus in *Writing Culture*. As Gina Ulysse argues, this crisis "is and has always been a crisis of position."[114]

It is, perhaps, the politics of positionality that must be explored further if we are to understand precisely what is at stake for Jamaican and Haitian Pentecostals in self-identifying through musical practice. By strategically distinguishing themselves from religious and cultural "Others," they not only gain a sense of spiritual empowerment, but also strive to maintain their dignity and self-respect, often in the face of debilitating poverty and sociopolitical strife. I contend that musical practice serves as a vital tool for Pentecostals in the African Caribbean to phenomenologically situate themselves favorably in relation to both their immediate local contexts, and also the broader transnational arenas in which they observe their faith and embrace religious forms of cultural nationalism.[115]

I have employed the notion of transcendence, in one sense, to refer to the transnational identities of churchgoers who either travel to and from the United States to visit natural and spiritual kin, or maintain links to those living abroad through monetary remittances and various forms of communication. Transcendence suggests the "cutting across" of national boundaries by Pentecostals who often share a class identity based largely on their style of religious practice, ethnicity (or race), and socioeconomic status within their respective societies. The transmigration of church music through these channels helps to connect Pentecostals in the United States and the Caribbean by providing shared sonic material for use in worship services. By indexing translocal places through North American gospel songs, Pentecostals self-identity as members of a global community of believers and imaginatively cross national boundaries often viewed as restrictive. Music also functions as a means through which believers transcend the self to experience divine joy and power through the Holy Spirit. This multifaceted role of Pentecostal music contributes significantly to its efficacy and popularity among African Caribbean believers.

I have also found transcendence a convenient trope through which to examine the multiple boundaries that are negotiated through Pentecostal musical practice. Through musical practice, Pentecostals are able to draw lines between a number of contested positions: sacred and profane, holy and worldly, church and dancehall, local and foreign, African Caribbean and North American, black and white, Self and Other, human and divine. By sharing my experiences with popular music and transcendence among Jamaican and Haitian Pentecostals, I hope to have shed light on how these dichotomies continue to be constructed through the expression of national, cultural, and religious identities within localized forms of charismatic Christian practice.

Notes

1. Cf. Karen Fog Olwig, *Global Culture, Island Identity: Continuity and Change in the Afro-Caribbean Community of Nevis* (Amsterdam: Harwood Academic Publishers, 1993), 9.

2. Michel-Rolph Trouillot, "The Caribbean Region: An Open Frontier in Anthropological Theory," *Annual Review of Anthropology* 21 (1992): 34.

3. Pentecostalism has recently been described as "a repertoire of recognizable spiritual affinities which constantly breaks out in new forms" across the globe—David Martin, *Pentecostalism: The World Their Parish* (Oxford: Blackwell Publishers, 2002), 176. Since the 1990s, scholars have begun to devote greater attention to the worldwide Pentecostal movement. For example, Martin L. Hollenweger, *Pentecostalism: Origins and Developments Worldwide* (Peabody, Mass.: Hendricks, 1997) provides a thorough synopsis of Pentecostalism as it has spread, during the twentieth century, from very few to approximately five hundred million adherents. Poewe and Coleman also provide comprehensive overviews of Pentecostal and charismatic churches from a global perspective—see Karla Poewe, "Introduction: The Nature, Globality, and History of Charismatic Christianity," in *Charismatic Christianity as a Global Culture*, ed. Karla Poewe (Columbia: University of South Carolina Press, 1994) and Simon Coleman, *The Globalisation of Charismatic Christianity: Spreading the Gospel of Prosperity* (Cambridge: Cambridge University Press, 2000). Coleman's study of charismatic Christianity differs from my own in that he is primarily concerned with "Word of Faith" churches that emphasize obtaining financial prosperity through faith and sacrificial giving.

4. In Haiti, the same is believed to be true of musics associated with Vodou, rara, and "heavenly armies"—see Melvin L. Butler, "Songs of Pentecost: Experiencing Music, Transcendence, and Identity in Jamaica and Haiti" (PhD diss., New York University, 2005).

5. Catherine Bell, *Ritual Theory, Ritual Practice* (New York: Oxford University Press, 1992), 74.

6. Mimi Sheller, *Consuming the Caribbean: From Arawacs to Zombies* (London: Routledge, 2003), 165-166.

7. William B. Seabrook, *The Magic Island* (New York: Harcourt, Brace, and Company, 1929), 42; quoted in Charles Arthur and Michael Dash, eds., *A Haiti Anthology: Libete* (London: Latin American Bureau, 1999), 323; Margarite Fernandez Olmos

and Lizabeth Paravisini-Gebert, eds., "Introduction: Religious Syncretism and Caribbean Culture," in *Sacred Possessions: Voodoo, Santeria, Obeah, and the Caribbean* (New Brunswick, N.J.: Rutgers University Press, 1997), 7.

8. Seabrook, *Magic Island*, 123; quoted in Arthur and Dash, *A Haiti Anthology*, 261.

9. Roger Bastide, *African Civilization in the New World* (New York: Harper and Row, 1971), 138. In April 2003, Haitian president Jean-Bertrand Aristide issued an executive order in which he referred to Vodou as "an essential part of [Haitian] national identity." Throughout the subsequent months, the statement was picked up by the Associated Press and published by several newspapers in the United States—see, for example, Michael Norton, "Haiti Officially Sanctions Voodoo," *New York Times/The Associated Press*, 2003, http://www.wehaitian.com.

10. J. Michael Dash, *Culture and Customs of Haiti* (Westport, Conn.: Greenwood Press, 2001), 51. Dash elsewhere provides an excellent historical discussion of literary representations of Haiti as they relate to the propagation of stereotypes in the United States—see J. Michael Dash, *Haiti and the United States: National Stereotypes and Literary Imagination* (New York: St. Martin's Press, 1997). See also Robert Lawless, *Haiti's Bad Press: Origins, Development, and Consequences* (Rochester, Vt.: Schenkman Books, 1992), for a comprehensive, yet somewhat idealized, contestation of negative media portrayals of Haitian expressive culture.

11. Clinton Eugene Lain, "Church Growth and Evangelism in Haiti: Needs, Problems, and Methods" (PhD diss., Asbury Theological Seminary, 1998), 72; Andre J. Louis, "Catholicism, Protestantism and a Model of Effective Ministry in the Context of Voodoo in Haiti" (PhD diss., Fuller Theological Seminary, 1998), 197.

12. Austin-Broos argues persuasively that Pentecostalism in Jamaica has become indigenized, as Jamaicans have adapted North American Pentecostal practice to fit their cultural needs—see Diane J. Austin-Broos, *Jamaica Genesis: Religion and the Politics of Moral Orders* (Chicago: University of Chicago Press, 1997). Toulis focuses on the ways in which Jamaican Pentecostals in England negotiate their identities through religious practice—see Nicole R. Toulis, *Believing Identity: Pentecostalism and the Mediation of Jamaican Ethnicity and Gender in England* (Oxford: Berg-Oxford International Publishers, 1997). However, studies on other aspects of Jamaican religion are considerably more prevalent. For example, anthropological studies of Jamaican Revival include Simpson's early study—see George Eaton Simpson, "Jamaican Revivalist Cults," *Social and Economic Studies* 5, (1956), as well as Joseph G. Moore, *The Religion of Jamaican Negroes: A Study of Afro-American Acculturation* (Evanston and Chicago: Northwestern University, 1953), Edward Seaga, "Revival Cults in Jamaica: Notes Toward a Sociology of Religion," *Jamaica Journal* 3 (1969): 3-13, and Barry Chevannes, "Revivalism: A Disappearing Religion," *Caribbean Quarterly* 24, no. 3/4 (1978): 1-17. Brathwaite and Chevannes have researched Kumina and Rastafarianism, respectively—see Edward Kamau Brathwaite, "Kumina: The Spirit of African Survival," *Jamaica Journal* 42 (1978): 44-63 and Barry Chevannes, *Rastafari: Roots and Ideology* (Syracuse, N.Y.: Syracuse University Press, 1994). John Barton Hopkin's short essay is the only existing music-centered study of Pentecostal church music in Jamaica—see John Barton Hopkins, "Music in the Jamaican Pentecostal Churches," *Jamaica Journal* 12 (1978): 23-40.

13. Rastafarianism gets its name from Ras Tafari, who was crowned King of Ethiopia in 1930. After his coronation, he adopted the name Haile Selassie and became the inspiration for many Jamaicans who formed a new religious sect. Rastafarians view Selassie as a black Messiah whose rise to power represented a fulfillment of biblical

prophecy—see Philip Sherlock and Hazel Bennett, *The Story of the Jamaican People* (Kingston, Jamaica: Ian Randle Publishers, 1998), 395-398, and Chevannes, *Rastafari*. Austin-Broos draws insightful comparisons between Rastafarianism and Pentecostalism in Jamaica—see Austin-Broos, *Jamaica Genesis*, 239-242.

14. Leonard E. Barrett, *The Rastafarians* (Boston: Beacon Press, 1997), 17.
15. George Eaton Simpson, *Black Religions in the New World* (New York: Columbia University Press, 1978), 112.
16. Barrett, *The Rastafarians*, 20.
17. Sherlock and Bennett, *The Story*, 177.
18. Simpson, *Black Religions*, 33.
19. Cf. Sherlock and Bennett, *The Story*, 180; Simpson, *Black Religions*, 42; Richard D. E. Burton, *Afro-Creole: Power, Opposition, and Play in the Caribbean* (Ithaca, N.Y.: Cornell University Press, 1997), 37.
20. Burton, *Afro-Creole*, 37.
21. Sylvia R. Frey and Betty Wood, *Come Shouting to Zion: African American Protestantism in the American South and British Caribbean to 1830* (Chapel Hill: University of North Carolina Press, 1998), 130.
22. Frey and Wood, *Come Shouting*, 131.
23. Simpson, *Black Religions*, 42.
24. Sherlock and Bennett, *The Story*, 182.
25. Sherlock and Bennett, *The Story*, 181.
26. Simpson, *Black Religions*, 42; Burton, *Afro-Creole*, 37.
27. Frey and Wood, *Come Shouting*, 132.
28. Sherlock and Bennett, *The Story*, 180.
29. David Patrick Geggus, *Slavery, War, and Revolution: The British Occupation of Saint Domingue, 1793-1798* (Oxford: Clarendon Press, 1982), 87-88.
30. Geggus, *Slavery, War, and Revolution*, 93.
31. See Geggus, *Slavery*, 95, for a more extensive treatment of the social, economic, and political impact of the Haitian Revolution on Jamaican society.
32. Frey and Wood, *Come Shouting*, 136-138; Simpson, *Black Religions*, 39-40; Barrett, *Rastafarians*, 20; Burton, *Afro-Creole*, 37.
33. Simpson, *Black Religions*, 9.
34. Simpson, *Black Religions*, 40.
35. Simpson, *Black Religions*, 40.
36. Sherlock and Bennett, *The Story*, 181.
37. Barrett, *Rastafarians*, 20.
38. Barrett, *Rastafarians*, 20.
39. Geggus, *Slavery*, 87, 95.
40. Burton, *Afro-Creole*, 40.
41. Edward Brathwaite, "Kumina," 61.
42. Burton, *Afro-Creole*, 37-8.
43. Burton, *Afro-Creole*, 43.
44. Burton, *Afro-Creole*, 37.
45. Austin-Broos, *Jamaica Genesis*, 43.
46. Burton, *Afro-Creole*, 101.
47. Burton, *Afro-Creole*, 101.
48. Cited in Barrett, *Rastafarians*, 18-19.
49. Barrett, *Rastafarians*, 19.
50. Kenneth M. Bilby, "The Caribbean as a Musical Region," in *Caribbean Con-

tours, ed. Sidney W. Mintz and Sally Price (Baltimore: Johns Hopkins University Press, 1985), 188 and 262.

51. See Bilby, "The Caribbean," 187-188, for a more in-depth discussion of African Jamaican popular religions and musics.

52. Abigail B. Bakan, *Ideology and Class Conflict in Jamaica: The Politics of Rebellion* (Montreal and Kingston, Canada: McGill-Queen's University Press, 1990), 57.

53. Burton, *Afro-Creole*, 37.

54. Like many prior uprisings, the Baptist War took place around December 25. Therefore, it is also referred to as the "Christmas Rebellion." See Burton, *Afro-Creole*, 86-88, for a full account of this event.

55. Burton, *Afro-Creole*, 86, 89.

56. Burton, *Afro-Creole*, 42, 97.

57. Lain, *Church Growth*, 66-67; Rayford W. Logan, *Haiti and the Dominican Republic* (London: Oxford University Press, 1968), 181.

58. Logan, *Haiti*, 182.

59. The brown class of "coloreds" or mulattoes in both Haiti and Jamaica also played a significant role in the socio-religious development of each locale. Sherlock and Bennett provide a helpful summation, in which they highlight the impact of color and class on the development of religion and social change in these two African Caribbean contexts.

> These differences [between Jamaican and Haitian contexts] become clear: the Evangelical Movement [started by Wesley in England], largely rooted in the Protestant world, contributed significantly to social change in Jamaica but not in Haiti; the people of colour in Haiti suffered the same civil disabilities as those in Jamaica, but their political and social aspirations were opposed by a much larger body of resident whites, both rich and middle class, than in Jamaica, where the mulattoes were essentially conservative. They [the Jamaican mulattoes] shared the "terrified consciousness" of the whites for the blacks. The Enlightenment reinforced the anti-slavery movement in England, but it did not provide Jamaican browns with a battle cry. The Evangelical movement was concerned with religious principles and man's conversion. The Enlightenment dealt with the principles of government and the rights of man. Each movement exercised a powerful influence in the Caribbean, one through the work of Lisle and Baker in Jamaica, the other through the Friends of the blacks and the Black Jacobins in Haiti.—Sherlock and Bennett, *The Story*, 189.

60. Logan, *Haiti*, 163.

61. Logan, *Haiti*, 182; Selden Rodman, *The Black Republic, the Standard Guide to Haiti* (Old Greenwich, Conn.: The Devin-Adair Company, 1980), 76; Lain, *Church Growth*, 67.

62. Logan, *Haiti*, 182.

63. According to Lain, the Adventist Church arrived in Haiti in 1871—see Lain *Church Growth*, 68. However, Austin-Broos states that the Adventist Church was founded in Kingston in 1894—see Austin-Broos, *Jamaica Genesis*, 55. The Baptist Convention in Haiti may have begun in the early 1860s, but Lain argues that they did not receive official recognition from the American Baptist mission until 1928—see Lain, *Church Growth*, 67; cf. Johnson 1970, 21.

64. Austin-Broos, *Jamaica Genesis*, 55.

65. Austin-Broos, *Jamaica Genesis*, 55-59; Simpson, *Black Religions*, 112; Barrett, *Rastafarians*, 22.

66. Austin-Broos, *Jamaica Genesis*, 71 and 59.

67. See Larry Fred Ward, "Filled with the Spirit: The Musical Life of an Apostolic Pentecostal Church in Champaign-Urbana, Illinois" (PhD diss., University of Illinois at Champaign-Urbana, 1997), 34-35.

68. Austin-Broos, *Jamaica Genesis*, 61-63.

69. Joseph M. Murphy, *Working the Spirit: Ceremonies of the African Diaspora* (Boston: Beacon Press, 1994), 126 gives a vivid account of the trumping of Revival Zion groups of spiritual dancers known as the "band" or "bands."

70. Ward, *Filled*, 63.

71. Austin-Broos, *Jamaica Genesis*, 62

72. For discussions of the relationship between religion and social respectability in Jamaica and Barbados—see respectively Diane Austin, "Culture and Ideology in the English-Speaking Caribbean: A View from Jamaica," *American Ethnologist* 10, no. 2 (1983): 232, and George Gmelch and Sharon Gmelch, *The Parish Behind God's Back: The Changing Culture of Rural Barbados* (Ann Arbor: University of Michigan Press, 1997), 148-156.

73. Gmelch and Gmelch, *The Parish*, 75-76.

74. Frederick James Conway, *Pentecostalism in the Context of Haitian Religion and Health Practice* (Ann Arbor, Mich.: American University, 1978), 163.

75. Conway, *Pentecostalism*, 163.

76. Myrthil Bruno, *Le Denominationalisme protestant et son action social en Haiti. Licence es-Sciences Anthropologiques* (Thesis, Faculté d'Ethnologie, Université d'Etat d'Haiti), 58; cit. Conway, *Pentecostalism*, 163.

77. Edner A. Jeanty, *Le Christianisme En Haiti* (Port-au-Prince, Haiti: La Presse Evangelique, 1989), 76.

78. Jeanty, *Le Christianisme*, 79-80; Conway, *Pentecostalism*, 164.

79. Jeanty, *Le Christianisme*, 80 and 164.

80. Jeanty, *Le Christianisme*, 82.

81. Austin-Broos correctly notes that the Azusa Street Revival was "especially significant" for Pentecostals of African descent because it involved William Seymour and his fiancée, Jennie Moore, both of whom were African American. However, she exaggerates the Revival's impact on black racial identity by claiming that "this event has become a charter myth for black Pentecostals, who deploy it as a statement of the spiritual ascendancy over whites that they propose for New World Africans"—see Austin-Broos, *Jamaica Genesis*, 99. In any event, the Azusa Street Revival did help to spread the message of Pentecostalism across the globe, emphasizing speaking in tongues as evidence of being filled or baptized with the Holy Spirit.

82. David Martin, *Pentecostalism: The World Their Parish* (Oxford: Blackwell Publishers, 2002), 5.

83. Jeanty writes that the Church of God arrived in 1937—see Jeanty, *Le Christianisme*, 56. However, Lain maintains that this church arrived three years prior "through Haitians returning from Cuba"—see Lain, *Church Growth*, 69. The majority of Haitian Pentecostals I encountered from 2000 to 2004 claimed membership in the Church of God.

84. Conway, *Pentecostalism*, 164. Like most scholars, Conway fails to distinguish Protestant from Pentecostal practice, using the term "Protestant" to designate both.

85. Michel S. Laguerre, *The Military and Society in Haiti* (Knoxville: University of Tennessee Press, 1993), 78.

86. Conway, *Pentecostalism*, 165-166; cf. Bruno, *Le Denominationalisme*.

87. Conway, *Pentecostalism*, 166 and 168.

88. See above Lain, *Church Growth*; and Louis, *Catholicism*.

89. "Pentecostal" and "Holiness" churches were difficult to distinguish early on because the Jamaican census conflated these two categories (cf. Austin-Broos, *Jamaica Genesis*, 91 and 98-101).

90. See Austin-Broos, *Jamaica Genesis*, 46-48 and 111-112 for a fuller discussion of the Anansi character and its roots in West African Ashanti cosmology.

91. Cf. Robert D. Pelton, *The Trickster in West Africa: A Study of Mythic Irony and Sacred Delight* (Berkeley: University of California Press, 1980); Victor Turner, *The Forest of Symbols: Aspects of Ndembu Ritual* (Ithaca, N.Y.: Cornell University Press, 1967); Victor Turner, *The Ritual Process: Structure and Anti-structure* (Chicago: Aldine Publishers, 1969).

92. Turner, *The Ritual Process*, 95; cited in Austin-Broos, *Jamaica Genesis*, 46.

93. Austin-Broos, *Jamaica Genesis*, 47; cf. Arnold Van Gennep, *The Rites of Passage* (Chicago: University of Chicago Press, 1960).

94. Austin-Broos, *Jamaica Genesis*, 46.

95. Found in B. Carradine, J. C. Fowler, and W. J. Kirkpatrick, *The Best of All* (Indianapolis, Ind.: Christ Temple, n.d.), 32.

96. McClurkin's version of this chorus, recorded live in London in 2000, is intriguing for a number of reasons. In my dissertation, I explain the tension between "Jamaican" and "African-American" musical styles and discuss the ways in which the piece's reggae-like accompaniment differs from that used among most Pentecostal congregations in Jamaica—see Butler, *Songs of Pentecost*.

97. Cf. Cheryl Sanders, *Saints in Exile: The Holiness-Pentecostal Experience in African-American Religion and Culture* (New York: Oxford University Press, 1996).

98. Pseudonyms are used throughout this section in place of the actual names of congregations and individuals I encountered during fieldwork.

99. Interview, Liliput (St. James), Jamaica. March 25, 2002.

100. "In the church, I can't express myself, so I'm not staying in the church. I'm going to the dancehall where I can express myself."

101. The cultural politics of Jamaican nationalism has contributed to ongoing tensions between social classes and their dynamic concepts of blackness, Jamaicanness, and Africanness—see Deborah A. Thomas, "'Tradition's Not an Intelligence Thing': Jamaican Cultural Politics and Ascendence of Modern Blackness" (PhD diss., New York University, 2000). The creolist ideology of Jamaica's national motto ("Out of Many, One People") was sometimes articulated to me by Pentecostals in response to the suggestion that blackness defines Jamaican culture.

102. The term "anointing" is generally used to refer to the effectual presence and power of the Holy Spirit in the life and ministry of a believer.

103. Among African American and Jamaican Pentecostals the word "shouting" often refers to a type of "holy dancing" that is most often done to musical accompaniment.

104. For discussions of religious dancing among African American worshipers as it relates to West and Central African expressions of spirituality—see Albert J. Raboteau, *Slave Religion: The "Invisible Institution" in the Antebellum South* (New York: Oxford University Press, 1978), 68-74, and Murphy, *Working*, 147-151 and 198-199. In addition to citing Melville Herskovits' landmark work, Murphy draws on the research of Stuckey and Creel who posit significant parallels between African-American holy dancing and African ceremonies involving initiation and ancestor invocation—see Melville Hersko-

Herskovits, *The Myth of the Negro Past* (Boston: Beacon Press, 1990); Sterling Stuckey, *Slave Culture: Nationalist Theory and the Foundations of Black America* (New York: Oxford University Press, 1987), 10-17; and Margaret Washington Creel, *"A Peculiar People": Slave Religion and Community Culture among the Gullahs* (New York: New York University Press, 1988), 296-302. For a concise summary of debates on the topic of African retentions in the New World—see Sidney W. Mintz and Richard Price, *The Birth of African-American Culture: An Anthropological Perspective* (Boston: Beacon Press, 1976), vii-xiv.

105. My stints with Haitian konpa bands began in February 1994 and continued steadily until September 1997, when I cut back on my saxophone playing in order to focus on my increasing obligations in school and church. For a succinct history of Haitian konpa—see Gage Averill, "Toujou Sou Konpa: Issues of Change and Interchange in Haitian Popular Dance Music," in *Zouk: World Music in the West Indies*, ed. Jocelyne Guilbault (Chicago: University of Chicago Press, 1993), 68. I detail the relationship between my research, musical activities, and church involvement in my doctoral dissertation—see Butler, *Songs of Pentecost*.

106. Averill, "Toujou," 89.

107. I am aware that the concept of a duality between absolute good and evil—God and Satan—stems from a particular Christian perspective in which these figures are seen as mutually exclusive opposing forces impacting the world. As an African-American Pentecostal scholar, my challenge is always to operate discursively on a scholarly level of analysis that both recognizes and contextualizes Christian doctrines in relation to a much broader array of theological, ontological, and epistemological stances. My conception of evil in the form of the "Satanic" is clearly informed by my own indoctrination into Protestant and Pentecostal Christian ways of thinking, knowing, and being that have shaped my worldview from childhood.

108. Here, I have in mind a particularly explicit form of couple dancing known as *ploge*, which refers to "dancing in a very tight embrace with the man's arms holding the woman's buttocks"—see Gage Averill, *A Day for the Hunter, A Day for the Prey: Popular Music and Power in Haiti* (Chicago: University of Chicago Press, 1997), 243.

109. Psalm 100.

110. Likewise, I very rarely mentioned my gigs with jazz, blues, and R&B artists among Pentecostals in the United States. It was much easier to discuss my work with Haitian bands, which are largely unknown to African American Pentecostals.

111. Timothy Rommen, "Nationalism and the Soul: Gospelypso as Independence," *Black Music Research Journal* 22, no. 1 (2002): 53.

112. Michael Eric Dyson, *Open Mike: Reflections on Philosophy, Race, Sex, Culture and Religion* (New York: Basic Civitas Books, 2003), 12.

113. Renato Rosaldo, *Culture and Truth: The Remaking of Social Analysis* (Boston: Beacon Press, 1993), 169.

114. Gina Ulysse, "Uptown Ladies and Downtown Women: Informal Commercial Importing and the Social and Symbolic Politics of Class and Color in Jamaica" (PhD diss., University of Michigan, 1999).

115. Glick Schiller and Fouron show that for Haitians living abroad, "the [Haitian] nation is an extension of the family, and that both family and nation can extend long distances and across the borders of states"—see Nina Glick Schiller and Georges Eugene Fouron, *George Woke Up Laughing: Long-Distance Nationalism and the Search for Home* (Durham, N.C.: Duke University Press, 2001), 90.

Bibliography

Arthur, Charles, and Michael Dash, eds. *A Haiti Anthology: Libete*. London: Latin American Bureau, 1999.

Austin, Diane. "Culture and Ideology in the English-Speaking Caribbean: A View from Jamaica." *American Ethnologist* 10, no. 2 (1983): 223-239.

Austin-Broos, Diane J. *Jamaica Genesis: Religion and the Politics of Moral Orders*. Chicago: University of Chicago Press, 1997.

Averill, Gage. "Toujou Sou Konpa: Issues of Change and Interchange in Haitian Popular Dance Music." Pp. 68-89 in *Zouk: World Music in the West Indies*, edited by Jocelyne Guilbault. Chicago: University of Chicago Press, 1993.

———. "'Se Kreyol Nou Ye'/'We're Creole': Musical Discourse in Haitian Identities." Pp. 157-179 in *Music and Black Ethnicity: The Caribbean and South America*, edited by Gerard Behague. New Brunswick, N.J.: University of Miami North-South Center, 1994.

———. *A Day for the Hunter, A Day for the Prey: Popular Music and Power in Haiti*. Chicago: University of Chicago Press, 1997.

Bakan, Abigail B. *Ideology and Class Conflict in Jamaica: The Politics of Rebellion*. Montreal and Kingston, Canada: McGill-Queen's University Press, 1990.

Barrett, Leonard E. *The Rastafarians*. Boston: Beacon Press, 1997.

Bastide, Roger. *African Civilizations in the New World*. Translated from the French by Peter Green. New York: Harper and Row, 1971.

Bell, Catherine. *Ritual Theory, Ritual Practice*. New York: Oxford University Press, 1992.

Bilby, Kenneth M. "The Caribbean as a Musical Region." Pp. 181-218 in *Caribbean Contours*, edited by Sidney W. Mintz and Sally Price. Baltimore: Johns Hopkins University Press, 1985.

———. "Jamaica." Pp. 143-82 in *Caribbean Currents: Caribbean Music from Rumba to Reggae*, edited by Peter Manuel. Philadelphia: Temple University Press, 1995.

Brathwaite, Edward Kamau. "Kumina: The Spirit of African Survival." *Jamaica Journal* 42 (1978): 44-63.

Bruno, Myrthil. "Le Denominationalisme protestant et son action social en Haiti. Licence es-Sciences Anthropologiques." Thesis, Université d'Etat d'Haiti (Faculté d'Ethnologie), 1967.

Burton, Richard D. E. *Afro-Creole: Power, Opposition, and Play in the Caribbean*. Ithaca, N.Y.: Cornell University Press, 1997.

Butler, Melvin L. "Songs of Pentecost: Experiencing Music, Transcendence, and Identity in Jamaica and Haiti." PhD diss., New York University, 2005.

Carradine, B., J. C. Fowler, and W. J. Kirkpatrick. *The Best of All*. Indianapolis, Ind.: Christ Temple, n.d.

Chevannes, Barry. "Revivalism: A Disappearing Religion." *Caribbean Quarterly* 24, no. 3/4 (1978): 1-17.

———. *Rastafari: Roots and Ideology*. Syracuse, N.Y.: Syracuse University Press, 1994.

Clifford, James, and George E. Marcus, eds. *Writing Culture. The Poetics and Politics of Ethnography*. Berkeley: University of California Press, 1986.

Coleman, Simon. *The Globalisation of Charismatic Christianity: Spreading the Gospel of Prosperity*. Cambridge: Cambridge University Press, 2000.

Conway, Frederick James. "Pentecostalism in the Context of Haitian Religion and Health

Practice." PhD diss., Ann Arbor, Mich.: American University, 1978.

Creel, Margaret Washington. *"A Peculiar People": Slave Religion and Community-Culture among the Gullahs.* New York: New York University Press, 1988.

Dash, J. Michael. *Haiti and the United States: National Stereotypes and the Literary Imagination.* New York: St. Martin's Press, 1997.

———. *Culture and Customs of Haiti.* Westport, Conn.: Greenwood Press, 2001.

Dyson, Michael Eric. *Open Mike: Reflections on Philosophy, Race, Sex, Culture and Religion.* New York: Basic Civitas Books, 2003.

Frey, Sylvia R., and Betty Wood. *Come Shouting to Zion: African American Protestantism in the American South and British Caribbean to 1830.* Chapel Hill: University of North Carolina Press, 1998.

Geggus, David Patrick. *Slavery, War, and Revolution: The British Occupation of Saint Domingue, 1793-1798.* Oxford: Clarendon Press, 1982.

Glick Schiller, Nina, and Georges Eugene Fouron. *Georges Woke Up Laughing: Long-Distance Nationalism and the Search for Home.* Durham, N.C.: Duke University Press, 2001.

Gmelch, George, and Sharon Gmelch. *The Parish Behind God's Back: The Changing Culture of Rural Barbados.* Ann Arbor: University of Michigan Press, 1997.

Herskovits, Melville J. *The Myth of the Negro Past.* Reprint Edition. Boston: Beacon Press, 1990.

Hollenweger, Walter J. *Pentecostalism: Origins and Developments Worldwide.* Peabody, Mass.: Hendricks, 1997.

Hopkin, John Barton. "Music in the Jamaican Pentecostal Churches." *Jamaica Journal* 12 (1978): 23-40.

Hurston, Zora Neale. *Tell My Horse: Voodoo and Life in Haiti and Jamaica.* New York: Harper and Row, 1990.

Jeanty, Edner A. *Le Christianisme En Haiti.* Port-au-Prince, Haiti: La Presse Evangelique, 1989.

Laguerre, Michel S. *The Military and Society in Haiti.* Knoxville: University of Tennessee Press, 1993.

Lain, Clinton Eugene. "Church Growth and Evangelism in Haiti: Needs, Problems, and Methods." PhD diss. Asbury Theological Seminary, 1998.

Lawless, Robert. *Haiti's Bad Press: Origins, Development, and Consequences.* Rochester, Vt.: Schenkman Books, 1992.

Logan, Rayford W. *Haiti and the Dominican Republic.* London: Oxford University Press, 1968.

Louis, Andre J. "Catholicism, Protestantism and a Model of Effective Ministry in the Context of Voodoo in Haiti." PhD diss., Fuller Theological Seminary, 1998.

Martin, David. *Pentecostalism: The World their Parish.* Oxford: Blackwell Publishers, 2002.

Mintz, Sidney W., and Richard Price. *The Birth of African-American Culture: An Anthropological Perspective.* Boston: Beacon Press, 1992.

Mintz, Sidney, and Michel-Rolph Trouillot. "The Social History of Haitian Vodou." Pp. 123-147 in *Sacred Arts of Haitian Vodou*, edited by Donald Cosentino. Los Angeles: University of California, Fowler Museum of Cultural History, 1995.

Moore, Joseph G. "The Religion of Jamaican Negroes: A Study of Afro-American Acculturation." Thesis, Northwestern University, 1953.

Murphy, Joseph M. *Working the Spirit: Ceremonies of the African Diaspora.* Boston: Beacon Press, 1994.

Norton, Michael. "Haiti Officially Sanctions Voodoo." *New York Times/The Associated Press*. 2003. http://www.wehaitians.com (accessed November 3, 2004).

Olmos, Margarite Fernandez, and Lizabeth Paravisini-Gebert. "Introduction: Religious Syncretism and Caribbean Culture." Pp. 1-12 in *Sacred Possessions: Vodou, Santeria, Obeah, and the Caribbean*, edited by Margarite Fernandez Olmos and Lizabeth Paravisini-Gebert. New Brunswick, N.J.: Rutgers University Press, 1997.

Olwig, Karen Fog. *Global Culture, Island Identity: Continuity and Change in the Afro-Caribbean Community of Nevis*. Amsterdam: Harwood Academic Publishers, 1993.

Pelton, Robert D. *The Trickster in West Africa: A Study of Mythic Irony and Sacred Delight*. Berkeley: University of California Press, 1980.

Poewe, Karla. "Introduction: The Nature, Globality, and History of Charismatic Christianity." Pp. 1-29 in *Charismatic Christianity as a Global Culture*, edited by Karla Poewe. Columbia: University of South Carolina Press, 1994.

Raboteau, Albert J. *Slave Religion: The "Invisible Institution" in the Antebellum South*. New York: Oxford University Press, 1978.

Rodman, Selden. *Haiti: The Black Republic, the Standard Guide to Haiti*. Old Greenwich, Conn.: The Devin-Adair Company, 1980.

Rommen, Timothy. "Nationalism and the Soul: Gospelypso as Independence." *Black Music Research Journal* 22, no. 1 (2002): 37-63.

Rosaldo, Renato. *Culture and Truth: The Remaking of Social Analysis*. Boston: Beacon Press, 1993.

Sanders, Cheryl. *Saints in Exile: The Holiness-Pentecostal Experience in African-American Religion and Culture*. New York: Oxford University Press, 1996.

Seabrook, William B. *The Magic Island*. New York: Harcourt, Brace, and Company, 1929.

Seaga, Edward. "Revival Cults in Jamaica: Notes Toward a Sociology of Religion." *Jamaica Journal* 3 (1969): 3-13.

Sheller, Mimi. *Consuming the Caribbean: From Arawaks to Zombies*. London: Routledge, 2003.

Sherlock, Philip, and Bennett, Hazel. *The Story of the Jamaica People*. Kingston, Jamaica: Ian Randle Publishers, 1998.

Simpson, George Eaton. *Black Religions in the New World*. New York: Columbia University Press, 1978.

———. "Jamaican Revivalist Cults." *Social and Economic Studies* 5 (1956): 321-403.

Stokes, Martin, ed. *Ethnicity, Identity and Music: The Musical Construction of Place*. Oxford: Berg Publishers, 1997.

Stuckey, Sterling. *Slave Culture: Nationalist Theory and the Foundations of Black America*. New York: Oxford University Press, 1987.

Thomas, Deborah A. "'Tradition's Not an Intelligence Thing': Jamaican Cultural Politics and the Ascendence of Modern Blackness." PhD diss., New York University, 2000.

Toulis, Nicole R. *Believing Identity: Pentecostalism and the Mediation of Jamaican Ethnicity and Gender in England*. Oxford: Berg-Oxford International Publishers, 1997.

Trouillot, Michel-Rolph. "The Caribbean Region: An Open Frontier in Anthropological Theory." *Annual Review of Anthropology* 21 (1992): 19-42.

Turner, Victor. *The Ritual Process: Structure and Anti-structure*. Chicago: Aldine Publishers, 1969.

———. *The Forest of Symbols: Aspects of Ndembu Ritual*. Ithaca, N.Y.: Cornell University Press, 1967.

Van Gennep, Arnold. *The Rites of Passage*. Chicago: University of Chicago Press, 1960.

Ulysse, Gina. "Uptown Ladies and Downtown Women: Informal Commercial Importing and the Social and Symbolic Politics of Class and Color in Jamaica." PhD diss., University of Michigan, 1999.

Ward, Larry Fred. "Filled with the Spirit: The Musical Life of an Apostolic Pentecostal Church in Champaign-Urbana, Illinois." PhD diss., University of Illinois at Champaign-Urbana, 1997.

5

Maarit Forde

Rituals, Journeys, and Modernity: Caribbean Spiritual Baptists in New York

The global movement of people in late capitalism has generated a plethora of concepts and theories which seek to make sense of the relocations of labor and the implications of the current mobility to culture, society, and the nation state. Many writers, and not least significantly those who have long studied the capitalist world system, have emphasized the need to place contemporary migrations and transnationalism into a historical perspective. Whereas some theories of globalization contrast the present fluidity with an alleged stasis of modern nation-states and bounded ethnic groups, forced and voluntary migrations have been an integral part of the world order since the dawn of capitalism. Sidney Mintz[1] puts it simply: "The massive movement of people globally is centuries old," whereas Jonathan Friedman[2] suggests that rather than a unique phenomenon, current globalization might be regarded a cyclical phase in the capitalist world system. In this chapter, I explore the theme and practices of traveling in a Caribbean creole religion with the purpose of analyzing contemporary Caribbean transnationalism as part of the centuries-long history of Caribbean capitalism and modernity. In addition to giving it historical depth, I seek to thicken my description of Caribbean transnationalism by focusing on an area that has merited very little scholarly attention, namely religion and cosmology. Studies of transnationalism have largely concentrated on its economic and political aspects, but in migrants' lives, the role of religion and religiously motivated transnational practices and networks may appear even more significant than economy or politics.

Modernity, as a "regime of social experience," has a long and specific history in the Caribbean.[3] Industrial production of sugar and links to global trade made Caribbean plantation societies modern in certain ways since the sixteenth century, as Mintz has shown in his extensive work on the region. Along with the production of sugar and rum, slavery and the practices of plantation economy made possible the production of modern selfhood. According to Mintz, slaves in the Caribbean were unfree industrial workers, part and parcel of world trade.[4] In similar vein, Michel-Rolph Trouillot investigates slaves' ways of carving modern, individual selfhoods through patterns of material production and consumption.[5] Sensibility to time and recognition of heterogeneity and sociocultural difference were other attributes of early Caribbean modernity. Modern selves were molded under extremely harsh conditions in the Caribbean, and the boundaries that demarcate such selves—ethnic, class, gender, and other social identities—have been formulated in strictly hierarchical and unequal social formations. Institutions such as patriarchy, colorism, heteronormativity, and ethnically divided political parties mark present-day Caribbean societies.

But along with the rigidity of the plantation society and its classifications, the cultural notion and practice of traveling has developed in this region of islands, shores, and harbors. The history of Caribbean societies is one of traveling and border-crossing. The routes of colonizers, slaves, and indentured workers connected the Caribbean to distant corners of Europe, Asia, and Africa, and the population of contemporary Trinidad, for example, consists of descendants of African slaves and indentured Indian laborers, but also of Chinese, Portuguese (mainly from Madeira), English, Irish, Scottish, German, French, American, and West Indian migrants. Also, movement within the region—the transfers of slaves from one colony to another, the journeys of seamen and adventurers, or the mobile livelihood of *higglers* (inter-island marketers) and workers seeking better standard of living—has been emblematic of the post-Columbian Caribbean.[6] The twentieth and twenty-first centuries have witnessed voluminous labor migrations from the Caribbean to North American and European cities. Instead of unilinear streams of people, these migrations pulsate back and forth as people travel between old and new homelands or visit their family members in Northern metropolises. Tourism, of course, brings along yet another layer of movement linking the Caribbean to North America and Europe.

The movement of people has produced specific societies, nations, and nationalisms in the region. Heterogeneity as well as creolization, ability to produce novel cultural forms on the foundation of various intertwining and merging traditions, characterize Caribbean modernity.[7] Not unlike the itineraries of migrants and travelers that, according to Charles Carnegie, "breach the nation-state's ideological and political claims and reach," ritual and cosmological transitions blur the contours of modern subjectivity.[8] Throughout the brutal regimes of colonial plantation societies, Caribbean people have had their God, their spirits, saints, *orishas* and *lwa*, connections to cosmologies that extend far beyond local realities. It is in this regard that I seek to replenish Mintz's and Trouillot's analyses of modern Caribbean selves and suggest that "relational" may better describe Caribbean personhood than "individual." Drawing on ethnographic data of Spiritual Baptist migrants in New York, I am going to discuss their cosmology and ritual practice in relation to Caribbean modernity. The research is based on multi-sited fieldwork: three months in New York in 2004, twenty-four months in Trinidad and Tobago between 1996-2004 and shorter visits to West

Indian neighborhoods in New York and Toronto in 2001 and 2002. In New York my family and I lived in Flatbush, Brooklyn, and I worked mainly there as well as in other West Indian neighborhoods, such as East Flatbush, Crown Heights, and East New York.

Spiritual Baptists

The global connections that characterize Caribbean history are evident in the fascinating cosmology of the Spiritual Baptist religion.[9] This creole religion developed in St. Vincent and Trinidad at the turn of the twentieth century, but it draws on centuries-old African and Christian traditions. It is practiced in Trinidad and Tobago, St. Vincent, Grenada, Guyana, Barbados, on the Venezuelan coast, and in the main destinations of Caribbean migrations in North America and Great Britain. An indigenous Christian church amidst countless European and North American denominations as well as Hinduism and Islam, Spiritual Baptists have always appealed to the poor and oppressed. In his celebrated novel *The Wine of Astonishment* Earl Lovelace captures the magic that has continued to draw "the little people" into Spiritual Baptist churches, even when their religious practice was deemed illegal in St. Vincent and Trinidad and Tobago: "We have this church where we gather to sing hymns and ring the bell and shout hallelujah and speak in tongues when the Spirit come; and we carry the Word to the downtrodden and the forgotten and the lame and the beaten, and we touch black people soul."[10]

Along with twentieth century migrations, the Spiritual Baptist religion has spread from the Caribbean to the United States, Canada, and the United Kingdom, and today, church members as well as resources, ritual items and ideas travel across borders and oceans. The Spiritual Baptist Church as an institution of national and transnational scale has no administrative center. It consists of hundreds of individual churches in the Caribbean, North America and England, some of which are affiliated with *dioceses* (I use italics to indicate Spiritual Baptist terminology). These churches, however, have in common a hierarchy of positions with only little variance in the statuses and titles. Also, the basis for this hierarchy, accumulation of religious knowledge, is a universally embraced principle. The structure of the church is therefore solid and well-established, and also rare among Afro-Caribbean creole religions: the elaborate hierarchy of statuses and relevant titles is absent from Orisha, Santería, or Vodou, and also alien to the Pentecostal churches prevalent in the region. The ritual representations and cosmology of Spiritual Baptists have a familiarity with other creole religions, like Orisha or Santería, but show more Protestant influence than these. Different manifestations of the Holy Spirit are central in the ritual practice. Such manifestations are performed in styles that reflect specific spiritual *nationalities*, cosmological fields of symbols, which I am going to describe later on in this chapter. Cosmological exegeses and ritual representations are strikingly similar all about the transnational Spiritual Baptist community, although the church has no written canon.

Religious transnationalism

Journeys are emblematic to the Spiritual Baptist religion. Spiritual Baptists travel in the sense of migrating abroad or visiting foreign countries in order to attend or conduct religious rituals. Moreover, sacred journeys are an integral part of their religion: church members participate in rituals that take the form of a journey, and most significantly, they make spiritual voyages in a symbolic universe called the *Spiritual world*. To unfold these multiple layers of movement and border-crossing, I first look into Spiritual Baptists' transmigrations.

The Spiritual Baptist church has been fluctuating and transnational from the start, as leaders and members have moved between different Anglo-Caribbean colonies, mainly from "small islands" such as St. Vincent or Grenada towards the more industrialized Trinidad to find work and a better standard of living.[11] Since the late 1960s, thousands of Spiritual Baptists have taken part in the voluminous movement between the Caribbean and the United States and to a lesser extent Canada, and today there are Spiritual Baptist churches in many North American metropolises as well as in England. The first Spiritual Baptist church in the United States, Sons and Daughters of Zion Spiritual Church, was founded in Brooklyn in 1967, and today there are more than one hundred churches in New York alone. Most of them are small storefront churches in the West Indian neighborhoods of Flatbush, Crown Heights and East New York. Many have been built in the basements of private homes in residential areas in Brooklyn or Queens, and some function in private living-rooms: to quote Bishop Charles, a senior Spiritual Baptist leader in Brooklyn, churches are built "in any hole in de wall." Some of these churches have been registered at the County Clerk's office, but many exist without official recognition.[12] Most members of the congregations are migrants from the Anglophone Caribbean—mainly from Trinidad and Tobago, St. Vincent, Grenada and Guyana, but also from countries in which the religion is not widely practiced, like Jamaica, Antigua, and Panama. There are some U.S. citizens with Caribbean parentage, and visitors from the Caribbean. Very few Americans without kinship ties to the Caribbean belong to this church, or even know about its existence. In the Caribbean, Spiritual Baptists have traditionally been lower class people with little education. Today, one can find practitioners with academic degrees, professional careers and solid incomes in many congregations. In migrant churches, members with middle class backgrounds are more common, but the majority of the congregants represent the urban working class. Most female practitioners in New York work in the lowly paid private service sector, either in health care or as home aids and housekeepers in private homes, whereas transportation, security services, and construction sites are among the main employers of Spiritual Baptist men.

For many Spiritual Baptist migrants, particularly newcomers, the church represents a home away from home: a place to meet one's countrymen and—women, to speak in one's own dialect, to dress and behave as if one was attending a church back home. In the private service sector, working hours tend to be long and holidays few. Those who are in the country without residence permits or valid visas may have to succumb to working conditions far below legal standards. Many Spiritual Baptist women who work in private households told me that the church was their only social activity, the only place they spent time in apart of the workplace, shops, and home. It was not uncommon to see the same people in different rituals at their church three or four times a week. Gillian, a Tobagonian Spiritual Baptist migrant in her early thirties, lives in the country without a green card and works as a live-in housekeeper in a wealthy household in Long Island. In the summertime, when ritual activities abound in local Spiritual Baptist churches, she could spend her entire weekend—her only time off—in different rituals: go to a *baptism* on Friday evening and go home to sleep early in the morning, then go on a *pilgrimage* for the whole day on Saturday, and still attend the regular Sunday service. In Tobago, elders admire the dedication of "American Baptists" in comparison to the perhaps less keen attendance in their own churches.

Spiritual Baptist migrants are part of the late capitalist political economy and cultural logic, and their lives and trajectories are fine examples of the transnationalism[13] so typical of today's Caribbean. They move to the United States for the same reasons as most Caribbean migrants—to work, perhaps to study, and to improve their standard of living, often with the ultimate goal of building their own house or starting their own business back in their country of origin. But they cross borders for religious reasons, too. Ritual specialists, lay members, resources and ideas travel between the Caribbean and the United States or Canada. This cross-border traffic moves along already-existing transnational social fields,[14] for example networks of kin, friends, and former neighbors that stretch across state borders. Religiously motivated journeys also create new transnational connections and widen the spatial arrangement of transnational networks. Many church members based in North America travel back home to undergo central rites of passage. For example, Sister Sandra who has lived in Toronto for over twenty years but visits her native Tobago every two years, got a calling to get baptized in the Spiritual Baptist church when she was in her early forties. Instead of going to one of the numerous churches in the Greater Toronto Area, she flew to Trinidad for the initiation. Later she also got married in a Spiritual Baptist church in Tobago, and plans to go through a demanding rite of passage called *mourning* in her native country as well.

In addition to this Caribbean-bound movement, church members travel northward for ritual purposes. Non-migrant ritual specialists are invited by church leaders in Brooklyn or Toronto to visit them and to conduct important rituals in their churches. Mother Cleorita is a Tobagonian Spiritual Baptist elder and an experienced and respected ritual specialist, and has been running St. Philomen Spiritual Baptist Church in Tobago with her husband for over thirty years. Like most Tobagonians, her family is transnational: two of her children and six of her grandchildren live in the United States. They keep in contact by calling each other, by writing letters and by traveling back and forth, once there is enough money and the necessary documents—visas and residence permits—are in order. Mother Cleorita travels to New York at least biannually. However, visiting family and friends is not the only reason for the Mother to pack her suitcases and board the "Bee Wee," the British West Indian Airlines, to JFK. Her *spiritual family*, as Spiritual Baptist congregations are called, is also transnational, as a few of the members live in the USA. When Mother Cleorita travels to New York, she visits her *spiritual children* (people who have been baptized in her church) and attends local Spiritual Baptist churches with them. At times Mother Cleorita's *spiritual children* invite her to come and work as the ritual specialist in important rites of transition they want to undergo in their new home towns. In summer 2004, when she was in New York, one of her *spiritual daughters* who resided in Philadelphia heard that "Mummy" was in the country and called her up. She asked her to come to Philadelphia and work as the ritual specialist, *Pointer*, in a *mourning* ritual there. Local Spiritual Baptist leaders have also invited her to attend special rituals. When King Shepherd, a Tobagonian-born leader who runs a church in the basement of his house in the Queens, had a *robing* ritual in which forty members of his church gained new statuses in the church hierarchy, he "needed a person to do it who had the authority." He thus invited Mother Cleorita (his aunt) and Bishop Daniel (who is married to his cousin), both from Tobago, to come and conduct this rite of transition. Many Tobagonian elders have told me of baptisms as well as *mourning* and *thanksgiving* rituals they have conducted in American churches. From the migrants' point of view, to have a Caribbean-based ritual specialist conduct the service adds to the value and the "authenticity" of the ritual.[15]

While most of these ritual travels are conducted by individual church members, some collective efforts have emerged to bring together Spiritual Baptists from different countries. Annual Spiritual Baptist Liberation Day celebrations in Trinidad, and since 2004, the Spiritual Baptist Recognition Day in New York every July draw notable numbers of participants from the Caribbean, North America and Britain. The recently founded United Ecclesiastical Order of Spiritual Baptists aims at providing an umbrella organization for the hundreds of small, independent churches and dioceses spread around the hemisphere. The Order organizes annual meetings, in which large numbers of church leaders from different countries meet to discuss common policies and dogmas and to *praise the Lord* together.

Not only people, but money, goods, and airline tickets flow across state borders, as church members who work in the United States or Canada send money to their home churches in the Caribbean prior to big annual rituals, like *thanksgivings* or *harvests*, or as church elders based in different countries organize a ritual together.[16] Ritual items, like brass bells and pots, candles, material for clothes, books, and scented oils and waters travel along with people. Caribbean church leaders shop in religious stores that abound in Flatbush and Crown

Heights when they visit their family members in New York and pack their suitcases with ritual paraphernalia to carry to their churches back home, whereas migrants running religious stores in Brooklyn bring in necessary ritual emblems such as calabashes or herbal medicines from the Caribbean. Caribbean foodstuffs, used in many Spiritual Baptist rituals both as ritual items and festive food, are shipped in huge quantities to Brooklyn supermarkets. In Brooklyn, it is quite easy to buy almost any Caribbean product one fancies.

Most Caribbean migrants send remittances to their family members, and many send goods like clothes, shoes, school equipment or kitchen appliances in barrels and as airline cargo.[17] Similar gift exchange takes place in *Spiritual families*, the networks of religious kinship within the Spiritual Baptist religion. *Spiritual families* in practically all Tobagonian churches are transnational: some of the children have migrated or travel back and forth as transmigrants or visitors. Spiritual children residing overseas are expected to send money for their home church, or more specifically to their Spiritual parents, for large annual rituals like church *harvest* and church *thanksgiving*. It is also recommendable to assist one's Spiritual Mother or Father in their personal lives as well, for example by giving money for their possible medical expenses.

Ritual journeys

Collective ritual journeys form another layer of voyages in the Spiritual Baptist religion. Although most Spiritual Baptist services are conducted in the church, there are important rituals in each church's ritual cycle that take the form of a journey. A *pilgrimage* is a service arranged in a location other than the church, and the transition to the destination of the pilgrimage is part of the ritual. A pilgrimage can head to a fellow Spiritual Baptist church in another town or even abroad; or the destination may be a park, a community center, a square, or a beach. In New York, as in other Northern cities with Spiritual Baptist churches, summertime is a ritually active season compared to colder parts of the year. Pilgrimages take place in the summer months, and as many churches organize one each year, there are pilgrimages criss-crossing the North-Eastern coast almost every weekend from May until October. In each service I have attended in Brooklyn, church secretaries have read invitation letters sent to their church by other Spiritual Baptist congregations to come and join their pilgrimage. For example, at a service at Judah House of Prayer Spiritual Baptist Church in August 2004 the secretary announced three upcoming pilgrimages: Sacred Heart Spiritual Baptist Church's pilgrimage to a Massachusetts church, with tickets selling for $50; Mt. Hope Spiritual Baptist Church's pilgrimage to a Toronto church in September, $160 for the trip, accommodation and dinner; and Mt. Moriah Spiritual Church's pilgrimage to upstate New York, tickets for $40. Pilgrimages are festive services and lively get-togethers for church members, but also fund-raisers. The organizing congregation normally uses the money to the mortgage or the upkeep of the church. The funds can also be given to charity: when King Shepherd, the Tobagonian-born Leader in the Queens, was hospitalized in New York, a Tobagonian Spiritual Baptist organization arranged a pilgrimage on the island to raise funds for his expenses.

The churches hire buses for the transportation. Two or three busloads of festively dressed church members comprise a normal pilgrimage, but huge entourages with so many participants that even up to fourteen buses are needed have taken place. The journey is an integral part of the pilgrimage ritual, and the hours spent on the road from New York to Philadelphia, Boston, Upstate New York, Toronto or some other popular destination are spent by singing, praying, and making music. I traveled to Philadelphia with the pilgrimage crowd of Mt. Tabor Spiritual Baptist Church in August 2004, and the prayers began at 8:30 in the morning as we left the corner of Bergen and Nostrand in Crown Heights. When we reached the highway, Bishop Charles *surveyed* the bus—invited the Holy Spirit by pouring libations and ringing a brass bell, as is customary in all Spiritual Baptist services. Crossing the New Jersey countryside, our busload of sisters wearing long white church dresses and red head ties and brothers in white knee-long shirts and pants kept on singing: solemn Anglican hymns, but also passionate, almost ecstatic spiritual songs and chants, like *When the hurricane blow, hold me in yuh hand, hold me blessed Jesus, hold me in yuh hand*; and *Children walk the road, it's ah lonesome road, children of Zion walk the Heavenly road*. There were no drums this time, but the pilgrims made music by clapping hands and shaking maracas and tambourines. We ate pieces of *coconut bake* filled with dasheen, a typical Trinidadian breakfast item; sisters had stayed up late on the previous night and baked at the church. Finally in Philadelphia, we parked near St. Anthony Spiritual Baptist Church and began the service there around noon. After six hours of preaching, praying, and singing we climbed back in the bus, exhausted, but still kept on singing all the way home to Brooklyn.

Missions are services kept on the roadside in order to deliver a message from God to passers-by, or to generally preach the Word of God. In a vision, God may order an individual practitioner to deliver a message, like the Tobagonian Leader Brothers who traveled to Grenada to preach on village crossroads and warn people of an upcoming hurricane. A church can also arrange a mission as a collective, in which case several people, sometimes even twenty, go *on the mission road* together. In Brooklyn, missions often take place in busy corners, like Nostrand and Church Avenue or on Eastern Parkway. Dressed in the church clothes, women in ankle-long dresses, aprons and head ties, men in long dashikis, sashes and headbands, a group of church members set up a small altar on the pavement, stick a tall, wooden Shepherd's Rod and a cross on stands, and begin a service in the middle of the busy city scene. Specifically Spiritual Baptist features of the service, like the practitioners' appearance and paraphernalia, their shouting out of sermons or *catching power* (spiritual manifestations) give the *mission* its unique character among many other groups' proselytizing efforts in New York.

The theme of movement emerges not only in Spiritual Baptist ritual forms, but also in their speech. The ritual language of the Spiritual Baptist religion is saturated with metaphors and images of traveling. *Journey* is a metaphor frequently used by elders and members of the congregations alike when referring to rituals and connections with the *Spiritual world*. Various references to journeys are used in different services, but most often in *thanksgivings* and rites of passage. They can be applied in sermons, prayers or in non-ritualized speeches.

Most often such metaphors imply traveling by foot. *Being on the road* and *traveling* are metonyms for the *mourning* ritual as well as for fasting and praying, during which Spiritual revelations are received. Another common image is the boat. After one long thanksgiving service, the conducting Leader announced that "all passengers have come ashore" and that "this is a deep water harbor." He meant that those who were in the Spirit had returned from the *Spiritual world* back to the harbor, the church. A visiting Mother then concluded the service in similar metaphors, stating that "the ship left and headed into some deep waters, but now the tide has changed so I won't preach—some other time." "We are lifting the anchor," "we are in the open seas," "we will reach various ports tonight," "hold on to the balance wheel," "chart and compass," "reaching Africa shore" or "going to India land" are phrases heard in thanksgiving services. Once Leader Gerald of St. Philomen church in Tobago warned us of "skylarking" in the thanksgiving service, lest "the ship sink." He meant that if participants kept on talking instead of taking part in the ritual proceedings in the proper manner, the Spirit would not arrive and the service would not succeed—the boat would go down. And finally, most churches have a *Captain* whose duties include "steering the boat off the harbor" at the beginning of the service, meaning that the Captain helps to start the service in such a way that the congregation becomes detached from their *carnal* preoccupations and Spiritual connections become possible. In addition to maritime metaphors, aviation can also serve as a suitable allegory. "We are about to take off—fasten your seatbelts, sit back and relax," Mother Cleorita once addressed her *Spiritual family* at the beginning of the church thanksgiving. Mother Carol of the New Jerusalem Church in Malabar, Trinidad, used similar rhetoric when opening a service of evening prayers: "switch off all ungodly things," "Jesus is the pilot tonight," "observe the non-smoking signs."

Journey metaphors also emerge in several popular hymns and choruses. Given the flexibility of the Spiritual Baptist service, anybody can start a hymn during the prayers or the preaching. Therefore the hymns do not reflect the choices of the conducting minister alone, but portray general associations that Spiritual Baptists have in connection to their rituals as journeys. *We Are Walking in the Light, Marching to Zion, We Are Climbing up Mt. Zion Hill, Two Roads Before You, Jordan We Are Going down, Lead Us Heavenly Father, Steal Away to Jesus, Carry Me through over yonder, I Am on My Way, Where He Leads Me I Will Follow, This Train is a Holy Train*, and *I'm Building a Bridge* are among favorite songs sung in rites of passage. Some hymns refer to a destination rather than the journey itself: *Marching to Zion, Jerusalem Jerusalem,*

We Are Climbing up Mt. Zion Hill, or *Coming All the Way from Africa Land*. Sea-related hymns with different sea and boat metaphors and references are common, too: *Hold on to the Balance Wheel, In the Sea by and by, I See the Lighthouse*, or *Michael Row the Boat Ashore* correspond to the importance of the watery element in the rituals and the cosmology of the faith. There are also songs like *Roll Jordan Roll, Jordan River So Chilly and Cold* and *Lay Your Burden down by the Riverside* that can be linked to the *Spiritual world* as well as to the physical locations of Spiritual Baptist rituals.

Traveling in the spirit: Cosmology

Exceptionally intriguing in the Spiritual Baptist religion are the themes of movement and border-crossing in its cosmology. They emerge as spiritual journeys in an extraordinary universe that reflects the colonial history of the Caribbean. I continue by depicting this universe, the *Spiritual world*, and its reproduction in rituals.

The houses and gardens in the quiet neighborhood on Brooklyn's Tilden Avenue look more or less the same. One may well pass Mother Molly's house without noticing three cotton flags flying on short poles in the corner of the yard, or a colorful statue of a saint standing by the side door. A simple sign over the back door reads *Jehova in Emmanuel Spiritual Baptist Church*. Inside the fenced back yard and in the basement, however, it is as if one had entered a different world. There is ritual paraphernalia that can be found in most Spiritual Baptist churches—*lotas*, brass pots filled with water, leaves and flowers, and *tarias*, brass plates laid with grains; flowers and candles, bottles of olive oil, talcum powder and scented waters. Numerous statues portraying saints, (Native American) Indians and Buddhas, printed pictures of Hindu gods and goddesses add to the seemingly indiscriminate multitude of symbolism in this small, sacred space. As will be seen, cross-cultural symbolic references such as these follow a specific cultural logic in materializing Spiritual Baptists' cosmology.

In July 2004 I climbed down the steps to the church with my one-year-old son, as I had done a few times before. Mother Molly, a Vincentian-born Spiritual Baptist elder and the head of the church, was celebrating her birthday by arranging a ritual called *Indian Prayers*. Around two o'clock on Sunday afternoon the church was packed to capacity with close to forty people, mostly women. The members of the congregation, Afro-Caribbean migrants and visitors mainly from St. Vincent and Trinidad, looked outstanding in their festive outfits: they were wearing brightly colored saris, long dresses and loose pants decorated with gold and silver embroideries, and had completed the regalia with flowers and jewelry. All the women wore head ties, as is normative in Spiritual Baptist services. There were yellow and orange chrysanthemums, marigolds, daisies and roses in pots and vases around the ritual space, the most lavish bouquet placed on a table in front of the altar. The colors of the flowers and clothes—yellow, orange, gold—are connected to a spiritual place called *India* in Spiritual Baptist ritual symbolism. Pictures of Hindu deities had been added to the regular ritual paraphernalia on the table—candles, bottles of oil, scented waters and perfumes, talcum powder, *lotas* and *tarias* (brass emblems used in rituals).

As Mother Molly prayed, standing in front of the altar in the crowded church room, the Spirit came and she began to shout in an unknown tongue while the congregation was humming a sad but beautiful tune. I had heard the same language and the same melody countless times in Spiritual Baptist churches in New York, Tobago, Trinidad, Grenada, and Toronto. They, like certain colors and emblems, manifest *India* in ritual representations; the statues of Native Americans and Buddhas in the church yard belong to this same cultural category of *Indianness*, an indication of the *bricolage* quality of religious creativity. The particular form in which the Spirit manifested itself during the Mother's prayer was St. Francis, an *Indian* entity in the Spiritual Baptist cosmology. The Mother, with a mask-like expression frozen on her face, danced with small, delicate steps with a *lota* pot on top of her head, Francis perceptible in her gestures. For a while, she no longer was an Afro-Vincentian grandmother, but had become an *Indian* man in this sacred, intense ritual. The service lasted for several hours, and the Spirit manifested many times in its *Indian* form during the prayers and the singing. In the evening the sisters served a delicious meal of Indo-Caribbean delicacies to all participants.

Imagine the crowd in the hot basement church, this group of Afro-Caribbean migrants dressed in bright Indian clothes entertaining the Spirit, as they say, to the rhythm of a djembe drum and to the clapping of hands in a middle-class neighborhood in Brooklyn. Mother Molly's birthday prayers were held at a crossroads of several exoduses, movements of people in different times and through very different routes. The participants, West Indian women and men who have come to New York to work their way to a better future, are part of the huge waves of migration from the Caribbean to North American metropolises. The cosmology of their religion, however, is an exquisite model of the global, colonial connections to distant regions and homelands that created the Caribbean as we know it. The *Spiritual world*, as the cosmology is called by the practitioners themselves, consists of spiritual locations or *nations*[18] called Africa, India, China and Syria, as well as Biblical cities and regions and local Caribbean sites. It is inhabited by anthropomorphic personifications of the Holy Spirit and other spiritual beings in human or animal form. Among these entities are a number of saints, biblical figures like Abraham, and characters from Caribbean folklore; the Holy Spirit is always clearly distinguished from lesser spirits and evil entities.[19] Earliest observations of this creole cosmology were made by Melville Herskovits in Toco, Trinidad, in 1939, but elders with whom I have worked assume that the Spiritual world has been part of the religion throughout its history.

The Spiritual world is reproduced in Spiritual Baptist rituals. It is an environment in which members of the church make spirit journeys, particularly in the central rite of passage called *mourning* which is aimed at conducting a journey to one or more of the *nations* in the Spiritual world. In spite of its name, *mourning* is not a funerary rite and does not imply actual physical death. Death symbolism, however, is emblematic to the liminal space that the ritual produces. As voluntary intensification of one's initiation to the Spiritual Baptist religion, *mourning* is a ritual of self-denial and sensory deprivation during which a *pilgrim* (initiate) travels in the Spiritual world, seeking "wisdom, knowledge and understanding" through prayers and meditation. *Mourning*, and the Spiritual journeys conducted within it, link the Spiritual Baptist religion strongly to shamanistic traditions found in various different cultures.[20] The journey begins as ritual specialists take the initiates, *pilgrims*, into a small room in the church compound, the *mourner room*, where they lay on their back for usually at least seven, but seldom more than twenty-one days. During this time they are blindfolded, not allowed to speak, bathe, eat or drink, save restricted amounts of liquids. They lay on the stony floor with a stone as their pillow. In the Caribbean, *mourner rooms* may have earthen floors, which is said to make the ritual more efficient and valuable. In North American churches, the *mourner rooms* are either small rooms connected to the church hall, or if the church is quite small, as is often the case, *mourners* lay on the church floor.

After their journey is complete, the *pilgrims'* return to the world is normally embedded in a Sunday service, where they finally recount their *tracks*, important parts of their journey, to the rest of the congregation. *Mourning* is essential in unfolding the mysteries of the faith, learning about the various symbols, the Spirit, good and evil. Disconnected from profane society, the *pilgrims* learn about the Spiritual world and their own position in it. As they travel to one or several Spiritual nations, their specific spiritual inclination becomes clear. Depending on where they travel and which Spiritual entities they meet, either Africa, India or China stands out as their personal Spiritual "nationality." Should a *pilgrim* travel to India, converse with an Indian personification of the Spirit, and receive Indian clothes, emblems, colors, and the skill to dance and speak unknown tongues in the Indian way, she is prone to rejoice with the Indian Spirit later on in the various services she attends. Experienced *mourners* have traveled all about the Spiritual world and communicated with many different spiritual entities there, and are thus able to entertain the Spirit in all its different forms.

Although personal experiences of Spiritual traveling form the basis of Spiritual Baptist religious knowledge and practice, the cosmology is not only a system of knowledge, separate from sensible and embodied social interaction. The Spiritual penetrates the daily lives of church members, and the intertwining of Spiritual knowledge and physical experiences blurs the boundaries between social and cosmological. The Spiritual Baptist cosmology becomes concrete and perceptible in ritual practice. To quote Clifford Geertz, "In a ritual, the world as lived and the world as imagined, fused under the agency of a single set of symbolic forms, turn out to be the same world."[21] Spiritual Baptist ritual symbolism includes colors, clothes, dance styles, rhythms, songs, ritual paraphernalia, glossolalia (speaking in tongues) and foodstuffs. The Spiritual Africa, India, and

China become perceptible by consistent usage of these symbols in ritual practice. Each nation is represented by specific symbols. Participants in rituals can see Africa or India in the colors of the clothes, tablecloths and shelf-cloths, in the candles, flowers, and iced cakes, in the paraphernalia used; the nations are there in the manifestations, the rhythms and the music, in the unknown tongues and dances, in the food served after the service—everyone present, not just the ones who *entertain* the Spirit, but also the observers, can see, hear, feel, smell, and taste Spiritual Africa and India, sometimes also China.[22]

Through the more materialistically motivated journeys of Caribbean migrants, the Spiritual world has traveled quite unchanged to the big cities on the East Coast of the United States, as well as to London, Toronto, Montreal, and other destinations of West Indians. In rituals held in Brooklyn or in suburban Toronto Spiritual Baptists make journeys to Africa, India and China just as they do in the Caribbean.[23] Mother Molly's birthday prayers is only one example of countless spiritual voyages that connect present-day Brooklyn to other times and places, to the colonial history of the Caribbean and the creole societies it has produced.

Spiritual journeys to Caribbean modernity

The topography of the Spiritual Baptist cosmology reflects a fairly modern way of looking at the world. The nations, Africa, India, China, and Syria, seem like bounded, separate units, and their respective, homogeneous populations each portray unique appearances, languages, customs, knowledge, music, food, and so forth.[24] One can encounter similar stylized, even stereotypical portrayals of each nation in rituals all about the transnational Spiritual Baptist community: the languages, dance steps, hand gestures, guttural sounds, and chants that represent, say, the Chinese Spirit, are the same in each church. The Spiritual world resembles nineteenth century nationalisms rather than the nation-building ideologies in the Anglophone Caribbean, where leaders of newly independent nations have propagated an anti-colonial creole culture as a necessary unifying principle for the various groups of people imported and migrated to the Caribbean during the colonial era. The phrase *All ah we is one* and metaphors such as *Callaloo country* or *Rainbow country* in Trinidad and *Out of many people, one nation* in Jamaica reflected the conviction of a single, homogenized culture amalgamating Afro-, Indo-, Euro-, Sino-, Luso- and other Creoles.[25] However, the objective of forging an indigenous, creole cultural identity not directly traceable to any Old World culture never materialized in a way that would have been equally satisfactory to all the ethnic groups. For example, Munasinghe shows how in the nation-building process of Trinidad and Tobago the concept creole was taken to signify Afro-Trinidadian cultural forms as an antithesis to the European colonizing cultures.[26] Indo-Trinidadians were largely left outside the melting pot, their version of creolization not accepted in the national narrative unless they adapted to the Afro-Trinidadian culture. In similar vein, Jamaican national culture is predominantly black, and Jamaicans with Indian, Middle Eastern, Chinese or other forefathers stand out as *different*.[27] Like in contemporary Caribbean societies, ethnic identities in the Spiritual Baptist cosmology are constructed in juxtaposition to different, separate Others. Although the vast majority of Spiritual Baptists are Afro-Caribbean, the category "African" in their cosmology and ritual representations is no less stereotypical than "Indian," "Syrian" or "Chinese." This is not to belittle the influence of African religious traditions in Spiritual Baptist beliefs and practices, but to suggest that portrayals of *Africanness*, as performed and uttered by church members, are specific cultural products and tell us as much, if not more, about the Caribbean as about Africa. Instead of unchanging African cultural continuums, the Spiritual Baptist religion exemplifies the creativity of creole culture, developed on the basis of various intertwining heritages.

The act of ritual and spiritual traveling and border-crossing, however, challenges the modern constellation of separate nations in the cosmology. In keeping with Caribbean cultural metaphors, journeys to Africa, India, and other Spiritual places could be seen as a sort of *marronage*.[28] In Caribbean plantation societies, *marronage* meant escaping from slave plantations and forming secluded communities of fugitives, maroons, sheltered by forests or mountains. Carnegie makes use of the concept to analyze escapes that took place in the colonial Caribbean, escapes from "the neat demarcations of place and person that define the modern subject."[29] He argues that the hegemony of the economic and political units of the plantation societies—plantations, colonies, and so forth—could be challenged by the subaltern population by traveling. Traveling enabled seemingly powerless and highly controlled people to craft their own identities and to escape prevailing classifications, which assorted people according to place and race. Thus "sailors, army conscripts and deserters, tavern operators, free people of color, runaway slaves, peddlers, and marketers" moved away from the geographical place as well as from the racial identity allotted to them by the political-economic power structure. They did not stay put in the "distinctive, unambiguous attachments to particular identities and locations" that modern subjects should embrace.[30] Michael Kearney, writing about transnational subjects more generally, also uses the word "escape" as he suggests that transnational identities cannot fit the "either-or classifications" and "unitary identities" typical of modern anthropological analyses.[31] Aside from these longer journeys, the plantation as a modern social formation also entailed an arrangement that enabled slaves to temporarily leave behind the oppression, racism and violence of their daily lives, as Holger Henke has shown.[32] In many Caribbean colonies, slaves grew their own food on small provision grounds in the hills surrounding the plantations. Like Mintz and Trouillot, Henke notes the significance of these provision grounds as a breach in the totalitarian regime of plantation societies and argues that in addition to their economic and recreational significance, provision grounds offered the slaves a space for expressing and experiencing their spirituality and religiosity. Henke sees the weekly journey from the plantation to the provision grounds as transition from slavery to freedom, as if the Middle Passage in reverse. "The notions of voyage in space and time, displacement, and home-coming" are integral to the "truly spiritual, transcendental and metaphysical culture" of Caribbean societies, he writes.[33]

Journeys to Spiritual nations and their ritual representations enable Spiritual Baptists to manipulate cultural categories and performances of ethnic and gender identities that have grown in thoroughly modern situations. Their journeys, both in the sense of worldly migrations and religious or Spiritual traveling, are part and parcel of the modern, capitalist world order and Caribbean modernity. However, Spiritual journeys offer avenues to subjectivities larger than those assigned by modern personhood and its clear-cut categories of gender, ethnicity, age and class. In the Spirit, a group of Afro-Trinidadian and Afro-Vincentian migrants packed in a Brooklyn basement, all dressed in saris, can sway their arms gracefully like temple dancers and shout in Indian language, or an uneducated Afro-Caribbean grandmother can become a respected Chinese male doctor.[34] These are radical transgressions from the classificatory structures of modern identity. The cultural creativity inherent in creolization enables people to challenge those normative categories that restrict the definitions and expressions of their identities, both in the Caribbean and in New York. Here I agree with Peter Hitchcock, for whom "Caribbeanness" is "about process, about an intercultural and transcultural dynamic," and who locates in it "a matrix of political possibilities."[35] It would be facile functionalism to reduce Spiritual Baptist ritual practice merely to an escape from the often harsh realities of migrants' lives; their religion is, most certainly, much more complex than that. However, one of the motives for these migrants' keen dedication to their religion could be that in their ritual practice, West Indian Spiritual Baptists whose ethnic and class status in the United States place them at the lower end of most social hierarchies can vastly expand their identities and capacities.[36]

But such transgressions are not teleological acts performed by Hegelian "self-defining subjects."[37] Whereas the economic activities described by Mintz and Trouillot, and the marronage discussed by Carnegie, can surely be taken as examples of modern, self-defining, individual subjectivity, in the spiritual realm selves are relational rather than autonomous. A Vincentian-born babysitter in Brooklyn who attends church week after week and entertains St. Francis, a popular personification of the Holy Spirit that is unmistakably male and Indian, is hardly a case-in-point of a modern self-sustained individual, defined only in terms of internal attributes. Spiritual connections transform practitioners' lives in thorough ways, as they receive religious knowledge and wisdom from God during their journeys in the Spiritual world, and then put it in practice in their mundane as well as religious lives. The cosmology and the spiritual identities they perform in ritual situation have a bearing on these migrants' perceptions of selfhood and of the world also outside the church. The continuous presence of the divine cannot be overlooked in analyses of Caribbean modernity and modern personhood. In his insightful study of Melanesian modernity, Edward LiPuma suggests that persons are never either completely individual or relational, but that in each society, they "emerge from [the] tension between dividual and individual aspects/relations."[38] LiPuma's formulation allows for cultural and historical variation in the modes of conceptualizing personhood and is helpful when thinking about Caribbean versions of modernity and personhood.

Conclusion

The Spiritual Baptist community fluctuates in and between the various national territories where West Indian migrations have reached—the Caribbean, North America, and Great Britain. Spiritual Baptist migrants and their traveling ritual specialists are typical of late capitalist world order and the globalized world of the twenty-first century. However, they are engaged in frequent, regular, and very time-consuming religious activities that reproduce cosmological imagery very different from the transnational realities they live in. Rather than delocalized ethnoscapes, their Spiritual atlas echoes the modern world with its nations and ethnic categorizations.[39]

In the long and demanding rituals conducted in hot basements and modest church rooms, Spiritual Baptists draw on the richness of their histories, the global networks that brought together myriad of traditions for new cultural creations to grow upon. The religion is emblematic of Caribbean modernity: its cosmology reflects colonial labor migrations and the merciless force of global capitalism that drew people to the Caribbean from distant corners of the world, and its rituals connote the centuries-long practice of transitions, traveling and border-crossing that characterizes the region. But however modern the framework of Spiritual Baptist traveling, their Spiritual journeys can be interpreted as sort of *marronage* from modern categories of ethnicity, class, and gender. The intimate and profound connections to a cosmology outside the practitioners' individual selves serve as avenues towards identities larger than those imposed on Caribbean migrants in the urban North. As transitions and transgressions of borders and boundaries, Spiritual journeys lead away from rigid definitions of modern personhood as self-sustained and self-designed. As a final note, worthy of further inspection elsewhere, I should point out the sharp contrast between the freedom of movement in ritual traveling and the stagnancy of many Spiritual Baptists, who live in New York as undocumented or "illegal" migrants. Having overstayed their visa, they are unable to travel back to their native countries in the Caribbean without risking the possibility to ever return to the United States. Their only option is to work wherever they can and wait for several years to either gain legal residence or to save enough money to go back home for good. For these church members, rendered immobile by impenetrable state borders, journeys in the Spiritual world—not only to the foreign Nations, but also to rivers, beaches, and forests back home in their own country—may offer an invaluable refuge and source of strength.

Notes

1. Sidney W. Mintz, "The Localization of Anthropological Practice: From Area Studies to Transnationalism," *Critique of Anthropology* 18, no. 2 (1998): 131.
2. Jonathan Friedman, "From Roots to Routes. Tropes for Trippers," *Anthropological Theory* 2, no. 1 (2002): 33.
3. Jonathan Friedman, "Modernity and Other Traditions," in *Critically Modern. Alternatives, Alterities, Anthropologies*, ed. Bruce M. Knauft (Bloomington: Indiana University Press, 2002), 289.
4. Sidney W. Mintz, *Caribbean Transformations* (New York: Columbia University Press, 1989), 47.
5. Michel-Rolph Trouillot, *Global Transformations. Anthropology and the Modern World* (New York: Palgrave Macmillan, 2003), 41-43.
6. See for example, Charles Carnegie, *Postnationalism Prefigured. Caribbean Borderlands* (New Brunswick: Rutgers University Press, 2002).
7. Simon Gikandi, *Writing in Limbo. Modernism and Caribbean Literature* (Ithaca: Cornell University Press, 1992), 16; Wilson Harris, "Creoleness: The Crossroads of a Civilization?" in *Caribbean Creolization. Reflections on the Cultural Dynamics of Language, Literature, and Identity*, ed. Kathleen M. Balutansky and Marie-Agnes Sourieau (Gainesville: University Press of Florida, 1998).
8. Carnegie, *Postnationalism*, 83.
9. On the Spiritual Baptist religion, see Stephen Glazier, *Marchin' the Pilgrims Home. Leadership and Decision-Making in an Afro-Caribbean Faith* (London: Greenwood Press, 1983); Maarit Laitinen, *Marching to Zion. Creolisation in Spiritual Baptist Rituals and Cosmology* (Helsinki: Research Series in Anthropology, University of Helsinki, 2002); Patricia Stephens, *The Spiritual Baptist Faith. African New World Religious History, Identity & Testimony* (London: Karnak House, 1999); Wallace W. Zane, *Journeys to Spiritual Lands. The Natural History of a West Indian Religion* (New York: Oxford University Press, 1999).
10. Earl Lovelace, *The Wine of Astonishment* (Portsmouth, N.H.: Heinemann, 1982), 32.
11. C.M. Jacobs, *Joy Comes in the Morning. Elton George Griffith and the Shouter Baptists* (Port of Spain, Trinidad and Tobago: Caribbean Historical Society, 1996); Laitinen, *Marching to Zion*.
12. Registered churches may offer help to their members in certain immigration problems as well as a wider variety of rites of transition.
13. By transnationalism I refer to processes, activities, and networks that surpass the borders of at least one nation-state, involving individuals and social groups, but also the state or states as actor(s) that shape such processes—see Nina Glick Schiller, "Transnational Urbanism as a Way of Life: a research topic not a metaphor," *City & Society* 17, no. 1 (2005): 50.
14. By transnational social field I refer to a network of social relations that cross the borders of at least one nation-state.
15. Maarit Forde, "Pilgrimages to Brooklyn. Transnationalism in Afro-Caribbean Rituals and Cosmology," *Journal of the Finnish Anthropological Society* 28, no. 2 (Spring 2003): 24-35.

16. See Forde, "Pilgrimages."

17. See for example, *Sending Money Home: Remittance to Latin America and the Caribbean* (Report of the IADB Multilateral Investment Fund, May 2004), 4 and 11.

18. The term *nation* is common in Afro-Caribbean cosmologies. It usually refers to West African peoples, "nations" like the Yoruba, the Congo, or the Igbo; in religions like the Big Drum ritual in Carriacou, Vodou in Haiti or Santería in Cuba such nations (*nacion, nanchon*) are regarded as the ancestral origins of the contemporary Afro-Caribbeans and as sources of their religious traditions. Similar connotations are attached to the word nation by Spiritual Baptists as well, when the discourse draws close to the Rastafarian terminology of "tribes." The twelve tribes of Israel (Acts 26:7, James 1:1) have been equated to African tribes, in the Rasta case Ethiopians—Leonard Barrett, *The Sun and the Drum. African roots in Jamaican folk tradition* (Kingston, Jamaica: Sangster's Book Stores, 1976), 111. There is a global Rastafari organization called the Twelve Tribes of Israel—Barry Chevannes, "Rastafari and the Exorcism of Racism and Classism in Jamaica," in *Chanting Down Babylon. The Rastafari Reader*, ed. Nathaniel Samuel Murrell, William David Spencer and Adrian Anthony McFarlane (Kingston, Jamaica: Ian Randle Publishers, 1998), 55-71. In Spiritual Baptist discourse, however, the reference is made to unspecified African nations. However, the term nation is more often used when discussing regions or countries in the spiritual world, namely Africa, India, China, and Syria.

19. Laitinen, *Marching*; Wallace W. Zane, *Journeys to Spiritual Lands. The Natural History of a West Indian Religion* (New York: Oxford University Press, 1999).

20. Zane, *Journeys*, 122-138.

21. Clifford Geertz, *The Interpretation of Cultures: Selected Essays* (New York: Basic Books, 1973), 112.

22. Very few Spiritual Baptist rituals, if indeed any, are arranged around one single nation theme. In African thanksgivings there are always one or two *lota* pots and a *taria* among the multitude of African symbols, and vice versa, a calabash on an otherwise Indian table. Elders state that in a service, one must always be prepared to entertain the Spirit in all possible forms.

23. Kenneth Bilby, "Neither Here Nor There: The Place of 'Community' in the Jamaican Religious Imagination," in *Religion, Diaspora, and Cultural Identity*, ed. John W. Pulis (Amsterdam: Gordon and Breach, 1999), 322—Bilby reports that American spirits have emerged in the pantheon of the Jamaican Convince religion as practiced today in Chicago. It seems that transnationally practiced Caribbean creole religions differ in regard to cosmological adjustment and inclusiveness.

24. The nations are not strictly exclusive, however. Popular destinations on spiritual journeys, Biblical locations like Zion, Jerusalem, Canaan, River Jordan, Egypt and Israel, are not necessarily separate from the main spiritual nations of Africa, India and China. Also, the distances between two places in the spiritual world vary, and they can be reached by different routes; sometimes they are just across the border, but sometimes the journey seems endless, as one has to climb mountains, find one's way in a thick forest or sail across an ocean.

25. See for example, Eric Williams, *History of the People of Trinidad and Tobago* (London: Andre Deutsch, 1964).

26. Viranjini Munasinghe, *Callaloo or Tossed Salad? East Indians and the Cultural Politics of Identity in Trinidad* (Ithaca, N.Y.: Cornell University Press, 2001).

27. Carnegie, *Postnationalism*, 31.

28. James Clifford, *The Predicament of Culture. Twentieth Century Ethnography, Literature, and Art* (Cambridge, Mass.: Harvard University Press, 1988), 181. Aimé Césaire introduced the verb *marronner* in his "poetics of cultural invention." James Clifford reads this not only as escaping, but also as "reflexive possibility and poesis."

29. Carnegie, *Postnationalism*, 117.

30. Carnegie, *Postnationalism*, 137.

31. Michael Kearney, "The Local and the Global: The Anthropology of Globalization and Transnationalism," *Annual Review of Anthropology* 24 (1995): 558; the Martinican poet Edouard Glissant, who celebrates "creative marronage" in Caribbean literature, points out that the plantation as a socio-economic unit produced a specific way of conceptualising time and connections, because it was "always multilingual and frequently multiracial tangle [that] created inextricable knots within the web of filiations." Western unilinearity in time and memory has therefore not taken root in Caribbean literary production—Edouard Glissant, *Poetics of Relation*, tr. by Betsy Wing. (Ann Arbor: University of Michigan Press, 1997), 71-72.

32. Holger Henke, "Mapping the "Inner Plantation": A Cultural Exploration of the Origins of Caribbean Local Discourse," *Social and Economic Studies* 45, no. 4 (1996): 51-75.

33. Henke, "Mapping," 62-63.

34. Laitinen, *Marching*, 176-177.

35. Peter Hitchcock, *Imaginary States. Studies in Cultural Transnationalism* (Urbana: University of Illinois Press, 2003), 31-32.

36. C.M. Jacobs, *Joy Comes in the Morning. Elton George Griffith and the Shouter Baptists* (Port of Spain, Trinidad and Tobago: Caribbean Historical Society, 1996), 151 and Laitinen, *Marching to Zion*, 46. In the Caribbean, ritual journeys and experiences of the Spirit in its various manifestations have enabled Spiritual Baptists to break away not only from ethnic, class, and gender categories and hierarchies, but also from actual persecutions. The Spiritual Baptist religion was illegal in Trinidad and Tobago in 1917-1951 and in St. Vincent in 1912-1965, and practitioners had to hide from informers and the police. Many were arrested, beaten, and taken to court during the Prohibition Ordinance. In order to keep on practising their religion, Spiritual Baptists—*Shouters* (Trinidad and Tobago) or *Shakers* (St. Vincent), as they were called, had to build makeshift churches in the bush, far away from villages.

37. Georg W. F. Hegel, *The Philosophy of History*, tr. J. Sibtree (New York: Dover, 1995).

38. Edward LiPuma, *Encompassing Others. The Magic of Modernity in Melanesia* (Ann Arbor: University of Michigan Press, 2001), 132.

39. Arjun Appadurai, *Modernity at Large: Cultural Dimensions of Globalization* (Minneapolis: University of Minnesota Press, 1996).

Bibliography

Appadurai, Arjun, *Modernity at Large: Cultural Dimensions of Globalization*. Minneapolis: University of Minnesota Press, 1996.

Barrett, Leonard. *The Sun and the Drum. African roots in Jamaican folk tradition.* Kingston, Jamaica: Sangster's Book Stores, 1976.
Bilby, Kenneth. "Neither Here Nor There: The Place of 'Community' in the Jamaican Religious Imagination." Pp. 311-336 in *Religion, Diaspora, and Cultural Identity*, edited by John W. Pulis. Amsterdam: Gordon and Breach, 1999.
Carnegie, Charles. *Postnationalism Prefigured. Caribbean Borderlands.* New Brunswick, N.J.: Rutgers University Press, 2002.
Chevannes, Barry. "Rastafari and the Exorcism of Racism and Classism in Jamaica." Pp. 55–71 in *Chanting Down Babylon. The Rastafari Reader*, edited by Nathaniel Samuel Murrell, William David Spencer and Adrian Anthony McFarlane. Kingston, Jamaica: Ian Randle Publishers, 1998.
Clifford, James. *The Predicament of Culture. Twentieth Century Ethnography, Literature, and Art.* Cambridge, Mass.: Harvard University Press, 1988.
Forde, Maarit. "The Global Cosmology of a Local Religion: A Caribbean Twist in Discourses of Diaspora." *The CLR James Journal: A Review of Caribbean Ideas* 9, no. 1 (Winter 2002/2003): 147-171.
———. "Pilgrimages to Brooklyn. Transnationalism in Afro-Caribbean Rituals and Cosmology." *Journal of the Finnish Anthropological Society* 28, no. 2 (Spring 2003): 24-35.
Friedman, Jonathan. "Modernity and Other Traditions." Pp. 287-314 in *Critically Modern. Alternatives, Alterities, Anthropologies*, edited by Bruce M. Knauft. Bloomington: Indiana University Press, 2002.
———. "From Roots to Routes. Tropes for Trippers." *Anthropological Theory* 2, no. 1 (2002): 21-36.
Geertz, Clifford. *The Interpretation of Cultures: Selected Essays.* New York: Basic Books, 1973.
Gikandi, Simon. *Writing in Limbo. Modernism and Caribbean Literature.* Ithaca, N.Y.: Cornell University Press, 1992.
Glazier, Stephen. *Marchin' the Pilgrims Home. Leadership and Decision-Making in an Afro-Caribbean Faith.* London: Greenwood Press, 1983.
Glick Schiller, Nina. "Transnational Urbanism as a Way of Life: a research topic not a metaphor." *City & Society* 17, no. 1 (2005): 49-64.
Glissant, Edouard. *Poetics of Relation.* Translated by Betsy Wing. Ann Arbor: University of Michigan Press, 1997.
Jacobs, C.M. *Joy Comes in the Morning. Elton George Griffith and the Shouter Baptists.* Port of Spain, Trinidad and Tobago: Caribbean Historical Society, 1996.
Harris, Wilson. "Creoleness: The Crossroads of a Civilization?" Pp. 23-35 in *Caribbean Creolization. Reflections on the Cultural Dynamics of Language, Literature, and Identity*, edited by Kathleen M. Balutansky and Marie-Agnes Sourieau. Gainesville: University Press of Florida, 1998.
Hegel, Georg W. F. *The Philosophy of History.* Translated by J. Sibtree. New York: Dover, 1995.
Henke, Holger. "Mapping the "Inner Plantation": A Cultural Exploration of the Origins of Caribbean Local Discourse." *Social and Economic Studies* 45, no. 4 (1996): 51-75.
Hitchcock, Peter. *Imaginary States. Studies in Cultural Transnationalism.* Urbana: University of Illinois Press, 2003.

Kearney, Michael. "The Local and the Global: The Anthropology of Globalization and Transnationalism." *Annual Review of Anthropology* 24 (1995): 547-565.

Laitinen, Maarit. *Marching to Zion. Creolisation in Spiritual Baptist Rituals and Cosmology.* Helsinki: Research Series in Anthropology, University of Helsinki, 2002. Also available at http://ethesis.helsinki.fi/julkaisut/hum/kultt/vk/laitinen/.

LiPuma, Edward. *Encompassing Others. The Magic of Modernity in Melanesia.* Ann Arbor: University of Michigan Press, 2001.

Lovelace, Earl. *The Wine of Astonishment.* Portsmouth, N.H.: Heinemann, 1982.

Mintz, Sidney W. *Caribbean Transformations.* New York: Columbia University Press, 1989 (1974).

———. "The Localization of Anthropological Practice: From Area Studies to Transnationalism." *Critique of Anthropology* 18, no. 2 (1998): 117-133.

Munasinghe, Viranjini. *Callaloo or Tossed Salad? East Indians and the Cultural Politics of Identity in Trinidad.* Ithaca, N.Y.: Cornell University Press, 2001.

Sending Money Home: Remittance to Latin America and the Caribbean. Report of the IADB Multilateral Investment Fund. May 2004.

Stephens, Patricia. *The Spiritual Baptist Faith. African New World Religious History, Identity & Testimony.* London: Karnak House, 1999.

Trouillot, Michel-Rolph. *Global Transformations. Anthropology and the Modern World.* New York: Palgrave Macmillan, 2003.

Williams, Eric. *History of the People of Trinidad and Tobago.* London: Andre Deutsch, 1964.

Zane, Wallace W. *Journeys to Spiritual Lands. The Natural History of a West Indian Religion.* New York: Oxford University Press, 1999.

6

Carol Bailey

Performing "Difference": Reading Gossip in Olive Senior's Short Stories

Olive Senior's extensive use of Caribbean orality in her short stories has captured the attention of many in the critical community, with reviews and articles focusing on her deft representation of a range of speech genres and linguistic registers on the page.[1] Senior's turn to the oral-performance traditions of the Caribbean is the primary means by which she inscribes the voices of girls and women, particularly those from the working class. Her female speakers typically have limited access to education or official means of communication such as newspapers, which prevents them from participating in official public discourse.[2] Of course, such women have always been actively involved with public issues, but their contributions have often gone unrecognized. Senior's stories in *Summer Lightning* (1986), *Arrival of the Snake Woman* (1989), and *Discerner of Hearts* (1995) offer community-inspired accounts of events. They are shaped by oral forms women have always used to talk about the issues that concern them. Senior uses these same forms to critique the women's participation in the structures that they deplore.

In this essay, I analyze Senior's use of oral forms, specifically gossip, to address issues such as class distinctions that are pertinent to postcolonial Caribbean societies. Senior de-familiarizes domestic performance spaces in ways that invite the audience to rethink some views of these traditionally private spaces, and understand the discourses that occur within them as central to postcolonial critical discussions. The prominence of these spaces as sites of the performance in Senior's stories foregrounds that segment of the community of Caribbean women (from different class groups) who constitute her subjects.

Senior's use of a wide range of genres within the broad category of personal narratives facilitates an "inward turn" whereby her fictive characters contest and examine questions about Caribbean social relations that are pertinent to the nation, region and postcolonial diaspora.[3] In the discussion that follows, I examine Senior's use of gossip as her primary narrative strategy in the stories "Real Old

Time T'ing," (*Summer Lightning*) the first section of "Lily, Lily" (*Arrival of the Snake Woman*) and "The Lizardy Man and His Lady" (*Discerner of Hearts*). I read Senior's use of gossip in these stories as a discursive tool for challenging the investment of persons from different strata of society in "difference" as a primary basis of social organization in colonial/modern Jamaica. The speakers in these stories use gossip as a means of foregrounding the self, and in so doing call into question their own investment in the systems they interrogate.

While many sociological, anthropological and linguistic studies have noted diverse social, political and other uses of gossip, this form is still generally regarded as a negative communication genre, and its impact thought to be destructive or at best frivolous.[4] Roger Abrahams notes that while gossip is seen as "an inevitable performance of everyday life," persons in his study disapprove of the practice, and suggest that it leads to fights and other conflicts. In Jamaica, gossip is regarded in much the same way the participants in Abrahams' study view it, that is, as a negative mode of communication. Yet, gossip is widely used and understood as inevitable. People gossip in work places, in various public spaces such as markets, shops, rum bars. Yards, in which women often gather, are among the main domestic spaces in which gossip occurs. Importantly too, as Senior's stories illustrate, more often than not gossip occurs between people of similar social status, and is often about those in "higher" social classes. Gossip often operates as an alternative to other forms of communication, especially among those on the lower rungs of the social ladder. Since women are generally believed to have a stronger predilection to gossip, it is not surprising that the association between women and gossip presents another opportunity for essentializing women and censoring their behavior.[5] Indeed, societies' and individuals' attempts to control women often involve restricting speech.

In evoking gossip as her central aesthetic, Senior challenges the negative perceptions of the genre as well as its function among women. By exploiting some inherent features of gossip, she demonstrates how this form, used in its usual informal social context offers possibilities for interrogating the values and mores of the larger society. "Talking about other people's business," Abrahams suggests, is "a technique for maintaining community control through the elucidation of public morality."[6] Making a similar point, Simpson notes that, "Gossip can prove [. . .] beneficial in terms of its use to affirm social codes and values within a community."[7] But beyond maintaining control and exposing social codes, gossip also operates as a means of affirming one's subject position. Simultaneously, gossip reveals a subject's own insecurities and investment in the system she critiques. In reading gossip as one of a number of "alternative performance strategies," I suggest that Senior deploys the genre to challenge some commonly held views of gossip, as she exploits its subversive potential.[8] At the same time, Senior uncovers the social investment that gossip both reveals and embodies.

A word on difference

Set primarily in the home and other domestic areas, these stories explore relationships among females who share these spaces. Invariably, the stories call attention to differences of age, morality, skin color, hair texture and other markers of difference so central to the position one occupies in this society. Ultimately then, the stories cast a critical look at the region's history of the domination of some over others, that continue to manifest itself in an emphasis on racialized and other colonial-related social markers. The region's history of slavery, indentureship and colonialism continues to inform how Caribbean societies think about and organize themselves. Thus, in many ways, modern life is shaped by colonial ideologies. One aspect of life in the Caribbean that continues to show traces of colonialism is a class structure based originally on race and color, and later on other indices such as education and material possessions, which were and to some extent are still tied to race and color. Therefore, I find a concern with "difference" that emerges from a colonial outlook as the thematic nexus of these stories. My use of the concept of "difference" derives from Frantz Fanon's and Edward Said's writing. I also draw on Homi Bhabha's further elaborations on the centrality of difference in the colonial framework.

In *Orientalism*, Said names "what is believed to be radical difference" as the basis of entities that coexist in a state of tension. He argues that the apparent genuine divisions—of race, cultures, histories—among humans serve as the basis of oppression. Said writes: "Such divisions are generalities whose use historically and actually has been to press the importance of the distinction between some men and some other men."[9] I also find Said's notion of "*positional* superiority" a useful concept for talking about particular manifestations of "difference" in the Caribbean context. According to Said, "Orientalism depends for its strategy on this flexible *positional* superiority, which puts the Westerner in a whole series of possible relationships with the orient without ever losing him the relative upper hand."[10] Here, Said calls attention to certain kinds of placing of one over the other, in this instance the European over the "Oriental." Other institutions that depend on the placing of people include some association with "*positional* superiority." Similarly, Fanon notes "divisions into compartments" as central to the structure of colonial institutions; in so doing he names a specific way in which "difference" is applied on the ground in colonial and postcolonial societies. Fanon notes: "The first thing the native learns is to stay in his place, and not to go beyond certain limits."[11] It is the idea of "radical difference" as conceptualized and propagated by the West that informs the creation of different "places" for the "different" groups in colonial and postcolonial societies.

Homi Bhabha builds on the writings of Fanon and Said in his discussion of stereotypes and discrimination in his essay "The Other Question." Bhabha explores the importance of difference in colonial discourse, noting the centrality of the body, particularly "skin," as a site of differentiation and discrimination. He writes: "Skin is the key signifier of racial and cultural difference [. . .] is the most visible of fetishes."[12] Bhabha's attention to physical features is particularly relevant to my discussion of Senior's work, because while other markers of social status are important in the Jamaican class structure, physical features—skin color, hair type, the size of one's nose and others—remain critical characteristics in the determination of one's place in this society. And often, other markers of class such as education and occupation depend on these physical characteristics.

In Senior's stories "difference" is represented as a generic idea that informs the social structure of postcolonial Caribbean societies; this understanding of difference is also the principle that determines individuals' "place[s]" in society, a fact that finds resonance in Fanon's observations about the colonial subject's understanding of "[her or his] place." But beyond representing some ways in which an understanding and imposition of "difference" inform life in postcolonial Caribbean societies, Senior's stories focus on manifestations of "difference" that are often elided in some traditional masculinist discourses.[13] Both Said and Fanon use language that talks about the colonial encounter as a meeting between the male native and male colonist. Senior's writing demonstrates that it is not sufficient to accept the masculine pronoun as an inclusive given; indeed, her stories focus on the specific manifestation of difference in the lives of girls and women. Also, like many other Caribbean writers, Senior's treatment is more targeted in the sense that it "turns inward," that is, she focuses on the manifestation of "difference" in relations among the formerly colonized, rather than between colonized and colonizer. Thus, she addresses a particular strain of difference as the organizing principle of the class structure, a direct spin-off from the racism of the colonial experience.[14] As I hope to show in the ensuing discussion, Senior's stories also go beyond an exploration of the differences as a given, and focus on difference as a façade: she shows how the "seemingly genuine differences" in humanity to which Said refers, are used to create a constructed set of differences.

Gossip as narrative strategy

Gossip tends to focus on people; often speakers report details ranging from ordinary descriptions of what others wear, eat, to extended critiques of behaviors; yet this focus on people often involves, albeit implicitly, an engagement with ideological constructs. While it appears that Senior maintains this preoccupation with people, close attention to her stories indicates that the preoccupation with people is a veneer for uncovering a number of entrenched beliefs and values that constitute the dominant culture in postcolonial Jamaica. Senior uses gossip to expose the society's anxieties about difference, particularly differences of race, class, overall social status and a related concern, morality.

"The Lizardy Man and His Lady" illustrates the usefulness of gossip in the domestic performance space where women at the lowest rung of the social ladder in Jamaica converse, and in the process, analyze and expose their and the society's acceptance of social hierarchy. An overt example of Senior's deployment of gossip, this story is told as a monologue. Although the speaker's use of performance keys indicates that there is an interlocutor (another domestic helper), the audience hears only one voice. The speaker's talk is interspersed with dialogue between the women's charges as the latter play.[15] The ostensible subject of gossip in this story is Ella, one of the women's young employers, who has fallen into a life of moral decadence. The speaker's discourse begins in medias res, and hers and the society's preoccupation with difference are immediately apparent:

> As I was saying, Miss Ersie, and this is the Lord's own truth, if it wasn't for the little there, me would leave long time, you know. Go right back to mi owna yard [. . .] Seh what? Yes mi'dear. Getting worse every day [. . .] Sometimes you can't predict how things will turn out ee? Like when you see what can happen to some people good good pickney. A walla-walla with bad company. Me seh, her mother would have belly-come-down pain if she could see the class of people fe har pickney a mix with these last days.[16]

The speaker's location in the performative tradition of gossip is well illustrated in her insertion of a number of stock features of the genre, including the expressions "yes mi' dear" and "seh what." She further authenticates her statements with "[t]his is the Lord's own truth" to embellish her discourse, another stock phrase that exemplifies the features of gossip that permeate this story. The speaker's distress at her young mistress's fall into "bad company" indicates her acceptance of the differences that her society stresses. Her reference to Ella as "people good good pickney" acknowledges Ella's "pedigree" and implies that there are others in the society who may be described in other less socially favorable terms. It is worth noting that the speaker connects social "superiority" with morality, another traditional conflation which I take up in greater detail later.

As often occurs in gossip, the speaker's lament over the young woman's poor judgment and her descent into "low life" fleshed out below goes beyond the apparent subject:

> Well, me stick wid her through thick and thin, move up and down with her, for who else she have to look after little Shelly-Ann? and me not lying, sometimes there she don't even have money to pay mi wages. From she leave the husband she suck salt, I tell you. Suck salt. From one man to the next till she meet up with this one [. . .] Well, him seem to have plenty money. Give her more gold chain and ring. Plenty food pon table.[17]

And further stressing her pedigree, the speaker juxtaposes this new low life against Ella's former high class life:

> Mi tell you. You see her there a mix up herself with every kind of riff-raff. You wouldn't believe what a pretty pickney she used to be. The class of family that girl come from. Born in mi hand, you have to say. Is me raise and grow her.

> And when she get married, is me the mother beg to go with her to set up house [. . .] I go with Miss Ella. For is big man she marry, you know. Expecting her to entertain all twenty people.[18]

The speaker celebrates Ella's former (and in her mind present) social superiority as she details Ella's past: "You wouldn't believe how pretty she used to be" and "[i]s big man she marry, you know." "Pretty" here is a likely reference to complexion and hair quality, and according to the speaker, with such looks Ella should have avoided "mixing up with riff-raff," the latter being the opposite of "people good good pickney." Since Ella's looks render her superior, the speaker reveals that in this community one's looks are part of what determines whether she or he is considered a "riff raff." Yet, this speaker reveals, through the candor that characterizes gossip, that these differences are often more perception than reality. For example, in spite of Ella's breeding and presumed socioeconomic superiority, her economic status is sometimes not very different from those of the working class, including her employee: She "suck salt" and "sometimes don't even have money to pay [. . .] wages."[19] The speaker also mentions that Ella moves "from one man to the next," a revelation that equates the upper-middle class young woman with those working class "others" whom the society believe are predisposed to sexual immorality.

So while the speaker seems preoccupied mainly with lamenting her employer's fall and celebrating her high breeding, the genre she employs allows her to undercut the very social system she upholds. In seeking to preserve Ella's difference, she ends up removing the veil of difference that conceals commonalities among the various class groups in that society. Here we see as well, that the tendency to be preoccupied with people or "people business" is not the limit of gossip. Often, people and their business are the starting points for explorations of more general concerns and fears. In this case the subject of gossip is not Ella, but the social system of which the speaker and others are products and victims. Therefore the intrinsic disruptive potential of gossip which Abrahams notes is evident here, because the speaker has an audience that is a "social equal" and is in a safe and comfortable space that allows her to critique the system that relegates her to a position of "social inferiority."

The intertwining of people's "business" and other concerns is further explored in "Real Old Time T'ing." This is a story ostensibly about Patricia, the daughter of an aging widower who takes it upon herself to remodel her father's house; much of the story also focuses on Patricia's obsession with antiques, and her materialism. The opening paragraph reveals a lot, not just about the apparent subject of the story, but also the speaker's and society's anxieties about class differences, especially as difference is manifested in the move to modernity: "Is the one name Patricia did start up bout how Papa Sterling need a new house for it look bad how her father living in this old board house it don't even have sanitary convenience. Sanitary convenience! So it don't name bath house any more?"[20]

The Gossip employs the genre's well-known malicious tendencies noted in her use of "is the one name Patricia," and the general tone of the passage. But this passage also hints at the speaker's concern over a change that has already taken place, and will occur in a small community. "Sanitary convenience! So it don't name bath house anymore," is a jab at Patricia's new fangled ideas, particularly her use of language that marks her off as now different from the community in which she grew up. Further, if Papa Sterling gets a new, more modern house, he will no longer be like the others in the community, all of whom are likely to live in similar board houses. The speaker's cynical outburst of "sanitary convenience!" confirms her anxieties about the possible change, which will likely result in Papa' Sterling's movement into another, higher social class. This idea is reinforced in her later comments: "Let me tell you not a thing wrong with Papa Sterling house except it need a little fixing up here and there. True, he getting old and could do with a little more comfort."[21] The speaker's admission that the house "need[s] a little fixing up here and there" affirms Patricia's concern, but at the same time shows the former's desire to have the house fixed up just enough, but not with the kind of elaborate modern renovation that Patricia envisions, and which would signal Papa Sterling's social mobility.

The speaker's subsequent descriptions of Patricia confirms that this is a speaker concerned about class differences, and one who fears changes that would accentuate her economic marginalization:

> Anyway, nuh Papa Sterling big girl the one that did marry the lawyer fellow from Kingston that always get him name in Gleaner. Big big lawyer. Name Akeson. But we won't going to all the ups and downs she did have before that piece a luck drop in her lap. And is luck fi true mi dear. The guy have money and he drive big car and he good looking can't done.[22]

Not only does she share the value system of her society about what constitutes luck—"big car," "money" and a lucrative profession—she betrays her insecurities through the backhanded compliments, "the ups and downs she did have." She takes something away from Patricia as a way of bringing her back a little closer to the community she has (socio-economically) left behind. Social advancement of some reinforces or creates differences which most in the society agree render some superior to others. The speaker endorses these ideas, and the concerns she expresses about Patricia's effort to modernize her father's house are indicative of her own insecurities about class barriers that marginalize her.

The implication of the value placed on socioeconomic differences and class distinction is explicitly expressed in "Lily Lily" (*Arrival of the Snake Woman*). In this story Senior evokes at least three oral forms, but for this discussion I focus on the first long section which appropriates gossip. Unlike "Real Old Time T'ing" and "The Lizardy Man," which focuses on working class speakers, the Gossip in "Lily, Lily" is an upper middle-class woman who candidly shares with her interlocutor of similar ilk, her anxieties about the threat to the erosion of the class system that honors their difference.[23] This story too begins in media res, and the speaker not only "micro-divides;" she also unmasks some inconsistencies and follies of the insistence on difference. Additionally, as Gossips tend to do, she reveals more than she intends or realizes:[24]

> the three little girls going to church? Elma, Sadie and Lily [. . .] Elma and Sadie are above reproach, children of the first family so to speak dressed simply [. . .] but impeccably, with manners to match (and you can't fault these refined, educated black people you know) [. . .] and Lily? Oh Lily's background is even finer than the teachers' children for how else would she get to walk with the teachers' children? Lily is the daughter of Mr and Mrs Dasilva, solid, respectable people. O yes. Mr Dasilva owns the sawmill over at rock road and makes a good living from it too.[25]

Aside from the obvious repetition of the marking of class that I noted in the other stories, this speaker also exposes a society blind to the inconsistencies in its value system. The children are on their way to *church*, yet, even there, where all are presumably equal, class differences matter, since as she reveals, it is Lily's "fine background" that makes her suitable company for these other girls on their way to church. Therefore, like the working class speaker in "The Lizardy Man and his Lady," this middle class Gossip tacitly critiques the system that she obviously upholds and seeks to keep intact.

But as the preceding examples indicate, the difference that material prosperity, class and social mobility ensure breeds insecurity and in this case the middle-class Gossip exposes her anxiety about the slippery ground on which difference is built:

> As I was saying Mrs Dasilva is the most prominent lady in our town, though nowadays with all this travelling back and forth that's taking place [. . .] there is a whole new breed of people who have money and little else, certainly no respect for manners or graces. One of these women from right here in our town, who not so long ago was walking the streets barefoot, looking for work as an ordinary domestic [. . .] got it into her head to take off to Colon as a higgler if you please and you are not going to believe it, but a year later the same woman is back wearing silk and satins [. . .] and this creature was actually rude to Mrs Dasilva only last week in Agostina shop. She objected to Mrs Dasilva being served ahead of her because she said she was there first.[26]

This Gossip shares the anxieties of the one in "Real Ole Time T'ing." While the speaker in "Real Old Time T'ing" is concerned that modernity and acquisition of material comforts threaten the equality among the working class people of her community, this middle-class Gossip is anxious about the possibility of her own privilege being erased by the upward mobility of some. "The whole new breed of people" to whom she refers are those who, through education or in the specific case she mentions, access to wealth and exposure to the outside world, threaten the comfort of those who, based on the class structure, enjoy positions of privilege. In both cases, Senior exploits the tendency among Gossips to inadvertently reveal their deepest insecurities to underscore the pervasiveness of the obsession with difference in postcolonial Jamaica. Her inclusion of speakers from different social classes is itself commentary on difference as an illusion, because the stories indicate that these women share a value system. This example illustrates the attention Senior draws to the fact that in many instances the differences between class groups are more perceived than real. Both speakers understand the importance of difference, and fear any change in these differences because it could affect each one's place in the social structure.

Talking about the other: revealing the self

My brief sketch of some ways in which Senior deploys gossip, and how she exploits some characteristic features of the genre to call attention the community's preoccupation with class differences rooted in racism, opens space for more general observations about this oral genre. For example, it becomes clear that while gossip is often ostensibly about other people, as Senior's use indicates, frequently, the Gossip is the real subject of the discourse. Particularly in the examples from "Real Old Time T'ing" and "Lily Lily," the fear and insecurity engendered by a society rooted in difference are inadvertently revealed. Further, this tendency of gossip makes the genre a fertile one for addressing some of the concerns in postcolonial societies that are still haunted by the preoccupation with difference that created them.

Much of the early scholarship on gossip that was the basis of further research and theorizing about the form centered on its use for individual and community interests. In "What is Gossip? An Alternative Hypothesis" Robert Paine departs from the dominant notion that gossip is "a property of the group" and that its function is primarily to maintain group integrity. Instead, Paine proposes that gossip serves individual interests, more than it does group interest. There is clearly great value in each of these positions, but here I am more interested in Paine's idea that gossip focuses significantly on the self. Paine's suggestion that gossip often promotes self-interest dovetails with my idea that in each of the stories I read above, the speakers use gossip to affirm and reclaim individual subjectivity. But, as I try to show in the analysis that follows, gossip is equally a tool for self-revelation, and it is this capacity of gossip that allows Senior to explore the characters' investment in difference.

As I have argued, Gossip's inclination towards foregrounding the self also presents the possibility for persons who are otherwise denied a voice in the mainstream to affirm their subjectivity.[27] This is particularly true for working class women with limited access to education, and little opportunity to participate in public discourse. For example, in "The "Lizardy Man," the speaker, a middle-aged woman who has been a domestic helper since she was a teenager, and whose entire life is characterized by relative subservience, is able to affirm the role of women like herself in ensuring stability or the façade of stability in the lives of the middle and upper class families they serve, showing that often it is the work of these women that holds these dysfunctional families together. She poses the rhetorical question, "Who else she have to look after little Shelly-Ann?" which implicitly states that Ella is an inadequate mother. The speaker also digresses to point out that she had to continue being this young woman's helper because the girl was "expected to entertain all twenty people to dinner party" which is in effect saying *I* had to entertain all these people. Here we are presented with a side of the story that hardly gets told: The work of domestic helpers is often taken for granted, and their role in all aspects of national development ignored. Because the speaker loosens her tongue in a domestic space in which she is comfortable, she is able to affirm her subjectivity and self-worth and acknowledge the personhood of these often forgotten community builders.

In situations in which people consider their humanity to be threatened, they usually find ways of reclaiming what may be regarded as an intrinsic personhood. Abrahams argues that gossip is "a tool by which the gossiper exercises personal control over the person talked about, if only because he is licensed to call the person's name."[28] In "The Lizardy Man" and "Real Old Time T'ing" the speakers gossip about other women that the social structure deems their superior. In each case, the speakers use gossip as a leveling device because they not only exercise their name calling license; they are also able to present information that indicates to their interlocutors and larger audience the similarities between themselves and their presumed superiors.

Gossip also allows these women to present themselves as informed persons fully aware of the challenges of a new modern society, and more than ignorant drudges. In "Real Old Time T'ing" for example, the speaker confronts and engages with the coexistence of tradition and modernity, and offers her views on a creolized existence, noting the complex experience of those who straddle the two worlds. She juxtaposes Patricia's desire to modernize her father's old house against an obsession with antiques. The speaker suggests: "Then if she so hot on sanitary convenience why she down here a buy up all the old water goblet and china basin she can find a talk say is real country this and how she just finding her roots."[29] Here the speaker confronts and calls her audience's attention to the cultural schizophrenia that many of the new black middle-class experience. She also seems uneasy about Patricia's romanticizing of her past and the essentialist view she has of "real country." Here again, Senior calls attention to the sophisticated analysis of which these women are capable, as well as the discursive potential of gossip, and uses these fictional characters to show how the society's emphasis on superficial differences exclude some, and their worldview from the mainstream.

In another passage the speaker makes a similar observation, ridiculing Patricia's comment that the "old time t'ings" remind her of her "happy childhood."[30] The Gossip's comment is: "You ever hear anything like that bout happy childhood? As if she couldn't wait to turn her tail on the place." "Turning [ones] tail on the place" is the decision many of the working class make out of necessity, since social mobility often requires physical movement from rural communities in order to access higher education, and other prerequisites of "advancement." Beyond envy that often accompanies gossip, the speaker's bitterness calls attention to the natural feelings of exclusion that many who do not have access to the scarce resources that foster social mobility experience. Gossip then allows her to reclaim her self worth, through both the calling out of Patricia's name, and calling attention to the latter's faults. The speaker also reports on the comic effect that news of Papa Sterling's house renovation has on the community as a way of diffusing her own insecurities. While she is not sympathetic to Patricia's cultural dilemma, her observation of, and engagement with the phenomenon invites further consideration from the audience, and contributes to critical discussions related to cultural change in new and emerging modern societies. It is noteworthy that the speaker is irritated both by Patricia's nostalgia for the past and her move towards modernity. Her choice to make both situations material for gossip betrays her own cultural ambivalence, and again, shows the tendency of gossip to expose more about the speaker than she often intends.

Gossip as performance

In referring to gossip as "one of the many inevitable performances of everyday life," and a type of "stylized encounter," Abrahams indicates that gossip belongs to a particular performance tradition that is governed by rules related to vocality and bodily involvement.[31] Senior evokes many of the performative features of gossip to explore how gossip is used to foreground the self. Richard Schechner defines performance as "restored behavior," "twice behaved behavior," "repeated behavior" and "behavior always subject to revision."[32] "Restored behavior" draws attention to the fact that performance always involves recourse to a set of agreed upon behaviors that locate the specific act within a particular tradition and at the same time contributes to the aesthetic value of the act. "Restored behavior" therefore entails drawing upon a set of both somatic and verbal resources. Gossip invariably includes "restored behavior" which the speaker evokes to attract and hold the attention of an audience. And specific kinds of behavior are also "restored" in order to establish credibility and embellish the story.

In gossip "restored behavior" often includes an evocation of particular ways of speaking, or the use of a number of stock phrases. For example, Senior includes expressions such as, "let me tell you," "hear this" "mi tell you" "see here" in these and other stories. These performance keys are especially effective in generating interest from the audience, getting them excited and at the same time calling attention to the speaker's authority over the material, and her importance in that performance space at the moment of performance. It is noteworthy that in each of the above phrases the first person singular is either explicitly stated or implied, a stylistic choice that addresses the function of these stock phrases in the role of affirming the self, since the possession and control of information are central to gossip, and equally crucial in the foregrounding the self.

Important too, is the bodily involvement that the inclusion of these stock expressions suggests. And here the outside audience (that is the person(s) reading the text), is invited to participate at another level. The inclusion of these phrases alerts any reader to the somatic dimensions of the form; and the reader familiar with the performance tradition that Senior evokes is likely to imagine more specific bodily involvement such as arms akimbo or eyes widening. Senior's stories are replete with similar linguistic cues that invite the audience to imagine the somatic dimension of the form. The bodily gestures mentioned above are usually restricted to informal spaces such as the yard and the street, and are usually associated with women such as those whose voices Senior inscribes. In alluding to these bodies and behaviors Senior accentuates the disruptive presence of some whom the society has tried to marginalize by limiting access to education and public discourse.

Senior's use of gossip also facilitates further consideration of the concept of "restored behavior" in a context in which difference is both performed and contested. Through their performances within the gossip tradition, the speakers restore not only some stock characteristics of the form to foreground the self: they also restore behaviors and ideologies that have been central to their own marginalization. As each of these women bare their insecurities about the constructed differences that limit them, they restore and keep intact, the differences that colonialism both fostered and relied on for its success. Therefore, Senior's "inward turn" necessarily involves calling out her subjects for the ways their performances contribute to maintaining colonial structures. Thus, Senior speaks to the fact that agency among women does not necessarily translate into positive engagement with the problems that plague both women and the wider community. As Rhonda Cobham shows in her essay "Revisioning our Kumblas," Caribbean women writers also expose in their works how "women themselves have participated in reproducing the system and that the power they now have to challenge the system has often been won by their complicity within it." Gossip effectively exposes this complicity.[33]

The performative dimension of gossip is most extensively illustrated in the interactive features of the narratives, where speakers demonstrate what performance studies scholars refer to as "responsibility to an audience." Dell Hymes formulated "responsibility to an audience" as a defining feature of performance from Erving Goffman's theorization, and as Marvin Carlson notes, "this reformulation [. . .] places the responsibility of performance, and its agency, squarely back upon the performer."[34] In all the stories in which gossip is used, the speakers address the immediate audience directly. For example, they use "Let me tell you," "Yu are not going to believe it" and "Where were we?" in direct reference to the interlocutor. These phrases also serve as reminders of the interdependence that characterizes performances, and the dialectical relationship between performer and audience that these stories affirm. In other examples, interaction with the addressee is even more direct as the addressee is named. For instance, the speaker in "The Lizardy Man and His Lady" says, "As I was saying Miss Ersie." The strong interactive tendencies are also related to the "performance keys" and the evidence of "restored behavior" discussed above, because these are stock linguistic tools that the speakers evoke to place themselves in an already established performance tradition, and constantly call attention to the self.

In both form and meaning, Senior's stories address the tensions between coloniality and modernity that constitute life in contemporary Caribbean (and other) societies. The association between orality and backwardness and conversely writing and sophistication, so central to modernity has been well documented, with writers locating its genesis in the era of European expansion. The marginalization of orality has resulted in what Walter Mignolo calls "subalternization of knowledge," a term which speaks to the exclusion of some and their points of view from the mainstream.[35] Senior's use of gossip facilitates a foregrounding of these knowledges since this form also privileges the point of view of marginalized groups. In writing stories that combine orature from the folk culture, with the short story, an established literary form, Senior creates texts that embody the coexistence of modern/colonial that is part of the stories' subject. However, since the short story has close ties with oral forms, these oral-written texts also perform the interconnectedness and overlaps of the colonial/modern twin.

Notes

1. See for example, Velma Pollard, "An Introduction to the Poetry and Fiction of Olive Senior," *Callaloo* 36 (Summer 1988); Richard F. Patteson, "The Fiction of Olive Senior: Traditional Society and the Wider World," *Ariel* 24, no. 1 (1993); Hyacinth Simpson, "'Voicing the Text': The Making of an Oral Poetics in Olive Senior's Short Fiction," *Callaloo* 27, no. 3 (2004).

2. I do not mean to suggest that women were "silent" or completely missing from public discussions. As Forbes notes, "The female silence of which feminist discourse speaks is [. . .] problematic in the West Indian context." Forbes also notes that the matter of silence is often based on whether one is represented in the public/written/academic document. My focus is on how postcolonial writers such as Senior, foreground oral forms that women have always used to include their voices in public discussions—see Curdella Forbes, *From Nation to Diaspora. Samuel Selvon, George Lamming and the Cultural Performance of Gender* (Kingston, Jamaica: University of the West Indies Press, 2005), 215.

3. I use the term "inward turn" in reference to a number of writers' critical examination of how formerly colonized peoples have themselves maintained the structures of colonialism, in ways that render the "post" in "postcolonial" criticism a misnomer (if one takes "post" to mean that the colonial climate has passed). The problems raised by the "post" in postcolonial studies have been addressed by many writers in the field. For example, Anne McClintock argues that the "post" in "postcolonial" is paradoxical, and she expresses her unease with its complicity with "linear, historical progress" as well as the failure of some writers to recognize the nuances of the experiences as well as responses to it. It is noteworthy however, that McClintock does not advocate dispensing with the

term; she accepts that there is "theoretical substance" in the field, and agrees that there are circumstances in which "postcolonial" can be used "judiciously." Others, such as Ella Shohat also raise pertinent questions about the term and the scholarly field it describes. See Anne McClintock, "The Angel of Progress: Pitfalls of the Term 'Post-Colonialism'," *Social Text* 10, no. 31/32 (1992): 84-98; Ella Shohat, "Notes on the 'Post-Colonial'," *Social Text* 10, no. 31/32 (1992): 99-113.

4. See for example, Roger Abrahams, "A Performance-Centered Approach to Gossip," *Man* 5, n. s., 2 (1970); Nancy B. Kurland and Lisa Hope Pelled, "Passing the Word: Toward a Model of Gossip and Power in the Workplace," *The Academy of Management Review* 25, no. 2 (April 2000): 428-38., and Robert Paine, "What is Gossip About? An Alternative Hypothesis," *Man* 2, n. s., 2 (1967): 278-285.

5. One of the findings Abrahams reports from his study of gossip among Vincentians is that men discourage friendship among women, and restrict their gathering in yards, since these friendships provide a community for gossip, and the yard is the space where gossip among women is likely to take place.

6. Abrahams. "A Performance-Centered Approach," 190.

7. Simpson, "Voicing," 841.

8. I refer to gossip as an example of "alternative performance strategies" to underline the marginal position that this form occupies as a medium for critical discourse. Robert Paine concurs with this categorization in his note that in gossip, "the channels of communication are selected . . . as alternatives to available official ones." In the stories I read here, gossip is all (or virtually all) that is available to these women. See Paine, "What is," 283.

9. Edward Said, *Orientalism* (New York: Vintage, 1994), 44.

10. Said, *Orientalism*, 7.

11. Frantz Fanon, *The Wretched of the Earth* (New York: Globe Press, 1963), 52.

12. Homi Bhabha, *The Location of Culture* (New York: Routledge, 1994), 78.

13. Many male writers from the Caribbean pay attention to how colonialism has impacted women. However, feminist scholars have consistently called attention to Caribbean women writers' important interventions in writing female experiences, and have noted how their treatment goes beyond that of male writers.

14. In *The Development of a Creole Society in Jamaica 1770-1820* (Oxford: Clarendon Press, 1971) Edward Kamau Brathwaite presents the status of the different racial groups in colonial Jamaica, and details the micro-division according to various shades as a manifestation of the ways in which color determined social status or "place." This categorization has always loomed large in the Jamaican consciousness and social structure, and is the context within which Senior explores "difference."

15. Formerly referred to as "maids," domestic helpers are (usually) women employed to perform a number of domestic tasks primarily in middle and upper-middle class families in the Caribbean. Arrangements range from one day agreements, weekly forty hour arrangements, to live-in arrangements in which the employee is almost constantly at the employer's disposal.

16. Olive Senior, *Discerner of Hearts* (Toronto: McClelland & Stewart, 1995), 94.

17. Senior, *Discerner*, 94.

18. Senior, *Discerner*, 95.

19. To "suck salt" is to suffer, experience dire need or see really hard times.

20. Olive Senior, *Summer Lightning* (Essex, England: Longman, 1986), 54.

21. Senior, *Summer Lightning*, 54.

22. Senior, *Summer Lightning*, 54.

23. I use "gossip" as a noun in two ways throughout this essay. When written with an uppercase "G" Gossip refers to a person, and when written with a lower case "g" it refers to gossip as an oral-performance genre.

24. My coinage "micro-divide" describes this speaker's representative delineation of minor variations in skin color, income and education as the basis for differentiation. This is typical of postcolonial Jamaica where every variation of skin color makes the individual a little more or less valued or privileged.

25. Olive Senior, *Arrival of the Snake Woman* (Harlow, UK: Longman, 1989), 112.

26. Senior, *Arrival*, 114.

27. I use the term "voice" here in the way Carole Boyce Davies and Elaine Savory use it in reference to "the absence of a specifically female position on major issues such as slavery, colonialism, decolonization, women's rights and more direct social and cultural issues ... or articulation that goes unheard"—see Carole Boyce Davies and Elaine Savory Fido Davies, eds., *Out of the Kumbla. Caribbean Women and Literature* (Trenton, N.J.: Africa World Press, 1990), 1.

28. Abrahams, "A Performance-centered Approach," 300.

29. Senior, *Summer Lightning*, 54.

30. Senior, *Summer Lightning*, 60.

31. Abrahams, "A Performance-centered Approach," 292.

32. Richard Schechner, *Between Theater and Anthropology* (Philadelphia: University of Pennsylvania Press, 1985), 36.

33. Rhonda Cobham, "Revisioning Our Kumblas: Transforming Feminist and National Agendas in Three Caribbean Women's Texts," *Callaloo* 16, no. 1 (1993), 51.

34. Marvin Carlson, *Performance: A Critical Introduction* (New York: Routledge, 1996), 42.

35. Walter Mignolo, Introduction. "On Gnosis and the Imaginary of the Modern/Colonial World System," in *Local Histories/Global Designs: Coloniality and Subaltern Knowledges and Border Thinking* (Princeton, N.J.: Princeton University Press 2000), 4.

Bibliography

Abrahams, Roger D. "A Performance-Centered Approach to Gossip." *Man* 5, n. s., 2 (1970): 290-301.

Bauman, Richard. *Verbal Arts as Performance*. Prospect Heights: Waveland Press, 1977.

Bhabha, Homi. *The Location of Culture*. New York: Routledge, 1994.

Brathwaite, Edward Kamau. *The Development of a Creole Society in Jamaica, 1770-1820*. Oxford: Clarendon Press, 1971.

Carlson, Marvin. *Performance: A Critical Introduction*. New York: Routledge, 1996.

Cobham, Rhonda. "Revisioning Our Kumblas: Transforming Feminist and National Agendas in Three Caribbean Women's Texts." *Callaloo* 16, no. 1 (1993): 44-64.

Davies, Carole Boyce, and Elaine Savory Fido, eds. *Out of the Kumbla. Caribbean Women and Literature*. Trenton, N.J.: Africa World Press, 1990.

Fanon, Frantz. *The Wretched of the Earth*. New York: Globe Press, 1963.

Forbes, Curdella. *From Nation to Diaspora. Samuel Selvon, George Lamming and the Cultural Performance of Gender*. Kingston, Jamaica: University of the West Indies Press, 2005.

Kurland, Nancy B., and Lisa Hope Pelled. "Passing the Word: Toward a Model of Gossip and Power in the Workplace," *Academy of Management Review* 25, no. 2 (April 2000): 428-38.

McClintock, Anne. "The Angels of Progress: Pitfalls of the Term 'Post-colonialism,'" Pp. 291-304 in *Colonial Discourse and Postcolonial Theory: A Reader*, edited by Patrick Williams and Laura Chrisman. New York: Columbia University Press, 1994.

Mignolo, Walter D. "On Gnosis and the Imaginary of the Modern/Colonial World System." Pp. 3-45 in *Local Histories/Global Designs: Coloniality, Subaltern Knowledges, and Border Thinking*. Princeton, N.J.: Princeton University Press, 2000.

Paine, Robert. "What is Gossip About? An Alternative Hypothesis." *Man* 2, n. s., 2 (1967): 278-285.

Patteson, Richard F. "The Fiction of Olive Senior: Traditional Society and the Wider World." *Ariel* 24, no. 1 (1993): 13-33.

Pollard, Velma. "An Introduction to the Poetry and Fiction of Olive Senior." *Callaloo* 36 (Summer 1988): 540-545.

Said, Edward. *Orientalism*. New York: Vintage, 1994.

Schechner, Richard. *Between Theater and Anthropology*. Philadelphia: University of Pennsylvania Press, 1985.

Senior, Olive. *Arrival of the Snake Woman*. Harlow, Essex, UK: Longman, 1989.

———. *Discerner of Hearts*. Toronto: McClelland & Stewart, 1995.

———. *Summer Lightning*. Essex, England: Longman, 1986.

Shohat, Ella. "Notes on the 'Post-Colonial.'" *Social Text* 10, no. 31/32 (1992): 99-113.

Simpson, Hyacinth. "'Voicing the Text': The Making of an Oral Poetics in Olive Senior's Short Fiction." *Callaloo* 27, no. 3 (2004): 829-843.

7

Lyndon Phillip

"This Is My Vibes": Legitimizing Vernacular Expressions in Caribana

Hip hop cultural forms stretch what traditionally stands for Caribbean carnival in Toronto. The arrival of global hip hop into the authenticating spaces of the transnational Trinidadian carnival raises a number of difficult issues that are useful considerations in the continued debates over questions of cultural continuity and change. Specific to understandings of Caribana, questioning continuity and change have singularly focused on broad issues of declining Afro-Trinidadian hegemony over the representative control of ideological uses of carnival throughout the African diaspora. Since the mid-1990s expressions of global hip hop within carnival have disrupted a hegemonic discourse, which tries to enunciate a particular version of the Trinidadian transnation through carnival performances. The central question I asked in this essay is "what role is hip hop culture playing in the context of a carnival that has banned it?" The strategy of this essay is to push at the limits of the academic literature that conceptually centers understandings of Caribbean carnival as tightly taking place on the performance of the Trinidadian transnation.[1]

Discussing Caribana and the nation

In Canada, multiculturalism is an official policy that acts to assemble ethnic diversity. In other words, since multiculturalism was introduced as a policy solution in 1971 to the issue of cultural disparities between English and French cultures and later the growing number of non-white ethnic groups relocating to major Canadian urban centers, the policy tried to create the social conditions that regulate the conduct of Canadian residents and citizens. Canadian multiculturalism, like other forms of dealing with racial and ethnic diversities is a form of ordering cultural experience into particular modes of coherence. Caribana then, emerging in the period of the late 1960s and early 1970s comes to be lived out under various forms of ordering. As such, Caribana is a cultural practice that produces contradictory ethnic meanings that veer toward and stray from the social institution of official multiculturalism. In other words, through the structures of Canadian multiculturalism, Caribana has marked out, designated and formalized a set of signifying practices that produce meanings that assimilate and integrate it into the national imagination.

What has happened is the available set of signifying practices that give order to the experience of Caribana has profoundly narrowed in wake of challenging economic times. During the period of the 1990s there has been a tremendous assumption that is articulated in the relationship between the formations of Caribana with respect to official multiculturalism. It assumes that ethnic and cultural identities are fully formed within the nation, particularly in those moments when financing the celebration is stabilized.

My interest in multiculturalism and Caribana, in this period, is to argue that the cultures of hip hop that occupy space in Caribana contradict this assumption. It does so by elaborating another set of signifying practices in relation to the representational forms that stabilize Caribana to the nation. Hip hop destabilizes the representational forms that signify ethnic coherence, or to put it differently the reading that we most often get about hip hop in Caribana is intended to show how it constrains, contests and breaks down the meaning making practices that describe the performance of traditional carnival. Instead I argue the practice of hip hop in Caribana is constructed as problematic and destabilizing because it points to the gaps of the social institution and the inadequacy of leaning on the nation as the sole modality to think through the festival. I take the position that cultural practices of hip hop in Caribana challenge the idea that there is a particular interest with regard to understanding the festival under the terms of the social institution that youth must inherit and continue.

Caribana is a popular black performance that enables multiple ethnic and identity positionalities. In the Canadian context, it is read in two broadly defined ways. These two signifiers of Caribana work in tension to either inscribe or destabilize a particular view through class, gender and race.

First, Caribana is an expression of Caribbean Canadian ethnic formation. This is the demand developed through elite structures such as multiculturalism and by a group of festival stakeholders to reproduce the Caribbean in Canada in simplified terms. This view insists on simplifying rather than complicating how the Caribbean is read in Canada. A number of stabilizing narratives circulate to police and fold back into traditional ways of being attempts to stretch the festival past its symbolic commitment of representing ethnic diversity and an imagined Caribbean regional identity successfully making itself visible in Canada.

In light of this view, I maintain that narrating ethnic stability actually points to the inadequacy of a term like Caribbean Canadian to describe the ways in which the cultures of hip hop are reinventing Caribana. I take this position because the performance of Caribbean Canadian is an invention partially drawing legitimacy from inside of the social institution. Caribana in other words makes particular investments in the legitimacy that ethnic groups might acquire within the structures of multiculturalism.

Caribbean Canadian as a signifying category operates to ignore shifting ethnic formations by way of shoring up the volatility. The effort made to make visible a Caribbean Canadian social figure within Caribana is a primary tool that has a dual effect. It generally serves to imagine a particular hybrid relation to Canada in the post-World World II era. However, a particular version of the Caribbean Canadian attempts to inscribe its performance within the transnational project of managing Caribana as an authentic reflection of the dominant Trinidadian carnival.

The dominance of Afro-Trinidadian identities in shaping four decades of Caribana has narrowed the practices of the Caribbean Canadian figure in Caribana as expressive of Trinidadian transnationalism in the broadest sense. Historian David Trotman notes "those of Trinidad origin see this [carnival] as their finest cultural export, an activity that signifies their cultural existence as a nation and that allows them to distinguish themselves from other peoples of the Caribbean." In contrast, Trotman notes that others have broadened the discussion beyond a narrow focus on Trinidad, offering carnival "as an example of the cultural hybridity of the Caribbean and evidence of something defined as 'Caribbean culture.'"[2]

These tensions suggest that Caribana is both rooted and routed within the cultures of the black north Atlantic. Second, Caribana is read as an associational slate for making black Canadian identities. The practice of widely affiliating other kinds of popular music to Caribana shapes another expressive space within the festivity. Often youth are taken as the quintessential representation of this emergent Caribana performance. Their activities, particularly under conditions of growing dissatisfaction with festival management of money and content programming, show both continuous and discontinuous meanings of ethnicity and identity formation.

At a conceptual level, I am interested in understanding the impact that other music has on facilitating specific ethnic identities. In what ways does music help us understand Toronto's Caribana as a Caribbean carnival? How does music enable us to imagine Caribbean identities in Caribana? How do festival organizers and bandleaders view the politics of music and the challenges that are created for maintaining Caribana as a continuous form of Trinidadian carnival? Why should this be the case for a Canadian celebration? At issue then is to understand how the pillars of carnival—steelpan, calypso and masquerade—continue to be the representative artistic traditions that explain Caribbean ethnicity, with respect to Caribana, in Toronto. In my view, the debates over the way that global hip hop has tried to create a relationship with Caribana by stretching the definitions of who can bring a masquerade band to the parade is a useful development in which to have these discussions.

In the remainder of the chapter I build my discussion around the following issues. Music is the primary social arena by which Caribana participants show continuity and discontinuity. It is an interventionist space that articulates sharp critiques centered on young people's music. The intervention foregrounds a process in which both Caribana and hip hop are being creolized. What I am most interested in doing is to understand the interaction of two forms of black popular culture (global hip hop and global carnival) as a creolizing encounter on a redefined carnival road.

Making hip hop in Caribana

Canadian hip hop artists such as the Baby Blue Sound Crew, Choclair, Kardinal Offishal, The Rascalz and iconic superstars like Sean Combs, Wyclef Jean and infamous stars like Luke Skywalker from the much maligned 2 Live Crew have each contributed cultural aesthetics of hip hop to the performance of Caribana. Romeo Jacobs is among this group and offers a chance to have an extended conversation about what hip hop does for reading Caribana. Jacobs is one of rap music's "wickedest" emcees. Born in Antigua, in the late 1970s, he migrated to Canada as a child and then soon settled into the small and close knit hip hop community in Vancouver at the age of sixteen.

He is better known across Canada and internationally as Red One, a member of the award winning group the Rascalz. After more than a decade of making albums, worldwide tours and supporting children's rights in Ghana and Sierra Leone, Red One is considered a Canadian hip hop pioneer. Noted for their celebration and respect of elemental hip hop, meaning a commitment to deejaying, emceeing, break dancing and grafitti designs, the Rascalz have been exemplary in declaring a Canadian presence among U.S. dominance of North American hip hop music.

In July of 2002, as organizers prepared to stage Toronto's annual Caribana, the Rascalz were likewise preparing to be atop the truck in the Jessie Matthews & Associates masquerade band. However, in the wake of organizers declaring that urban music, by which they meant rap and dancehall, was banned from the masquerade competition, the Rascalz took to the television airwaves to voice their disagreement. The point of organizer's dismissals was to reclaim the spirit of carnival masquerade and celebrate the artistry of costume making, steelpan and calypso, something that was in decline since the 1997 performance by hip hop mogul Sean Combs signaled urban music's arrival and a cultural subversion that did more to raise concerns that it was the sense of Canada in Caribana that was being threatened by American cultural imperialism. Red One publicly reacted against the decision and issued a political challenge to the mostly youth viewers that staging a phone-in protest was a sensible method to express their dissatisfaction.

The decision to ban rap music is a serious statement about what it means to remove and control what particular black bodies are allowed to do during the parade. It shows what is at stake for the preservation of "institutionalized ethnicity" in Caribana's relationship to the nation and to the commitment of traditional Caribbean carnival. Before a national audience of mostly youth viewers, Red One used the language of global hip hop to explain the issues of home, movement and longings for a Caribbean. His yearnings were summarized within music and by a particularly romantic call for the *vibes*. Reading the vibes as a particular claim of belonging and as an assertion that youth make different things out of Caribana contests the idea that there is an authoritative view.

> I was just talking to Kardinal [another Canadian rapper], and I'm saying, he just wanted me to remind everybody, you know what I'm saying, we have to phone in and write in and let people know that hip-hop [...] we're here for the Caribana Vibe also, you know what I'm saying. And they really ain't trying to let hip-hop be part of Caribana this year. So we want people to know that, you know, they're trying to not let hip-hop be part of the Caribana. We want people to know that's wrong, because I'm from the Caribbean and Caribbean music influences everything I do and how I put my vibes down to the people. That's a big part of what I'm saying Caribana music is. I just want to let people know that, and they have to hit up the committee or something because that can't go on.[3]

The narration of Caribana is polyvocal. Multiple views of the festivity converge to work out the details of its community aspirations. *This is my vibes* is one narration. It attempts to rewrite home, place and space in what anthropologist Patricia Alleyne-Dettmers locates as "this global vortex of migratory flows" that paradoxically, "construct[s] the bridge that redefines the margins for the recreation of other new spaces." Alleyne-Dettmers adds, "Carnival mas is a powerful symbol within the global system for the attainment of territorial power and it becomes the cultural medium for mobilizing migrant subordinate groups."[4] "This is my vibes" is a discourse about creating linkages and marking affinities, as a technique to translate experiences. It enunciates belonging as a set of claims that desires to have standing and a sense of being within Caribana. In closing the interview Red One offered:

> I want you to know we're here for Caribana and we'll be at Spy Lounge this Friday, but, yo, phone in your radio stations, Muchmusic, everybody, let them know that you want hip-hop a part of Caribana. This is a real serious issue. You know what I'm saying. Let them know you ain't down with that and you down with hip-hop, for real. I'm saying, whether you from the West Indies or not, but pick it up, everybody, album in stores, "reloaded," came out yesterday.[5]

This is my vibes is a narrative performance aimed at critiquing the performance of mainstream or centered Caribana. Around the same time that Red One spoke to the nation about his views of Caribana, music critic Errol Nazareth also made a difficult connection between global rap and nationalizing aesthetics within Caribana, with respect to the participation of Red One and Sean Combs. Nazareth writes:

> With P-Diddy once again skedded (sic) to grace a float at the upcoming Toronto International Carnival (the parade formerly known as Caribana), we must figure out a way of replacing him with Rascalz.[6]

Nazareth's comments about replacing American rappers with Canadian emcees "tenuous[ly] shift[s] or play[s] between the national and outernational," and this play Rinaldo Walcott suggests "is crucial to reading the emergent vernacular youth cultures of black Canada."[7] Red One is more to the point stressing that "America ain't all the world; there's the rest, the other 90% of the world."[8]

The demand and claim issued by Red One "does not determine the formation of social and cultural identities in any mechanistic way, but it supplies a variety of symbolic, linguistic, textual, gestural and above all musical resources that are used by people to shape their identities, truths and models of community."[9] "This is my vibes" may not be as attractive or have the same force as this is "we ting" but its appeal for belonging does provide youth another mode for imagining black space within the Caribbean experience of Caribana.

Red One's call for mobilization against what he viewed as closure of black youth's desire to enjoy Caribana on terms they create were more symbolic than actually intended to stand as a viable platform for action. His critique of the organizer's decision to remove rap music from the parade criticized the hierarchical arrangement of identity performances in the festivity. Nevertheless, as an intervention into debates about the terms of participation and membership within the community he proposes an interesting strategy for negotiating a position of entry into the essentialized performance of the community. Identity as suggested by Red One's comments is relational. It is not a clean and absolute entity that one steps into, something the dominant discourse of Caribana culture promotes. Wrapping his argument against the banishment of rap around the affinities expressed in "my vibes' is mostly an attempt to "elude the heavy handed approach to ethnic authenticity in official multiculturalism by unraveling the intercultural story."[10]

Hip hop and Caribana Friday Night

A defiant act that occurs outside the scope of official Caribana, which is neither sanctioned nor sponsored by the organizers are the parties simply referred to as "Caribana Friday Night." During the Friday night before the traditional Saturday Caribana parade Toronto's Yonge Street is transformed into a massive partyzone by black youth. The youth are there looking to have a pre-party bash as a kick-off to their long-weekend revelry. The party is developing into a regular event for thousands of youth. The Friday night street party is the first event that many youth think of as comprising "Caribana weekend" or the "unofficial but official black Canadian holiday." Youth attend this street celebration in far greater numbers than any other competition event leading up to the masquerade. Yonge Street, mostly between King and Carlton streets, is transformed into an urban black playground. It's a six block area in which youth blast music, flash style and profile from inside cars. Most importantly, youth show off their fashions by walking the street.

The party zone is defined by the Yonge-Dundas square. The square, an open concrete expanse, is the premiere tourist intersection in the city of Toronto. The location features a concert stage, permanently installed seating and a column of geyser-like waterspouts for aesthetic ambiance. The square's skyline is enclosed by commercial billboards advertising some of the biggest national and global media corporations and their related branding strategies. Youth fill the area, while police officers try to keep the crowd moving, incidentally treating the whole affair as if it were a licensed city parade. An account of the 2004 Caribana Friday Night described it thus:

> Roughly 100,000 people—many from the [United] States—poured onto the strip from Bloor to King for the city's biggest unofficial, unscripted street party. The main activity? Checking each other out ("It's basically a runway," one 18-year-old [city of] Vaughan resident explained).[11]

However, in relation to the project of Canadian heritage and the demands of staging a state-regulated Caribana, the annual Friday night mash-up sits well outside what constitutes the proper celebration. Instead a typical reading of it suggests Friday's events are synonymous with danger, violence, rampant sexualities and the encroachment of hip hop's morally debased forms. In other words, it is a reference used by organizers to explain the cultural losses of Caribana among youth. The "unscripted" party and the "bordertown" atmosphere of these parties, I read as an elaborate masquerade that features the performances of heterosexual desire, dominant masculinity and displays of material wealth. In other words, the performance has particular views of sexuality and materialism that make it continuous with the next day's official masquerade. For instance, black males generally take up a location against buildings forming a perimeter in which black females meander in front of the sidewalk.

> Gaggles of teenage girls—hair freshly sprayed, eyebrows severely tweezed—walked up and down until their stilettoed feet gave out (or curfews drew near).[12]

Moreover, flashy cars with eye-popping rims and ear-shattering hip-hop and dancehall reggae music provide the soundtrack to the party that begins sometime after ten and extends well into the morning hours, as weary bodies and the ever-present police dismiss the crowd.

> Guys in souped-up SUVs inched through traffic, their windows down, hip-hop thumping in the muggy air. The vibe was part high school dance, part music video set, part bordertown shopping mall (the hottest product being members of the opposite sex).[13]

One Toronto rapper, his moniker is Rochester, used "Caribana Friday Night" themes in a video-shoot. A source described that "He especially wanted that unique Caribana Friday experience." The same source described that:

> Toronto native Rochester, aka Juice, taps into his Caribbean background for the song and video to "Do It (Like We Do It)." [. . .] the video's concept is based around Caribana's "pick-up" night. "Rochester really wanted that kind of feel—a unique Toronto experience and Caribana offers that," says director Randall Thorne.[14]

Stretching the sites of Caribana to include the Friday night fêtes on Yonge Street suggests that the role hip hop plays in Caribana is to further creolize both expressions within the pop-culture economies of North America by broadly elaborating blackness as a representative sign constitutive of both expressive forms.

Fusion and diaspora entanglements

Hip hop cultural forms stretch what traditionally stands for Caribbean carnival in Toronto. Several recent academic discussions have signaled this issue. Philip Scher's notion of the transnation usefully discusses the overlapping political, economic and social networks that highlight the tensions between readings of the carnival festivity as strictly performed national celebrations and simultaneous diasporic encounters. Much of this argument emphasizes the inability of disentangling issues of the nation from those which apparently accrue from diasporic locales. Cultures of hip hop provoke this and offer a reading against the fixtures within diaspora.

Caribana organizers introduced several events throughout the 1990s that invoked representations of the nation and the diaspora. All of these efforts reflect the declining commitment among governments for the festival against the increased commitment by organizers to address the differences that operate within Toronto's heterogeneous Caribbean community. This is also to say that the social environment of the 90s in which the relevancy of Caribana to the nation shifted, evident by the declining efforts to fund the celebration, is also the period in which new claimants arrive on the scene desiring something else and something more from traditional Caribana.

Organizers developed *new* events to accommodate the growing number of third and fourth generation participant desires in the festival. The re-introduction of the calypso tent competitions to the festival attempted to fulfill nostalgic and new desires. The tents were a dual reference to an earlier moment in which Caribana hosted such events and it was also a way to re-create it as a Trinidadian tradition within Toronto. At an ideological level the tent competitions served as another performance site in which Afro-Caribbean people (not exclusively) in Toronto expressed their ethnicity.

Competitions were hosted in tents across the city. Traditional calypsonians perform their compositions that described the imagined Caribbean Canadian identity that takes shape within the interstices of the nation and the Caribbean diasporas. Hip hop was also part of the competitions. Artists rapped about a variety of themes that relationally emphasized an ethnic formation informed by diasporic connections.

The efforts of Caribana organizers in giving first, second and third place prizes for best rap song were haphazardly awarded. Organizers in their attempts to monitor the thematic content of rappers lyrics put in place the criteria that rappers' storytelling must be free of expletives and speak to the practice of carnival. The calypso component of the tent competitions suffered because the shows were poorly organized and the awarding of prizes fell subject to favoritism and other partisan acts. The judging of best rap was more nebulous. Having far less knowledge in terms of judging the quality of rap songs, organizers could do little but to award prizes based on whimsical assessments rather than on careful assessment of composition, delivery and timeliness of the satire. Remaking the tent competitions as a space in which to include hip hop expressiveness is, I argue, about the difficulties of localizing the performance of transnational carnival in Toronto.

Critic Ford-Smith thinks about performance and she notes that excesses, strategic collusions, contradictions and absences mark the practice of African diasporic celebrations. I agree with the general thrust of her argument. However, my position is to emphasize the decentering of the dominant script of Caribana by hip hop and to view the tent as a creolizing representational space. The challenges of thinking through the elaboration of Caribana by hip hop are disruptive of any guaranteed reading of ethnicity the festival claims to put forward. In an interesting way then, the performances of hip hop and calypso in the tents is an illumination of the tensions against fixing both fiercely rooted and unwieldy routed senses of diaspora.

Her statement suggests that other forms of blackness may emerge to compete as one of the constitutive elements and coalescing ideologies of ethnic community making. In his attempts to argue the emergent forms of blackness in Canada, Rinaldo Walcott emphasizes the "echoes and traces" to elsewhere, which are crucial to understanding the continuously changing representations of being black in Canada within particular socio-economic conditions. In the 1990s hip hop, albeit within difficult circumstances, has fostered notions of diasporic connections sonically in tune with the roots and routes of a carnival experience. The excesses as Ford-Smith suggests describe the "instability that allowed subjects from diverse social locations to grasp alternative social possibilities and elaborate these in terms of the particular marginalization or exploitation that they face."[15]

Exhorting the *vibes* as a particular sensibility shaped in response to the socio-economic and cultural exclusions youths faced during the 90s suggests that Caribana's cultural politics are waged within forms of representational cultures. Drawing upon Belinda Edmondson's notion of the "decorous" and "vulgar" spectacles of Caribbean diaspora performances[16] as a framework, I argue that the tent competition is an interface in which seemingly contradictory styles try to inhabit the same place under a singular meaning of Caribana. Edmondson theorizes that reading public performances as either decorous or vulgar spectacles is a representational strategy in which proper display and social distance often signify the middle class and elite notions of the nation. I read the 1996 tent competitions as an attempt to bring together a range of community identifications and subjective positions that try to coalesce around the festival.

The tent, in my view, is a site invested in the concrete imagining of the Caribbean in Toronto. It played host to desires of dis-identification that repress the investment in something that eagerly desires to display itself as a dominant community within Caribana. In other words, imagining regional ethnic identities into Caribana is shaped by and through the denials that a series of performances exists within Caribana. What the tent, illuminated for me, is the notion that broadly performing Caribana does not require a specific repeatable subject that is able to recite over time.

My reading of the tent thinks about it as a creolizing performance. Caribana and hip hop cultures within the modes of calypso and rap music enables me to think about how Canadian discourses of heritage centers Caribana around a legitimate expression of the Caribbean. Canadian discourses of heritage exhibit utopian longings for a home scripted as elsewhere and outside of the nation. This experience is deeply symptomatic of the ambivalence that being black and belonging to Canada carries. Caribana is exemplary of this articulation and bears that ambivalent burden of having to do the nation's work.

Ruptures of diaspora

However, in jettisoning the tightness of the nation, I view global hip hop as a cultural site that tries to deal with the ruptures of blackness within carnival practices. In other words the ruptures of blackness are also a correspondence articulating a difficult and new practice. Harvey Neptune suggests something about this in his discussion of the African American rapper Jay-Z's (Shawn Carter) contentious presence during carnival 2000 in Trinidad. Stressing that Jay-Z is representative of an ambivalent positioning of the African American figure in diasporic practices and performances, Neptune's argument is about the tensions that arise in terms of an encounter between these two global African diasporic forms. The transnational Trinidadian carnival encounters global hip hop in terms of commercializing effects. Neptune notes that in Trinidadian history, "the persistence of African Americans' ambivalent place within the global black community . . . outlines how their circulation continues to generate intradiasporic conflict."[17]

> Jay-Z was a wildly inspiring icon of a cultural style central to the construction of an imagined international black community; for others, the black American was no more than an imperious visitor corrupting local standards.[18]

Jay-Z's commercialized relationship to the transnational carnival impacted the 2005 Caribana celebration. This instance of hip hop insurgency into the authenticating spaces of the transnational festival points to the overlapping issues of commercialization, authenticity and disciplinary practices. In the tradition of the all-inclusive Trinidadian fêtes, Jay-Z hosted a pricey party, charging over $80 Canadian dollars to attend a *jump up* featuring himself and fellow recording artists Kanye West in the Toronto parking lot of the Much Music television station. Hundreds of youths showed up and about the same amount were turned back. The expensive affair subverted normative carnival within another dominant discourse of black popular culture. At a conceptual level, the impact of taking seriously the destabilizing effects of global hip hop upon global carnival is to think beyond the idea that the nation is the primary cultural space for understanding how this new performance is practiced.

The efforts of Canadian rap artists to create an expressive zone in which to link up a viable space within the parade reflects the overlap between narratives of Caribbean-Canadian and an emergent sense of black Canadian identities. Hip hop culture is exemplary of the ruptures within this zone. To borrow from Alleyne-Dettmers, the zone is "an emergent third diaspora space"[19] in which the contest over representing Caribana takes place in the site institutionally set up to make, claim or absorb a *proper* Caribbean Canadian identity as a convergence.

The controversy over Caribana's soundscape—the attempts to play other sounds—reveals the limitations of dominant ethnicities to account for creolizing effects. At the moment, hip hop emerges as a vulgar and contradictory performance that struggles to pass into the decorous strictures of representing Caribana. It remains on the outside of key Caribana performance sites, notably the Saturday parade and the tent competitions because it undermines the practice of ethnicity within these specific contexts. In other words, the transformations of Caribana's soundscape reflect the "crumbling of familiar texts and the textures about community."[20] In the most simply senses then, in the context of a Caribana celebration that has apparently banned hip hop music, it still remains one of the key enactments in which to operationalize readings of the black diaspora within Toronto.

Red One's desire for hip hop in Caribana is a dual claim. It falls back on a particular reading of the Caribbean Canadian as a distinctive identity, buttressed by enactments within Canadian multiculturalism and as a visible performance within the parade. At the same time, his claim also expresses how certain identifications with global blackness push him outside of the Caribbean Canadian category, making popular expressions of multiculturalism invisible to the institutionalized forms that Caribbean Canadian identities fasten onto with respect to the parade. This tension is about the inability of hard notions of Caribbean Canadian to make sense as a viable explanation of the association that Red One advocates. In virtually all of Caribana's ethnic performances a claim for reading authentically Caribbean Canadian identities is made.

Red One gestures toward some important issues about the challenges of cultural continuity and the protectionist attitudes that monitor the site and the proper displays of its cultural symbols. He demonstrates that living political lives is not bounded in, nor dictated by, continual returns and renewals in primeval identities. He shows a political desire to think beyond the limit of nostalgic black diasporic discourse and to insist on reading practices that heuristically bring in the future-directed discourses of diaspora as a thinking strategy for writing black culture.[21]

In my view, in stretching the limitations of the festival, hip hop signals the slips, slides and complicated meanings of performing blackness in Toronto's Caribana among youth. Addressing the slides is to experience Caribana in both its attempts to remain fundamentally committed to the idea of "*overseas*" Trinidadian carnival[22] and to take note of the liquidated and brash presentations of spectacular play AnneMarie Gallaugher,[23] in writing about the *hood* as a discursive space within Caribana, suggests that scripting the vibes of the hip hop hood as a crisis of public morality threatens the socially instituted status of the celebration.

However, my position is that the hood in Caribana can only be read as disconnecting Caribana from the national text insofar as one attaches an absolute sense of how ethnicity operates. And moreover one must read the hood as existing outside of the constitutive Caribana celebration. Keeping it there, where it can be used to explain a continual moral debasement of youth and Caribana, must in my view mechanically present Caribana as being totally creolized by hip hop and absolutely ignore the fact that Caribana also works to creolize hip hop. At the same time that *my vibes* declares a particular embrace of Caribana authenticity, there is also a subversive demand that is resistant and endeavors to recreate another association.

Notes

1. See for example Philip W. Scher, *Carnival and the Formation of a Caribbean Transnation* (Gainesville: University of South Florida Press, 2003).
2. David Trotman, "Transforming Caribbean and Canadian Identity: Contesting Claims for Toronto's Caribana," *Atlantic Studies* 2, no. 2 (2005): 177.
3. Red One, *Much Music transcript* (July 31, 2002).
4. Patricia T. Alleyne-Dettmers, "The Relocation of Trinidad Carnival in Notting Hill, London and the Politics of Diasporisation," in *Global, Diaspora and Caribbean Popular Culture*, ed. Christine G.T. Ho and Keith Nurse (Kingston, Jamaica: Ian Randle Publishers, 2005), 75.
5. Red One, *Much Music*.
6. Errol Nazareth, *Eye Weekly*, 25 July 2002.
7. Rinaldo Walcott, "Caribbean Pop Culture in Canada; Or, the Impossibility of Belonging to the Nation," *Small Axe* 9 (March 2001): 137.
8. Source of comments is http://www.unb.ca/bruns/0203/06/entertainment/rascalz.html (accessed August 2005).
9. Paul Gilroy, "Roots and Routes: Black Identity as an Outernational Project," in *Racial and Ethnic Identity: Psychological Development and Creative Expression*, ed. Herbert W. Harris (London: Routledge, 1995): 25.
10. Kobena Mercer, "Ethnicity and Internationality: New British Art and Diaspora-Based Blackness," in *The Visual Culture Reader*, ed. Nicholas Mirzoeff (New York: Routledge, 2002): 197.
11. Sarah Fulford, "Camera: Yonge Street, U.S.A.," *Toronto Life* 38, no. 10 (2004).
12. "Camera: Yonge Street, U.S.A."
13. "Camera: Yonge Street, U.S.A."
14. See http://www.muchmusic.com/music/videofact/index.asp?vfAssetID=6817.
15. Honor Ford-Smith, "Unruly Virtues of the Spectacular: Performing Engendered Nationalisms in the UNIA in Jamaica," *Interventions* 6, no. 1 (2004): 18.
16. Edmondson, Belinda, "Public Spectacles: Caribbean Women and the Politics of Public Performance," *Small Axe* 13 (March 2003): 3.
17. Harvey Neptune, "Manly Rivalries and Mopsies: Gender, Nationality, and Sexuality in United States—Occupied Trinidad," *Radical History Review* 87 (2003): 90.
18. Neptune, "Manly Rivalries and Mopsies," 90.
19. Patricia T. Alleyne-Dettmers, Patricia, "The Relocation of Trinidad Carnival in Notting Hill, London and the Politics of Diasporisation," in *Global, Diaspora and Caribbean Popular Culture*, ed. Christine G.T. Ho and Keith Nurse (Kingston, Jamaica: Ian Randle Publishers, 2005), 76-77.
20. Alleyne-Dettmers, "The Relocation," 75.
21. See also Jenny Burman, "Masquerading Toronto Through Caribana: Transnational Carnival Meets the Sign 'Music Ends Here,'" *Identity: An International Journal of Theory and Research* 1, no. 3 (2001): 273-287; and Walcott, "Caribbean Pop Culture in Canada."
22. Keith Nurse, "Globalization and Trinidad Carnival: Diaspora, Hybridity and Identity in Global Culture," *Cultural Studies* 13, no. 4 (1999): 662.
23. AnneMarie Gallaugher, "Constructing Caribbean Culture in Toronto: The Representation of Caribana," in *Reordering of Culture: Latin America, the Caribbean and*

Canada, ed. A. Ruprecht and C. Taiana (Ottawa: Carleton University Press, 1995), 397-407.

Bibliography

Alleyne-Dettmers, Patricia T. "The Relocation of Trinidad Carnival in Notting Hill. London and the Politics of Diasporisation." Pp. 64-90 in *Global, Diaspora and Caribbean Popular Culture*, edited by Christine G. T. Ho and Keith Nurse. Kingston, Jamaica: Ian Randle Publishers, 2005.

Burman, Jenny. "Masquerading Toronto Through Caribana: Transnational Carnival Meets the Sign "Music Ends Here." *Identity: An International Journal of Theory and Research* 1, no. 3 (2001): 273-87.

Edmondson, Belinda. "Public Spectacles: Caribbean Women and the Politics of Public Performance." *Small Axe* 13 (March 2003), 1-16.

Ford-Smith, Honor. "Unruly Virtues of the Spectacular: Performing Engendered Nationalisms in the UNIA in Jamaica." *Interventions* 6, no. 1 (2004): 18-44.

Fulford, Sarah, "Camera: Yonge Street, U.S.A." *Toronto Life* 38, no.10 (2004).

Gallaugher, AnneMarie. "Constructing Caribbean Culture in Toronto: The Representation of Caribana." Pp. 397-407 in *Reordering of Culture: Latin America, the Caribbean and Canada*, edited by A. Ruprecht and C. Taiana. Ottawa: Carleton University Press, 1995.

Gilroy, Paul. "Roots and Routes: Black Identity as an Outernational Project." Pp. 15-30 in *Racial and Ethnic Identity: Psychological Development and Creative Expression*, edited by Herbert W Harris. London: Routledge, 1995.

Mercer, Kobena. "Ethnicity and Internationality: New British Art and Diaspora-Based Blackness." Pp. 190-204 in *The Visual Culture Reader*, edited by Nicholas Mirzoeff. New York: Routledge, 2002.

Nazareth, Errol. "The Rascalz Dancehall Return." *Eye Magazine Weekly* (Toronto, Ontario), July 25, 2002 web edition at http://www.eye.net/eye/issue/issue_07.25.02/thebeat/sample.php (accessed March 15, 2007).

Neptune, Harvey. "Manly Rivalries and Mopsies: Gender, Nationality, and Sexuality in United States—Occupied Trinidad." *Radical History Review* 87 (2003): 78-95.

Nurse, Keith. "Globalization and Trinidad Carnival: Diaspora, Hybridity and Identity in Global Culture." *Cultural Studies* 13, no. 4 (1999): 661-90.

Red One, Interview by MuchMusic Transcripts posted July 31, 2002 at http://www.muchmusic.com/music/artists/transcripts.asp?artist=142.

Scher, Philip W. *Carnival and the Formation of a Caribbean Transnation*. Gainesville: University of South Florida Press, 2003.

Trotman, David. "Transforming Caribbean and Canadian Identity: Contesting Claims for Toronto's Caribana." *Atlantic Studies* 2, no. 2 (2005): 177-198.

Walcott, Rinaldo. "Caribbean Pop Culture in Canada; Or, the Impossibility of Belonging to the Nation." *Small Axe* 9 (March 2001): 123-139.

III

WRITING SELF, OTHER, AND (TRANS-)NATION IN THE TRANS-CARIBBEAN

8

Wendy Knepper

Patrick Chamoiseau's Seascapes and the Trans-Caribbean Imaginary

Increasingly, we find ourselves in a world where local and global economies, cultures and imaginaries are highly permeable, influencing and influenced by one another. Arjun Appadurai describes this fundamental transformation as producing a "complex, overlapping, disjunctive order," which is no longer to be understood in terms of "existing center-periphery models."[1] What then might serve as a model for understanding these changes? One approach is to consider the trans-Caribbean experience as both a precursor to and embodiment of the changes taking place in today's global cultural economy. With its multifarious economic flows, histories of mobility and displacement, uneven creolization processes and political transformations, the Caribbean is a particularly relevant example of the interactions among various local and global flows. Notably, the Martinican author and Creolist Patrick Chamoiseau sees a vital connection between globalization and creolization, arguing that the contemporary world is "undergoing a process of Creolisation." In his view, the Caribbean experience can help us to grapple with contemporary global transformations.[2]

Nonetheless, Chamoiseau also sees differences between creolization in the form of cultural intermixture as a positive force for change and the negative aspects of globalization. In his view, we are living in an era of "furtive domination," which makes him wary of the "great communicative circuits that link up the world today," such as the internet.[3] Consequently, he has identified the need for a warrior figure, a *guerrier*, who "can recognize that the battle against oppression and domination has moved into the realm of the imaginary."[4] While it remains a deeply contested sphere, the domain of the imaginary is an "absolutely fundamental theater for resistance" against homogenizing global forces.[5] Chamoiseau's critique of creolization and concept of the local shapes his theory of vernacular modernity in the Caribbean and informs his vision of a counter-hegemonic global imaginary.

155

In this chapter, I will explore Chamoiseau's critique of the connection between creolization and globalization. As we shall see, Chamoiseau's theory of the local underpins his embattled stance toward all forms of domination, including the negative aspects of a top-down understanding of globalization. Instead, Chamoiseau argues for a more dynamic relationship. He argues that what happens in small, out-of-the-way places can have a more significant impact on humanity, on the imaginary than what occurs in large metropolitan centers such as New York or Berlin.[6] Concerned with the need to protect and foster a sense of the local as a way of relating to other local cultures, he defends a "Place-centred perception of the world, its changes and exchanges (*the world must have a shimmering fabric of Places undergoing inter- and retro-action*)."[7] The complexities of the global cultural economy demand a profound investigation into one's own place with a special attentiveness to how the past, present and emerging forces can change the ways in which we understand the meaning of place.

Simple as it sounds, this endeavor involves a highly complex, sometimes difficult, confrontation with the flows and forces of Martinican history both past and present. In Chamoiseau's fictional writing and theory, the result is a fluid poetics, nascent in *Texaco* but fully evident in his journalism and works such as *Ecrire en pays dominé, L'esclave vieil homme et le molosse, Emerveilles* and *Biblique des derniers gestes*. In these works, he pursues a new kind of poetics; he introduces figures and concepts that demonstrate the inter-retro-active imaginary at work. In seeking to describe how this poetics functions, I will put forward a theory of Caribbean seascapes as way of articulating what seems to me to be a uniquely trans-Caribbean theory of global flows. An ongoing commitment to the poetics and politics of seascapes is needed to fuel the Caribbean struggle to maintain local culture in face of global forces and flows. At the same time, such a theory opens new horizons and networks of affiliation with other local cultures, thus inviting a new way of imagining community and solidarity in an increasingly mobile, interdependent world.

The "-scapes" of modernity

Appadurai's critique of modernity is my point of departure for considering the flows and mobilities of the Caribbean experience. In the modern world, Appadurai observes that "[n]either images nor viewers fit into circuits or audiences that are easily bound within local, national, or regional spaces."[8] To describe the effects of these uneven, disjunctive flows, he introduces the idea of "-scapes," including ethnoscapes, mediascapes, technoscapes, financescapes and ideoscapes.[9] He notes that the "suffix *-scape* allows us to point to the fluid, irregular shapes of these landscapes."[10] These terms "also indicate that these are not objectively given relations, that look the same from every angle of vision but, rather, that they are deeply perspectival constructs, inflected by the historical, linguistic, and political situatedness of different sorts of actors."[11] In the contemporary world, an analysis of "-scapes" serves as the basis for articulating alternative or vernacular modernities, that is to say the particular ways in which local culture has experienced modernization as well as the ways in which it might offer an alternative account of modernity.

This topographical, fluid approach to the flows of influence seems at first glance ideally suited to an analysis of the Caribbean experience. In the case of the trans-Caribbean experience, perhaps the most immediately striking "-scape" of analysis is the ethnoscape or the "landscape of persons who constitute the shifting world in which we live."[12] The flows of peoples in and out of the Caribbean, the influx of tourism, the history of migration and the diasporic experience of many Caribbeans living abroad all play a role in this transnational space. The migration of Caribbeans is sometimes described as "colonization in reverse." This phrase, coined by Louise Bennett, refers to the counter-flow of Caribbean migrants to former colonial centers, such as Jamaicans migrating to the United Kingdom, and can be understood more generally as describing the diffuse influence of Caribbean culture on the postcolonial concept of nation.[13] Outward flows into the global imaginary from the Caribbean, particularly in the case of music, language and religion, as well as through mediascapes and ideoscapes have the potential to transform the global imaginary. Iconic Caribbeans, such as Ernesto "Che" Guevara and Bob Marley, as well as intellectuals, such as Marcus Garvey, C.L.R. James, Aimé Césaire, Frantz Fanon, and Édouard Glissant, have come to play an important role in theorizing trans-Caribbean and diasporic identities. The global popularity of reggae music and the pervasive, circulating image of Che (on T-shirts, jeans, posters and even appropriated for Madonna's rebel stance on the cover of *American Life*) are evidence of the deterritorialization of the Caribbean in the global imaginary. This "consuming" of Caribbean influences may be evidence of the local on the global imaginary, but it is also a phenomenon that can be situated in a history of ongoing attempts to ingest the Caribbean. Tracing a history of such endeavors, Mimi Sheller calls attention to the ethical and intellectual risks of tropicalization as well as of the appropriation of creolization for the discourses of global culture.[14]

Let me offer another example of the risks entailed by taking the Caribbean experience of transformation and interculturation as a precursor for globalization. Today, it is often argued that the global economic flows dominate the local as is evidenced in the rate of imports to versus exports from the Caribbean. However, there are also discontinuities, shaped by the persistence of the local Creole cultural economy as a force that continues to operate in a supposedly "modern" economy. For instance, in Martinique, the *djobeur* of the past (whose travails are described in *Chronique de sept misères*) is the forefather of the *débrouillard*, a person who seeks a measure of autonomy and liberty in his or her labor by working in today's informal economy.[15] This in turn is often linked to the post-emancipation desire for the right to choose one's own mode of labor. Attitudes toward the economy and labor continue to be touched by the residual experience of slave labor. With respect to the uneven temporal and political flows of the region, Chris Bongie refers to the "post/colonial" experience of the Caribbean, a world described as one in which "two words and worlds appear uneasily as one, joined together and yet also divided in a relation of (dis)continuity." This approach affords ways of critiquing not only colonial hegemonies but their residual, disruptively experienced influence in ways of thinking about community, identities and global flows.[16]

Consequently, I view Appadurai's theory of "-scapes" as useful insofar as it prompts one to consider the various disjunctive flows in, through and away from the Caribbean. Yet, such a theory is insufficient in that it fails to take into account the ways in which globalization intersects with other pre-existing modes of mobility, transformation and modernity. How does this new global imaginary impact an area such as the Caribbean, which underwent earlier forms of mass migration, multicultural contact and international circulations? In *The Repeating Island*, Antonio Benítez-Rojo sees the plantation experience as the "big bang of the Caribbean universe" whose "slow explosion throughout modern history threw out billions and billions of cultural fragments in all directions."[17] In his view, these fragments continue to be pulled apart and come together in an ongoing, destabilized process of creolization and cultural creativity. The idea that Caribbean culture is grounded in fragmentation has been the source of creative and destructive as well as positive and negative interpretations of Caribbean culture. Instead of a deterritorialized theory of "-scapes" or an anachronistic application of theories of relativity, I would like to forward a historically situated trans-Caribbean theory of seascapes as a way of reconceptualizing the work and networking of the global imaginary.

Time for a sea change: Caribbean seascapes

My theory of seascapes recognizes the importance of vernacular modernities as experienced in the Caribbean. Stuart Hall refers to "vernacular modernities" as the processes of globalization that are not articulated solely through capitalism but through a commitment to local cultural practices and identities. In Hall's view, what emerges from such vernacular modernities is a "new kind of 'localism' that is not self-sufficiently particular, but which arises *within*, without being simply a simulacrum of, the global."[18] To understand what he means by this it is useful to recall the meanings of the "vernacular." Etymologically, "vernacular" can be traced to *vernaculus*, a word that refers to a slave born in a master's house. A second meaning of the vernacular is to express oneself in a local idiom, whether this is linguistic, architectural or cultural. In a conversation on the topic of vernacular modernities, Hall insists on the importance of slavery in shaping local culture and as a force for disrupting a hegemonic concept of modernity. He observes: "Slavery itself, within capitalism, is not the older form of slavery, but it is an older, archaic, differentiated form, enclosed within and intimately linked to the development of the modern mode. It constitutes the possibility of a kind of modernity from below."[19] Significantly, Hall argues: "This localism is no mere residue of the past. It is something new—globalization's accompanying shadow; what is left aside in globalization's panoramic sweep, but returns to trouble and disturb globalization's cultural settlements."[20] Our approach to vernacular modernities needs to take into account a critique of slavery and its legacies. What has been exiled from the local needs to be reconstituted in the quest for an alternative account of modernity.

Seascapes constitute the historical and ongoing significance of the discourse of the sea as a theory of mobilities and flows within the Caribbean as it has and continues to be invoked or resurfaces as a way to negotiate a relationship to time, place and identities. Vernacular culture, including literary works, plays an important role in reconstructing the past and present as well as renegotiating creolized identities as the new tides of globalization enter into this tumultuous flow. In the context of seascapes, one might recall Paul Gilroy's image of the ship, which he describes as a "living, micro-cultural, micro-political system in motion."[21] He notes that ships "immediately focus attention on the middle passage, on the various projects for redemptive return to an African homeland, on the circulation of ideas and activists as well as the movement of key cultural and political artefacts."[22] The sea—a reminder of the Middle Passage or more generally of the fluidity of identity formations in the Caribbean—is for many Caribbean writers and theorists, notably Derek Walcott, Bob Marley and Saint-John Perse, a landscape through which other -*scapes* are often investigated. For Walcott, the image of the ship bears the idea of Antillean culture as a "shipwreck of fragments."[23] The image of the sea plays an important role in *Omeros* or *The Gulf*. In *The Schooner Flight*, Shabine says: "I'm just a red nigger who love the sea, / I had a sound colonial education, / I have Dutch, nigger and English in me, / and either I'm nobody, or I'm a nation."[24] In the song entitled "Exodus," Marley refers to the movement of the Israeli people out of slavery and the crossing of the Red Sea as a symbol of the Caribbean movement of liberation. Thus, the biblical reference to the sea of history is given a new currency of meaning in the context of Jamaican history and the quest for liberation. Seascapes refer to the fluidity of identities that were shaped through forced mobilities and envisioned through desires or fantasies of chosen migrations and flows.

To understand the Caribbean experience, which is already trans-Caribbean in its formation, we need to consider the impact of its outward flows. Antonio Benítez-Rojo suggests the importance of these flows when he observes that the "Antilleans' insularity does not impel them toward isolation, but on the contrary, toward travel, toward exploration, toward the search for fluvial and marine routes."[25] Following Glissant's lead, J. Michael Dash argues that the Caribbean Sea is not "an inland, centralizing body of water but one that explodes outward, thereby dissolving all systems of centering or totalizing thought."[26] This is also what I mean when I say that the trans-Caribbean vernacular functions as a "seascape": the uneven experience of modernity as mobility—a phenomenon that consists of the flows into, through and out of the Caribbean as a consequence of its own particular vernacular experience. Such a change would then trace not only the flows of the Middle Passage, the underground currents traversing the

Caribbean, from the sea to the land, but also pay attention to the flows from the land, the shores, outward once more. Seascapes function as the return of the repressed or the revival of elements of a forgotten local history, which have been marginalized by hegemonic accounts of Caribbean identity and modernity. These shipwrecked fragments are to be rescued and repurposed by the Caribbean imaginary. A theory of seascapes also considers the Caribbean experience in trans-Caribbean terms: as one in a network of many places that give evidence to vernacular constructions of modernity and introduce new possibilities for imagining an alternative theory of global flows.

Chamoiseau's seascapes: the inter-retro-actions of place

In the case of Chamoiseau, a theory of seascapes helps us to grapple with the author's concept of the inter-retro-active imaginary, which is simultaneously interactive and retroactive in its workings. The inter-retro-active perspective is evident in his description of the necessity to undergo a meditative return to the places of the past as the foundations of the future. He observes:

> J'écris en *devenir*, donc je me projette dans le monde qui vient dans le futur. Et c'est parce que je me projette dans le monde qui vient que je comprends que nous avons un problème de fondation, à assurer la fondation du lieu. Et c'est pourquoi, apparemment, la plupart de mes textes explorent une période qui à mon avis est une période fondatrice, comme l'esclavage, comme ce qui s'est produit après, parce que si nous ne parvenons pas à assurer cela nous ne pouvons pas vivre le désordre du monde.[27]

> I approach writing as *becoming*, thus I project myself into the world that will be in the future. And because I project myself in the world to come that I understand that we have a fundamental problem: to ensure the foundation of place. And this is why, apparently, most of my texts explore a period that in my opinion is a founding period, slavery and that which it produced afterwards. If we cannot recognize this, we will not be able to live the disorder of the world.

The problem of finding one's place in the modern world requires a thorough analysis of the foundations of modernity in Martinique. He argues that what makes for the modernity of a literary text as well as for its future is its ability to explore a relevant problematic for a particular place.[28] Chamoiseau like Hall, pursues a theory of "modernity from below" by investigating the experience of slavery. Unlike Hall, this investigation takes a fictional form as part of a quest for a new kind of vernacular.

Chamoiseau's evocation and critique of this seascape is evident in his screenplay for the film, *Passage du Milieu*, which was adapted for American viewers by Walter Mosley under the title *The Middle Passage*. The abyss of the hold, the sea as a grave and the transformation of identities are documented in this account of the Middle Passage. Notably, it is the image of the water rather than the ship that comes to dominate the film, particularly as the kidnapped African dives into a watery grave rather than accept enslavement. Édouard Glissant sums up this relation to water in concisely worded, haunting language when he notes: "In actual fact the abyss is a tautology: the entire ocean, the entire sea collapsing in the end into the pleasures of sand, make one vast beginning, but a beginning whose time is marked by these balls and chains gone green."[29] The land and the sea, past and present, the flows of time and imagination are thus conjoined through the slave trade. This conjoining is ever problematic, disrupted as it is by the "gouffre" of the Middle Passage. In *Ecrire en pays dominé*, Chamoiseau observes that Glissant's image of a "submarine carpet of corpses" is a trope of the Caribbean imaginary, evident in Walcott, Kamau Brathwaite and others, citing "[t]he unity is sub-marine."[30] The result of this destructive sea experience is something profoundly creative, disruptively fluid:

> Défait par l'expérience du gouffre, l'imaginaire qu'ils mobilisent pour se décrire, et pour décrire leur île liée à la mer, et pour vivre la mer comme aire de relations, miroite d'une mosaïque imaginaires. Pour se dire, ces poètes mobilisent l'Afrique, l'Europe, le monde amérindien, l'Inde, le Levant . . .[31]

> Undone by the experience of the abyss, the imaginary Caribbean poets mobilized to describe themselves, and to describe their island linked to the sea, and to live the sea as the area of relation, refracts from a mosaic imaginary. To express themselves, these poets mobilized Africa, Europe, the Amerindian world, India, the Levant . . .

The imaginary is transformed through this and subsequent migration experiences with revolutionary consequences for and in the vernacular forms of Caribbean writers.

In terms of modernity, this profound rupture of the vernaculars (idioms, cultures, localities, etc.) serves as the painful rebirth or genesis experience of the inhabitants who come to dwell in this "New World." Chamoiseau observes that the *gouffre* or abyss of the slaver's hold was not simply a place of torture or transitory dehumanization:

> And one of the most amazing things is that the abyss spared no one. Of course, it deconstructed those who found themselves in the depths of the hold in such terrible conditions (which makes this period the time of one of the greatest crimes against all humanity), but it also affected the sailors, the ships' captains and the European ship-owners. [. . .] Master and slave were bound together in the same process of dehumanisation and, without knowing it, embarked on a restructuring which neither could escape.[32]

Not one, but multiple geneses are experienced in relation. For Chamoiseau, modernity is characterized by this vernacular, local experience of creolization: "the bringing together of peoples, languages, races, world views and cosmogonies on a massive, accelerated scale" within the colonial plantation, under colonization, saw an open worldview born in a closed, oppressive system.[33]

For the Creolists, vernacular modernities or this "modernity from below" stems not only from the hold in the slave ship (literally below deck) but also from the experience of the storyteller on the plantation: that *vernaculus* or slave born (if not literally) in the master's house (*Lettres créoles*). In addition to storytelling, the Creole language serves as a force to reconstitute memory and find self-expression. Created through contact, exchange and dialogue, the etymology of words helps us to understand the history of economic and cultural flows. For instance, in *Texaco*, the flows between master and slave, slavery and forced labor are traced through linguistic transformation:

> Ils disaient avec leurs mots: *l'esclavage*. Pour nous c'était entendre: *l'estravaille*. Quand ils le surent et dirent à leur tour *Lestravaille* pour nous parler en proximité, nous avions deja raccourci l'affaire sur l'idée de travail[34]

> With their words, they would say: *l'esclavage*, slavery. But we would only hear: *l'estravaille*, travail. When they found out and began to say *lestravaille*, to speak closer to us, we'd already cut the word down to travail, the idea of plain toil[35]

More generally, the flows of traffic and trade through the area are seen as important to the act of naming. The name "Texaco" itself, which is that of a multinational, is appropriated as the space of a local community that evolves through creole culture and local building techniques, prompting at least one critic to view the community as a heterotopia or "a local, rehumanized postmodern community which strangely, nostalgically, attempts to redefine city and country and to restore the lost balance between them."[36] In the film *Biguine*, the name of this genre of music is explained as originating with the sailor's shouts that the music should "begin," which traverses the seas of language to become "beguine." Music is portrayed as the product of exchange between Western classical and local Creole folk music traditions: it is the product of migration, trade and cross-cultural exchange. *Chronique de sept misères* offers another approach to this question of mobility and labor in its portrait of the extinction of the *djobeurs* (a person who does odd jobs) and the decline of the market as a vernacular tradition, where local products and genres of exchange (commercial and cultural) dominated. The changing rhythm of the novel reflects the gradual sense of stasis as the metropolitan comes to dominate the local: sanitizing and straightening the routes and flows of traffic, and in Chamoiseau's view stifling the path to an alternative vernacular modernity in an imagined world that is not subject to departmentalization. In literature, cinema and theory, Chamoiseau's works can be seen as engaging in a critique and self-conscious reproduction of how various local and global flows interact within the Caribbean as a mode of creolization.

An inter-retro-active engagement with the meaning of place (Lieu) allows us to better understand the interactions of the local and global imaginaries.

Readers of *Ecrire en pays dominé* will be familiar with the notion of place as a mode of diversity, transversal memory and relation to the network of other places in the global imaginary.[37] Re-membering the land and its place in the world occurs through a polyphony of personal memories, a task that Chamoiseau pursues in *Guyane: traces-mémoires du bagne, L'esclave vieil homme et le molosse, Ecrire en pays dominé* and *Biblique des derniers gestes*, where in various ways he signals the important role of "les Traces-mémoires." Édouard Glissant's idea of "memory traces" refers to "les traces" or the colonial roads that cut through the tropical forest of Martinique. Chamoiseau initially explored this theme in speeches and articles in the press addressed to a local audience of Martinicans. One notable example is the 1993 article titled "Contre la mémoire et l'histoire" (which is a transcription of an oral presentation), published in *Antilla*. For Chamoiseau, this term refers to a space forgotten by History and by single Memory, because it bears witness to the original diversity and tends to preserve this diversity.[38] Memories, forgotten or disavowed by History, are characterized as collective and individual, of the community and trans-communal, immovable and mobile.[39] Chamoiseau describes the ways in which place and territory are opposed concepts in a catalogue that touches on the role of history and memory:

> Le Lieu est traversé de racines multiples, qui s'étendent, qui s'étalent; le Territoire est arc-bouté sur une racine unique.
> Le Lieu vit en réseau; le Territoire dispose d'un centre et de périphéries.
> Le Lieu vit de la poétique de la diversité; le Territoire s'arme de la pensée de l'Unique.
> Le Lieu participe à la Diversalité; le Territoire invoque l'Universalité.
> Le Lieu a des histoires, le Territoire a une Histoire.
> Le Lieu a des mémoires, le territoire a une Mémoire.[40]
>
> Place is traversed by multiple roots, which extend, which spread out; Territory is the sprouting arch of a single root.
> Place lives in a network; Territory is composed of a centre and peripheries.
> Place lives the poetics of diversity; Territory invokes Universality.
> Place has stories, Territory has one History.
> Place has memories, Territory has one Memory.

Place is associated with the poetics of diversity, a multiplicity of memories and multiple roots. In a public lecture almost a decade after his speech in Martinique, speaking to an audience in Bordeaux, he observes that "place is trans-multilingual, transmulticultural, transmulti-identitarian, transmultiracial, trans-multi-religious."[41]

Fostering a deeper sense of place is a positive mode of adapting to the effects of globalization, where increasingly we are witnesses to the fact that (in an echo of the Middle Passage): "Nous avons le sentiment d'être sur le même bateau. Que le destin de l'un est lié à celui de l'autre" / We have the feeling that we are on the same boat. That the destiny of one person is linked to that of the other.[42] Chamoiseau argues the concept of *Lieu* or place enables us (meaning

Martinicans) to constitute ourselves in networks of solidarity, of cultures, of exchanges, that traverse nations and territories, and to get rid of the "detestable idea that we are on the periphery of the world."[43] He insists on the importance of narrating Martinique through stories as a means to preserve interior diversity and to better live in the diversity of the world.[44] Chamoiseau's concept of place entails an open relation between local and global flows. He argues for a "[p]lace-centered perception of the world, its changes and exchanges (*the world must have a shimmering fabric of Places undergoing inter- and retro-action*)."[45] This requires an ability to balance the interaction and retro-action of global and local flows, an ability that demands reconfiguring place in time and history in a fluid yet concrete way. This inter-retro-active view is both rooted and rhizomatic: "We reject this kind of evanescent world citizenship which is a desertion of Place. [. . .] *True world citizenship is multi-citizenship in a multiplicity of Places.*"[46] This is not a Kantian notion of citizenship, but rather a notion of the citizen as someone who participates in a multiplicity of real and imagined communities. Citizenship is understood as an active effort of imagination and memory that seeks to relate and reconstitute one's own local conditions in dialogue with those of others.

The seascapes of *Ecrire en pays dominé*

This inter-retro-active approach to space and place is explored in *Ecrire en pays dominé*, a text that is part memoir, part history, part cultural topography and part theory. Chamoiseau asks the question, "Comment écrire dominé?"[47] The domination he speaks of stems from the residual influence of the colonial past in postcolonial society as well as the sources of domination present in contemporary Martinique, both from the metropolitan centre of France and from the increasing influence of global society at the local level. Richard Watts notes that for Chamoiseau departmentalization is primarily experienced through the domination of television and the supermarket.[48] Subsequently, "[s]ites of exchange were transformed into sites of distribution and sites of participation were replaced by sites of passive consumption."[49]

Chamoiseau the narrator begins with a critical view of Martinique as a place of "colonial modernity."[50] Addressing himself in the second-person, he adopts a retrospective view of the writerly self in the history of literary protest:

> Tu n'es pas de ceux qui peuvent dresser des cartes de goulags, ou mener discours sur les génocides, les massacres, les dictateurs féroces. Tu ne peux pas décrire des errances de pouvoir dans des palais stupéfiés, ni tenir mémoire des horreurs d'une solution finale. Autour de ta plume, aucun spectre de censure ni de fil barbelé.[51]

> You are not among those who can draw a map of gulags or lead a discourse on genocide, massacres, fierce dictators. You cannot describe the wandering course of power in stupefying palaces, or recall memories of the horrors of a fi-

nal solution. Surrounding your pen, there is neither a specter of censorship nor of barbed wire.

In an almost nostalgic tone, Chamoiseau seems to lament the lack of clearly identifiable evil forces against which to pit his writerly energies. Instead, he suggests that the contemporary Martinican writer confronts more insidious forms of domination.[52]

In resistance to the subtle and stealthy forms of domination that trouble the contemporary world, Chamoiseau envisions a warrior of the imaginary. Capable of all kinds of resistance, this warrior nourishes and protects dominated peoples everywhere.[53] This trans-Caribbean warrior figure confirms Chamoiseau's suspicions that his liberty is only apparent and that he must seek true liberty through a new art of resistance.[54] In dialogue with the warrior, the narrator unleashes a critique of the global imaginary that finds its force in a history of vernacular modernities and an analysis of various forms of domination in Martinique and elsewhere. Chamoiseau discloses the need to explore critically one's place in the world and to embrace a trans-local perspective as a mode of resistance. His disruptive narrative rewrites History as it has come to be known in Martinique by retelling it through the mediating effects of personal memory and dreams. The narrative presents multiple perspectives in time and place, shifting among these perspectives in a way that reflects the uneven account of vernacular modernities in Martinique. This inter-retro-active narrative approach to the trans-Caribbean imaginary serves as a model for transforming the global imaginary through a critique of the local.

While it is not the purpose of this chapter to investigate fully the complex critique presented in *Ecrire*, I will offer some examples of how Chamoiseau's engagement with the local recognizes the complexities of vernacular modernities. The tripartite structure of *Ecrire en pays dominé* with its "Anagogie par les livres endormis," "Anabase en digenèses selon Glissant" and "Anabiose sur la Pierre-Monde" functions as a critique of master narratives, a demonstration of the importance of the local and an argument for a vision of a new kind of democracy. In the "Anagogie," Chamoiseau's postcolonial critique of hegemonic thinking includes a kind of Foucauldian attack of institutions, examining the ways in which religion, education and healthcare function as modes of dominating body and spirit by ignoring the local. Thus, the underlying ideoscapes of colonization, relying on Enlightenment rationalization are subject to attack. The warrior is a witness to the devastating effects of colonial education in Vietnam, India, Algeria, Senegal, Cambodia, the Congo, the Antilles and other places.[55] A critique of the domination begins with a global catalogue, situating the Caribbean experience in a trans-Caribbean flow. Simultaneously, Chamoiseau provides an account of his own childhood and adolescent reading habits, suggesting how reading served to help him release his imaginary from the prison of French-thinking. In a gesture typical of this text, which plays with the relations among various registers and sites of meaning, he extends the signification of his literal experience working in the French penitentiary system to the symbolic level.

In "Anabase" (an introspective journey), Chamoiseau maps what Appadurai refers to as an ethnoscape or "the landscape of persons who constitute the shifting world in which we live."[56] Chamoiseau shares Appadurai's view that "tourists, immigrants, refugees, exiles, guest workers, and other moving groups and individuals constitute an essential feature of the world and appear to affect the politics of (and between) nations to a hitherto unprecendented degree."[57] Appadurai argues that the warp of stable communities and networks is "everywhere shot through with the woof of human motion" with the result that "moving groups cannot afford to let their imaginations rest too long, even if they wish to."[58] For Chamoiseau, self-identification is inseparable from the history of migrating peoples who make up the trans-Caribbean self. If for some, migration produces a fluid, restless imaginary, perhaps even a sense of drifting, Chamoiseau proposes another alternative. In response to this discourse of domination, he turns to the task of dreaming the land (*rêver-pays*) as a means to undo the colonial chains that place constraints on everyday realities.[59]

Following Perse's lead in *Anabase*, Chamoiseau's "Anabase" begins with an interior voyage where he catalogues vernacular culture with its stories, proverbs, marvels, Creole language and local traditional objects, such as the *yole* or boat.[60] He envisions the "landscape of persons who constitute the shifting world in which we live" as an "anthropological magma" or as a diagenetic model of self.[61] Diagenesis is the process by which sediments of rock become fused as sedimentary rock. Transported and deposited, the rock undergoes a process of compaction as the grains are forced together and then cemented into one. The mode of transport and deposition leaves visible signs or clues in the sedimentary rock. Chamoiseau applies this model to creolization, which also entails a process of transport, compaction and transformation. Tracing the accumulation of migratory groups to Martinique as the sedimentary layers of himself, he creates his own cultural geology: describing how these fluid layers, subject to the pressures of the New World, are transformed into a sedimentary, solid yet fluid, rock-like identity. The result is a diagenetic self, including the *moi-colons, moi-amérindiens, moi-africains, moi-indiens, moi-chinois, moi-syro-libanais* and *moi-créole* / colonial-me, Amerindian-me, African-me, Indian-me, Chinese-me, Syro-Lebanese-me and Creole-me. Creolization then is imagined as a diagenetic process where each identity traverses the other, producing a composite yet distinctive self.[62] This vernacular experience of modernity, formulated as a fluid geology of selfhood and communal identities, has implications for the trans-Caribbean imaginary.

In his third movement, titled "Anabiose," Chamoiseau's critique of technology plays a particularly influential role in describing the trans-Caribbean imaginary. Chamoiseau describes the influx of communications technologies in Martinique and elsewhere, noting the rapid-flash communications of cable, satellite, Minitel, fax, fibre optics, modem, telephones, etc.[63] The *guerrier* observes: "Les circuits de communications s'étaient agrégés en réseaux, les réseaux en mégaréseaux, les mégaréseaux en un rhizome technotronique qui couvrait l'ensemble de la terre, et me plongeait, à chaque instant de ma vie" / Circuits of communication were aggregated in networks, networks in mega-networks, mega-networks in a technotronic rhizome that covers the entire world, and engulfs me, at each moment of my life.[64] Chamoiseau expresses an ambivalent view of technology: at the same time that technology enables the sharing of local knowledge, it also functions as a diffuse system of domination.[65] Chamoiseau's warrior notes that technology is not equally accessible and is even sometimes subject to abuse, often mirroring and even promulgating systemic inequities.[66] For Chamoiseau, "the centre / periphery problem and the balance of forces which are implicit therein did not disappear but only changed form."[67]

Chamoiseau's discussion of the rhizome contrasts the concepts of cyberspace to Glissant's Poetics of Relation.[68] Gilles Deleuze and Felix Guattari first introduced the term rhizome in order to articulate a poststructuralist idea that there is not simply one root or origin but multiple, reproducing roots that exist in a proliferating networked system. This notion has been applied to the Internet or "world wide web" as a model of decentralized, circulating flows of information. It has also been taken up by Glissant as a model for the Poetics of Relation, in which "each and every identity is extended through a relationship with the Other."[69] For Chamoiseau, the rhizome is a neutral concept, capable of being experience in both negative and positive ways. At the local level, the rhizome can be experienced as a mode of domination. Such is the case when globalization is driven by the logic and energy of the "jungle" of Western centers, particularly when the media, political powers, economic forces, financial powers and cultural powers overlap with and constrain one another.[70]

The warrior's comments about the need for a new kind of imaginary interrupt the narrative flow. Eventually, these comments flow into the main discourse and transform Chamoiseau's own narrative as he begins to react to and acknowledge the force of this sub-narrative. Chamoiseau's narrator documents the stultifying effects of departmentalization on the collective imaginary. He observes that departmentalization has led to a profound self-alienation, observing that an ejection from oneself, from one's biological, geographic, cultural and mental realities, began with this change.[71] Simultaneously, the warrior interjects remarks concerning the dangers of technological flows. These two separate narrative threads, one a critique of colonial modernity and the other a critique of homogenizing global forces, converge in the figure of the sea, the marooned slave and cyberspace.

Despite his admiration for Perse, Chamoiseau observes that the poet's construct of the sea, which is seen as an element of power and a source of knowledge, is indicative of the Western imaginary at work.[72] By contrast to the presumptuous spirit of the Westernized imaginary, Chamoiseau admires the imaginary as represented by the marooned slave: this is a figure who is arrested by the sea as the great unknown.[73] Several pages later, Chamoiseau's warrior reconstructs the marooned slave as a hacker who circulates in this rhizomatic space as a rebel figure.[74] Thus, he retroactively imagines the marooned slave as a hacker. This hybrid figure is a product of various temporal and spatial flows, including local cultural memory and the flows of the internet. The local and global flows of the imaginary, past and present, merge to create a new figure of resistance. The "Négre-marron du rhizome-de-réseaux" or "negro-maroon of the rhizome of networks" follows an impulse to confront the unknown and to seize on the imaginary as a virtual space of wandering.[75] This glocalized figure is an example of the inter-retro-active imaginary at work. This rebel and warrior is imagined through a self-conscious dialogue with local and global impulses, past and present.[76]

Chamoiseau uses the notion of cyberspace or virtual identities to introduce his virtual hero and reality: the warrior of the imaginary and the world of the *Pierre-Monde*. Linguistically, the *Pierre-Monde* can be seen as an alternative to the Glissantian notion of the *Chaos-Monde*, but the concept also has other roots. The *Pierre-Monde* finds its etymology in the alchemical idea of the Philosopher's Stone, the result of turning base metals into gold. In this sense, the *Pierre-Monde* is a way of reconceptualizing the diagenetic model of creolization whereby multiple cultures (base metals) undergo a cultural alchemical process of transformation. The Caribbean experience of creolization is a precursor to the discovery of the *Pierre-Monde*, an imagined world grounded in a relational concept of identities. The self as warrior of the imaginary embraces a relational mode of being. The warrior puts forward a view of democracy that fosters relations of diversity and allows for equilibrated communions between modernity and tradition.[77]

The trans-Caribbean vision of the *Pierre-Monde* is a way of reconceptualizing vernacular modernities as a model for a rhizomatic approach to globalization. Chamoiseau sees an attachment to place as a necessary precursor to entering the *Pierre-Monde*.[78] The vision of the *Pierre-Monde* enables the writer to find a virtual niche: a space that unifies the imaginary of places and instructs one about the proliferation of roots.[79] The circulating discourse forms an open textual landscape that traverses multiple genres and languages in order to embrace a "transversal fluid" form.[80] Stylistically, the text thematizes its multiplicity of sources through the cross-cutting of literary citations, which serve to disrupt the chronological flow of the text. These interruptions are inter-retro-active because the unfolding narrative about the initiation of the warrior of the imaginary contains insights that are accumulated in the process of writing the text. Thus, through authorial interventions, the discourse proves to be a self-reflexive, inter-retro-active construction.

Furthermore, the sense of wandering through a virtual space is fostered by the structuring of the text into three sections, each of which functions as a kind of niche or virtual reality: "Anagogie," "Anabase" and "Anabiose." Within these niches, the reader can meander through the text, following its textual flows in achronological and atopical ways, all the while traversing through narrative fragments that nonetheless offer analyses of "real" histories and places. In these sections, as we have seen, the writer pursues an internal voyage, one that includes chronological and topographical and analyses of the self as a site of plural identities, shaped by experiences past and present as well as local and global. Thus, the text functions to recreate for the reader an experience that has already transpired and has yet to take place: the readerly experience is both situated and dislocated. The reader is prompted by these metatextual cues to circulate through the text, exploring a dialogic narrative that exposes uneven chronologies and shifting topographies. *Ecrire en pays dominé* is a compelling example of inter-retro-active imaginary at work; whereby that which was effaced from the history of modernity resurfaces and transforms the perception of global flows.

The work of the inter-retro-active imaginary

Finally, I would like to return to the question of how Chamoiseau perceives the connection between creolization and globalization. In what ways does the local Martinican experience become useful as a mode of analysis for the global imaginary? Like Hall, who views cultural hybridity as an agonistic, ongoing and undecidable process, Chamoiseau argues that creolization, a process taking place around the world, is accompanied by dynamic diversity and flux.[81] Chamoiseau notes the world today is experienced as "a complexity in which contrarieties and antagonisms are balanced in a constantly renegotiated dynamic."[82] What is required is not a fixed position on modernity or domination but a "capacity to relate to others" as a mode of self-definition.[83] A new concept of identity is required: identities "will no longer be stable but at the same time fluid and permanent—like a river which is in a constant state of flux while remaining itself in an irresistible process of transformation."[84] As the Caribbean experience has shown, the process of creolization brings with it changes and challenges in terms of conceptualizing one's place in the world. Describing the Philosopher's Stone World or the *Pierre-Monde* as he calls it in French, he argues:

> We need to regard the world not as a tablet on which we read a message, but as an entity as opaque and unpredictable (though potentially fruitful) as the old philosopher's stone of the alchemists. We are learning to live in the enigma of the world—what I call "the Philosopher's-Stone World."[85]

In his view, the principles of place and the harmonious relating of preserved diversities are essential aspects of the *Pierre-Monde* as a model of vernacular modernity in Martinique as well as for a trans-Caribbean articulation of globalization. In *Emerveilles*, Chamoiseau states that the challenge of contemporary literature is to agitate a consciousness of the Glissantian concept of the *Tout-monde*.[86] He perceives the global imaginary as a network of locales. He notes that peoples, cultures, races, gods, traditions, languages, explanations of the universe are more than ever connected to one another. Local cultures influence one another, are experienced relative to one another and transform one another. Individuals are no longer enclosed in the absolute of one's village, culture and language.[87] In his view, writing should encourage and prepare individuals for this new experience of the interrelated local and global imaginary.

This philosophy is dramatized in *Biblique des derniers gestes*, an epic tale of a hero who lives through ages of domination and anti-colonial conflict. In this text, the tropical forest of Martinique functions as a rhizome, an entry or relay point into the field of global resistance. The raids of Balthazar Bodule-Jules in Bolivia, the Congo, Vietnam and Algeria serve to link Martinique to a history of domination and resistance. Thus, *Oiseau de Cham* (the bird of the field, a nickname for Chamoiseau) draws the reader into a new field of the imaginary through the local experience of Martinique. Richard Watts describes the effect of this experience in *Biblique des derniers gestes* as a liquification of the narrative: "The overall effect is that the ground of the narrative is never solid, which conditions the reader to receive the other liquid elements of the novel."[88] Such a strategy reflects an awareness of the fluidity of the real, with its global and local flows, its places that articulate a complex, multiply situated alchemical chronotope where "space becomes charged and responsive to the movements of time, plot and history."[89] Thus, attachment to the local as a place of imaginary battle serves to prepare the writer for the global struggles to affirm solidarity through a shared commitment to defending the specificities of place, memory and culture. Chamoiseau maps a global imaginary among various locales, recognizing their distinctive yet shared struggles to defend the vernacular in face of various forms of domination.

As a political activist, Chamoiseau has shown how a trans-Caribbean vision of globalization might simultaneously be imagined via a commitment to the local. At the same time, local struggles for autonomy can be supported through a new kind of global imaginary. This point is exemplified by Chamoiseau's written response to political unrest in Corsica. In this piece, he defends a radical concept of democracy as a mode of government that risks chaos in order to defend freedom of speech. He observes that democracy is an ocean of contrary forces, all the more sane because it boils at a temperature close to its dissolution. In so doing, he draws on the lava-like imagery of an ocean of fire to express his vision of citizenship. He argues that the democrat should tend the flames of democracy.[90] Expressing solidarity with Corsicans, Chamoiseau describes an imagined landscape of fluvial forces. Violence in Corsica is re-envisioned through the haunting imagery of the terror, destruction and rebirth that followed the eruption of the volcano, Mount Pelée. Eruptive energies, of lava and waves, past and present, converge in apocalyptic geneses that also function as an ecological, organic model of community. Chamoiseau affirms that he is a Corsican because he is an Antillean. In this renewed space of the trans-Caribbean imaginary, grounded in vernacular solidarities, where various places are interrelated in the global imaginary, Chamoiseau argues for a vision of the world where "tout le monde" is transformed into a warrior battling for the preservation of diversity.[91] Through the imaginative extension of his own local Martinican experience, Chamoiseau negotiates the seascapes of the Caribbean. These waters prove to be salient beyond the region as this vernacular washes up on other shores, disrupting the notion of insular identities through acts of elective affinities.

Notes

The author acknowledges funding provided in support of this research by the Social Sciences and Humanities Research Council of Canada.

1. Arjun Appadurai, *Modernity at Large* (Minneapolis: University of Minnesota Press, 1996), 32.
2. Patrick Chamoiseau, "In the World of the Philosopher's Stone," in *The Creolisation of Culture*, trans. Simon Knight (Zurich: ProHelvetica, Arts Council of Switzerland, 2000), 14.
3. Lucien Taylor, "Créolité bites: A Conversation with Patrick Chamoiseau, Raphaël Confiant, and Jean Bernabé," *Transition* 7, no. 2 (74) (1998): 140.
4. Taylor, "Créolité bites," 140.
5. Taylor, "Créolité bites," 140.
6. Chamoiseau, "In the World," 16.
7. Chamoiseau, "In the World," 15.
8. Appadurai, *Modernity*, 4.
9. Appadurai, *Modernity*, 33.
10. Appadurai, *Modernity*, 4.
11. Appadurai, *Modernity*, 33.
12. Appadurai, *Modernity*, 33.
13. Mimi Sheller, *Consuming the Caribbean* (London: Routledge, 2003), 177-181.
14. Sheller, *Consuming*, 195.
15. Katherine E. Browne, "Creole economics and the Débrouillard: From slave-based adaptations to the informal economy in Martinique," *Ethnohistory* 49, no. 2 (Spring 2002): 374-375.
16. Chris Bongie, *Islands and Exiles: The Creole Identities of Post/Colonial Literatures* (Stanford, Ca.: Stanford University Press, 1998), 13.
17. Antonio Benítez-Rojo, *The Repeating Island* (Durham, N.C., and London: Duke University Press, 1996), 55.
18. Stuart Hall, "Conclusion: The Multicultural Question," in *Un/Settled Multiculturalisms. Diasporas, Entanglements, Transruptions*, ed. Barnor Hesse (London and New York: Zed Books, 2000), 261.
19. Stuart Hall, "A conversation with Stuart Hall," *The Journal of the International Institute* 7, no. 1 (April 1999), http://www.umich.edu/~iinet/journal/vol7no1/Hall.htm (accessed July 25, 2005).
20. Hall, "Conclusion," 216.
21. Paul Gilroy, *The Black Atlantic: Modernity and Double Consciousness* (Cambridge, Mass.: Harvard University Press, 1993), 4.
22. Gilroy, *The Black Atlantic*, 4.
23. Derek Walcott, *The Antilles: Fragments of Epic Memory* (New York: Farrar, Strauss and Giroux, 1993), 11-12.
24. Derek Walcott, *Collected Poems: 1948-1984* (New York: The Noonday Press, 1994), 346.
25. Benítez-Rojo, *The Repeating Island*, 25.
26. Michael J. Dash, *The Other America* (Charlottesville and London: University Press of Virginia, 1998), 14.

27. Quoted in Maeve McCusker, "D'une poétique du territoire à une poétique du lieu: un entretien avec Patrick Chamoiseau," *The French Review* 73, no. 4 (April 2000): 726-727 (my translation).
28. McCusker, "D'une poétique du territoire," 727.
29. Edouard Glissant, *Poetics of Relation* (Ann Arbor: University of Michigan Press, 1997), 6.
30. Patrick Chamoiseau, *Ecrire en pays dominé* (Paris: Gallimard, 1997), 265 (my translation).
31. Chamoiseau, *Ecrire*, 265.
32. Chamoiseau, "In the World," 6-7.
33. Chamoiseau, "In the World," 7.
34. Patrick Chamoiseau, *Texaco*, (Paris: Gallimard, 1992), 65.
35. Patrick Chamoiseau, *Texaco*, trans. Rose-Myriam Réjouis and Val Vinokurov, (New York: Vintage International, 1998), 47.
36. Roy Chandler Caldwell, Jr., "For a theory of the Creole City: *Texaco* and the Postcolonial Postmodern," in *Ici-Là: Place and Displacement In Caribbean Writing in French*, ed. Mary Gallagher (Amsterdam and New York: Editions Rodopi, 2003), 30, 37-38.
37. Chamoiseau, *Ecrire*, 227.
38. Patrick Chamoiseau, "Contre la mémoire et l'histoire," *Antilla* no. 557 (October 29, 1993): 31.
39. Chamoiseau, "Contre la mémoire," 31.
40. Chamoiseau, "Contre la mémoire," 27 (my translation).
41. Quoted in Dominique Deblaine, "Rencontre avec Patrick Chamoiseau," *La lbrarie Mollat* February 6, 2002, http://www.msha.fr/CELFA/recherche/auteur/chamoiseau/chamoiseau.htm (accessed July, 25, 2005).
42. Chamoiseau, "Contre la mémoire," 30 (my translation).
43. Chamoiseau, "Contre la mémoire," 31 (my translation).
44. Chamoiseau, "Contre la mémoire," 31.
45. Chamoiseau, "In the World," 15 (my translation).
46. Chamoiseau "In the World," 15-16 (my translation).
47. Chamoiseau, *Ecrire*, 17.
48. Richard Watts, "The 'Wounds of Locality': Living and Writing the Local in Patrick Chamoiseau's *Ecrire en pays dominé*," *French Forum* 28, no. 1 (Winter 2003): 115.
49. Watts, "The 'Wounds of Locality,'" 116.
50. Chamoiseau, *Ecrire*, 17.
51. Chamoiseau, *Ecrire*, 17 (my translation).
52. Chamoiseau, *Ecrire*, 18.
53. Chamoiseau, *Ecrire*, 21-22.
54. Chamoiseau, *Ecrire*, 23.
55. Chamoiseau, *Ecrire*, 49.
56. Appadurai, *Modernity*, 33.
57. Appadurai, *Modernity*, 33.
58. Appadurai, *Modernity*, 33-34.
59. Chamoiseau, *Ecrire*, 106.
60. Chamoiseau, *Ecrire*, 108.
61. Chamoiseau, *Ecrire*, 110 (my translation).

62. Chamoiseau, *Ecrire*, 233 (my translation).
63. Chamoiseau, *Ecrire*, 238.
64. Chamoiseau, *Ecrire*, 238 (my translation).
65. Chamoiseau, *Ecrire*, 261-262.
66. Chamoiseau, *Ecrire*, 290-291, 295-296.
67. Helmtrud Rumpf, "Technology-based Orality: A Force for Social Change in the Caribbean," in *A Pepper-Pot of Cultures: Aspects of Creolization in the Caribbean*, ed. Gordon Collier and Ulrich Fleischmann. *Matatu* 27/28 (Amsterdam and New York: Editions Rodopi, 2003), 274.
68. Kathleen Gyssels, "The World Wide Web and Rhizomatic Identity: *Traité du tout-monde* by Édouard Glissant," *Mots pluriels*, August 2001, http://motspluriels.arts.uwa.edu.au/MP1801kg.html (accessed July 25, 2005).
69. Édouard Glissant, *Poetics of Relation* (Ann Arbor: University of Michigan Press, 1997), 11.
70. Chamoiseau, *Ecrire*, 280.
71. Chamoiseau, *Ecrire*, 247.
72. Chamoiseau, *Ecrire*, 263.
73. Chamoiseau, *Ecrire*, 264.
74. Chamoiseau, *Ecrire*, 286.
75. Chamoiseau, *Ecrire*, 286.
76. Chamoiseau, *Ecrire*, 286.
77. Chamoiseau, *Ecrire*, 334.
78. Chamoiseau, *Ecrire*, 337.
79. Chamoiseau, *Ecrire*, 339.
80. Chamoiseau, *Ecrire*, 340-341 (my translation).
81. Hall "Conclusion," 226; Chamoiseau, "In the World," 13-14.
82. Chamoiseau, "In the World," 13.
83. Chamoiseau, "In the World," 13.
84. Chamoiseau, "In the World," 13.
85. Chamoiseau, "In the World," 16.
86. Patrick Chamoiseau, *Emerveilles* (Paris: Editions Gallimard Jeunesse, 1998), 126.
87. Chamoiseau, *Emerveilles*, 126.
88. Richard Watts, "'Toutes ces eaux!': Ecology and Empire in Patrick Chamoiseau's *Biblique des derniers gestes*," *Modern Language Notes* 118 (2003): 902.
89. M.M. Bakhtin, *The Dialogic Imagination* (Austin: University of Texas Press, 1990), 84.
90. Patrick Chamoiseau, "Mon journal de la semaine. Enrayer la violence en Corse," *Libération*, November 27, 1999.
91. Deblaine, "Rencontre."

Bibliography

Appadurai, Arjun. *Modernity at Large*. Minneapolis: University of Minnesota Press, 1996.

Bakhtin, M.M. *The Dialogic Imagination*. Edited by Michael Holquist. Translated by Caryl Emerson and Michael Holquist. Austin: University of Texas Press, 1990.

Benítez-Rojo, Antonio. *The Repeating Island*, translated by James E. Maraniss. Durham, N.C., and London: Duke University Press, 1996.

Bongie, Chris. *Islands and Exiles: The Creole Identities of Post/Colonial Literatures*. Stanford. Ca.: Stanford University Press, 1998.

Browne, Katherine E. "Creole economics and the Débrouillard: From slave-based adaptations to the informal economy in Martinique." *Ethnohistory* 49, no. 2 (Spring 2002): 373-403.

Chamoiseau, Patrick. *Texaco*. Paris: Gallimard, 1992.

———. "Contre la mémoire et l'histoire." *Antilla* no. 557 (October 29, 1993): 25-31.

———. *Ecrire en pays dominé*. Paris: Gallimard, 1997.

———. *Emerveilles*. Paris: Editions Gallimard Jeunesse, 1998.

———. *Texaco*. Translated by Rose-Myriam Réjouis and Val Vinokurov. New York: Vintage International, 1998.

———. "Mon journal de la semaine. Enrayer la violence en Corse." *Libération* (November 27, 1999).

———. "In the World of the Philosopher's Stone." Pp. 4-18 in *The Creolisation of Culture*. Translated by Simon Knight. Zurich: ProHelvetica, Arts Council of Switzerland, 2000.

———. *Biblique des derniers gestes*. Paris: Gallimard, 2002.

Chandler Caldwell, Jr., Roy, "For a theory of the Creole City: *Texaco* and the Postcolonial Postmodern." Pp. 25-39 in *Ici-Là: Place and Displacement In Caribbean Writing in French*, edited by Mary Gallagher. Amsterdam and New York: Editions Rodopi, 2003.

Dash, J. Michael. *The Other America*. Charlottesville and London: University Press of Virginia, 1998.

Deblaine, Dominique. "Rencontre avec Patrick Chamoiseau." *La librarie Mollat*. February 6, 2002. http://www.msha.fr/CELFA/recherche/auteur/chamoiseau/ chamoiseau.htm (accessed July 25, 2005).

Gilroy, Paul. *The Black Atlantic: Modernity and Double Consciousness*. Cambridge, Mass.: Harvard University Press, 1993.

Glissant, Édouard. *Poetics of Relation*. Translated by Betsy Wing. Ann Arbor: University of Michigan Press, 1997.

Gyssels, Kathleen. "The World Wide Web and Rhizomatic Identity: *Traité du toutmonde* by Édouard Glissant." *Mots pluriels*. August 2001. http://motspluriels.arts.uwa.edu.au/MP1801kg.html (accessed July 25, 2005).

Hall, Stuart. "A conversation with Stuart Hall." *The Journal of the International Institute* 7, no. 1 (April 1999). http://www.umich.edu/ ~iinet/journal/vol7no1/Hall.htm (based on a faculty seminar held on April 15, 1999) (accessed September 1, 2005).

———. "Conclusion: The Multicultural Question." Pp. 209-241 in *Un/Settled Multiculturalisms. Diasporas, Entanglements, Transruptions*, edited by Barnor Hesse. London and New York: Zed Books, 2000.

McCusker, Maeve. "D'une poétique du territoire à une poétique du lieu: un entretien avec Patrick Chamoiseau." *The French Review* 73, no. 4 (April 2000): 724-733.

Rumpf, Helmtrud. "Technology-based Orality: A Force for Social Change in the Caribbean." Pp. 261-276 in *A Pepper-Pot of Cultures: Aspects of Creolization in the Car-

ibbean, edited by Gordon Collier and Ulrich Fleischmann. *Matatu* 27/28. Amsterdam and New York: Editions Rodopi, 2003.

Sheller, Mimi. *Consuming the Caribbean*. London: Routledge, 2003.

Taylor, Lucien. "Créolité bites: A Conversation with Patrick Chamoiseau, Raphaël Confiant, and Jean Bernabé." *Transition* 7, no. 2 (74) (1998): 124-161.

Walcott, Derek. *The Antilles: Fragments of Epic Memory*. New York: Farrar, Strauss and Giroux, 1993.

———. *Collected Poems: 1948-1984*. New York: The Noonday Press, 1994.

Watts, Richard. "The 'Wounds of Locality': Living and Writing the Local in Patrick Chamoiseau's *Ecrire en pays dominé*." *French Forum* 28, no. 1 (Winter 2003): 111-129.

———. "'Toutes ces eaux!': Ecology and Empire in Patrick Chamoiseau's *Biblique des derniers gestes*." *Modern Language Notes* 118 (2003): 895-910.

9

Karl-Heinz Magister

"A Local Habitation and a Name": Travelers, Migrants, Nomads of "Caribbean New York" in Colin Channer's *Waiting in Vain*

"On the day he met Sylvia, Fire woke up in Blanche's arms with a numbness in his soul."[1] The novel's opening sentence presents his protagonist Fire, a Jamaican writer, as a volatile traveler, who is used to rapidly darting around the globe, as well as an eager lover never lacking a female companion wherever he moves between his homeland and exiles. Variable locations and women bridge his time and space or are transitory. For the "nomadic" artist, the space of time and spatial distances are permanently shrinking or nearly dwindling away:

> He checked his watch. It was eleven. Air Jamaica was leaving at three; and they were always on time. He would be in New York at seven.
> [. . .] "New York," [Blanche] began. "How long are you going to be there?" "Just the weekend," he said. "Then you go to London. And you're coming back when?" "The end o' August." "Three months."[2]

The narrative discourse is governed by male temporal calculations: while he is in command of (his) time and destinations, his female Jamaican partner is offered the role of accepting and confirming his strong-willed and ruthless announcements of leaving her for a long time. On the same night in New York, Fire thinks he needs to rush his date with his new lady Sylvia and squeeze their relationship into a short stay in the metropolis, "because he lived in Jamaica to begin with, and would be leaving New York in two days."[3] While staying in London for some months, he confuses Sylvia on the telephone in a similarly arbitrary way by promising to see her "tomorrow," and surprises her with his sudden appearance shortly afterwards, giving her a blunt explanation for his speediness: "In the fullness of time. Everything happens in the fullness of time."[4] The global traveler is thinking casually in real time dimensions, when mysteriously competing with the velocity of a phone call and unexpectedly turning up in New York only a couple of hours later.

The Afro-Caribbean migrant of the jet age is leaving his Jamaican capital for the North American metropolis within one day—turning up "almost" simultaneously in Kingston and New York, being at the same time both traveler and dweller, resident and diasporic, and in the company of two different women within only a few hours. The migrating male subject's arbitrary decisions unleash hectic traveling activities across geographical, temporal, national, ethnic and sexual boundaries. West Indian upper-middle class migrants in the eighties and nineties, while remaining deeply rooted in the Caribbean, developed a cosmopolitanism which still kept its strong ties to their homeland. Colin Channer[5] represents a generation of migrant intellectual West Indians/Jamaicans in the late nineties who gave rise to a complex culture of travel and migration. They developed a new, complex attitude towards the North American metropolis, which may testify to vital West Indian-American relationships and the strong repercussions of the lifestyle of metropolitan diasporas on the culture of the Caribbean island.

I want to argue, firstly, that increasing ethnic dichotomies and racial segregations at the turn of the twentieth century have led to a radical reconceptualization of migration, a division and ramifications into different migratory customs and subjects of traveling and exile. Secondly, the postcolonial traveler is thought of less as being embedded within the geographical limits of urban neighborhood communities, but more as living in an "in-between" space, or in many places, that is, in a state of "nomadology," or within the global space of "transnational diasporic cultures."[6] Thirdly, Channer subverts old binary distinctions between the global and the local, the transnational and the national, blurring the difference between traveling and walking; that is, the increased mobility of the "Pilgrims from the Sun"[7] begins already within city limits. Walking—here in conspicuous opposition to "modern" transport like driving, as well as to other forms of modern technology—becomes the prevailing mode of "traveling" within the city. The traveling subject develops a variety of pedestrian practices to get acquainted with the city, what Anne D. Wallace called "the 'peripatetic' mode of signification,"[8] which is "based on the cosmopolitan flux of the modern metropolis."[9] They are inscribed by a host of words of movement varying the act of walking and visualizing the strange, as it were, non-Western forward locomotion of the Jamaican dreadlocked (and not self-described) Rastaman Fire. And the fourth step will investigate the metaphorical grounding of traveling and walking, or—as de Certeau puts it—the "enunciative function" of writing and "walking" footnotes, which should make the urban space for the city traveler more knowable and habitable. The fifth point will be the relation of the Caribbean migrants' pervasive West Indianness or Jamaicanness to their underlying cosmopolitanism. And sixth, Caribbean traveling practices are gendered, usually male-centered, as Isabel Hoving argued: men are shown as travelers, women as dwellers, staying at home, being "domesticated" by male supremacy and violation.

Genealogies of West Indian exile and migration

For Channer's West Indian intellectual traveler, the North American metropolis becomes a site of arrivals and departures, of encounters between cosmopolitan migrants and their frequent global dispersals. West Indian migrations are characterized by an essential splitting up into different migratory subjects: the traveler against the dweller, the economic migrant or worker against the homeless person, the exile against the expatriate, the refugee against the religious convert, the tourist against the anthropologist or explorer, the pilgrim against the postcolonial figure of the nomad. In Western metropolitan centers as in New York City, Toronto, London (as well as in Havana where Fire used to study), privileged migrant subjects performed a shift from the displaced exile to the postmodern cosmopolitan diasporic dweller and traveler. While exile was traditionally considered emblematic of human estrangement and loss, Channer employs a variety of meanings and functions of a privileged West Indian exile—far beyond the colonial "forced exile," transcending also the Euro-American myth of exile. Moving from the postcolonial "peripheries" to the metropolitan "center," the male Jamaican traveler is pitted against, and has to negotiate, other forms of exile and migration in New York. His North American and British metropolises display a differently established multi-racial community of exiles, who contend—or already negate, and partly disagree with, ban, slander—patterns and subjectivities of deprived Third World migration. *Waiting in Vain* can be subsumed in—what Günter H. Lenz called—the "'new ethnic novel,' as it portrays and constructs ethnicity and the migratory experience and diasporic cultural identities of its protagonist in a way completely different from the traditional pattern of the immigrant novel and of the 'originary,' 'essentialist' notion of 'ethnic identity.'"[10]

The three main cohorts of West Indian migration to New York City within the last century[11] each display unique modes of locating migration. The migrant literary subject of the first wave of West Indian immigration, say, in Claude McKay's fiction, oscillates between deep "dislocation" and a passionate confession to New York's cityscape with its black working class.[12] In *Home to Harlem* (1928) or *A Long Way from Home* (1937), the traveling author, organizing his autobiographical writing around a departure-return trope, negotiates his repeated returns to Harlem (from Europe, from Jamaica) as "a sense of being at home" and as "a site of rebirth" or as "a sense of territorial at-homeness." McKay's migration from his homeland to the United States "is a journey from country to city, from 'colonial backwater' to the metropolitan center; it is a journey across national boundaries from one diasporan space to another."[13] Migration before independence could also serve as "a means of resistance against colonial domination and exploitation" and as "a symbol of the newly gained freedom [to travel]." At the height of their nationalist period in the 1960s, West Indian writers were confronted with "two Caribbean myths closely intertwined with the search for identity, namely the myth of return [to the Caribbean] and the myth of [national] independence."[14] The Brooklyn-born author Paule Marshall, of Bajan descent, fictionalized in her first novel *Brown Girl, Brownstones* (1959) the migration of the second wave, which may be positioned between a state of "dislocation" and of "dual location," characterized by "her joint membership in two worlds simultaneously."[15] Equally, the Bajan author George Lamming migrating to Britain, in *The Pleasures of Exile* (1960), negotiated cultural alienation in terms of "exile and displacement," and of an aesthetic strategy and political program of decolonization and of accommodation to the new home. Lamming emphasized "the *presence* of a multiply centered Caribbean culture" beyond national boundaries and "a Caribbean presence—community in territory—as a place of return, of homecoming."[16] For Simon Gikandi, exile and its concomitant displacement—in the late colonial period—constitute the basis of West Indian literature, "its radical point of departure; exile generates nationalism and with it the desire for decolonized Caribbean spaces."[17]

Shortly following independence, V. S. Naipaul defined exile and displacement in relation to Britain as "one's lack of representation in the world; one's lack of status."[18] For the Indo-Caribbean traveler to London in *The Mimic Men* (1967), exile meant "homelessness and unbelonging, personal alienation and hopelessness" and fragmentation.[19] On the other hand, Naipaul belongs to those "West Indian male writers, writing from England in self-imposed exile, [who] gained a certain kind of literary authority by their particular negotiation of the space between 'home' and 'exile.'"[20] In contrast to the Anglo-Trinidadian author, the Antiguan writer Jamaica Kincaid entered the North American metropolitan society not as an intellectual exile, and not as a "literary exile" for that matter, but as a domestic laborer, before she began to write. While viewing her own emigration as an act of liberation from poverty, familial narrowness and the nightmarish postcolonial devastation of natural environments by tourism (in *A Small Place*, 1988), she replaces the lost Caribbean self with a new one—that of becoming a female West Indian-American author: "For Kincaid, therefore, exile becomes an essential component in the construction of the modern Caribbean self."[21]

The intellectual migrant of the eighties and nineties, during the third wave, seems to have lost feelings of expatriation and ethnic displacement. The state of "dual location" might still be applied to Marshall's *Daughters* (1990), as young Ursa Beatrice travels routinely between her metropolitan home and the West Indian homeland of her father. By the alternating settings of New York City and the Caribbean island, the traveling discourse in the novel is "blurring the boundary between the United States and the Caribbean, in order to emphasize the wave-like movement of cultures and peoples."[22] The postcolonial nomad subject of the late nineties could be defined as migrating between multiple locations. The nomads are moving from place to place. They have no home. Or, put it in the words of Hugo St. Victor of the twelfth century, which were quoted by Erich Auerbach and Edward Said and used as a "postcolonial" message of exile and a cosmopolitan alternative:

Delicatus ille est adhuc cui patria dulcis est; fortis autem iam, cui omne solum patria est; perfectus vero, cui mundus totus exilium est.

The man who finds his homeland sweet, is still a tender beginner; he to whom every soil is as his native one is already strong; but he is perfect to whom the entire world is a foreign land. The tender soul has fixed his love on one spot in the world; the strong man has extended his love to all places; the perfect man has extinguished his.[23]

The postcolonial Afro-Caribbean writers demystify the "Euro-American modernist trope of exile as authorship," the artist as a nomadic prototype of exile and displacement, and the "concept of exile as aesthetic gain."[24] However, they still foster a nostalgia for the past, for the native soil, for collective identities of family and nationhood, and for home. While the American travel writers' dreams of escape to modernist European cities of the earlier period had spurred their illusion of creativity just under the auspices of displacement, the travelogues of the West Indian-American author of the later post-independence period can be read against the grain of feelings of estrangement. They may realize a cosmopolitanism with new benefits and losses, reaching beyond issues of the displacement of the colonized; the postcolonial migrant shares a range of particularized practices and identities with other subjectivities like those of the exile, the tourist, the refugee, the nomad etc.

New York's multi-racial metropolitan community challenges the prevailing homogeneous mainstream American discourses of ethnic purity and segregation. Channer makes the case for the coexistence of heterogeneous ethnic groups within spaces of encounter or so-called *contact zones*, as opposed to what he calls "comfort zones,"[25] where issues of color and ethnicity are fading. His *contact zones* consist of a mixture of black and white people: of white Americans fitting smoothly into this community, but displaying various signs of patronizing the racial other (Phil: "I'm clearly not a nigger"[26]); of Africans or Italo-Africans (Virgil Pucy) who strive to pass for whites and condescendingly call Blacks "niggers"; of African-Americans who disparage their own ethnicity and that of Afro- and Indo-Caribbeans (Adrian Heath [Fire] and Ian Gore); and of Anglo-West Indians. The African-American Lewis reduces a black woman like Sylvia, a talented female West Indian fiction writer doing secretary work for him in the publishing field, to a mere mechanical "word processor." Predominantly belonging to the upper-middle class in *Waiting in Vain*, they are travelers: traveling globally between the West Indian archipelagos and the American and British metropolises, but also socially moving or 'traveling' upward. They have connections with "filmmakers, congressmen, musicians, and bankers."[27] And they are privileged and conservative migrant intellectuals: their hierarchical thinking testifying to the "bourgeoisification of Third World elites," fostering an "opportunistic Third-Worldism"[28] and an adoption to social and cultural values of the white "First World," which again reduces Channer's globalized multi-racial community concept to a homogenized "cosmopolitanism" (contrary to James Clifford's "discrepant cosmopolitanism").

Adrian Heat, with his nickname Fire, stands out of this heterogeneous diasporic community, taking on the role of an intruder, who incorporates a variety of migratory practices and positions. At times he is a traveler, but soon becomes a metropolitan dweller and walker, signifying the inverse of traveling: he is a tourist and a walking exile, a traveling writer and a nomad, whose activities signify "absolute movement." The transience and volatility of migratory positions designate the traveling West Indian subject as a symbol of mobility and hybridity. In terms of political, social, cultural and religious convictions, he is a figure of non-commitment and non-alignment: he subscribes to no party and no religion, he is strongly devoted to all kinds of arts, but with no deep affection for any particular lifestyle. He has connections and personal contacts with the Rastafarian movement on the island, and feels some sympathy for it, incessantly oscillating between indifference and affiliation, but without any deep engagement in Rastafarianism itself, although benefiting from its culture ("I'm not a rastaman... And love is bigger than religion").[29] He denies any commitment to communism, which his three-year stay in Cuba might suggest, but confesses his *weltanschauung* to be "leftist" and socialist. His character wavers between softness and the heroic, the commonplace and the fastidious, between hesitancy and spontaneity of decision. Fire's volatile character accounts for his girlfriend Sylvia's futile attempt to appropriately define him:

> He was Jamaican, obviously. Educated and middle class from his accent. And had spent some time abroad—at college perhaps—most likely in the States.
> Age-wise he was thirty, thirty-two... and lived where now? Well, that would depend on what he did. He was involved in the arts somewhat—but not to the point where it paid his bills. [...]
> But which art?
> There was a thing about him—a sense that dirt didn't disturb him—that made her think "sculptor" or "painter." He wasn't a dancer, for sure. His posture didn't say that.
> Graphic designer was a maybe... Web sites and that kind of thing. Those guys often dressed like that. [...] She considered 'writer' briefly, then chucked it away. [...] He was a musician... or did something related to music. [...] He was connected to The Wailers somehow.[30]

Fire could be everything—the spectrum of presumed professions ranging from a painter to a sculptor or musician to a graphic designer with special interest in computing—or rather, he is not really any of these at all. Although posing as a renowned novelist, not very much of his narrative subject or activities in fiction writing is disclosed; his authorship is more or less defined by his allegiance and devotion to other literary and musical celebrities and movements and by his intimate knowledge of West Indian (and other) arts and writings. He mentions in passing his acquaintance with Bob Marley, as if he were—quite naturally—entitled to permanently and personally consort with such distinguished

Jamaican compatriots. Though hailing from an educated family—his father was a professor of art history in Kingston and New York City, his uncle I-nelik a dentist and a reggae musician with The Wailers, and the famous Jamaican politician of the seventies, Michael Manley, his godfather—he never flaunts his breeding and education, but casually plays it down. The narrative discourse projects a privileged artistry of a well-traveled and experienced all-round talent with the noble air of a leisurely aristocratic creativity, who takes his doings lightly and without great efforts. To his female companion Fire presents his non-career, non-materialistic, jobless lifestyle without ambition in a negligent—nearly irresponsible—manner, alleging a modesty and simplicity in his way of living:

> "Well, and what are you doing now?"
> "A little o' this and a little o' that? A little writing, a little farming." [. . .]
> "Writing, traveling, painting . . ."
> "Don't you worry about money?"
> "No. [. . .] Because my needs are pretty simple. [. . .] A place to live. Food to eat. Good friends. Good health. That kinda thing."[31]

Fire's evasive and vague manner of answering Sylvia's questions pertaining to his concrete work puts Sylvia between doubtfulness and admiration. "How does he function in the modern world? She wonders."[32] Fire is—as it were—"out of modernity," as he consciously avoids instruments of modern technology and transport (no computer, no car in New York), and is consistently walking instead of driving in the city. His random lifestyle corresponds with some kind of fatalistic behavior. His "alternative" and "leftist" views hide a social conservatism, deeply embedded in a hierarchical belief in the fateful, the inevitable. Expressed in these fatalistic terms, "life is a game of luck," he calls himself "a lucky sperm"—contrary to his friend Ian, an Indo-Caribbean figure, a despised "coolie," who is ethnically and culturally pitted against Fire's "lucky sperm" as a "denatured sperm."[33]

To Sylvia he appears as "a new man"—differing from the greedy and opportunistic multi-racial group he encounters in New York. She takes his persona of a detached and noble behavior, of an unpredictable and unreadable biography, as a disposition for a natural "magic" and "genius": "There was something compelling in his madness, though . . . something inspirational . . . something noble in his pursuit. Because he was someone with choices."[34] The character's performance of "magic," cosmopolitanism, nobleness, distinctiveness and detachment from reality, which distinguishes him from the rest of humanity, exempts him from any dependence on home and from responsibility, particularly towards women (he leaves Blanche in Jamaica and, temporarily, Sylvia in New York). Given the material independence bestowed on him by his parents' prosperity, his feelings of not-belonging and unrestraint pave the way for a life of random traveling—traveling as life. Channer conceptualizes travel as a constitutive of his cultural lifestyle. There is arbitrariness in Fire's traveling motions. He makes a dazzling appearance at Sylvia's after he had just called her from London a few hours ago: "freshly shaven, his hair brushed back, dressed in a white linen shirt that was open at the neck, and black dress pants and square-toed shoes that shone like the wheels of a new Mercedes."[35] His "magic" omnipresence is defined as a conspicuous attribute of his emphasized maleness. He makes a special point of claiming virtues and values of "intelligence, courage, and imagination" for a Rasta-informed ideal of "manhood."[36]

Eventually, the male protagonist takes on a mystic aura when compared by her with Jamaica's icon Bob Marley; his "resemblance becomes uncanny," emanating a sensual and "spiritual magnetism . . . as if he were a shaman . . . as if he had the power to draw people out of themselves into the new space"—with the author's ellipses between his thoughts to let his masculinity fully expand.[37] Channer negotiates a set of Rastafarian symbols of "Caribbean iconography that contains external messages and internal contestations" of culture, gender and ethnicity, of comparisons between masculinity and femininity.[38] Typically, his "resemblance" of Rasta signs becomes all semblances, make-believe. His insinuations at Bob Marley and his devotion to reggae music do not make him a Rastafarian nor even a musician, just as his empathy towards the underprivileged does not make him a political combatant, and his possession of Claude McKay's writing desk and typewriter ("his Underwood manual, a 1930 No. 5"[39]) does not convert him into an heir of the anti-colonial independence movement. On the contrary, when Fire intrudes on Sylvia's life with his fatalistic views, he totally negates her frail position as a black woman in a male society, requiring her to let herself fully give up to fate and ignore harsh reality:

> We can't choose our histories. When we come into this life the greater part of our history is already in place—race, class, gender, religion, sexual preference, wealth, access . . . the things that remain pretty much constant throughout our lives. [. . .] So why kill up yourself? Come home, sweet girl . . . even for a day . . . to sit by a river and eat a mango and say that God is good.[40]

Travel *as* culture and Trans-Caribbean nomads

For privileged Fire, traveling appears to be taken for granted, and a natural symbol of freedom and independence. James Clifford propounds a concept of the traveler as "someone who has the security and privilege to move about in relatively unconstrained ways" as a "travel myth."[41] Fire's "freedom" is partially restricted by the United States immigration bureau because of his frequent sojourns in Cuba. What the trans-Caribbean discourse of migration here withholds is the difference between the fictitious Jamaican writer traveling from Kingston or Montego Bay to the United States, and the real chances of present-day Jamaican-North American migration. Usually, West Indian writers' residences are not located in the Caribbean, but in American and European metropolises. Moreover, the native Caribbean artist Fire, as the fictive character and writer of his own fiction, contrary to the West Indian-American real author as well as to his permanent New York residency, begins his journey from the West Indian island, transcending national, racial, cultural and global boundaries. Fire is both islander and exile, always returning to his Jamaican home after some months (as detailed in the second part of the novel), then traversing the island from south to the north in a quest for his childhood and the aboriginal landscape. Channer's West Indian-American voyages oscillate between transnational traveling and island nativity.

New York City and London, as well as Jamaica's capital Kingston, are all dealt with as sites either of residence or of transience and transition. Being "in town" (of New York) means, for Fire, walking around for a few days or rushing through it to the next location. "'What do you mean *in town*?'" His girlfriend Sylvia asks him, when they were both going "home" to Brooklyn. "'You don't live in New York?' 'I live in [Kingston] Jamaica,' he said, smiling. 'And I'm going to London at eight in the morning.' 'Well ... call me ... whenever ... you're in town,' she replied, trying to hide her disappointment."[42] And, we may add, he is coming back for a short visit just to see her before leaving again for his Jamaican hometown. But during his short relationship with Sylvia, Brooklyn has become his home, too. Equally, women are dealt with as sites of sojourn and of transience or transition. For the cosmopolitan male traveler, home can be everywhere. In this dialogue, tropes of departure and return, of traveling and residing, are overlapping. And departures of the protagonist in *Waiting in Vain* are depicted as escapes from women: "the act of writing travel means fleeing the feminine sphere of domestication."[43] As a diasporic traveler of post-independence Jamaica, Fire is arriving at, leaving and returning to the metropolises as well as to Kingston in ongoing interactions with hidden fears and vague expectations, with different cultures, urban locations and intellectual diasporas. He is both traveler and dweller, in whom the cultural figure of the traveling "native" and the resident migrant with the writing nomad intertwine. He encounters "a community of interchangeable travelers and dwellers, islanders and exiles."[44]

Channer's postcolonial, non-white traveling and migration activities are conceptualized beyond aestheticized notions of modern exile and displacement as transnational and trans-Caribbean. He constantly emphasizes the non-career, non-materialistic structure of his traveling subject, the emergence of—what Guattari and Deleuze call—a "nomadic subjectivity." Channer's migration is "a nomadic way of traveling or signifying, not the imperialistic one that would be aimed at settling and appropriating."[45] Its nomadism is related to a "deterritorialized" condition of "freedom," contrary to Western middle-class traveling and tourism. In Channer's transnational narrative the trope of journey and the trope of mobility become markers of transcending boundaries between the colonial and the postcolonial world.[46]

"Post-migratory" narratives of the late twenty-first century (after the earlier anti-colonial independence movement) subvert Western notions of writing about travel and migration—without totally escaping it—by the use of such concepts as "nomadology" and "deterritorialization," and by the postcolonial figure of the nomad, descended from the modern figure of the "flâneur." In their famous treatise *Nomadology. The War Machine*, Deleuze and Guattari distinguish the figure of the nomad clearly from that of the migrant or exile:

> The life of the nomad is the intermezzo [the in-between] [...] The nomad is not at all the same as the migrant; for the migrant goes principally from one point to another [...] the nomad only goes from point to point as a consequence and as a factual necessity: in principle, points for him are relays along a trajectory.[47]

The trajectories of the deterritorialized nomad are without specific points, paths or land. He/she does not become territorialized. He or she moves between local urban and global spaces—not "with a purpose" but (physically, spatially, intellectually) "as purpose,"[48] which clearly distinguishes him/her from modernist concepts of the migrant subject. Nomads occupy, as it were, a "smooth space," being not confined by national boundaries and cultural restrictions. Nomads have "absolute movement," as Caren Kaplan argues: "the generalized figure of the nomad as a symbol of hybridity, mobility, and flux [...] the metaphorical nomad and theories of nomadology counter assertions of purity, fixed dwelling or being, and totalitarian authorities and social practices."[49] Channer's postcolonial migrant protagonist is a member of the privileged diaspora of writers, artists, and professionals who may well be understood in terms of Deleuze's "nomadism"; but certainly, the majority of Caribbean migrants who are exiled in order to make a living for their families back home could not be characterized as nomads; without possessing multiple passports and a high level of income they have few means to travel beyond national boundaries.

The notion of "nomadic citizenship," which Channer's West Indian subject could be identified with, negotiates an extended transnationality and imaginative geography; it challenges "the coherence of national boundaries and is transnationally linked to informal networks of kinship, migrancy, and displacement, opening up circuits of dependency between communities in Canada, Britain, or the United States and communities in East Africa." The "nomadic" concept engenders a "pan-national identity in opposition to Western-determined conceptions of state and citizenship"[50]; it makes possible new racial, ethnic, gender, transnational alliances and identities, transcending fixed regional formations and existing structures of nationhood. The authority of the Western nation-state is challenged, and the actual white predominance and multi-racial characteristics of New York's diasporas are made invisible. The metropolitan refugees in the 1950s/60s—say, in Sam Selvon's *The Lonely Londoners*, or in V. S. Naipaul's *The Mimic Men*—still suffer from feelings of homelessness and displacement, from the fragmentation of diasporic communities and the destruction of the Black self; but Channer's male nomadic subject undermines such negative dispositions. While preferring ethnic Brooklyn and Brighton for his transitional residences in New York and London, Fire still harbors a strong desire for home and indigenous cultures; although this is not necessarily tied up with a fixed national and racial belonging. "Nomadic citizenship," Joseph maintains, "delegitimizes the state as arbiter of identity and citizenship. [. . .] Nomadic citizenship fractures coherent categories of belonging."[51] Fire and his companions move indiscriminately between their Caribbean hometown and the American and European metropolises without having a special national and cultural claim on either of them.

In this context, "nomadism" serves as a metaphor which opens up directions and destinations, and occupies transnational, multi-racial, trans-cultural in-between spaces. It signifies "the inverse of dwelling or being and celebrates the *intermezzo* zone," and "the opposite of Euro-American metropolitan modernity" of the early twentieth century. The nomad is a central figure in postmodern thought.[52] Contrary to nationalist or modernist strategies, postmodern critics negotiate the figure of the nomad "as a symbol of utter and complete deterritorialization" and "of hybridity, mobility, and flux; in short, the metaphorical nomad and theories of nomadology counter assertions of purity, fixed dwelling or being, and totalitarian authorities."[53] Deleuze and Guattari employed "the nomad as a figure of resistance" to authoritarian state discipline and fixed spatiality, even as a metaphor of rioting, revolution, guerilla warfare, and social change. In Fire, the step from the migrant to the mobile icon of the nomad is exemplified, highlighted by the history of the modern metropolis to the postmodern hub of mobility in the world of international airports: "The experience of the airport traveler and the contemporary Western intellectual [. . .] are not dissimilar. The *flâneur* becomes the *plâneur*."[54]

Urban walking as a "peripatetic signification"

In Channer's migrant, the two figures of the "plâneur" and the "flâneur" alternate constantly, and at ever shorter intervals. He feels as much at home in the domain of Jamaica's airline, where coincidentally his mother is employed, as on the streets of New York City or London. "He checked his watch. It was eleven. Air Jamaica was leaving at three; and they were always on time. He would be in New York at seven."[55] During the flight, the location quickly changes from the contemplative tropical cityscape of Kingston's scenic surroundings to the bustling metropolitan vista of New York. Shortly after his arrival at JFK Airport, he climbs up from the subway tunnels to walk in the streets of downtown Manhattan:

> Chinatown collides with Soho and Tribeca at Canal and West Broadway, chucking chi-chi bistros against hardware stores, stereo shops, and purveyors of fake Chanel. As the clock closed in on midnight, Fire stepped out of the subway and strayed through the gates of love. Dressed in a red T-shirt and slack-fitting jeans, he forded the truck-polluted stream of Canal and strode up West Broadway in his tough, scuffed boots past cafés and bars whose faces were pressed

together like a Polaroid of friends from prep school. [...] For all its pretensions, he liked Soho. The brickwork reminded him of London and the ironwork reminded him of older parts of Kingston. He liked the scale of it. It was low. One could see the sky without trying.[56]

The traveler has changed from airborne and driving locomotion, to walking. Fire is a powerful walker. In the streets of New York City, he persistently prefers walking to driving. His choice of urban locations and his choice of a diversified rhetoric of human mobility (in conjunction with his deliberately "old-fashioned" way of writing) shed light on the traveling subject's preference for a pre-modern, if not anti-modern, habitual lifestyle. He emerges from the underground not, say, onto the touristy areas of downtown's Twin Towers, but in Manhattan's fashionable Soho and Tribeca near West Broadway. He moves around in the streets of the low-scale nineteenth century buildings of Soho rather more than within postmodern surroundings.

The sight of metropolitan architecture reminds the West Indian walker of similar urban architectural views in London and in his Caribbean hometown. Cities of different geographical, political and social worlds and ethnic spaces are juxtaposed with comparable cultural and architectural memories of urban modernity. And Soho and Chinatown are also by name (in London and New York) doubly bound metropolitan spaces. These areas are—similar to those in other metropolises—easily recognizable and readable as culturally rich and variable architecture, which invites pedestrians to watch and to walk. Here, in the streets of Brooklyn and Manhattan, the air passenger becomes a walker. The postcolonial author foregrounds traveling and walking as transnational practices—as a new "culture *as* travel," and travel as a site and a constitutive of culture and migration.[57] Traveling between different worlds of the globe finds its pedestrian pendant in the urban walking between different ethnic and social areas and districts of the metropolis. Walking is like "traveling" between various social and cultural "worlds" or "cities" within the city. The *narrative* discourse concerns itself with walking procedures between and within metropolitan spaces and their ethnic diasporas and segregations. It creates a genealogy of migration and traveling and a new diversified rhetoric of walking. The *geographical* discourse is mapping the city, supplying the walking subject with names and connecting lines; the *walking* discourse as a "peripatetic mode of signification" sketches out legends of a detailed cityscape. The *metropolitan* discourse signifies spatialities in an allegedly hierarchical order—privileging or neglecting urban areas. Fire's mobility contains an underlying Rastafarian informed discourse that creates an unrestricted, indigenous West Indian *vernacular culture of walking*. A latent *poetic* discourse delineates walking as some kind of an artistic activity: captured by a pedestrian aesthetics.

Channer's genealogy of traveling and walking harks back to an earlier history of West Indian migration to New York. In *Home to Harlem* (1928), the Jamaican novelist Claude McKay, while traveling between the Caribbean, Europe and the United States, presented an exciting picture of his island's exiles in New York during the first immigration wave in the 1920s. His urban narrative displays the Blacks' identification and infatuation with the metropolitan settlement. The bourgeoning of the African-American and Afro-Caribbean community is charged by the jazz ecstasy of syncopated and rhapsodic African rhythms in the midst of the heavy street traffic. The West Indian exile is inspired by a Creole-tinged rhetoric of walking, and enthralled by an exuberantly celebrated topography of street and avenue names and home numbers. The walking and narrating ethnic protagonist interacts with the bustling urban space as an object of new geographical discovery after his long absence; the urban itself becomes a subject in motion:

> Harlem! Harlem! Little thicker, little darker and noisier and smellier, but Harlem just the same. The niggers done plowed through Hundred and Thirtieth Street. Heading straight foh Hundred and Twenty-fifth. Spades beyond Eighth Avenue. Going, going, going Harlem! Going up! Nevah befoh I seed so many dickty shines in sich swell motor-cars. Plenty moh nigger shops. Seventh Avenue done gone highbrown. O Lawdy! Harlem bigger, Harlem better . . . and sweeter. Street and streets! One Hundred and Thirty-second, Thirty-third, Thirty-fourth. [. . .] Thirty second, Thirty-third . . . Only difference in the name. All the streets am just the same and all the houses 'like as peas.[58]

The urban location itself pushes ahead by impetuous incitements to be "going, going, going Harlem." The urban Jamaican Creole invokes a sense of being at home in the new space of immigration, which functions as a site of rebirth. It is enhanced into a frantic apotheosis of modern urbanity. Having returned to Harlem after years of migration to England and Russia, McKay confesses a passionate attachment to New York's cityscape, to the black working class, and an identification with a new feeling of pan-Caribbean African transnationalism beyond national boundaries.

The postmodern urban image of multi-ethnicity within "a new spatial order" during late twentieth century immigration reflects the radical changes of migratory trajectories between the Caribbean homeland and New York City. There are racial movements and fluctuations in patterns "of separate clusters of residential space"[59] or heterotopic "Islands in the City"[60] within the American metropolis itself. In Paule Marshall's novel *Daughters* (1992), the new migratory patterns of the eighties of frequent flying and a new freedom of traveling between the West Indies and New York City have also changed the view of homogeneous diasporic communities within excluded, segregated racial enclaves. Ethnic boundaries are transcended and traditional West Indian locations like Crown Heights and East Flatbush in Brooklyn become subsidiary scenes of action, as the Jamaican traveler moves easily between all of New York's urban districts. The migrants' attention is focused on the metropolitan tourist area of the Upper West Side. Masses of people on Columbus Avenue around Columbus Circle invoke a multitudinous "walking in the city" and produce a multi-cultural sight of many races, ages, classes and ethnic groups—merging with streets, places, landmark buildings, stores, bars and street cafés:

> The change in the weather has swelled the weekend crowd on the avenue. The entire Upper West Side, it looks like, is either strolling along with them in the direction of Eighty-sixth Street, their cutoff point a dozen blocks ahead, or moving in an opposing tide downtown, toward the Chagall murals and the fountain at Lincoln Center. Couples, small groups, lovers, friends—all of them in as many different combinations as there are races and sexes—are window-shopping in front of the boutiques, book-stores and antique shops that line the street. They throng the bars, the gourmet food stores, the twenty-four-hour Korean fruit stands, and are still crowding into the restaurants although it's less than an hour from midnight. [...] The faces flow by, black, white, Latina, Asian but mostly white, the Young and the Restless Upwardly Mobiles [...].[61]

Marshall celebrates a metropolitan image of an anonymous mass of people, who are like a big multi-racial family immersed in New York's spectacular vibrant midtown nightlife and enjoy walking around and visiting various places; they are "window-shopping" and "crowding" and "strolling along" fashionable tourist sites.

In contrast, Paul Auster, in his New York trilogy, displays a totally devastated picture of the metropolis and its roaming subjects in the eighties. It is the individual who is getting lost in the city, which is metaphorized as "junk"; it is to become the writing subject's main artificial destination:

> I have come to New York because it is the most forlorn of places, the most abject. The brokenness is everywhere, the disarray is universal. You have only to open your eyes to see it. The broken people, the broken things, the broken thoughts. The whole city is a junk heap. It suits my purpose admirably. I find the streets [...] an inexhaustible storehouse of shattered things.[62]

Here it is the mystery author Daniel Quinn, who is mistaken for the private detective Paul Auster and hired to find out about the secret ways and purposes of a mysterious figure named Stillman, and to follow him around the town. Consistent with the idea of the city as "a junk heap," the fictive "Paul Auster" defines his own person as "a man with no interior, a man with no thoughts."[63] The postmodern "man without qualities" (echoing Robert Musil's "Mann ohne Eigenschaften") needs a blank mind with no bad memories to retreat to, and to fight off his disgust and his anxieties, and thus to be able to fix his attention on this bizarre figure of Stillman. While he is drawing his urban paths, walks, tracks, traces in his notebook, he sketches obscure figures, letters, diagrams as enigmas and mysteries to be deciphered, unraveled. Stillman's walking habits and "walked" figures are mysteries, puzzles:

> More than anything else, however, what he liked to do was walk. Nearly every day, rain or shine, hot or cold, he would leave his apartment to walk through the

city—never really going anywhere, but simply going wherever his legs happened to take him.

New York was an inexhaustible space, a labyrinth of endless steps, and no matter how far he walked, no matter how well he came to know its neighborhoods and streets, it always left him with the feeling of being lost. Lost, not only in the city, but within himself as well. Each time he took a walk, he felt as though he were leaving himself behind [. . .]. Motion was of the essence, the act of putting one foot in front of the other and allowing himself to follow the drift of his own body. By wandering aimlessly, all places became equal, and it no longer mattered where he was. On his best walks, he was able to feel that he was nowhere. [. . .] New York was the nowhere he had built around himself, and he realized that he had no intention of ever leaving it again.[64]

Quinn's ("Auster's") meanderings through town mean walking about without any direction, with no intended destination but getting "lost," lost in a double sense: to lose direction and destination, and to lose his mind and memories. In the *City of Glass* it is the single protagonist who gets lost. Moving through the city means walking not *on* purpose, but *as* purpose, walking as "the essence."

Against Marshall's highlighted metropolitan multi-racial nightlife and Auster's lost walker in "a junk heap" city of "nowhere," Colin Channer posits New York beyond theories of racial segregation, crime and street violence, as a symbol of a "walkable" and "habitable city," authorizing his identity as a West Indian traveler. Mixed lifestyles of luxury and distressed diasporic cultures are depicted as existing side by side everywhere in the City. Fire moves indiscriminately between different racial and cultural areas and transcends urban boundaries—and highlights them all with a similar vernacular (Rasta) visibility. Flatbush Avenue is looked upon as "a broad street clogged with shops and traffic—lumbering buses, sharkish livery cabs, and an assortment of coupes, sedans." And through West Forty-Ninth Street "the aroma of marijuana sweetened the air against the pungency of tobacco, boiled corn, jerk chicken, and floral perfumes. [. . .] There were a few rastas sprinkled in, steadfast in righteous drabness in the fashion Babylon [. . .]. Patois swirled and collided in mid-air, and burst into sparkles."[65] Contrary to "Auster's" walking distinctly without purpose, Fire transforms walking into a—linguistically and kinetically—visible and active performance of movement. The practice of an ethnically informed walking and the reflection on it engender "a counter-discourse of the urban." Fire's walking renders the city ethnically readable and produces its own texts and expressions of motion and conduct: "Perhaps the metaphor of walking possesses the power to unsettle the narrative of (post)modern urban decay and civic disarray?"[66] Channer's primary walking discourse, not primarily located in a junk city of nowhere nor in urban areas of decay and public disturbances, discloses his admiration for landmark architecture and grand plazas. But it may also function as an emancipative metaphor of New York's urban street culture, which Sharon Zukin called "the vernacular culture of the powerless"[67]:

[the] neighborhood shopping streets are the site of vernacular landscape. Sometimes local merchants represent the vernacular of the powerless against the corporate interests of chain stores and national franchises. [. . .] The transformation of shopping streets from vernacular diversity to corporate monoculture is also a reflection of the global and national economies.[68]

Fire's "map" of the city has neither a spatial order nor a choice of locations. His *vernacular* walking discourse is non-hierarchical, without rankings of spatiality or preferences of locations. But this in no way contradicts his penchant for some rather more first-world urban spaces. Jamaican immigrants are commonly seen to turn up in the bustling West Indian locations like crime-ridden Crown Heights, East Flatbush and Bedford-Stuyvesant, or Harlem, for that matter. This is different with Fire; he pays only a cursory attention to those areas. His walking spirit traces alternative indigenous cultures in the neighborhood shopping streets of Brooklyn Heights. But the ethnic and spatial differences between the separate parts of the city's boroughs are blurred, or not made explicit. Our walking hero's special attention is focused instead on representational high culture and his admiration for landmark buildings, which receive much more investment by the political administration.[69] He expresses a distinct liking for Soho's low-scale "brickwork" and "ironwork" and the gentrified areas around Prospect Park. From the elevated locus of his "hotel chronotope" of the *Fulton Inn*, "a place of transit, not of residence,"[70] the Jamaican traveler gets an enrapturing view of Brooklyn's fascinating environment, of Prospect Park and Brooklyn's historic landmark architecture, and he wonders, "why he liked this part of Brooklyn so." He is deeply impressed with the sight of Grand Army Plaza, "the triumphal arch at the roundabout . . . the grand boulevard with the old shade trees" and Brooklyn Museum, because of its shining example of high-cultured European representation of beauty and form and its "Order. Practicality. Efficiency."[71] Contrary to this enhanced metropolitan site of the classical cityscape, Fire's fancy walking areas are the neighborhood shopping streets of "the old Lebanese quarter along Atlantic Avenue near Smith Street"; he immerses himself in the indigenous Arabic culture of sidewalk cafés and stores, and "edged around barrels of bulgur wheat and fava beans, and squeezed by counters lined with five-gallon jars of dates and figs and nuts and sun-dried fruit," and on his way back "he picked up a shirt, some socks and some boxers at the Gap on Montague Street"[72] in fashionable Brooklyn Heights. We are taken to South Elliot, DeKalb and Myrtle Avenues, where the narrator is getting hazily anticipatory by informing us that the ethnic residences around Fort Greene Park, "the home of acclaimed and emerging figures in music, fine art, and literature. The historic district of "Filmmakers. Architects. Choreographers" is regarded as "the manger of African America's future,"[73] or—in Stuart Hall's words—"the 'imagined community' of Africa."[74] Fire's and Sylvia's walks are mapping out tourist guides with detailed locations and conditions of streets, buildings, inhabitants near Brooklyn and Manhattan Bridge at the East River:

After walking down a hill through the urban campus of the Watchtower Society, they came to Old Fulton Street, whose old brick buildings had been turned into restaurants and bars. [. . .] They walked down the gradient toward the river and the old ferry landing, which was marked by a lighthouse and a jetty—a narrow strip of planks [. . .] they walked on cobblestones crisscrossed by trolley tracks. Passing under the Brooklyn Bridge, they slithered past the skeletons of old warehouses and rehabbed factories, occupied now by photographers and artists, and filed beneath the Manhattan Bridge, continuing now along silent streets with broken hydrants and pavements overgrown with weeds.[75]

Channer's geographical discourse of Brooklyn Heights and its adjacent ethnic neighborhoods turns paths and tours into "maps" and narratives in the walking subject's mind, which may be traced on New York's city maps; Fire's walking practices become legends, immersed in the West Indian-American narrative of traveling, walking, and of reconnoitering urban topographies and inhabitants' residences.

The migrant's inclination to walking is permanently mapping alternative, unwonted West Indian pathways. A genealogy of linguistic ramifications and subdivided word modifications represents a metropolitan *pedestrian other*. The experience of going on foot is constantly redefined by different modes of perambulation through the city. The vivid diasporic urban discourse develops a diversified language of walking: "Fire edged through the mob, swiveling left and right, his eyes skimming the horizon like a periscope, his body pressed on all sides. [. . .] As the crowd began to evaporate from the narrow, cracked sidewalk, he drifted down the street to the stage door."[76] Beyond the casual use of "walk" or "walking," frequently more expressive synonyms are used. Fire "edged," "swiveled," "squeezed by," "pressed," "drifted down." When he arrived in Manhattan after his flight, he "stepped out" of the subway, "forded" the stream of Canal, "strayed" through the gates, and "strode up" West Broadway. He is apparently strolling and roaming aimlessly, but his pedestrian movement is an ethnically, linguistically, and politically informed walking and navigating through various municipal districts, and an inconsiderate transcending of the city boroughs' boundaries—a locomotion that often resonates with rites and rituals and the music of Jamaican Rastafarian culture. The West Indian's walking engenders a *vernacular rhetoric* of taking possession of metropolitan locations, a peculiar kind of what Stuart Hall called "vernacular modernity" that conspires with "the modernity of hybrid black music in its enormous variety throughout the New World—the sound of marginal people staking a claim to the New World."[77] Channer's "vernacular" approach to a metropolitan Rasta mobility is intensified by his figures' occasional use of Jamaican Creole, which is, at other times, denounced as "the nihilistic ghettocentric rhetoric." Fire and Sylvia speak Kingston's patois with each other to reassure themselves of their mutual local roots in the Caribbean, and Fire returns to an unused accent as "he'd worked so hard to unlearn, the near-British cadence of old Jamaica [. . .] the voice of the legendary barristers and parliamentarians [. . .] the voice of breeding,"[78] to signify social and cultural superiority and authority when opposing the corrupt post-colonial administration in Jamaica.

It signifies an empowered, offensive manner of a challenging Rasta walking: the Jamaican is "picking" his way through the crowd, "edging" between cars, "jerking" along the street; Rastafarians self-confidently "saunter," "loiter" or take their strolls and amblings through the city. Here, Fire's "drifting down the street" can be compared with "Quinn/Auster's" random locomotion, which follows "the drift of his own body," sketching figures on the map through walking.[79] This verb seems to be best suited to a West Indian walker; "to drift" or "derive" (Fr.) as "side walk" in Fire's unconventional moving around suggests some kind of controlled spontaneity and reconnaissance by an intuitive walking. The urban nomad's walking proceeds in a form of de-touring. Fire never reads a map; he thus never follows official or tourist directions and public stratagems of a straight way to destinations, but rather by-paths, turnings, bents, diversions. The "dérive helps to invest the city with human meaning"[80] as it makes spaces more recognizable and habitable and less predetermined by strict regulations through strange authorities. But Fire's walking also reminds us of a much deeper and more metaphorical meaning in West Indian colonial history. Bob Marley sings in his famous song *No Woman, No Cry*: "My feet are my only carriage so I got to push on through."[81] And Fire's Rasta kind of "walking" procedure may be imbued with the historical meaning of "walking" or running away from slavery—in the emancipation movement of the so-called marronage, when the maroons took refuge from the plantations in the inner parts of the island.[82]

Fire's West Indian emancipative Rasta walking *as purpose* is clearly differentiated from that of his friend Ian, who roves and rambles around in town *without* any purpose or destination. Ian has wasted his artistic talents during his traveling adventures. Having been much more at home in Kingston's ghetto than Fire, the reason for his unhappiness as a "denatured sperm" and his lack of self-confidence seems to be due to his East-Indian descent as a "coolie," which some Afro-Caribbeans still look down upon. His deep depression and feeling of alienation leading to his suicide is already looming large in his random urban walks:

> He walked a lot that night, moving in a hunched-over shuffle like a laborer carrying a sack of cement. And he stopped in at many places. Illegal gambling dens. Warehouse raves. Strip clubs. Churches. Crack houses. Poetry readings in performance spaces. Artists' studios. Cafés. Liquor stores. Record shops.—He walked around until he could find nowhere else to go, then walked back home.[83]

Ian has been cut off from his childhood ghetto life. Without getting fairly recognized by his ethnic other, he has lost his bearings as well as any feelings for his Caribbean homeland, as he has got used to the western lifestyle of the well-to-do diasporas in the United States. There he is treated just as condescendingly because he is not a West Indian. In many ways he has become a homeless person everywhere. Ian is doubly exiled: he is a nomad without a message as well as a nomad without a place.

The creative West Indian walking discourse tries to construct a dialogue between the migrant and his/her metropolitan locations. There is meaning in urban spaces, which the subject has to extract: "He'd never known New York to be indifferent. There was always something calling out to the lonely. Good things and bad things, novelties and fixtures, bright lights and dark places, saviors and con men. But tonight, though, the city just went about its business."[84] By varying the words of locomotion, the walking subject exerts a distinctive spatial augmentation within the city and beyond—significantly not by transportation or the modern media of telecommunications, but by the body's physical extension through its moving capacities. Here, the word "peripatetic," derived from the Greek, or the phrase of "the 'peripatetic' mode of signification" for intense and expressive pedestrian activities in the city, may incur a dialogic relationship between the walking West Indian and his urban surroundings, based on a cosmopolitan flux of the modern metropolis. Walking challenges the territorialization of urban space, pedestrians manipulate routes and take short cuts, tell stories through their choices of urban areas they prefer or avoid. "Thus, the ordinary activities of everyday life, such as walking in the city, become acts of heroic everyday resistance. The nomad is the hero(ine)."[85] For the West Indian traveler, the predominantly male Rastafarian-informed walking becomes a challenge to any ordinary or self-satisfied walking. His West Indian walking subverts a materialized locomotion by tourism—say, the production of tourist space by (walking or bus) tour guides through the city.[86] Channer's migratory concept invokes the dynamic and democratic dimensions of walking, and an invitation to everybody to join in.

Against the long decline of the "walking city" in North America, going on foot appears to be a challenge to the omnipresence of cars and communication media, as the automobile never turns up in his New York text. Channer's metropolitan walks are immersed in incessant streams of information about urban life, locations and geographical names; his urban world excludes today's images of "wired sleepwalkers" or "technomads" ambling in cultural blindness, "communicating" only with their "walkmen." The car poses an invisible threat to the walker, who otherwise is regarded as an outcast just for strolling in the street, notably in U.S. cities like Los Angeles and Miami.[87] Channer's walking discourse invokes new visions of a car-free metropolis and dreams of a pedestrianization of the urban traffic. In the fall of 2006, a competition held by the History Channel in the Grand Central Terminal called for the ideal design of a twenty-second century "City of the Future" in 2106. The "Terreform" group was the architectural team with the best presentation, which won the competition "with a proposal that involved elimination of privately owned cars in Manhattan; it predicted that sixty percent of the city's population would be walking to work by 2038."[88]

Writing spaces and walking "footnotes"

Walking is actively interrelated with, and informed by, speech and writing: "The act of walking is to the urban system what the speech act is to language or to the statements uttered." Discourses of the city like legends, narrations, memories, dreams "make habitable or believable the place they clothe with a word."[89] Narrations create and employ a rhetoric of walking, and walking itself develops an enunciative function in a poetical narrative. The interrelation of "linguistic and pedestrian enunciation," of "spatial and signifying practices"[90] pushes the walking rhetoric far beyond the confines of the local urban and spans the metropolitan and the Caribbean location. Sylvia, while waiting for Fire on Brooklyn Bridge, reads West Indian poetry by Derek Walcott. Both are walking from Old Fulton Street past Brooklyn Bridge to a subculture hip-hop venue in the club "Rio" in an old warehouse beneath Manhattan Bridge, listening to new poems: "The poem is a walk."[91] Sylvia recites her own poem with the title of "Exile," expressing an Americanized desire for her strange Caribbean home, thus connecting the activities in the metropolis with the tropics. Fire's and Sylvia's walking as "derive" or side-walks becomes a poetic performance: they are both performing (in) the city. The trans-Caribbean poetic counter-discourse of the city becomes a "long poem of walking"[92] that manipulates metropolitan spaces and challenges predominant, misanthropic, car-centered concepts of the urban. Sylvia's walk-poem is the aesthetic result of their poem-walk, of their pedestrian activities in the Brooklyn Heights neighborhoods. By walking from neighborhood to neighborhood, an intimacy and familiarity with their communities is established. The writing traveler creates a meaning by his choice of locations and the calling-up of street names, thus by his spatial and signifying practices transforming the urban into a habitable space. Channer's poetic images of urban spaces, signified by low-scale brickwork architecture without cars and glaring advertisings, promulgate human habitability; they are harking back to premodern or early modern poetic concepts of visualizing, denominating and taking in possession unfamiliar locations in non-possessive ways: "The poet's eye," says Duke Theseus in Shakespeare's *A Midsummer Night's Dream* [V,1,12-17]),[93] "Does glance from heaven to earth, from earth to heaven; And as imagination bodies forth/The forms of things unknown, the poet's pen/Turns them to shapes, and gives to airy nothing/A local habitation and a name."[94]

The city dweller's going on foot and designating locations creates a "foot-writing," which leaves a trail of "footnotes" along those more spectacular urban tourist rides. The act of (non-commercial, non-consuming) walking achieves a signifying practice of reading the names of locations, of streets, places, land- and cityscapes. The signifying walking practices of the exile on foot transform the "walking city" into a "habitable city." With the decline of the "walking city" and of public spaces the "enunciative function" of walking vanishes—a function which this text endeavors to resuscitate. West Indian walking manners create a special nomad "foot-writing." His/her walking habits and local preferences denote and "enunciate" the West Indians' familiarity or identification with urban ethnic neighborhoods. Sylvia's walks are guided by her poetic activities and literary interests—while "waiting in vain" for Fire she reads Walcott on Brooklyn Bridge, and reads her own poem *Exile* in a hip-hop club. After crossing Union Square and walking along Broadway to Twelfth Street, she heads for New York's prime second-hand bookshop "Strand" to buy Fire's novel *The Rudies*. Later she meets with Margaret and Phil in the "Blue Note" for a jazz session. Fire indiscriminately traces Brooklyn's landmark architecture and multi-racial shopping neighborhoods along Atlantic Avenue as well as Soho's and Tribeca's gentrified modernist buildings and midtown Manhattan's tourist sites, moving between both boroughs without further ado. He expresses his admiration for the metropolitan glamour by patching it with myths and memories from his own cultural heritage; first-world metropolitan life is easily clad in third-world popular culture. Walking towards Forty-second Street, the heavy traffic captures the imagination of the West Indian traveler as the spectacular "bacchanal" of "the carnival" of Times Square, whereas later on, an Americanized estrangement from the indigenous culture is revealed, when the real carnival of the West Indian-American Day Parade is derided as "a lava flow of rum-loosened revelers in fringes, sequins, and feathers—hissed across the TV screen like a beckoning smile of a femme fatale."[95] From the remote metropolitan view, the island walker in the streets of New York City acquires a critical—if not disparaging—judgment of his tropical homeland. As traditional modes of West Indian migratory behavior and lifestyle are challenged, different concepts of an ethnic narrative are required. The West Indian-American writer is searching for a new approach to the urban space, in order to "elaborate narratives of city life that no longer claim to represent 'the urban' but, instead, are *stories* from the city."[96]

Whereas Kingston in *Waiting in Vain* is portrayed as the location of West Indian creative repose and an alternative space for a privileged intellectual lifestyle, the American metropolis becomes a site of walking and of global encounters between locals and foreigners—a favorable place for "the emergence of a cosmopolitan subject as celebrity author."[97] Channer's West Indian-American artist flaunts his celebrity authorship by giving an insight into his West Indian character's pretentious choice of readings and arts, his devotion to Jamaica's reggae tradition, and by aligning himself indiscriminately with artistic and political luminaries of various fame and reputation—"like Marcus Garvey and Bob Marley and Michael Manley and Harry Belafonte and Colin Powell and Claude McKay and Peter Tosh."[98] The author's namedropping list of his favorite writers maps a cosmological authorship by crossing political, racial, geographical, continental, and epochal boundaries, varying the late European modern with 'other' modernities of Latin American, Afro- and Indo-Caribbean, and West Indian-American origin: "'Well, Updike, as I said. Naipaul. Henry Miller. Márquez. Carpentier [. . .] but I'd have to add Toni Morrison and D. H. Lawrence. In poetry, now, there's Walcott, Neruda, Guillén, Yeats, Rita Dove, Philip Larkin . . . Kwame Dawes down in

South Carolina ... different people for different moods."[99] Incidentally, he adds African-American names like James Baldwin, Margaret Walker, Langston Hughes, and of Zora Neale Hurston. Fire shows a negligible interest in "ethnic" modernity, considering on the one hand his father's influence, "a master draftsman and composer in the Western realist tradition," and on the other his own education at Yale, where he "began to imbibe the ink of Derek Walcott," and the impact of Mexican muralists and Cuban art during his three-year Cuban sojourn. The West Indian-American author Channer equips his author subject Fire, living "in between" his Caribbean homeland and two First World metropolises, with a "swirling" vision of his own life "that he recognized as neither past, present, nor future [. . .] as his head filled up with thoughts and memories. After sorting and stacking and counting and filing and cross-referencing for date and subject and characters and ideas, he was as unclear about his compulsion as he'd been at the beginning."[100] The migrant's self-fashioned artistry consists of an arbitrary patchwork of references "traveling" across the boundary lines of arts, media, temporalities, multi-racial communities, urban spaces, sexualities, walking and writing practices, and of geographical locations, reaching from Brazil to the United States and to Canada; his aesthetic concept reverberates a universal, nondescript notion of literature, claiming a cross-cultural, multi-racial, transnational, cosmopolitan understanding of different worlds and arts. John Updike's novel *Brazil*—discussed by some immigrants as a commentary on their own failed inter-racial relationship among Channer's fictive West Indian community, by others heavily criticized as an unrealistic Cinderella story—serves as a metaphor of overlapping races, cultures and geographies, and of the Americanization of Third-World cultures: "Imagine if *Brazil* were set in the contemporary American West, and Isabel were the daughter of a white municipal banker, and Tristao a homeboy named Tyrone, from Harlem." The novel of the white American John Updike is looked upon from the point of view of its cultural transfer and its translatability into other languages: "the book almost reads like it was translated from Portuguese or Spanish."[101]

Fire is manipulated into the figure of a West Indian celebrity author, who fashions himself as a Somerset Maugham Prize winner, having been short-listed for the Booker Prize. For a writer in Jamaica he seems amazingly well-off, having already become famous with a million and a half copies of his book sold in the whole Commonwealth, and having purchased a house in Kingston when he sold its film rights. Not much is disclosed about his real writing capacities, though, and we are not told a lot about his novel *The Rudies*: "an epic about the rise and fall of a Jamaican gang in London [meaning 'Brixton']"[102] nor about his practice of producing Rasta fiction; although, "while researching *The Rudies* he'd met and befriended many gunmen and posse leaders."[103] Fire's connection to the Rastafarian diasporic history in Britain, as well as to Jamaica's Rastas, remains nebulous, vacillating between intimate commitments to its reggae culture and renouncing strictly any personal Rastafarian identification.

The time of Fire's socialization in the 1970s coincides with the explosion of Rastafarianism in Jamaica, when the first independent national motion picture

The Harder They Come (1972) by Perry Henzel and Trevor Rhone, and its novelization by Michael Thelwell eight years later, as the movement's two outstanding narrative and cinematic documents stirred the emotions of the Jamaican people.[104] Radicalized and violent sections of the Rude Boys, whose activities as drug dealers and cop killers were styled on the stereotyped model of the American Western as "badmanism," had already been migrating to Britain since the 1950s.[105] In the 1980s/90s, Jamaican posses increasingly migrated to the United States. Phillip Baker in his novel *Blood Posse* (1994, comparable to the Jamaican film *Shottas*) renders a glorified picture of Jamaican Rude Boy gangsterism, drug trafficking and gun violence, portraying young migrant criminals as heroes on the streets of "Caribbean New York"—in Brooklyn's West Indian diasporas.[106] Channer is concerned with none of this. Fire keeps himself aloof from the matter of the radical Jamaican exiles. The narrator's world of Rastafarian migration is a space which his author does not want to share with his readers; it is a world from which he is actually far removed and which—for all his asserted deep-rooted affiliations to it—is an alien one to him.

Fire's world is determined by ways of pretending, feigning, and imagining. His urban walking habits, while effacing the sphere of metropolitan transport and locomotion, correspond with his anti-modern rituals of writing. In a world of computers and telecommunications, which he avoids, he is in possession of Claude McKay's original typewriter and desk, using them as touchstones of authenticity. Comparable to the procedure of "foot-writing" or leaving "footnotes" by walking, Fire prefers conventional instruments and materials of moving and writing, thus conspicuously slowing the pace of everyday processes and activities; his impetuous migratory activities are not ruled by signs of velocity. Channer's walking and writing procedures echo the classical critique of the acceleration of modernity by Johann Wolfgang von Goethe, who denounced the impatience and volatility of his age as "alles veloziferisch" (his coinage "velociferic" from the Latin word "velocitas").[107] Fire sends Sylvia letters in longhand, and "a handmade book, twenty-four pages of heavy-gauge paper bound with needle and embroidery thread," with a dried rose affixed to the cover, "a series of warmly impressionistic streetscapes" in ink and gouache and a love poem done in calligraphy on the inside back cover.[108] Here, Fire's alternative "foot-writing" matches his meticulous procedure of creative hand writing: "But the ritual of writing—the choosing of the paper, the finding of the pen, the convening of the thoughts, the drawing of the letters—was an intimate act."[109] Fire lacks all utensils of the modern technomads—no car, no computer, no e-mails, no TV, he never had a real job, has always done "this and that": just "writing, traveling, painting," which prompts his girlfriend Sylvia to ask: "'How does he function in the modern world'"?[110] He does not want or need to "function" at all. His pre-modernist practices, part and parcel of his brand of migrant or nomad artistry, have no place in post-modern society; they create a fictitious post-migratory and transnational representation of intellectual, socially privileged lifestyle in West Indian-American urban in-between spaces. Fire pursues an ethnic, artistic and cultural patchwork lifestyle—interrelating or ethnic, artistic and cultural patchwork lifestyle—interrelating or mixing together various arts, media, writing modes, sexual practices, and celebrities of arts and politics of different levels and ideologies, temporalities, ethnic communities, urban locations, metropolitan and Jamaican legends. Although the Jamaican migrant has developed a whole range of intellectual instruments and facilities to deal with the intricacies of the postmodern metropolis, he displays—after leaving New York for Kingston—a much greater sympathy and intimacy with his post-colonial Caribbean homeland, which the writing subject praises in a poetical style.

Transnational West Indianness

> The sea dived away from the land and the hills ran away from the road and the road collapsed its width, and suddenly the expansive Rockfort Road was the rowdy, crowded Windward Road, where goats loitered between overcrowded minibuses, and unemployed youths sat on broken fences, and old women sat on stools in shop pizzas hawking bad fruit and loose cigarettes, and men pushed homemade carts with stuff nobody wanted to buy, and reggae thundered from the speaker boxes set up outside record shops, and people crossed the street against the traffic lights, and the pungent smell of jerk chicken wafted from smoky pans set up in front of the kind of bars where the only mixed drink was rum and water, and the beautiful homes with their shingled roofs and hardwood floors had become ugly tenements. [. . .] then headed north, ascending in a steady incline toward prosperity past the stadium, a small bowl overlooked by grand villas on Beverly Hills, along Old Hope Road, past the old mansions converted to administrative use, up, up past the Sovereign Center, a Miami-style shopping mall [. . .] through the commercial bustle of Liguanea [. . .] past the botanical gardens and the two universities, up into the fern-draped foothills of the tall Blue Mountains, [. . .] green hillsides dotted with brightly painted houses that from a distance looked like plastic thumbtacks.[111]

The second part of the novel (chapter 10) opens with the return of the trans-Caribbean travelers to their West Indian home—evoking a hymn on the scenic cityscape of Jamaica's capital as well as memories of Ulysses's return to his Greek lands. The text celebrates "the beauty of the drive." After the long flight from New York, the fascinating sight from Harbour View towards the city of Kingston with its hillside and the Blue Mountains and the rainforest as its backdrop, renders a totally different image from the one Fire envisioned when he climbed up from the subway station in downtown Manhattan. From the Jamaican travelers' vantage point, the city of Kingston is defined more by its scenic surroundings than by the dire living conditions of its native people. The Caribbean landscape and its urban architecture add another shade to the definition of transnational West Indianness. But the beauty of the landscape soon collapses with the growing ugliness of the urban environment and the decaying of the postcolonial civilization in the downtown areas. At the first moment, Ian and

Fire are both "overwhelmed by the sense of space and freedom"[112] which this New-World landscape conveys after their long sojourn in the Old World metropolises of London and New York. Their movement through the city perfectly maps a crooked and crowded journey through the urban geography of Kingston; the drive from "Norman Manley Airport" follows the path through dilapidated downtown Kingston to its stylish uptown and the hilly and green outskirts of the city, where Fire has taken up residence. Channer's travel discourse circumscribes the urban changes in terms of an apparent transformation of its adjacent landscape: due to the industrialization and suburbanization towards the coastline, the town seems to have moved away from the seaside and up into the hills. Or, he asks undecidedly, has "the sea dived away from the land"?

Despite the initial promises of their tropical homeland, the migrants' views of Jamaica's capital are, from the beginning, diverging tremendously from each other. The narration presents two conflicting images of the city: the beauty of its surrounding landscape cannot conceal "squalid Kingston." Ian, as a frustrated migrating artist, has not returned to his home, but to a strange past; he rejects the tourists' opinion of his country: "Wasn't this supposed to be paradise?"[113] On arriving from France via New York at the airport after fifteen years' absence, he enters his country doubly alienated: as an immigrant to his own homeland and as a descendant of Indo-Jamaican indentured slaves, obvious to his African-descended countrymen as a coolie—"a coolie with a French passport." Ian suffers terribly from his East Indian origin: "Like the nigger in America, the coolie in Jamaica is invisible."[114] Different political and national commitments are due to different memories of their social and ethnic past (Ian's as a "coolie" in Kingston's ghetto against Fire's Afro-elite social status). A dispute between the two men about transnational relations and ethnic prejudices concerns financial advantages and disadvantages, economic efficiencies, different lifestyles, and crime rates between Third-World and First-World nations, between First-World comfort and Third-World insecurity, between Afro and Indo West Indian nationhood and mentalities.[115] Whereas the self-confident upper-middle class Fire, even after his long absences, has freely chosen Jamaica for his home, Ian's negative attitude towards his home country still echoes the old colonial's attitude to his homeland, which was that "the best of us had to run away."[116]

While driving along the seaside and the harbor through the city, the shocking changes in post-independence Kingston with its American-styled commercial centers and shopping malls become visible, heavily contrasting with images of the past of the Jamaicans' ramshackle residences in Trenchtown. The drive through the Third-World cityscape clearly reverses metropolitan modes of movability and visibility. In Kingston, Fire's walking habits have radically changed, and he customarily drives a car, signifying his status as a U.S. Jamaican who, by virtue of his distinct metropolitan behavior, could possibly be recognized as such by indigenous Jamaicans. The difference between the flâneur of New York City and the motorist in Jamaica's Kingston surely is resonant of a problematic socio-political infrastructure and the critical usage of public spaces in the postcolonial city. The urban landscape of Kingston is determined by a conspicuous divide between ravaged downtown (with the ill-fated Rastafarian Trenchtown) and the hermetically sealed hillside suburbs of uptown (with the administrative New Kingston and the area of the University of the West Indies in Mona). Fire cannot negotiate these social, cultural, and geographical boundaries as a flâneur; he cannot traverse the city except in the mode of just passing through.[117]

The West Indian travelers' nomadic migrations between postcolonial Jamaica and the North American and European metropolises demolish any cohesive notion of what Joyce Pettis, with regard to Caribbean-American authors, called the interaction between the "the physical place and the psychological space,"[118] which means, between a stationary geographical location of the migrant diasporas and the space of their psychological and ethnic designation as West Indians in New York. They establish a changeable, variable and volatile *West Indianness*. The old conflict of colonial immigration between exile and return, between the ultimate loss of homeland and the futile dream of seeing it again, apparently seems to have dissolved or dwindled into insignificance. The novel testifies to transformations of local communities into transitory, nomadic spaces for post-independence migration. The extensively traveled migrant Fire is "at home" in multiple locations. His West Indianness—as pitted against a denied or forfeited "Americanness" in the British and North American metropolises—always travels along with him. The West Indian-American author, who himself has already been living in New York for many years, invests his migrant subject with the dream of preserving his West Indian identity. For Fire Jamaica is his real homeland, where he can enjoy all the West Indian tastes and penchants along with the privileges and advantages of the upper-middle-class society:

> for me Jamaica is the place. I mean I miss London y'know, but when I was there I missed Jamaica. And when the urge take me now, I jump on a plane and go where I feel like go. But this is my base, Ian. This is where I'm rooted. I'm a Jamaican, Ian. Yardie to de *bloodclaat* core. I love stout more than wine. I love cricket more than baseball. I love rice more than pasta. And I love Bob Marley more than Beethoven or Count Basie. I call women I don't know "darling." When a fight start I look to throw a stone quicker than a punch.[119]

Channer's discourse of West Indian migration "travels" from the geography of urban space to the vibrant topography of the Afro-Caribbean migrant's face. Fire's physiognomy is a space where multiple ethnicities intersect:

> As [Blanche] watched him [Fire] pick up the mango, she marveled anew at his face. Like reggae it was a New World hybrid, a genetic mélange of bloods that carried in their DNA memories of the tribes that fought and fucked on the shores of the Americas—Chinese and Arab, English and Scotch from his father's side; and from his mother's, Dutch and Portuguese Sephardic Jew. But the final combination—brown like sun-fired clay, cheeks high and spread apart; nose narrow with a rounded tip; lips wide and fluted—was vibrantly Yoruba and Akan.[120]

Fire's Jamaican mate Blanche maps a multi-racial physiognomy that resonates with a transnational lifestyle, ultimately making the traveler's descent negligible. The postmodern West Indian nomad subject "is recreated as a homeless traveler who no longer constructs meaning by relating to his/her origins."[121] The mapping of a European, American, African, AmerIndian history exhibits a modernized, mobile, charismatic West Indianness—drawing from the rich heritage of the colonial past and a national culture of emancipation and independence. Channer conceptualizes "West Indianness" not only as a geographical location of "that island," but as a gendered habitation, the place of the female members of his (disrupted) family: "to me West Indian women were my mother, my aunts, my cousins, my teachers, the first girls I fell in love with."[122] To negotiate West Indianness and Jamaicanness as a female space, beyond the postcolonial definition of displacement, is not a sign of loss but of procreation and national transformation, and of new migratory subject positions.

But Fire's hybrid physiognomy testifies to a much more heterogeneous, global vision of West Indian nationality. Behind the multi-racial physiognomy, the female perspective uncovers distinct signs of a genuine Jamaican artistry. Fire's face reminds Sylvia of Bob Marley's image on the cover of a famous disc: "You look like the picture on *Natty Dread.*"[123] Sylvia's fascination with Fire and his shining example transforms the ingenious reggae musician into her talented friend; both figures' physiognomies merge into one, and Fire takes on the mysterious features of an exalted Bob Marley image: "I'd never seen such a charisma in my life." He had "a spiritual magnetism . . . as if he were a shaman."[124] And Fire himself completes, self-reflectively, the list of an outstanding West Indian character: Marley was "(i)ntrospective. Listened more than he talked, and pretended to know less than he did. [. . .] he was roots but cosmopolitan, tough but humble, thrifty but generous, workaholic but laid back [. . .] he understood love in all its forms—spiritual, fraternal, and romantic."[125]

Channer negotiates his compatriots' national and cultural authenticity and ingenuity by engendering a new West Indian pride and self-confidence. Fire and his uncle "represent an essential Jamaicanness or Caribbeanness that embraces a left-wing perspective on social inequities, a hands-on relationship to experience, a reveling in the natural and organic rather than the artificial."[126] From the hills surrounding Kingston, Fire declares for himself an extensive West Indian nationhood that is neither tied to a fixed geographical location nor restricted by national, ethnic and cultural boundaries. In the cosmopolitan diasporas located in so-called second cities—Brooklyn, Brixton, or Kingston's ghetto of Trenchtown and other marginalized postcolonial urban spaces—Fire invalidates stereotyped and homogenized notions of West Indian identity: "'Being West Indian matters?' Ian asked. 'Not anymore [Fire replies]. But I must admit that it used to. [. . .] being West Indian isn't so critical to me anymore. Today everybody has to step outside themselves and learn about other people, other ways of thinking.'"[127] Fire reinvents an unrestrained, unpretentious register of ethnic identity with a programmatic narrative:

You make ice cream and drinks with peanut butter, but you never put it on bread with jelly [...] You think steak is a waste of good meat; you would rather cut it up and stew it with potatoes or curry it and have roti [...] You wash and rinse plastic utensils and cups that can be used again [...] You say "tree" and "ting" instead of "three" and "thing" [...] You point with your lips.[128]

Besides landscape and the colonial and pre-colonial heritage, food becomes an essential marker of West Indianness. Fire's choice of food and his culinary procedures prove him a cosmopolitan. He usually serves transnational tastes of Middle Eastern and West Indian food, cooks a vegetarian rice pilaf in London, with eggplant tossed in olive oil and a vegetable stock seasoned with onions, garlic, cinnamon and allspice.[129] He spreads a blanket in the garden for Sylvia and makes a Trinidadian *buljol*, a salt cod in thyme, olive oil and garlic as a healthy breakfast, with diced tomatoes, onions, baked unleavened bread, avocado slices, feta cheese, and water with sugar and crushed ice. In his Kingston home Fire makes fried fish "in coconut oil, then stewed them with tomatoes and allspice while boiling rice and making a salad of avocados, cucumbers, carrots, and watercress" and eats it with Ian.[130] Usually, his art of cooking is intended to stimulate an atmosphere of understanding and cordiality, or to inflame a love relationship. Supplying food and cooking are one of Fire's favorite activities. But they are also undermining the female role of the Black mother as a kitchen dweller.

Gender and migrating sexualities

Fire expresses his love for Sylvia, based on an imaginary construct of a West Indian female. But Sylvia's ardent desire for her Jamaican homeland is determined by an urbanized detachment from her national belonging: she has already long been Americanized. Both lives' experiences, that of the metropolitan diaspora and the more or less unfamiliar of her homeland, seem to exclude each other rather than be complementary. Thus, Fire's character-study is rather nebulous: "She's not big-headed about being smart . . . and with all that she is, at her core she's really a cool West Indian girl."[131] Fire expects her also mentally and emotionally to be of West Indian descent and strongly wishes for her to come and live with him in Jamaica. But her own desire to be a *Jamaican* woman author—expressed in her poem *Exile*—is contradicted by her estrangement from home and her native culture (as Fire discovers the lack of contemporary and Caribbean literature in her library). But in spite of his love confession, which does not include a respect for her writing talent, he maintains that he "won't be waiting in vain" for Sylvia[132]—with an allusion to Bob Marley's line "I don't wanna wait in vain for your love" (from his song *Waiting in Vain*), which sheds a light on their unequal love positions: Fire's women are always waiting in vain for him.[133]

Channer's gender images present a female authorship which is regarded as distinctly inferior to the male one; as a woman, she suffers heavily from a general social and sexual discrimination by males, irrespective of their color. Sylvia lacks the freedom to travel and to walk in town that Fire enjoys. In spite of her successful career as a magazine editor and a writer, being a "black woman over thirty, a member of the demographic group that was least likely to be married"[134] she is given no other choice but total subordination to the male world. Instead of being acknowledged as a creative writer by men, she gets deeply insulted when they compare women like her with a "word processor."[135] Her deranged and confounded writing process resonates with her disrupted inner self: "'I've rewritten my novel so many times. It's gone from serious fiction to mystery, then back to serious fiction, then somehow it became a thriller one time . . . and now I think it's a contemporary romance. You know what? I really don't know what the fuck it's about. I don't even know what *I'm* about.'"[136] Just as her exile from her homeland has been the consequence of the bitter devastation of her Jamaican family and her own harassment, her traveling or roving across the literary genres expresses frustration rather than creativity. She wants to write a love story, set in her alien Jamaica, which will never be finished. Writing becomes a way of, or a replacement for, traveling. She writes (in her poem *Exile*) about her futile desire for the tropics and her home—a place of her birth and early childhood, which she has lost any memory of, and which she is not supposed to experience as "home" again.

In contrast to the (upper-middle class) mobility of men, female traveling is subjected to male prejudices, suffering much more from gender confinements: "Often, men are cast in the role of travelers; women are deemed to be passive residents by nature."[137] Sylvia's migration to New York was determined by her mother's will and by poverty, violation, rape and the loss of her childhood. And the loss of her parents eliminates any reason to return. Sylvia's short biographical data conceal what she has suffered—her "homeland" Kingston has become a place of no return. The process of her "Americanization" has doubly exiled her: alienated as a black woman in New York, and separated her from home and family in Jamaica. After he has met her, Fire cannot exactly define her ethnic identity, but offers a lot of choices instead: "On her looks she could be many things"—which she actually is not (in opposition to Fire who has multi-racial features). "Latina. North African. Native American," and he even conjectures "East Indian." Sylvia sees herself "a spoilt New Yorker," although "I don't feel like I belong here."[138]

Lovemaking is represented as a sexualized form of traveling. For Sylvia, Fire "was more than a giver of pleasure. He was a giver of life."[139] Fire's fingers and tongue travel over and map the space of the female body as a space of male supremacy reflecting/highlighting his own virile muscular body. While the male subject is defined by his compelling self-styled towering masculinity donating sexual vitality and desires to females, Sylvia is required to submissively embrace it and to succumb to male rules of sexuality; for that purpose she is expected—though already being "Americanized"—to fully embroil herself in the magic of an Afro-Caribbean carnival figure: "Now you must ride to meet your dragon [. . .] you must slay the dragon."[140] The carnival image is turned into an image of female submission. When relations with women are fading, Fire imposes on himself celibacy and sexual abstinence (from Blanche, from Sylvia), which signals male supremacy and his power to regulate and organize or curb their love relationships by distance of space and time (between Kingston, New York and London). Sylvia has always been at the mercy of men abusing her body. Having freed herself from the sexual harassments of her uncle by killing him, she has entered into a state of constantly being dominated by lovers. Fire is the woman-whisperer (which is not a far cry from the violent womanizer Ian), who dreams the male dream of a female sexual subconscious and obedience to his persuasive power. His actions echo the author's view of the relationship between Jamaican men and women in a male dominated culture: "Jamaican women have a way of making their men feel like princes. That is something on the order of magic, they take the sexual satisfaction of their men as something of a royal charter." In this interview by Settimana, Channer conceives of his discursive interplay between eroticism and pornography as a natural issue of the indigenous reggae culture, from which he claims to have achieved his narrative criteria:

> I am very much influenced by reggae. And in the world of reggae there is no crisis in being popular and artistic at the same time. Reggae worked out a way to create a kind of narrative art that was simultaneously sensual, political and of the spirit. [. . .] It means that I am a writer of real ambition who presumes that his characters are going to fuck or make love and that the readers will find it interesting if there is proper motivation and if the fucking or love making is presented in a fresh, original way in language.[141]

This quotation does not take issue with the frivolous and male dominated usage of a sexualized language that, under the pretense of artistic representation, serves to disparage women and leaves them with no other role than that of subjection. In these cases, but not throughout the book, the author-narrator obviously seems to expose himself to populist opinions of a commercialized permissiveness and sexism, harking back to West Indian (male) values of a distorted reggae culture. Concessions like these might make it more likely to be embraced by the metropolitan publishing industry.

Like the author as the self-styled "high priest of love," his protagonist fashions himself as the troubadour wanderer, whose "women" are at the mercy of his male sex appeal. And when love dies, Fire leaves the location for another place and love. Travel and migration are not conducive to love relationships. Or they are simulated by modern techniques of a transmission of desires and consummation by telephone calls. The burlesque scene of Fire's phone sex with Sylvia[142] reverses the sex industry's commercial service and gender positions. They both make it a game between London and New York, performing virtual presence and immediate satisfaction of sexual desires—rather more hers than his. Fire only gives directions and encouragements to spur her libido, while Sylvia comments on the progress of their sexual intercourse leading towards *her* orgasm—simultaneously feigning and performing it in terms of the common understanding: "An orgasm, at its core, is a mind thing."[143] Fire promises to change his imaginary presence into a real one, and magically turns up the next day in person, to "really" meet her in New York. Fire's gender game of manipulating female sexuality and male presence/absence confuses the "here" and "there," the "now" and "then," the "virtual" and the "real," fact and make-believe; it simulates simultaneous presence in two global cities, playing omnipresence and dominance, and pitting space against time. Migrating sexualities and traveling gender relations result in a male-preoccupied culture of travel.

Coda

Waiting in Vain delineates migratory experiences and diasporic cultural ethnicities, represented by a Jamaican-American protagonist in a "new ethnic novel" that challenges traditional patterns of immigrant narrative and "essentialist" identities.

The West Indian-American cohort of travelers and dwellers in New York City constitutes a heterogeneous and multi-racial cosmopolitan diaspora of elitist intellectual and literary exiles. Their diasporic behavior deconstructs representations of cohesive ethnic urban neighborhoods. Idealized concepts of community life and imaginary homelands in metropolitan centers during the post-independence period are challenged. Stuart Hall refers to the diaspora as a scattered and dispersed people who can neither return to their home nor easily settle down in their exile.[144] The postcolonial West Indian discourse of traveling and writing subverts the myths of "the Euro-American modernist trope of exile," its "romanticizations of the metropolitan experience" during the large wave of expatriation of American intellectuals after the First World War.[145]

Channer conceptualizes "travel as culture" and "culture as travel." Traveling between the Caribbean home and the North American and British metropolises, or dwelling at either place for some time, becomes the migrating male subject's main purpose, and a prerogative of upper-middle class intellectual sections in Caribbean diasporas.

Waiting in Vain posits a privileged metropolitan vantage point of a West Indian-American diaspora making frequent roundtrips between the "First" and the "Third World" and using their homeland as a cheap and attractive permanent or intermediate residence, irrespective of the duration of the stay. The Jamaican-born narrator negotiates transnational traveling and island nativity.

But the novel also feeds the late twentieth's century postcolonial character's illusion of independence and freedom, when Fire fashions himself as the new self-confident "black man" on "that island," who "waited for scraps at no one's table. He was no one's scapegoat. No man's Sambo."[146]

There is a postcolonial shift from the modernist expatriation and exiles to the postmodern cosmopolitan diasporas that spatializes Caribbean migration as a transnational practice: the "culture of travel" as a late twentieth century phenomenon. From an ethnographical point of view, James Clifford reverses bourgeois—scientific, anthropological, commercial, aesthetic—"Traveling Cultures" and questions rigid European-American notions of traveling by positioning "culture *as* travel." He exerts a complex cultural studies approach to "everyday practices of dwelling *and* traveling: traveling-in-dwelling, dwelling-in-traveling"; the great urban centers are to be understood as specific powerful sites of "stories of dwelling-in-traveling."[147]

Caribbean migrant groups are conceived of as multi-racial configurations of a West- and East Indian-American, African American and Italian American community in New York. The narrative discourse of nomadism captures an exceptional diasporic world, in which essentialist concepts of race, ethnicity, nation and home are made negligible by frequently changing space relations and cross-cultural connections between the two worlds.

Channer's nomad is a pedestrian. By walking through many different locations, Fire creates an urban fabric of New York City and a meaning between the activity of walking and its signifying practice. The peripatetic discourse emphasizes the *enunciative* function of walking. Fire is constantly transgressing temporal, special, ethnical, cultural, social and diasporic boundaries between West Indian local habitations in Brooklyn and postmodern skyrocketing Manhattan.

Fire's pedestrian activities mark him out as a spectator and explorer in the city, whose walking activities create a path to reading streets and places as an urban text. In a way, this makes him a cultural descendant of the aesthetic *flâneurs* of European literary modernity like James Joyce (Leopold Bloom in *Ulysses*) and Walter Benjamin in the early twentieth century; Fire has become a postmodern walking writer in the late twentieth century's North American global city.

Normally, he would be a stranger in the postmodern metropolitan American world: the walker is out of space! But walking in New York keeps the body *in* space. Thus we may, with David Macauley, ask whether walking subjects are "post-ambling" today, that is, "wandering away from walking and drifting toward a post-ambling society?" In Channer's text we observe a linkage between walking, the city and the text: "the convergence, collaboration, and confluence of the body, mind, and place."[148] This makes up the richness of the character: his walking activities are closely interrelated with metropolitan culture and topography.

Notes

* I am deeply indebted to the Research Institute of Literary and Cultural Studies in Berlin, and the support by its director Sigrid Weigel, for working on this project of West Indian migration to New York City within the research group "New York's 'Other' Modernities: Urban Spaces as Contact Zones of Cultural Translation" between 2001 and 2005, subsidized by the *Deutsche Forschungsgemeinschaft (DFG)*. The project was headed by Günter H. Lenz, Humboldt University (Berlin), who encouraged me and has given me many valuable suggestions to write this text. I also want to thank Colin McCabe (Glasgow) very much for the close reading and his corrections of my text. A short version of this chapter was delivered at the conference "City Life in Caribbean History: Celebrating Bridgetown" at the University of the West Indies, Cave Hill Campus, Barbados, in December 2003. Finally, I am grateful for the permission to quote materials from *Waiting in Vain* by Colin Channer, copyright © 1998 by Colin Channer. Used by permission of Ballantine Books, a division of Random House, Inc.

1. See Colin Channer, *Waiting in Vain* (New York: One World / The Ballantine Group, 1998), 3.
2. Channer, *Waiting in Vain*, 5.
3. Channer, *Waiting in Vain*, 27.
4. Channer, *Waiting in Vain*, 107.
5. Born in Kingston, Jamaica, in 1963, Colin Channer came to New York in 1982 at the age of eighteen. Having worked as a journalist for some time, he became interested in writing fiction about young intellectuals migrating from the Caribbean to New York City. Although he has been living most of the time—and, as a naturalized American, considers himself to be based—in Brooklyn, New York, he remains fundamentally grounded in Jamaica. And since leaving, he has maintained strong ties to his homeland, where he has become the founder and artistic director of the annual Calabash International Literary Festival. Besides *Waiting in Vain*, Channer has written short fiction and two other novels: the novella *I'm Still Waiting*, published in *Got to Be Real* (2000), *Satisfy My Soul* (2002), *Passing Through* (2004), and *Iron Balloons: Hit Fiction from Jamaica's Calabash Writers' Workshop* (2006). Cf. http://aalbc.com/authors/colin.htm (accessed December 11, 2006).
6. Mary C. Waters, *Black Identities. West Indian Immigrant Dreams and American Realities* (New York: Russell Sage Foundation; Cambridge, Mass., and London: Harvard University Press, 2001), 90.
7. Ransford W. Palmer, *Pilgrims from the Sun. West Indian Migration to America* (New York and London: Twayne Publishers, 1995).
8. Anne D. Wallace, *Walking, Literature, and English Culture: The Origins and Uses of Peripatetic in the Nineteenth Century* (Oxford: Clarendon Press, 1993), deals with walking as a "historical construct," with its origins in Wordsworth's poetry, maintaining that "transport revolution" (from coach- to train-travel) made walking respectable, culturally meaningful, and "peripatetic" as a socially cultivating and individually renovating labor.
9. Cf. Steve Pile and Nigel Thrift, *Mapping the Subject. Geographies of Cultural Transformation* (New York: Routledge, 1995), 19.
10. Günter H. Lenz, "New EthniCities: Recodifying Urban Spaces and Intercultural Translation in New York Fictions of the 1990s," in *CinematoGraphies. Fictional*

Strategies and Visual Discourses in 1990s New York City, ed. Günter H. Lenz, Dorothea Löbbermann, and Karl-Heinz Magister (Heidelberg: Universitätsverlag Winter, 2006), 254.

11. Cf. Waters, *Black Identities*, 15-43.
12. Heather Hathaway, *Caribbean Waves. Relocating Claude McKay and Paule Marshall* (Bloomington and Indianapolis: Indiana University Press, 1999), 12-13.
13. Sandra Pouchet Paquet, *Caribbean Autobiography: Cultural Identity and Self-Representation* (Madison: University of Wisconsin Press, 2002), 100, 78, 88.
14. Raimund Schaeffner, "'At times, home is nowhere': Migrancy in Caryl Phillips's *The Final Passage* and *A State of Independence*," *Journal of Caribbean Studies* 17, no. 1 and 2 (Summer and Fall 2002): 14.
15. Hathaway, *Caribbean Waves*, 87f.
16. Paquet, *Caribbean Autobiography*, 77.
17. Simon Gikandi, *Writing in Limbo. Modernism and Caribbean Literature* (Ithaca, N.Y., and London: Cornell University Press, 1992), 33.
18. Quoted by Gikandi, *Writing in Limbo*, 34.
19. Schaeffner, "At times, home is nowhere," 16.
20. Belinda Edmondson, "Jamaica Kincaid and the Genealogy of Exile," *Small Axe* 5 (March 1999): 76.
21. Edmondson, "Jamaica Kincaid," 79.
22. Hathaway, *Caribbean Waves*, 145.
23. See Hugo of St. Victor, *Didafcalicon*, Liber Tertius, Caput XIX, quoted in Aamir R. Mufti, "Auerbach in Istanbul: Edward Said, Secular Criticism, and the Question of Minority Culture," *Critical Inquiry* 25 (Autumn 1998): 97f.
24. Karen Kaplan, *Question of Travel: Postmodern Discourse of Displacement* (Durham, N.C.: Duke University Press, 1996), 49, 41.
25. Colin Channer: "America's fascination with racial purity is too much of an easy target to ignore. I create multiracial characters to take people out of their comfort zones. Black people don't always act like black people. White people don't always act like white people. [. . .] Caribbean people accept the fact of racial mixing. The national motto of Jamaica is, 'Out of many, one people'." http://aalbc.com/authors/colin.htm.
26. Channer, *Waiting in Vain*, 194.
27. Channer, *Waiting in Vain*, 26.
28. Kaplan, *Questions of Travel*, 107.
29. Channer, *Waiting in Vain*, 320.
30. Channer, *Waiting in Vain*, 37-38.
31. Channer, *Waiting in Vain*, 136-137.
32. Channer, *Waiting in Vain*, 138.
33. Channer, *Waiting in Vain*, 237.
34. Channer, *Waiting in Vain*, 138.
35. Channer, *Waiting in Vain*, 106.
36. Channer, *Waiting in Vain*, 143.
37. Channer, *Waiting in Vain*, 145.
38. Cf. Patricia Mohammed, "The Emergence of Caribbean Iconography," in *New Caribbean Thought. A Reader*, ed. Brian Meeks and Folke Lindahl (Jamaica, Barbados, Trinidad and Tobago: University of the West Indies Press, 2001), 236.
39. Channer, *Waiting in Vain*, 238.
40. Channer, *Waiting in Vain*, 132.
41. James Clifford, "Traveling Cultures," in *Cultural Studies*, ed. Lawrence Grossberg, Cary Nelson, and Paula Treichler (New York: Routledge, 1992), 107.

42. Channer, *Waiting in Vain*, 63.
43. Gary E. Holcomb, "The Persistence of Nomadism and the Matrilineal Link: Shiva Naipaul's Right to Travel," *Journal of Caribbean Studies* 13, no. 1 nd 2 (Summer and Fall, 1998): 38.
44. Paquet, *Caribbean Autobiography*, 79.
45. Hoving, *Praise of New Travelers*, 37.
46. Cf. Hoving, *Praise of New Travelers*, 32.
47. Cf. "nomadic subjectivity" by Deleuze and Guattari with Carole Boyce Davies' notion of a Black female "migratory subjectivity," in *Black Women, Writing and Identity. Migration of the Subject* (London and New York: Routledge, 1994).
48. Ian Buchanan, *Deleuzism. A Metacommentary* (Durham, N.C.: Duke University Press, 1985), 71.
49. Kaplan, *Questions of Travel*, 92.
50. May Joseph, *Nomadic Identities. The Performance of Citizenship* (Minneapolis: University of Minnesota Press, 1999), 2, 9.
51. Joseph, *Nomadic Identities*, 17.
52. Tim Cresswell, "Imagining the Nomad: Mobility and the Postmodern Primitive," in *Space and Social Theory. Interpreting Modernism and Postmodernism*, ed. Ulf Benko and George Strohmayer (Oxford: Blackwell Publishers, 1997), 362.
53. Kaplan, *Questions of Travel*, 89, 90, 92.
54. Gilles Deleuze and Félix Guattari, *Nomadology: the War Machine* (New York: Semiotext(e), 1986), 365-366.
55. Channer, *Waiting in Vain*, 5.
56. Channer, *Waiting in Vain*, 13.
57. Cf. James Clifford, *Routes: Travel and Translation in the Late Twentieth Century* (Cambridge, Mass.: Harvard University Press, 1997), 24-29.
58. Claude McKay, *Home to Harlem* (New York: Harper & Brothers, 1928), 25f.
59. Peter Marcuse and Ronald van Kempen, *Globalizing Cities: A New Spatial Order?* (Oxford: Blackwell, 2000), 3.
60 Nancy Foner ed., *Islands in the City* (Berkeley, Los Angeles, and London: University of California Press, 2001).
61. Paule Marshall, *Daughters* (New York: Plume; London: Penguin Books, 1992), 51-52.
62. Paul Auster, "City of Glass," in *New York Trilogy* (New York and London: Penguin Group, 1987), 94.
63. Auster, "City of Glass," 75: "To be Auster meant being a man with no interior, a man with no thoughts."
64. Auster, "City of Glass," 3-4.
65. Channer, *Waiting in Vain*, 57, 59.
66. Benjamin Rossiter and Katherine Gibson, "Walking and Performing in 'the City': A Melbourne Chronicle," in *Companion to the City*, ed. Gary Bridge and Sophie Watson (Oxford, and Malden, Mass.: Blackwell Publishers, 2000), 439.
67. Cf. Sharon Zukin: "On the streets, the vernacular culture of the powerless provides a currency of economic exchange and a language of social survival. In other public places—grand plazas, waterfronts, and shopping streets reorganized by business improvement districts—another landscape incorporates vernacular culture or opposes it with its own image of identity and desire." In *The Cultures of Cities* (Oxford: Blackwell Publishers, 1995), 46.

68. Sharon Zukin, "Space and Symbols in an Age of Decline," in *Re-Presenting the City: Ethnicity, Capital and Culture in the Twenty-First-Century Metropolis*, ed. Anthony D. King (London: Macmillan, 1996), 56.

69. Zukin, "Space and Symbols in an Age of Decline," 56.

70. The image of the "hotel chronotope," first used by Mikhail Bahktin, suggests "relevant sites of cultural encounter and imagination," or an "older form of gentlemanly Occidental travel;" see James Clifford, "Traveling Cultures," 96, 105.

71. Channer, *Waiting in Vain*, 49.

72. Channer, *Waiting in Vain*, 123.

73. Channer, *Waiting in Vain*, 174.

74. Stuart Hall, "Negotiating Caribbean Identities," in *New Caribbean Thought*, 35.

75. Channer, *Waiting in Vain*, 140-141.

76. Channer, *Waiting in Vain*, 59.

77. Hall, "Negotiating Caribbean Identities," 34.

78. Channer, *Waiting in Vain*, 229.

79. Auster, "City of Glas," 4.

80. David Macauley, "Walking the Urban Environment: Pedestrian Practices and Peripatetic Politics," in *Transformations of Urban and Suburban Landscapes: Perspectives from Philosophy, Geography, and Architecture*, ed. Gary Backhaus and John Murungi (Lanham, Md, and Oxford: Lexington Books, 2002), 213.

81. I owe this reference to Bob Marley's song "No Woman, No Cry" to Holger Henke's considerations about West Indian walking in the Summer of 2004.

82. Michael Stone (Princeton University) made this suggestion of the runaway slaves after emancipation.

83. Channer, *Waiting in Vain*, 185.

84. Channer, *Waiting in Vain*, 118.

85. Michel de Certeau, *The Practice of Everyday Life*, trans. Steven Rendall (Berkeley: University of California Press, 1984), 363.

86. Cf. Dorothea Löbbermann, "Productions of Ethnic Space: Tourism's Narrations," in *Postmodern New York City. Transfiguring Spaces—Raum-Transformationen*, ed. Günter H. Lenz and Utz Riese (Heidelberg: Universitätsverlag Winter, 2003), 57.—I would like to thank Dorothea Löbbermann very much for her close reading and for her many valuable suggestions and corrections in the text.

87. Cf. Macauley: "Pedestrian Practices and Peripatetic Politics": "the car degrades the pedestrian to a threatened second-class citizen" and produces a "diminished status of peripatetic life in the United States," 201.

88. Pogrebin, Robin, "Visions of Manhattan: For the City, 100-year Makeover," *New York Times*, November 4, 2006, sec. B, p. 7, vol. 6.

89. de Certeau, "Walking in the City," 97, 105.

90. de Certeau, "Walking in the City," 99, 105.

91. 91. Cf. A. R. Ammons, "A Poem is a Walk," quoted in David Macauley, "Pedestrian Practices and Peripatetic Politics," 217.

92 de Certeau, "Walking in the City," 101.

93 See William Shakespeare, *A Midsummer Night's Dream*, V, 1, 12-17 (Cambridge: Cambridge University Press, 1984), 116.

94. Channer uses Shakespearean phraseology, underscoring Fire's privileged position as a West Indian-American urban observer, cf. *Waiting in Vain*, 230: "With his poet's eye, he saw in this a metaphor: life is a game of luck. Some people are pawns and some are kings."

95. Channer, *Waiting in Vain*, 172.
96. Sally Westwood and John Williams, eds., *Imagining Cities. Scripts, Signs, Memory* (London: Routledge, 1996), 6.
97. Hoving, *In Praise of New Travelers*, 123.
98. Channer, *Waiting in Vain*, 282.
99. Channer, *Waiting in Vain*, 128.
100. Channer, *Waiting in Vain*, 86.
101. Channer, *Waiting in Vain*, 128.
102. Channer, *Waiting in Vain*, 79.
103. Channer, *Waiting in Vain*, 243.
104. Cf. Karl-Heinz Magister, "Trans-Caribbean CinematoGraphic Narratives in Jamaican Urban Diasporas," in *CinematoGraphies. Fictional Strategies and Visual Discourses in 1990s New York City*, ed. Günter H. Lenz, Dorothea Löbbermann and Karl-Heinz Magister (Heidelberg: Universitätsverlag Winter, 2006), 191-218.
105. The so-called X-Press novels offer a severe criticism of an authoritarian and racist London Metropolitan Police Force, which has been shaped by the media and the political administration. Both novels speak to the British-born generation of Jamaicans who retain strong ties to their Caribbean homeland. *Cop Killers* includes a detailed description of Brixton as the black capital of Europe with a global view of diasporic locations. Cf. Loretta Collins (2001), "Raggamuffin Cultural Studies: X-Press Novels' Yardies and Cop Killers Put Britain on Trial," *Small Axe* 9 (March 2001): 70-96.
106. About cinematic representations of ethnic strife with other ethnic minorities, say, with Jewish residents of Brooklyn in Marc Levin's film *Brooklyn Babylon* (2000), cf. Holger Henke, "Brooklyn Babylon: The Reproduction, Reinvention, and Consumption of Cosmological and Epistemological Space in New York City," in *CinematoGraphies. Fictional Strategies and Visual Discourses in 1990s New York City*, ed. Günter H. Lenz, Dorothea Löbbermann, and Karl-Heinz Magister (Heidelberg: Universitätsverlag Winter, 2006), 161-189.
107. Cf. Manfred Osten, *"Alles veloziferisch" oder Goethes Entdeckung der Langsamkeit. Zur Modernität eines Klassikers im 21. Jahrhundert* (Frankfurt am Main: Insel Verlag, 2003).
108. Channer, *Waiting in Vain*, 96.
109. Channer, *Waiting in Vain*, 49.
110. Channer, *Waiting in Vain*, 138.
111. Channer, *Waiting in Vain*, 209-210.
112. Channer, *Waiting in Vain*, 209.
113. Channer, *Waiting in Vain*, 207.
114. Channer, *Waiting in Vain*, 209, 173.
115. See Nancy Foner, *From Ellis Island to JFK*, 150: "The term West Indian refers here to people of African descent from the English-speaking Caribbean [. . .]. I do not include the growing number of Trinidadian and Guyanese immigrants of East Indian descent, whose ancestors were brought to the Caribbean as indentured laborers to replace slaves after emancipation. East Indians [. . .] typically attempt to establish an Asian identity in New York as a way to avoid being labeled black."
116. Channer, *Waiting in Vain*, 207.
117. I owe these revealing comments on the barriers to walking in the city of Kingston to a talk with Nadi Edwards in December 2003 at the University of the West Indies, Mona (Kingston, Jamaica).

118. Joyce Pettis, *Toward Wholeness in Paule Marshall's Fiction* (Charlottesville and London: University of Virginia, 1995), 38.
119. Channer, *Waiting in Vain*, 213.
120. Channer, *Waiting in Vain*, 6.
121. Hoving, *In Praise of New Travelers*, 37.
122. Channer, *Waiting in Vain*, 253.
123. Channer, *Waiting in Vain*, 145.
124. Channer, *Waiting in Vain*, 144f.
125. Channer, *Waiting in Vain*, 146.
126. See Faith Louis Smith, "You Know You're West Indian if . . .': Codes of Authenticity in Colin Channer's *Waiting in Vain*," *Small Axe* 10, vol. 5, no. 2 (Sept. 2002): 56. I owe numerous important suggestions to this brilliant article, as well as to a talk by Faith Smith at the MLA convention in New Orleans in December 2001.
127. Channer, *Waiting in Vain*, 252.
128. Channer, *Waiting in Vain*, 213.
129. Channer, *Waiting in Vain*, 79-80.
130. Channer, *Waiting in Vain*, 244.
131. Channer, *Waiting in Vain*, 252.
132. Channer, *Waiting in Vain*, 250.
133. Channer's devotion to Marley is made a point of with the novel's title, which is taken from his song "Waiting in Vain." Fire uses the phrase in the same sense: he does not want to wait in vain for his love.
134. Channer, *Waiting in Vain*, 165.
135. Channer, *Waiting in Vain*, cf. 30, 33, 50.
136. Channer, *Waiting in Vain*, 145.
137. Hoving, *In Praise of New Travelers*, 4.
138. Channer, *Waiting in Vain*, 130.
139. Channer, *Waiting in Vain*, 65.
140. Channer, *Waiting in Vain*, 156-157.
141. Helena Settimana, "The High Priest of Love." An Interview with Colin Channer, July 12, 2004 (http://www.erotica-readers.com/ERA/SL-ColinChanner.htm).
142. Channer, *Waiting in Vain*, cf. 98-101.
143. Channer, *Waiting in Vain*, 103.
144. "They are people who belong to more than one world, speak more than one language (literally and metaphorically); inhabit more than one identity, have more than one home; who have learned to 'negotiate and translate' between cultures and who [. . .] have learned to live with, and to speak from difference. They speak from the in-between of different cultures, always unsettling the assumptions of one culture from the perspective of another, and thus finding ways of being both the same as and different from the others amongst which they live. [. . .] They represent new kinds of identities—new ways of 'being someone' in the late modern world." Stuart Hall, "New Cultures for Old," in *A Place in the World: Places, Culture and Globalization*, ed. Doreen Massey and Pat Jess (Oxford: Oxford University Press, 1995), 77-78.
145. Kaplan, *Questions of Travel*, 29, 31.
146. Channer, *Waiting in Vain*, 77.
147. Clifford, Traveling Cultures, 103, 108.
148. Macauley, Practices and Peripatetic Politics, 197-199, 219.

Bibliography

Auster, Paul. *"City of Glass." The New York Trilogy.* New York: Penguin Books, 1987.

Buchanan, Ian. *Deleuzism. A Metacommentary.* Durham, N.C.: Duke University Press, 2000.

Certeau, Michel de. "Walking in the City." Pp. 91-110 in *The Practice of Everyday Life,* translated by Steven Rendall. Berkeley: University of California Press, 1984.

Clifford, James. *Routes: Travel and Translation in the Late Twentieth Century.* Cambridge, Mass.: Harvard University Press, 1997.

———. "Traveling Cultures." Pp. 96-116 in *Cultural Studies,* edited by Lawrence Grossberg, Cary Nelson, and Paula Treichler. New York: Routledge, 1992.

Collins, Loretta. "Raggamuffin Cultural Studies: X-Press Novels' Yardies and Cop Killers Put Britain on Trial." *Small Axe* 9 (March 2001): 70-96.

Cresswell, Tim. "Imagining the Nomad: Mobility and the Postmodern Primitive." Pp. 360-382 in *Space and Social Theory. Interpreting Modernism and Postmodernism,* edited by Ulf Benko and George Strohmayer. Oxford: Blackwell Publishers, 1997.

Davis, Carole Boyce. *Black Women, Writing, and Identity: Migrations of the Subject.* London: Routledge, 1994.

Deleuze, Gilles, and Félix Guattari. *Nomadology. The War Machine.* Translated by Brian Massumi. New York: Semiotext(e), 1986.

Edmondson, Belinda. "Jamaica Kincaid and the Genealogy of Exile." *Small Axe* 5 (March 1999): 72-79.

———. "Public Spectacles: Caribbean Women and the Politics of Public Performance." *Small Axe* 13 (March 2003): 1-16.

Foner, Nancy, *From Ellis Island to JFK. New York's Two Great Waves of Immigration.* New Haven, Conn., and London: Yale University Press; New York: Russell Sage Foundation, 2000.

———. ed. *Islands in the City. West Indian Migration to New York.* Berkeley, Los Angeles, and London: University of California Press, 2001.

Gikandi, Simon. *Writing in Limbo. Modernism and Caribbean Literature.* Ithaca, N.Y., and London: Cornell University Press, 1992.

Hall, Stuart. "Negotiating Caribbean Identities." Pp. 24-39 in *New Caribbean Thought. A Reader,* edited by Brian Meeks and Folke Lindahl. Kingston, Jamaica: University of the West Indies Press, 2001.

Hathaway, Heather. *Caribbean Waves. Relocating Claude McKay and Paule Marshall.* Bloomington and Indianapolis: Indiana University Press, 1999.

Henke, Holger. "Brooklyn Babylon: The Reproduction, Reinvention, and Consumption of Cosmological and Epistemological Space in New York City." Pp. 161-189 in *CinematoGraphies. Fictional Strategies and Visual Discourses in 1990s New York City,* edited by Günter H. Lenz, Dorothea Löbbermann, and Karl-Heinz Magister. Heidelberg: Universitätsverlag Winter, 2006.

Holcomb, Gary E. "The Persistence of Nomadism and the Matrilineal Link: Shiva Naipaul's Right to Write Travel." *Journal of Caribbean Studies* 13, no. 1 and 2 (Summer and Fall 1998): 35-57.

Hoving, Isabel. *In Praise of New Travelers. Reading Caribbean Migrant Women Writers.* Stanford: California University Press, 2001.

Joseph, May. *Nomadic Identities. The Performance of Citizenship.* Minneapolis: University of Minnesota Press, 1999.

Kaplan, Caren. *Questions of Travel: Postmodern Discourse of Displacement*. Durham: Duke University Press, 1996.

Karlene, "Interview with Colin Channer." *Jamaicans.com*. http://www.jamaicans.com/articles/0203_colin_channer.htm (accessed March 15, 2006).

Lenz, Günter H. "New EthniCities: Recodifying Urban Spaces and Intercultural Translation in New York Fictions of the 1990s." Pp. 241-270 in *CinematoGraphies: Fictional Strategies and Visual Discourses in 1990s New York City*, edited by Günter H. Lenz, Dorothea Löbbermann, and Karl-Heinz Magister. Heidelberg: Universitätsverlag Winter, 2006.

Löbbermann, Dorothea. "Productions of Ethnic Space: Tourism's Narrations." Pp. 111-136 in *Postmodern New York City: Transfiguring Spaces—Raum-Transformationen*, edited by Günter H. Lenz and Utz Riese. Heidelberg: Universitätsverlag Winter, 2003.

Macauley, David. "Walking the Urban Environment: Pedestrian Practices and Peripatetic Politics." Pp. 193-226 in *Transformations of Urban and Suburban Landscapes: Perspectives from Philosophy, Geography, and Architecture*, edited by Gary Backhaus and John Murungi. Lanham, Md, and Oxford: Lexington Books, 2002.

Magister, Karl-Heinz. "Trans-Caribbean CinematoGraphic Narratives in Jamaican Urban Diasporas." Pp. 191-218 in *CinematoGraphies: Fictional Strategies and Visual Discourses in 1990s New York City*, edited by Günter H. Lenz, Dorothea Löbbermann, and Karl-Heinz Magister. Heidelberg: Universitätsverlag Winter, 2006.

Marcuse, Peter, and Ronald van Kempen, eds. *Globalizing Cities: A New Spatial Order?* Oxford: Blackwell, 2000.

Marshall, Paule. *Daughters*. New York: Plume; London: Penguin Books, 1992.

McKay, Claude. *Home to Harlem*. New York: Harper & Brothers, 1928.

Mohammed, Patricia. "The Emergence of a Caribbean Iconography." Pp. 232-266 in *New Caribbean Thought. A Reader*, edited by Brian Meeks and Folke Lindahl. Kingston, Jamaica: University of the West Indies Press, 2001.

Mufti, Aamir R. "Auerbach in Istanbul: Edward Said, Secular Criticism, and the Question of Minority Culture." *Critical Inquiry* 25 (Autumn 1998): 95-125.

Osten, Manfred. *"Alles veloziferisch" oder Goethes Entdeckung der Langsamkeit. Zur Modernität eines Klassikers im 21. Jahrhundert*. Frankfurt am Main: Insel Verlag, 2003.

Palmer, Ransford W. *Pilgrims from the Sun. West Indian Migration to America*. New York and London: Twayne Publishers, 1995.

Pettis, Joyce. *Toward Wholeness in Paule Marshall's Fiction*. Charlottesville and London: University of Virginia, 1995.

Pile, Steve, and Nigel Thrift, eds. *Mapping the Subject. Geographies of Cultural Transformation*. New York: Routledge, 1995.

Pouchet Paquet, Sandra. *Caribbean Autobiography. Cultural Identity and Self-Representation*. Madison: University of Wisconsin Press, 2002.

Rossiter, Benjamin, and Katherine Gibson. "Walking and Performing in 'the City': A Melbourne Chronicle." Pp. 437-447 in *Companion to the City*, edited by Gary Bridge and Sophie Watson. Oxford, and Malden, Mass.: Blackwell Publishers, 2000.

Schäffner, Raimund. "'At times, home is nowhere': Migrancy in Caryl Phillips's *The Final Passage* and *A State of Independence*." *Journal of Caribbean Studies* 17, no. 1 and 2 (Summer and Fall 2002): 13-31.

Settimana, Helena. "The High Priest of Love." An Interview with Colin Channer, July 12, 2004 (by Helena Settimana). http://www.erotica-readers.com/ERA/SL-ColinChanner.htm (accessed March 15, 2006).

Smith, Faith Louis. "'You Know You're West Indian if . . .': Codes of Authenticity in Colin Channer's *Waiting in Vain*." *Small Axe* 10, vol. 5, no. 2 (Sept. 2002): 41-59.

Stone, Maureen. *Black Women Walking. A Different Experience in World Travel*. Bournemouth: BeaGay Publications, 2002.

Wallace, Anne D. *Walking, Literature, and English Culture: The Origins and Uses of Peripatetic in the Nineteenth Century*. Oxford: Clarendon Press; New York: Oxford University Press, 1993.

Waters, Mary C. *Black Identities. West Indian Immigrant Dreams and American Realities*. New York: Russell Sage Foundation; Cambridge, Mass., and London: Harvard University Press, 2001.

Westwood, Sally, and John Williams, eds. *Imagining Cities. Scripts, Signs, Memory*. London: Routledge, 1996.

Zukin, Sharon. *The Cultures of Cities*. Malden, Mass., and Oxford: Blackwell Publishers, 1995.

———. "Space and Symbols in an Age of Decline." Pp. 43-59 in *Re-Presenting the City: Ethnicity, Capital and Culture in the Twenty-First Century Metropolis*, edited by Anthony D. King. London: Macmillan, 1996.

10

Elaine Savory

Playing Both Home and Away: National and Transnational Identities in the Work of Bruce St. John

> Fuh if Limey born in Wahkiki,
> He swear to God that 'e English;
> An' Bajan Lolita gran-chil'
> 'Cause he pulp out in England, he English.
> Bruce St. John, "Nationality," (1982, 14)

Barbadian poet Bruce St. John (1923-1995), significantly contributed to the development of respect for indigenous language and culture in Barbados from the early 1970s until the mid-1980s.[1] However, as is often the case with oral or performance poetry, his work has been little known outside the places he performed (mostly Barbados and Canada), and has rarely been performed since 1987.[2] But it is a mistake to assume that the intensely local nature of oral poetry (especially in the Caribbean, with its plethora of markedly different nation languages) means that the concerns of the poetry are parochial. This chapter considers the ways in the local (national) in St. John's work often references the transnational (whether the regional Caribbean or the Caribbean or African diaspora), or is informed by the wider world.

St. John began his work as an oral poet in his late forties in Barbados during a moment both intensely regional (following the quick dissolution of the 1958 West Indies Federation) and national (following Barbados' Independence from Britain in 1966). The Anglophone Caribbean's federal project preceded the birth of the Barbadian post-colonial nation. Then because of migration and exile, the concept of the nation in the Caribbean is generally rather complicated. "Nationality," (quoted above) makes the point that a British expatriate, if born in Hawaii, would retain his English identity whereas the grandchild of a Barbadian, born in England, would want simply to be English. This catches a moment when early Barbadian immigrants to Britain in the 1950's hoped for full integration into the "Mother Country," an expectation often thwarted by British racism and parochialism. Subsequently, as Caribbean-British writers have often demonstrated, Caribbean immigrants have developed a plural identity. Many hope to return to the Caribbean in retirement. St. John's poem however reflects the complexity of nationalism at the moment of a still powerful imperial hegemony, (wanting to acquire English nationality), which is at the same time a moment of nationalism in the Caribbean.

There is a good deal of interesting work on the formation of the nation in post colonial societies.[3] The new postcolonial nation was both a key rallying point for anti-colonial politics and chance for neo-colonial elites to continue many of the economic arrangements of colonialism under a new flag: postcolonial Caribbean politics reflect both. But its citizens were not oblivious to the wider world. As Errol Barrow, first Prime Minister of independent Barbados, pointed out in a major speech, Barbadians (and other West Indians), out of economic necessity and because of volunteering to serve in wartime, had gone out into the world and made a difference (in the British armed forces, for example, or building the Panama Canal).[4] The Barbadian nation, like many other Caribbean nations, was and is at the same time a coherent entity and an elastic space, locally made up of people at home and people "from away," returning exiles, descendants of native-born citizens, or expatriates from the Caribbean and beyond who stay to be naturalized. It is conscious of its many communities retaining national identity and culture whilst established overseas. Though each country has its own particular population and history, the common historical experience of transatlantic slavery, racism and colonialism makes the Caribbean deeply connected. There has also long been constant interaction between the local and regional in the form of intra-regional migrations and intermarriages, now being actively encouraged in the Anglophone Caribbean by the recent formal institution of a new economic common market.

The idea of regional federation of some kind has long been an important goal, because it reflects the interconnectedness of Caribbean countries (at least those relatively close to each other), through generations of migration and intermarriage. Gordon Rohlehr reminds us that it was seriously pursued from the time of the Roseau Conference of 1932, and taken to heart by most of the population, including of course writers and artists.[5] He specifically mentions several in relation to this: Derek Walcott, St. Lucia, Eric Roach, Trinidad and Tobago, and Louise Bennett, Jamaica.[6] The federal dream never died (though it receded) during the late twentieth century. But as long ago as 1958, the West Indian Federation, though short-lived, delighted those who desired Caribbean unity, and subsequently CARICOM provided an opportunity for cooperation between small nations.[7] Yet what broke up the Federation were tensions essentially between larger and smaller countries over the ways in which economic and political power was to be shared and managed. These national interests were each separately engaged in the struggle for independence from Britain.[8]

Then there are powerful diaspora connections. Ancestrally, these are predominantly African, and in the Eastern Caribbean, also significantly Asian, as well as European, for the minority of whites. European colonialism established its own cultural norms and mores as the official identity of its various Caribbean colonies. But since the middle of the twentieth century, the Anglophone Caribbean has seen huge migration to the United Kingdom, the United States, and Canada which has made another more immediate sense of diaspora, as many of those who migrated keep strong ties to home and despite having adopted other nationalities, retain a strong sense of original national identity.

Like his nation, St. John was simultaneously aware of and concerned about the local, the regional and the international. He was a cosmopolitan person who was educated in Barbados, the United Kingdom, and Canada, taught Spanish at the tertiary level and traveled whenever he could. He was trained as a conservatoire singer (in a European style), and like most Caribbean people, could speak both international English and deep Creole. When St. John started to perform his poetry (1970), the U.S. Civil Rights struggle and Black Power were issues of the day in Barbados. Importantly, it was the impact of international Black politics which made an oral poet out of St. John, specifically the visit of Trinidad born, pan-Caribbean and Black activist Stokely Carmichael (later Kwame Ture), to Barbados in 1970 (and the reaction of the Barbadian authorities to it) and the death of Martin Luther King (1968).[9] St. John wrote that it was not a close knowledge of the reasons for Carmichael's visit or his speeches which caused this, but rather that Carmichael was known to be a persuasive speaker and many West Indian governments banned him from entry. St. John felt that the banning made Carmichael far more powerful, and that he wanted to be permitted to hear the man speak, especially since he had been allowed to do so in Guyana.[10] What is clear here is the intersection of working class frustrations, Carmichael's black radicalism and the government's response of nervousness. Writing was St. John's own political response to the situation (and it was by no means a simple one).

He was nine years old at the time of the Roseau conference which began serious talks about West Indian political union, and thirty five when the West Indies Federation began. Hilary Beckles notes that it was only in 1947 at the Montego Bay, Jamaica, conference that Barbados was seriously represented, led by Grantley Adams, who was to become the first premier of the Federal Government in 1958. That government was sited in Trinidad, but after serious divisions amongst the largest participating countries, and political shifts in terms of mass support within them, Federation was formally ended in 1962.[11]

The period from the mid-1930s until the mid-1960s in Barbados saw the struggle for full adult suffrage (achieved 1950), as well as the foundation of new political parties and the ending of political domination of the country by the white plantocracy. This was the same period in which Bruce St. John grew up and matured, in a country which was highly aware of regional and international news and concerns, as well as local development and identity, because of the quality of its educational system and its press.[12]

St. John was forty-three when Barbados became an independent country in 1966, and about to find his voice as a poet. Like all Barbadians, at and after

1966, he considered what it meant to speak of Barbadian culture and language, first in the newly created independent nation, but also in the Caribbean region and the postcolonial world. There is no doubt that he felt his work contributed to the quest for national identity, nor that the nationalist movements of the Caribbean, the focal point of the struggle to end colonial rule, strongly shaped the Caribbean literature emerging in the mid-twentieth century (just as "English Literature" was strongly informed by and often served the national/imperial project).

But whilst St. John's language might be particularly local in phrasing and intonation (necessarily since he was an oral poet committed to performing in Barbadian), the political issues he raised were often transnational and generally post-imperial. He couched his vision of Barbadian language at the opening of a long biographical, cultural and critical essay in the following broad global terms: "If oppressed people are denied their own language, the ensuing difficulty of learning another language causes them to invest simple words and sounds of the imposed language with multiple meanings."[13]

Furthermore, he was aware that critical (if at the time he was writing, just becoming recognized) cultural identities within Barbados derived from the African diaspora. Barbados's population is mostly of African descent. Politician and journalist Wynter Crawford, in his memoirs, comments that its white population was historically high enough and owned enough of economic resources to make effective racial separation possible, unlike other Caribbean countries.[14] Certainly Barbados had a rigid racial hierarchy through the colonial period.

Independence meant rethinking this history of racial and economic division which resulted directly from slavery and the plantation, and as part of that, re-evaluating the role of the working class, both urban and rural. African cultural identities in Barbados were systematically erased from public acknowledgement until the work of important writers, academics and activists in the 1970s and 1980s.[15] St. John was never explicitly an activist, but nevertheless his work was importantly political and demonstrated to diasporic audiences of Barbadians and others in Canada and elsewhere his serious respect for all the diverse elements of Bajan language. As early as 1982, in her preface to St. John's collection *Bumbatuk*, Kathleen Drayton paid tribute to the significance of St. John's contribution, saying that he "records what is truly indigenous and what we are in danger of losing- the culture of the folk."[16] As the persona in Jamaican Valerie Bloom's "Language Barrier" explains, it is easy to take for granted what is local and familiar until someone from outside fails to understand: "An den im call attention to / Some things im sey soun' queer, / Like de way wi always sey 'koo yah' / When we really mean 'look here.'"[17] St. John's self-set mission was to explain Barbadian language not only to outsiders, but to Barbadians as well.

He saw himself as coming from the folk, sharing their language. He grew up in a family without much in the way of material resources, and had a strong sense of working class Barbadian culture, which he embraced. But as was quite common in Barbados when he was growing up, his family's limited income did not mean poverty of the mind. He grew up with people who were particularly interested in the power of words and music and gifted in using them. In his autobiographical essay, "Introduction," St. John wrote: "(my) father, besides being a newspaper reporter, was a musician. He played the piano, the pipe organ, and violin. Both classical music and dance music appealed to him, but both yielded so little, that low wages made him oscillate between being a church organist and a band leader."[18] This conscious embrace of both local rhythms and European musical styles was an example which St. John followed himself. Sophisticated, learned and well written discussions of musical performances by visiting musicians (a number of whom were African American) and of concerts witnessed overseas were frequent in the Barbadian press in the early twentieth century, and though it is not possible to identify exactly what St. John's father wrote for the local papers, because almost all the local contributors used pseudonyms, it is tempting to imagine that Clement St. John, who himself avoided sounding too indigenous in his speech, might have authored some of these columns.[19] The press, despite its white patronage, was also acutely aware of overseas events of interest to the black majority of Barbados, such as the trial of Marcus Garvey (no doubt with mixed motives).

St. John however did not immediately seek a profession which would involve him in writing or performing. He was first a physical education teacher, which gave him a discipline of the body and an understanding of its intelligence, which would be a crucial basis for his later performance ability, along with his voice training.[20] He was trained in England. One of his memories of this experience was a white woman telling a shopkeeper that St. John was ahead of him in the queue, something he was not used to happening in the Barbados in which he grew up. His own advanced education, profession as an academic, cosmopolitanism and wide ranging tastes in literature and music could have meant that he might have used international English as his primary creative medium, but his major affiliation remained the working class from which he came and whose voices he wanted to portray in his work. Middle-class voices in his poems are usually either bewildered expatriates or culturally elitist educators (he especially portrays women in this role as enemies of Bajan language and working class spirit).

Though St. John said that his grandmother, mother and father "were always poor financially," they were each clearly strong personalities, and he remembered that his grandmother and his father both emphasized academic study greatly.[21] From all three, he understood words to be important, especially as weapons or defenses. His father wrote, and was also verbally outspoken; his mother "spoke the dialect with some originality" and could also effectively disarm a verbal combatant in an argument, and his grandmother was "aggressive and outspoken."[22] St. John therefore grew up understanding words to have great power to protect and attack, but also to lance both social and personal wounds far more effectively than physical violence, as is a theme in other Caribbean poems. John Agard's "Listen Mr Oxford Don" plays cleverly with the sublimation of violence into words: "I ent have no gun / I ent have no knife / but mugging de Queen's English / is the story of my life," thus neatly skewering both

English literary and colonial dominance and the racist stereotype of the young black mugger.[23]

St. John's "With Respect" is one of the most vehement of his poems, expressing rage against someone "red," or light-skinned; it opens: "You stop red man or you done."[24] The curse is a subgenre of Caribbean poetry (as evidenced in a section of the Caribbean poetry anthology *Voice Print* 1989). Jamaican Pamela Mordecai's "Last Lines" is a similar direct verbal threat to the male abusers of young girls, "This is the last line I draw."[25]

St. John's acknowledged influences in Barbados are both colonial and anti-colonial in their voices. He says in "Introduction" that when he began to write he had read the poetry of Barbadians Hilton Vaughan and Frank A. Collymore, as well as the early work of Kamau Brathwaite.[26] Collymore's "Hymn to the Sea" is one of his most well known poems: it begins "Like all who live on small islands / I must always be remembering the sea / Be always cognizant of her presence; viewing / Her through apertures in the foliage."[27] His late Victorian tone, characteristic of the Barbadian middle-class and of scribal poetry of the early twentieth century, is shared by H.A. (Hilton) Vaughan. Vaughan was born in 1901 and was deeply involved in progressive politics and public life, eventually becoming a magistrate.[28] His "To the Unborn Leader" has the tone of technically and thematically conventional English poetry of the late nineteenth and early twentieth century: "You who may come a hundred years / After our troubled bones are dust, / Farseeing statesman, born to lead, / And worthiest of people's trust, / Turn these few pages in that hour / When by dark doubts you are assailed."[29]

The arrival of Kamau Brathwaite's early poetry in *The Arrivants* (the first volume of which came out in 1967) is the beginning of an entirely new era. It is unmistakably cosmopolitan in tone and outstandingly original in form and content, using both international English and Barbadian language to convey the African diaspora: "It is not / it is not / it is not enough to be free / of the red white and blue / of the drag, of the dragon."[30]

St. John's views on these three poets are interestingly suggestive of the choices he would make for his own work. In his long essay, "Introduction," he mentions Vaughan's empathy for the disadvantaged but also comments "there are those who would wish that Vaughan's language were different, but nobody can deny that this poet looked with an uncondescending eye at his environment and found worthy material in the local flora and fauna."[31] Vaughan's work, rather colonial in form but local in content, contrasts with that of Collymore, of whom St. John says he has a different eye: "One gets the impression that this eye looked at the local materials, then looked far away over the horizon. And that in this back and forth movement, the eye either did not capture the local drama or it looked away from it toward a lyricism far beyond the limits of the viewer of Mt. Hillaby."[32] Mt. Hillaby is the highest point in Barbados. But if Collymore's horizons were too distant, Brathwaite's African diaspora vision impressed St. John because it had focus and penetration, and beyond that a "powerful stream of partly hidden anger, an anger that resides in the rhythms and

and the rich phonic arrangement of sonorous consonants."[33] It is the combination of political resistance and linguistic pitch and tone, sheer poetic skill and acute political insight, seamlessly fused, which spoke to St. John.

One of Brathwaite's most famous and loved poems in Barbados, "The Stone Sermon" (*The Arrivants* 1973; *Islands* 1969), represents a preacher, catching the identity of Bajan language but in a way which is accessible to non-Barbadian readers: "We is goin' to leave / this vale o'shame / an' narrow minded- // ness an' breathe agen / the vivid hair o' God's / blue fields an' mountain."[34] In "Horse weebles" in *Mother Poem*, Brathwaite moves even closer to capturing the actual sounds of Bajan being spoken: "how you? How / you, eveie, chile? / you tek dat miraculous bush / fuh de trouble you tell me about? . . . / uh bet-'cha feelin less / poorly a' ready! / i int know, pearlie, / man, any- way, de body int dead" (How are you? How are you, Eveie, child? You took that miraculous bush. For the trouble you told me about? I bet you are feeling less poorly (ill) already. I don't know, Pearlie, man, anyway, the body isn't dead).[35]

Some passages in *Sun Poem* (1982), are even more difficult at first sight for someone unfamiliar with spoken Bajan: "*then he sit pun de edge a de pier wid de tread in e hann*" (then he sat on the edge of the pier with the thread [cotton thread for fishing] in his hand)[36]; "*yu know de lath letter yu senn me i loothe it*" (You know the last letter you sent me I lost it).[37] But Brathwaite's voice also pulls right back from the local: in *X/Self*, "Titan" begins: "Now they burn west/across the christian ocean humming high above the high drift of the harmattan/lights blinking on/and off/in touch with the stars."[38] His work demonstrates, as does that of novelists Barbadian George Lamming and Barbadian-American novelist Paule Marshall, the continuum between deep Creole and international English which marks Barbadian writing as it does the rest of the West Indies.[39]

The biggest challenge of this pioneering generation was to translate the oral into the scribal. In that continuum of their linguistic registers lies the complex range of affiliations to nation (and village or town within it), region, diaspora and world. Caribbean writers of fiction and scribal poetry have constantly worked to put the demotic on the page, but as most Barbadian (and West Indian) novelists have been published in the United States, the United Kingdom, or Canada, this has to work both for the local and the foreign reader. Like them, St. John's content and concerns are often cosmopolitan, he wrote essays in international English and in one poetry collection he uses a Barbadian inflected international English register.[40] His desire to fashion a poetic rendering of Bajan demotic which expressed an unsentimental appreciation and close observation of "the local drama" is far more central to his work than to other Barbadian writers of his generation. It was not only facilitated by his awareness of the local, however, but also of the interplay between Barbados, the Caribbean and the world.

Barbados has had a fateful geography, in the sense that the Trade Winds, which facilitate the slave ships sailing from West Africa to the Caribbean, made first landfall there. It is an island eighty miles to the east of the island chain with a large sheltered harbor on the leeward side. This has made of Barbados a key element in the brutal history of transatlantic slavery, a key economic underpinning of British imperialism. As Richard Sheridan has said, it has had many firsts, most of them associated with transatlantic slavery and the plantation system: it was the "first island to attract English settlers in considerable numbers, the first to introduce sugar cane and successfully market its raw sugar in international markets, the first to transform its society from a small-holder, semi-subsistence base to a slave plantation, near mono-culture regime which was dominated by a class of wealthy sugar merchants."[41] This gave it undue influence in terms of settling colonies within the Caribbean, and as far away as the Carolinas.[42] In its early export of planters, slaves and the plantation system, its later investment in education and export of teachers across the colonial world, as well as the migration of Barbadians to the United Kingdom, the United States, and Canada, as well as the Caribbean, the island has had a strongly international dimension as well as the reputation of being a closely knit, small island society with its own identity and culture.

As an overcrowded island, with relatively flat topography (because it is coral limestone), and by itself to the east of the island chain, Barbados was hard for slaves to escape from or even rebel openly within: uprisings could easily be suppressed because there were few places to really hide. The long term result has been an island accused of being the most colonized of all the former British Caribbean colonies. But slave rebellions did occur, most importantly that of Bussa, indicating a vehement underground resistance (which was made the more necessary by the violent response on the part of the local authorities to any challenge to their power). Though strong verbal expressions of opinions are common in Barbadian culture, the economic heritage from slavery and the plantation system is still largely in place, a majority of economic resources remaining in the hands of a small white or very light-skinned minority. But political power has moved from the white minority to the black majority as a result of successive challenges to the status quo led by remarkable political leaders. In this, the use of effective words has been key.

Linguistic skills, key to West African cultures from which the slaves came, became generally central to resistance in Caribbean colonies. Peter Roberts, in his study of colonial experience in the British Caribbean titled *From Oral to Literate Culture* (1997), gives an account of the importance of verbal skills (story-telling, proverbs, speech-making and music [including satirical songs]) among slaves in the West Indies, as strengtheners of community and reminders of African ancestry, as entertainment and as political tools.[43] Oral skills of this kind were important in Barbados, but there was also an early emphasis on printing. A printer was working in Barbados as early as 1730.[44]

St. John understood that his language, whilst being in effect an English "patois" (his chosen term), has a history going back to Africa also (another and very important sense of the transnational). In West Africa, where drum languages could traverse wide spaces too hard for people to communicate across otherwise, the human voice and the voice of the drum can be coded together. That coded use of sounds could also be crucial in planning rebellion or other forms of resistance on the Caribbean plantation if slaves still retained both the knowledge and the drums themselves, but the drum was therefore often banned.[45] African influence in the Caribbean has survived in the constant creation of sound *as* sense, parallel to the ways in many African tonal languages that units of sense and sound can be combined, recombined and layered inventively to create fresh ways of communicating. Caribbean Creoles are notoriously challenging to entrap convincingly on the page partly because they, too, are always on the move, creating and recreating words and phrases. As Roberts notes, creative writing and political rhetoric were read side by side in newspapers (almost entirely in colonial English, not Creole). By the twentieth century, he argues, a "consistently recurring comment made by authors presenting West Indian language and especially folklore is that words or the text are those of the speakers, exactly as they were said, or that the author has given those characters their normal speech. This seemingly innocent comment, often made with great sincerity, is extremely misleading [. . .] the interpretation of every word that is written varies [. . .]" according to many factors.[46] The poet is given both more freedom and more difficulty by this, regardless of which Caribbean territory he or she is from.

Precisely because St. John's father wrote for the newspapers in Barbados and called himself a journalist to his son, it is important to understand their importance. Newspapers were important from early in the colony. Roberts points out that the idea of "making paper talk" was seen even by the slaves as "advantageous," though he also makes the point that newspapers reinforced the dominance of English as a colonial language.[47]

From the late nineteenth century and especially during the twentieth century in Barbados, serious respect for education as a possible path to political power as well as economic advancement led to a high literacy rate, which enabled an important role for newspapers in the political life of the masses. In 1919, the *Barbados Herald* was founded by Clement Innis, and Hilary Beckles records that it was described as "providing for the first time in the colony's history biting, acerbic, working class views."[48] St. John was born four years after the paper was founded, into a society in which the black majority working class felt it had a public voice through the press. Their struggle was informed by information and by leadership which was aware of Caribbean and U.S. struggles for economic and political justice. They also found cosmopolitan leaders, such as Charles Duncan O'Neale (1879-1936) who, as Hilary Beckles recounts, returned to Barbados from his British medical education and early practice in Trinidad in 1924, and was dismayed by the poor health and infant mortality rates of the working class. As a another sign of Barbados connection to affairs in the wider world of African diaspora politics, Marcus Garvey's Universal Negro Improvement Association (UNIA) established itself strongly in Barbados (from 1920) despite the income and property qualifications then required in order to vote.[49] Garvey himself founded a paper, in New York City, *The Negro World,* for which many West Indians wrote (political essays and poetry were the most popular genres) Newspapers were very important for diasporic African political movements, including Garvey's highly successful movement. Though newspapers in the Caribbean have a long history, Garvey's influence cannot be discounted as assisting the growth of a network of journalists in the 1930s which was pan-Caribbean. Politician Wynter Crawford (1910-1993), described by Barbadian historian Woodville Marshall as "one of the giants of the movement for political and social enfranchisement that culminated in the independence of Barbados in 1966," founded the *Barbados Observer* in 1934, when Bruce St. John was eleven, and edited it until it terminated in 1975.[50] The working class also had access after World War II to Rediffusion, a radio system originating in Britain which provided affordable service via receivers mounted on the wall of the house and rented by the month and which provided not only news and music but many programs on culture and local events and issues. This was the world into which St. John was born, in which cultural and political uses of language were closely linked, and the politics of island, region and world were understood to be importantly connected.

But journalists who spoke out against vested interests could risk a good deal. Clennell Wickham, often identified as the greatest journalist Barbados has ever produced, always put his name to his column and as the well established editor of the *Barbados Herald*, 1930, supported a candidate in a by-election. Walter Bayley, a prominent local businessman and rival candidate, lost that election, and then refused to continue advertising in *The Herald*. Wickham made negative comments about him in the paper, and Bayley then brought a successful libel case against Wickham. The financial penalty leveled against Wickham was enormous, ruined him, and caused the paper to change hands. The connection between politics and the word was cemented by the role of the newspaper in the 1920s and 1930s, as it was in many colonies beginning to fight for an end to colonial rule.

The 1930's were a difficult time for poor Barbadians. There were riots in Barbados in 1937 as in other Caribbean countries. In his summary of the report of the Dean Commission of Enquiry into the 1937 "disturbances" in Barbados, G. Addinton Forde writes: "(the) report paints a grim picture of a Barbados which in 1937 was an island of economically disenfranchised people."[51] By 1937, Clement Payne, a young Barbadian born in Trinidad and recently returned, began to agitate for better conditions. He was subsequently deported to Trinidad after a charge of making a false statement to immigration (he had claimed to be born in Barbados). His many followers rioted, and nine people were killed, thirty wounded.[52] Beckles comments: "Payne succeeded in combining the incisive sociopolitical analysis of Wickham with the organizational drive of O'Neale."[53] Payne spoke eloquently: "Barbadians are sleeping giants, they are ragged and starving and yet no consideration is given them."[54] He also saw literature as involved in the fight for economic and social justice: "The days of uncle Tom's Negroes are dead [. . .] your elementary schools in this Island are always teaching children about great white men They should be taught the Black literature."[55]

However, newspapers could also present political and social material less confrontationally through wit and humor. St. John was very much aware of the popular Bajan characters Lizzie and Joe, who first appeared in the *Barbados Recorder* long before his birth, and then reappeared in the mid-1930s in the *Herald*, when St. John would have been in his teens. Their voices were heard via ballad style poems on largely local topical issues- and most importantly they spoke in Bajan.[56] These verses were the precursors of the popular Barbadian language columns and essays which appear in the press to this day, usually commenting on topical local issues. Austin "Tom" Clarke, the Barbadian novelist resident in Canada, wrote columns in Bajan on local topical concerns for the island press for a long time in the 1980s.[57] The work of Frank Collymore (1955) and St. John strengthened respect for Barbadian language locally, helping dislodge some of the middle-class prejudices against it: those prejudices were determinedly dismissive of the capacity of the local for international awareness or breadth of intellectual interest.

This was aided by the fact that in St. John's childhood and youth, one of the biggest problems was the lack of Barbadian language in schools (where many teachers and administrators were British expatriates who did not speak it or approve of it), as well as a lack of dictionaries, grammars, histories and other descriptive and analytical tools to help standardize it for use as an educational medium. In his important *Dictionary of Caribbean English* (1996), Richard Allsopp notes that "[a]s home-made, the Caribbean linguistic product has always been shame-faced, inhibited both by the dour authority of colonial administrators and their written examinations on the one hand, and by the persistence of the stigmatized Creole languages of the labouring populace on the other."[58] This construction of the local *lingua franca* in a colonial/postcolonial situation as inferior to the metropolitan language is not confined to the Caribbean, of course. In 1974, Loreto Todd, though she cited an example of dismissal of Creole by a scholar in 1971, said hopefully:

> In the past, pidgins and creoles with lexical affinities to European languages were often misunderstood and disparaged. Because they were associated with populations which had been enslaved or with peoples whose cultures differed radically from those of western Europe, they were regarded as inferior languages, the use of which was often seen as a reflection of inferiority.[59]

As late as 1986, Hubert Devonish commented that denying the right of Creole children to speak their own language in the classroom was an extension of the denial of respect for Creole as an adult language.[60] In St. John's childhood, Barbadian (Bajan) language was mostly considered "bad English" in the eyes of the educated, despite being, to a great or lesser extent, the lingua franca of the entire locally born population (include most of the whites).

Thus Frank Collymore's 1955 (reprinted 1970) glossary of Barbadian words and phrases is extremely important, especially as he also offered general comments on the importance of pronunciation (location of stresses), and other key issues in the language.[61] St. John knew Collymore's work, and cited it in his introduction to his poems in *Revista De Lettras* (1972). Hubert Devonish describes Collymore as offering a remarkably detailed analysis of Bajan for a non-linguist.[62] Collymore notes that "Barbados has always been British; and it is to be expected therefore that there are few words in our dialect of foreign origin: what is remarkable, however, is the fact that there seem to be so very few words of African origin."[63] If African words are rare (such as unna and wunna, meaning all of you, or as St. John puts it "the plural of you is wunna") certain coinages and emphases are not.[64] In his section called "Compound Redundant," Collymore lists "to(o) besides," "back-back" (to go back), out-out (extinguish), play-play (make-believe).[65] The repetition is usually an intensifier (as in "small, small"). Of course such duplications are also familiar in West African pidgins and, in fact, Todd remarks that (re)duplicated forms exist in all of the English-based pidgins and creoles.[66] Her examples are from both the Atlantic and the Pacific; from the Atlantic, for example, "kraikrai" (cry continuously), "sansan" (sand), and from the Pacific, "waswas" (go to wash), lukluk (stare at, see). But it is important to realize that, as Peter Roberts argues, Barbadian language, like other West Indian languages, has its own unique complexity. In the early slave period, "West Indian societies were dominated by a mass of language learners in a way no normal society is," as slaves from different African cultures struggled to communicate in English, having lost their own connection to their linguistic roots.[67] Not only that, but Caribbean whites came from England, Scotland and Ireland, with their own patterns of English speech.[68] Barbados's "Scotland District" marks the historical presence of poor whites from Scotland who formed a particular community.

Given the lack of formal education for slaves and also most indentured servants, inventiveness with regard to words became more important than trying to follow the structures of a language necessarily apprehended via individual intelligence and understood inventively. Collymore gives examples of local "echo words" (onomatopoeia) such as "bruggadung" (a loud percussive noise) and "plashow" (splashing); such inventions have been common and vivid in Barbadian language.[69] Collymore and St. John both have "bellyologist" (glutton) and "busylickum" (busybody) as well as vivid phrases, such as "in duck's guts" (in bad trouble) or "fire one" for drinking strong liquor. St. John has "spaulboogle" (flabbergasted) and "wampAh" (cutlass).[70] St. John also explains how sometimes a word is emphasized by the addition of a preposition as in play up or dirty up, rest off (if tired) or lick up (for an accident).[71] He gives examples of pronouns: "I am leaving" is "uh gone"[72] and offers "Soah" as the pronunciation of "so" and "noah" for no.[73] Many words have currency for only a certain time. St. John himself invented words, as did his mother.

Both Collymore and St. John try to codify stress patterns. In thinking about British versus Barbadian pronunciation, Collymore gives the example of Scotland. Pronounced with a slight emphasis on land, as the English (not the Scots) say it, it means "the country north of England," but "*Scot*-land is the hilly district to the north of Barbados."[74] In his talk "Barbadian Dialect" (August 16,

1971, University of Ottawa), St. John demonstrated the difference between Barbadian and British English pronunciation of certain words (Standard English cArpenter, Barbadian English, carpentEr; similarly gArage, garaGe, Educated, educAted, Afternoon, afternoOn).[75] He also pointed out that there are exceptions, where English and Barbadian have the same emphases (LEcture, CAtholic, LIterature.[76] Overall, he argued, "There is then, a tendency towards rhythmic syncopation in words which have a two beat rhythm" ("Introduction" 3).[77]

Where they appear to differ is on a particular group of words which means both relative and member of a church depending on pronunciation (brother, father, or sister or mother). For Collymore, "brother" is a relative and "*bro*-ther" is a member of a church (and so on for sister and the others). St. John says: "A son has a mOther, but he may be taught at a Roman Catholic school by a nun who is called a mothEr, or by a priest who is called a father."[78] SistEr is at church, SIster is the family relative.[79] The issue of how to describe Barbadian pronunciation of bi-syllabic words is more complicated. Barbadian linguist Peter Roberts says "the prominent features of Barbadian speech are mainly in pronunciation."[80] But this is not simply in the way stresses are aligned. Roberts also lists, among a number of other identifying features, nasalization and glottalization ("swallowing the ends of the words" or, more precisely, under-articulating consonants").[81] Certain consonants are replaced in Barbadian, such as "f" or "v" replacing "th," as in "paf" for path, and "teeving" for teething.[82]

But what complicates all of this is "pitch and tone" which subtly interact (low pitch and high stress could happen in the same syllable, as Devonish points out). St. John, with his musical training, was acutely aware of this. In speaking about the ways in which an oppressed people would find a way to communicate in their oppressor's language, he said:

> This is done by the greater use of pitch and tone. Other sounds are created which may arise from the language of the oppressed, or which may be the result of attempts to copy sound from the language of the oppressors. In the poetry, one must be very conscious of the sound, and fairly cautious with the printed word or sign, especially if these are to be repeated, since what may appear to be dull monotony may be very eloquent variety.[83]

It is therefore hard to designate the exact pronunciation of Bajan on the page without highly accurate linguistic symbols, although Hubert Devonish,[84] a linguist himself, seems to accept Collymore's description of the process by which Barbadian intonation is achieved: "but by over emphasizing this accent, holding on to it, as it were, making the slightest of pauses thereafter and then allowing the voice to rise ever so slightly for the second syllable, quite a different intonation is achieved, and too, a word with quite a different meaning."[85]

The political undertones are even more difficult to transcribe onto the page, and often require knowledge of the local moment, just as calypso often does. There is a rich resource here for irony, a deliberately subversive doubleness of meaning perhaps inevitably a part of anti-colonial resistance. In his comparative study of Anglophone postcolonial poetry, Ramazani identifies strong irony in the poetry of Jamaican Louise Bennett (Mis' Lou): his list of other Anglophone Caribbean poets who use irony includes Walcott, Brathwaite, Mervyn Morris, Dennis Scott, Lorna Goodison, Grace Nichols, Michael Smith and David Dabydeen.[86] We should add St. John.

It was in 1984 that Brathwaite's term "Nation Language" began to have a great effect in reducing prejudices against Caribbean demotics. In his framing of the term in "History of the Voice" (1979/81), Brathwaite argued that in the oral tradition, for which nation language is the means of expression, "the noise and sounds that the poet makes are responded to by the audience and returned to him."[87] But, in a kind of parallel to St. John's affiliation by training to patterns of European music which somehow aided him in a totally different "music" in his work, Brathwaite also argues that "what T. S. Eliot did for Caribbean poetry and Caribbean literature was to introduce the notion of the speaking voice, the conversational tone."[88] That is, a creative imagination brought up on British literature could reconfigure Eliot's example as a doorway into Caribbean poetics, and leave behind both the colonial idea that Eliot was superior because of being associated with the imperial center *and* its natural retort, which would be not to see any use in Eliot at all in a post-colonial poetics. Similarly, when St. John, seven years older than Brathwaite, and just as much a child of the high point of British global imperialism, was trained in European music, he saw that it could teach him how to utilize tone in a very different context, to hear and deliver the precise nature of tonality in Bajan speech.

Listening to any outstanding performer of Barbadian language (such as Alfred Pragnell or calypsonian The Mighty Gabby) proves the point that the range and potential relationship of pitch and tone available to the canny practitioner is very rich and also offers opportunities to create new combinations, which a Barbadian audience, at home or overseas, picks up on immediately. It is well to remember that what looks like international English in a Barbadian text might be intended to be read in a subtle local accent. All Barbadians shift linguistic registers according to locale, although this will obviously differ from class to class and person to person. The late Alfred Pragnell, the well known Barbadian radio commentator and oral performer, demonstrated this very clearly (and not only with his voice); he offered visitors two kinds of tea, served in china cups, "white people tea" (black tea) and "we tea" (made from herbs from his garden). He read Frank Collymore's well known patriotic poem about Barbados, "This Land," in his "BBC English" voice, which as a key radio announcer, he used for reading the news and for doing the commentary for important national occasions. His reading of "This Land" is included in his CD, *Skylarkin'* (n.d.). This very English voice was in sharp contrast to the demotic in which most of his performances were conducted (he used to leave amusing Christmas holiday telephone answering service messages in the persona of a disgruntled Barbadian servant who always had some criticism of "Mr PrAgnell"). He had an large expressive vocabulary which included not only words but very precisely pitched sounds and groups of sounds, some onomatopeic and some not, but all easily recognized as meaningful by a Barbadian audience, though they were often exaggerated for wonderful comic effect. The shifts in tone in Pragnell's delivery emphasized nuances of meaning in the material (he often used a bus stop or telephone conversation between two gossipy women as a vehicle for his most expert delivery of Barbadian).[89] In Barbados today, newspapers almost always carry columns on current issues written in Barbadian. Jeannette Layne-Clarke is particularly well known and wrote much of Pragnell's material. Richard Hoad, a white Barbadian farmer, writes a comic column. In the 1980s, Austin "Tom" Clarke, the eminent Barbadian novelist long resident in Canada, wrote regular features in one of the newspapers.

St. John's advice to poets was to compose their poems as if they were musicians: "try to isolate melodies from words, and rhythmic patterns from words. Try hard to develop a drum-beat language and a melodic language. Strip your poems bare to the skeleton of the drum-beat, later dress the skeleton with the flesh of melody, and finally clothe it with the finery of words."[90]

It is very difficult in general to capture the full identity of oral poetry outside of its performance, just as a musical score does not capture the actual interpretative performance. Jamaican poet and critic Mervyn Morris remarks in an essay titled "Printing the Performance": "We can never put the performance in print [. . .] Why then bother with the book? Because the best performance poets are poets, and the dance of language is central to what they do."[91] St. John himself said, "The identification of the rhythmic structure is a type of 'open sesame' to the poems [. . .] the written word on the page will be for many a libretto only."[92] The setting down of sounds on the page, especially in cultures where dictionaries of local languages do not exist, must somehow hope for a basic comprehension of the possibilities inherent in variations of tone or emphasis, because the performer is likely to be portraying a particular persona, or dramatic voice, which plays against a wide range of inventive language use in a local, largely oral community. Kamau Brathwaite's inventive "video style," in which print types and spaces on the page are key in delineating the speaking voice, has tried to bridge this gap.

Though Barbados was thought of as a particularly colonized culture where the written word was central, at least for all educated people, one of the most popular entertainments there before the First World War was the "tea-meeting," which Collymore describes as "a sort of prolonged concert whose main features were songs, both solo and choral, and abundance of refreshments, and a type of oratory that delighted in the display of resounding polysyllabic words (some of them specially coined for the occasion) and elaborate alliterative allusions to the great names of history and literature."[93] Such an event took both planning and rehearsal and began at 9pm with an "oration" by the vice-chairman, after a welcoming period during which a choir sang. The chairman would follow, and then the program was outlined by the vice-chairman. Each item would receive commentary from the chairman, and then at midnight, a two hour break would begin, and cold snacks and desserts would be served, with tea and chocolate. Then the program would continue until dawn. This tradition helped strengthen the local tradition of love of words which drew both on the strong West African ancestral love of orature and the British colonial emphasis on literature via the dramatic voice of Shakespeare, among other writers.

So St. John's dramatic poems and his view of them as "songs" seems to suggest he was building on such a Barbadian tradition in which words and music were indivisible. There was a musical syncopation to a St. John reading which owed everything to his vocal training so that he could precisely pitch his voice and exactly articulate his words and phrases, even (and this was his preferred performative location) sitting down at a table, perfectly still except for an occasional turn of the head or movement of a hand in the air.[94]

Key to understanding St. John's work is to understand his attention to the minutest detail of the meaning of language (heightened after his training in Spanish language and his graduate work in Spanish poetry) and its sounds in performance (resting on his musical training). He did not exclude white Barbadians in thinking about the language. In his address on Barbadian language at the University of Ottawa in 1971, he said it

> flows through the lips of persons who are visibly Caucasian, who are visibly African, and who combine admixtures of all the hues and structural characteristics which a blending of what is meant by these terms [. . .] can mean. Barbadian "song" may be sung by representatives of all professions, trades and classes.[95]

St. John advised that his poems ("songs" as he called them) in *Foetus Pains* and *Foetus Pleasures* (1974) should be read/performed as an entire cycle.[96] Curwen Best's analysis of St. John's poems relates their rhythms to the indigenous music of the Barbadian "tuk" band, with its penny whistle and drums (bass and "snare" or kettle drum), and triangle.[97] This band has a long history, going back to slave times when, as Best demonstrates, the colonial repression of drumming by African slaves in Barbados caused innovative substitutions to be found and used as percussive instruments (such as clay pots). Best argues that Archie and Boysie, St. John's two dramatic characters, might be seen as representing the different drums of the tuk band: certainly St. John's own directive to poets suggests he heard the tuk drums clearly whilst composing. But it is also important to consider what he distinguishes as "melodic" and "drum-beat" language, and I would argue that these represent the traditions of European and African music and language which he saw as always interacting in Barbadian culture. He used both in some poems and sometimes only one. In his "Saturday Night at the Exhibition," the short lines and heavy repetitive rhythm convey the happy chaos of many people in a room during a popular event: "People like pigeon peas / People like san' / Heavy an' skinny / Country an' town / Onion an' aloes / An' rotten grapefruit / Musk an' Avon."[98]

St. John understood that proverbs are not only a functional part of contemporary Barbados, but carry, as proverbs always do, a social history. They are also highly rhythmic and imaginatively figurative, therefore of great use to a poet. Their history in Barbados goes back to both slavery (proverbs are so important in West African cultures, though Roberts comments that the forms of them of course had to change as they came into English), and colonialism, which brought British proverbs into local usage.[99] They are then both intimately local and ancestrally international.

St. John's poem "Bajan Litany" contains a number of proverbs: "Wuh sweeten goat mout bu'n 'e tail"; "De higher de monkey go, de more he show 'e tail"; "Follow pattern kill Cadogan"; "Choke 'e collar, hang 'e 'tie, trip 'e up trousers, t'row 'e down boots"; "Stop friggin' spiders fuh twice de increase"; "Wuh in ketch yuh en pass yuh."[100] Richard Allsopp's collection of Afric Caribbean proverbs demonstrates that the first two of these are widespread in the Caribbean.[101] He includes two pages of proverbs involving goats, about half of which are known in Barbados.

One subsection is devoted to a widespread Caribbean proverb referring to "goat-mouth," which Allsopp attributes to a West African origin, because of the centrality of the goat to West African cultures. Goats are commonplace in Barbados and the local black-bellied sheep is often mistakenly thought to be a goat by inexperienced viewers. "Wha(t) sweeten goat-mout(h) does bu(r)n (h)e tail" is listed as a Barbadian and Grenadian version of the proverb.[102] St. John's slightly revised version opens this section. It marks the goat's willingness to eat almost anything regardless of the consequences in digestion, but also acts as a warning against temptations for people which might have terrible consequences. Variant forms of this proverb exist, as Allsopp's collection proves, in Antigua, Jamaica, Tobago, Guyana, the U.S. Virgin Islands and Trinidad, and Allsopp has a version in Krio (Sierra Leone). Allsopp lists eighteen proverbs involving monkeys, and the one St. John uses is very widespread in the Caribbean. It suggests climbing (socially or professionally) will reveal the crude reality of a person. Again, St. John's version is slightly different from the one Allsopp lists "The higher the monkey climb, the more he show he tail," showing how the proverb, like Bajan language itself, was inclined to change formation slightly in common usage (and when a poet like St. John uses a proverb it will need to serve the poem in its rhythm).[103] The last four proverbs which St. John used in this poem appear to be only Barbadian (Allsopp has a Barbadian variation of "Follow pattern kill Cadogan" as "Follow-pattern kill a man an(d) mek a monkey break (h)e han(d).[104] "Follow pattern kill Cadogan" reinforces resistance to group fashions or dictates.

The last three proverbs in St. John's poem are not present in Allsopp's collection. "Choke 'e collar, hang 'e 'tie, trip 'e up trousers, t'row 'e down boots" is a vivid rendition of someone dressed, as in colonial days, in clothing suitable for a cold climate, in search of higher status. "Stop friggin' spiders fuh twice de increase" is hard to explain, but it has the sense of an absolutely pointless effort. "Wuh in ketch yuh en pass yuh"—this clearly is about not thinking you are free of a danger in the immediate moment of escaping it. All of these proverbs have vivid language and their rhythm is very distinct: they appear to be particularly local.

St. John's use of call and response is another key aspect of his use of rhythm, and this is again both local and a key part of African diaspora cultures. St. John often used argument or dialogue in his poems, but the call and response is more ritualized, with a main speaker and a refrain. His use of "Litany" in the titles of two key poems is evidence of his awareness of the ritualized form of the church litany as useful for political poetry. Once again here, he presents local expression of widespread Caribbean and diasporic concerns.

The slaves of a small island, like Barbados, where the plantation system employed both open coercion and successful hegemony, had to find a layered way of simultaneously expressing and concealing. St. John, belonging to a generation in which, at least among the working class, traces of African tonality still survived, deliberately employed nuanced tone and pitch in refrains in his poetry so the same words could signify very different meanings (and so be coded for insiders and outsiders). In "West Indian Litany," "Da is true" is repeated eight times.[105] The first six are by no means the same response to the statements of the "caller." To the assertion that "Stokeley (sic) like he mad" the response is a strong reinforcement, so "Da" is stressed heavily (the stress here would be high-low-medium). To the next assertion of Stokely being out of touch with the West Indies, all three words are slightly less stressed, as in the accusation that he isn't discreet. But when it comes to be that he "can' be 'pon we side" there is room for questioning in the refrain, so true becomes a little more pronounced, and the accusation of Stokely working for the whites would either be something which restores a confident affirmation (providing a sense of security) in the respondent, or which continues to be a little disturbing. However the next accusation, that whites "thrive 'pon we division," would be instantly supported. Then the caller turns and says "So dey won' leh 'e talk!" and the respondent says "Wuh da?," shocked. Then comes a question, repeated twice, "Suppose he right though?" and the response each time, "Da is true" should be at first a little less confident and then very confident. By this strategy, St. John shows two Barbadian voices considering all the options, offering statements which can have multiple shades of meaning simply caught by an adroit lifting or lowering of the voice. Those who simply hear the plain word miss the point.

Sometimes St. John was explicit in directions. He worried that later generations would no longer hear tone so exactly, or even at all. "Bajan Litany" has a stage direction for performers at the beginning (unusually for St. John's work), which is like a pace notation on sheet music:

(*Fast*) Follow pattern kill Cadogan	Yes, Lord.
America got black power?	O, Lord.
We got black power.	Yes, Lord.
Wuh sweeten goat mout bu'n 'e tail.	O, Lord.
Bermuda got tourism?	Yes, Lord.[106]

Twice in subsequent sections the instruction is to become louder, so that the poem rises to a crescendo. But as St. John would read it, the nuances of tone in both the questions and statements of the first speaker and the refrain of the second were always shifting within the gradually rising volume overall. The content of this poem, referencing U.S. Black Power, Bermuda, Jamaica, Trinidad and England, conveys Barbados's need to avoid imitating other countries: the whole effect lies in the changes of response, from a perky agreement to a weary sigh to a forced agreement to an exclamation of alarm.

The ironically titled "Truth" has the refrain *"You lie! You lie!"* repeated twemty-one times as the respondent emphatically denies the caller's statements until the caller says "Uh lie? Uh lie?" and then proceeds to ask questions of the respond- ent, the answers to which affirm the caller's point.[107] After which, the caller goes back to his accusations and the respondent goes back to rebutting them. "Privilege" has far less repetition in the responses, but there is enough to make it also a call and response poem, though this is also a dialogue between St. John's characters Archie and Boysie: "Boysie boy—trouble in town" "Wuh happen?" Wuh happen?"/"Trouble boy trouble-trouble, trouble, boy, trouble" "Wuh happen?" "Wuh happen?"[108] In all of these examples, the first syllable of the refrain is generally stressed (in "Truth", the refrain "You lie" has almost equally stressed syllables and is emphatic").

St. John's major themes, education, race and class, are all expressed in his work in local, regional and international contexts via the local context expressed through his use of Bajan language. Education, one of St. John's passions, both in his career and in his poetry, is deeply engaged with the politics of language and liberation in the Caribbean in general and Barbados in particular. Though St. John was partially educated in England, he regarded those for whom that was a colonial stamp of approval with contempt. In the school system, some of the most disapproving teachers were women of the middle-class, at whom St. John directed this poem called "Bajan language":

> Yuh know what wrong wid she?
> 'Cause she fahduh did a wring-neck dentis'
> Could afford she study in Englant
> When we res' cou'n' go
> She t'ink we en' know
> Wuh we own talk 'bout? [. . .]
>
> Bajan language is a damn funny language
> Piece o' English, piece o' African tongue,
> Mix Carib an' Arawak to save damage
> An' de cook-up is a beautiful soun'.[109]
>
> (You know what is wrong with her?
> Because her father is a wring-neck dentist
> Could afford for her to study in England
> When the rest of us could not go
> She thinks we don't know
> What our own talk about?

Bajan language is a damn funny language
Piece of English, piece of African tongue,
Mix Carib and Arawak to save damage
And the cook-up is a beautiful sound.)

The image of a "wring-neck" dentist (conjuring up the red rooster neck, so suggesting light-skinned elite status, plus a professional standing), and the references to Carib and Arawak, who lived in Barbados before European colonization (they are now widely thought to have been the same people), mark the poem as particularly local, though the poem refuses the idea of Barbadian language as having any single primary identity or source. This was less easy to see when St. John started writing that it is today. Barbados is clearly less historically diverse than many other Caribbean nations (Trinidad and Tobago, for example, has formative Spanish, French, English, African and Asian identities and their constant interaction has fuelled cultural development). Derek Walcott's poetic persona famously says in "The Schooner Flight," "I have Dutch, nigger, and English in me / and either I'm nobody, or I'm a nation."[110] But St. John was always clear that it was a mistake to simplify Barbadian cultural norms.

Many of St. John's poems have a pair of voices, and one often provokes ideas by asking a lot of questions. This is a popular Barbadian mode for considering important ideas, a more or less friendly argument in which one or more of the speakers demonstrates learning, wit, linguistic resourcefulness and the desire to knock down the opposition's position with or without offending them. "Education" is an excellent example of this, in which St. John's characters, Archie and Boysie begin:

"Studyation beat eddication."
"Man, Archie man, what you talkin'?
'Studyation' ent even a word."

"Studyation ent even a word?
It ent a word in a damn dictionary,
But um is a good, good Bajan word.

Eddication is a lot a lot o' paper,
Studyation is 'nough 'nough brain.
A book in yuh han' an' trash bone in yuh head,
You better lef' de bloody book in de bag'."[111]

and eventually concludes with Archie's triumphant assertion:

"Studyation beat eddication,
Studyation boss eddication
Studyation plus eddication
Is wisdom, Boysie boy, wisdom."[112]

In "Introduction," St. John explains the word "Studyation" and its role in the opening phase of the poem:

> The word "Studyation" like many others is formed by the folk-addition of the suffix –ation to a word. The new word is invested with greater authority by the two additional syllables. It becomes a "big word," and it is admitted into the family of important words like *education, transportation, emigration, elevation* etc. Boysie's reaction is typical: the concept is avoided, as Boysie has to be one up. So he attempts to use "English" to defeat Archie. This sets alight the Barbadian in Archie, who has become resentful over the importation of foreigners as advisors in every field, in spite of the reputation Barbados has for its fine educational system.[113]

The image of the trash bone (the middle of the cane blade) is particularly local, but in the next line the commonplace British swearword of the era, "bloody," demonstrates the language's absorption of words both coined locally and brought from overseas.

Archie's indignation as it develops is wonderfully rhythmic and effective, as he protests the presence of the foreign "expert" (pervasively a part of colonialism and its aftermath):

> Buhbados eddication is de bes'?
> Den why, why so many expert in de town?
> Expert fuh salary, expert fuh tax,
> Expert fuh teachin', expert fuh man,
> Plan plan fuh dis, plan plan fuh dat.[114]

This willingness to argue freely in the street or the rum-shop frequently disappeared in the neocolonial classroom. "Higher Learnin'" explores the ways in which learning to be a scholar, at Cave Hill, the Barbados campus of the University of the West Indies, involves learning to respect major theories and arguments which are imported. The University of the West Indies has facilitated interaction between students and faculty from the entire Anglophone region and the Barbados campus particularly, in its early days, drew students from the whole Anglophone Eastern Caribbean, as well as having the law school for the whole of the Anglophone Caribbean region.[115]

The world over, learning ideas which are generated externally to the student's most intimate original culture marks them with the surface habits of educated elites. Barbadians have a verb for this process: "middle-classing." In postcolonial situations (at least in the early decades after Independence), there is an even more insidious possibility, where books are mostly still written by foreigners, and grand-sounding theories might well impress the student enough to persuade him or her to ignore the inherited wisdom of the community. The Caribbean has succeeded in impressing the world often enough with its intellectuals who have conquered foreign or colonial knowledge and used it for their own creative purposes (for example, Frantz Fanon, Aimé Césaire and Nobel Laureates, both from St. Lucia, Derek Walcott and Sir Arthur Lewis [shared with Theodore W. Schultz]).

The speaker in "Higher Learnin'" is impatient with the kind of book-learning which reduces individual self-confidence and confidence in the local:

> Talk 'bout history, talk 'bout economics,
> I mek history a plenty in dis village,
> But de way you talking,' you en able to write um . . .
>
> Yuh get papers and prizes so I realize
> Dat at leas' yuh di'n' wastin' muh crop-time money
> But now yuh in yuh twenties an' still playin' echo,
> I wonderin' if yuh evah goin' t'ink fuh yuhself . . .
>
> I ben'in' me ol' back wid dis fork puttin' in good
> Labour pullin' out bettah money fuh keep you up de
> Hill an' you rollin' down big word like
> Goat rolls rattlin' 'pon galvanize tinin![116]
>
> (Talk about history, talk about economics
> I make history a great deal in this village
> But the way you are talking, you won't be able to write it . . .
>
> You get papers and prizes so I realize
> That at least you aren't wasting my crop-time money
> But now you are in your twenties and still playing echo
> I wonder if you are ever going to think for yourself . . .
>
> I'm bending my old back with this fork putting in good
> Labour pulling out better money to keep you up the
> Hill and you are rolling down big words like
> Goat rolls rattling on a galvanized tin.)

Goat rolls are goat droppings and the image is of them (small hard objects) rolling down a piece of galvanized tin ("tinin" in Barbadian), the most common roofing material for wooden houses in Barbados, houses usually inhabited by the working class.

Race is a complicated terrain in Barbados, as in the whole of the Caribbean, because it is deeply implicated not only in the history of slavery but also postcolonial hierarchies and economic disparities.[117] St. John neither ducks the hard truths about race in Barbados nor refuses to be inclusive. Kathleen Drayton said in her preface to St. John's collection, *Bumbatuk 1*, "Race has divided our societies but St. John reminds us 'All o' we is Bajan . . . / Bajan black, Bajan white.'"[118] In his poem "Nationalism" the confident anticolonial voice "We goin'shake up dis place boy," is mocked by the cynical realist "*Da is if yuh white.*"[119] Despite the divisions of race and of shade (so connected to class), which caused such pain and deprivation in Caribbean cultures, the transition from white plantocracy to universal suffrage was achieved through political means, and so both a sense of racial grievance and a sense of racial inclusion can be simultaneously deeply felt by the same person. St. John's poems collectively demonstrate that through his Barbadian poetic personae. It is this ability to hold both positions at once which marks not only Barbadian but Caribbean reality.

St. John both acknowledged and challenged the racial and concomitant economic and political divisions in postcolonial Barbados. Backra is local whites, the assembly is the House of Assembly, or parliament. He embraced the idea that dividing the nation along racial lines was foolishness, as his poem "Who Is We?" makes clear: "Bajan black, Bajan white, / Bajan hair curly, Bajan hair straight, / Yo' brother red, yo' sister brown, Yo' mother light skin, yo' father cobskin. / Strike back to morning,' strike back to evenin'."[120] "Red" is very light brown; "cobskin" signifies dark skin and dark, straight hair, often understood as mixed African and Indian ancestry. He also however reflected his society by being not only acutely aware of the white / black socio-economic disparities directly resulting from the history of a plantation system built on racial slavery, but also the implications of differences in shade within people of color. He also sometimes used an edgy humor (present often in Caribbean portrayals of race). Such comic effect is intended as a social corrective or at least to cause awareness of racial tensions. At other times, whilst the poem might have an outrageous tone on the surface, there is an evident underlying seriousness. St. John's poetic personae have a wide range of emotional tones.

Layne-Clarke's comic "Shades of Spades" is an interesting comparison with St. John's more sober "Colour." She devotes a stanza in this long poem to a different "shade" of skin and its cultural significance:

> You evah stop to study
> Hummuch shades Buhbajans got?
> Rangin's from black to backra-
> Startin' wid "black-as-de-pot"? . . .
>
> Between jet-black an' brown-skin
> Is a mob-o'-ton o' shades . . .
> Ef some person black an' shine
> Duh like "de ess-o'-spades"! . . .
>
> Ef duh hair got li'l pretentions
> To sof'ness, an' it light-
> Yuh calls dat body "sof'-skin"
> "Smood-skin" wun be right![121]

The nation has shades from backra (local white), to black. Darkest shades are designated "black as the pot," "jet-black," black as "the ace of spades." If hair has "little pretentions" to softness, and is light, the person would be called "soft skin" (as opposed to smooth skin). After smooth skin comes "clean-skin," then "cob-skin," then "light-skin," then an even more peculiar designation:

> Somewhey in-between dey is grizly . . .
> We's call somebody so a grey-goose;
> Da'h when duh complexion like khaki
> Mix wid a shade looking' like lime-juice . . .[122]

After which comes brown-skin (the most admired of all), then red, high-brown, clear, and if the hair is a little reddish, the person might be called "snuffy." But mulatto is not, the poem explains, to be confused with high-brown: "Now ef yuh tek 'high-brown' fuh mulatto, / Believe me-yuh will be errin' . . ./ A mulatto is strickly a cross-bread- / Nieder fish, foul nor red-herrin'!"[123] After high-brown comes "fair-skin" (able to pass for white), and if this person is freckled, they might be a "backra-johnney," a "red-leg" (a particular subset of local whites descended from indentured white laborers and still largely poor and marked by the sun as they have worked the land for generations in poverty). Lastly there is a "real white Bajan." The poem ends: "B'looka life- wid all dem shades, / Bajans en know no hate! / We en ha' nuh time for prejudice- / We does only discriminate.[124]

This is a very adroit treatment of simultaneous shade consciousness and denial of "prejudice," in which people claim to be only observing difference (the pun on discriminate is effective however), not erecting barriers. Not all these terms are merely local, as those familiar with racial designations in the rest of the Caribbean and the United States will be aware.

Layne-Clark's poem is very much pitched at the local level, whereas St. John's "Colour" is playfully aware of race as a global issue. His poem is less formally constructed, and more complicated in its attitudes to the race/shade question: in the end, race is about power:

> Dis black an' white business
> Um en as easy as um soun',
> Um en as easy as um look;
> Good an' bad black an' white
> Blue an red gold an' lead;
> Duh had a macaroni man name Mackya Velly.
> He did very good fuh some an' bad enough fuh de res'.
> *He did white if any o' we white.*
>
> (This black and white business
> Is not as easy as it sounds
> Is not as easy as it looks
> Good and bad black and white
> Blue and red gold and lead
> They had a macaroni man called Machiavelli
> He did very well for some and bad enough for the rest.
> He was white if any of us are white.)
>
> Den duh had a Frenchy call Trousseau or
> Rousseau, I en sure wuh sort o' so;

He did so so for some
But 'e di'n' so so fuh all;
Some o' we reapin' wuh he sow
Some o' we still eatin' macaroni.
He did white, if any o' we white.

(They had a Frenchman called Trousseau or
Rousseau, I'm not sure what sort,
He did so so for some
But he didn't do so so for all
Some of us are reaping what he sowed
Some of us are still eating macaroni
He was white if any of us are white . . .)

We man up in Haiti-
Toussaint L'Ouverture-
He over throw dem pow'ful Frenchman,
Change de colour o' rulin' power.
But wuh happen after dat?
He di'n' white, if any o' we black.

(Our man up in Haiti-
Toussaint L'Ouverture-
He overthrew those powerful Frenchmen
Changed the color of the ruling power
But what happened after that?
He was not white, if any of us are black.)

Nkrumah, God res' 'e, did a pow'ful, pow'ful man
But . . .
Martin Luther King, a son a' God if evah dey was one,
A peaceful peaceful man
But . . .
Dem did black, if any o' we black . . .

(Nkrumah, God rest him, was a powerful, powerful man
But . . .
Martin Luther King, a son of God if ever these was one,
A peaceful, peaceful man
But . . .
They were black if any of us are black.)

De trouble en in colour,
De trouble is in power . . .
So down, so deep down, dat . . .
Colour! Um en colour, um en colour,
Um is power dat cuttin' we ass.

(The trouble is not color,
the trouble is with power . . .

So deep, so deep down that . . .
Color! It is not color, it is not color,
It is power that's biting us in the ass.)[125]

More provocatively, and perhaps curiously, St. John broached the tension between African and Asian populations, a major factor in Guyana and Trinidad, but not in Barbados (though some local anxiety apparently existed about the extent of possible Asian migration to Barbados at the time the poem was written). "Truth" sets out to address racial tensions in the wider Caribbean:

De coolie tekin' over	You lie! You lie!
I say de coolie tekin' over!	You lie! You lie!
Dem strong in Guyana!	You lie! You lie!
Strong in Trinidad!	You lie! You lie!
Dem-coming in Buhbadus!	You lie! You lie!

The poem ends with the refutation still hurled at the speaker:

De coolie tekin' over!	You lie! You lie!
An' you cynan' see de coolie!	You lie! You lie!
De coolie tekin' over!	You lie! You lie!
De coolie tekin' over!	You lie! You lie![126]

In his explanation of this poem, St. John said it really referred to Guyana and Trinidad, and that the term "coolie" in Barbados meant something different:

> In Barbados, there have been Asians for a very long time, but never in large proportions . . . For the Barbadian, the word "coolie" does not include Chinese; it was really a term used for describing Middle East and Far East itinerant sellers of clothing who began by walking around the country districts with a valise, who practiced a hire purchase system on a small scale . . . The poorer people were enabled to possess clothing by this type of vendor, since credit for them in Bridgetown stores was impossible. There was therefore, and probably still is, among Barbadian folk, no animosity in the term "coolie."[127]

He also argued that the term "nigger" tends to raise a smile in Barbados rather than to suggest violence: "There are red niggers and white niggers too, since the word 'nigger' connotes a certain type of behaviour."[128] Both terms are clearly racist and were originally used for people of Asian or African descent by whites, and that "a certain type of behaviour" is associated with "nigger" simply confirms its hegemonic and racist identity. But there has long been a widespread usage of it in Barbados, where it is assumed to have a different connotation, one which St. John intends.

But key to understanding the rhetorical construction of the poem is that "you lie" is a Barbadian folk expression which can mean both "I do not believe you" and "I believe you"—the meaning will be taken from the tone of voice.[129] In the poem, the caller is not always telling the truth, and the responders, though saying the same words, do not always mean them the same way. St. John connected Stokely Carmichael to this poem, which is the last in the *Pains* cycle: "although Stokely is not mentioned in *Truth*, he informs the poem as a probable narrator at whom listeners of all ethnic groups hurl their refutation, 'You lie!'"[130]

Carmichael was also central to "West Indian Litany," which begins "Stokeley (sic) like he mad!"[131] St. John said that "Truth" expressed the fear in "certain thinkers" that "the African in the West Indies be overcome by the Asian."[132] Stokely Carmichael is a presence in the whole "Pains" cycle of ten poems, St. John adds, "for there is the constant question to the African which asks 'What are you doing in the West Indies to establish yourself as the owner and maker of your destiny.'"[133] St. John's delivery of this inflammatory material is risky, but his dramatization of working class fears and resentments was never deliberately divisive, but rather sought to present what was being thought and said outside the circles of the powerful (of whatever color). He had both sympathy and resistance to Black Power, seeing it as betrayal of a complex national and regional cultural identity which has to transcend race and, at the same time, a necessary corrective to racist and economic denial of the contribution and abilities of people of African descent.

Humor is a very important aspect of Barbadian popular culture, which St. John recognized well. In his unpublished essay, "Laughter," he argued that laughing may be a "personal release, a racial release or a national release."[134] This is a very Caribbean (or West Indian) position, especially in the idea that laughing about race may alleviate tensions over it. Also, he thought that all persons in authority are laughed at, in response to their generating tension which must be released if it is not to become hatred (by that time laughter is not a possible relief). It is in fact another poet, W. H. Auden, who is quoted by St. John as saying "when we really hate someone, we cannot find them comic."[135] St. John also knew that "since laughter is human, it must have its imperfections."[136] He connects laughter to oppression in a particular way, "since oppressed communities are in everyday life often subjected to tensions," theater may be one of the few places which provides a release from tension by laughter.[137] This would explain the laughter by West Indian audiences in what theater professionals might consider the wrong places in a play, or the enduring popularity of comic shows which utilize social stereotypes and raucous interactions of characters, because St. John sees this type of laughter as reversing social roles and subjecting those in authority (which may be those trying to impose an "elite" play on the masses) to being laughed at and therefore becoming inferior for a moment.

In his "Introduction," he writes "[t]he Barbadian buffer is humour, a humour that often results in hearty laughter, a sound which carries a complexity of meanings: happiness, relief, resentment, embarrassment, understanding, doubt, to mention a few . . . a humour in which irony abounds."[138] And further "[i]n addition to humour, oppressed peoples often have to resort to silence as a method of communication, but this is for the most part accompanied by gesture, grin, sigh, smirk, smile or simper. One should therefore, in the poetry of such peoples, of such folk, expect some eloquence in pauses of unusual length, and one should pay attention to the reader's gestures."[139]

In short, the political life of a people unable to voice their discontents may be discovered in the tiniest of gestures and expressive sounds, as evidenced in performers such as St. John and Pragnell. Comic writers in Barbados, from those who have created the long-running annual topical drama of working class life, "Laff It Off," as well as Layne-Clarke (whose very successful radio series "Okras in de Stew" began in the 1970s), prove how St. John's work was part of a wider cultural use of humor as a vehicle for the airing of difficult subjects. Across the West Indies as a whole, performers have used humor to do this as in the work of Paul Keens-Douglas (Trinidad and Tobago), and Louise Bennett (Mis' Lou) and Trevor Rhone (Jamaica).[140] Like Caribbean humor, African-American humor also makes great use of physical and vocal nuancing, as well as layering of meaning, irony, and the exploitation of working-class expressions.

St. John's poetry is often ironical or suffused with a sly humor which is sympathetic even when making fun of someone.

Thus in "Wisdom," the rhetorical questions expose political naivety (as when South African's cricketers were refused entry to Barbados because of apartheid, but the counter banning blocks world class black sportsmen like Arthur Ashe (the American tennis player) and Gary Sobers (the Barbadian cricketer) as well:

> Yuh t'ink we foolish?
> We gine ban South Africa an' invite the U.S.A.,
> We gine kill apartheid an' lick up black power,
> Ashe cyan' play nor Sobers needuh
> You t'ink we foolish?[141]

In "Letter to England," a mother in Barbados is both grateful for her child sending money and gifts from away, but also very willing to use manipulation to extort more:

> Uh paint up de place an varnish de furnitures
> An' Lord mek peace dat t'ief charge muh so
> High dat I ain' got a cent lef' to brighten
> Muh face, so de Lord will bless yuh
> Don' fo'get you ol' muddah, lonely
> An' t'ankful wukkin' she fingers to de
> Bone, she soul-case droppin' out, Wuh Lord!
>
> (I paint up the place and varnish the furniture
> And Lord make peace that thief charge me so
> High that I haven't got a cent left to brighten
> My face, so the Lord will bless you
> Don't forget your old mother, lonely
> And thankful working her fingers to the
> Bone, her soul-case dropping out, Wuh Lord!)[142]

Again, though the expression is Barbadian, as in "her soul-case dropping out" and "Wuh Lord" (an untranslatable expression of concern or exasperation), the situation is a pan-Caribbean one, with so many adult children away working in Canada, the United States or Britain, trying to remit money and keep in touch with elderly parents (and most especially elderly mothers). In "Jamaica," a son is leaving to study there, and the father gives advice about the strange ways of Jamaicans, "Jamaica West Indian but um far far from we." "Li'l ignorant wid a capital H comin' to food / Callin' eddoe cocoa an' christophene chocho, / Decent dunks coolie plum an' ackee one guinep / Dem ackee is fowl egg growin' pun a tree."[143]

Cricket is a crucial part of Barbadian and West Indian culture, a game which the English brought as their own imperial expression in sports, but which was turned into an opportunity to literally beat them at their own game by West Indian players, and thus became an iconic part of anti-colonial politics, especially since black working class boys could enter this sport and dominate it, when others, like tennis, which depended on particular facilities, were available only to whites. C. L. R. James's classic text on the role of cricket in his own young life and in the West Indies as a whole, *Beyond the Boundary* (1963), began an intellectual tradition of seeing the sport as a series of metaphors by which to read social and political history. He said, "I haven't the slightest doubt that the clash of race, caste and class did not retard but stimulated West Indian cricket."[144] The West Indies Test team is made up of the best players from across the region and cricket has been one of the most important ways that the West Indies has developed a collective consciousness and still provides a clear route to focusing the cricket world's attention on the Anglophone Caribbean and to significant interaction between the local and the global (Barbadians listen or watch cricket at whatever time it is being played by West Indians, in Australia, India, Pakistan, the United Kingdom, etc.).

Both St. John and Brathwaite have written "cricket poems." Brathwaite's "Rites" and St. John's "Cricket" each present the game not just as a national ritual but as moral teacher and serious business (a local development of the British belief that something not fair is "not cricket").[145] In "Rites," the narrator, a tailor talking whilst he sews in his shop, says, in a deliciously ironical way: "this isn't no time for playin' / the fool nor makin' no sport; this is cricket![146] The poem reiterates that "when things goin' good, you cahn touch / we; but leh murder start an' you cahn fine a man to hole up de side" (a prophetic position given the way the West Indies has collapsed as a world leader in cricket in recent years).[147] In St. John's "Cricket," the folk philosopher Archie holds forth on the game, "De lord got som'ting to do wid cricket. / De wicket does remin' me o' de Trinity / God in de centre of de three, / Holy Ghost pun de lef' and Jesus / Pun de right an' de bails like a crown / Joinin' dem an' mekkin' dem Three in One"[148] and that being the case, Archie eventually concludes:

> Cricket is de game o' de Lord
> Cricket is de game o' de Master

> Play de game right, Boysie boy
> An' you stan' a good chance hereafter.[149]

Brathwaite's poem is not only conversational (with a slightly heightened repetition which both portrays ordinary speech and reinforces its embedded patterns), but captures onomatopoeic sounds in Bajan language, a key aspect of indigenous speech, very much on view in the kinetic excitement of witnessing a game in progress and understood by everyone:

> Lambert went in, play-
> in' he know all about it as us'al
> an' *swoosh!* there he go fan-
>
> nin' outside the off-stump an'
> is *click!* ...
>
> but leh murder start an' *bruggalungdung!* ...
>
> [...]
>
> He bowlin' off-breaks.
> Int makin' no fuss
> jus' toss up de firs'
>
> one an' *bap!*[150]

St. John's poem also captures the game in energetic process, with a tight shift of sounds within lines, requiring careful attention of both performer and listener, a heightened version of the expert cricket commentator delivering the game from a distant location to the imaginations of rapt fans listening to the radio:

> De "Holy Ghost" stretch down de wicket
> An' 'e jook an' 'e poke like t'ings tight,
> All of a sudden 'e step back
> An' e' stretch up in de air an' 'e smack!
> A fielder pun de boundary pounce
> Like a cat! Down de han' 'pon de ball
> An' de ball twis' out 'e han' an' de man
> Eatin' grass an' de ball hit de board
> An' bounce back![151]

Brathwaite's poem utilizes more repetition (perhaps because it is less formal in structure), which helps capture the way cricket can seem itself repetitive (to the non-believer, slow, but to the absorbed supporter, absolutely gripping in its ball by ball detail):

> Firs' ball ...
> "N ... o ... o"

back down de wicket to Wardle.
Secon' ball . . .
"N . . . o . . . o"

back down de wicket to Wardle.[152]

St. John's rhythms are at times strong, "Big Joe David did de captain / An' So-So Johnney open de bowlin'. . . ."[153] but he varies them considerably to depict the turns in the game, sometimes rhyming internally, and sometimes using a loose couplet structure in which two lines are fairly similar in length and pattern:

De "Father" did a master 'pon de bat
Nuh lot o' crack no lot o' smack but de grace when 'e place,
Divine like de dawn foreday mornin',
Three men pun de off stan' in' close,
An 'e drive t'rough de covers smooth an' sweet
Duh get so close dat dem butt up an' fall down.[154]

Christianity and cricket, the one the major formal religion in Barbados and the other a cultural "religion" are brought together in St. John's poem. In the same way, cricket is a powerful expression and symbol across the Anglophone Caribbean, and the composition of the West Indies Test team is always a source of intense interest and debate in the region (especially if they lose a major series).

Even the poem "Kites," which might seem at first sight particularly local, has a broader significance. The Trade Winds, always playing across Barbados in varying intensities from breeze to storm, (the same agency which made the slave ships' passage possible) provide the air flows to permit kite-flying to be an art form in which all of Barbadian life can be expressed from sacred to profane. Though kite-flying is associated with the celebration of Easter (as emblem of colonial Christianity), in St. John's childhood they were usually home-made, again providing an outlet for poor children to express their creativity and resourcefulness. In the poem, he demonstrates that every kite "got it own personality."[155] The "square kite wid snaky tail" is female and "she does ben' down to right, she does ben' down / To de lef', roun' head to de tail, / Pon de right to the tail, pun de lef."[156] A popular sport is described in popular language, "Now doan forget de good ol' shop-paper kite, / A scissors an' a couple o trash bone / Bring joy to lots o' poor chil'ren heart; / Humble an' dumb but tough."[157] The underlying concern of the poem (which clearly flirts with a sentimental affirmation of working class culture) is that local inventiveness is likely to be assaulted by incoming materialism and reliance on store-bought goods, a concern understood right across the Caribbean, because its position at the crossroads of modernities, and its small economies, always makes the region vulnerable to outside economic and cultural pressures.

St. John's work is grounded in the local, which required more attention in Barbados, when he began to write, than did the transnational, and sometimes his work entirely focuses on the connection between Barbados as a place and the ways of her people. In "Reason," he plays with the kind of argument he sees as a fundamental element in Bajan culture, a kind of emotional correlate to its topography, as he explains in "Introduction":

> In folk life, there is a phenomenon which in some way corresponds to the reactions caused by the sudden appearance of steep hills, steep but short. Quarrels occur suddenly. Some are caused by a glance, especially one called "cutting the eye," which is a pronounced turning of the eye away from another person's glance. (This action is accompanied by a frown.) Others are brought about by a word, a gesture, a particular inflection of the voice or by the closing of a window of door "in the face of the onlooker." Some of these quarrels "rise sharply"; bystanders gather, and very often a heated argument ends quickly through some humorous remark, said by one of the bystanders or by one of the original contenders.[158]

Barbados is, as a coral island, flat compared to the steep sides of volcanic islands such as Dominica or Grenada. It has a series of ridges, which are indeed steep but short, as well as one more serious hill, called "Mt. Hillaby."

"Reason" is short enough to include here in full, because the dynamic of the argument is an important illustration of St. John's playful view of conflict in Bajan life: here the conflict is not serious, but amusingly about the need for one person to argue a "right" position over something trivial.

> "Man, yuh wrong,"
> "Man, uh right!"
> "No, yuh wrong"
> "Oh, Christ!"
> "You see yuh wrong?"
> "What yuh mean?"
> "Yuh swear."
> "I know uh swear."
> "So yuh wrong!"
> "But . . ."
> "God say doan swear?"
> "Yes, but . . ."
> "Well yuh wrong."
> "But . . ."
> "Yuh wrong! Yuh wrong!"[159]

St. John's own interpretation of this poem demonstrates his understanding of the theatricality of Bajan argument. He describes how it begins in the middle of a confrontation where one character "in anger, swears in true Barbadian (West Indian fashion), calling the Lord's name in vain, and how this proves to be his undoing, for the other character, playing upon the religious ethos of the country, breaks his opponent down on this Christian malpractice, and thus wins the argument that took place outside the poem."[160] Religion is very important in Barbadian and West Indian culture, and here it dominates the argument. But there is also the determination to win the verbal exchange, the core of the argumentative strain which St. John perceives as particularly Barbadian.

Though many of St. John's poems are arguments, a form he utilized with great skill and variety, he often ended with a question rather than an answer (for example, see the ending of "West Indian Litany," "Political Progress," "Courage."[161] The latter was more about leading the audience (both fictional and actual), to complicate positions. Dialogue, frequently a conversation but sometimes a call and response (a single voice and an audience, as in a church service), utilizes voices which present different points of view. By adroitly using these, St. John mapped a great many oppositional forces within Barbadian and West Indian culture and society (racially and culturally, black/white/brown/red; male/female; elite and working class, confident pronouncement and questioning doubt, intellectualism and savvy street smartness, powerful and powerless, parent and child). This is true whether he was using "dialect" or a more international inflection of English. St. John's first paired cycles of poems, *Foetus Pains* and *Foetus Pleasures* were intended to be heard together. In the cycle *Pains*, he said, he intended to convey a "certain unpleasantness in the English speaking West Indies in general" (though some of the poems are focused on Barbados). Similarly, St. John's *Pains* and *Pleasures* should not be read separately, or as opposed, because one is intertwined with the other. This happens not only between the two cycles but within individual poems (see, for example, the upbeat note in "Bajan Litany"[162] and the seriousness of "Art": "Painter doan paint studyation, / Painter doan paint worryation, / Painter doan painter paint de nation").[163]

St. John also saw that violence and death are:

> a necessary part of living at all times of the year. One has to kill ants, spiders, houseflies, cockroaches, centipedes, caterpillars, snails and slugs with or without insecticide. Cats, dogs and frogs are struck and crushed by vehicles daily. Womenfolk cut the throats of chickens, ducks and turkeys, butchers "stick" pigs, goats and sheep in backyards. Urban methods of butchering have reduced these home practices considerably, but have not yet eliminated them. Violence, therefore, has a place in folk speech.[164]

Thus strong argument may be a reflection of the violence, accidental and deliberate, which is in every part of nature and of human life still lived close to it, which was the experience of most ordinary Barbadians and West Indians in St. John's childhood and youth. Similarly, in "Bajan Language," Barbadian speech is imaged as a hearty pot of soup, with yam, potato, dumplings, eddoes, beets, carrots, pig tail, okra, salt and pepper.[165]

St. John's work came at a crucial moment to help establish respect for local language and culture (in an island where the international and the foreign was often seen as innately superior to the local, though local people often inventively realigned them for their own use). He built on Collymore's pioneering work and demonstrated his theories of language via his excellent performances of his work. He was a theorist who put his ideas into practice, and a poet who thoughtfully analyzed what his poetry attempted to achieve. This is marked in the juxtaposition of essay and poems in *Revista De Letras*.[166] He understood that the language itself is the living composite of everything which has happened in Barbados and the West Indies, and that ways of using it (say in an argument) reflect that history. By paying Barbadian language that respect, he continued the local and regional tradition of verbal skill used as political discourse with the express aim of decolonizing the culture and protecting the indigenous with its unique capacity to express Barbadian experience and identity. By recording the idiosyncratic tones and pitches of the Bajan language with which he grew up, St. John left a record of a particular moment (because like any language, Barbadian, and other West Indian languages change over time, and with increasing globalization, are now increasingly impacted by foreign influences through the media and technology). Perhaps it is only through strong local identities that island peoples can come together in a unity which does not ignore difference. Thus it is important that St. John's work is deeply local, but also aware of the region and the world. Even his international English poems are, as Curwen Best has pointed out, inflected with a local accent.[167] Also there is the international register, less frequently obvious but definitely there, as in the importance of Stokely Carmichael, or in the poem "African Diaspora," or the unpublished play "The Vests," in which two vests hanging on a line consider their "Boss" and his travels overseas. Finally, the forms of his poems (for example, call and response) are a demonstration of the vitality of the culture of the working class, both specially Barbadian and generally Caribbean, and both local and transnational in their recognition of Caribbean verbal skill.

Notes

1. The dates of St. John's death and the end of his writing life are different. He died December 4, 1995, but was ill from 1987 with Alzheimer's, and so wrote no more once the illness took hold. I am grateful for permission to quote from his work from the executors of his literary estate. I am presently editing a collection of St. John's work.

2. Despite the importance of his work, he was largely forgotten except by those who had witnessed his performances and read his work. In early 2003, a small symposium was held at the University of the West Indies, Cave Hill, organized by Marcia Burrowes and myself, to celebrate the work of Bruce St. John and introduce him to a new generation of young Barbadians who had never heard of him. The symposium was able to present restored video and audio tapes of St. John reading, scholarly papers, personal reminiscences, a display of his publications and a final performance of his work which was developed in conjunction with the National Cultural Foundation of Barbados and directed by Harclyde Walcott of the University of the West Indies. This show brought together older performers, including the late Alfred Pragnell (d. 2004), and young people who did not know St. John's work. It was chosen to be Barbados's contribution to Carifesta in Surinam (late 2003), where it was very well received, thus clearly establishing the quality of St. John's work and the importance of bringing it back into public view.

3. Brennan notes the impact of international electronic media on traditional cultures, which was precisely St. John's concern in relation to the fading of tonality in Barbadian speech—see Timothy Brennan, "The National Longing for Form", in *Nation and Narration*, ed. Homi Bhabha (London: Routledge, 1990), 67. The tensions between national and international and white, middle-class black and poor black strongly inform St. John's work.

4. Yussuff Haniff, ed., *Speeches by Errol Barrow* (London: Hansib Publishing, 1987).

5. Gordon Rohlehr, *A Scuffling of Islands: Essays on Calypso* (San Juan: Lexicon Trinidad, 2004), 22.

6. Rohlehr, *A Scuffling*, 22.

7. The West Indies Federation brought together Barbados, Jamaica, Trinidad and Tobago, Dominica, Grenada, Jamaica, Montserrat, St. Kitts-Nevis-Anguilla, St. Lucia and St. Vincent. Barbadian Grantley Adams became the first Federal Prime Minister, with the political capital of the Federation situated in Trinidad. Gary Lewis writes, "[. . .] the Adams federal government was condemned to rule a federation, isolated in its Trinidad headquarters, that was by design weakly constituted and which would soon come to be seen by the larger, richer islands as an obstacle to their own economic development and aspirations for political independence"—see Gary Lewis, *White Rebel: The Life and Times of TT Lewis* (Mona, Jamaica: The Press University of the West Indies, 1999) 173. Errol Barrow, first Prime Minister of Barbados as an independent country, was both pro and con Federation at different times, hopeful for its future and bitter about its breakup, (the latter he blamed on the British—see Haniff, *Speeches*. However in early 2006, a new economic union was established among Anglophone Caribbean nations, which will ultimately permit their nationals to live and work in any participating country.

8. The West Indies Federation dissolved in 1962, the same year that both Jamaica and Trinidad became independent.

9. Carmichael was of course associated with establishing the term "Black Power," and when he tried to tour the Caribbean in 1970, various Caribbean governments were alarmed. His Pan-Caribbean politics could be said to rest partially on his sense of being a Pan-Caribbean man (his maternal grandmother was from Montserrat, his mother was born in Panama, his maternal grandfather was from Antigua, his paternal grandmother was born in Tobago, his paternal grandfather was from Barbados). He identified a special connection to Barbados in his memoir with Michael Thelwell—see Stokely Carmichael (with Ekueme Michael Thelwell), *Ready for Revolution: The Life and Struggles of Stokely Carmichael, (Kwame Ture)* (New York: Scribner, 2003). It should be noted that St. John spelled the name Stokely as Stokeley, perhaps as a natural response to his poetic rhythms.

10. Bruce St. John, "Introduction" (unpublished essay), 31.

11. Hilary McD Beckles, *A History of Barbados* (Cambridge: Cambridge University Press, 1990), 194-96.

12. Gary Lewis argues that "it is impossible to underestimate the importance which Barbados as a society has attached to building its social capital through educational attainment [. . .] Since independence, the island's alternating governments have routinely given the lion's share of public spending, typically one fifth of the government's total budget, to educating its citizens [. . .] The island still devotes a larger proportion of total annual income to education than any other country in the Western hemisphere"—Lewis, *White Rebel*, 174.

13. St. John, "Introduction," 29.

14. Woodville Marshall, ed., *I Speak for the People: The Memoirs of Wynter Crawford* (Kingston, Jamaica: Ian Randle, 2003), 17.

15. This includes Elombe Mottley, who founded a cultural center devoted to the recognition of African cultural inheritance in Barbados, called Yoruba House, in the mid-1970s. Kamau Brathwaite however has done more than anyone to rehabilitate consciousness of and pride in African ancestry in Barbados. Barbados' population is different in composition from that of Trinidad and Tobago or Guyana, which both have large Asian populations, and also cultural inheritances from colonial rule by multiple European countries. Barbados was solely British from 1637 until Independence. The population is of African or mixed descent, with the exception of a tiny minority of local whites.

16. Kathleen Drayton, "Introduction," in *Bumbatuk 1*, Bruce St. John (Bridgetown, Barbados: Cedar Press, 1982), viii.

17. Valerie Bloom, "Language Barrier," in *Voiceprint: An Anthology of oral and related poetry from the Caribbean*, ed. Stewart Brown, Mervyn Morris, and Gordon Rohlehr (Harlow, UK: Longman, 1989), 108.

18. St. John, "Introduction," 14.

19. I am very grateful to Ruby St. John for the detail of Clement St. John's reservations about speaking Bajan, and for many other details and affirmations or clarifications of information during the research for this essay. She read the last draft of this essay also. I also thank Joy St. John and Christopher St. John, Bruce St. John's children and literary executors, for permission to quote from his unpublished and published work.

20. St. John says in "Introduction" that he began to study singing in 1953, after being a choir boy. He studied at the Royal Conservatory of Music in Toronto in 1956, one year after giving his first recital, and was encouraged to think of a career in singing. He sang as a soloist in public or at his own recitals 1957-1962, and found that singing in public made him comfortable with audiences, as well giving him a "deeper appreciation for consonants and vowels," which clearly helped his oral poetry to develop—St. John, "Introduction," 14.

21. St. John, "Introduction," 4.

22. St. John, "Introduction," 4.

23. John Agard, "Listen Mr Oxford Don," *Voiceprint: An Anthology of oral and related poetry from the Caribbean*. ed. Stewart Brown, Mervyn Morris, and Gordon Rohlehr (Harlow: Longman, 1989), 109.

24. Bruce St. John, "With Respect," in *Bumbatuk* (Bridgetown: Cedar Press, 1982), 33-35.

25. Pamela Mordecai, "Last Lines," in *Journey Poem* (Kingston, Jamaica: Sandberry Press, 1989), 53.

26. St. John, "Introduction," 17-18.

27. Brown, Morris, and Rohlehr, *Voice Print*, 264.

28. H.A. Vaughan was born in Santo Domingo—see Kenneth Ramchand and Cecil Gray, eds., *West Indian Poetry* (Burnt Mill, Harlow, UK: Longman, 1971), 45. There is an interesting portrait of him in Marshall, *I Speak*, 63-64 and 82-83.

29. John Figueroa, *Caribbean Voices: An Anthology of West Indian Poetry*, vol. 1, (London: Evans, 1966), 59.

30. Kamau Brathwaite, "Negus," in *The Arrivants: A New World Trilogy (Rights of Passage, Masks, Islands)* (Oxford: Oxford University Press, 1973), 222.

31. St. John, "Introduction," 17.

32. St. John, "Introduction," 17.

33. St. John, "Introduction," 18.

34. Kamau Brathwaite, "The Stone Sermon," in *The Arrivants: A New World Trilogy (Rights of Passage, Masks, Islands)* (Oxford: Oxford University Press, 1973), 254.
35. Kamau Brathwaite, *Mother Poem* (Oxford: Oxford University Press, 1977), 39.
36. Kamau Brathwaite, *Sun Poem* (Oxford: Oxford University Press, 1982), 31.
37. Brathwaite, *Sun Poem*, 79.
38. Kamau Brathwaite, "Titan," in *X/Self* (Oxford: Oxford University Press, 1987), 61.
39. Brathwaite, Lamming and Marshall, Barbados's most eminent writers, all made their reputations outside Barbados. Barbadians have long complained about lack of government support for the arts and about the difficulty of being a professional artist of any kind in such a relatively small community of less than 300,000 people, but now there are literary competitions sponsored both by the National Cultural Foundation and various other bodies, such as the Central Bank. But many writers still to this day go overseas, mainly to the United States, Canada or the United Kingdom, where there are not only more publishing opportunities but employment opportunities (for example, in creative writing departments of universities).

Lamming (b. 1927) left Barbados for Trinidad in 1946 and then migrated to the United Kingdom in 1950 where he became a novelist and a wide-ranging journalist. He came back frequently to the Caribbean from 1956 and has for many years now spent a part of the year in Barbados. Pouchet Paquet notes when he returned from the United Kingdom in 1956 on assignment for *Holiday Magazine*, he was involved in political platforms in Trinidad—Sandra Pouchet Paquet, *The Novels of George Lamming* (London: Heinemann, 1982), 9. For Lamming, there was an early interconnection between words and politics.

His first novel, *In the Castle of My Skin* (1953), is set in a Barbadian village, but his later work reflects his own cosmopolitan experience. He grew up working class, and being only four years younger than St. John and three years older than Brathwaite, knew an identical Barbados as a child. Richard Drayton comments that the 1937 Riots in Barbados, responses to terrible conditions of poverty which were shared across the region, were decisive in Lamming's formative years. Drayton comments rightly that "the labour movement and mass politics" had their origins in the Riots, "and their mark is clear in all of Lamming's mature work"—Richard Drayton, "Introduction," *Conversations: George Lamming: Essays, Addresses and Interviews 1953-1990*, edited by Richard Drayton and Andaiye (London: Karia Press, 1992), 18. Like St. John, he is acutely aware of class:

> Class, to one degree or another is an informing influence on the imagination of every serious writer who tries to record and interpret the content of an individual relationship . . . knowledge is never passive. It is always intended to be put in the service of some specific intention.—George Lamming, *The Sovereignty of the Imagination* (Kingston, Jamaica: Arawak Publications, 2004), 17

As his work developed, Lamming created fiction about the West Indian migrant community in Britain (*The Emigrants*, 1954), or a composite, fictional West Indian country he called San Cristobel (*Of Age and Innocence*, 1958, *Season of Adventure*, 1960), or a slave ship in the seventeenth century (*Natives of My Person*, 1982). Barbados demotic is central to *Castle*, but it is made phonetically available for the foreign reader, or even just the reader of a novel, reading alone and not wanting to be held up by having to make out the writer's phonetic equivalences of Bajan on the page. The following examples give no trouble to most readers of English: "But there wus another rumour that she wus a funny woman, used to work with spirits an' that sort of thing, an' we start to wake up . . ."—

."—George Lamming, *In the Castle of My Skin* (London: Longman, 1970), 134; "You can't pitch or play bat-an'-ball when you like 'cause there's a chil' to feed, an' this to do an' that to do, an' when you ask what the bloody hell she wus doin' or would 'ave to do if you din't come along and put yuhself in all that, she up an' tell you; don't trouble trouble till trouble trouble you"—Lamming, *In the Castle*, 142. Lamming's later fiction continues this, expanding the geographic range to include characters from different West Indian countries (*The Emigrants*) as well as Europeans (*Natives of My Person*). The range of his linguistic registers, from seventeenth century English to twentieth century Barbadian reflects the range of educated Barbadian speech and awareness of language registers.

Marshall, born in 1929 of Barbadian parents who emigrated to New York before her birth, learned Bajan in her family home in Brooklyn, and in her fiction, which is about the connections, both positive and negative, between the West Indies and the United States, she catches Bajan expression as something which can travel beyond the island and still survive. In her first novel, *Brown Girl, Brownstones* (1959), a *bildungsroman* about a young girl's growing up Bajan in Brooklyn, this is the voice of the girl's mother, Silla: "'But be-Jesus-Christ, what kind of man is you, nuh?' [. . .] 'But what kind of man he is, nuh? Here, every Bajan is saving if it's only a dollar a week and buying house and he wun save a penny. He ain got nothing and ain looking to get nothing'"—Paule Marshall, *Brown Girl, Brownstones* (Old Westbury, N.Y.: The Feminist Press, 1981), 22. This is the father, Deighton: "Yuh see yuh mother there, lady-folks? That's the way she was when we was courting. Never a hard word. A look on her face that did make you think of Jesus meek and mild."—Marshall, *Brown Girl*, 118. In *The Chosen Place, The Timeless People* (1969), despite many of the major characters either being foreign or having significant experience out of the island, Marshall gives her supporting characters language which shows Marshall has an insider's ear. But they speak in a way which is not hard for the foreign reader, as in the following brief examples: "Who the person is?"—Paule Marshall, *The Chosen Place, The Timeless People* (New York: Vintage, 1969), 25; "I'm studying Vere too bad"—Marshall, *The Chosen*, 27; "But what to do"—Marshall, *The Chosen*, 411; "Somebody that don't seem to have no uses a-tall a-tall for women"—Marshall, *The Chosen*, 311. These characters are, respectively, Leesy, great-aunt of Vere; Stinger and Elvita. Like Lamming, Marshall writes mainly in an available and well crafted narrative voice, portraying both African American and Barbadian speech in her fiction. A number of her major characters, such as Merle Kibona in *The Chosen Place, the Timeless People*, are transcultural, with experience of the African diaspora.

40. See Curwen Best, *Roots to Popular Culture: Barbadian Aesthetics: Kamau Brathwaite to Hardcore Styles* (London: Macmillan, 2001). The collection is *Joyce & Eros and Varia* (1976).

41. Richard B. Sheridan, *Sugar and Slavery: an Economic History of the British West Indies 1623-1775* (Barbados: Caribbean Universities Press, 1974), 124.

42. Barbadian language has been influential wherever it has settled outside the island, as in the connection between Gullah, spoken on Carolina's Outer Banks. Devonish points out that Barbados was the original colony/plantation society which influenced, through migration of both planters and slaves, Jamaica, Surinam, and Carolina, as well as exporting labor and with it language practices, to many other places—Hubert Devonish, *Talking Rhythm, Stressing Tone: The Role of Prominence in Anglo-West African Creole Languages* (Kingston, Jamaica: Arawak Publications, 2002), 177. He sees Barbados as the most likely source of influence on particular aspects of Sierra Leone's Krio, because Barbados exported people all over the Caribbean and then in 1792, "eleven hundred ex-slaves from the British colonies in the Americas" arrived in Freetown, Sierra Leone—

Devonish, *Talking Rhythm*, 178. Many of them might well have had Barbadian ancestry or have been influenced by Barbadian migrations.

43. Peter A. Roberts, *From Oral to Literate Culture: Colonial Experience in the English West Indies* (Mona, Jamaica: The Press University of the West Indies, 1997), Chap.3.

44. For an excellent discussion of the impact of printing in the early history of the West Indies—see Roberts, *From Oral*.

45. Gordon Rohlehr notes the importance of music, dance and calypso in the political history of Trinidad, and the banning of the Calinda drums there by colonial authorities. He also writes that Barbadians were the largest group of nineteenth century immigrants, bringing with them a strong tradition of "Sunday dancing, work songs and at times rebellion." In Barbados, there were "the same laws against dance assemblies, horns and drums, and the same call-and response style of singing, and polyphonic drumming"—Gordon Rohlehr, *Calypso and Society in Pre-Independence Trinidad* (Tunapuna, Trinidad: Gordon Rohlehr, 1990), 18. St. John's call and response poems continue this long tradition of combining music and words to express urgent social and political issues. After the Bussa Rising of 1816 (Easter Sunday, 14th April), the only slave rebellion of any size, which was suppressed in three days, Governor Leith reported by September that a hundred and twenty-three people were sentenced to be transported to Sierra Leone, a hundred and forty-four had been executed under martial law, and seventy were under sentence of death—Beckles, *A History*, 79. But still strong resistance was felt by the slaves to the plantocracy and to the British as colonial rulers. In his account of the Bussa rebellion, Beckles cites a white Barbadian's sense of the situation after the rebellion was crushed (the quotation comes from an anonymous letter, dated June 6, 1816, in Colonial Office archives [28.85], as cited by Beckles). In the quoted extract, the slaves are described as "sullen and sulky," and as seeming to "cherish feelings of deep revenge," which leads the writer to conclude that the West Indies is held by the British very tenuously, and only by military force—Hilary McD Beckles, *Rewriting History: Bussa: The 1816 Barbados Revolution* (Bridgetown, Barbados: Barbados Museum and Historical Society, 1998), 40. Since language was the one area of slave culture which was impossible for the whites to control, it became an important medium for resistance, especially as Barbados had no topography to permit a Maroon community to develop, as in Jamaica and to some extent, Trinidad. In terms of the impact of repression on Barbadian language, it is worth retelling here the wry story by the late Earl Warner, the groundbreaking theater director from Barbados, who when trying to explain how to reproduce the Barbadian accent for a class in the United Kingdom, discovered that as he put it, to produce a genuine Barbadian accent, "you first need to clench your teeth" (which he explained as all of the anger which had been suppressed in Barbados for so long). However, St. John's delivery of his poems, in meticulously pronounced and very clearly projected Barbadian is something of a rebuttal to Warner's comment, except that few people have had the kind of vocal training which enabled such a performance of the language.

46. Peter A. Roberts, *West Indians and their Language* (Cambridge: Cambridge University Press, 1988), 135.

47. Roberts, *West Indians*, 270 and 269 respectively.

48. Hilary McD Beckles, *Chattel House Blues: Making of a Democratic Society in Barbados: From Clement Payne to Owen Arthur* (Kingston, Jamaica: Ian Randle, 2004), 185.

49. Hilary McD Beckles, *Great House Rules: Landless Emancipation and Worker's Protest in Barbados* 1838-1938 (Kingston, Jamaica: Ian Randle, 2004), 186-187.

50. Marshall, *I Speak*, xiii.
51. G. Addinton Forde, *The 1937 Disturbances of Barbados* (Bridgetown, Barbados: G. Addinton Forde, 1999), 12.
52. See Forde, *The 1937 Disturbances*.
53. Beckles, *Chattel House*, 7.
54. Forde, *The 1937 Disturbances*, 42.
55. Forde, *The 1937 Disturbances*, 42.
56. "Lizzie and Joe" were characters first created in the *Weekly Recorder* newspaper by Edward Cordle (1857-1903), and then recreated subsequently because they were so popular with readers, by Archie C. Greaves, after Cordle's death, for the *Herald* newspaper—see Paula Burnett, *The Penguin Book of Caribbean Verse* (Harmondsworth, UK: Penguin, 1986), 375, and also for several examples of the Cordle series. Bruce St. John gave me photocopies of some of the poems from a collection edited by Greaves, explaining their importance to him. The "Lizzie and Joe" poems were written in four line rhyming stanzas (aa bb), generally with fourteen syllables a line, in iambic meter. They were often topical, as when Lizzie praised a new gas stove she had bought. "Lizzie and Joe in Court" demonstrates the social comment which these poems often contained, "Uh nebah cross dese courts agen ess uh live un hundred yares / Yuh nebah gets no justice, how dese false witnus swares / An dem dat got fuh try you en eben wut deh pay / Uh wud back me Josif gence dem in law-wuk enny day"—Burnett, *The Penguin Book*, 17. Brathwaite comments in his poetic autobiography that Cordle's 1903 *Overheard*, of Lizzie and Joe poems is one of the earliest examples of "dialect [I cannot yet say nation language] in the English-speaking Caribbean"—Kamau Brathwaite, *Barabajan Poems* (New York: Savacou North, 1994), 90.
57. St. John, "Introduction," 14.
58. Richard Allsopp, *Dictionary of Caribbean English Usage* (Mona, Jamaica: University of the West Indies Press, 2003), xvii.
59. Loreto Todd, *Pidgins and Creole* (London: Routledge and Kegan Paul, 1974), 87.
60. Hubert Devonish, *Language Liberation: Creole Language Politics in the Caribbean* (London: Karia Press, 1986), 119.
61. Frank A. Collymore (1893-1980) was a poet and a teacher at Combermere School in Barbados and founder and editor of the legendary literary magazine, *Bim*, in which so many Caribbean writers of the 1950s and 1960s were first published.
62. Devonish, *Talking Rhythm*, 176.
63. Frank Collymore, *Barbadian Dialect* (Bridgetown, Barbados: Barbados Tourist Board, 1970).
64. Bruce St. John, "Barbadian Dialect A Brief Introductory Sketch" (unpublished talk given at University of Ottawa, Aug 16, 1971), 5.
65. Collymore, *Barbadian Dialect*, 26.
66. Todd, *Pidgins*.
67. Roberts, *From Oral*, 73.
68. Roberts, *From Oral*, 73.
69. Collymore, *Barbadian Dialect*, 36.
70. St. John, "Barbadian Dialect," 7.
71. St. John, "Barbadian Dialect," 8.
72. St. John, "Barbadian Dialect," 4.
73. St. John, "Barbadian Dialect," 5.
74. Collymore, *Barbadian Dialect*, 84.
75. St. John, "Barbadian Dialect," 3.

76. St. John, "Barbadian Dialect," 3.
77. St. John, "Introduction," 3.
78. St. John, "Introduction," 4.
79. St. John, "Introduction," 5.
80. Roberts, *West Indians*, 92.
81. Roberts, *West Indians*, 92.
82. Roberts, *West Indians*, 92.
83. St. John, "Introduction," 29.
84. Devonish, *Talking Rhythm*, 176.
85. Collymore, *Barbadian Dialect*, 84.
86. Jahan Ramazani, *The Hybrid Muse: Postcolonial Poetry in English* (Chicago: Chicago University Press, 2001).
87. Kamau Brathwaite, "History of the Voice," in *Roots*, Kamau Brathwaite (Ann Arbor: University of Michigan, 1993), 273; key here are the terms "noise" and "sound": by which is meant words, echoes of words, sounds which communicate a feeling without words or sounds which mimic a familiar noise. Brathwaite's poem "Angel/Engine," which appears in different versions in *Mother Poem* (1977), *Barabajan Poems* (1994), and *Ancestors* (2001), is a brilliant demonstration of one set of sounds (the singing of hymns in Barbados) translating into another (the Yoruba god Shango becoming manifest in the singing), and his performance of this poem makes words into noise and sounds with a quite other signification from their original meaning.
88. Brathwaite, "History," 286.
89. For example, in "Telephone Conversation" (Alfred Pragnell's CD, *SkyLarkin!*, Track 1), utilizes tone brilliantly, from high pitched exclamations, sly emphases, long drawn out exaggerated syllables and sighs or laughs. There are many complex sounds in Barbados in extensive popular use which convey a great deal. Of these the most ubiquitous is the "chupse." Collymore explains it as "a sound made by pouting the lips and sucking in air between the teeth; indicative of distrust or sulking" and includes a reference to Richard Allsopp's argument that such sounds exist in East and West African languages (he does not know if these convey the same emotions)—Collymore, *Barbadian Dialect*, 22. Collymore adds that he was criticized by a leading journalist for such a narrow version of the contribution the "chupse" makes throughout the West Indies, to convey amused tolerance, self-criticism, disdain, disgust, abuse of someone else, or provocation—Collymore, *Barbadian Dialect*, 23.
90. St. John, "Introduction," 30.
91. Mervyn Morris, *Is English We Speaking and Other Essays* (Kingston, Jamaica: Ian Randle Publishers, 1999), 45, 50.
92. St. John, "Introduction," 51.
93. Collymore, *Barbadian Dialect*, 107.
94. Occasionally, as when he performed at Kairi House in Trinidad, his simple request for a table and a chair caused anxiety as to how theatrical he could be, until he began to perform—see Bruce St. John, "Bruce St John at Kairi House," *Kairi* 4/5 (1974): E3.1 (Introduction). His vocal training gave him excellent breath control, and as he sat with a straight back and only rarely moved his hands in a very discreet way to emphasize a point now and then, the vitality of the poetry as he delivered it was a stunning contrast.
95. St. John, "Barbadian Dialect," 1.
96. St. John, "Introduction," 30.
97. See Best, *Roots*.
98. Bruce St. John, "Saturday Night at the Exhibition," in *Bumbatuk* (Bridgetown, Barbados: Cedar Press, 1982), 23.

99. Roberts, *From Oral*, 44.
100. Bruce St. John, "Bajan Litany," in *Bumbatuk* (Bridgetown, Barbados: Cedar Press, 1982), 9.
101. See Richard Allsopp, *A Book of Afric Caribbean Proverbs* (Kingston, Jamaica: Arawak, 2004).
102. Allsopp, *A Book*, 89.
103. Allsopp, *A Book*, 145.
104. Allsopp, *A Book*, 79.
105. Bruce St. John, "West Indian Litany," in *Bumbatuk*, 2.
106. St. John, "Bajan Litany," 9.
107. Bruce St. John, "Truth," *Bumbatuk*, 12.
108. Bruce St. John, "Privilege," *Bumbatuk*, 38.
109. Bruce St. John, "Bajan Language," *Bumbatuk*, 53, 55.
110. Derek Walcott, "The Schooner 'Flight,'" in *Collected Poems: 1948-1984*, Derek Walcott (New York: Farrar, Straus and Giroux, 1986), 346.
111. Bruce St. John, "Education," in *Bumbatuk*, 3.
112. St. John, "Education," 4.
113. St. John, "Introduction," 43.
114. St. John, "Education," 3.
115. The University of the West Indies has however provided centers in Law (Barbados), Medicine (Jamaica) and Agriculture and Engineering (Trinidad and Tobago) which facilitate intra-Caribbean student connection.
116. Bruce St. John, "Higher Learnin," in *Bumbatuk*, 31-32.
117. In his essay, "Independence and the Social Crisis of Nationalism in Barbados" Hilary Beckles quotes St. John's "Political Progress," a poem about the white Barbadian retreat from direct involvement in government into business—see Hilary McD Beckles, "Independence and the Social Crisis of Nationalism," in *Caribbean Freedom: Economy and Society from Emancipation to the Present*, ed. Hilary Beckles and Verene Shepherd (Princeton, N.J.: Markus Weiner Publishers, 1996), 528-539. After Independence, a comfortable black middle class was mostly willing to maintain the status quo, in which whites controlled the economy.
118. Drayton, "Introduction," vii.
119. Bruce St. John, "Nationalism," in *Bumbatuk*, 48.
120. Bruce St. John, "Who Is We?" in *Bumbatuk*, 6.
121. Jeannette Layne-Clarke, "Colour," in *Bajan Badinage*, Jeannette Layne-Clarke (Bridgetown, Barbados: Impact Productions, 1993), 19-21.
122. Layne-Clarke, "Colour," 19-21.
123. Layne-Clarke, "Colour," 19-21.
124. Layne-Clarke, "Colour," 19-21.
125. Bruce St. John, "Colour," in *Bumbatuk*, 51-52.
126. St. John, "Truth," 12.
127. St. John, "Introduction," 36.
128. St. John, "Introduction," 36.
129. St. John, "Introduction," 36.
130. St. John, "Introduction," 32.
131. St. John, "West Indian Litany," 2.
132. St. John, "Introduction," 31-32.
133. St. John, "Introduction," 32.
134. St. John, "Laughter," 1.

135. St. John makes a clear distinction between what is funny and what is comic in this essay. Auden's essay, he notes, is from "Notes on the Comic," an essay published in 1965.

136. St. John, "Laughter," 4.
137. St. John, "Laughter," 3.
138. St. John, "Introduction," 26.
139. St. John, "Introduction," 28-29.

140. Keens-Douglas and Bennett both perform their own material as individual performers; Rhone's work scripts in play form. The dramatic is evident in any portrayal of Caribbean Creole, which is so often demonstrated in performance through dialogue, argument, call and response, or a dramatic monologue.

141. Bruce St. John "Wisdom," in *Bumbatuk*, 10.
142. Bruce St. John, "Letter to England," in *Bumbatuk*, 44.
143. Bruce St. John, "Jamaica," in *Bumbatuk*, 49.
144. C. L. R. James, *Beyond A Boundary* (New York: Pantheon, 1983), 72.

145. The University of the West Indies now has the *C. L. R. James Institute for the Study for Cricket*, which sponsors research into all aspects of the game and its contribution to West Indian culture.

146. Kamau Brathwaite, "Rites," in *The Arrivants. A New World Trilogy*, Kamau Brathwaite (Oxford: Oxford University Press, 1973), 198.

147. Brathwaite, "Rites," 201.
148. Bruce St. John, "Cricket," in *Bumbatuk*, 17; bails are the top of wicket.
149. St. John, "Cricket," 19.
150. Brathwaite, "Rites," 200-201.
151. St. John, "Cricket," 19.
152. Brathwaite, "Rites," 200.
153. St. John, "Cricket," 17.
154. St. John, "Cricket," 19.
155. Bruce St. John, "Kites," in *Bumbatuk*, 20.
156. St. John, "Kites," 20.
157. St. John, "Kites," 21.
158. St. John, "Introduction," 26-27.
159. Bruce St. John, "Reason," in *Bumbatuk*, 2.
160. St. John, "Introduction," 37.

161. St. John, "West Indian Litany," 2; Bruce St. John, "Political Progress," in *Bumbatuk*, 5; Bruce St. John, "Courage," in *Bumbatuk*, 8.

162. St. John, "Bajan Litany," 9.
163. St. John, "Pleasures," in *Bumbatuk*, 14.
164. St. John, "Introduction," 28.
165. St. John, "Bajan Language," 53-56.

166. See Bruce St. John, "Bruce St. John/Bumbatuk (Poems in Barbadian Dialect)," *Revista De Lettras*, 16 (December 1972): 540-585.

167. Best, *Roots*, 76.

Bibliography

Agard, John. "Listen Mr Oxford Don." Pp. 109-110 in *Voiceprint: An Anthology of oral and related poetry from the Caribbean*. edited by Stewart Brown, Mervyn Morris, and Gordon Rohlehr. Harlow, UK: Longman, 1989.

Allsopp, Richard. *A Book of Afric Caribbean Proverbs*. Kingston, Jamaica: Arawak, 2004.

———. *Dictionary of Caribbean English Usage*. Mona, Jamaica: University of the West Indies Press, 2003.

Beckles, Hilary McD. "Independence and the Social Crisis of Nationalism." Pp. 528-539 in *Caribbean Freedom: Economy and Society from Emancipation to the Present*, edited by Hilary Beckles and Verene Shepherd. Princeton, N.J.: Markus Weiner Publishers, 1996.

———. *Chattel House Blues: Making of a Democratic Society in Barbados: From Clement Payne to Owen Arthur*. Kingston, Jamaica: Ian Randle, 2004.

———. *Great House Rules: Landless Emancipation and Workers' Protest in Barbados 1838-1938*. Kingston, Jamaica: Ian Randle, 2004.

———. *A History of Barbados*. Cambridge: Cambridge University Press, 1990.

———. *Rewriting History: Bussa: The 1816 Barbados Revolution*. Bridgetown: Barbados Museum and Historical Society, 1998.

Best, Curwen. *Roots to Popular Culture: Barbadian Aesthetics: Kamau Brathwaite to Hardcore Styles*. London: Macmillan, 2001.

Bhabha, Homi. "Introduction: narrating the nation." Pp. 1-7 in *Nation and Narration*, edited by Homi Bhabha. London: Routledge, 1990.

Blake, William. "Songs of Innocence and of Experience." Pp. 15-60 in *Blake's Poetry and Designs*, edited by Mary Lynn Johnson and John E. Grant. New York: Norton, 1979.

Bloom, Valerie. "Language Barrier," Pp. 108 in *Voice Print*, edited by Stewart Brown, Mervyn Morris, and Gordon Rohlehr. Burnt Mill: Longman, 1989.

Brathwaite, Kamau. *Ancestors*. New York: New Directions, 2001.

———. *The Arrivants: A New World Trilogy (Rights of Passage, Masks, Islands)*. Oxford: Oxford University Press, 1973.

———. "Negus." Pp. 222-24 in *The Arrivants: A New World Trilogy (Rights of Passage, Masks, Islands)* Oxford: Oxford University Press, 1973.

———. "Prelude." Pp. 28-29 in *The Arrivants: A New World Trilogy (Rights of Passage, Masks, Islands)* Oxford: Oxford University Press, 1973.

———. "Rites." Pp. 197-203 in *The Arrivants: A New World Trilogy (Rights of Passage, Masks, Islands)* Oxford: Oxford University Press, 1973.

———. "The Stone Sermon." Pp. 254-57 in *The Arrivants: A New World Trilogy (Rights of Passage, Masks, Islands)* Oxford: Oxford University Press, 1973.

———. *Barabajan Poems*. New York: Savacou North, 1994.

———. *Mother Poem*. Oxford: Oxford University Press, 1977.

———. "Angel/Engine." Pp. 97-103 in *Mother Poem*. Oxford: Oxford University Press, 1977.

———. "Horse weebles." Pp. 38-40 in *Mother Poem*. Oxford: Oxford University Press, 1977.

———. "History of the Voice." Pp. 259-304 in *Roots*. Ann Arbor: University of Michigan, 1993.

———. *Sun Poem*. Oxford: Oxford University Press, 1982.

———. *XSelf*. Oxford: Oxford University Press, 1987.
———. "Titan." Pp. 61-63 in *X/Self*. Oxford: Oxford University Press, 1987.
Brennan, Timothy. "The National Longing for Form." Pp. 44-70 in *Nation and Narration*, edited by Homi Bhabha. London: Routledge, 1990.
Burnett, Paula, ed. *The Penguin Book of Caribbean Verse*. Harmondsworth, UK: Penguin, 1986.
Carmichael, Stokely, with Ekueme Michael Thelwell. *Ready for Revolution: The Life and Struggles of Stokely Carmichael (Kwame Ture)*. New York: Scribner, 2003.
Collymore, Frank. *Barbadian Dialect*. Bridgetown: Barbados Tourist Board, 1970.
———. "Hymn to the Sea." Pp. 264-265 in *Voiceprint: An Anthology of oral and related poetry from the Caribbean*. edited by Stewart Brown, Mervyn Morris, and Gordon Rohlehr. Harlow, UK: Longman, 1989.
Cordle, Edward. "Lizzie and Joe in Court." P. 17 in *The Penguin Book of Caribbean Verse*, edited by Paula Burnett. Harmondsworth, UK: Penguin, 1986.
Devonish, Hubert. *Language Liberation: Creole Language Politics in the Caribbean*. London: Karia Press, 1986.
———. *Talking Rhythm, Stressing Tone: The Role of Prominence in Anglo-West African Creole Languages*. Kingston, Jamaica: Arawak Publications, 2002.
Drayton, Kathleen. "Introduction." in *Bumbatuk 1*, Bruce St. John. Bridgetown, Barbados: Cedar Press, 1982.
Drayton, Richard. "Introduction." Pp. 18-20 in *Conversations: George Lamming: Essays, Addresses and Interviews 1953-1990*, edited by Richard Drayton and Andaiye. London: Karia Press, 1992.
Figueroa, John, ed. *Caribbean Voices: An Anthology of West Indian Poetry*, vol. 1. London: Evans, 1966.
Forde, G. Addinton. *The 1937 Disturbances of Barbados*. Bridgetown, Barbados: G. Addinton Forde, 1999.
Haniff, Yussuff, ed. *Speeches by Errol Barrow*. London: Hansib Publishing, 1987.
James, C. L. R. *Beyond A Boundary*. New York: Pantheon, 1983.
King, Bruce. *Derek Walcott and West Indian Drama*. Oxford: Oxford University Press, 1995.
Lamming, George. *Of Age and Innocence*. London: Michael Joseph, 1958.
———. *In the Castle of My Skin*. London: Longman, 1970.
———. *The Emigrants*. Ann Arbor: University of Michigan Press, 1994.
———. *Natives of My Person*. London: Longman, 1972.
———. *Season of Adventure*. London: Allison and Busby, 1979.
———. *The Sovereignty of the Imagination*. Kingston, Jamaica: Arawak, 2004.
Layne-Clarke, Jeannette. "Colour." Pp. 19-21 in *Bajan Badinage*, Jeannette Layne-Clarke. Bridgetown, Barbados: Impact Productions, 1993.
Lewis, Gary. *White Rebel: The Life and Times of TT Lewis*. Mona, Jamaica: The Press University of the West Indies, 1999.
Marshall, Paule. *Brown Girl, Brownstones*. Old Westbury, N.Y.: The Feminist Press, 1981.
———. *The Chosen Place, The Timeless People*. New York: Vintage, 1969.
Marshall, Woodville, ed. *I Speak for the People: The Memoirs of Wynter Crawford*. Kingston, Jamaica: Ian Randle, 2003.
Mordecai, Pamela. "Last Lines." Pp.53-54 in *Journey Poem*, Pamela Mordecai. Kingston, Jamaica: Sandberry Press, 1989.
Morris, Mervyn. *Is English We Speaking and Other Essays*. Kingston, Jamaica: Ian Randle Publishers, 1999.

Pouchet Paquet, Sandra. *The Novels of George Lamming*. London: Heinemann, 1982.
Pragnell, Alfred. "Skylarkin'!" CD of performance of Barbadian stories, songs and poems. Christ Church, Barbados: CRS Music, n.d.
Ramazani, Jahan. *The Hybrid Muse: Postcolonial Poetry in English*. Chicago: Chicago University Press, 2001.
Ramchand, Kenneth, and Cecil Gray, eds. *West Indian Poetry*. Burnt Mill, UK: Longman, 1971.
Roberts, Peter A. *From Oral to Literate Culture: Colonial Experience in the English West Indies*. Mona, Jamaica: The Press University of the West Indies, 1997.
———. *West Indians and their Language*. Cambridge: Cambridge University Press, 1988.
Rohlehr, Gordon. *Calypso and Society In Pre-Independence Trinidad*. Tunapuna, Trinidad: Gordon Rohlehr, 1990.
———. *A Scuffling of Islands: Essays on Calypso*. San Juan: Lexicon Trinidad, 2004.
Sheridan, Richard B. "The Condition of Slaves in Barbados." Pp. 31-50 in *Inside Slavery: Process and Legacy in the Caribbean Experience*, edited by Hilary McD Beckles. Kingston, Jamaica: Canoe Press, University of the West Indies, 1996.
———. *Sugar and Slavery: an Economic History of the British West Indies 1623-1775*. Barbados: Caribbean Universities Press, 1974.
St. John, Bruce. "African Language." P. 30 in *Joyce & Eros and Varia*. Bridgetown: Benin Books, 1976.
———. "Bajan Language." Pp. 53-56 in *Bumbatuk*. Bridgetown: Cedar Press.
———. "Bajan Litany." P. 9 in *Bumbatuk*. Bridgetown: Cedar Press.
———. "Barbadian Dialect. A Brief Introductory Sketch." Unpublished talk given at University of Ottawa, August 16, 1971.
———. "Bruce St. John/Bumbatuk (Poems in Barbadian Dialect)." *Revista De Lettras* 16, (December 1972): 540-585.
———. "Bruce St John at Kairi House." *Kairi* 4/5, (1974): E3.1 (Introduction).
———. *Bumbatuk 1*. Bridgetown, Barbados: Cedar Press, 1982.
———. "Colour." Pp. 51-52 in *Bumbatuk*. Bridgetown: Cedar Press, 1982.
———. "Courage." P. 8 in *Bumbatuk*. Bridgetown: Cedar Press, 1982.
———. "Cricket." Pp. 17-19 in *Bumbatuk*. Bridgetown: Cedar Press, 1982.
———. "Education." Pp. 3-4 in *Bumbatuk*. Bridgetown: Cedar Press, 1982.
———. "Higher Learnin." Pp. 31-32 in *Bumbatuk*. Bridgetown: Cedar Press, 1982.
———. "Introduction." Unpublished essay.
———. "Jamaica." P. 49 in *Bumbatuk*. Bridgetown: Cedar Press, 1982.
———. *Joyce and Eros and Varia*. Bridgetown: Benin Books, 1976.
———. "Kites." Pp. 20-22 in *Bumbatuk*. Bridgetown: Cedar Press, 1982.
———. "Laughter." Unpublished essay.
———. "Letter to England." P. 44 in *Bumbatuk*. Bridgetown: Cedar Press, 1982.
———. "Nationalism." P. 48 in *Bumbatuk*. Bridgetown: Cedar Press, 1982.
———. "Nationality." P. 14 in *Bumbatuk*. Bridgetown: Cedar Press, 1982.
———. "The Other Woman." Pp.15-16 in *Bumbatuk*. Bridgetown: Cedar Press, 1982.
———. "Pleasures," P. 14 in *Bumbatuk*. Bridgetown: Cedar Press, 1982.
———. "Political Progress." P. 5 in *Bumbatuk*. Bridgetown: Cedar Press, 1982.
———. "Privilege." P. 38 in *Bumbatuk*. Bridgetown: Cedar Press, 1982.
———. "Reason." P. 2 in *Bumbatuk*. Bridgetown: Cedar Press, 1982.
———. "Saturday Night at the Exhibition." P.23 in *Bumbatuk*. Bridgetown: Cedar Press, 1982.
———. "Truth." P. 12 in *Bumbatuk*. Bridgetown: Cedar Press, 1982.

―――. "The Vests." Unpublished verse play.
―――. "West Indian Litany." P.2 in *Bumbatuk*. Bridgetown: Cedar Press, 1982.
―――. "Who Is We?" Pp. 6-7 in *Bumbatuk*. Bridgetown: Cedar Press, 1982.
―――. "Wisdom." P. 10 in *Bumbatuk*. Bridgetown: Cedar Press, 1982.
―――. "With Respect," Pp. 33-35 in *Bumbatuk*. Bridgetown: Cedar Press, 1982.
Todd, Loreto. *Pidgins and Creoles*, London: Routledge and Kegan Paul, 1974.
Vaughan, H. A. "To the Unborn Leader." P. 59 in *Caribbean Voices: An Anthology of West Indian Poetry*, edited by John Figueroa. London: Evans Brothers, 1966.
Walcott, Derek. "The Schooner 'Flight.'" Pp. 345-361 in *Collected Poems: 1948-1984*. New York: Farrar, Straus and Giroux, 1986.

11

Tanya Shields

The Amerindian Transnational Experience in Pauline Melville's *The Ventriloquist's Tale*

Pauline Melville's first novel, *The Ventriloquist's Tale*, offers a model to investigate some of the ramifications of globalization, transnationalism, and integration in the Anglophone Caribbean with specific reference to the rights of indigenous peoples in a development context.[1] In Guyana, a state plagued by ethnic, economic, and environmental duress and political stalemates, solutions that push the boundaries of all citizens are crucial. Power sharing is one suggestion dynamically argued in the Caribbean by David Hinds.[2] Hinds's position on power sharing, while primarily limited to Afro and Indo Guyanese, is one political approach on coexisting in plural societies rife with ethnic and racial violence. While these Guyanese are trying to coexist in their fracturing nation-state, transnationalism for indigenous people has meant that nation-states have been built on their territories. While they have always belonged to a particular nation with its own practice, colonization has meant that their nations now exist within other states. Their transnational practice does not necessarily involve migration and travel in the accepted sense (that is, outside of their national borders), but rather negotiation between their nations and the states that have cut across their communities to establish themselves. Essentially, this has made them transnational before the terminology of transnationalism emerged.

The Ventriloquist's Tale focuses on the lives of the Amerindian McKinnon family, their interactions with each other, the Guyanese state, and the larger global order. The novel juxtaposes worldviews that are Amerindian, European, and "Coastlander"—a mix of African, Asian, and European. Economic hardship forces Chofy McKinnon, the protagonist, from the savannahs to the coastal capital, Georgetown. Chofy's journey between these landscapes highlights contemporary conflicts within Amerindian communities, and among the settler communities that surround them. Leaving behind his wife, Marietta, and their son, Bla-Bla, Chofy temporarily resettles in Georgetown with his Aunt Wifreda, who needs a cataract operation. There he works in a library and has an affair with Rosa Mendelson, a British researcher investigating writer Eveyln Waugh's visit to Guyana. Chofy's relationship with Rosa leads to harmful disclosures for his family. Their affair, which takes place in the contemporary world, parallels the sexual relationship between siblings Danny and Beatrice, which unfolds in the early twentieth century as part of McKinnon family history. These relationships signal the personal, historical, and contemporary challenges faced by indigenous communities. Tenga, the protagonist's cousin, puts it succinctly: "We are destroyed if we mix and we are destroyed if we don't."[3] The essence of survival for Melville is posed in the simple question of exogamy or endogamy—to mix or not to mix—which?[4] Examining the novel for Caribbean positions on globalization and transnationalism, one notes that they are mired in these two poles of mixing, which can narrowly be applied to Amerindians but also, more broadly, to the region. To mix or not to mix, or rather *how* to mix; on whose terms does and will the region and its people participate with each other and in the wider world?

In this intersectional space, let me define my groundwork and larger project on Caribbean integration. I use political scientists Anthony Payne and Paul Sutton's definition of integration, which characterizes it as a political process through which countries and citizens accept that greater regional good may occasionally predominate over local and national concerns.[5] I refer to this utopic undertaking as another El Dorado—a quest for citizenship in a globalized world. This quest means asking and finding solutions for the hard questions of multiracial and multiethnic coexistence in economically developing areas. Mixing for the Wapisiana people in the novel illustrates the larger problems for the integration debate—the unity of the nation-states, their specific national personalities, as well as finding a place for ethnic, religious, economic, and sexual difference in a politically integrated state.

To theoretically move toward this, I have developed, what I call, Amerindian Postmodernism,[6] a framing that acknowledges the Amerindian trace and the commonalities between the often obliterated native and the enslaved African.[7] These commonalities emerge from a shared relationship and characterization of the natural environment and foster integration through access to these rhizomatic[8] latent roots. Amerindian Postmodernism is constructed around four guiding principles: enlarging visionary capacity; reclaiming stories languishing in [H]istorical[9] ruptures; rehearsing, or prismatic re-readings of the past; and concretizing these into action through theater and/or theatrical methods. The attempt of uniting the epistemological legacies of science and alchemy suggests an approach to reality which looks for truth somewhere beyond linear realist stories. These narratives present themselves when we consider Caribbean colonial history and the formation of independent nation-states.

To connect the political process of integration with the social, economic, and emotive processes of mixing, Amerindian Postmodernism creates mutual spaces, where "enemies" can congregate around shared bias/es, to unite science,

European quest for order, with alchemy, unification of order and disorder through transformation. Science privileges discovery, while alchemy recognizes that all-knowing is impossible—thus, uniting contradictory elements. To this end, Amerindian Postmodernism distinguishes itself from 1960s manifestations of postmodernism because of its direct and material link to the past, an indigenous past, and the myths that help to explain the existence and attitudes of these groups.

Caribbean citizenship, for the purposes of this discussion, is divided into five areas: local, national, regional, diasporic, and transnational. The most narrowly defined area local refers to is kinship ties—fictive and biological—and their immediate community. National encompasses the state and its governing apparatus, the actual infrastructure of resource distribution, rather than an ethnic nation. Regional citizenship is constructed territorially around Caribbean geography. Diasporic citizenship operates on several levels: first, those who have left their national communities; in other words, those who left their own state by migrating to one or more Caribbean states; and second, those who absent themselves from the geographic Caribbean entirely. The final category, transnationalism, has similar demarcations, but the primary difference is that transnationals are engaged with minimally two national spaces simultaneously, for example, Amerindians who belong to an "ethnic" grouping or nation as well as to European sanctioned states.

Throwing voice[10]

The Ventriloquist's Tale offers several parallel love stories with which to discuss issues of belonging and citizenship. Chofy and Rosa, a Wapisiana man and his British lover; Danny and Beatrice, an incestuous brother-sister relationship, between Chofy's uncle and aunt, which results in a child, Sonny; and patriotic love of community or nation as expressed by Tenga, Chofy's cousin, and Olly Sampson, the fictional Guyanese finance minister. This novel enables readers to participate with a history, more than likely not their own, by throwing voice and experience through fiction.

Fiction and history seem to be strange bedfellows. Collaboratively, they are the sharpest lenses through which to view the experiences of marginalized groups and attempt an understanding of the psychosocial aspects of "the other." Fiction complicates history's truths by expressing the latter's own narrative process since the fluid elements of character and metaphor saturate any documented fact. Still, given the weight of [H]istorical writing, those who have constructed history through non-scribal means have had to make meaning against these hegemonic notions of the past and use fiction as an intervention.

Amerindians, who horizontally construct themselves across the borders of Venezuela, Guyana, and Brazil, rupture Guyana's vertical territorial space, and complicate any notion of Caribbean national communities operating as psychosocial homelands for postcolonial Caribbean people. Due to the treaties signed by various colonial powers, "Amerindians enjoy certain entitlements linked to their status as first inhabitants of Latin American countries. Amerindians are free to cross the borders between the different ex-colonies in South-America,"[11] indicating the lasting transnational nature of indigenous communities and reminding the contemporary Caribbean of its origins in something more enduring than the colonial paradigm. Outside the purview of nation-states, Amerindian citizenship and sovereignty are grounded in smaller notions of community and history—primarily ethnicity and tradition. In Melville's novel, Tenga, Chofy's ideological foil, clearly articulates this position, "We Amerindian people are fools, you know. We've been colonized twice. First by the Europeans and then the Coastlanders. I don't know which is worse . . . by companies, scholars, aid agencies, tourists or politicians . . . Amerindians have no chance in this country [Guyana]."[12] Tenga's response is to leave the corrupters and colonizers of the European and Coastlander varieties alone. As the Coastlanders and the wider Caribbean communities with which they are aligned consider notions of homeland and the effect of transnationalism, studying the experiences of often forgotten Amerindian groups allows for a deeper understanding of Caribbean realities than might be obtained from studying the space exclusively from the perspective of its colonial inheritance.

On the question of surviving in the margins, economist Samir Amin puts forth one controversial view of *how* those who are so marginalized might ensure survival on their own terms. He suggests "delinking" as a strategy, arguing that the developing world has nothing to lose by withdrawing politically and/or economically from the West, or more precisely from Western corporations and institutions. Amin defines delinking as "not autarky, but the subordination of outside relations to the logic of internal development and not the reverse."[13] Amin is asking for an examination and foregrounding of how national and personal "interests" are constructed. Why and how do the interests of the West or its hegemonic minority/ies (the "black-skinned, white-masked" minorities) in developing countries become global interests? While Amin's ideas could be construed as unreasonable or unrealistic, he is proposing in the realm of *hard* reality what *The Ventriloquist's Tale* discusses in fiction for Amerindian communities and for Guyana. To invoke Amin's solution in this novel is to delink and focus on Amerindian and Wapisiana concerns above all else.

According to Melville's fictional portrayal, Tenga's retreat from the "states,"—Guyana, most clearly—is one endogamous response. It asserts the power of delinking from the margins of the Guyanese state, since Guyana cannot or does not address Amerindian concerns. It is in Amerindian interests to help themselves by foregrounding their priorities. In reality, outside of the world of the novel, Amerindians prioritizing their own interests led to a coalition with ranchers in which the two groups were part of "the aborted January 1969 Rupununi Uprising" which Prime Minister Forbes Burnham characterized as an insurrection [which] was planned, organized and carried out by the ranchers of the Rupununi—the savannah aristocrats [. . .] And which was drawn mainly, but not exclusively from the Hart and *Melville* families [. . .] Such Amerindian citizens as were involved were employed in a secondary capacity and appeared generally to have acted under duress and in response to the orders of their rancher employers [. . .] the Venezuelan press were reporting an Amerindian uprising . . . and suggesting that it arose out of the wish of these Guyanese citizens to come under the sovereignty of Venezuela[14] (emphasis added).

This comment underscores the intersections of Melville's personal history and Amerindian agency, and illustrates the relevance of these issues which then and now influence Guyanese economic and socio-political realities.[15] While Burnham categorizes Amerindian participation as secondary, and one operating under rancher duress, the fact of the matter is that Amerindians were negotiating with his administration for land title and recognition of rights. Through linguistic sleight-of-hand, this negotiation allowed Amerindians land titles for "those areas occupied by [them] at the time of independence"[16] rather than the unreasonable fifty percent of Guyana's land mass that approximately fifty thousand Amerindians were claiming as their ancestral lands.[17] This concession reiterates the fluidity of sovereignty between indigenous populations and settler communities.

In Guyana, Amerindian claims are viewed not only in the context of conquest, colonialism, and neocolonialism, but also under the rubric of human rights. As human rights constituencies recognized by the United Nations (UN) and other international organizations, indigenous groups have been acceded the right to ancestral lands that allow for the perpetuation of their ways of life. In fact, Article 15 of the UN's "Universal Declaration of Human Rights" states that, "everyone has the right to a nationality."[18] Ultimately, invoking this Article could lead to more isolated and autonomous Amerindian enclaves. In Melville's fictional work, though, Tenga advocates privileging Amerindian boundaries and knowledge systems; he does not argue for total isolation from settler communities. The novel begs the question: what is the impact on political, economic, and cultural values for communities living at the crossroads of other nations and other worldviews?

The idea of the crossroads becomes primary when examining transnational practice in an age of globalization and in the context of Caribbean integration. Simply stated, economic globalization is an expansion and integration of markets in an age of rapid technological advancement. Although this process affects other aspects of life and cultural production, its impact on Caribbean development is primarily economic, political, social, and cultural. The inequities inherent in the process of globalization are rife and are concentrated in the arenas of access and distribution. The world's poor have limited or no access to the technological freeway, yet some middle- and many upper-class elites benefit from the increasing disparity in global poverty. Paget Henry calls this dismantling of the "third world capitalist [welfare] state, savage globalization [or] the West's new imperialism."[19] This "new imperialism" is the backdrop for Third World development issues, particularly diversity, equality, and citizenship.

In the novel, issues of purity and contamination emerge in the sometimes binary relationship between Tenga and Chofy, cousins who have different notions of racial, cultural, and intellectual integration with the Guyanese state. Melville interrogates the meaning and usefulness of interaction with the outside world. Via the contentious relationship between Professor Michael Wormoal and the researcher Rosa Mendelson, she highlights the issue of who owns and controls knowledge about the Amerindians. Both these European experts want information from indigenous people, since Rosa's need is not directly related to the Amerindians themselves, but is about a visit to Guyana once made by the *Brideshead Revisted* writer Evelyn Waugh, she feels superior to Wormoal, an anthropologist who is invested in his superiority to the native populations— Amerindian and Coastlander. Wormoal contends that he "probably know[s] more about the Amerindian peoples than they know about themselves;" and laments that "Indian culture is disintegrating these days—contaminated mainly by contact with other races."[20] Wormoal's quest is another form of plunder that allows him to explain the Amerindians to the larger world, because he will not share his collected data with them.[21] The Professor's need to know, catalog, and categorize defines Europeanness against nativeness and concretely illustrates Tenga's point on double colonization and complete exploitation.

However, the knowledge shared between Europeans proves dangerous to the locals. Rosa, Chofy's British lover, reveals the meaning of his name to Wormoal,[22] who, shares it with the executives and engineers of the U.S. drilling company, Hawk Oil.[23] This leads, as argued by April Shemak, to misinterpretations and misrepresentations by outsiders. The death of Chofy's son, Bla-Bla, exemplifies[24] Shemak's point and illustrates how knowledge ferreted out and shared *among* Europeans, even when based on fact, can be a disrupting influence in native communities, "Chofy translates his name as 'explosion of rapids or fast-flowing waters,' [which] by the time the oil workers use it to warn Bla-Bla the meaning has become merely 'explosion.' Chofy's decision, as a native informant, to share the meaning of his name with Rosa sets off the series of events that lead to Bla-Bla's death, thus translation becomes a space of violent disruption and dislocation."[25] This misinterpretation of the native catapults the Wapisiana into another enactment of the Conquest and the continual occupation of their lands by foreigners. The quest for foreign "gold," defined here as knowledge, continues to infect indigenous people. Here Melville introduces the idea of knowledge as gold, another hallmark of globalized and transnational economies.

In the Caribbean, economic globalization has manifested in its typical fashion in the global South. It is an experience of moderate to extreme wealth for capitalism's collaborators and penury for the rest. The Caribbean middle class, a sector of service workers in managerial, government, and small business posts, as well as educators is on the ropes similar to middle classes elsewhere. Moreover, local economic and political elites, those who own wholly or in-part businesses that are necessary to the country's economy—like tourist resorts—or are government ministers and officials who set policy, are part of the class of global professionals who manage the movement of goods, services, and if need be, politics, in service of multinational corporations.[26]

In the novel, Tenga, reacting against the interference of outsiders, wants to reassert a pre-colonial space, where intellectual and material resources are out of foreign reach. He proclaims, "I am not Guyanese, I am Wapisiana."[27] For him, this means ignoring the Guyanese state and its borders. The Wapisiana nation—which predates the contemporary states of Venezuela, Brazil, Suriname, and Guyana—spills across these borders, *undermining* them all. The border as a site of flux and contemporary contestation is reinforced. The deterritorialized border, which for economic globalization is transparent, while similarly invisible in this case, is problematic especially for the surrounding states. The pre-colonial Wapisiana nation can claim the rights to its sovereignty across this vast territory. Its claim rests primarily on constructions of indigenous identity, while delinking advocate Samir Amin finds identity politics problematic, the in-between spaces that the Wapisiana and other indigenous groups occupy allow for other notions of belonging (an Amerindian nationalism) and organizing.

Yet, an integrated, and I must stress, *defacto* Wapisiana state based solely on Amerindian identity, is more of a threat to Guyanese territorial borders than are the endless border claims made by Brazil, Suriname, and Venezuela. This is mainly because claims made by these states seek legal restitution and acknowledgement, while the Wapisiana do not. Well, not quite. When aligned with a state, the Wapisiana do seek the legal acknowledgement of their land claims and human rights as indigenous people within the state. However, if they do not acknowledge the state, they do not seek its validation in any respect.[28] In Amin's parlance, they have delinked; and as symbolized by Tenga, *ignore* outsiders and construct and represent themselves and their nation on their own terms. The difference between them and the Guyanese state is that they have never had pretensions to participation in the international economic order. Thus, the Amerindian ability to imagine and practice indigenous communities and nation-building continues to challenge the postcolonial state from *within*, while economic globalization challenges the sovereignty of the postcolonial state from *without*.

As globalization challenges the legal limits and sovereignty of European ordered and endorsed states, the Wapisiana nation reasserts its right to nationhood across borders and beyond legal administrative structures of the West. In fact, between Suriname and French Guiana (Guyane) this movement of Amerindians, Maroons, and Haitians into these states continue to undermine these borders.[29] The organization of Amerindian societies thus provides a space of refuge for outcasts from the contemporary postcolonial nation state. The Wapisiana and other Amerindian communities in the Guianas never relinquished their land rights to colonizers such as the British by "conquest, cession, treaty or papal bull, yet [the British] asserted sovereignty over them,"[30] enshrining a policy of assimilation over Amerindian objections.[31] Paget Henry argues that "the colonial state is an illegitimate formation in local political discourses, and so also is the authority of the foreign cultural elites. Yet the stability of the larger hegemonic order requires that these illegitimate formations be made to appear legitimate."[32]

In the novel, Tenga tries to delegitimate European-drawn borders by ignoring them. His is the most narrow, familial form of citizenship. In essence, it is the citizenship of the blood. The second possibility is of participation within these states and therefore a demand for recognition of Amerindian human rights and land claims. This is the perspective of an internal transnational citizen—one who belongs to two nations. Fundamentally, it is one who claims citizenship beyond kinship, ethnic, and racial lines.

Large and small states are increasingly servicing the agendas of transnational corporate power.[33] In Melville's novel, Hawk Oil Company, a U.S. conglomerate looking for black gold in Wapisiana territory, best represents the concrete manifestations of globalization.[34] The favored status of the fictional Hawk Oil Company mirrors the real-life situation. The Guyanese government, in direct contradiction of Amerindian desires, granted this very same access to Rupununi lands to Migrate Mining Company of South Africa.[35]

The Ventriloquist's Tale facilitates a conversation about contamination, purity, and citizenship. The landscape one "belongs to" conditions one's participation in politics, both formal and informal. In speeches to the Amerindian Leaders Conference in February and March of 1969, Burnham spoke to Amerindian leaders about loyalty. His speech, coming just seven weeks after the Rupununi Uprising,[36] spoke directly of citizenship and Amerindian marginalization. Burnham reminded Amerindians that the patronizing British had characterized them as "children of the forest," and that they would, if they could, beggar them. He reiterated that his administration was the only one in the neighboring region to recognize Amerindian land claims. And he asked Amerindians to acknowledge that they were citizens of Guyana and that the "riches of the interior are the riches of the nation." He reminded them that "those who come with Bibles and leave with diamonds" have neither their interests nor the interests of the Guyanese nation at heart.[37] Burnham's intention was preservation of Guyana as a state with access to the management and exploitation of natural resources. Thus, the Guyanese state recognized Amerindian rights within its territory, but not Amerindian desires to organize across the borders of the Guyanese state. The postcolonial reality was the ascendancy of the nation state and given that reality, Amerindian transnationalism could not be allowed to violate the sovereignty of the state.

Michel Laguerre argues that transnational citizenship means not being a minority because one remains connected to a homeland.[38] Desrey Fox sociologist and Akawayo, one of the aboriginal communities in Guyana, expresses this position as well:

> We as indigenous peoples, should get together and do something about our plight because the whole Indian question is a problematic question in the South [. . .] we should get ourselves organized like the Caribbean Organisation of Indigenous Peoples [or the] World Council of Indigenous Peoples and some other brother organizations like the Mezquito organization in Nicaragua and really talk about what the Amerindian people want in the future, what they want for their progress. [Because] we find links in Belize—the Garifuna of Belize. I was just there [and] I thought that I was there before; the familiarity was there.[39]

Fox observes that organizing across boundaries is the way to Amerindian empowerment and her project incorporates the global South, not just Guyana or Central America. In reconfiguring indigenous identities in a global framework, Fox recognizes the importance of a "whipped up consciousness [that enables me] to merge what I learned [in sociology courses] with my own Amerindian experience [and utilize the knowledge] from both cultures."[40] Fox's solution to potential marginalization or in-between status of Amerindian cultures is to find spaces of accommodation. She posits that Amerindian cultural abandonment has been an impediment, "We tend to see it a little wrong, I mean my own people too. After they have been introduced to this modern, contemporary education [and lifestyle] they tend to go aside with the dominant culture, leave their own culture [. . .] and try to develop that way, but then you realize that you are neither here nor there."[41]

It is through confronting this space of in-betweenity, "neither here nor there," that *The Ventriloquist's Tale* explicitly examines notions of citizenship within Amerindian communities and the larger world. As Desrey Fox's observations note, constructing Amerindian citizenship across not just conjoined borders, but all borders, is a conversation Amerindians are actively pursuing. Melville's Tenga, though the primary proponent of an endogamous lifestyle, lives in a non-Wapisiana Amerindian village near the capital and is theoretically (or imaginatively), rather than physically, aligned with the open vistas of the savannah. The savannah's remoteness from the capital and the overall physical environment of the country maintains the illusion of exclusivity and exacerbates the multi-national feeling generated in Guyana. Human interaction has affected the savannahs and, like other areas, they have changed. People have not tamed them, in the sense of cultivation, but access to the forests and subsoil has transformed the land. Whether this change is permanent is debatable—the landscape repeatedly reclaims the changes man has made, but drilling, deforestation, and other human interventions affect the land and its inherent viability.

In such a physical space, Tenga's position makes sense. Amerindian traditions evolved through an interaction with a reclaiming nature, one in which the natural cycles of flooding eradicated whatever changes were made to the land. Amerindians found a way to live within the limits of the natural environment. The Guyanese government and the multi-national corporations (MNCs) have eroded these sustaining traditions by trying to exploit the region's resources. In an Enlightenment sense, they believe that they can control, mitigate, and deal with natural flows in ways Amerindians technologically were unable to. Tenga's position becomes not only a discussion on Amerindian culture and notions of citizenship, but also one that foregrounds the ecological (historical and social) nature of citizenship and this discussion in an environmentally unstable world. Tenga's ally, strangely, is the expatriate researcher Professor Wormoal, who believes that "the purity of the nation [. . .] has its attractions."[42]

Thanks largely to colonialism and globalization, Tenga's Amerindian world is one of conflict. He lives with other Amerindians in land occupied by Coastlanders and multinationals whose worldviews, to his mind, are genocidal. With Chofy, the potential enemy most like his mirror-self, Tenga shares landscape, biology, and traditions. Tenga's preferences are based on his understanding of how Wapisiana history and culture have been corrupted:

> Look at this shop. Before it opened, people used to fish and share everything with the other families here. Now they take the fish to sell in Georgetown for money to buy things in the shop. And did you see the well outside? Some people came and asked us what we wanted. We didn't know. We just said a well. They built it for us. But people missed going down to the creek to fetch water and talking to each other. It destroyed the social life of the village. And the well water tastes different—horrible—like iron. Then somebody shat in the well or children threw rubbish in it and half the village got poisoned.[43]

These development initiatives were external and, while not exactly imposed, "destroyed the social life of the village." For Tenga, development and technology are at odds and he has no plan for rectifying this problem. Because of this, his beliefs on returning to an imagined Wapisiana purity are still conflicted. "You say we should mix,' said Tenga bitterly. 'What to do? We're destroyed if we mix; and we're destroyed if we don't'."[44] The novel does not explicitly answer these questions and Melville confesses that she, too, is ambivalent about the possibilities.[45] Two central unanswered questions in the novel are how to proceed—how to accommodate the endogamy/exogamy question and how to deal with these accommodations across race, ethnicity, and nationality. However, what is valuable about the novel's approach is the continued *interplay* between these issues. The recognition that no one space, or text, can provide a panacea, but radically fusing, sometimes disparate elements, disparate epistemologies, to reconfigure new ventriloquisms.

Citoyen power

Since the Enlightenment, two traditional distinctions have emerged in Western citizenship discourse: the *citoyen* and the burgher. Bart van Steenbergen argues that the ideal citizen, or *citoyen*, is active in public life and willing to sacrifice for the greater good. The burgher, or economic citizen, "generally lacks the feeling of responsibility and public spirit."[46] Transnationally, these categories systematize class relationships. The *citoyen* can be found across class lines, but can reproduce class concerns within its public manifestation. Burgher citizens are not only Richard Falk's transnational economic elites, which in the Caribbean have traditionally been absent planters or investors, but also those who migrate for [sometimes meager] economic opportunities and whose responsibilities are more narrowly tied to households rather than municipalities.

Similarly, Mahmood Mamdani examines the roles of race and ethnicity in the postcolonial state. Mamdani posits that imperial governments had two policies for defining colonial citizenship. First, direct rule fostered a race-based political identity, which distinguished between settlers and natives. Settlers had the power to govern and shape policy, while natives were limited to an economic arena, where they were rarely owners or managers, but wage earners. In the second scenario—indirect rule—political identity was "fractured along ethnic lines."[47] Therefore, under direct rule, the civilizing project, linked concretely to the law, distinguishes the colonizer from the colonized and encourages the development of a class that can participate in the civic (civilizing) sphere.[48] As a result, the notion of civilization is connected to whether one is *worthy* of citizenship.

Like his Guyanese enemies from Chofy to the Coastlanders, Tenga grapples with the idea of mixing. Though he values the ideal of Wapisiana purity and wants Wapisiana unity, he recognizes the impossibility of achieving it. However, he sees both—inter-ethnic mixing and its opposite—as resulting in crisis. Similarly, in Guyana, Trinidad, and other Caribbean nations with significant "ethnic" populations, prejudices and racist attitudes about "other" ethnic groups are evident. While governments push the "national" identity—"We are all Surinamese, Cuban, etc."—the material realities based on a history of colonial governments pitting groups against one another on the ground have resulted in access inequities and have bred resentments which continue to foster, at minimum, injustice.

For Tenga, reconnecting science and alchemy, or making the harmonizing epistemological link between colonial and Amerindian knowledge, is as paralyzing as all other options. Because mixing or not mixing yields the same result, Tenga is maintaining the status quo. Taking an active stance in one direction or another is too great a commitment for him. According to this Wapisiana citizen, full integration of Amerindians into Guyanese society means a literal poisoning of cultural wells. Limited integration, what is currently in place, is a slow poisoning of indigenous people. Tenga's reference to the rum shop, which he names Jonestown, invokes the idea of a foreign incursion, a place where people go to disappear.[49] Jonestown invokes the memory of the massacre of nine hundred and fourteen people lead by charismatic U.S. evangelist and leader of the People's Temple, Jim Jones. Jonestown, the site of Kool-Aid sweetened salvation or murder disappeared under an overgrowth of weeds and vines; Jonestown, as fact and metaphor, is another encroachment of foreigners bringing death and doom through their refreshing beverages. However, Tenga and Chofy avail themselves of the drinks in Jonestown, the bar.[50]

In the framework of Amerindian Postmodernism, Tenga's inability to unify, or at least engage with, science and alchemy indicates that he cannot shape a hopeful space from the chaos and despair of the contemporary circumstances of indigenous people. He cannot fashion a mutual space. In the postcolonial space of native peoples Amerindians are faced with the challenge of transforming traditional notions of citizenship. One can argue that this site is still not *post* colonial given the continual colonization that some (Tenga) might argue indigenous people still experience from the Guyanese state, currently formulated as African and Indian. Tenga cannot transcend his Amerindian national space or (even transgress, as he would see it, into) the national spaces of the nation-states that enclose Wapisiana territory.[51]

Constructing narratives and subjectivities is one way to move beyond narrow identity formation. There must be interaction across narrow national borders. These narratives, as Benedict Anderson argues, are key to national development and identity formation and are a critical component of nationalism and citizenship discourses.[52] Transnationalism is defined by Basch, Schiller, and Blanc "as the process by which immigrants forge and sustain multi-stranded social relations that link together their societies of origin and settlement,"[53] the important factors being "post" colonialism and deterritorialization. Thus, issues of transnationalism and transnational identities as considered in this project not only concern immigrants outside their national borders, but as is the case with Amerindians, natives within their own territory that were consumed and cobbled into states by outsiders in the colonial process. That is one aspect of the postcolonial condition as it regards citizenship; the other is, of course, the economic effect of colonialism that breeds dependency. Central to this discussion on citizenship is how identity is used to cultivate belonging and how, as Mamdani argues, political citizenship and identity have been subsumed to cultural and sometimes economic identities.

In Melville's novel, Chofy, unlike Tenga, goes out to the primary Guyanese landscapes, the coastal areas of the capital. Georgetown supports eighty percent of the Guyanese population and it is there that Chofy tries to recoup his economic losses and send remittances to the Rupununi. There are clear parallels with the migration of Caribbean people to Europe and the United States., and the return of remittances repatriated to assist with specific economic need. After suffering financial reversals because his cattle were killed from bat bites which drained their blood, Chofy travels to the city to make some money. In this solitary and uneasy[54] landscape Chofy is stifled, and describes the city as an empty, foreign place with a spatial structure that indicates the messy madness of mixing, "It was as if the architects and builders had attempted to subdue that part of the coast with a geometry to which it was not suited and which hid something else [. . .] Even the width of the streets produced melancholy amongst the European colonists, used to the narrow cobbled alleys and uproarious slums of their own capital cities."⁵⁵ Georgetown, the "city built of space," with elastic buildings, is a grid of contradictions full of stuffy offices and narrow streets. Stabroek Market, once a slave market, is a maze of stalls unlike the savannahs. Georgetown is a place of racial mixture, heat, humidity, and rot. In a sense, the city is representative of a "larger world," one closer to the West. The city, like other colonial cities, especially one built on the foundations of Dutch slave markets and engineering that is an ode to European technology and efficiency, is the link to Western values, ethics, and knowledge. It is no accident that the writer has Chofy working in a library, arranging, and restocking validated bits of European knowledge. Libraries, like museums, have been spaces in which Amerindians have generally been the objects of study; Chofy as an arranger in this environment inverts the idea of who owns and arranges knowledge.

But like Chofy's stay in the city, a hermetic place in which he finds love with a Marxist, Jewish, British researcher, Georgetown also offers a contradictory reading as a site of Western connection. While it is spatially the most technologically and structurally Western space in Guyana, it is also "contaminated" by the mixtures of Western colonialism, a mixture that fosters the "tingalinga tingalinga" culture and history of the steel pan, a drum invented in 1930s Trinidad and Tobago.⁵⁶ Georgetown, an enclosed space, because of limited road and rail infrastructure, is isolated from the rest of the country. Such containment from the hinterlands has made it a site of mixing or contamination, depending on one's perspective. The contradiction of Georgetown is that it too, while Western, is alienated from the West. It is stuck in a colonial mode of imitation and reaching for something it can never be, either in spatial or temporal terms. Even as space is technized and subdued, as with the taming of the landscape to make a city, it is a space that reiterates Amerindian unbelonging and alienation. Instead, their salvation is linked, somewhat romantically, to the open vistas and "brown clumps of grass" of the savannahs.⁵⁷ Georgetown for Amerindians is a place where they are teased, tormented, and on the fringe. They are not part of the coastal nation. Chofy's sojourn in the city illustrates that Georgetown's possibilities of love (Rosa) and, inversion of knowledge (his job in the library) can only be temporary.

After Chofy begins an affair with Rosa Mendelson, he argues the positives of mixing with other communities. Disagreeing with Tenga, he says, "We [Amerindians] have to mix; otherwise we have no future. We must get educated. We can't go backwards. Guyana has to develop."⁵⁸ Of course, Chofy means education in a formal, European sense. In this instance, integration seems to be the obvious correct *progress*ive answer. Chofy and his family are products of mixing fostered by colonization and globalization. Retreat for them is, if nothing else, genetically impossible.

Paula Burnett posits that Chofy "is one of the Wapisiana, who inhabit a zone of exchange between the constantly hybridizing cultural communities of the coastal strip and the unmodified traditional cultures of the interior."⁵⁹ In part, Burnett's argument seems to be that Chofy's singularity, his entrance into the zone, is made possible by his racial mixture, a heritage not all Amerindians can claim. Therefore, his genetic identity enables him to enter this buffer zone where he negotiates two cultures. While I agree with this, recognizing that this exchange zone is one way of characterizing transnational citizenship, I disagree with Burnett's assessment that Amerindian culture is unmodified. While Tenga would hope so, the fact is that interior cultures have changed precisely because people like Chofy exist.[60] Furthermore, there is no original Caribbean culture to which to return if the contemporary mix is rejected.

Chofy's buffer zone also embodies Amin's ideas: delinking from his Wapisiana home, which he considers territorially part of the Guyanese nation-state, from his wife, Marietta, to pursue Rosa, and from Wapisiana notions of education, as indicated by his belief that the Amerindian "must get educated." Chofy's disassociation from a pure Wapisiana home and identity is, like the rest of the novel, mitigated by his return to the savannahs because of his son's death—a return that prizes cultural identifications over political ones.

Moreover, Chofy's temporary disconnection from his Wapisiana world presents one delinking alternative. Temporary delinking highlights the privileging of shifting priorities. Removal from his Wapisiana world made it possible for Chofy to have other experiences, primarily a love affair with Rosa. Chofy may have remained indefinitely in the city if not for his son's tragic death, which calls for his immediate removal from the metropolis to the savannah. Initially Melville's vilification of the city heightens the restorative properties of the savannah. Yet, this, too, is undermined.

Though Chofy eventually leaves Georgetown and Rosa, his return to the Rupununi is not celebratory. It is with a heavy heart that he is compelled to return to his former life, "[a]s Chofy stared at the stern and exhausted little face, he felt a crushing pain in his chest and his arms seemed to lose their life. The expression on Bla-Bla's face was a sneer of accusation. It seemed to accuse him of many things: of abandoning his family, deserting his son, of not being able to keep the land safe for his children. With shock, he felt that he had lost not only a child but a whole continent."[61] Chofy's return and Bla-Bla's death are weighted with blame, "Tenga blames Chofy for deserting his own people . . . [and he was] silenced by the guilt."[62] For Chofy, the landscape is poisoned with "evil dripping from the thatch."[63] Eventually, however, it facilitates his recovery, "The great, unchanging open spaces gave him time and a frame in which to think. Despite the grief and guilt, in the savannahs his son's death seemed contained within a certain order of things and not just an extra, random confusion, as everything was in the city. From a distance, the affair with Rosa began to seem like a sort of bewitchment, something unreal."[64] The contradiction of Chofy's choice continues when juxtaposed with other concrete events; Bla-Bla's death and Aunt Wifreda's sight all belie the dream Chofy wants to fulfill. Indeed, as Rosa had been warned, "nothing keeps in the tropics," reiterating the reality of tropical impermanence and the predisposition to rot.[65] Thus, the Guyanese territory—Amerindian and Coastlander—seems only capable of temporary encounters.

Every event is a "bewitchment," which will not last. Every event demands detachment and delinking, in other words, constant reevaluation. The lesson in Chofy's response to the landscape (territory) is that nothing is permanent *except change*. Essentially, there is nothing to lose by reassessing one's relationship to one's thatched house, a capital city, or nation-state.

By juxtaposing city and savannah, though she seems more authorially predisposed to the savannah, Melville begins a conversation about models and reevaluation—which models of citizenship and nation are best suited for the Wapisiana, which should they reconsider. In the long run, it is a lesson also valuable at the national level. The buried (or not so buried) contradiction is that as Europe becomes more regional, the Caribbean and other underdeveloped regions need to consider maximizing the power of their resources or addressing the lack of them through equitable, mutually sustaining regional options—not to mimic European regionalism, but to construct the promise of the nation embedded in Caribbean geography.

Caribbean regionalism, like Chofy's stay in the city, underscores his transnationality. He, unlike Tenga, sees himself as both Wapisiana and Guyanese. Textually, transnationalism is another option for the Wapisiana, though it is clearly one of the most painful (Bla-Bla's death) and costly choices. Nonetheless, Chofy's experience constructs the transnational citizen internal and external to the region. Chofy's struggles emphasize new and complex representations of Amerindians in a globalized and technologized world, while also highlighting groups excised from or romanticized in the construction of the nation—historically and politically.

As for the spaces Chofy shares with the enemy, initially they are centered on the idea of development. Chofy, like Coastlanders and foreign investors, believes there is value in education and mixing. In fact, he argues that it is the only way Amerindians will survive. Yet, by the novel's end, Chofy recants this earlier position and because of Bla-Bla's death returns to the vast and soothing openness of the Rupununi. Chofy's loss of his son, a child who, after the accident would have been paralyzed had he lived, represents continual depletion of Amerindian "blood-stock," and to a degree, Amerindian "choice" over their nation and future. However, Chofy's retreat to the savannahs—and especially their characterization in such romantic terms—reads a bit too neatly. Upon his return, Chofy is thrown into the creek by his horse and is chided by his wife, Marietta, "You been away too long. Don' you remember that horse? You have to do his girth up tight because he pushes his belly out when you saddle him . . . Chofy, soaking wet, stood on the banks . . . while Marietta sat and cried with laughter."[66] I am especially intrigued, however, by Chofy's earlier position as an internal transnational straddling two different communities with mixed agendas. This dilemma of the transnational, of where to put one's loyalty: in which "home"; in which publics to participate becomes a core question in the project of advancing a larger Caribbean community. Did Chofy, as Tenga claims, betray his people and his family by going to the city? He certainly betrayed his wife,

Marietta, who *is* aligned with the Wapisiana nation and characterized as the archetypal mother of the nation. How is Chofy's earlier transnationalism reconciled with his retreat to the savannahs? It is a dilemma Melville also claims not to have resolved. In a 2001 talk, she said, "I am still trying to decide how I feel about the issue of to mix or not to mix. I'm still not sure about it."[67]

Despite Melville's uncertainty, her life as a writer moving between the United Kingdom, the Caribbean, and various Wapisiana territories, across the borders of Guyana and Brazil, suggest a possible model both for the Wapisiana and a Caribbean searching for a less fractured sense of self. Danny, Chofy's uncle, moves across the same terrain, and there is also Chofy's move between city and savannah, all point to the transient, migratory aspects of life for fictional and real characters. In a transnational world, this type of movement becomes a necessary part of life. Entrance into systems of exchange in the global order has necessitated the acquisition of money and skills that in turn foster the inherent portability in peoples' lives. In an age of aeronautic travel, migration has created transnational citizens who belong to more than one place and actively participate in and comment on several "local" communities. Transnationalism is shaped by many factors;[68] and in the novel, transnationalism is formed by the semi-autonomous Amerindian spaces, which endogamous advocates such as Tenga, would like to be independent.

Melville's "soulful epistemology" juxtaposes "modernness" with an Amerindian way of being. She reconnects science, Enlightenment strategies to uncover and "know," and alchemy, indigenous classification strategies that recognize chaos and the unknowable, by showing that science is no better than alchemy and, may in fact, be less useful. Yet, the characters she uses to illustrate this point are themselves invested in "science" and other modern methods despite the fact that these approaches fail them. Mainly, these characters reside permanently or temporarily in the city, a contaminated location removed from the purity and "rotting" romance of the savannahs. The urban characters Rosa and Olly share this category,[69] of those invested in Western disciplines, structures, and knowledge strategies; while Father Napier, the missionary, homosexual priest and Alexander McKinnon, the patriarch of Chofy's family and the savannah oligarch, represent this pole in the interior.

Incest and indigeneity

Like the rest of the novel, the Wapisiana national construct does not provide a romantic refuge. The incestuous relationship of Chofy's aunt and uncle, Danny and Beatrice, is emblematic of the lack of romantic answers. They are the ultimate manifestation of Tenga's position, since it is difficult to be more introspective and endogamous than a sexual relationship between siblings. Their family, the larger Wapisiana community, and other Amerindian communities treat the relationship with various levels of discomfort and horror.[70] Familial and national splits further manifest in their parents' reactions. Alexander McKinnon, Beatrice and Danny's father, leaves the savannah, because "after twenty-five years, he realized that he did not belong."[71] McKinnon, based on the "fertile person of H.P.C. Melville"[72] and the most liberal incarnation of a European, is ruptured by his children's relationship.

In contrast, Maba, Danny and Beatrice's mother, has perhaps the more complicated response to her children's affair, "I know it's not good, what Danny and Beatrice are doing, but it is not the worst thing in the world. It's happened before." Maba's matter-of-fact response reiterates Amerindian worldviews—in which the incest myth is a myth of *accepted* contradiction and harbinger of change.[73] In Amerindian folklore and in this family, incest tied to the eclipse, is a form of obliteration, which leads, according to Walter Roth, former Chief Protector of Aborigines in North Queensland, Australia, to metamorphosis.[74] Danny's uncle Shibi-din tells the story of the loss of Wapisiana immortality, in which the killing of a deer and herbicide is followed by an eclipse:

> "You killed a deer. You killed a creature," they screamed.
> "Keep away from us." He cut more plants and they screamed. That day, a bite seemed to be taken from the sun [. . .] When the eclipse was over and the sun became itself again, we Wapisiana people had lost our immortality and we could no longer speak to the plants and animals.[75]

As Danny and Beatrice travel the savannah, other Amerindians refer to their incestuous relationship as "living close," to the confusion of Father Napier, who does not understand the implication of this phrase. Around the campfire, Wario[76] tells the Wai-Wai version of the incest myth: "'A long time ago, Nuni made love to his sister. Yes, he made love to his own sister . . . He left his spirit to play the flute and let his body come to her. He came over and over again.'"[77]

Another Amerindian incest myth coming from the Taruma has the brother becoming "the sun [and the sister] becoming the moon. He is still chasing her round the sky. Whenever he catches her and makes love to her there is an eclipse."[78] In the text, the incest and eclipse myths are characterized as deeply internal or endogamous but generative beginnings of the world *and* as the beginning of [sexual] awareness. The stories allow characters and tribes to travel inward to reveal truths of desire, conflict, and the forbidden. These incest and eclipse narratives reveal what Amerindians have lost and gained. In Shibi-din's tale, the loss of immortality leads to the story, which becomes a way to carry life, a way to immortality. While incest—the ultimate endogamous position—fractures the family and community, it functions, in the novel, as an effective vehicle to engage with questions and rivalries of nations coming to terms with complicated histories forged in desire, conflict, and taboo. These stories of loss bring recognition, but not harmony for indigenous and non-natives who participate in the story, either through listening to it or reading it. As a textual strategy, incest is about reflection before engagement.

What change does the incest-eclipse signal? First, there is a clear indication that Amerindians, despite policies and assumptions to the contrary, were not obliterated; they did not become museum relics, but they have been changed. Within these incestuous tales of forbidden love (mythical siblings, Danny/Beatrice, and Chofy/Rosa) a process of destruction, exposure, unmasking, separation, and eventually transformation is metaphorically rendered, as well as stories of belonging through shared perspectives and common histories of indigenous people. The metaphorical process that uses stories as a gateway to transformation is the most critical component in these tales. These stories also emphasize sacrifice and loss since both Danny and Beatrice leave the Wapisiana community, other indigenous nations, as well as the Guyanese state, abandoning their family and larger communal constructs. The incest stories—of Wapisiana, Wai-Wai, and Taruma—emphasize the unity among Amerindian peoples and foster an Amerindian nationalism. However, this nationalism is unsustainable.

By the novel's end, Sonny, the child of [consensual] incest, slyly reveals that he is the god Makunima[79] manifesting an Amerindian worldview that is able to find redemption in even the most taboo and unredeemable relationships and situations. "Sonny," the silent son, disappears into the bush—an unknown territory. The textual weight of an incestuous relationship birthing a god seems inescapable validation of endogamy and Wapisiana internalization. The trio eventually leaves the savannah: the brother and sister because their relationship could not be sanctioned in this space and the son to fully embody his Makunima identity. This character, Chico/Sonny/Makunima/narrator, juxtaposes Western, "American" (Brazilian), and Amerindian constructions of indigenous peoples in this hemisphere.

To begin with, Sonny's initial silence could be read as idiocy or retardation, a not unexpected consequence of incest.[80] In Melville's text and in Amerindian lore, the tale told by an "idiot," the mute, possibly retarded Sonny is not *only* full of sound and fury as, "Imbeciles are regarded with awe by the Indians, for according to their traditions, these are in close intimacy with good Spirits, and hence their words and actions are regarded as signs of divinity."[81] The narrator, as device and characters (Chico, Sonny, and Makunima), connects Amerindian, Western, and mixed value systems. Characters intimately tied to Amerindian epistemologies offer stark expressions of internalized traditions that do not serve them well. They do not transcend; they escape.

Cream suits and coffee

In the prologue, Chico speaks of his love for the lie and for the cream suits he likes to wear—the embodiment of the jet-set gigolo. This is no one's noble savage—staid, naked, and native. The narrator's ability to see the world as a stage, perform, and then return to his origins indicates two things. One, that the trope of performance is as crucial for indigenous people of the Americas as it is for non-Amerindian Caribbean people; and two, in his soliloquies—the prologue and epilogue—the narrator clarifies that he is rectifying a past of Caribbean, Brazilian (non-Amerindian), and European distortions and misrepresentations of indigenous people. Sonny's ability to transition beyond the boundaries of his origins means that he transcends local and national identities. To leave his Wapisiana family he goes into the bush, where he is transformed into or embraces his identity as Makunima. This character wears several masks throughout the text, each revealing limited information—at his discretion—and co-mingling factual lies and ultimate truth. However, Sonny's transcendence of boundaries does not foster regionalism, rather his project seems to be taking on the larger, global postcolonial world. It engages with the political agenda of this adaptable and outrageous being who does not respect constructions of space and time as they are generally understood, who is a master of disguise, a lover of women and his people, and a god. Sonny's crucifixion of history as a discipline, his use of art, culture, and language are the typical concerns of a postcolonial.

The mutual spaces that the siblings Danny and Beatrice, and their offspring, Sonny, share with the enemy are, as is the case with other characters, both internal and external. For this trinity the internal enemy is most forcefully displayed. Instead of consuming a morsel that will reveal an external enemy, they need to acknowledge that the enemy is already within. Their function is to move beyond consuming to synthesizing and understanding how this enemy operates and how to mitigate its negative influences or convert them to strengths.

Because Beatrice and Danny leave, they forfeit their citizenship in the Wapisiana nation. Sonny, though constantly on the move, still claims the South American landscape as his. Though he eschews the hard work of citizenship, his articulation of fiction as a lens or technology used to establish and critique notions of belonging is the clearest and most vociferously stated. Sonny claims that writing, in the Western sense, based purely on causal, "logical" relations, is a toothless fiction, with heroes too pedantic to enchant, and the legacy of triumphal [Western] rationality. Sonny's understanding of fiction and the function of heroes is a cultural and political understanding entwined with manifesting his worldview. As he dismisses Western fictions, he celebrates another—the venerated lie.[82]

Sonny's explicit articulation of this power is the most exultant in the book and is ironically, the most closely linked to issues of citizenship, transnationalism, and globalization. Sonny's migratory movement is that of a deterritorialized citizen, though the "rain forest" is his only home. Critically, this broader construction of homeland is a necessary condition of regional citizenship. Citizens should, like Sonny, care about the region, but need to see beyond narrow nationalistic ties. As he claims the entire rainforest—no matter where it may fall—he does so because he sees himself beyond Wapisiana boundaries, partly because he embraces the mythic and grandiose manifestations of himself—Makunima. This is not to advocate abandonment of one's local space, but to argue for the need to work at balancing it with a regional sensibility—this is about the *simultaneity of belonging*. This character for a time, especially in the epilogue, is a transnational citizen in the traditional sense (participating in two localities across two nation-states). Yet even this deity is overwhelmed by integration and the genocides that separatism generates. This question of how to mix and if to mix proves too much for Sonny/Makunima and in the novel's last line he retreats to his place among the stars.[83]

States fall apart

Another character who dramatically transcends his nation is Olly Sampson, the novel's Westernized finance minister. After thirty-nine years of "independence" in 2005, Guyana is as ruptured as a state can get without an official declaration of war. One of Melville's funniest and, sadly, truest moments in the novel is after Olly, discarding "the idea of turning the whole country into an enormous theme park for tourists . . . [where] history would be created as a spectacle,"[84] fantasizes about dissolving the Guyanese state at the United Nations:

> Ladies and Gentlemen, I should like to inform you, on behalf of the nation state of Guyana, that we are going to resign from being a country. We can't make it work. We have tried. We have done our best. It is not possible. The problems are insoluble . . . The nation will disperse quietly, a little shamefaced but so what. We had a go.
>
> Different people have suggested different solutions. Do it this way. Try that. Let me have a go. Nothing works. We are at the mercy of the rich countries. A team of management consultants from the United States could not find the answer, and for not finding the answer, we had to pay them an amount that substantially increased our national debt. We give in, gracefully, but we give in.[85]

In the shadow of Samir Amin, Olly Sampson posits an outrageous alternative. Sampson's fantasy highlights the fragility of Western models and exposes their failure, especially in the Guyanese context. Therefore, why keep investing in national models that have not worked? Why keep fighting for territorial integrity when there is little integrity elsewhere?[86] In the context of fictional Guyana, Melville's text suggests that the supposed nation does not exist for a substantial portion of its citizens. Internal racial strife is an indication that, "ideology don't win elections in this country. Race is the thing."[87] This issue, combined with oppressive international debt and limited economic development, means that Guyana continues to stagnate. Amin's delinking, subordinating external desires and relations to/for the benefit of internal development, becomes more attractive when looking around and seeing that models of correct behavior are corrupt colonial and neo-colonial entities such as Great Britain and the United States. These models are preferred not for their moral superiority but for the economic and military might that buttresses them.

Olly Sampson, the clearest representation of the Guyanese state, knows that not only is the state about to collapse, but believes that it should be proactive in its own dissolution. Like Tenga, Sampson does not see the value of the Guyanese state continuing because it has already failed to function. Guyana should cut the pretense, he advises, and resign from being a country. Sampson's critique is powerful because he represents the educated, economic, political, and social elites who are still invested in and can profit from going through the motions of running a dysfunctional state.

As a patriotic citizen, Sampson has been invested in the state as a manifestation of national aspirations. Yet he realizes that the Guyanese state does not function and he has no alternative to put forth—the gaping debt, IMF conditionalities, and dicey elections all contribute to his despair. Olly Sampson has seen the enemy—corporations and the very structure of government, but he is paralyzed by the problems. He does not see a way out. Sampson retreats to a world of fantasy because he cannot construct any real world solutions while still bound by and to the apparatus of an admittedly failed state.

Antonio Gramsci's notions of hegemony and capitalist seduction are relevant in this context because the belief that external products are better than local ones continues in the economic and political arena. The inherited system of governance and the management experts were both imported. In Guyana attempts at changing the system are met with resistance, primarily from the party in power. Currently, the predominately Indian People's Progressive Party (PPP) is in power and unwilling to entertain new conceptions of governing this increasingly miserable plot. David Hinds argues that power sharing is a way forward because it combats the entrenched governmental gridlock of the last sixty years.[88] According to Hinds, a political lightening rod on the Guyanese political scene, the advantages of power sharing is that for plural societies, it is the most obvious step towards fairness and participation. To share power means forming a grand coalition of political actors, a mutual veto system, proportional representation, and local autonomy.[89] Hinds goes on to propose a multi-person executive, a coalition cabinet and "a bicameral legislature including an elected People's House of Representatives and an appointed Chamber of Civil society [. . .] which will include representatives of the bar association, the council of churches, women's organizations and the private sector commission" to name a few.[90] While Hinds has an equal number of detractors and supporters, he has at least delinked from entrenched political systems and partisan politics long enough to imagine an alternative solution.

Conclusion

Pauline Melville's *The Ventriloquist's Tale* is an interesting commentary on the state of the Guyanese nation, as the problem of establishing and stabilizing internal legitimacy plagues not only the citizens at the national level but anything a government would embark on at the regional level.[91] The novel does not provide neat and tidy answers to the questions on mixing. The twofold question that faces Guyana and the rest of the Caribbean is not how to function as individual nation-states, but what exactly does that (a Caribbean nation-state) look like in a globalized world? David Hinds echoes Melville's observation that the polemicized nation-state of Guyana is on the verge of collapse. He further states that "Caribbean nations as such have never been nations—they have always been in the pre-nation state." In terms of governance, they have always been in a state of imitation or degenerative mimicry[92] developing no institutions independent of Europe. While I do not believe that the region must disclaim its European inheritances, I would argue that as it has done in the arts, the inheritance must be *adapted* (more perfectly) to regional particularities.

The region cannot continue to employ methodologies that cripple it, which, I believe, happens when governments continue flawed imitations of Westminster and Washington, D.C. While the Guyanese state and, indeed every (Caribbean) state, might be invested in territorial borders, when fictional truth, reflecting real situations, invites us to dissolve these borders it is imperative to then explore cooperative potentials such as power sharing because these strategies can be effective at the local, national, and regional levels. A Caribbean nation will have to grapple with various manifestations of mixing—racial, economic, and linguistic, to name a few. In each instance, delinking to enlarge visionary capacity by examining the competing interests of various sectors—from the peasantry and working class communities to the hegemonic minorities and their Western, often corporate allies—is vital. For these communities living at the crossroads of colonial impositions and their own (emerging) visions of themselves, the novel provides a space to engage with the self and the other as well as the competing epistemologies of science and alchemy.

Melville's novel has great promise as a guide for the conversations and considerations needed in the integration debate. Though Melville slyly revisits the race question through an examination of Amerindian realities, I would stress that overtly addressing the broader issue of race in the Caribbean is a necessity. Amerindians represent race, indigeneity, and minority perspectives. In the text, Chofy interacts with his East Indian landlords, and the black Coastlanders who were a threat to the community in Danny's mind and who, in their various ways, *perform* as colonizers. Yet, the day-to-day tensions between Afro and Indo Guyanese are not fully explored and are only tangentially referenced. However, dealing with this tension in Guyana, Trinidad, and other countries is critical given the role racism and ethnic strife play in all Caribbean societies. Foundational to the colonial project were European notions of white supremacy which continue to haunt and corrode these territories. While Melville's narrator recognizes that separatism has led to genocides in Europe,[93] perhaps like the romantic depiction of the savannahs, Melville felt the region had problems aplenty without adding this. Additionally, in the larger Caribbean context, language reconfigures race and new racial constructs give way to new challenges, for example, the mulatto class in Haiti functions as a non-black class of people in that space. Racial nuances, but not necessarily racism, are coded differently in the Spanish-speaking Caribbean, which in the larger Caribbean nation will be a majority space.

The sense of ethnic strife and the raw, naked, corrosive elements of power—even at the smallest scales—as it is exercised and expressed in the story, revisit the concerns of Samir Amin and Mahmood Mamdani—that identification along ethnic lines is a divide and conquer strategy that keeps the indirect rulers in power indefinitely. The new Caribbean quest for citizenship cannot continue models of governance and democracy that maintain winner take-all systems. Part of this challenge to combat ethnic and cultural divisions is to have more inclusive proportional models of democracy by revisiting power-sharing strategies suggested by David Hinds.

Pauline Melville's *The Ventriloquist's Tale* speaks to issues of definition in an era of globalization that is not new; in fact, it is built on age-old structures that colonized people recognize. This novel raises questions that are important to Caribbean states, and to the development of *a* Caribbean nation. The novel challenges the rhetoric of unity, not because poverty and race are not enough to engender solidarity, but because the connection between these things, survival, and building community is not always overtly stated or dealt with complexly. Therefore, harnessing and cultivating viable and lasting coalitions means deeply and consciously acknowledging and working through differences of embedded and imagined power. In fact, the novel serves as a model for the conversations and approaches that will be valuable in a regional nation-building project. It calls attention to the provocative nature of art that allows us to imagine beyond our borders and limitations for innovative and creative solutions both in terms of rearticulating colonial inheritances and as a way to imagine through and beyond very concrete issues of survival/surviving. The novel asks that reader-participants not lose themselves in easy rhetorical spaces, but through the lens of an ancient technology—fiction—grasp the differences, and deal with them. Differences are grasped by beginning the conversation with the story, which puts these issues in the public sphere and ask for two things: first, using the characters as tools to discuss the issues; and second, thinking of the characters as ourselves. Therefore, there is a platform for discussion and change—the text has created a mutual space that fosters realigning science and alchemy.

Using the framework of Amerindian Postmodernism with this novel widens the scope of belonging while examining the mutual spaces where enemies and the fatigued citizens of fragmenting states can come together. Amerindian ideas on belonging, citizenship, and sovereignty help the larger Caribbean to interrogate what it means to *belong* to local communities, states, and regional bodies—through various ideological undertakings of the nation, the state, and the transnation. *The Ventriloquist's Tale* utilizes the often unstable in-between space within the text and the reader's world. Melville's narrative suggests that Guyana, and by extension the region, must practice simultaneity in power relations, extending its "hands" inward and outward—like the knot at the center of a tug-of-war rope.

Notes

1. My sincerest appreciation to Professor Merle Collins for her suggestions and guidance throughout this process.
2. David Hinds, "Power Sharing: Towards a New Political Culture," http://www.guyanacaribbeanpolitics.com/commentary/hinds_ps.html (accessed May 28, 2004).
3. Pauline Melville, *The Ventriloquist's Tale* (London: Bloomberg, 1997), 55.
4. Paula Burnett claims that Melville constructs these two poles—endogamy (incest) and exogamy (trans-racial interaction) in a zone of exchange—see Paula Burnett, "'Where else to row, but backward?' Addressing Caribbean Futures through Re-Visions of the Past," *Ariel* 30, no. 1 (January 1999): 24-25.
5. Anthony Payne and Paul Sutton, *Charting Caribbean Development* (Gainesville: University Press of Florida, 2001), 174.
6. My framework is largely influenced by Wilson Harris's philosophical contextualization of the Carib bone flute—see Wilson Harris, "Judgment and Dream" in *The Radical Imagination: Lectures and Talks*, ed. Alan Riach and Mark Williams (Liège, Belgium: Université de Liège, 1992), 22-23.
7. Peter Hulme and Neil Whitehead have contributed greatly to (re-) reading the indigenous experience in the Americas. While I acknowledge their foundational contributions, they are not currently my focus. However, Hulme's work is particularly valuable—see Peter Hulme, *Colonial Encounters: Europe and the Native Caribbean, 1492-1797* (London: Routledge, 1992).
8. This term, made famous by French theorists Gilles Deleuze and Pierre-Felix Guattari, is used by Martiniquan Edouard Glissant to articulate philosophical work that values multiple non-hierarchical points-of-view. I engage with Glissant's deployment of the term.
9. Glissant divides history into two categories—[H]istory, master narratives and [h]istory, the stories of others lost in the ruptures of [H]—see Edouard Glissant, *Caribbean Discourse. Selected Essays*. (Charlottesville: University of Virginia Press 1989), 61-65.
10. Melville is also an intertextual ventriloquist and like her characters who throw voices within the text, she throws voice between texts from Mário Andrade's *Macunaíma*, and Michael Swan's *The Marches of El Dorado*, to Evelyn Waugh's travelogue *Ninety-Two Days* and his novel, *A Handful of Dust* —see Mário de Andrade, *Macunaima* (New York: Random House, 1984); Michael Swan, *The Marches of El Dorado* (London: Jonathan Cape, 1958); Evelyn Waugh, *Ninety-Two Days: A Journey in Guiana and Bra-*

zil, *1932* (New York: Penguin, 1986); Evelyn Waugh *A Handful of Dust* (New York: Back Bay Books, 1999).

11. NDS Secretariat, "Guyana National Development Policy," Chapter 22, "Amerindian Policies." *Guyana Ministry of Finance* October 15 1996, http://www.guyana.org/NDS/chap22.htm (accessed October 13, 2004).

12. Melville, *The Ventriloquist's Tale*, 34-35.

13. Samir Amin, *Capitalism in the Age of Globalization* (London: Zed Books, 1997), 40.

14. See Robert H. Manley, *Guyana Emergent: the Post-Independence Struggle for Nondependent Development* (Cambridge, Mass.: Schenkman Publishing Company, 1982), 51; Forbes Burnham, *A Destiny to Mould: Selected Speeches* (New York: African Publishing Corporation, 1970), 172-174.

15. As recently as 1999 the South African mining company *Migrate Mining* received permission from the Guyanese government over the objections of Amerindian people to "conduct reconnaissance surveys over 8 million acres of land"—http://www.sdnp.org.gy/apa/southafricancompany.htm (accessed November 20, 2004).

16. Marcus Colchester, *Guyana: Fragile Frontiers* (Kingston, Jamaica: Ian Randle Publishers, 1997), 135.

17. Manley, *Guyana Emergent*, 53.

18. United Nations. "Universal Declaration of Human Rights 1948-1998." http://www.un.org/Overview/rights.html (accessed March 10, 2005).

19. Paget Henry, "Philosophy and the Caribbean Intellectual Tradition" (paper presented at the annual meeting of the Caribbean Studies Association, St. John's, Antigua, 1998).

20. Melville, *The Ventriloquist's Tale*, 77-78.

21. It might be worth noting that Melville's Wormoal could be a challenge to intellectuals and/or academics in relevant fields to consider whether it is worthwhile to share the intellectual spoils of their research with those communities they constantly place under the microscope.

22. Melville, *The Ventriloquist's Tale*, 78.

23. Melville, *The Ventriloquist's Tale*, 309.

24. April Shemak, "Doing What We Ask It To Do: Native Transmutation in Pauline Melville's *The Ventriloquist's Tale*" (paper presented at the annual meeting of the Caribbean Studies Association Conference, Belize City, Belize, May 2003).

25. April Shemak, "Alter/Natives: Myth, Translation and the Native Informant in Pauline Melville's *The Ventriloquist's Tale*," *Textual Practice* 19, no. 3 (2005): 353-372.

26. Falk posits that this growing technocratic transnational elite of finance capital shares a "global culture of experience, symbols, infrastructure, food, and music that constitute [their] way of life." Increasingly, neither national nor regional identity holds sway for the "deterritorialized and homogenized elite global [citizen whose] culture is becoming extremely influential as a social force driving the political and economic systems of the world." The economically rickety portion of this transnational house, are those citizens who cross borders in search of financial stability and who send "remittances" to their home or family space. Deterritorialization and homogenization are veering from one extreme to another; while there are advocates of purity, there are others seeking greater integration between groups and nations.—See Richard A. Falk, "The Making of Global Citizenship," in *The Condition of Citizenship*, ed. Bart van Steenbergen (London: Sage, 1994), 134.

27. Melville, *The Ventriloquist's Tale*, 54.

28. Because of their special status as indigenous people, Amerindians are entitled to make claims on these states.

29. See Michaëlla L. Pèrina, "French Guiana," in *African Caribbeans: A Reference Guide*, ed. Alan West-Durán. (Westport, Conn.: Greenwood Press, 2003), 88-89; and Alan West-Durán, "Suriname," *African Caribbeans: A Reference Guide*, ed. Alan West-Durán. (Westport, Conn.: Greenwood Press, 2003), 176-177. For both these writers, especially Pèrina, this border-crossing raises questions about local identity. She asks, "How does Guiana reconcile these migrations with the political and economic challenges it faces? Is Guianese culture only a mirror of society or can it help create a new model for social harmony and development"—Pèrina, "French Guiana," 88?

30. Colchester, Marcus. *Guyana*, 129.

31. Colchester, Marcus. *Guyana*, 129-130.

32. Henry, "Philosophy," 17.

33. Within these states, elites who benefit from economic and political power pursue these policies despite their destabilizing risks to the masses of people at home and abroad.

34. Melville, *The Ventriloquist's Tale*, 327.

35. See "South African Company Gets Reconnaissance Survey Permit in Regions 7, 8 and 9," in *APA Newsletter* no. 2, http://www.sdnp.org.gy/apa/southafricancompany.htm (accessed November 20, 2004).

36. Burnham, *A Destiny*, 171.

37. Burnham, *A Destiny*, 141-143.

38. Rose-Marie Chierci, "Caribbean Migration in the Age of Globalization: Transnationalism, Race, and Ethnic Identity," *Reviews in Anthropology* 33 (2004), 48.

39. "Transcript of an interview with Desrey Fox," *Banyan Productions* Georgetown, Guyana, 1989, http://www.pancaribbean.com/banyan/desrey.htm (accessed January 15, 2005).

40. "Transcript of an interview with Desrey Fox."

41. "Transcript of an interview with Desrey Fox."

42. Melville, *The Ventriloquist's Tale*, 79.

43. Melville, *The Ventriloquist's Tale*, 55.

44. Melville, *The Ventriloquist's Tale*, 55.

45. Pauline Melville, "The Caribbean Experience in London" (notes taken during a class visit at University of London, August 2001).

46. Bart van Steenbergen, "Introduction," In *The Condition of Citizenship*, ed. Bart van Steenbergen. (London: Sage, 1994), 1-2.

47. Mahmood Mamdani, *When Victims Become Killers: Colonialism, Nativism, and Genocide in Rwanda* (Princeton, N.J.: Princeton University Press, 2002), 24.

48. Mamdani, *When*, 24-26.

49. Melville, *The Ventriloquist's Tale*, 53.

50. Melville, *The Ventriloquist's Tale*, 53.

51. Because Amerindians vacillate between being characterized as native minority groups within the states they inhabit or as autonomous states or independent enclaves within larger states, integration into the larger society by both sides has been a struggle, one example is Dominica.—see Anthony Layng, "The Caribs of Dominica: Prospects for Structural Assimilation of a Territorial Minority," in *Caribbean Ethnicity Revisited*, ed. Stephen Glazier, (New York: Gordon and Breach Science Publishers, 1985), 130-133.

52. Benedict Anderson, *Imagined Communities: Reflections on the Origins and Spread of Nationalism* (London: Verso, 1991), 29, 36, 46.

53. Linda Basch, Nina Glick Schiller, and Cristina Szanton Blanc, *Nations Unbound: Transnational Projects, Postcolonial Predicaments and Deterritorialized Nation-States* (Langhorne, Pa.: Gordon and Breach Science Publishers, 1994), 7.
54. Melville, *The Ventriloquist's Tale*, 34.
55. Melville, *The Ventriloquist's Tale*, 35.
56. Melville, *The Ventriloquist's Tale*, 31.
57. Melville, *The Ventriloquist's Tale*, 39.
58. Melville, *The Ventriloquist's Tale*, 55.
59. Burnett, "'Where," 11-37, 25.
60. Amerindian cultures, like all others, are ever evolving. Wilson characterizes the idea that indigenous people are inauthentic for participating in non-indigenous spaces as a "damaging myth." Focusing his comments on Island Caribs, he writes that to argue "that modern Island Caribs somehow are not 'real' Caribs . . . is a peculiar way of looking at things, and one that does not make sense: human cultures are constantly changing, and if Island Caribs today do not live as their ancestors did five hundred years ago, neither do people who came from Africa or Europe"—Samuel M. Wilson, ed., *The Indigenous People of the Caribbean* (Gainesville: University Press of Florida, 1997), 197. Forte explores how native peoples around the world are using emerging technologies, like the Internet. "In the case of Guyana, the Amerindian Peoples Association has a Website (APA 2001) which was produced and is maintained as a result of an initiative between the Government of Guyana and the United Nations Development Program—and this is a site with a strong political and economic focus that is not centered on the 'we are not extinct' since this is not a predominant perception of the state of Guyana's Amerindians."—Maximilian C. Forte, "'We are not extinct': The Revival of Carib and Taino Identities, the Internet, and the Transformation of offline Indigenes into online 'N-digenes,'" *Sincronía* Spring 2002, http://www.kacike.org/cac-ike/notextinct.htm (accessed February 15 2006).
61. Melville, *The Ventriloquist's Tale*, 345.
62. Melville, *The Ventriloquist's Tale*, 343-344.
63. Melville, *The Ventriloquist's Tale*, 345.
64. Melville, *The Ventriloquist's Tale*, 348-349.
65. Melville, *The Ventriloquist's Tale*, 346-347.
66. Melville, *The Ventriloquist's Tale*, 350.
67. Melville, "The Caribbean Experience."
68. Basch et al., *Nations Unbound*, 9.
69. Rosa, while like Wormoal in pursuit of knowledge, is uncomfortable with the idea of possessing knowledge, control and the colonial project. Rosa characterizes Wormoal's ideas on knowledge as the "new" colonial project—Melville, *The Ventriloquist's Tale*, 80. However, control of knowledge in accumulation, distribution, and characterization is an old mainstay of imperial and colonial powers. Because Rosa's knowledge accumulation focuses on citizen of the empire rather than a subject, her research seems less nefarious. But she too shares a sense of possessing Chofy (through sex) that Wormoal gets from books. Similarly, Alexander McKinnon's pride in his rationality is fractured by the incestuous relationship between his children, Danny and Beatrice—see Melville, *The Ventriloquist's Tale*, 213.
70. Melville, *The Ventriloquist's Tale*, 200.
71. Melville, *The Ventriloquist's Tale*, 210.
72. Michael Swan, *The Marches of El Dorado* (London: Jonathan Cape, 1958), 125. Swan, in his 1950s search for El Dorado, recounts with relish the story of H.P.C. Melville, who moves from prospector to land and cattle baron in the late nineteenth cen-

tury Rupununi. The Wapisianas made him their "Chief." Characterizing the relationship with his wife, Swan writes, "[she] had borne him fine children. He treated her with a certain indifference, I gathered, and their relationship had little in it of Captain Smith's idyll with the Princess Pocahontas. He taught the Indians many things that were of use to them, and they, besides giving him their allegiance, sharpened arrow points so fine [. . .] he was able to use them as gramophone needles. He found them a meek, utterly passive people who accepted whatever fate brought them"—Swan, *The Marches*, 125. Chronicling his relationship with his two partners, Mamai Mary, his Wapisiana wife and an unnamed Patomona wife, Swan illustrates Mamai Mary's lack of resentment, since she reportedly said, "She can have him. I had the best of him"—Swan, *The Marches*, 126. Swan concludes Melville's history, which like McKinnon's does not end in the savannahs, "Old Melville did not die on the savannahs; in fact the end of his story is a little disappoint, an unromantic acceptance of the values of civilization. No wonder there is a slight mystery about it. He put his two wives to live with their children and sailed away to the Scotland his father left so many years before. Here he married at the *kirk*, and here, in or about the year 1930, he died . . . It was interesting, as I traveled all over the savannahs and met the Melville children and many of the hundred or so grandchildren of the old man, to see the Mendelian sports that the mixed bloods had played. And I felt at the end that those powerful Scottish genes would be active till the end of time"—Swan, *The Marches*, 127.

73. Melville, *The Ventriloquist's Tale*, 215.
74. Walter E. Roth, *An Inquiry into the Animism and Folk-lore of the Guiana Indians* (London: Johnson Reprint Company Ltd., 1970), 198; see also Robert Manne, "The Colour of Prejudice," http://www.miramax.com/rabbitprooffence/ (accessed March 15, 2002).
75. Melville, *The Ventriloquist's Tale*, 122-123.
76. This young Wai-Wai narrator is perhaps another incarnation of Makunima.
77. Melville, *The Ventriloquist's Tale*, 191.
78. Melville, *The Ventriloquist's Tale*, 193.
79. The name Makunima means "one that works in the dark"—Roth, *An Inquiry*, 130. This makes sense for a child of the eclipse.
80. William.Shakespeare, *Macbeth*, (Folger Shakespeare Library edition), ed. Barbara A. Mowat and Paul Werstine (New York: Washington Square Press, 1992), 177-179 (Act V, Scene V, lines 22-33).
81. Roth, *An Inquiry*, 166
82. April Shemak also discusses the veneration of the lie in her presentations and publications of this novel.
83. Melville, *The Ventriloquist's Tale*, 357.
84. Melville, *The Ventriloquist's Tale*, 324.
85. Melville, *The Ventriloquist's Tale*, 325.
86. This debate on the role of accountable government rages on in Guyana after the flooding of early 2005 and the state's inability to provide services.
87. Grace Nichols, *Whole of Morning Sky* (London: Virago Press, 1986), 72.
88. Hinds, "Power Sharing."
89. Hinds, "Power Sharing."
90. Hinds, "Power Sharing."
91. Norman Girvan, "Reinterpreting the Caribbean," in *New Caribbean Thought: A Reader*, ed. Brian Meeks and Folke Lindahl (Kingston, Jamaica: University of the West Indies Press, 2001), 16.

92. Derek Walcott, "The Caribbean: Culture as Mimicry?" *Journal of Inter-American Studies and World Affairs* 16 (February 1974), 3-13. Walcott addresses this idea as both a positive and a negative. In addressing Naipaul, Walcott says that "our pantomime is conducted before a projection of ourselves which in its smallest gestures is based on metropolitan references. No gesture, according to this philosophy, is authentic, every sentence is a quotation, every movement either ambitious or pathetic, and because it is mimicry, uncreative"—Walcott, "The Caribbean," 6. Walcott acknowledges that this would indeed be a paralyzing phenomena, one he characterizes as not just West Indian, but American. Walcott goes on to argue that mimicry, but mimicry by design is what the Caribbean needs: "Mimicry is an act of imagination [. . .] endemic cunning [. . .] Camouflage [. . .] is mimicry, or more than that, it is design. What if the man in the New World needs mimicry as design, both as defense and as lure"—Walcott, "The Caribbean," 10. Degenerative mimicry would be that imitation without design. That imitation that is neither a tool nor a weapon, but the "crippling [. . .] uncreative [. . .] pantomime"—Walcott, "The Caribbean," 6.

93. Melville, *The Ventriloquist's Tale*, 355.

Bibliography

Ahmed, Belal. "The Impact of Globalization on the Caribbean Sugar and Banana Industries." *The Society for Caribbean Studies Annual Conference Papers*, vol. 2, 2001, edited by Sandra Courtman. http://www.scsonline.freeserve.co.uk/olvol2.html (accessed January 15 2004).

Amin, Samir. *Capitalism in the Age of Globalization*. London: Zed Books, 1997.

———. "Imperialism and Globalization." *Monthly Review* 53, no. 2 (June 2001). http://www.monthlyreview.org/0601amin.htm (accessed March 2003).

Anderson, Benedict. *Imagined Communities: Reflections on the Origins and Spread of Nationalism*. London: Verso, 1991.

Andrade, Mário de. *Macunaíma*. Translated by E. A. Goodland. New York: Random House, 1984.

Basch, Linda, Nina Glick Schiller, and Cristina Szanton Blanc. *Nations Unbound: Transnational Projects, Postcolonial Predicaments and Deterritorialized Nation-States*. Langhorne, Pa.: Gordon and Breach Science Publishers, 1994.

Burnett, Paula. "'Where else to row, but backward?' Addressing Caribbean Futures through Re-Visions of the Past." *Ariel* 30, no. 1 (January 1999): 11-37.

Burnham, Forbes. *A Destiny to Mould: Selected Speeches*. Compiled by C. A. Nascimento and R. A. Burrowes. New York: African Publishing Corporation, 1970.

Chierci, Rose-Marie. "Caribbean Migration in the Age of Globalization: Transnationalism, Race, and Ethnic Identity." *Reviews in Anthropology* 33, no. 1 (January-March 2004): 43-59.

Colchester, Marcus. *Guyana Fragile Frontiers*. Washington, D.C.: Latin America Bureau, 1997.

Ellwood, Wayne. *The No-Nonsense Guide to Globalization*. Toronto: New Internationalist/Between the Lines Press, 2003.

Falk, Richard A. "The Making of Global Citizenship." Pp. 127-140 in *The Condition of Citizenship*, edited by Bart van Steenbergen. London: Sage, 1994.

Fanon, Frantz. *Black Skin, White Masks.* Translated by Charles Lam Markmann. New York: Grove Press, 1967.

Forte, Maximilian C. "'We are not extinct': The Revival of Carib and Taino Identities, the Internet, and the Transformation of offline Indigenes into online 'N-digenes.'" *Sincronía* (Spring 2002), http://www.kacike.org/cac-ike/notextinct.htm (accessed February 15 2006).

Fox, Desrey. "Continuity and Change among the Amerindians of Guyana." Pp. 9-104 in *Ethnic Minorities in Caribbean Society*, edited by Rhoda Reddock. St. Augustine, Trinidad and Tobago: The University of the West Indies, Sir Arthur Lewis Institute of Social and Economic Studies, 1996.

Girvan, Norman. "Reinterpreting the Caribbean." Pp. 3-23 in *New Caribbean Thought: A Reader*, edited by Brian Meeks and Folke Lindahl (Kingston, Jamaica: University of the West Indies Press, 2001).

Glissant, Edouard, *Caribbean Discourse. Selected Essays*. Charlottesville: University of Virginia Press 1989.

Gregoire, Crispin et al. "Karifuna: The Caribs of Dominica." Pp. 107-171 in *Ethnic Minorities in Caribbean Society*, edited by Rhoda Reddock. St. Augustine, Trinidad and Tobago: The University of the West Indies, Sir Arthur Lewis Institute of Social and Economic Studies, 1996.

Guyana National Development Policy. Chapter 22, "Amerindian Policies." October 15 1996. http://www.guyana.org/NDS/chap22.htm (accessed October 13, 2004).

Harris, Wilson. "Judgment and Dream." Pp. 17-31 in *The Radical Imagination: Lectures and Talks*, edited by Alan Riach and Mark Williams. Liège, Belgium: Université de Liège, 1992.

Henry, Paget. "Philosophy and the Caribbean Intellectual Tradition." Paper presented at the annual meeting of the Caribbean Studies Association, St. John's, Antigua, May 1998.

Hinds, David. "Power Sharing: Towards a New Political Culture." http://www.guyanacaribbeanpolitics.com/commentary/hinds_ps.html (accessed May 28, 2004).

Hulme, Peter. *Colonial Encounters: Europe and the Native Caribbean, 1492-1797.* London: Routledge, 1992.

Kurlansky, Mark. *A Continent of Islands: Searching for the Caribbean Destiny.* Reading, Mass.: Addison-Wesley Publishing Company, 1992.

Layng, Anthony. "The Caribs in Dominica: Prospects for Structural Assimilation of a Territorial Minority." Pp. 125-138 in *Caribbean Ethnicity Revisited*, edited by Stephen Glazier. New York: Gordon and Breach Science Publishers, 1985.

Mamdani, Mahmood. *When Victims Become Killers: Colonialism, Nativism, and Genocide in Rwanda.* Princeton, N.J.: Princeton University Press, 2002.

Manley, Robert H. *Guyana Emergent: the Post-Independence Struggle for Nondependent Development.* Cambridge, Mass.: Schenkman Publishing Company, Inc., 1982.

Manne, Robert. "The Colour of Prejudice." www.miramax.com/rabbitprooffence/ (accessed March 15, 2002).

Meeks, Brian. "Envisioning Caribbean Futures." Paper presented at the annual meeting of the Caribbean Studies Association, Belize City, Belize, May 2003.

Meeks, Brian and Folke Lindhal, eds. *New Caribbean Thought: A Reader.* Kingston, Jamaica: University of the West Indies Press, 2001.

Melville, Pauline. *The Ventriloquist's Tale.* London: Bloomberg, 1997.

———. "The Caribbean Experience in London," Notes taken during a class visit at University of London, August 2001.
NDS Secretariat. "Guyana National Development Policy." Chapter 22, "Amerindian Policies." *Guyana Ministry of Finance* October 15 1996. http://www.guyana.org/NDS/chap22.htm (accessed October 13, 2004).
Nichols, Grace. *Whole of Morning Sky.* London: Virago Press, 1986.
Payne, Anthony, and Paul Sutton. *Charting Caribbean Development.* Gainesville: University Press of Florida, 2001.
Pèrina, Michaëlla L., "French Guiana." Pp. 88-89 in *African Caribbeans: A Reference Guide*, edited by Alan West-Durán, Westport, Conn.: Greenwood Press, 2003.
Reddock, Rhoda. *Ethnic Minorities in Caribbean Society.* St. Augustine, Trinidad and Tobago: The University of the West Indies, Sir Arthur Lewis Institute of Social and Economic Studies, 1996.
Roth, Walter E. *An Inquiry into the Animism and Folklore of the Guiana Indians.* London: Johnson Reprint Company Ltd., 1970.
Shemak, April. "Doing What We Ask It To Do: Native Transmutation in Pauline Melville's *The Ventriloquist's Tale.*" Paper presented at the annual meeting of the Caribbean Studies Association Conference, Belize City, Belize, May 2003.
———. "Alter/Natives: Myth, Translation and the Native Informant in Pauline Melville's *The Ventriloquist's Tale.*" *Textual Practice* 19, no. 3 (2005): 253-372.
Sizer, Nigel. *Profit Without Plunder: Reaping Revenue from Guyana's Tropical Forests Without Destroying Them.* Washington, D.C.: World Resources Institute, 1996.
"South African Company Gets Reconnaissance Survey Permit in Regions 7, 8 and 9." *APA Newsletter* no. 2. http://www.sdnp.org.gy/apa/southafricancompany.htm (accessed November 20, 2004).
Steenbergen, Bart van. "Introduction." Pp. 1-9 in *The Condition of Citizenship*, edited by Bart van Steenbergen. London: Sage, 1994.
Swan, Michael. *The Marches of El Dorado.* London: Jonathan Cape, 1958.
"Transcript of an interview with Desrey Fox," *Banyan Productions* Georgetown, Guyana, 1989, http://www.pancaribbean.com/banyan/desrey.htm (accessed January 15, 2005).
United Nations. "Universal Declaration of Human Rights 1948-1998." http://www.un.org/Overview/rights.html (accessed March 10, 2005).
Walcott, Derek. "The Caribbean: Culture as Mimicry?" *The Journal of Inter American Studies and World Affairs* 16, no. 1 (February 1974): 3-13.
Waugh, Evelyn. *Ninety-Two Days: A Journey in Guiana and Brazil, 1932.* New York: Penguin, 1986.
———. *A Handful of Dust.* New York: Back Bay Books, 1999.
West-Durán, Alan "Suriname." Pp. 171-184 in *African Caribbeans: A Reference Guide*, edited by Alan West-Durán. Westport, Conn.: Greenwood Press, 2003.
Wilson, Samuel M., ed. *The Indigenous People of the Caribbean.* Gainesville, FL: University Press of Florida, 1997.
Wynter, Sylvia. "Rethinking 'Aesthetics': Notes Towards a Deciphering Practice." Pp. 237-179 in *Ex-Iles: Essays on Caribbean Cinema*, edited by Mbye Cham. Trenton, N.J.: Africa World Press, Inc., 1992.

12

Raphael Dalleo

Readings from Aquí y Allá: Music, Commercialism, and the Latino-Caribbean Transnational Imaginary

Like any epochal shift, the passage in the Caribbean from colonialism to postcoloniality has been fraught with contradictions and complications.[1] This essay will look at two texts from a pivotal moment in this history: the album *Siembra*, released in 1978 as one of the first and most successful collaborations of Panamanian *salsero* Rubén Blades and Nuyorican bandleader Willie Colón; and a novel published two years earlier, *La guaracha del Macho Camacho* by Puerto Rican author Luis Rafael Sánchez. Reading these texts together will allow a close examination of the 1970s as part of the passage in the Caribbean from the colonial framework of binary separation and hierarchy to a postcoloniality defined by globalization as political, economic, and cultural interpenetration on a new scale. This decade marks a particularly important moment of shift and flux in the Caribbean, from the possibilities promised by the liberation struggles against European colonialism to the realities of a U.S.-dominated postcoloniality. Looking at the 1970s also allows us to see how this political and social transition has coincided with a cultural one: just as literature was finding its role in the public sphere in question, the decade witnessed the golden age of salsa with socially engaged performers like Héctor Lavoe, Rubén Blades and Willie Colón and the rise of reggae in both local Jamaican politics and the imagining of an international black diaspora.[2]

It is within the context of these shifting priorities that contemporary music and literature from the Caribbean must be discussed. In a European colonial system which privileged high culture, anticolonial writers like José Martí, C. L. R. James, and Aimé Césaire sought to inhabit the written word as a cultural weapon in the battles for decolonization.[3] Postcoloniality has brought an uncertainty about that system of values; as a result, we see an increased movement into cultural studies for Caribbean writers and critics alike, as popular culture forms, and music in particular, become the sites for intellectuals to channel the utopian aspirations once invested in the literature. The field of cultural studies follows the attempts made in *testimonio* and dub poetry to turn to popular culture as the last authentic repository of Caribbean identity in the face of cultural imperialism, at precisely the moment in which international culture industries have become dominant in the production and circulation of visual and aural forms.[4] The rise of Caribbean cultural studies, as a postcolonial response to the unfulfilled promises of anticolonialism, is part of the context for the interventions of Blades, Colón and Sánchez.

After establishing the critical move away from literature and towards cultural studies, the essay will turn to two major texts from the Caribbean and its diaspora that both thematize and illustrate elements of a residual anticolonial and emergent postcolonial world. Listening to and reading *Siembra* and *La guaracha del Macho Camacho*, one crafted in New York and the other in San Juan, will allow us to trace out the contours of the cultural exchanges between Puerto Rico and its U.S. diaspora, affirming and interrogating a transnational understanding of cultural identity. This essay presents readings along the axis of what Lisa Sánchez González calls the "p'acá y p'allá dialectics" of Caribbean transnationalism, the shifting space not coinciding precisely with the territory or culture of either the United States or the "Other America" but existing in both, in between both, and in the movement between both.[5] Putting these two texts into dialogue shows how they speak directly to the contradictions and paradoxes of postcolonial Caribbean cultural production, addressing in particular how the contemporary intellectual move into popular culture displays simultaneously the desires to move past and to reconstitute the utopian horizons of the anticolonial project. This chapter will show how Blades and Colón, in the song "Plástico," and Sánchez, in *La guaracha del Macho Camacho*, draw on this nostalgia for the anticolonial even as they attempt to imagine new functions for cultural products in the postcolonial marketplace and new roles for the committed artist in contemporary Caribbean society.

The forms and content of postcolonial cultural products such as "Plástico" and *La guaracha del Macho Camacho* can be best understood within the context of a postcolonial literary field in which the value of the written word can no longer be taken for granted. This movement, from literary criticism to a criticism centered around music and popular culture, begins to be seen in the 1970s in the work of influential literary critics such as Gordon Rohlehr. Rohlehr emerged as a major authority on West Indian literature during the "*Savacou* debate" of the early 1970s, in a series of essays about the nature of West Indian poetry and the relationship of literature to orality and the subaltern folk.[6] His work directly engages the question of what the passage from the colonial to the postcolonial means for Caribbean cultural production. He describes his collected writings from the 1970s and 1980s as "concerned with the relationship between upheaval and making, the vortex of old worlds going out of and the turmoil of new worlds coming into existence"; that is, the unfulfilled promises of West Indian independence.[7] In the two volumes of his collected essays, Rohlehr writes about most of the major male West Indian novelists and poets from the post-war generation: George Lamming, Martin Carter, Derek Walcott, Sam Selvon, Eric Roach, Roger Mais, and many others.

In addition to these two volumes of essays on literature, as well as a monograph on Kamau Brathwaite's *The Arrivants*, Rohlehr's career is noteworthy for another major strand: since the 1960s, he has published numerous essays on calypso and popular music, frequently in local newspapers and regional journals. This facet of his career culminated in the publication of his more than 600-page *Calypso and Society in Pre-Independence Trinidad* in 1990. Describing music as "one of the surest guides towards an understanding of our milieu and our moment," Rohlehr adopts the techniques of textual analysis to show the dialectical relationship of cultural production and the society in which it is produced.[8] Rohlehr's dual interest, in literature as well as music, makes him an important pioneer in the trend towards cultural studies which emerges full-blown during the 1990s amongst Caribbean literary critics such as Juan Flores, Carolyn Cooper, and Lisa Sánchez González.[9]

The socio-cultural factors that form the context for this movement into cultural studies can be seen in the introduction to Juan Otero Garabís' recent study *Nación y ritmo*. He argues that technological and political developments now mean that literature no longer articulates the nation. Otero Garabís begins from Benedict Anderson's concept of the nation as an imagined community; he summarizes Anderson's argument that "the appearance of newspapers was fundamental to the creation of the 'horizontal comradeship' that we call nations."[10] If print-capitalism, in particular the newspaper and the novel, was during the eighteenth and nineteenth centuries the most important vehicle for transmitting the form and content of the nation, Otero Garabís wonders if "the growth of what Walter Benjamin calls the 'age of mechanical reproduction'—what would later become an age of mass communication—implies a reconfiguration of the groups who participate in nation building."[11] He continues to reflect on the new forms that dominate our contemporary imaginary, and what kinds of communities they might be imagining: "in this sense, the appearance of the film industry, the music industry, radio and television provoked and promoted new forms of social representation which affected the ways in which national communities conceived (of) themselves."[12] Finally, Otero Garabís links these reflections to Doris Sommer's idea of the centrality of the novel to nation-building in Latin America: "These means of communication will be the new producers of 'foundational fictions' they will construct new national imaginaries which reflect changing relations . . . between social groups."[13]

Meditating on the historical place of various cultural forms and modes of production in their respective societies and historical moments leads Otero Garabís to posit popular music as the form through which the contemporary Caribbean transnation is imagined. Similar to other critics, Otero Garabís locates popular music, in contrast to the cultural elitism of the experimental novel, as an art form created by and for the "pueblo."[14] Music, because of its wide dissemination by the culture industry, travels more effectively across boundaries of nation, language and class, and is more effective in producing transnational and sometimes translinguistic communities. As his argument proceeds, Otero Garabís moves away from literary texts to suggest that the salsa of Willie Colón, the *nueva trova* of Silvio Rodríguez and the hybrid rhythms of Juan Luis Guerra are the forms in which Puerto Rican, Cuban and Dominican transnationalism are today simultaneously challenged and imagined.

Imbuing the field of literary criticism with models and methods learned from popular culture is thus a primary strategy for giving postcolonial Caribbean criticism a voice in the public sphere. Indeed, mourning the culture industry's emasculation of an anticolonial literature able to participate in political and collective action, while trying to reinstitute that presence by investing the printed word with the sounds of popular music, becomes a major theme of contemporary Caribbean literature.[15] Yet if, as the impulse towards cultural studies suggests, music is the best site for understanding the ways that transnationalism is imagined, my readings of "Plástico" and *La guaracha del Macho Camacho* will emphasize how these articulations run along the circuits of multinational capitalism.[16] Readings of these texts reveal how the turn to music as more "transgressive" or resistant than literature relies on two forms of nostalgia: the idea of popular culture as pure and uncorrupted, as well as nostalgia for the anticolonial ideal of culture as a weapon in decolonization struggles.[17] Rather than substituting music into literature's former position as privileged cultural medium, this essay brings together a literary and a popular text as a way to advocate for a critical practice that takes account of cultural production as a field of diverse practices occupying distinct positions in relation to one another as well as economic, political, and social structures.[18]

The positions taken in *Siembra* and *La Guaracha del Macho Camacho* point to the seductions but also the dangers of the intellectual's entry into the commodified public sphere. On the album *Siembra* (1978), Rubén Blades and Willie Colón claim the roles of spokesmen and social critics that during the 1970s were increasingly unavailable to literary practitioners. Blades and Colón explicitly envision themselves as successors to the anticolonial writers of the 1950s and 1960s. An examination of the first track, "Plástico," shows most clearly how the song's language and stance allow the *salsero* to connect to Caribbean legacies of revolutionary resistance. "Plástico" is a critique of neo-colonialism and cultural imperialism, beginning with the threat of foreign contamination and ending with a call to arms for the working masses to defend Latin essence. This faith in what might be referred to as the "folk" or "pueblo" as a redemptive agent, coupled with a positioning of the intellectual as able to articulate his people's aspirations and thus lead them forward, show Blades and Colón's project to be a renewal of anticolonial literary modernism through the medium of music. A reading of "Plástico" will point to how this resistant *salsero* persona is forged, and the complications of a musician adopting this anticolonial stance in the context of postcoloniality.

The album opens by laying down a funky disco-like track, whose beat and instrumentation mark it as decidedly un-Latin. The synthesizer and drum-track opening quickly give way to the rhythm, brass section, and beat identifiable as salsa, but not before this overture has introduced the questions of cultural authenticity and contamination that will be the song's themes. Disco is here invoked as product of a U.S. culture industry, a threat to Latin American indigenous culture and self-determination as identified by theories of neo-colonialism through cultural imperialism. From this opening, Blades and Colón will advocate the position Néstor García Canclini attributes to "the adherents of dependency theory" who "accus[e] the bourgeoisie of a lack of loyalty to national interests."[19]

After the overture allusively introduces these themes, the song's first lines launch into a Spanish-language critique of the commodification of everyday life. Although the first few stanzas contain few obvious historical or geographical markers, the sense of "us" and "them" comes from the framing of the problem as "those over there," like the "chica plástica" who is subject of the first stanza.[20] What makes this woman "plastic" is an obsession with social status and the acquisition of material things to mark that status. As a result, she and her social circle—the feminized, "elegant" man introduced in the song's next stanza—are allowing commodity relations to corrupt simple human activities such as conversation (talking only about car makes and models), friendship (avoiding anyone below them on the social scale) and love (marrying someone from the right family and with the right profession).

In the following stanzas, the critique extends to the plastic cities that these plastic people inhabit, heartless and emotionless places that worship only the cold symbol of the dollar. Instead of a generalized lament about money, this mention of the dollar brings the song's historical specificity into more obvious focus, presumably locating the setting in a place that uses the dollar for its currency (in this context, likely the United States or Puerto Rico). Along with the reference to "those over there," this localization invokes the Latino-Caribbean experience of the divided nation. Unlike "Pedro Navaja," the most famous track from Siembra, which strongly identifies its setting as Latino/a New York—it features the line "I like to live in América" and ends with a fictional news broadcast mentioning "two people killed in New York"—"Plástico," by not identifying its locale, occupies a transnational, in-between positioning, appealing to Caribbean people at home and abroad, "aquí" and "allá."[21]

From this point, "Plástico" shifts to a different movement, breaking from the rhythmic and lyrical pattern established in the first four stanzas. This middle section acts musically and narratively as a bridge between the initial, descriptive stanzas, and the didactic latter half of the song. Forming this bridge is crucial for an anticolonial politics, moving from identifying the problem to articulating a solution:

> Listen Latino, listen brother, listen friend,
> never sell your destiny
> for gold or for comfort.
> [...]
> Let us all go forward so that

> together we can end
> the ignorance
> that makes us susceptible
> to imported models
> that are not the solution.

Blades speaks here directly to his listeners: "Oye Latino, oye hermano, oye amigo." This address establishes the alliance that is meant to stand up to and oppose "plasticization." Different levels of solidarity are implied; of these forms of identification (the nation of brothers, the sympathy of friends) the first term in Blades' address ("oye Latino"), extends the boundaries of brotherhood or casual friendship. This constituency, frequently articulated in Blades' songs as an all-encompassing diaspora including Latin America as well as the Spanish-speaking United States, unites the two possible interpretations of the first part of the song—that the "plastic people" are a U.S. bourgeoisie, or their Puerto Rican counterparts—branching out, as the end of the song will make explicit, to incorporate all of the Americas. As a transnational text, "Plástico" is addressed to the victims of the commodification of all aspects of life, whether in metropolitan centers or postcolonial margins.[22]

"Plástico" ends with an impassioned appeal to the people of the Americas to come together against "imported models" threatening traditional, organic cultures throughout the hemisphere. This second half of the song is performed as chorus and improvisational response, offering suggestions couched in at first biblical ("From dust we all come and we all will return"), and increasingly political, language. The language of the second half of the song clearly signals its indebtedness to radical movements in both U.S. Latino/a and Caribbean communities. "P'alante" invokes the publication by the same name of the Young Lords, a radical pro-independence and anti-capitalist Nuyorican organization from the early 1970s.[23] Other lines directly borrow from the slogans of the Cuban Revolution—"Seguiremos unidos y al final venceremos", "Vamos todos adelante"—slogans that were disseminated to U.S. Latino/as through radical organizations like the Young Lords.

Cuba acts as an inspiration for the kind of pan-American solidarity imagined in "Plástico." The song finally posits an honest and hard-working laboring class as the subject of this pan-American revolution, "a people of flesh and blood" with "faces of work and of sweat":

> But ladies and gentlemen, amidst the plastic
> hopeful faces are also seen;
> proud faces that are working for a united Latin America
> and for a tomorrow of hope and freedom.
> We see the faces of work and sweat;
> of a people of flesh and bones who have not been sold;
> of a people working and searching for a new path, proud of their inheritance
> and to be Latin(o);
> of a race, united, like Bolivar dreamed of.

"Plástico" closes with a role call of Latin American nations who, in the late 1970s, it was still possible to imagine participating in the search for a "new path" between U.S. imperialist capitalism and Soviet-style communism. The last "nation" in this role call, as "Plástico" fades out, is "El Barrio," the song closing with the incorporation of the diaspora and a hope for its radical potential in the liberation of the hemisphere.

Reading "Plástico" against *La guaracha del Macho Camacho* highlights how Blades and Colón never engage with the complexities of their own positioning, as Latino/a artists addressing Latin America and telling them to free themselves from U.S. cultural imperialism, while doing so through the medium of a cultural form created in the United States and distributed via U.S. economic circuits. "Plástico" is part of a rich tradition of Latino/a intellectuals taking advantage of the position of enunciation enabled by their U.S. location, beginning with José Martí's organizing of anti-Spanish and anti-U.S. support for Cuban independence through the channels of U.S.-based newspapers and organizations, and continuing in works like *Once Upon a Time in Mexico* by Chicano Robert Rodríguez, a Hollywood blockbuster that is also a clear indictment of U.S. imperial adventures south of the border. Indeed, this is indicative of the contradictory positioning of the Latino/a, as potential spokesperson for Latin America and the Caribbean embedded in what Martí famously called "the belly of the beast" and thus having privileged access to the ear of power. Blades and Colón, as much as any *salseros*, position themselves as this kind of organic intellectual, translators for their native cultures who occupy a hinge, presumably able to speak and listen to both sides of the dialogue; it is no coincidence that both Blades and Colón have tried to run for elected office, Blades in Panamá and Colón in New York. Yet the desire to occupy the space of the spokesperson, in presuming to speak for his or her people, removes the representative from the experience of the subaltern and threatens to become complicit in their silencing.[24]

The choice of Spanish as medium is one way in which Blades affirms his allegiance to "the Other America," even while sacrificing some of his efficacy in speaking truth to an Anglophone power. "Plástico" establishes itself from the beginning as a bilingual text, both in the initial use of disco music, and in its opening line deploying "Chanel Number Three" in English. Although this code-switching is not pursued for the rest of the song, its presence at the outset is a nod to a Latino/a discursive based in Spanglish. At the same time, the song's attitude towards bilingualism, I would like to suggest, is less a "Spanglish" aesthetic than an "espanglés," linguistically based in a Spanish substrate and only occasionally complemented with English words and phrasings. This "espanglés" is the Puerto Rican flip-side of the "Spanglish" favored by Nuyorican poets during this time period as a way of decentering English dominance in their writing. In both "Plástico" and *La guaracha del Macho Camacho*, this "espanglés" is both derided as a contaminated and imperfect corruption of proper *español*, and yet utilized with artistic license, as a way of creating hybrid new cultural forms engaging with, but not entirely given over to, a U.S.-based culture industry.

Luis Rafael Sánchez's novel *La guaracha del Macho Camacho* (1976) speaks directly to the project laid out in "Plástico." The novel is similarly concerned with the effects of materialism on the Caribbean language and culture, but it expresses certain reservations with U.S.-based interventions in Puerto Rican culture and politics, casting doubt on whether the notion that the *salsero* can carry forward the legacy of anticolonialism is even possible under the regime of postcoloniality. More explicitly than Blades and Colón, Sánchez identifies Puerto Rico as primary front in the hemispheric battle against U.S. cultural imperialism. As the novel makes clear, Puerto Rico's location, at the leading edge of spreading U.S. commercialism, has made the island especially ambivalent about its relationship to cultural products originating from its diaspora in the United States.

La guaracha del Macho Camacho appeared in 1976 as a landmark event in Puerto Rican literature. Efraín Barradas speculates: "I don't think that in the history of Puerto Rican literature there had been another novel as commented upon by its contemporaries in the initial moment of its publication as *La guaracha*."[25] Politically, the mid-1970s in Puerto Rico were marked by the first popularly elected pro-statehood government; public intellectuals like Rafael Sánchez were struggling to define their place in this society, while at the same time, salsa was experiencing its *edad de oro*, a "golden age" with performers like Eddie Palmieri, Héctor Lavoe, Blades and Colón. For writers and critics envious of the public voices of these *salseros*, *La guaracha del Macho Camacho* suggested the possibility that literature could have something to say, that it could reach a broad public sphere as well as music. Arcadio Díaz Quiñones writes of the effect the novel had on Puerto Rican intellectuals in his introduction to the edition republished in 2000: "*La guaracha* had immediate repercussions [. . .] It allowed a considerable number of Puerto Ricans to intervene, from literature or criticism, in cultural debates."[26]

For such a challenging novel, the plot of *La guaracha del Macho Camacho* is quite straightforward. The duration of the novel lasts only a few minutes and contains almost no action: the narrative shifts between a traffic jam where we find Senator Vicente Reinosa and his son, stuck in separate cars; a mistress awaiting the Senator, alternately called La China Hereje and La Madre; and the Senator's wife, Graciela. The narrative revolves around the consciousnesses of these four main characters, focusing on the relationship between Senator Reinosa and his mistress; Graciela's sessions with her therapist; the conversations between La Madre and her friend Doña Chon; and the events of the traffic jam. The novel treats the predatory relationship between the Senator and La China Hereje as symbolic of Puerto Rico's relationship to the United States; Reinosa, explicitly aligned with the United States as part of the island's pro-statehood party, acts as local bourgeois politician whose wealth and position of power allow him to take advantage of La China, the lower-class woman who needs his money. Just as in the first verse of "Plástico," then, imperialism can be read on the body of the "native" female.

The enormous traffic jam, the *tapón* which is part and parcel of Puerto Rican and U.S. industrialization and modernization, frustrates the drivers at the same time that it freezes everyone in their place. It stops the action and ensures that virtually nothing happens throughout the novel; even the suggestion of change or mobility in this world appears unthinkable. This stasis is especially marked when contrasted with one of Sánchez's other major works, *La guagua aérea* (1983). *La guagua aérea*, in contrast to *La guaracha del Macho Camacho*, is organized around movement; the entire story takes place on a flight (an air bus, as the title calls it) between San Juan and New York, and has become a founding text for the in-between Latino/a community defined by that border crossing.[27] Far from the world of *La guagua aérea*, *La guaracha del Macho Camacho* captures in its language and form the social stasis of a world in which movement is *not* available to all: amidst the standstill, the novel's energy comes not from its plot, but from its language, which twists and contorts as it incorporates the sounds of the street and the radio. The novel's most memorable moments come from how the language of television commercials, of *telenovelas*, and of radio DJs mingles with the performances of Macho Camacho himself, the singer whose *guaracha* crosses class-lines and seems to be the only thing capable of circulating inside the traffic jam.

Lisa Sánchez González and Juan Otero Garabís are two of the critics who *La guaracha del Macho Camacho* has allowed to, as Díaz Quiñones puts it, "intervene in cultural debates." Both critics use readings of the novel to make their move away from literature and towards music as the articulation of the transnation. Sánchez González ends *Boricua Literature* with the chapter "*Ya deja eso*: Towards an epi-fenomenal approach to Boricua cultural studies," which takes its title from *La guaracha del Macho Camacho*. Sánchez González arrives at her "epi-*fenomenal*" approach, of displacing literary with cultural studies, through her reading of *La guaracha del Macho Camacho*. Despite the novel's literariness, Sánchez González's reads the novel as signaling the extraliterary direction in which she takes her work. She writes:

> Macho Camacho's guaracha gives voice, in an unmistakably Puerto Rican accent, to a collectivizing realization . . . the shared experience of hearing it . . . provides its characters—and its readers—a dynamic moment for making it ontological, for assuming the epi-*fenomenal* posture of "ya deja eso"—enough already—and re/turning to what has been perhaps the only genuinely inclusive national articulation in Puerto Rico's history: popular music.[28]

Sánchez González argues that *La guaracha del Macho Camacho* "is less a novel than a poetically inscribed invitation to dance, the music being everywhere implied but never representable."[29] The novel's stylistic resemblance to popular speech and music allows it to be "anti-canonical" as it breaks down hierarchies between the spoken and written word.[30] The novelist, she contends, totally subverts the hierarchical division between high and low cultures by creating a novel which is actually a song.

Like Sánchez González, Otero Garabís gives *La guaracha del Macho Camacho* a primary place in his argument in *Nación y Ritmo*, also using a reading of the novel as a transition into analyses of musical texts. Yet while Sánchez González sees the novel opening up new spaces for academic study of Latino/a popular culture, Otero Garabís understands it as an effort to close down and control the threats of the U.S. culture industry on Puerto Rican identity. Otero Garabís reads Luis Rafael Sánchez's resistance to the contaminated world of popular music as the privileging of experimental literature as an autonomous space, independent of market concerns: "the novel aspires to create with the reader an intelletual community that, although contaminated with the play of mass culture, maintains the necessary distance to write."[31] Citing an interview in which the author of *La guaracha del Macho Camacho* posits "Puerto Rican literature as a wall against the unbearable vulgarity of assimilation," Otero Garabís argues that the novel allows Sánchez to critique the growth of commercialism and offer the lettered city as a bastion against foreign penetration and the dilution of a literarily constructed, Spanish-speaking *puertorriqueñidad*.[32]

Reading *La guaracha del Macho Camacho* as an elitist, anti-popular attack on the contaminated culture of the masses leads Otero Garabís to the same place as Sánchez González, to an abandonment of literature as inescapably tied to upper class forms of knowledge. Although they arrive at a similar position, Sánchez González and Otero Garabís represent the two opposing poles that critics have generally chosen in discussing *La guaracha*: the novel either seeks to subvert or reinforce the position of high culture; it accomplishes this through the adoption or critique, respectively, of the language and techniques of popular culture. I would like to suggest that these approaches breakdown into a rough, perhaps stereotypical "readings from aquí/readings from allá" binary.

Along with Sánchez González, other "diasporic" approaches to the novel have tended to emphasize the liberatory potential of popular culture. Frances Aparicio, for example, reads in the novel "a stylistic revolution based in the poetics of vulgarity and in the subversive presence of Caribbean popular rhythms."[33] On the other side, the reception from the island has usually been to view the novel as an Adornian critique of mass culture as mass deception, emphasizing the deterioration of Puerto Rican identity in light of U.S. cultural domination. Arnaldo Cruz, for example, writes that "*La guaracha* is essentially a novel about Puerto Rico's mass culture and its complex relationship with American colonialism," and as such, it is "a searing indictment of Puerto Rico's colonial reality and the role of the American-controlled mass media in maintaining this colonial status."[34] The "diaspoRican" reading and the "island *independentista*" reading each betrays elements of self-interest; the diaspoRican approach hardly wants to see in the novel a critique of the contaminating influence of U.S.-made, Latino/a culture like salsa; the *independentistas* want the novel to be a defense of a "pure" Puerto Rican identity against foreign culture industries.[35] The divergent interpretations of these two orientations, both wanting to claim the novel for their own cause, typifies the ongoing schisms between independence movements on the island, defining themselves against U.S. imperialism, and radical movements originating in the diaspora.[36]

La guaracha del Macho Camacho can lend itself to both of these positions because of the in-between positioning which actually undermines many of the central assumptions of each. On the one hand, the novel mocks island elitism, having the Senator's Hispanophile wife express her belief that art should be "elevated and refined," that literature shouldn't be about "people who sweat."[37] *La guaracha del Macho Camacho* is surely not what Graciela has in mind; the novel is peopled with characters sweating and cursing, and shot through with the English of television commercials and political sloganeering, all clearly unsuited for her idea of high literature. At the same time, as much as the diasporic reading wants the novel to celebrate salsa as the culture of the transnational Puerto Rican working classes, the novel repeatedly describes Macho Camacho's *guaracha* as an outside force which "infiltrates," "invade[s]," or "has taken over" the country.[38]

This language of a foreign threat appears to echo Blades and Colón's suggestion that being "plastic" is an unnatural state for the Caribbean: "Plástico" accuses its characters of adhering to "imported models," but holds on to hope that the foreign will eventually "melt" in the tropical sun. Yet Sánchez's novel provides no such outside space from which to construct an authentic, uncontaminated Latino/a or Puerto Rican culture. Colón's early albums depict the *salsero* as a resistant subjectivity, capable of "starting riots" in the words of one of his more famous album covers, *La Gran Fuga/The Big Break*. On that album, Colón is pictured in an FBI Most Wanted poster, along with text describing him as "armed with trombone" and adding that he and singer Héctor Lavoe, "are highly dangerous in a crowd and are capable of starting riots: *people immediately start to dance*."[39] In this formulation, the *salsero* as spokesperson is also revolutionary: dancing and improvisation are identified as a challenge to the status quo, a communal activity that puts the *pueblo* in motion and hints at a threat to established power.

In the novel, the DJ repeatedly identifies Macho Camacho as this resistant *salsero*, talking at one point about how Macho Camacho is "into salsa."[40] The DJ emphasizes Macho Camacho's allegiance to the ghetto, in particular through his blackness:

> What Macho Camacho has put into his guaracha is his soul, that heart of his that's also the great heart of a man who's gone hungry. Yes, ladies and gentlemen, friends, gone hungry the way a man does who's sweaty and poor and bears the mark of the color of sufferance. Because he's no mulatto, black is what he is, pitch black and let's leave it at that.[41]

The DJ's discourse locates in Macho Camacho's cultural product, the *guaracha* which his supposed suffering has produced, a form of resistance in opposition to or outside of the empty shell presented by the culture industry.

But at other points, the novel suggests that this may be an overly utopian reading of popular music, that in fact the DJ, and the packaging of Macho Camacho, is only another layer of commodified culture as instrument of control. Contrary to the DJ's characterization of Macho Camacho as spokesman of the subaltern, within the scope of the novel the *guaracha* appears to be as hollow and as much a part of the disciplinary system as the upper class's elitist conception of culture. The system which creates and disseminates the *guaracha* aspires to totalitarian control; the song is described as establishing "absolute rule," and "a regime of absolutism."[42] The DJ calls Macho Camacho himself "the priest or pastor or preacher of the thing," suggesting his song's complicity in the religious deification of commodities, the "thingification" of Puerto Rican society.[43] In Macho Camacho's *guaracha*, life is a thing ("la vida es una cosa fenomenal"), a depthless phenomenon without context or consequence. The *guaracha* paints a picture of life as nothing but hip music, dancing, and sex, a notable distance from the violence, poverty and frustration which the characters actually experience as life.

In one of the rare moments in which someone inside the novel sees through this surface and speaks with some lucidity, the *guaracha* enters to subdue and silence the protest. The scene is observed by La China Hereje on a bus: "The country doesn't work," proclaims another passenger on the bus, repeating it over and over "facing a red traffic light that was black because the traffic signal wasn't working."[44] He arrives at his conclusion through sustained thought about the situation, moving from observing the basic phenomenon, to a higher understanding of the superstructural cause: "Because the light has gone, because the light goes every afternoon, because the afternoon doesn't work, because the air conditioning doesn't work, because the country doesn't work." His protest is greeted with two reactions:

> The passengers signed up in two opposing parties: one a minority of timid people in agreement and the other a vociferous majority who proceeded to intone with a verve reserved for national anthems Macho Camacho's irrepressible guaracha *Life Is a Phenomenal Thing*, the deeper tones provided by the driver: wiry and skinny, a wild guarachomaniac; the bus afire with the shrieks and roars of the majority party, the bus afire with the torches of happiness held high by the passengers of the vociferous majority party: happy because with the neat swipe of a guaracha they had crushed the attempt at dissidence.[45]

As this passage illustrates, the *guaracha* serves the quasi-religious function of a national anthem in Sánchez's novel. The song's inane lyrics and irresistible beat induce La China Hereje and her neighbors to ignore the social *tapón* which has them trapped, and instead dance their troubles away.

The Adornian reading of *La guaracha del Macho Camacho* might see the complete domination of this disciplinary system; the novel, though, suggests that control is never absolute. The guaracha may be mass produced as a means of pacifying the population, but the ends to which people put the song are beyond the control of this culture industry. While protests may appear to come from a minority, that minority is never silenced. The *tapón* which has immobilized and ossified Puerto Rican society makes resistance as social movement appear futile, but the multitude nonetheless insists on resisting and keeping moving. Although it achieves no obvious purpose, countless drivers loudly protest their frustration by blowing their horns: "Foreseen and collective and conscious recognition of the uselessness of protest but: a chorus of horns proceeds, altogether, *todos a una* . . . the enwheeled multitude brakes, guarachas, advances, brakes, guarachas, advances, brakes, guarachas, advances."[46]

The *tapón* opens up the possibility for lucidity for some of the characters, such as the man on the bus who realizes that the country doesn't work. As the *tapón* persists, the drivers begin to leave their cars and move towards understanding the reality of their circumstances: "All chaufferdom, the whole passagerial flock, had risen up onto the car roofs in order to find out what the fuck is going on up ahead: a swirl of asking asked by those who have no access to the privileged positions from where one can appreciate what the fuck is going on up ahead."[47] Only by standing on their cars, these potentially atomizing prisons, can those down below begin to see through false consciousness to the nature of their situation. Although the *guaracha* enters again in this scene to deflate the tension, the threat has been established that unrest will incite the multitude to more than permanent partying.[48]

In this moment, *La guaracha del Macho Camacho* demonstrates its affinities with the imagined project laid out in "Plástico": in both cases, the goal is for greater insight, to be able to see the transnational spaces interpolating the "Other America" and the United States. Even so, the distance between the two suggests the very different positions of literature and music today. Lacking the assured revolutionary vision that anticolonialism provides in "Plástico," *La guaracha* nevertheless refuses to resign itself to postcolonial pessimism, insisting instead on the space between these oppositions. Taken together, then, these two texts point to the possibilities and contradictions opened up for Caribbean culture by the passage from colonialism to postcoloniality; a culture that is always already a commodity, but can use its place within economic circuits to reconstitute a postcolonial public sphere.

Rather than celebrating the decentering of literature as a blow against the cultural monasticism of an elite upper class or lamenting this deprivileging as the loss of an idealized literary public sphere of rational exchange, both "Plástico" and *La guaracha del Macho Camacho* seek to interrogate popular music as the medium for a postcolonial public sphere. Imagining new roles for postcolonial Caribbean art leads both of these texts to highlight especially the transnational spaces interpolating the Caribbean and the United States. Blades and Colón figure this mutual implicatedness as an underlying connection, best seen from the trans-ghetto—"busca al fondo y su razón," they tell us. Sánchez imagines the connections as overarching, floating through the air in television commercials and radio broadcasts—a system of control the people below can't see without a more privileged vantage point. Like Spanglish and espanglés, these are the two different faces of globalization: the spread of corporate America to the south, bringing the people of the "Other America" to the north. This in-between and in-motion positioning of Latino-Caribbean culture offers the possibility of seeing the complicated mutual dependency of North and South the double vision that Blades, Colón, and Sánchez identify as the goal of transnational postcolonial art.

Endnotes

1. I distinguish between postcolonialism or postcolonial studies, as academic practice, and postcoloniality as a historical designator. Scott makes this distinction in David Scott, *Conscripts of Modernity: The Tragedy of Colonial Enlightenment* (Durham, N.C.: Duke University Press, 2004); see also Graham Huggan, *The Postcolonial Exotic: Marketing the Margins* (New York: Routledge, 2001).

2. Paul Gilroy reads the reggae star against this moment of flux and contradiction—Paul Gilroy, "Could you be loved? Bob Marley, anti-politics, and universal sufferation," *Critical Quarterly* 47, no. 1-2 (July 2005): 226-245.

3. My essay "Authority" examines how two Anglophone Caribbean writers dealt with their new relationship to the public sphere after anticolonialism—Raphael Dalleo, "Authority and the Occasion for Speaking in the Caribbean Literary Field: George Lamming and Martin Carter," *Small Axe* 20 (September 2006): 19-39.

4. In one of the foundational critiques of the field, Dorfman and Mattelart look specifically at Disney's mass produced comics as primary vehicle of cultural imperialism—see Ariel Dorfman and Armand Mattelart, *How to Read Donald Duck: Imperialist Ideology in the Disney Comic*, trans. David Kunzle (New York: International General, 1975). By contrast, a recent essay collection returning to the subject of Disney's role in cultural imperialism moves away from the critique of text to examine new media such as movies—see Brenda Ayres, ed., *The Emperor's Old Groove: Decolonizing Disney's Magic Kingdom* (New York: Peter Lang, 2003).

5. Lisa Sánchez González, *Boricua Literature: A Literary History of the Puerto Rican Diaspora* (New York: New York University Press, 2001), 168.

6. Rohlehr's contributions to these debates appear in: Gordon Rohlehr, *My Strangled City and Other Essays* (Port of Spain, Trinidad and Tobago: Longman Trinidad, 1992); "The Folk in Caribbean Literature," *Tapia Literary Supplement* 2, no. 11 (December 17, 1972): 7-8, 13-14; "The Creative Writer and West Indian Society," *Kaie* 11 (1973): 38-77; and "A Carrion Time," *Bim* 58 (June 1975): 92-109.

7. Gordon Rohlehr, *The Shape of That Hurt and Other Essays* (Port of Spain, Trinidad and Tobago: Longman Trinidad, 1992), vii.

8. Gordon Rohlehr, *Calypso and Society in Pre-Independence Trinidad* (Port of Spain: Gordon Rohlehr, 1990), vi.

9. Flores, Cooper, and Sánchez González display the postcolonial impulse towards suspicion of literature as part of the desire for indigenous cultural forms: for each critic, literature is aligned with the high culture of the Caribbean's ruling classes and foreign imperial powers, whether England or the United States. The novel, with its "assimilationist proclivities," can no longer represent a Caribbean form of knowledge to use against the metropole—Juan Flores, *From Bomba to Hip-hop: Puerto Rican Culture and Latino Identity* (New York: Columbia University Press, 2000), 183. The critics thus ironically

repeat the same desire we will see in *La guaracha del Macho Camacho*: focusing on music becomes part of an attempt to "turn history upside-down," to give political significance to literary endeavors and to create a public role for an increasingly privatized literary field—Carolyn Cooper, *Noises in the Blood: Orality, Gender and the "Vulgar" Body of Jamaican Popular Culture* (Durham, N.C.: Duke University Press, 1995), 174; for more on this tendency in Latino/a Studies—see the introduction and first chapter of Raphael Dalleo and Elena Machado Sáez, *The Latino/a Canon and the Emergence of Post-Sixties Literature* (New York: Palgrave Macmillan, 2007).

10. Juan Otero Garabís, *Nación y ritmo: "descargas" desde el Caribe* (San Juan, P.R.: Ediciones Callejón, 2000), 15—translations are my own.

11. Otero Garabís, *Nación*, 15.

12. Otero Garabís, *Nación*, 15.

13. Otero Garabís, *Nación*, 16.

14. Otero Garabís, *Nación*, 155-56.

15. These contradictory impulses are perhaps best illustrated in Earl Lovelace's novel *The Dragon Can't Dance*.

16. Sylvia Wynter, in a remarkably prescient essay written in 1968, notes:

> The concept of "people," better expressed by the Spanish "pueblo," is vanishing fast. The writer who returns from exile at the metropolitan centre to "write for his people" . . . must come face to face with the fact that his 'people' has become the "public." And the public in the Caribbean, equally like the public in the great metropolitan centres, are being conditioned through television, radio, and advertising, to want what the great corporations of production in the culture industry, as in all others, have conditioned them to want.—Sylvia Wynter, "We Must Learn to Sit Down Together and Talk About a Little Culture: Reflections on West Indian Writing and Criticism. Part I, *Jamaica Journal* 2, no. 4 (December 1968): 25.

Wynter distinguishes between the anticolonial ideal of the people as collective actors, and the postcolonial reality of a public as a collection of private individuals, linking this discontinuity explicitly to the growth of a broader mass production of culture and communication in Caribbean society. She is interested, then, not only in slipping the yoke of the European literary tradition, but also of the political implications of replacing that tradition with a model of culture based on consumerism. As the postcolonial Caribbean's place in the world system shifts from that of a producer of raw materials to a consumer of foreign products, she suggests that Caribbean cultural studies becomes potentially complicit in following the logic of this new system. If Wynter's reservations towards popular culture appear reminiscent of certain works of the Frankfurt School, it is no coincidence that the only "non-Caribbean" text listed among Wynter's "Criticism Consulted" is *Prisms* by Theodor Adorno.

17. García Canclini identifies the first of these forms of nostalgia as the idealized view of popular culture "as the 'expression of the personality of a particular people,'" dependent on a "romantic" vision of the people "as a homogeneous and autonomous whole, whose spontaneous creativity represented the highest expression of human values and the way of life to which humanity should return"—Néstor García Canclini, *Transforming Modernity: Popular Culture in Mexico*, trans. Lidia Lozano (Austin: University of Texas Press, 1993), 21 and 22.

18. In *The Field of Cultural Production*, Bourdieu offers a description of the literary field in nineteenth-century France; while the specifics of this description are almost

entirely inapplicable to the contemporary Caribbean, the idea of cultural practices as a field is a useful place to begin imagining the relationships between literature, literary criticism, music, and the international market—Pierre Bourdieu, *The Field of Cultural Production*, ed. Randal Johnson (New York: Columbia University Press, 1993).

19. Néstor García Canclini, *Consumers and Citizens: Globalization and Multicultural Conflicts*, trans. George Yúdice (Minneapolis: University of Minnesota Press, 2001), 44.

20. Transcriptions and translations of the lyrics to "Plástico" are my own.

21. Duany's "Popular Music in Puerto Rico," a groundbreaking work in the academic analysis of salsa, devotes one of its sections to "Pedro Navaja," and features as an appendix a transcription of the song's lyrics—Jorge Duany, "Popular Music in Puerto Rico: Toward an Anthropology of Salsa," *Latin American Music Review* 5, no. 2 (Autumn-Winter 1984): 186-216.

22. The community Blades addresses remains grounded in language, as only listeners who understand Spanish will be able to follow his subsequent instructions ("nunca vendas tu destino," for example). Indeed, despite its hybrid and diasporic perspective, "Plástico" does tend at times to assert xenophobic and closed notions of cultural authenticity. For example, the opening sounds of "Plástico" clearly are meant to evoke disco as threat to authentic Latino/a culture; in so doing, the song depends on a construct of disco music as the monolithic product of a bourgeois culture industry, rather than the dynamic interaction of corporate record companies, potential music consumers from a variety of class and race positions, and the musicians themselves.

"Plástico" is not alone as a Latino/a text in tending to obscure internally marginalized and colonized aspects of U.S. culture and society, in particular of African Americans; Juan González, in *Harvest of Empire*, refers a number of times to "black and white America" as if both groups occupy the same relationship to Latino/as and Latin America, a surprising oversight considering González's experience working alongside African-American groups in New York City. Juan Flores and Lisa Sánchez González, on the other hand, take a very different perspective in *From Bomba to Hip-hop* and *Boricua Literature*, emphasizing the commonalities of these Nuyorican and African-American experiences in New York. Flores even calls Latino culture "black," in the sense of being integral to yet marginalized by the U.S. mainstream.

23. For more on the Young Lords—see Andres Torres and José Velázquez, eds., *The Puerto Rican Movement: Voices from the Diaspora* (Philadelphia: Temple University Press, 1998).

24. Mendieta's essay "Latinas/os" makes a case for the need for Latino/as to act as public intellectuals in representing the interests of Latin America in the United States—Eduardo Mendieta, "What Can Latinas/os Learn From Cornel West? The Latino Postcolonial Intellectual in the Age of the Exhaustion of Public Spheres," *Nepantla: Views from South* 4, no. 2 (2003): 213-233.

25. Efraín Barradas, *Para leer en puertorriqueño: Acercamiento a la obra de Luis Rafael Sánchez* (Río Piedras, P.R.: Editorial Cultural, 1981), 131—translations are my own.

26. Arcadio Díaz Quiñones, "Introducción," in *La guaracha del Macho Camacho*, by Luis Rafael Sánchez (Madrid: Cátedra, 2000), 15 — translations are my own.

27. Sandoval Sánchez represents this critical trend in identifying the air bus as the place where "the so-called 'floating identity' of Puerto Ricans is articulated not only between geographical spaces but also in the creations of a space in midair where identity intersects, overlaps, and multiplies"—Alberto Sandoval Sánchez, "Puerto Rican Identity Up in the Air: Air Migration, Its Cultural Representations, and Me 'Cruzando El

Charco,'" in *Puerto Rican Jam: Essays on Politics and Culture*, ed. Frances Negrón-Muntaner and Ramón Grosfoguel (Minneapolis: University of Minnesota Press, 1997), 197.

28. Lisa Sánchez González, *Boricua Literature: A Literary History of the Puerto Rican Diaspora* (New York: New York University Press, 2001), 165.

29. Sánchez González, *Boricua*, 165.

30. Sánchez González, *Boricua*, 165 and 166.

31. Otero Garabís, *Nación*, 75.

32. Otero Garabís, *Nación*, 55.

33. Frances Aparicio, "Entre la guaracha y el bolero: Un ciclo de intertextos musicales en la nueva narrative puertorriqueña," *Revista Iberoamericana* 162-163 (1993), 73—translations are my own.

34. Arnaldo Cruz, "Repetition and the Language of the Mass Media in Luis Rafael Sánchez's *La guaracha del Macho Camacho*," *Latin American Literary Review* 13 (1985), 35 and 36.

35. Lao traces some of the contours of the interactions between island and diaspora in his essay "Islands"—Agustín Lao, "Islands at the Crossroads: Puerto Ricanness Traveling between the Translocal Nation and the Global City," in *Puerto Rican Jam: Essays on Politics and Culture*, ed. Frances Negrón-Muntaner and Ramón Grosfoguel (Minneapolis: University of Minnesota Press, 1997), 169-188; see also Negrón-Muntaner's essay on how, even more recently, reactions to Puerto Rican Barbie break down into these two perspectives—Frances Negrón-Muntaner, "Barbie's Hair: Selling Out Puerto Rican Identity in the Global Market." in *Latino/a Popular Culture*, ed. Michelle Habell-Pallán and Mary Romero (New York: New York University Press, 2002), 38-60.

36. Whalen writes about the conflicted relationship between radical movements from the island and the diaspora—Carmen Whalen, "Bridging Homeland and Barrio Politics: The Young Lords in Philadelphia," in *The Puerto Rican Movement: Voices from the Diaspora*, ed. Andres Torres and José Velázquez (Philadelphia: Temple University Press, 1998), 107-123.

37. Luis Rafael Sánchez, *Macho Camacho's Beat*, trans. Gregory Rabassa (New York: Pantheon Books, 1980), 86.

38. Luis Rafael Sánchez, *La guaracha del Macho Camacho* (Madrid: Cátedra, 2000), 20 and 121. As Otero Garabís points out, these descriptions echo the resistance during the 1970s of the Puerto Rican Left towards salsa as a foreign and inauthentic musical form, and the revival of folkloric music as the true cultural expression of Puerto Rican identity—Juan Otero Garabís, *Nación y ritmo: 'descargas' desde el Caribe* (San Juan, P.R.: Ediciones Callejón, 2000). Also see the work of Quintero Rivera for more on the reception of salsa by Puerto Rican intellectuals during the 1970s—Angel Quintero Rivera, "Migration and Worldview in Salsa Music," trans. Roberto Márquez, *Latin American Music Review* 24, no. 2 (2003): 210-232 and "La gran fuga, las identidades socioculturales y la concepción del tiempo en la música 'tropical,'" in *Caribe 2000: Definiciones, Identidades y Culturas Regionales y/a Nacionales*, ed. Lowell Fiet (Río Piedras, P.R.: Universidad de Puerto Rico, 1997), 24-44.

39. Colón and Lavoe's album covers are analyzed in Otero Garabís, *Nación y Ritmo*, Quintero Rivera, "La gran fuga," and Valentín Escobar, "El Hombre que Respira Debajo del Agua: Trans-*Boricua* Memories, Identities, and Nationalisms Performed through the Death of Héctor Lavoe," in *Situating Salsa: Global Markets and Local Meaning in Latin Popular Music*, ed. Lise Waxer (New York: Routledge, 2002), 161-186.

40. Sánchez, *La guaracha*, 79.

41. Sánchez, *La guaracha*, 99.
42. Sánchez, *La guaracha*, 27 and 45.
43. Sánchez, *La guaracha*, 129. Aimé Césaire writes about the "thingification" of another postcolonial colony, Martinique, in his *Discours sur le colonialisme*: "No human contact, but relations of domination and submission which turn the colonizing man into a classroom monitor, an army sergeant, a prison guard, a slave driver, and the indigenous man into an instrument of production. My turn to state an equation: colonization = 'thingification'"—Aimé Césaire, *Discourse on Colonialism*, trans. Joan Pinkham (New York: Monthly Review Press, 1955), 21.
44. Sánchez, *La guaracha*, 11.
45. Sánchez, *La guaracha*, 11-12.
46. Sánchez, *La guaracha*, 51.
47. Sánchez, *La guaracha*, 122.
48. The guaracha is often described as "a guaracha that incites to permanent partying"—Sánchez González, *Boricua*, 61.

Bibliography

Aparicio, Frances. "Entre la guaracha y el bolero: Un ciclo de intertextos musicales en la nueva narrative puertorriqueña." *Revista Iberoamericana* 162-163 (1993): 73-89.

Ayres, Brenda, ed. *The Emperor's Old Groove: Decolonizing Disney's Magic Kingdom*. New York: Peter Lang, 2003.

Barradas, Efraín. *Para leer en puertorriqueño: Acercamiento a la obra de Luis Rafael Sánchez*. Río Piedras, P.R.: Editorial Cultural, 1981.

Blades, Rubén, and Willie Colón. *Siembra*. Fania Records, 1978.

Bourdieu, Pierre. *The Field of Cultural Production*. Edited by Randal Johnson. New York: Columbia University Press, 1993.

Césaire, Aimé. *Discourse on Colonialism*. Translated by Joan Pinkham. New York: Monthly Review Press, 1955.

Colón, Willie. *La gran fuga/The Big Break*. Fania Records, 1971.

Cooper, Carolyn. *Noises in the Blood: Orality, Gender and the "Vulgar" Body of Jamaican Popular Culture*. Durham, N.C.: Duke University Press, 1995.

Cruz, Arnaldo. "Repetition and the Language of the Mass Media in Luis Rafael Sánchez's *La guaracha del Macho Camacho*." *Latin American Literary Review* 13 (1985): 35-48.

Dalleo, Raphael. "Authority and the Occasion for Speaking in the Caribbean Literary Field: George Lamming and Martin Carter." *Small Axe* 20 (September 2006): 19-39.

Dalleo, Raphael, and Elena Machado Sáez. *The Latino/a Canon and the Emergence of Post-Sixties Literature*. New York: Palgrave Macmillan, 2007.

Dávila, Arlene. *Latinos, Inc.: The Marketing and Making of a People*. Berkeley: University of California Press, 2001.

Díaz Quiñones, Arcadio. "Introducción." Pp. 11-73 in *La guaracha del Macho Camacho*, edited by Luis Rafael Sánchez. Madrid: Cátedra, 2000.

Dorfman, Ariel, and Armand Mattelart. *How to Read Donald Duck: Imperialist Ideology in the Disney Comic*. Translated by David Kunzle. New York: International General, 1975.

Duany, Jorge. "Popular Music in Puerto Rico: Toward an Anthropology of Salsa." *Latin American Music Review* 5, no. 2 (Autumn-Winter 1984): 186-216.

Flores, Juan. *From Bomba to Hip-hop: Puerto Rican Culture and Latino Identity*. New York: Columbia University Press, 2000.

García Canclini, Nestor. *Transforming Modernity: Popular Culture in Mexico*. Translated by Lidia Lozano. Austin: University of Texas Press, 1993.

———. *Consumers and Citizens: Globalization and Multicultural Conflicts*. Translated by George Yúdice. Minneapolis: University of Minnesota Press, 2001.

Gilroy, Paul. "Could you be loved? Bob Marley, anti-politics, and universal sufferation." *Critical Quarterly* 47, no. 1-2 (July 2005): 226-245.

González, Juan. *Harvest of Empire: A History of Latinos in America*. New York: Penguin Books, 2000.

Huggan, Graham. *The Postcolonial Exotic: Marketing the Margins*. New York: Routledge, 2001.

Lao, Agustín. "Islands at the Crossroads: Puerto Ricanness Traveling between the Translocal Nation and the Global City." Pp. 169-188 in *Puerto Rican Jam: Essays on Politics and Culture*, edited by Frances Negrón-Muntaner and Ramón Grosfoguel. Minneapolis: University of Minnesota Press, 1997.

Mendieta, Eduardo. "What Can Latinas/os Learn From Cornel West? The Latino Postcolonial Intellectual in the Age of the Exhaustion of Public Spheres." *Nepantla: Views from South* 4, no. 2 (2003): 213-233.

Negrón-Muntaner, Frances. "Barbie's Hair: Selling Out Puerto Rican Identity in the Global Market." Pp. 38-60 in *Latino/a Popular Culture*, edited by Michelle Habell-Pallán and Mary Romero. New York: New York University Press, 2002.

Otero Garabís, Juan. *Nación y ritmo: "descargas" desde el Caribe*. San Juan, P.R.: Ediciones Callejón, 2000.

Quintero Rivera, Angel. "La gran fuga, las identidades socioculturales y la concepción del tiempo en la música 'tropical.'" Pp. 24-44 in *Caribe 2000: Definiciones, Identidades y Culturas Regionales y/a Nacionales*, edited by Lowell Fiet. Río Piedras, PR: Universidad de Puerto Rico, 1997.

———. "Migration and Worldview in Salsa Music." Translated by Roberto Márquez. *Latin American Music Review* 24, no. 2 (2003): 210-232.

Rohlehr, Gordon. "The Folk in Caribbean Literature." *Tapia Literary Supplement* 2, no. 11 (December 17, 1972): 7-8, 13-14.

———. "The Creative Writer and West Indian Society." *Kaie* 11 (1973): 38-77.

———. "A Carrion Time." *Bim* 58 (June 1975): 92-109.

———. *Calypso and Society in Pre-Independence Trinidad*. Port of Spain, Trinidad and Tobago: Gordon Rohlehr, 1990.

———. *My Strangled City and Other Essays*. Port of Spain: Longman Trinidad, 1992.

———. *The Shape of That Hurt and Other Essays*. Port of Spain: Longman Trinidad, 1992.

Sánchez, Luis Rafael. *La guaracha del Macho Camacho*. [1976] Madrid: Cátedra, 2000.

———. *Macho Camacho's Beat*. Trans. Gregory Rabassa. New York: Pantheon Books, 1980.

Sánchez González, Lisa. *Boricua Literature: A Literary History of the Puerto Rican Diaspora*. New York: New York University Press, 2001.

Sandoval Sánchez, Alberto. "Puerto Rican Identity Up in the Air: Air Migrations, Its Cultural Representations, and Me 'Cruzando El Charco.'" Pp. 189-208 in *Puerto Rican Jam: Essays on Politics and Culture*, edited by Frances Negrón-Muntaner and Ramón Grosfoguel. Minneapolis: University of Minnesota Press, 1997.

Scott, David. *Conscripts of Modernity: The Tragedy of Colonial Enlightenment*. Durham, N.C.: Duke University Press, 2004.

Torres, Andres, and José Velázquez, eds. *The Puerto Rican Movement: Voices from the Diaspora*. Philadelphia: Temple University Press, 1998.

Valentín Escobar, Wilson. "El Hombre que Respira Debajo del Agua: Trans-*Boricua* Memories, Identities, and Nationalisms Performed through the Death of Héctor Lavoe." Pp. 161-186 in *Situating Salsa: Global Markets and Local Meaning in Latin Popular Music*, edited by Lise Waxer. New York: Routledge, 2002.

Whalen, Carmen. "Bridging Homeland and Barrio Politics: The Young Lords in Philadelphia." Pp. 107-123 in *The Puerto Rican Movement: Voices from the Diaspora*, edited by Andres Torres and José Velázquez. Philadelphia : Temple University Press, 1998.

Wynter, Sylvia. "We Must Learn to Sit Down Together and Talk About a Little Culture: Reflections on West Indian Writing and Criticism. Part I." *Jamaica Journal* 2, no. 4 (December 1968): 23-32.

IV

THE (TRANS-)NATION (DIS-)EMBODIED

13

Patricia Mohammed

Like Sugar in Coffee: Third Wave Feminism and the Caribbean

I would like to connect with another generation of women and men, those who are already seriously engaged in feminism, gender and women's studies, those who flirt and flit on the margins, those who have inherited from the feminist struggles without recognizing what they may owe to these struggles, those who would stay the course to become the new scholars and activists in our midst, and those who may not ever avow feminism but in their daily lives and actions are eminent practitioners.[1] These ideas may not be universally shared by my Second Wave colleagues and friends. They come out of my own experience and perceptions of feminism in the Caribbean, relative to other societies.[2] Second Wave feminism was founded on sentiments and theoretical notions of "speaking one's piece," "the personal is political" and using a standpoint and reflexive methodology which brought us closer to a "truth" of the way things really are, however we define this truth in and out of the academy. My approach is lyrical at times, a stream of consciousness written as a conversation with an imaginary set of individuals, drawing in different trajectories.[3] It disputes some of the theoretical strands which emerged from Second Wave feminism and the burdens imposed by discourses such as "sisterhood" which presented limits on the question of difference.

"Like sugar in coffee"[4] describes my contemporary perception and measured optimism about feminism today. Unlike three or four decades ago, a gender consciousness, if not a feminist consciousness, has filtered throughout society. By "gender consciousness" I refer to the self awareness and confidence of one's rights and privileges as female or male in society, and an informed sense of the limits or oppressiveness which biological sex still imposes on each individual to realize their full potential. This sweetened moment of a permeated gender consciousness is not to be taken lightly or unadvisedly. If young women and men have benefited unwittingly from struggles waged by their foremothers and fathers so that they are aware of the rights and privileges which accrue to each sex, then what are their imperatives to avow feminism or to engage in old and new feminist concerns today, particular when it might seem that they have more to lose by joining this "ism"? It is always difficult to put oneself in the place of another. It is even more difficult to span the generational gap. Nonetheless, I attempt in this piece to speak through my (hopefully, our) experience to do just that. The sub-sections of this essay are titled after selected feminist authored texts of the First and Second Wave which have planted theoretical or programmatic issues still relevant to Third Wavers. Second Wave is also in the process of becoming Third Wave. Each wave is not just a chronology of events; it is continually engaged in a polemic with history, thought and action.

Of woman born

"Nana rolled herself another cigarette. I liked the smell of sulfur when she outed her match and was fascinated by the way she cupped the cigarette in both hands and sucked erratically before she got a good enough light." This vignette from Shani Mootoo's *Cereus Blooms at Night* rescues a memory of old Indian women I had known in the village in which I was raised in south Trinidad. These women were most unlike the svelte and sophisticated, young white lasses in the Virginia Slims ad—"You've come a long way, baby"—that we knew from American magazines. For one thing they smoked the harsh tobacco of Trinidad's Broadway cigarettes. Not unlike their rural menfolk, they generally bought two or five at a time from a jar on the shop counter. Then they would wrap the cigarettes in worn cotton handkerchiefs, and tuck them into the bosoms of their shapeless cotton frocks, to be retrieved for a smoke when they sat among their women friends. Interestingly, cigarette smoking was never a public activity for women in the Caribbean, and to this day is not, despite the passage of years and ideas.

Nonetheless, one wondered what long ways these women, like the Virginia Slims models, had come? Their eyes were full of mischief when they talked amongst themselves. Rheumy eyes, the twinkle kept wonderfully alive by shared memories. Their laughter and conversation would grow secretive when we came too close, switching to the Hindi which they knew we could not fully understand. I was too young to listen except in passing, as the young always are, too busy discovering life to recognize it unfolding in the everyday and commonplace events. Subconsciously, I expect, one constantly noticed things. I sided with these livelier souls especially when they were set against other women who were so bent over double by life that you could barely see their eyes. If you did catch sight of the latter's eyes, they were piercing, unflinching, almost accusing in their gaze, as if willing you to choose between two alternatives. Shani Mootoo recognizes these differences among the women. She called the irreverent one "Cigarette Smoking Nana," the other is dubbed "Bible Quoting Nana," of whom says her protagonist, "I couldn't bring myself to get too close to, nor she to me since I was not turning out to be boyly enough for her church going satisfaction."[5]

The Bible Quoting Nanas too had their stories to tell. Perhaps there were only two alternatives for women in the 1950s. After all, the choices were marriage or spinsterhood, motherhood or barrenness, acceptance or ostracism. Were you going to be a good serious woman, well respected in the community; or one of the fallen, who laughed too loudly, drank and smoke like men, dressed gaudily, wore too much eye makeup and Moscow red lipstick? Good women stayed by their men, loyal and faithful, in martyred polygamous unions as brides of Jesus Christ or the Prophet Mohammed or Krishna. Others had strayed from the paths of righteousness.

Many of these women, bible quoting and cigarette smoking both, would not have heard of feminism or gender as we talk about it freely today. Yet they would have made the most of their lives, flaunting or following rules when they had to. Let us not dismiss them as cardboard characters on a stage in which they played preordained roles. Any notions of gender equality which we, the generation who came of age in the wake of the 1960s women's liberation movement, entertained in our heads, were planted there by the examples of our foremothers and fathers. To speculate on what has influenced Third Wave feminism I think one should return to the mother lode: that of trying to figure out what is conveyed to each generation by the previous ones as they come of age. We should not also, in considering Third Wave feminism, think that it is only women who influence the shape of a feminist and gender consciousness. Such ideas are transmitted or influenced equally by the actions, or reactions, of men and masculinity.

Caribbean fiction, including women's writing which grew in stature in the last few decades of the twentieth century, is valuable in representing these coded messages between generations of women. There are fewer examples of the ways in which manhood and ideas of masculinity are being transmitted between men and men, although this is by no means an absent theme in the fiction of the region. Femininity had first to discover and map itself. The relationships between women—young and old, book educated and book-uneducated, rural and urban, mother and child, grandmothers and granddaughters, between women of different ethnic groups and classes—are never untroubled. Much of the fiction of the region which has dealt with coming of age, has pointed to the uneasy processes by which gender, race and class identities are ascribed, acquired and maintained.[6]

In the Martiniquan novel *The Bridge of Beyond*, Simone Schwartz-Bart deals with the competition between women, and, at the same time the wisdom gained from the knowledge of their physical bodies. Toussine was once a beauty: "when she was fifteen, she stood out from all the other girls, with the unexpected grace of red canna growing on the mountain, so that the old folk said she in herself was the youth of L'Abandonnee."[7] Her beauty is disturbing to the other women: "The breeze blowing over Minerva's (her mother's) cottage embittered the women, made them more unaccountable than ever, fierce, fanciful, always ready with some new shrewishness. What I say is Toussine's more for ornament than for use. Beauty's got no market value. The main thing is not getting married, but sticking together year in and year out."[8] When luck deserts Toussine, when she becomes a grandmother, she refuses to prop sorrow and instills in her grand-daughter Telumee the principles of self-reliance, which she has come to learn, because of and despite her beauty. Beauty is another curse for women to bear, even while it presents opportunities for happiness or sexual fulfillment. A 1970s U.S. pop song by Janis Ian comes to mind, "*I learnt the truth at seventeen, that love was meant for beauty queens, and high school girls with clear skin smiles, who married young and then retired.*" Beauty is not to be scoffed at, and young women are not fooled by the idea that "good looks"—however this may be constituted in their society—are not important. They have not been blindly cajoled that they can make up for good looks through academic achievements or by being sanctimoniously proper and therefore loved or chosen for themselves rather than their bodies. The young know that the currency of the body matters. Feminism has not provided a panacea for such social beliefs, and cannot do so, even while it creates the space for other possibilities for the feminine and masculine selves to emerge and find fulfillment.

In Olive Senior's "The Two Grandmothers" (1989) Grandma Del has baby chickens, lives in a pretty house with white lace curtains covering jalousied windows, sends her granddaughter to Sunday school, is appalled that she comes to visit her with only jeans and shorts and no respectable church dress. Grandma Del has no television, and so she tells her granddaughter stories at night. Grandma Elaine refuses to be called "grandma," dresses elegantly, is always rushing off to the gym, the pool, dinners and cocktails. While she is fun, she has no time for her granddaughter. Yet she makes her granddaughter very self-conscious about her darker skin and curly hair. The messages are mixed: the girl likes both grandmothers. The homely one who stifles yet comforts her, the other whose lifestyle suggests excitement but who is disquieting to her spirit.

Expanding the breadth of gender possibilities does not necessarily these choices easier. Today young women are faced with multiple choices: marriage, motherhood, a career, or all three. They therefore have a harder time in determining which avenues to choose. Marx's often cited quote, "the satisfaction of basic needs creates other needs" seems to hold equally true for feminism as it does for other material concerns. The fact that women have more possibilities of expressing their femininity today than the cigarette smoking and bible quoting nanas had in the past does not mean that they will yet comprehend the repercussions of their choices. One example of how this conflict of choice was understood in retrospect is valuable here. While women were busily proving equal performance in employment outside of the home, the burden of housework and childcare was not being similarly shared. The increasing satisfaction of a need for recognition as workers and professionals has not reduced the double burden most women still carry.

Older women recognize and celebrate the opportunities now available to younger women, compared to those they would have had in their lifetimes. "Befo' time," her Gran remarked towards nightfall, "Beka would never have won that contest . . . And long befo' long time, you wouldn't be at no convent school" writes Zee Edgehill in *Beka Lamb*.[9] Beka had just won an essay contest at St. Cecilia's Academy in Belize City, a victory which changed her overnight from "a flatrate Belize creole into a person with a high mind" in her family's view. Not only is educational access for girls recognized and treasured by older women, nationhood also represents the possibilities for their granddaughters to achieve the things never available to them. Education also marked out other territorial borders and boundaries for women. In Merle Hodge's *Crick Crack Monkey* (1970), Tee's winning of a scholarship draws her out of rural sanctity to experience discrimination by color and class at the hands of her urbanized Aunt Beatrice, cold comfort for progress after her country Tantie's enveloping warmth and unconditional love. In Claude McKay's *Banana Bottom*, Bita Plant is placed in a similar quandary. "Rescued" from poverty and a peasant class future by the English missionaries, educated in England and returned like polished fruit to her native environment, Bita's choices are between the identity and comfort of the native self and the presumed benefits of respectability, education and the church. Educational access created more barriers between women, more choices for how they adjust to the same women they have loved and depended on, but who now have become more distant. It has created more spaces between women, another basis for establishing gender oppression within the sex.

In Jamaica Kincaid's *Annie John*, the individuation of mother and daughter is a tortured path between childhood and adolescence. The sexual awakening of young girls is recurrently traumatic it seems, whether in fiction or real life, or precisely as fiction expresses reality. "As if that were not enough, my mother informed me that I was on the verge of becoming a young lady, so there were quite a few things I would have to do differently. She didn't say exactly just what it was that made me on the verge of becoming a young lady, and I was so glad of that, because I didn't want to know."[10] We are drawn palpably into this growing distance between mother and daughter at the onset of puberty and the utter self consciousness of the young girl at this time, in the spare prose of Jean Rhys' *Smile, Please*. "I remembered the dress she (her mother) was wearing, so much prettier than anything I had now, but the curls, the dimples surely belonged to somebody else. The eyes were a stranger's eyes. The forefinger of her right hand was raised as if in warning. . . . Why I didn't know, she wasn't me any longer. It was the first time I was aware of time, change and the longing for the past. I was nine years of age. Catching sight of myself in the long looking-glass I felt despair, I had grown into a thin girl, tall for my age. My straight hair was pulled severely from my face and tied with a black ribbon. I was fair with a pale skin and huge staring eyes of no particular colour."[11]

Edwidge Danticat, like Shani Mootoo, is representative of a Third Wave voice in feminist literature. In Danticat's *Breath, Eyes, Memory* (1994), the protagonist Sophie is excruciatingly forthcoming, more fitting to the times in which there is greater openness with the subject of sex and the possibilities of the sexual expression open to men and women. Yet for the Caribbean female protagonist in this novel, guarding, preserving, or discovering female sexuality is a painful business, both legacy and burden, to be passed from mother to daughter. How is this to be handled by mother and received by daughter?

> "When I was a girl, my mother used to test us to see if we were virgins. She would put her finger in our very private parts and see if it would go inside. Your Tante Atie hated it. She used to scream like a pig in a slaughter house. The way my mother was raised, a mother is supposed to do that to her daughter until the daughter is married. It is her responsibility to keep her pure. [. . .] My mother stopped testing me early," she said. "Do you know why?" [. . .] "The details are too much," she said. "But it happened like this. A man grabbed me from the side of the road, pulled me into a cane field, and put you in my body. I was still a young girl, just barely older than you."
> "You need to concentrate when school starts, you have to give that all your attention. You're a good girl, aren't you?"
> By that she meant if I had ever been touched, if I had ever held hands, or kissed a boy.
> "Yes," I said. "I have been good."
> "You understand my right to ask as your mother, don't you?"
> I nodded.[12]

Adrianne Rich's work, couched in the metaphor "of woman born", pointed to the new feminine ethic required of feminism and women. She writes, "Patriarchal lying has manipulated women both through falsehood and silence . . . and so we must take seriously the question of truthfulness between women, truthfulness among women. As we cease to lie with our bodies . . . (there) . . . is a truly womanly idea of honor in the making?"[13] Third Wave feminism must take this idea of honor in the making further, dispute by action rather than words the convenient patriarchal cliché, that women have been their own worst enemies, and push the boundaries of sisterhood further than Second Wave feminism did. We continue to be, both male and female, of woman born.

Vindication of the rights of women

By the beginning of the twenty-first century, gender awareness had placed its stamp on human self-consciousness, indelibly so. If in the nineteenth century the black ex-slave woman Sojourner Truth had the temerity to ask a group of white men and women "And Ain't I A Woman?" and the twentieth century dawned with the British suffragettes chaining themselves to Parliament railings to demand civil rights, then a high visibility of womanhood, if not unchained power, has been partially won. To the casual onlooker or observer, sexual difference as a conceptual tool of social analysis might not appear to be a valuable one, but it is one which cannot be ignored, just as we cannot take for granted the validity of different ethnic and cultural practices, imbalances in development between societies, political machismo, or the persistence of pockets of extreme poverty in an excessively wealthy contemporary world. The young are born today, in most societies, with entitlements and rights, including those accrued to them as members of a particular sex.

Mary Wollstonecraft, who authored *Vindication of the Rights of Woman* in 1792, is cited as the mother of First Wave liberal feminism. Despite the limits of her time, class and race, she established some common ideas which fed into the First Wave and remains on the agenda today, that apart from being given free access to education, women were not to be excluded, without a voice, from "a participation of the natural rights of mankind."[14] The first feminist wave was categorized as a movement for women to have rights within and alongside men, and other social movements. In both Europe and America this wave emerged out of abolitionist platforms, but also led to a demand for rights under liberalism and socialism.

The Second Wave has been viewed as the twentieth century movement for women to have legal rights and legal equality. The early Second Wave, from the Sixties to the Eighties, was perceived as a more intensive moment of social realization and change. It arose in a period of defined social movements, among them the socialist and Left struggles, the civil rights movement and the anti-Vietnam protests in the United States. The accomplishments of the Second Wave feminist movement include highlighting the demand for legal abortion and reproductive rights, equal employment laws, sexual offences bills, equal education, equal opportunity in the workplace, and the recognition of housework and childcare as unpaid labor. Again these may seem commonplace today because they have filtered into the everyday language, policy documents of companies and governments' political agendas. This wave also brought women and gender studies into the university classroom, and created both a globalized feminist movement and a thriving non-governmental business of feminist and women's organizations, which deal with matters ranging from ensuring rights for prostitutes or sex workers to training women for political leadership.

The emerging Third Wave appears more diffused and at present less confrontational than the first and Second Waves. It has been viewed as having already been co-opted by institutions, organizations and states, conservatively channeled into universities, non-governmental organizations, government bureaucracies and political agendas for votes, and international funders with tax-free funds to disburse. This reading however needs to be revised. What is less known is that feminist scholarship continues, as in the Second Wave, to be quietly subversive within the university curricula, disputing existing epistemologies, and inviting critical thought. This feature remains more elusive, not by choice, but by virtue of the project in which it engages—that of reconstructing androcentric knowledge and validating women's voices. The strength of the third wave Caribbean feminist project of reconstructing knowledge is its willingness to challenge the limits of Second Wave feminist thinking on issues of race and difference. Alissa Trotz and Michelle Murphy, for instance, argue that "racialization has not been part of the analytical trajectory that moved from Women in Development in the 1970s to Gender and Development by the late 1980s [...] if difference was rendered visible in these debates, it was conceived as existing between women and men. In fact, it was the poor who were and remain central to this focus."[15]

Third wave feminist writings began to enter more open and constructive debates than Second Wave feminist thinking, confronting issues that those of us heavily involved in the Second Wave assumed would wither away in the struggle for equal sisterhood. Trotz writes: "My initial reaction to what I was reading about Second Wave feminism and different was profoundly disjunctive given that the Caribbean/Guyanese context I was working in, difference, not similarity, was the point of departure and the Achilles heel that had to be confronted."[16] Issues of race and ethnicity and differences between rich and poor were to become far more vocalized in the writings which began to emerge in what may be constituted as third wave critiques, although many of these writers had been involved in early Second Wave initiatives. Among them Rawwida Baksh-Soodeen who argued in a seminal paper that "Feminist organizing had been largely viewed as the domain of African women, rather than as a space in which women of different racial/cultural identities and experiences interact." She observes that women of Indian, Chinese and European heritage have been left out, the latter primarily because the discourse has emerged from the standpoint of those who were enslaved by Europeans.[17]

Two other key components form part of the Third Wave. How this is being expressed is not yet quite clear. First is that young women today (admittedly not all but many that I know) are well aware and quite articulate about their gender rights in an everyday sense and are willing to stand up for these rights, in their homes, with their partners, in their workplaces. This has had its obvious effect in challenging masculinity on many fronts, and thus the third wave is equally the adjustments or retaliations being made by masculinity and men. Writers such as Linden Lewis, Mark Figueroa, Wesley Crichlow, Keith Nurse, Antonio de Moya and Aviston Downes have contributed to a volume entitled *Interrogating Caribbean Masculinities*, an already well-thumbed book that is used as a text-based reference for courses being offered in men and masculinities in the Caribbean.[18]

Based on the responses of male writers in deconstructing masculinity, as well as the increasing rapprochement between essentialism and constructivism in mainstream thought, the Third Wave has also benefited from another kind of diffusion, that of disrupting the essentialism of social, if not biological, gender. No longer can we hold on to notions of fixed gender and sexual roles and attributes. Ideas of transgender, transsexual identities and shifting gender identities throughout one's lifetime are already the currency of thought in gender and feminism.

Perhaps the main problem that first and Second Wave feminists have with the Third Wave is that there is less evidence of a militant organization around specific issues or themes, such as those which fed the struggles before. First and Second Wave feminism were grounded in praxis rather than theory and benefited from the articulated relationship between these. Second Wave feminism, as Mohammed described, spread across the globe like a virus, infecting women of almost every nation and uniting them through similar symptoms.[19] The dispersion of Third Wave feminist activisms and ideas in my view emerged because the effects of the first and Second Waves were widely felt and received. As one feminist ally reminded me over dinner one night, daughters today have grown up with mothers who taught them by their actions to expect a certain set of rights and possibilities as a way of life, without even questioning this, just as our mothers transmitted ideas of their generation to us.[20] Women today have more social freedoms, more privileges, more access to occupations, more scope for communicating dissatisfaction with social norms and expression of their sexuality than that allowed their mothers, grandmothers and great grandmothers. By the end of the Second Wave, masculinity had also begun a reconsideration, tentatively still at this stage, offering men further possibilities for performance of masculinity. Patriarchy has been forced into a new collective reckoning about gender roles because of women's agency in contemporary society.

At the root of these shifts are the changes in mode of production, technology and divisions of labor which have over time drawn men and women differently into the labor force, thus creating different needs of each sex at any time. The ideas of gender equality did not simply emerge from the ideological meanderings of a subversive minority. They were prompted by concrete factors. Among these have been women's demand for reproductive rights, for freedom from consistent child bearing and rearing and its effects on their health, for equal wages for work which they did outside of the home, many as heads of households, from the lived experience of oppressive acts such as domestic violence, and from the persistent threat of rape as social control over their sexuality. Ideas about gender equality are also fundamentally influenced by other social and political movements which demand freedoms of one sort or another. The emergence of the first and Second Wave movements cannot be delinked from received philosophical notions of development: that the level of "development" of a society may be measured by the status of its women.

But these new gender rights and reconfigurations in the twentieth century, though inalienable in many societies, are still alien in others. The un-education of girls in Afghanistan was counteracted by brave women within the society who worked underground, at the risk of death, to continue teaching young girls. Nor do we condone that a woman may be stoned to death under *sharia* law in Nigeria for committing adultery. She is castigated as a sinner, while the adulterous male walks free. Such clear instances of an absence of women's rights in "Third World" societies are transmitted across the globe on the internet and via media networks as evidence of underdevelopment of such societies. Third Wave feminism must be far more politically sophisticated and astute as to how these are used and misused in political agendas. Michelle Rowley comments personally on these two examples "even as we speak to Afghanistan and Nigeria, it is important to note simultaneously that these manifestations of misogyny are not only national but also tools in a geo-political battle where the West draws attention to the Rest as a way of re-establishing old political markers of Third World-ism. So it is not accidental that concern re-emerged for Afghanistan's women on U.S. based Women's Studies List Serves around the threat of terrorism. My point is that the notion of sisterhood is still riddled with sinister nationalistic agendas where the only thing of color in the 'south' that seems to matter to the West is the black of oil."[21] While Third Wave feminism will continue to rethink "what sisterhood means," it also has to consider how it may deal with cultural inconsistencies across the globe in respect of those rights that we now hold to be indisputable. What has Third Wave feminism to offer in those instances where rights once gained may be just as easily retracted?

"Woman's Consciousness, Man's World"

A short while after I had begun an activist and scholarly involvement in the area of socialism and feminism in the late Seventies, I was introduced to Sheila Rowbotham's *Woman's Consciousness, Man's World*. "When I was seventeen," wrote Rowbotham, "feminism meant to me shadowy figures in long old-fashioned clothes who were somehow connected with headmistresses who said you shouldn't wear high heels and make-up. It was all very prim and stiff and mainly concerned with keeping you away from boys. From dim childhood memories I had the stereotype of emancipated women: frightening people in tweed suits and horn rimmed glasses with stern buns at the back of their heads."[22] Although separated by miles of cultural differences in a little Caribbean island, I understood the sentiments. The images she evoked were similar to those I had of older, unmarried, Presbyterian female teachers at Naparima Girls High School in San Fernando, Trinidad. Among these were two elderly white Canadian teachers who earned my great respect, along with a youthful compassion for their singleness. I thought that although rewarded as career women, their lives must be very lacking without children and husbands and family outings. There were of course other married women on the teaching staff, some of whom looked happy, but others who looked harassed and tired in front of the classroom. Was this the burden of a career? Were these the new choices available to us when we grew up? Again, these were never clear-cut. The younger teachers on the staff were glamorous and seemed to lead very rich social lives, some not beyond reproach by the respectable, or so it seemed to the prurient young. Curiously, I was not put off by these contradictions; rather, life seemed to offer an exciting range of possibilities to the map of a future.

Looking at these female role models in the 1960s, I can understand Rowbotham's question and response: "Why did it take so long to make a movement like women's liberation? [...] To start with, we had consciously to recognize our femaleness and see through the existing versions of femininity which surrounded us."[23] Young women, and young men, in the beginning of the twenty-first century, are placed in a similar dilemma; they must navigate between old and new constructions of femaleness and maleness around them and come to terms with the convictions of their choices. Like all choices pertaining to identity building, these are not simple or linear ones, for they tread a path of great uncertainty and are still controlled by social sanctions about male and female roles which defy time. What are the imperatives to avow feminism today, either for the young woman or for the young man? Many argue and believe that younger women have far less to lose by becoming feminists, but what they have to lose may not be so clear to those already past their prime.

Fear of feminism

I think we need to examine carefully this seeming apathy to feminism among the young. I use "seeming" deliberately. There is far more here than meets the eye in the lifestyles of the young and restless. "Young women today have been profoundly affected by the demonization of feminism during [. . .] the time when they formed their understanding of political possibility and public life," writes Lisa Marie Hogeland. "Young women may experience their situation as extremely precarious—too precarious to risk feminism."[24] Hogeland argues that this fear of feminism is a fear of politics, the latter understood as "a fear of living in consequences, a fear of reprisals" as there are powerful interests opposed to feminism. What are these powerful interests against feminism or the ideas which feminism advances? It is not in the interest of men that women insist on abortion and reproductive rights. It is not in the interest of capitalism that women demand economic equality in the marketplace. It is not in the interest of consumer culture that women demand that their bodies are less exploited for sale of products. It is not in the interest of men that women demand an end to sexual abuse in the home and the workplace. It is not in the interest of men that women begin to compete evenly with them in the once male-dominated spheres of governance and politics, of high finance and corporate business. It is not in the interest of the family and the society that women choose careers over childbearing, and are more selective in their choice of partners. It is not in the interest of men that women ask them to give up the privilege of multiple partners (a "deputy" or "matie" being essential in the Caribbean) or the freedom from domestic routines which tie one partner, usually the female, to the home and the workplace.

There are other repercussions of Second Wave feminism now visited on the young. A declared feminist, unless otherwise known and proven to be heterosexual, is assumed to be a lesbian—the two go together as love and marriage once did with a horse and carriage. At a time in which the young are self-consciously involved in discovering and constructing their identities and when romantic and sexual relationships are primary arenas for selfhood, the institution of heterosexuality provides the safety net of normalcy. In their early 20s few young women have begun professional or community careers that provide another venue through which alternative identities can be shaped. They know that being a feminist limits their chances with the pool of men available for partnerships.

Engaging men

Masculinity, occupied in a defense of its patriarchal rights, is only slowly lowering its rose-colored lens on traditional ideas of companionship and sexual partnership. In the view of a young Canadian, Ramesh Dharan, the word feminism "strikes a chord of terror in the heart of young males. Images of an army of young feminist activists, clutching proposed legislative amendments and burning Barbie dolls in effigy, leap forth at night from the dark recesses of the male mind.... Though perhaps not strong enough to paralyze us with fear, accepting feminism is often an especially problematic proposal for many young males."

One young Caribbean man had a slightly different take on the subject: "I cyar mess with dem liberated woman. Dem want you to wash up and stay home with them and do everything they say. You cyar make a wrong note around them but they down on yuh case. I prefer woman I could fool a lil bit. I still want to feel like I'se man." Feminism appears to be a direct attack not on phallocentricism, but on the male phallus, an observation supported by Rhoda Reddock, that "One of the most intriguing, although little noticed developments on the 1998 calypso scene in Trinidad was a significant increase in the number of songs dealing with the phallus."[25] Reddock points out that references to phallic imagery have always been an important component in the calypso genre, yet from 1997, the songs dealing with the phallus "did not express that triumphal tone."[26] The angle had changed. The use of humor was now self-directed and unassertive, and for Reddock, pointing tenuously to a male reflection of current uncertainty affecting men in general.

It is not difficult to appreciate the male response: not all men are batterers, delinquents, bad fathers, parents and lovers. Not all men are powerful in the workplace or public sphere. While these qualifications of masculinity are implicit or explicit in feminist literature, particularly from the Caribbean where it was the systemic nature of patriarchy rather than individual males who were being targeted, the Second Wave feminist analysis of patriarchy was viewed as a collective attack on all manhood. Even today, the message that all feminism cannot be reduced to male bashing and the undermining of masculinity, has not migrated into popular understandings. The fear of "women taking over" looms large as a threat and seems to have merged with symbolic processes associated with manhood and emasculation. Dharan questions this response. "Having grown up in a post-civil rights, politically correct, and morally conscientious society, what could young males possible find fault with in feminism, at least in the most popular 'liberal emancipatory' part of the movement? I have come to realize that many of my male peers are uncomfortable and antipathetic to the continual advancement of feminism and the consequences of this advancement. The causes for this for the most part can be traced back to a common thread: a lack of understanding and a narrow-minded view of feminism, and the accompanying fear which the movement has made possible. . . . In my own personal experience, a typical response of teenage males when confronted with an expression of feminist views has been to dismiss the debate as irrelevant, since women and men supposedly possess equal rights and freedoms in our society."[27]

In the face of this debate, the young woman who publicly avows feminism runs the risk of being denounced as going against women's essential nature, therefore, not "wife material." Masculine methods of control over the freedoms now available to young women are both clever and efficient. One young woman in my gender studies class jokingly proffered that a favorite gift of young men to their girlfriends was a cellular phone. Why? "Miss, they could check up on you any time, anywhere." I suppose that in a rare case of gender equality, the opposite also obtains.

Michael Flood, who teaches Women and Gender Studies at the Australian National University, agrees that men's lives have changed in profound ways over the last three decades. "The women's movement and feminism have questioned the meanings given to being male and female," he writes. "Their efforts, plus other social changes, have shifted the possibilities of men's lives. Men now face new expectations from their girlfriends and partners, their friends, their sisters and daughters and other men. Some traditional forms of manhood—based on being emotionally shut-down, dominating others, work-obsessed and aggressive—are often seen as out-of-date and unhealthy. Men are being encouraged to change their behavior in the kitchen, the bedroom, the classroom and on the street. Men are expected to treat the women in their lives with respect and to avoid sexist behavior such as date rape and domestic violence."[28] Recognizing that this change is also being asked of Caribbean men, Linden Lewis observes that "social change presupposes some degree of concession and compromise, and it is very often accompanied by some notion—however articulated—of struggle and resistance."[29] Lewis suggests that given the imbalance of power between men and women, "It is fairly axiomatic that men ought to play a pivotal role in the reconfiguration of gender relations" since men everywhere, benefit from the "patriarchal dividend in society."[30]

If men are being asked to change their expectations of femininity, to reshape their practices of masculinity and so on, then what is being asked of young women in their own behavior and attitudes to young and older men? If one reads between the lines of what young women are saying, they have been presented with a gender consciousness of their equal status, a right to expect equality in all spheres, public and private, collectively and individually. But masculinity itself has not been fully primed or even collectively receptive to the kind of changes in gender relations that Lewis points to. Thus younger women, who are less experienced, are faced with the question of how to manage this new equality which has been offered to them. The younger men, some of whom appear to understand and respect these changes, are trying to adjust. Others react more harshly and resentfully; after all, the rights of the father were also expected by the son. The Freudian connections cannot be so summarily dismissed.

More feminist bogeys

For those who teach or work in gender studies or feminist organizations of one kind or another, feminism has not by any means been easy work. Both intellectual and activist work required much reading, thinking, time, energy and courage to defy accepted norms, to challenge institutional arrangements, and to take a leap of faith, if you like, that this was a valid enterprise towards engendering both new knowledge and new sources of empowerment for the young and the society at large. The study of gender, unlike many other disciplines which have emerged in the academy over centuries, is constantly forced to explain its relevance over and over again and to account for itself. I can think of no other discipline or sub-discipline offhand which has had so many critics from so many directions, from the popular as well as the academic; in the latter, on theoretical, epistemological and political grounds. Most unfortunately, it acquired a reputation in the early days of its introduction as a "soft" option, as if both the students and those who taught and worked in this area had compromised quality for some puttied quantity. In many ways, gender studies, like much of feminist activism, has become ghettoized. Why should we assume that young women and men will voluntarily sign up for the labeling, hardship, censorship, and reprisals associated with this area of work or study?

Women's studies and gender studies have now been part of the academy in the Caribbean for at least twenty years, more formally with the setting up of a Centre for Gender and Development Studies at each of the three campuses of the University of the West Indies in 1993.[31] Students who venture into the gender studies curriculum come with a range of misconceptions and simultaneously have to contend with a range of perceptions about themselves. Why on earth are they doing courses in gender studies, they are asked by female and male peers, parents and relatives? What are they going to do with this after university? The undertones are they must be closet lesbians or man haters to have made such a choice, foolhardy as gender studies is not a professional degree linked to an obvious occupational choice or career, or worst yet, simple minded as gender studies is soft and available for those who "cannot take learning." Needless to say, many have never bothered to discover the content of such courses but assume that the curriculum must be filled with male-bashing topics—a school for feminist scandal and intrigue. The questions we are faced with, those who teach and work in the area, and those who choose to follow, have become too tiresomely repetitive, but nonetheless gnawing and annoying.

In the context of the English-speaking Caribbean, features emerged at the end of the twentieth century that fuelled this fear of feminism and its proliferation through the teaching of women and gender studies. First among these has been the introduction of a clause related to marital rape in the Sexual Offences Act; and secondly, the establishment of the Domestic Violence Act in several societies. While in practice these pieces of legislation are by no means unproblematic in themselves, they serve the more profound purpose of signaling that age-old ideas thought to be founded on the "essential nature" of male and female can and do undergo change. The marital rape clause questions the conjugal rights of a man over a woman within the institution of marriage. In the case of the Domestic Violence Act, it is no longer possible for the court to dismiss domestic violence as "man-woman business" which should be settled outside of the judiciary and policing system. The signal to masculinity is loud, clear and frightening, destabilizing to what has constituted masculinity for centuries. Residual notions of chattel slavery which have "kept femininity in its place" are slowly eroding. For the layman and laywoman, this shift in what constitutes a woman's and a man's rightful place in society intimidating, raising everyday questions and concerns: How do we bring up our children? How must they be socialized? What moral values must apply to each sex? Who will be responsible for the home?

These are very legitimate concerns and questions, which First Wave feminism could not have anticipated, and Second Wave feminism assumed would be ironed out in provisions and services by state and community, by accommodations within households and by an increasing conscientized society which would accept the inevitability and logic of changing gender roles and ideologies. Third Wave feminism must consider carefully the implications of what real gender equality and equity means to relations between and among the sexes in general, the sexual division of labor in the family and the workplace and relations within the household. Third Wave feminism must also consider how ideologies, more than practices, are most resistant to change. The recent experience of Trinidad and Tobago in the battle to have a National Gender Policy for Equity and Equality passed by the government of the day is a good example. The policy was met with relative openness and support throughout its consultative and writing stages. When first tabled for public discussion, however, the major debates were not around the benefits that the policy could bring to real issues affecting both men and women, but the fear of some Christian-based groups that a gender policy challenged the nature of biological sex as it is known to exist traditionally, that is that a gender policy was the thin edge of the wedge in condoning homosexual freedoms.

The second feature, a global occurrence, is the entry of more women into the formal education system, particularly at secondary and tertiary levels. In the Caribbean, this increased visibility of women in education, albeit dominantly in the "softer" areas of humanities and social sciences and in professions such as teaching, law and medicine, has come under serious scrutiny, echoing perhaps the fear that eighteenth and nineteenth century educators had when they opened the schoolroom to women en masse. Ironically, the far fewer numbers of educated women until the last decades of the twentieth century created no such panic among policy makers and planners. The ideas of an assumed male marginality in the household have now been further underscored by a panic about the underachievement of men in education, and consequently, in the workplace and in public office. Both spoken and unspoken are the directives to women, that feminism has bred disfigurement and chaos to the natural order of society, that once again, like the biblical Eve in the Garden of Eden, women have compromised the "true course of nature." The convenient bogey is feminism, rather than the circumstances which have given rise to a new social order.

Gender consciousness versus feminist consciousness

The problem is not a lack of gender consciousness, but the lack of a feminist consciousness. To admit or embrace a feminist consciousness, by definition, one has to work actively and consciously at dealing with the problem, not just acknowledging it. More to the point, to admit a feminist consciousness requires moving beyond the clichéd ideas of supporting gender equity and equality, to more informed and articulated ideas of how these may be achieved—it demands a level of intellectual and political engagement to which few are prepared to commit. Gender as a concept has always appeared easily accessible because each individual possesses a body with biological sex organs and experiences the world in terms of their gender. Thus gender was viewed as learnt through the school of life, requiring no formal instruction about the systemic nature of gender discrimination or its cultural reproduction. So too ideas of feminism are thought to be easily understood; worse yet static, as if there has been no progression in theory and praxis over the last few decades.

Teresa de Lauretis (1989) observed that the technology of gender is both its presentation and re-presentation.[32] Once we become self-conscious of our gender identities, we are also busily engaged in consciously re-presenting it. This proceeds daily in many spheres, but the process is most obvious in the media industry. Contemporary television and big screen films are rife with examples of how gender representation has come a long way from the first half of the twentieth century. Films in the Eighties and Nineties that tackled women's issues, such as "An Unmarried Woman" (Jill Clayburgh) and "Working Girl" (Sigourney Weaver and Meg Ryan) have grown far more explicit and precise. Among these are the remaking of the old TV series "Charlie's Angels"; the Angels, though angelic, are by no means pushovers and docile pawns of the mysterious Charlie again. Series such as "Sex and the City," "Mind of the Married Man," "Queer as Folk" and "The L Word" dissect from different viewpoints the new morality which informs each sex, while "Will and Grace" take homosexuality, one of feminism's best bedfellows in activism, as its theme in a family situation comedy. Nor are these interrogations restricted to a white middle-class morality. Ideas of race and gender differences and representation have become generous fodder for the financially conscious mill of the film industry, tapping into new themes to engage the modern mind. If "Guess Who's Coming to Dinner?" forced the old white couple of the screen, Spencer Tracy and Katherine Hepburn, to accept the black Sidney Poitier as their daughter's spouse, Spike Lee's "She's Gotta Have it" examines the flexibilities allowed the young black woman of the 1980s in her choice of sexual partners. The more recent "Save the Last Dance" pits a young black man and a young white woman in a close encounter of another kind. The James Bond movie "Die Another Day" even admits the black femme fatale heroine in the form of Halle Berry, suggesting that black women too have come a long way. In the Western dominated media which influences the everyday consciousness of the young, these are not incidental in inscribing new symbols of gender, reshaping ideas and obfuscating yet representing new dimensions of race, gender and sexual relations.

Third Wave feminism is surfing in different waters than that of the Second Wave. There has emerged a gender confidence without an attendant political consciousness. Hogeland observes of the contemporary situation that "Gender consciousness is a necessary precondition for feminist consciousness, but they are not the same."[33] Others have suggested that this is actually the other way around: we need to separate gender consciousness and feminist consciousness, to understand the successes of the first as a victory of feminism itself, and the limits of the other as the limits of social movements themselves. Eudine Barriteau suggests that "gender has consumed its feminist mother." Third Wave feminism must continue to pose the question this raises: has gender consciousness been at the expense of a feminist consciousness? Is there a difference and is this difference key to the future of feminism?

"My mother who fathered me" and the rise of a new matriarchy

It is easy to blame the early feminists and founding mothers of feminism for this or that flaw in the feminist agenda. The reasons for this lack of obvious activism may lie outside feminism itself: Second Wave feminism actually emerged alongside a period of great social resistance and turmoil, including black power, civil rights and student movements, whereas Third Wave Feminism is emerging in a time that, though troubled, has no grand narratives of resistance or subordination such as capitalism versus socialism on which it could hang its hat. Nor has terrorists versus the rest convinced us that this is how the west must be won.

It is easy to blame the young women and men for lacking a feminist consciousness and for not becoming part of the "women's movement." But what is not clear to many of them is precisely what "movement" they should join. The Second Wave women's movement in the 1960s was admittedly a more defined and public feminism. There were visible characters, activities and public proclamations of varying sorts. But feminism has for some time now, in the popular discourse, become immersed with and consumed by an amorphous set of ideas and practices and less difficult to pin down other than in its most direct statements pertaining to women's continuing struggle for ascendancy to political power, equal treatment in the home and workplace, persistent fight against sexual violence, control of reproductive rights, and a growing dialogue with masculinity. As with all political change, some of the spokespersons are not convincing that they represent all women, even if this is not intended. As with all social change, each generation, by definition, challenges and resists the other, reinventing the wheel until they learn that the revolutions can simply continue if we add more spokes and spokespersons.

Within feminism the distance between older and younger women is more worrying because Second Wave feminism itself was built on ideas of sisterhood. "There is not enough continuity being built with a new cadre of up-and-coming feminist women leaders," writes Eudine Barriteau. We have to guard against mistrust hardening to the point it prevents our strategic solidarities around the agendas with which we identify. We the ones who are established, who have paid some dues, cling to power in all its manifestations and often frustrate younger women. Similarly, younger women, anxious and eager to make their mark, often arrive before they have reached. They dismiss the wisdom, the experiences, even the mistakes of the women who walked before them as irrelevant to feminist politics and scholarship of the twenty-first century."[34] There is need for understanding and appreciation on both sides, a willingness to share knowledge, power and resources, an openness to unlearn and to learn.

If feminism has perchance thrown up a new matriarchy, there are other female regimes and authority figures with which younger women and men have had to reckon. The relations between mother and son, mother and daughter itself has to be individuated. The power of the mother-in-law over new daughters-in-law, of first wives over younger wives—all of these are built on similar ideas of ascendancy through experience or the crucial roles one has played, as ways of establishing power bases. The rise of a new matriarchy in feminism may be read as both, with its problems but also its pathways. The resolution once more lies in the feminist solution. Many young women are mindful of the lessons of the past and are interested in the foundations laid by Second Wave Caribbean feminist thinkers. Trinidadian Gabrielle Hosein, for instance, writes: "I feel I need to know—about the gains won, the setbacks and the original issues that Caribbean women organized around—to be able to differentiate specifically Caribbean concerns. To tell the truth, as a young person, I have major concerns about how much more my generation needs to know about our history since independence—that history of what has been achieved and how and where we need to still follow through. I think this has major consequences for the future of the feminist movement and for changing generational roles." Jamaican Shakira Maxwell observes: "I think as feminists we cannot necessarily believe that our concerns are so vastly different from others around the world, despite the region or country they may come from. However, I do believe that Caribbean feminists have had to fight for the rights of Caribbean women in different ways than those which have been undertaken in First World countries. For instance, class and racial concerns have had to be tackled from a different standpoint, similar to that of countries such as Africa and Latin America and this I think binds us together."[35]

"From margin to center": Challenges for third wave feminism

The young have a lot to give. Many of them do not yet have the binding responsibilities of families or careers. They have energy, idealism and time. Feminist activism will nonetheless arise out of the specific experiences and problems which confront the present generation and will test their will and capacity to create change. Although I do not dare to speak for a new generation, it appears to me that some of the issues are already apparent. Among these are:

1. The paradox of choice

Women are presented with a range of acceptable choices, of motherhood or career, to have or to not have children and still lead full, productive lives, to be single, to have families in same-sex relations. Those who do have children are faced with the problem of feeling left out of the brave new world experienced by those who choose otherwise. With the freedom to choose comes the responsibility of this choice and of their future lives. The blame for unfulfilled professional or family lives cannot be put on men, or masculinity, or patriarchy, for that matter. This responsibility for self must be accepted by women. Women have been writing themselves out of the victimhood script, but what is the next scene?

2. Deconstructing masculinity

Feminism has shaken masculinity to its core. Masculinity is already rethinking itself. What are the implications for new, more equitable gender relations and for the reshaping of patriarchal structures? What are the benefits to masculinity for taking on such a challenge? In addition, will patriarchy, like the amoeba, recreate itself from the spore of a damaging masculinist discourse?

3. The institutionalization of feminism

Feminism has moved into the academy but what is its true goal in the academy? Is it about jobs for the girls or about reshaping epistemologies? That feminism has entered the classroom should not be viewed as conservatism but as a new site from which activism takes place. But what theoretical directions and guidance will academic Third Wave feminism bring to feminist thought and practice? Already, we face one challenge: how to move Caribbean feminist scholarship and indigenous material to the center from the margins where it still lingers.

4.   The geo-political challenge of feminism
The real political challenge of feminism, through its reconstruction of knowledge and understanding of power, is to intervene in global political and economic threats to peace and human security, to openly engage in issues that appear unrelated to specific gender interests. How might this be achieved and what new internationalist movements must this give rise to in feminism?

Epilogue

The title of the last section of this essay is an adaptation of bell hooks' book *Feminist theory: from margin to center*. hooks establishes a rewarding relationship between margin and center, a symbiotic one, as if to say the center is continuously shifting and cannot hold for all time. The margin too has its standpoint: "To be part of the margin is to be part of the whole but outside the main body." The Third Wave may be on the margins now, but it is part of the whole. The full effects of each wave are not felt until they have completely washed over us. We should not assume by an apparent lack of militancy that the present gender consciousness will not create another form of the feminist movement. Like sugar in coffee, feminism has dissolved throughout society. We should celebrate this as one of the Second Wave's victories, as we wait for the Third Wave to rise to its own crescendo.

Notes

1.   An earlier version of this paper was published in *Social and Economic Studies*, vol. 52, no. 3, September 2003, a thematic issue commemorating the 10th Anniversary of the Centre for Gender and Development Studies, University of the West Indies, Guest Editor: Rhoda Reddock. My thanks to SES editor Annie Paul and Rhoda Reddock for their agreement to publish a revisited version.

2.   I date my formal involvement in feminist activism in the Caribbean to 1977 when I began an M.Sc. Thesis in Sociology on Women and Education in Trinidad and Tobago, predating the advent of women or gender and development studies in the region. This was coupled with an activism that emerged alongside socialism from 1978 and with this the events that led to the formation of the Concerned Women for Progress by 1980, an early Second Wave feminist group of which I was one of the co-founders.

3. I am very grateful to Michelle Rowley, then Lecturer, Centre for Gender and Development Studies, UWI, Cave Hill campus, who carefully read the first draft of this chapter and gave me valuable comments on its structural improvements as well as some of its errors and contradictions. The views retained in this essay are, however, idiosyncratically mine, and do not represent a collective voice nor those of the institution to which I belong.

4. The title is borrowed from a line from Doris Anderson "Feminism's future is secure," an optimistic reading which I partially share, that if there is no future for feminism, then there is no future for the world, http://ww2.mcgill.ca/uro/Rep/r3105/anderson.html.

5. Shani Mootoo, *The Cereus Blooms at Night* (New York: Avon Books, 1996), 24.

6. This brief foray into the rich fiction of the region in no way can represent the complex themes dealt with by these writers. It is by way of homage to such writers of fiction who, some without claiming themselves feminists, have left profound legacies for us in the region.

7. Simone Schwarz-Bart, *The Bridge of Beyond* (London, Kingston, Jamaica, and Port of Spain, Trinidad and Tobago: Heinemann Caribbean Writer Series, 1982), 4.

8. Schwarz-Bart, *The Bridge*, 7.

9. Zee Edgehill, *Beka Lamb* (London, Kingston, Jamaica, and Port of Spain, Trinidad and Tobago: Heinemann, 1982), 1.

10. Jamaica Kincaid, *Annie John* (New York: A Plume Book, 1986), 26.

11. Jean Rhys, *Smile, Please* (London: Penguin Books, 1981), 19-20.

12. Edwidge Danticat, *Breath, Eyes, Memory* (New York: Vintage Books, 1994), 60-61.

13. Adrienne Rich, "On Lies, Secrets and Silences," in *Women's Studies, Essential Readings*, ed. Stevi Jackson (New York: New York University Press, 1993), 446.

14. Mary Wollestonecraft, *Vindication of the Rights of Woman* (Harmondsworth, U.K.: Penguin Books, 1992), 88.

15. Alissa Trotz and Michelle Murphy, "The Retreat from Race in Development Studies. Provisional Notes" (unpublished paper from Deconstructing Disciplinary Discourses of Development Interdisciplinary Seminar, University of Toronto, April 2005), 7.

16. Alissa Trotz, "Globalization and Transnationality: Pedagogical Possibilities from a Women's Studies Perspective" (paper presented to Adult Education Conference, Victoria, B.C., May 2004), 3.

17. Rawwida Baksh-Soodeen, "Issues of Difference in Contemporary Caribbean Feminism," in *Rethinking Caribbean Difference, Feminist Review* 59, (Summer 1998), 79.

18. Rhoda Reddock, ed. *Interrogating Caribbean Masculinities* (Kingston, Jamaica: University of the West Indies Press, 2004).

19. Patricia Mohammed, "Stories in Caribbean Feminism: Reflections on the Twentieth Century" (Fifth Anniversary Lecture of the Centre for Gender and Development Studies, U.W.I., St. Augustine, 1998), 17.

20. Conversation with Carla Foderingham—a self-evident point but worth noting since we forget the simplicity of how such ideas are transmitted on an everyday basis, and assume some mysterious process by which the young inherit their beliefs—it is not from the public sphere at first but primarily from their homes and families.

21. Extracted from comments by Michelle Rowley on a first draft of this chapter, June 2003.

22. Sheila Rowbotham, *Woman's Consciousness, Man's World* (Harmondsworth, U.K.: Pelican Books, 1974), 12.
23. Rowbotham, *Woman's Consciousness*, 3.
24. Lisa Maria Hogeland, "Fear of Feminism: Why young women get the willies," *Ms. Magazine*, (November/December 1994), 1.
25. Rhoda Reddock, "Man gone, man stay!: Masculinity, Ethnicity and Identity in the Contemporary Sociopolitical Context of Trinidad and Tobago," in *Caribbean Masculinities: Working Papers*, ed. Rafael Ramirez, Victor Garcia-Toro and Ineke Cunningham (San Juan: HIV/AIDS Research and Education Center, University of Puerto Rico, 2002), 161.
26. Reddock, "Man gone," 162.
27. Ramesh Dharan, "Feminism from the Sidelines: A young male's perspective," http://www.youthactionnetwork.org/forum/spring_summer1998/Feminism_from_the_Sidelines.html.
28. Michael Flood, "Can men be feminists?" in *Australian National University Women's Handbook* (Canberra, Australia, 2001)—see also: http://www.xyonline.net/Canmenbefeminists.shtml.
29. Linden Lewis, "Envisioning a Politics of Change within Caribbean Gender Relations," in *Gendered Realities: Essays in Caribbean Feminist Thought*, ed. Patricia Mohammed (Kingston, Jamaica: University of the West Indies Press, 2002), 512.
30. Lewis, "Envisioning," 513.
31. For further reading on the introduction of women's studies and gender studies into the academy in the Caribbean, readers are referred to Elsa Leo Rhynie, "Women and Development Studies: Moving from the Periphery" in *Gendered Realities: Essays in Caribbean Feminist Thought*, ed. Patricia Mohammed (Kingston, Jamaica: University of the West Indies Press, 2002), 147-163.
32. Teresa de Lauretis, *Technologies of Gender* (Bloomington: Indiana University Press 1989).
33. Hogeland, "Fear," 1.
34. Eudine Barriteau, "Issues and Challenges of Caribbean Feminisms" (Keynote address at Caribbean Feminisms Workshop: Recentering Caribbean Feminisms, University of the West Indies, Cave Hill, Barbados, June 17, 2002), 14.
35. Responses taken from emailed questionnaire sent in February 2003 to a group of scholars in Caribbean feminism and gender studies.

Bibliography

Barriteau, Eudine. "Issues and Challenges of Caribbean Feminisms." Keynote address at Caribbean Feminisms Workshop: Recentering Caribbean Feminisms, University of the West Indies, Cave Hill, Barbados, June 17, 2002.

Baksh-Soodeen, Rawwida. "Issues of Difference in Contemporary Caribbean Feminism." *Rethinking Caribbean Difference, Feminist Review* 59, (Summer 1998), 74-85.

Baumgardner, Jennifer and Amy Richards. *Manifesta: Young Women, Feminism, and the Future.* New York: Farrar, Straus & Giroux, 2000.

Danticat, Edwidge. *Breath, Eyes, Memory.* New York: Vintage Books, 1994.

De Lauretis, Teresa. *Technologies of Gende.* Bloomington: Indiana University Press, 1989.

Dharan, Ramesh. "Feminism from the Sidelines: A young male's perspective," http://www.youthactionnetwork.org/forum/spring_summer1998/Feminism_from_the_Sidelines.html.
Edgehill, Zee. *Beka Lamb*. London, Kingston, Jamaica, and Port of Spain, Trinidad and Tobago: Heinemann, 1982.
Flood, Michael. "Can men be feminists?" in Australian National University Women's Handbook. Canberra, Australia, 2001—also see http://www.xyonline.net/Canmenbefeminists.shtml.
Hodge, Merle. *Crick Crack Monkey*. London and Kingston, Jamaica: Heinemann Educational Books Ltd., 1970.
Hogeland, Lisa Maria. "Fear of Feminism: Why young women get the willies." *Ms. Magazine*, November/December 1994.
hooks, bell. *Feminist theory: from margin to center*. Cambridge, Mass.: South End Press, 1984.
Kincaid, Jamaica. *Annie John*. New York: A Plume Book, 1986.
Lewis, Linden. "Envisioning a Politics of Change within Caribbean Gender Relations." Pp. 512-530 in *Gendered Realities: Essays in Caribbean Feminist Thought*, edited by Patricia Mohammed. Kingston, Jamaica: University of the West Indies Press, 2002.
McKay, Claude. *Banana Bottom*. London: Pluto Press, 1986 (first pub. 1933).
Mohammed, Patricia. "Stories in Caribbean Feminism: Reflections on the Twentieth Century." Fifth Anniversary Lecture of the Centre for Gender and Development Studies, U.W.I., St. Augustine, 1998.
Mootoo, Shani. *The Cereus Blooms at Night*. New York: Avon Books, 1996.
Reddock, Rhoda. "Man gone, man stay!: Masculinity, Ethnicity and Identity in the Contemporary Sociopolitical Context of Trinidad and Tobago." Pp. 147-172 in *Caribbean Masculinities: Working Papers*, edited by Rafael Ramirez, Victor Garcia-Toro and Ineke Cunningham. San Juan: HIV/AIDS Research and Education Center, University of Puerto Rico, 2002.
———. ed. *Interrogating Caribbean Masculinities*. Kingston, Jamaica: University of the West Indies Press, 2004.
Rhys, Jean. *Smile, Please*. London: Penguin Books, 1981.
Rich, Adrienne. "On Lies, Secrets and Silences." Section 13.4, pp. 445-446 in *Women's Studies, Essential Readings*, edited by Stevi Jackson. New York: New York University Press, 1993.
Rowbotham, Sheila. *Woman's Consciousness, Man's World*. Harmondsworth, U.K.: Pelican Books, 1974.
Schwarz-Bart, Simone. *The Bridge of Beyond*. London, Kingston, Jamaica, and Port of Spain, Trinidad and Tobago: Heinemann Caribbean Writer Series, 1982.
Senior, Olive. *Arrival of the Snake-Woman and Other Stories*. Harlow, U.K.: Longman Caribbean Writers, 1989.
Trotz, Alissa. "Globalization and Transnationality: Pedagogical Possibilities from a Women's Studies Perspective." Paper presented to Adult Education Conference, Victoria, B.C., May 2004.
Trotz, Alissa, and Michelle Murphy. "The Retreat from Race in Development Studies. Provisional Notes." Unpublished paper from Deconstructing Disciplinary Discourses of Development Interdisciplinary Seminar, University of Toronto, April 2005.

Wollestonecraft, Mary. *Vindication of the Rights of Woman.* Harmondsworth: Penguin Books, 1992 (first published 1792).

14

Mimi Sheller

Work That Body: Sexual Citizenship and Embodied Freedom

Relational formations of "race," class, gender, ethnicity, nation and sexuality are currently one of the most dynamic fields of research in Caribbean Studies, especially in studies of slavery and emancipation, (post)colonial and neocolonial governance, citizenship and nation building, and critical legal studies.[1] Caribbean scholars both in the region and in the diaspora have contributed crucial scholarship to such relational analyses. Recent Caribbean feminist research and queer studies have especially addressed the questions of sex and sexuality in innovative and compelling ways, suggesting new empirical and theoretical questions around issues of embodiment and sexuality. Re-thinking how colonial representations of "the black body" (or bodies) continue to inform contemporary national, racial and sexual geographies also has been crucial to this political and theoretical work. Yet much of the work in the area of sexuality, embodiment and citizenship has been scattered across diverse disciplinary fields and its gathering significance across both trans-Caribbean and Black Atlantic studies has not been fully acknowledged.[2]

This chapter, drawing on work in progress,[3] is offered as a contribution to a genealogy of sexual citizenship across the trans-Caribbean, an examination of recent Caribbean feminist theorizations of sexual agency and "erotic autonomy," and a preliminary exploration of how analyses of the sexual and the erotic might inform a theory of embodied freedom in the context of postcolonial, transnational and what some would call neo-imperial restructuring processes. My aim is to elucidate a theory of freedom that begins from a relational context that is grounded in everyday bodily encounters in public and private spaces, as well as addressing the multi-scalar political structures (local, regional, national and transnational) that legislate, govern, and police particular embodiments and sexualities. Most studies of "freedom" in the Caribbean have been concerned with organized political movements such as collective resistance to slavery, group marronage, slave rebellions, revolution, formal processes of emancipation,

tion, peasant rebellions, pan-Africanism and anti-colonial independence movements. Occasionally "everyday" forms of resistance are acknowledged, and there are discussions of a "eudemonic of freedom" within popular religious cultures,[4] yet there have been no extensive studies of the meaning and practice of freedom at the bodily scale as it intersects with the (trans)national, especially in terms of what I shall describe as sexual agency.

My concern with elaborating a better account of embodied freedom brings into conversation three bodies of work that are not usually juxtaposed. First I will draw on queer/feminist theorizations of sexual citizenship, especially those emerging out of Black feminist theory, to reconsider the sexual dimensions of black popular publics in the post-slavery Caribbean. Post-slavery practices of embodied freedom, I argue, were crucial antecedents to contemporary efforts to bring the body into public political discourse, helping to make visible a bodily politics of race, class, ethnicity, gender and sexuality. Secondly, I will read the debates surrounding sexuality, gender and violence in the Blues, Dancehall, Ragga music and other African diasporic popular cultural forms in order to bring out their contribution to a theory of embodied freedom. I especially consider debates surrounding sexuality within Caribbean popular music because this has been one of the key sites for the most extensive trans-Caribbean public discussions of sexual agency. Finally, I turn to the concept of erotic agency as developed by several Caribbean feminist theorists in order to extend the horizon they have opened for thinking through the formation and transformation of sexual, racialized, and classed "inter-embodiments" (a term I discuss further below) as crucial aspects of "doing" freedom in contemporary trans-Caribbean cultures.

Theorizing trans-Caribbean sexual citizenship

The very concept of citizenship, many feminist theorists and historians have argued, excludes women, dependents, slaves, and racialized "others" precisely because their bodies were understood to be overly sexual, emotional, and incapable of the "higher" rationality of "disembodied" objectivity.[5] Feminist theorizations of embodiment offer a critique of the universal "disembodied" (white male) subject who animates Western philosophies of freedom through the disavowal and abjection of grotesquely "embodied" others (women and racialized others).[6] Yet many feminist analyses of embodiment and sexual identity do not necessarily pay attention to the racialized *trans*national contexts in which such bodies are performed and given meaning. As Nancy Leys Stepan argues, "the history of embodiment must be seen as part of the story of citizenship; [. . .] it is no accident that 'race' and 'sex,' in their modern, primarily naturalized or biological meaning, emerged in the eighteenth century, when the new political concept of the individual self and the individual bearer of rights was being articulated."[7] Individualization thus went hand-in-hand with positioning as a particular kind of national rights-bearing subject. Moreover, kind of national rights-bearing subject. Moreover, *racialized* understandings of gender and sexuality, and *sexualized* understandings of race and citizenship, were critical to the entire project of emancipation, freedom and national citizenship across the Atlantic world.

Citizenship, especially in post-slavery contexts, is profoundly implicated in what Michel Foucault called the "biopolitics" of state efforts to control racializations, sexualities, and procreation. To become a citizen is also to become a gendered, racialized and sexed subject. Forms of national participation, including immigration control strategies and citizenship law, are tightly linked to state policies governing sexuality, fertility and reproduction, which are the crucial elements in the production and reproduction of racially and ethnically differentiated populations. As Evelyn Nakano Glenn argues, "Citizenship has been a principal institutional formation within which race and gender relations, meanings, and identities have been constituted."[8] In the trans-Caribbean and the Americas generally we can trace state policies concerning the biopolitics of citizenship back to the period of slave emancipation, when racialized and subordinated populations had to be incorporated into the citizenry on a large scale. Recent work on gender and emancipation emphasizes the centrality of racial, sexual, and gender constructions of the embodied person in shaping post-slavery moral orders, legal systems, state practices, and everyday interaction.[9] Anglo-American and European concepts of citizenship and freedom were elaborated with and upon the disavowed abject body of the slave, while gendered racial and sexual discourses and inter-bodily relations together informed political power and the struggle over freedom in post-slavery societies, as I have explored for nineteenth century Jamaica and Haiti in particular.[10]

Recent historical studies of the Atlantic World suggest that ideas and practices "of masculinity and femininity [not only] shaped slaves' and abolitionists' understanding of the wrongs of slavery, [but also] consolidated notions of contract and liberalism, contributed to the organization of postemancipation wage labor and political economies, and influenced freedpeoples' dreams of freedom and family in racially charged postemancipation landscapes."[11] Citizenship can thus be understood as a set of intertwined practices and collective repertoires for defining, legitimating and exercising the rights of some bodies as against others. It is through these "institutionally embedded practices" and local "contexts of activation" of citizenship, as Margaret Somers puts it, that the surface effects and deeper reiterations of corporeal differences are performed.[12] Insofar as citizenship (and the forms of "freedom" that it underwrites) is an embodied performance that requires racial, ethnic, gender and sexual boundaries to be marked and articulated in public ways, its practice or activation is always in tension with state efforts to control sexuality, reproduction, family formation, kinship systems and labor systems.

At the same time, recent approaches to gender, sexuality, race, and ethnicity have moved away from "essentialist" or "primordialist" models of biological determinism in which bodies in any simple way pre-exist social or cultural contexts. Gender, racial, ethnic and sexual categories are always contingent and contextual—they do not precede social interaction, but arise as meaningful only out of social interaction. If race making "take[s] place in the interplay between bodies and their mobile habits of gesture, dress and speech,"[13] then the governance and regulation of racial, gender and sexual etiquettes, norms of dress, public demeanor, forms of respectability, speech acts, symbolic violence and obscenity, are all crucial aspects of embodied freedom. Public and private cultures of inter-bodily contact are the quotidian sites in which racial-sexual repertoires of citizenship are enacted and activated. Thus everyday "personal" relations between bodies in both public and private spaces underwrite forms of unequal freedom, while also affording opportunities for social change by allowing for occasional performative destabilization or revision of the conventional interplay between bodies, spaces, and racial, gender, and sexual norms.

Following on from this, the concept of sexual citizenship more specifically concerns the relationship between sexuality and politics; between bodies and governments; and between forms of embodied power and national and transnational "biopolitics." A theory of sexual citizenship begins from the placement of the body at the core of political analysis—a kind of shift of attention from "the body politic" to a "body politics," and a consideration of the relation between the two.[14] To think sex and citizenship together is to assert the insistently embodied *corporeality* of citizenship in everyday *practice*, as against the "disembodied," abstracted, juridical citizens of constitutional law who in fact are semantically and symbolically coded as white, male, propertied, and heterosexual.[15] Lauren Berlant and Elizabeth Freeman note that "crucial to a sexually radical movement for social change is the transgression of categorical distinctions between sexuality and politics, with their typically embedded divisions between public, private, and personal concerns. The multiplicity of social spaces, places where power and desire are enacted and transferred, need to be disaggregated and specified."[16] Insofar as forms of national participation are tightly linked to state policies governing sexuality, fertility and reproduction, we must be alert to the everyday aspects of physical life that are usually excluded from the political realm. At stake here, following the work of Jacqui Alexander, is how bodily sexual and erotic potentials are developed and deployed in contexts of constrained freedom, social inequality, and state regulation of "deviance" and criminality.[17]

To conjoin a politics of sex and citizenship is to insist not only on the primacy of inter-bodily relations as the basis for human dignity and freedom, but also on the importance of those aesthetic forms—whether poetry, music, dance, fashion, style—that "encourage awareness of the political character of sexuality" and offer "the possibility of understanding the social contradictions [people] embodied and enacted in their lives."[18] The metaphor of "performance" is a useful bridging concept between popular cultures of bodily expressivity and dramaturgic models of the public sphere as a stage. Michael Warner argues that counter-publics embody "not merely a different or alternative idiom, but one that in that in other [public] contexts would be regarded with hostility or with a sense of indecorousness."[19] Insofar as the public sphere is governed by modes of heteronormative, bourgeois sexual mores, queer publics seek to deploy "sociability, affect and play" in alternative "world-making projects," according to Warner, "in which intimate relations and the sexual body can in fact be understood as projects for transformation among strangers."[20] Sexual citizenship is not just about personal rights or individual empowerment, then, nor is it simply about state recognition of certain kinds of privacy, although it includes these; it is also concerned with collective processes, public spaces, and forms of interrelatedness which are sexual and/or sexualized. Performances, of course, are always reiterations that allow for a certain amount of improvisation and hence transformation, as Judith Butler (1990) has shown. The "everyday" and "personal" relations between bodies in both public and private spaces may enact forms of domination, yet also afford opportunities for social change through iterative play.

Sexual citizenship can thus be understood as a set of intertwined practices and collective repertoires for defining, legitimating and exercising the rights of some bodies as against others, which are thereby deeply implicated in *producing difference* at the surfaces of bodies. Sara Ahmed refers to such relations as "inter-embodiments" that produce "sites of differentiation." She asks:

> How do "bodies" become marked by difference? How do bodies come to be lived precisely through being differentiated from other bodies, whereby the differences in other bodies make a difference to such lived embodiment? Such questions require that we consider how the very materialisation of bodies in time and space involves techniques and practices of differentiation [. . .] To examine the function of cultural difference and social antagonism in the constitution of bodily matters is not to read difference on the surface of the body (the body as text), but to account for the very effect of the surface, and to account for how bodies come to take certain shapes over others, and in relation to others.[21]

What is called for, then, is a history of the techniques and practices of differentiation that produce differently marked bodies in particular relations with others. In relation to the trans-Caribbean, we might ask how the particular national, racial and sexual geographies that arose from post-slavery practices of instituting citizenship and embodied freedom are being revised within post-colonial transnational restructuring processes, producing "neo-imperial" and "neocolonial" inter-embodiments.[22]

Queer theorists of sexual citizenship have highlighted the intersections of queer sexualities and state practices in relation to nationalism, urbanism, and globalization.[23] More recently, this has extended into an interest in the production and lived experience of racial/sexual hierarchies that extend across national boundaries into diasporic or transnational spaces.[24] This work suggests that theories of sexual citizenship must not only move beyond the realm of the national, but also engage with the transnational formation of "race" and "ethnicity" if they are to fully account for the (trans)national production of racialized sexualities. Postcolonial historical studies also provide useful examples of research that explores racial/sexual formations across national borders. Recent studies of British imperialism, for example, employ critical perspectives on gender and racial formation that begin to bridge the once separate realms of "domestic" national histories and "imperial" world histories, effectively bringing sexuality into focus at a transnational scale.[25] Historical studies of specific colonial societies have also shown how processes of race-*ing* and gender-*ing* uphold colonial power through the intimate relations between different bodies.[26] Often drawing on Foucault's notions of biopower and of the disciplining of the body within sites such as "the hospital, the asylum, the police station, the museum, and even the colonial archive itself," these histories have made the micro-histories of bodies and sexualities, intimacy and conjugality, more central to understandings of macro-histories of power and domination.[27] There is also a growing interest in the intersections of gender, sexuality and race in studies of Latin America and the Hispanic Caribbean, in which the interplay between national and transnational processes is increasingly evident.[28]

From these approaches we can begin to formulate guiding questions that new research must address: How do racialized, gendered and sexualized bodies surface as social and political agents from the intersections of multiple forms of ordering, regulation, discipline and governance? And how do these "inter-embodiments" change across space and over time? As bodies move through space (locally, regionally, and transnationally), in what different ways can they (or must they) surface? The body as a colonial "contact zone" has been taken up as a way and a method "to see with particular vividness the variety of somatic territories that modern states have identified as the grounds for defining and policing the normal, the deviant, the pathological, and, of course, the primitive."[29] Focusing on the discursive and performative mobilization of citizenship as an embedded practice in various trans-Caribbean settings, I argue that intimate bodily encounters within counter-spaces of performance are crucial to understanding the national and transnational formation of gender, racial, ethnic and sexual subjectivities. I draw on traditions of "history from below," the study of subaltern counterpublics, and Black feminist and queer theorizations of "sexual citizenship" and "erotic agency" to develop an understanding of citizenship from the "bottom(s) up," as Carolyn Cooper puts it.[30] And I consider the ways in which counter-performances of citizenship can sometimes deploy sexual and erotic agency to "un-do" the gender, racial and sexual inequalities that uphold normative moral orders, legal systems, and state practices.

The questions animating this approach arise out of the intersection of studies of slavery and emancipation, colonialism and the intimate realm, and contemporary sexual citizenship in contexts of transnational migration, tourism, and mobility. What does it mean to lay claim to ones own body? And how is this connected to state practices of citizenship, il/legality and the problem of agency/autonomy within hegemonic processes? Just as claims to citizenship from below may inscribe political subjects more deeply into state "governmentalities," as Foucault argued, claims to sexual agency (especially hetero-sexual agency) evidently risk deeper inscription/insertion into the legalities and heteronormative cultures of contemporary sexuality.[31] And for Black men and women racialized histories of "hypersexuality" often seem to overdetermine any forms of sexual agency.[32] What scope is there, then, for "agency" and "autonomy" in negotiating these pitfalls? I begin in the following section with an analysis of the emergence of "the black body" in slavery and in emancipation, showing how particular racial-sexual economies have constrained citizenship yet also enabled some forms of counter-power to be deployed. I then turn to an analysis of forms of embodied freedom within trans-Caribbean popular cultures of music and dance. I conclude with some reflections on Caribbean theories of erotic agency, which I argue posit an alternative praxis of the embodied subject as a relational, polycentric, non-individuated, and intersectional point of generative energy.

Racial-sexual economies and counter-practices

In a prescient 1987 article, Hortense Spillers articulates a powerful theory of the body in slavery and in post-slavery societies. Spillers posits that the sociopolitical order of the New World "with its human sequence written in blood, *represents* for its African and indigenous peoples a scene of *actual* mutilation, dismemberment and exile. First of all, their New World diasporic plight marked a *theft of the body*—a willful and violent (and unimaginable from this distance) severing of the captive body from its motive will, its active desire."[33] One of the key outcomes of this theft of the body is the loss of gender distinctions between male and female bodies, which as "property" are placed outside the social systems of gender and kinship practices. As a result, she argues,

> 1) the captive body becomes the source of an irresistible, destructive sensuality; 2) at the same time—in stunning contradiction—the captive body reduces to a thing, becoming *being for* the captor; 3) in this absence *from* a subject position, the captured sexualities provide a physical and biological expression of "otherness"; 4) as a category of "otherness," the captive body translates into a potential for pornotroping and embodies sheer physical powerlessness that slides into a more general "powerlessness," resonating through various centers of human and social meaning.[34]

This physical expression of abject otherness can be understood as the polar opposite of European ideas of citizenship as a set of practices governing competent membership in society: captured flesh stands for the disavowed and abject body of the non-citizen, against which the concept of freedom is defined.

Spillers draws a crucial distinction between "the body" and "the flesh," which she argues is the central distinction "between captive and liberated subject-positions." Referencing the archival litany of "altered human tissue" in its horrific "laboratory prose" of "anatomical specifications of rupture"—the brutal laceration, rupturing, wounding, scarring and puncturing of the flesh by iron, whips, chains, knives, the canine patrol, the bullet, and the brand—she suggests that the "undecipherable markings on the captive body render a kind of hieroglyphics of the flesh whose severe disjunctures come to be hidden to the cultural seeing by skin color."[35] The shocking clarity of Spillers' vision of the stolen bodies, tortured flesh, and "captured sexualities" of New World slavery must inform any understanding of colonial, and postcolonial, sexual politics.

Spillers goes on to examine some of the perverse effects of the degendering of black women, the denial of black kinship and motherhood, and their vulnerability to a "gigantic sexualized repertoire" that informs the "incestuous, interracial genealogy" of slavery in the United States and marks the psycho-geography of racialized and gendered subject positions today.[36] Her delineation of the entanglements of living flesh and blood with gender and racial orders, with kinship systems, and with legal systems, shows precisely how intimacies of desire and sexuality are produced (and entrapped) within a transnational world economy in which black flesh was bought and sold, a national state system in which enslavement was legally codified and enforced, and regional practices in which slavery was normalized and made domestically intimate. When slavery ended, there were still entrenched techniques and practices of sexual domination and violence against the flesh which continued to be exercised in corporeal forms of private and public inter-embodiment that perpetuated existing racial, gender, sexual and class hierarchies. As I have argued elsewhere, in taking up positions as "free subjects" freed men and women at times had to (indeed wanted to) perform normative scripts of sexual citizenship such as the "good mother," the "respectable woman," or the "father of a family," which had the effect of delimiting freedom to particular embodied forms.[37] Black masculinity, furthermore, was distorted into hypermasculine forms in rebellious response to white supremacist rhetoric of the black male as symbolically castrated.[38]

Even (or especially) in emancipation, then, the body, sexuality, and sexual orientation remained contested terrains for the elaboration of freedom. National sexualites are rooted in politics, in relations of power, and in access to or exclusion from the rights of citizenship. And claims to citizenship are rooted in and enacted through sexual relations, including relations of domination through which those subjects with access to the legal protections and rights of citizenship can use their position to exploit non-citizens, as well as disciplinary relations in which non-normative sexualities are criminalized. Wherever "the heterosexual family played such a central role in the nation's public imaginings that motherhood could be viewed as a national service, female nonreproductive sexuality and female-female eroticism were constrained, as a consequence, to operate within the domestic (or at least the private) domain."[39] Alexander (2005) shows how a "homophobic exclusionary nationalism" emerges from the current neocolonial conjuncture, one that bars non-heteropatriarchal female sexualities in particular.[40] At the same time, heteropatriarchal reproduction of the nation through the "respectable" marital family rests on an extensive practice of non-conjugal sexual relations outside the family, with lower-status women, producing "illegitimate" children, who are excluded from the rights of legal personhood and citizenship.

Crucial to such maneuvers is the abstraction of the ideal citizen as a "disembodied" subject, yet one who is implicitly white, male and heterosexual. Lauren Berlant's work traces the fatal "dialectic between abstraction [the disembodied 'person' in the language of law] in the national public sphere and the surplus of corporeality of racialized and gendered subjects," and tracks "its discursive expressions, its erotic effects, its implications for a nationalist politics of the body."[41] A crucial question for Berlant concerns the "complex relation between local erotics and national identity," and hence the possibilities for corporeal enfranchisement in the American body politic. In contrast to the racialized and gendered bodies of those who are "overembodied," the "white, male body is the relay to legitimation, but even more than that, the power to suppress that body, to cover its tracks and its traces, is the sign of real authority, according to constitutional fashion." Thus she asks, "What would it take to produce the political dignity of corporeal difference in American culture, where public embodiment is in itself a sign of inadequacy to proper citizenship?"[42] In her reading of Harriet Jacobs' narrative *Incidents in the Life of a Slave Girl* (1861), Frances Harper's postslavery novel *Iola Leroy* (1892), and the Senate testimony of Anita Hill (1991), Berlant argues that Hill, Jacobs and Leroy produced "vital public testimony about the conditions of sexuality and citizenship in America," yet they each attest to "their previous failures to secure sexual jurisdiction over their bodies." These three texts re-narrate the perversities of American national citizenship and "break the sanitizing silences of sexual privacy in order to create national publics trained to think, and thus to think differently, about the corporeal conditions of citizenship."[43]

What happens, then, when embodied Black agents, male and female, straight and queer, make public discussion of sexuality into a political intervention? Creating public spaces and aesthetic forms for reclaiming and speaking one's own body and sexuality are crucial elements of cultures of freedom in the post-slavery Black diaspora.[44] Because racial politics is played out sexually and sex is played out through a racial politics, a politics of the body must be central to any liberation movement and to any praxis of freedom. Carolyn Cooper's tongue-in-cheek yet serious call for "bottoms-up history" reminds us of the "pubic" that is the root of the word "public" and of the "sexualised representation of the potent female bottom in contemporary Jamaican dancehall culture"—these nether-regions that are not spoken of in polite/political society.[45] In a controversial reading of "Slackness" (sexually explicit lyrics, performance, dress and dance) as "erotic play in the dancehall," Cooper argues that "[l]iberated from the repressive respectability of a conservative gender ideology of female property and propriety, these women lay proper claim to the control of their own bodies."[46] Janelle Hobson likewise calls for a reclaiming of the "batty" (or backside) as a "site of resistance" when Black women are able to reclaim agency and subjectivity in naming, valuing, and affirming the beauty of their own bodies.

Yet there is no simple way to re-present "the" "black" "body" that is not already inscribed within the biopolitics or racial and sexual inter-embodiments. In her analysis of the contrasting public spectacles of middle-class female respectability and working-class dancehall vulgarity in the Caribbean, Belinda Edmondson argues that the policing of women's public image was closely linked to various forms of nationalism since the nineteenth century. "English perceptions of the pathological masculinity of black Caribbean women, highlighted against other racialized femininities such as those of white and Asian women, were—and arguably still are—the basis for black (and later, Indo-Caribbean) nationalists to police the public images of their women, and this policing meant scrutinizing their public behavior."[47] Amongst those who were scrutinized and found wanting were the Trinidadian "jamettes," disreputable urban "black women associated with the barracks yards, gangs, and the streets," who were "also active as 'chanterelles,' or calypso singers, and their 'carisos,' songs, were habitually castigated as being lewd and erotic, and for allegedly instigating obscene dancing." Edmondson argues that nationalist concerns with social progress and proving their modernity/civility (within a racist international system that questioned the black capacity for self rule) led to anxieties about black women's performances in the public sphere that required "decorous spectacles" of black womanhood such as beauty pageants "as its antidote." She traces the emergence of an "eroticized yet decorous" performance of displays of "beauty" by middle-class black and brown women, which rendered their visibility in the public sphere more acceptable within national and global culture.[48]

Expressive use of the body in public performances of pleasure can never be a simple matter of freedom, for the bodily realm is always already disavowed in the national public. As bell hooks points out, "[t]he black body has always received attention within the framework of white supremacy, as racist/sexist iconography has been deployed to perpetuate notions of innate biological inferiority. Against this cultural backdrop, every movement for black liberation in this society, whether reformist or radical, has had to formulate a counter-hegemonic discourse of the body to effectively resist white supremacy."[49] Yet neither repressing and denying carnality nor embracing it in its existing racialized forms offers easy solutions. In her important study of Black Sexual Politics in the United States, Patricia Hill Collins observes that, "[s]exualized Black bodies seem to be everywhere in contemporary mass media, yet within African American communities, a comprehensive understanding of sexual politics remains elusive. In a social context that routinely depicts men and women of African descent as the embodiment of deviant sexuality, African American politics has remained curiously silent on issues of gender and sexuality."[50] This goes doubly for Caribbean sexual politics, or so it sometimes seems. Nevertheless, there is an emerging body of literature on Caribbean sexualities that has a great deal to offer in terms of theorizing a transnational sexual politics offering some scope for imagining embodied freedom.

In an extremely helpful recent overview of the subject, Kamala Kempadoo has shown how there is an extensive body of research on the "deviancy," "disorganization," and general pathology of Caribbean sexuality (including sociological and anthropological studies of the family, kinship, and child bearing practices in many different Caribbean societies) yet very little that addresses women's sexual agency, even within Caribbean feminist research.[51] Against the prevailing negative literature on Caribbean sexual practices, Kempadoo proposes a "bottom-up" approach in which "sexualized Caribbean bodies come forward in this study as self-actualizing and transformative—as sexual agents that shape and are shaped by larger political and economic forces, social structures and institutions, and relations of gender, ethnicity, and race."[52] She asks a crucial set of questions, which can serve as a guide for future studies of Caribbean sexuality:

> To what extent, I ask here, can we read the "excesses" or "vulgarity" of Caribbean sexuality not simply as European inventions that refract upon Europeanness and that negate or demean the history and agency of the Other, but also as sedimented, corporeally inculcated dispositions that are lived and practiced every day? Can we speak about embodied sexual practices, identities, knowledges, and strategies of resistance of the colonized and postcolonial subject without lapsing into notions of an essential native sexuality? Is it possible to explore the knowledge that is produced through Caribbean sexual praxis, and to ask whether sexual resistances offer a potential for a politics of decolonization or narratives of liberation?[53]

Through her research on prostitution and other forms of "transactional sex"[54] Kempadoo explores the "sexual economy" not only in terms of exploitation and oppression, but also in terms of the interplay of structural inequalities with possibilities for agency, autonomy, and potentially transformational praxis. From the era of slavery up to the contemporary global economy she shows how forms of labor engaging "sexual energies and parts of the body" are integral to Caribbean economies and have been crucial to national and transnational capitalism. Thus her important work enables us to connect the histories of Caribbean sexuality with questions of national citizenship, transnationalism, freedom, and agency as lived through the sexed and raced body.

Another exploration of Caribbean sexual praxis is Carolle Charles' study of poor and working-class Haitian women's discourses on the use of their bodies. Charles begins by noting the powerful social and political forces that are at play in "the regulation and control of women's bodies" and that "are reproduced and reinforced through patterns of behavior, forms of representation, and cultural practices." Her analysis of "body politics" calls for analysis of the "practices and dynamics of sexual politics and of sexuality as they relate to kinship relations and to racial and class practices inherited from slavery and transformed with the postcolonial state. It is also important to look at the impact of poverty in defining the relationship of sexuality to struggles for economic survival and strategies of social mobility."[55] In paying close attention to poor and working-class Haitian women's own accounts of their bodies and sexualities she offers a glimpse of an "alternative discourse" that gives new meanings to bodies. When such women describe their bodies as "my piece of land," as a "resource, an asset, a form of capital that can reap profits if well invested," Charles argues they are contesting hegemonic ideas and beliefs, redefining sexuality, creating possibilities for the negotiation of space, and some room for self-expression and empowerment. At the very least, this transactional view of sexuality, as in Kempadoo's work, is "an expression of consciousness of the existing relations of gender oppression and inequality."[56] Racial-sexual economies, then, are not simply sites of oppression in which bodies are marked and marketed as raced, gendered, sexed commodities, but are also arenas for self-definition, self-empowerment, and alternative performances of the self.

A final example of an alternative working-class Afro-Caribbean sexuality is found in Gloria Wekker's research on *mati* in Suriname, which she defines as "women who have sexual relations with other women but who typically also will have had or still have relationships with men, simultaneously. More often than not they will also have children."[57] Wekker connects "*mati* work" to a kind of critical agency within Suriname's Creole working-class culture, and also to a "multiplicitous, layered conception of subjectivity" which is at odds with the Western individualized notion of the subject. She understands "the *mati* work within a broad African American, sociocultural, constructivist perspective, that is . . . an elaboration of West African principles and ideas about personhood, gender, and sexualities."[58] She therefore reads it as a "culture of resistance" that challenges existing notions of the "modern subject," and cannot be interpreted in terms of Western categories such as "lesbianism." In order to even recognize the existence of such counter-practices at work within working-class sexualities, I suggest, we need to develop a more sensitive interpretation of embodied freedom as a post-slavery trans-Caribbean praxis. Such freedoms are grounded in struggles for citizenship, but also extend transnationally through popular cultures of music and dance. In the following section, I track in more detail arguments for an alternative, subaltern, or counter-hegemonic praxis of sexuality and sexual citizenship within trans-Caribbean popular cultures.

Working the body: Free bodies, embodied freedom

Against the forces of a world economy that commodified black bodies and the personal relations of domination that inflicted violence on black flesh, resistance has long taken the form of staking a claim not only in one's own body, but also in a community of bodies who re-claimed agency. In an essay on Caribbean women writers' "Body Talk," Denise Narain notes that "[c]ontemporary postcolonial critics have attempted to recuperate this battered black body and, increasingly, to utilise it as the source of empowerment and agency rather than continuing to represent it as the site of pain and victimhood."[59] First of all, studies of slavery suggest that women (of all colors) traded upon sexuality (including converting it into forms of either "respectability" or "reputation") to better their condition, thus deployments of sexuality were highly strategic. Barbara Bush adopts a Foucauldian approach to argue that despite Black women's sexual subordination under slavery, "sexuality constitutes a 'particularly dense transfer point for relations of power,' allowing for many varied strategies" such that "there are innumerable, diverse points of resistance which may even involve a temporary inversion of power relation." She reads the sexual relationships between enslaved black women and slave-owning and other white men, in particular, as "ambivalent" and the sexual power exercised within them as "not purely repressive."[60]

Charles follows Bush in noting that "black women slaves used their sexuality and their reproductive capacities as a means of gaining relative or temporary respite from the horror of their situation [. . .] It was not that sex [with white men] benefited women but rather that slave women could use sexuality to mediate and undermine race and class hierarchies."[61] Kempadoo likewise points out that the "exchange of sex for material benefits or money has been evident in the Caribbean region for several centuries. Under slavery such transactions were lodged at the nexus of at least two areas of women's existence: as an extension of sexual relations (forced or otherwise) with white men and as an income-generating activity for both slave and 'free colored' women." She shows how "transactional sex" historically served as a resource "for women to secure emancipation and economic security or to obtain freedom from violent and oppressive racial systems of labor" and more recently has enabled women to "autonomously improve their economic positions and survival chances."[62] Sexual "agency," then, has long been a two-edge sword, both implicating the sexual subject in relations of domination and subordination, and offering an economic route out of such relations, which may be seized as an enabling possibility.

The mere exercise of sexual agency within personal relations does not in and of itself overturn broader social structures of inequality, including unequal access to the rights and protections afforded by recognition as a citizen; however, it may enable some forms of maneuver, negotiation and exchange. But crucial to such bodily negotiations of freedom is the ability to drag them into the public sphere, in effect *to make public the pubic*. Against the privatization of violence, abuse, and terror within the household, the workplace, or the closed community, diverse forms of sexual agency in contemporary Caribbean and African-American popular cultural forms—and feminist readings of these forms—engage *in public* with these intimate embodiments of power. This tactic has something in common with the vulgar oraliteracies and "low theory" championed by Carolyn Cooper. "These vulgar products of illicit procreation," she suggests, "may be conceived—in poor taste—as perverse invasions of the tightly-closed orifices of the Great Tradition"[63] or, we might say, of the orifices and policed boundaries of national sexuality. Often this takes the form of an assertive public sexuality and what Berlant calls the "strategies of corporeal parody" in "camp," youth, sexual and ethnic subcultures, "that recast and resist the public denigration of the nonhegemonic 'other' body."[64]

Black counter-publics in many shapes and forms continue to work on the body, work with the body, and "work the body" as conduit to collective projects of liberation. In his study of culture, politics and the black working-class in the United States, Robin D.G. Kelley calls for a "history from below" that "emphasizes the infrapolitics of the black working class," one which includes "issues of economic well-being, safety, pleasure, cultural expression, sexuality, freedom of mobility, and other facets of daily life."[65] Beyond the formal institutions of "daylight" community organization such as churches or mutual benefit societies, he argues that we must also attend to what is hidden in the dark of "the night"— the dancehalls and juke joints, the barbershops and bars, the rich expressive cultures of the secular "forms of congregation" that "enabled African Americans to take back their bodies for their own pleasure rather than another's profit."[66] Many black critical theorists who have studied cultures of embodied freedom and sexual agency highlight the significance of popular music and its stylistic aesthetics. Here I want to focus on feminist readings of Black diasporic musical cultures that deal with issues of sexuality and sexual agency, for it is here that we can find the elements of a theory of embodied freedom that negotiates both intimate and transnational scales.

In her important study *Blues Legacies and Black Feminism*, Angela Davis argues that sexuality "was one of the most tangible domains in which emancipation was acted upon and through which its meanings were expressed. Sovereignty in sexual matters marked an important divide between life during slavery and life after emancipation."[67] The focus on issues of love and sex in the Blues repertoire was linked "inextricably with possibilities of social freedom in the economic and political realms"; thus "the personal and sexual dimensions of freedom acquired an expansive importance, especially since the economic and political components of freedom were largely denied to black people in the aftermath of slavery."[68] In her reading of the corpus of work of Gertrude "Ma" Rainey, Bessie Smith and Billie Holiday, Davis argues that:

> These blues women had no qualms about announcing female desire. Their songs express women's intention to "get their loving." Such affirmations of sexual autonomy and open expressions of female sexual desire give historical voice to possibilities of equality not articulated elsewhere. Women's blues and the cultural politics lived out in the careers of the blues queens put these new possibilities on the historical agenda.[69]

Davis further argues that women's blues also thematize male violence against women in ways that "suggest emergent feminist insurgency in that they unabashedly name the problem of male violence and so usher it out of the shadows of domestic life where society had kept it hidden and beyond public or political scrutiny."[70]

Hazel Carby likewise argues that the classic women's blues of the 1920s and early 1930s "is a discourse that articulates a cultural and political struggle over sexual relations: a struggle that is directed against the objectification of female sexuality within a patriarchal order but which also tries to reclaim women's bodies as the sexual and sensuous objects of song."[71] Both Davis and Carby further note that beyond themes of heterosexuality, some songs in this genre name female-to-female sexual relations and "engage directly in defining issues of sexual preference as a contradictory struggle of social relations."[72] As Collins also notes, it was through a blues culture that working-class black women rejected both archetypal "respectability" and the stereotypes of the debased jezebel, and instead "defined their sexual selves in terms much closer to erotic sensibilities about Black female expressiveness, sensuality, and sexuality." Urbanization of the southern rural African American population moreover allowed free women to escape "the sexual exploitation of slavery as well as the demands of having thirteen babies in insular Southern rural families," while at the same time fostering "the increased visibility of lesbian, gay, and bisexual (LGB) African Americans" in urban spaces such as Harlem.[73]

Paul Gilroy's analysis of black cultural forms also emphasizes that both soul and reggae music address "issues of gender conflict, sexuality and eroticism" and "the autonomous field of political action which they map out."[74] He examines the convergence of music and dance, the dialogic or interlocutory relation between performer and audience, and the attempt to blur distinctions between art and life in cathartic "collective processes" which may create an "alternative public sphere." The body is crucial here:

> In these cultural traditions, work is sharply counterposed not merely to leisure in general but to a glorification of autonomous desire which is presented as inherent in sexual activity. The black body is reclaimed from the world of work and, in Marcuse's (1972) phrase, celebrated as an "instrument of pleasure rather than labour." Sexuality stands therefore not only as an area of conflict in its own right, but as a symbol of freedom from the constraints of the discipline of the wage.[75]

Thus, in the African-American vernacular speech "the word work can mean dancing, labour, sexual activity or any nuanced combination of all three." Gilroy links the polysemy of "work" to a carnivalized space of the party, in which the bodily "residues of work" are "transposed into a source of collective pleasure"; parties challenge the chronotopes of capitalist wage labor as the "period allocated for recovery and reproduction is assertively and provocatively occupied instead by the pursuit of leisure and pleasure."[76] Denise Noble similarly argues that the "inversion of work to signify sexual activity can be seen as a valorization and assertion of the playfulness and recreational possibilities of Black bodies in defiance of [the] alienated corporeality" associated with enslavement.[77] Patricia Saunders uses the dual term "work/wuk" somewhat more critically to represent "the simultaneous connections and intimacies among labor, gender, sexuality, and commodification in Jamaican culture"; thus rather than simply celebrating the playfulness of this reversal of meaning, she instead calls for "an interpretive model that understands women as demanding both equality and full compensation (sexual and economic) for their work/'wuk.'"[78]

Just as the Blues did in the early twentieth century, Jamaican popular music in the late twentieth century provided one of the prime contemporary sites for an ongoing dialogue about sexuality and freedom within a transnational black counter-public. In contrast to Paul Gilroy's (1987) reading of the sexist and homophobic lyrics within Dancehall as politically conservative, Carolyn Cooper suggests that DJ slackness "can be seen to represent in part a radical, underground confrontation with the patriarchal gender ideology and the pious morality of fundamentalist Jamaican society." With sensitivity to the stylistics of slackness in Jamaica, she suggests that, "[i]n its invariant coupling with Culture, Slackness is potentially a politics of subversion. For Slackness is not mere sexual looseness—though it certainly is that. Slackness is a metaphorical revolt against law and order; an undermining of consensual standards of decency. It is the antithesis of Culture."[79] Are the vivid sexual displays and bodily gestures of Slackness a "corporeal parody" of the reigning moral order of Culture? Can "raw" language, lyrics, and sexual expression serve as a counterdiscourse to national sexuality, or does it merely feed into pre-existing pornographies of national and transnational racial and sexual commodification? How can anti-racist transnational feminism address the apparently misogynistic and homophobic lyrics of some genres of dancehall, ragga, gangsta rap and hip-hop?[80] The approaches of Cooper, Noble, Kelley, Davis and others suggest that a counterpublic discourse of erotic autonomy and sexual agency may potentially subvert what Spillers called the "capture of sexualities."

These are not simply theoretical questions, but are crucial to everyday practices and intra-communal conflicts. Debates over public displays of sexuality permeate the performance of class, color, and national distinctions in the Caribbean. Deborah Thomas, in her study of a community on the outskirts of Kingston, Jamaica, shows how "popular culture provides a space within which people perform, debate, and, to an extent, contest ideas about gender and sexuality."[81] She links middle-class "respectability" to the legacies of "creole multiracial nationalism" by which the brown middle-class positioned itself as a leader of the nation into independence by making a "respectable state" and legitimized their leadership by "reproducing the colonial value system."[82] Thus Thomas shows how contemporary popular discourses of sexuality and efforts to control the exercise of variant "vulgar" sexualities are closely tied to both colonial legacies and postcolonial nation-building efforts. The public emergence of what she calls "ghetto feminism" amongst "scantily clad and sexually explicit female" DJs like Tanya Stephens, Lady Saw, and Ce'cile, challenges "two primary aspects of the creole nationalist project—the pursuit of respectability and the acceptance of a paternalistic patriarchy." Through "its public affirmation of female agency, especially as this is related to sexual desire and fulfillment," such ghetto feminism "created a space for a new *public* advocacy [. . .] by women for women." Nevertheless, Thomas notes, black feminists especially in the United States "have been wary of condoning the use of erotic power as a means of battling sexism expressly because of the historical legacies enfolding black female sexuality." Thus it would behoove us to "make central the links between gender, sexual politics, and nationalist constructions of sexuality, which [. . .] have defined the contours of respectable citizenship."[83]

Denise Noble also wrestles with the ambivalent response of Black female audiences (especially in the diaspora) to the "often outrageously sexy, rude and unashamed enjoyment of Black female sexuality" in Ragga music, using it as an opportunity "to raise questions about eroticism and sexuality in Black life."[84] "The celebration of the Black female body is a particularly strong theme within Ragga music," argues Noble, although the "racist history of European ideas of sexuality complicates any attempt by Black women to assert their sexual selves in the public domain." Thus "the shame and discomfort that many Black women feel about the ways in which we are celebrated in Ragga centre [a]round its apparent demand for our complicity with a racist sexual iconography of the Black female body." Nevertheless, Noble contends that "the claiming of bodily integrity and autonomy through the celebration of uses of the body in pursuits of leisure and pleasure—song, dance, sport and sex; and the creation and claiming of public spaces of Black autonomy" can be understood as the foundations of sexual citizenship and erotic autonomy.[85]

Ragga lyrics, Noble argues, "typically emphasize Black women's sexual agency and advocate a libertarian individualism where women have autonomy from patriarchal marital domesticity and the cult of motherhood." She notes that "Ragga women engage in exhibitionism which is crude, vulgar, shocking, sexy and powerful":

> in dances which simulate clitoral masturbation and women in controlling and dominant sexual positions, and clothes that imprint the vagina on the observing gaze, the Ragga Queens construct a sexual subjectivity which is centred on the vagina as the locus of female sexual agency and generative power which does not tie it inevitably to reproduction, that is open and inclusive to a wide continuum of desire: autoeroticism, lesbian desire and an active powerful heterosexual eroticism. Through the elaboration of a gynocentric mode of signification, Ragga women create a gender symbolism that hints at what remains largely unspoken and unacknowledged in the vast majority of Ragga lyrics—that is, the possibility of a Black lesbian or bisexual presence in the dancehall and in Black identity.[86]

Thus, against the argument that Black popular cultures are simply in the service of capitalist commodity culture, the male gaze and heterosexism, Noble instead reads the Ragga queen's garish and loud appearance as a kind of kitsch "drag" in which "erotic style [is used] to play with the sexist gullibility of the male gaze." "Her style presents us with a highly processed, commodified appearance," she suggests, reveling in a kind of consumer fetishism in which women's consumption of style can signify personal economic agency, social power and sexual agency over the consumerism (sexual and material) of men."[87]

The argument for women's agency within the sexual cultures of the dancehall and "ghetto feminism" continues to be debated across national and transnational settings, further underlining the embroiling of sexuality within state practices and legal institutions. Patricia Saunders offers a complex reading of Ragga lyrics and sexual politics in Jamaica, in which she agrees with the "claim that dancehall lyrics can indeed be read as an affirmation of black female sexuality in Jamaica, [yet] we cannot deny the very limited freedom women have in constructing their own sexuality, controlling their resources (their bodies and their labor), and certainly in protecting themselves from economic, political and physical violence." Thus in an alternative and more politically complex reading of women's sexual agency within the dancehall, she suggests that:

> The cultural, economic and discursive linking of gender and sexual politics needs to be considered in relation to nationalist politics and nationalist constructions of sexuality.... The construction of sexuality in some dancehall lyrics effaces women as social, political and sexual beings, producing a masculinized narrative of unified national identity. From this perspective, workers in the global marketplace, women and their bodies are constructed as having no identity (no face, just body parts, or units of labor) and are constructed as absent from their sexual experiences and the "body politic" of the nation.[88]

Thus national/ist discourses of masculinity come to mediate public performances and popular discourses of appropriate male and female sexualities, and the "productivity" of women's work/sexuality is tied to the reproduction of masculinity, heterosexuality, and the nation. Saunders' reading of women's sexual agency demands that we also read their political agency, and above all their capacity to "*determine the meaning of equality and freedom.*"[89]

What is clear from both Noble and Saunders' analyses of Ragga is that the performance of racialized/sexualized black female power cannot be lifted out of capitalist "heteropatriarchal" economies that subordinate black women and subordinate Jamaica within global racial-sexual economies. The dancehall thus becomes a site for the activation and struggle over sexual citizenship and embodied freedom. Although not necessarily becoming a space of liberation, it nevertheless contributes to putting back the pubic in the public, that is to say, generating trans-Caribbean public debate about sexuality, class, and freedom.

As in other cases of struggle for citizenship, "discourses of resistance also work to reinscribe hegemonic practices," but this is not to say that such state practices are always determinative, since popular "unofficial" gender ideologies always intersect with state sanctioned ones and "show the fissures and contradictions in the locations and the narratives produced therein."[90] It is precisely such fissures and contradictions that Davis reads in the discourses and performances produced by the female Blues queens, and others read in the erotic gynocentric performances of the dancehall queens. A thorough discussion of the politics of sexual citizenship and sexual agency, then, would make central to public debate the inequalities of gendered, sexualized and racialized inter-embodiments, and above all their manipulations in national legal regimes and transnational economic regimes. These debates are already taking place, both nationally and transnationally. Yet the entanglements of sexual agency with formations of race, class and nation suggest that we must expand the notion of sexual citizenship beyond the national terrain and also include a notion of erotic empowerment that encompasses the wider realm of bodily needs, health, and well-being, which further implicates transnational power-structures through which some (wealthier) bodies exercise power over other (poorer) bodies. In the concluding section I want to explore how Black feminist/queer understandings of sexual agency and embodied freedom have developed into a deep account of the erotic dimension of freedom and the liberatory potential of erotic power.

Conclusion: Towards Caribbean erotic agency

With this understanding of sexual citizenship and embodied freedom grounded in an appreciation of the legacies of slavery and the insights of black feminist critical theory, I want to conclude by gesturing towards the theorization of "erotic autonomy" and "erotic agency" within Caribbean and Black lesbian feminist theory. Can a radical public politics of sexuality transform citizenship and governance? Can a radical sexual politics of the public citizen transform heteronormative and patriarchal sexualities as defined in both national and transnational arenas? While public discussion of lesbian, gay, bisexual, transgendered and other sexualities has emerged to some extent within Caribbean fiction and literary studies,[91] and to some extent in diasporic locations, the existence of a "queer Caribbean" theoretical position often seems silenced and might even seem to be unspeakable, unthinkable. Yet it is crucial.

A more explicit queering of Black and Caribbean feminist theory has been central to the recognition of the importance of embodied freedom in the post-slavery world, and it enables us to reconnect recent "queer theories" of sexual citizenship with the colonial histories of racialized and sexualized embodiment that mark contemporary inter-embodiments. For example, Noble's intervention in the debates over black embodiments and their historical "entanglements" allows her to reclaim the significance of queer Black feminism, including its often overlooked contributions to white lesbian feminist theory and the "emphasis

African-American lesbian writers have placed upon sexuality as a legitimate arena of attention for Black female empowerment and politics." She challenges Black women and feminists "to confront the repression and disavowal of desire and the Black female body as legitimate sources of Black female agency and oppositional subjectivity."[92]

The notion of erotic power is crucial in the work of several Caribbean and African-American feminist theorists, and derives from the practices of embodied freedom that emerged out of the African diaspora experience of enslavement. Audre Lorde (the daughter of Grenadian immigrants to the United States) was one of the first Black lesbian feminist theorists to theorize the erotic in her "Uses of the Erotic: The Erotic as Power," a talk originally delivered in 1978:

> The very word erotic comes from the Greek word eros, the personification of love in all its aspects, born of Chaos, and personifying creative power and harmony. When I speak of the erotic, then, I speak of it as an assertion of the life-force of women; of that creative energy empowered, the knowledge and use of which we are now reclaiming in our language, our history, our dancing, our loving, our work, our lives. In touch with the erotic, I become less willing to accept powerlessness [. . .] Recognizing the power of the erotic within our lives can give us the energy to pursue genuine change within our world, rather than merely settling for a shift of characters in the same weary drama.[93]

The erotic, then, is clearly more than the sexual, though it may encompass the sexual. It includes the power of love, knowledge, creativity and life-force itself. And it appears not only in the context of sexual relations, but also in the context of other forms of creativity, including work. It is also, crucially, connected not only to personal empowerment but also to social change. Erotic agency, in sum, is the antithesis of enslavement. It is an empowerment of the "I" but also a turning towards the "world" and, moreover, towards the divine. Erotic knowledge, according to Lorde, is the bridge between the spiritual and the political.

Jacqui Alexander further explores the work of the erotic as a sacred act as well as a political undertaking. She significantly adds to the lexicography of "work" as economic and sexual, discussed above, a third spiritual dimension: "the focus on spiritual work necessitates a different existential positioning in which to know the body is to know it as a medium for the Divine, living a purpose that exceeds the imperatives of these plantations. Put differently, it is to understand spiritual work as a type of bodily praxis, as a form of embodiment."[94] The struggle for bodily empowerment, therefore, is not simply a matter of sexual agency and sexual citizenship, but is more significantly also a matter of a Sacred praxis of the body. Alexander calls for the knitting together of mind, body and Spirit as experienced in what we call spirit possession, and for a bodily praxis that would become a "meeting ground of the erotic, the imaginative and the creative."[95] Public forms of sexual citizenship can contribute to the development of erotic agency as a practice of resistance to the constrained heteronormative sexualization and hierarchical racialization of citizenship. Erotic agency encompasses not just sexuality but forms of control of time, space, movement, labor, knowledge, kinship, and divinity. It is the larger life horizon in which existence flourishes. Thus it returns us to the very forms of embodied freedom that those "emancipated" from slavery were struggling for, and which so often remain unfulfilled today.

Erotic domination today continues to take the form of rules, norms, laws, and structures of inequality that force people to give up control over their own bodies, labor, time, space, movement, kin and spirit. In conclusion, we can see emerging out of trans-Caribbean theorizations of sexual citizenship, embodied freedom, and erotic agency a broad terrain of political struggle that encompasses the national, regional and transnational scales, yet locates agency and activism in the body, in the spaces of collective "work," and in the quotidian interactions between bodies in those erotically charged spaces of work, dance, sex, and sacred service. As I have attempted to show, this is a theoretical approach that can deal with colonial histories of enslavement and emancipation as fluently and effectively as it deals with contemporary neoimperial and neocolonial contexts. Indeed, it enables us to draw connections between the past and present in ways that may offer greater insight into both the continuities and the transformations within racial/sexual politics over several centuries. Finally, these emerging approaches enable a "queer Caribbean" theoretical project to bridge traditions of Caribbean women's studies, Black feminist theory, and transnational queer studies, to create a promising direction for future political work. Such work will have to navigate the confluences of national and transnational perspectives, sexual and economic relations, material and spiritual dimensions, and academic and activist engagements. But many are already doing this work and we have much to learn from them.

Notes

1. I use the term "relational" to signal "intersectional" approaches that show how structures of race, gender, class etc., cross-cut each other in complex ways and are experienced simultaneously, thus cannot be separately theorized and then "added" together. Indeed the intersectionality of these dimensions is arguably the prime theoretical paradigm driving the analysis of black diaspora cultural formations generally. See for example, Patricia Hill Collins, "It's All in the Family: Intersections of Gender, Race and Nation," in *Decentering the Center: Philosophy for a Multicultural World*, ed. Uma Narayan and Sandra Harding (Bloomington: Indiana University Press, 2000); Kimberley Crenshaw, "Mapping the margins: Intersectionality, identity politics and violence against women of color," in *The Public Nature of Private Violence*, ed. M. Albertson Fineman and R. Mykitiuk (New York: Routledge, 1993), 93-118; Elizabeth Spelman, *Inessential Woman: Problems of Exclusion in Feminist Thought* (Boston: Beacon Press, 1988).

2. See Verene Shepherd, Bridget Brereton and Barbara Bailey, eds., *Engendering History: Caribbean Women in Historical Perspective* (Kingston, Jamaica, and London: Ian Randle & James Currey, 1995); Patricia Mohammed, ed., *Gendered Realities: Essays*

in Caribbean Feminist Thought (Barbados: University of the West Indies; Mona, Jamaica: Centre for Gender and Development Studies, 2002); Linden Lewis, ed., *The Culture of Gender and Sexuality in the Caribbean* (Gainesville: University Press of Florida, 2003); Kamala Kempadoo, *Sexing the Caribbean: Gender, Race, and Sexual Labor* (New York and London: Routledge, 2004); and M. Jacqui Alexander, *Pedagogies of Crossing: Meditations on Feminism, Sexual Politics, Memory, and the Sacred* (Durham, N.C., and London: Duke University Press, 2005). On the "black body" more generally, see Thelma Golden, ed., *Black Male: Representations of Masculinity in Contemporary American Art* (New York: Whitney Museum of American Art, 1994); Dorothy E. Roberts, *Killing the Black Body: Race, Reproduction and the Meaning of Liberty* (New York: Pantheon, 1997); Radhika Mohanran, *Black Body: Women, Colonialism and Space* (Minneapolis and London: University of Minnesota Press, 1999); Patricia Hill Collins, *Black Sexual Politics: African-Americans, Gender and the New Racism* (London and New York: Routledge, 2004).

3. An earlier version of this chapter was presented to the annual meeting of the Society for Caribbean Studies (July 2006), whose participants are thanked for their comments. This chapter draws on my forthcoming book, *Citizenship from Below: Caribbean Agency and Embodied Freedom* (submitted to Duke University Press). I thank Sara Ahmed and Imogen Tyler for discussions, and the editors of this volume for comments.

4. Hilary Beckles, *Centering Woman: Gender Discourses in Caribbean Slave Society* (Kingston, Jamaica, Princeton, N.J., and Oxford: Ian Randle, Markus Weiner, & James Currey, 1999); Diane J. Austin-Broos, *Jamaica Genesis: Religion and the Politics of Moral Orders* (Chicago and London: University of Chicago Press, 1997).

5. Genevieve Lloyd, *The Man of Reason: "Male" and "Female" in Western Philosophy* (Minneapolis: University of Minnesota Press, 1984); Dorothy Smith, *The Everyday World as Problematic: A Feminist Sociology* (London: Open University Press, 1987); Carole Pateman, *The Sexual Contract* (Cambridge: Polity Press, 1988); Joan Landes, *Women and the Public Sphere in the Age of the French Revolution* (Ithaca, N.Y., and London: Cornell University Press, 1988); Nancy Fraser, *Unruly Practices: Power, Discourse and Gender in Contemporary Social Theory* (Minneapolis: University of Minnesota Press, 1989); Mary Ryan, *Women in Public* (Baltimore: Johns Hopkins University Press, 1990); Evelyn N. Glenn, *Unequal Freedom: How Race and Gender Shaped American Citizenship and Labor* (Cambridge, Mass., and London: Harvard University Press, 2002).

6. Iris M. Young, "Impartiality and the Civil Public: Some Implications of Feminist Critiques of Moral and Political Theory," in *Feminism as Critique: On the Politics of Gender*, ed. S. Benhabib and D. Cornell (Minneapolis: University of Minnesota Press, 1987); Judith Butler, "Variations on Sex and Gender: Beauvoir, Wittig and Foucault," in Benhabib and Cornell, *Feminism as Critique*; Judith Butler, *Gender Trouble: Feminism and the Subversion of Identity* (New York: Routledge, 1990); Denise Riley, *"Am I That Name?": Feminism and the Category of "Women" in History* (Minneapolis: University of Minnesota Press, 1988); Sidonie Smith, *Subjectivity, Identity and the Body* (Indianapolis: Indiana University Press, 1993).

7. Nancy L. Stepan, "Race, gender, science and citizenship," in *Cultures of Empire*, ed. Catherine Hall (Manchester: Manchester University Press, 2000), 65.

8. Glenn, *Unequal Freedom*, 18; and see Stuart Hall and David Held, "Citizens and Citizenship," in *New Times: The Changing Face of Politics in the 1990s*, ed. S. Hall and D. Held (London: Lawrence and Wishart, 1989).

9. Pamela Scully and Diana Paton, eds., *Gender and Emancipation in the Atlantic World* (Durham, N.C.: Duke University Press, 2004).

10. Sibylle Fischer, *Modernity Disavowed: Haiti and the Cultures of Slavery in the Age of Revolution* (Durham, N.C., and London: Duke University Press, 2004); Mimi Sheller, "Sword-Bearing Citizens: Militarism and Manhood in Nineteenth-Century Haiti," *Plantation Society in the Americas* 4, no. 2/3 (1997): 233-78; Mimi Sheller, "'Quasheba, Mother, Queen': Black Women's Public Leadership and Political Protest in Post-emancipation Jamaica," *Slavery and Abolition* 19, no. 3 (1998): 90-117; Mimi Sheller, *Democracy After Slavery: Black Publics and Peasant Radicalism in Haiti and Jamaica* (Gainesville: University Press of Florida, 2001); Mimi Sheller, "Acting as Free Men: Subaltern Masculinities and Citizenship in Post-slavery Jamaica," in Scully and Paton, *Gender and Emancipation*, 79-98; Mimi Sheller, "'Her Majesty's Sable Subjects': Subaltern Masculinities in Post-Emancipation Jamaica," *Political Power and Social Theory* 17, (2005): 71-99.

11. Scully and Paton, *Gender and Emancipation*, 1.

12. Margaret Somers, "Citizenship and the Place of the Public Sphere: Law, Community, and Political Culture in the Transition to Democracy," *American Sociological Review* 58 (October 1993): 587-620.

13. Caroline Knowles, *Race and Social Analysis* (London and New Delhi: Sage, 2003), 101.

14. Susan Bordo, *Unbearable Weight: Feminism, Western Culture and the Body* (Berkeley: University of California Press, 1993).

15. Landes, *Women and the Public Sphere*; Ryan, *Women in Public*; Nancy Fraser, "Re-thinking the Public Sphere," in *Habermas and the Public Sphere*, ed. Craig Calhoun (Cambridge, Mass., and London: MIT Press, 1992), 109-142; Michael Warner, "The Mass Public and the Mass Subject," in *The Phantom Public Sphere*, ed. Bruce Robbins (Minneapolis and London: University of Minnesota Press, 1993), 234-256.

16. Lauren Berlant, *The Queen of America Goes to Washington City* (Durham, N.C., and London: Duke University Press, 1997), 149.

17. M. Jacqui Alexander, "Not Just (Any) Body Can Be a Citizen: The Politics of Law, Sexuality and Postcoloniality in Trinidad and Tobago and the Bahamas," *Feminist Review* 48 (1994): 5-23; M. Jacqui Alexander, "Erotic autonomy as a politics of decolonization: an anatomy of feminist and state practices in the Bahamas tourist economy," in *Feminist Genealogies, Colonial Legacies, Democratic Futures*, ed. M. J. Alexander and C. Mohanty (New York and London: Routledge, 1997), 63-100; M. Jacqui Alexander, *Pedagogies of Crossing: Meditations on Feminism, Sexual Politics, Memory, and the Sacred* (Durham, N.C., and London: Duke University Press, 2005).

18. Angela Davis, *Blues Legacies and Black Feminism: Gertrude "Ma" Rainey, Bessie Smith and Billie Holiday* (New York: Pantheon, 1998), 179.

19. Michael Warner, "Publics and Counterpublics," *Public Culture* 14, no. 1 (2002), 86.

20. Warner, "Publics and Counterpublics," 88. Thanks to Imogen Tyler for bringing this article to my attention.

21. Sara Ahmed, *Strange Encounters: Embodied Others in Post-Coloniality* (London and New York: Routledge, 2000), 48, 42-43.

22. Alexander describes "neo-imperial state formations" as "those advanced capitalist states that are the dominant partners in the global 'order'" and "neo-colonial state formations" as "those that emerged from the colonial 'order' as the forfeiters to nationalist claims to sovereignty and autonomy"—see Alexander, *Pedagogies of Crossing*, 4; she

tracks the deployment of regulatory heterosexual practices across the colonial, neocolonial and neo-imperial nation-state, in the process showing the mutual interactions of national and transnational sexual politics.

23. David Bell and Jon Binnie, *The Sexual Citizen: Queer Politics and Beyond* (Cambridge: Polity, 2000); Jon Binnie, *The Globalization of Sexuality* (London: Sage, 2004); D. T. Evans, *Sexual Citizenship: The Material Construction of Sexualities* (London: Routledge, 1993); Andrew Parker et al., eds., *Nationalisms and Sexualities* (New York and London: Routledge, 1992); Shane Phelan, *Sexual Strangers: Gays, Lesbians and Dilemmas of Citizenship* (Philadelphia: Temple University Press, 2001); D. Richardson, *Rethinking Sexuality* (London: Sage, 2000); Jeffrey Weeks, "The sexual citizen," in *Love and Eroticism*, ed. Mike Featherstone (London: Sage, 1999).

24. See for example, Gayatri Gopinath, *Impossible Desires: Queer Diasporas and South Asian Public Cultures* (Durham, N.C.: Duke University Press, 2005); Eithne Luibheid and Lionel Cantu Jr., eds., *Queer Migrations: Sexuality, U.S. Citizenship, and Border Crossing* (Minneapolis and London: University of London Press, 2005); Cindy Patton and Benigno Sanchez-Eppler, eds., *Queer Diasporas* (Durham, N.C.: Duke University Press, 2000). Jacqui Alexander's early-1990s work in this area (reprinted in *Pedagogies of Crossing*) can be considered a precursor of this field of studies, placing the Caribbean at a central cross-roads of race, nation, migration/tourism and crises of sexual citizenship. For other early contributions to transnational studies of migration and sexuality see also *GLQ* 5, no. 4, Special issue on "Thinking Sexuality Transnationally" (1999); and *Social Text*, no. 52-53, Special issue on "Queer Transexions of Race, Nation and Gender" (Fall-Winter 1997).

25. Anne McClintock, *Imperial Leather: Race, Gender, and Sexuality in the Colonial Context* (New York and London: Routledge, 1995); Vron Ware, *Beyond the Pale: White women, racism and history* (London: Verso, 1992); Mary L. Pratt, *Imperial Eyes: Travel Writing and Transculturation* (London: Routledge, 1992); Simon Gikandi, *Maps of Englishness: Writing Identity in the Culture of Colonialism* (New York: Columbia University Press, 1997); Ann L. Stoler and Frederick Cooper, eds., *Tensions of Empire: colonial cultures in a bourgeois world* (Berkeley: University of California Press, 1997); Antoinette Burton, *Burdens of History: British Feminists, Indian Women, and Imperial Culture, 1865-1915* (Chapel Hill: University of North Carolina Press, 1994); Antoinette Burton, *At the Heart of Empire: Indians and Colonial Encounters in Late-Victorian Britain* (Berkeley: University of California Press, 1997); Catherine Hall, *Civilising Subjects: Metropole and Colony in the English Imagination 1830-1867* (Cambridge: Polity, 2002).

26. Catherine Hall, *White, Male and Middle Class: Explorations in Feminism and History* (Cambridge: Polity Press, 1992); Thomas Holt, *The Problem of Freedom: Race, Labor and Politics in Jamaica and Britain, 1832-1938* (Baltimore and London: Johns Hopkins University Press, 1992); Ann L. Stoler, *Race and the Education of Desire: Foucault's "History of Sexuality" and the Colonial Order of Things* (Durham, N.C., and London: Duke University Press, 1995); Ann L. Stoler, *Carnal Knowledge and Imperial Power* (Berkeley: University of California Press, 2002); Pamela Scully, *Liberating the Family? Gender and British Slave Emancipation in the Rural Western Cape, South Africa, 1823-1853* (Portsmouth, N.H.: Heinemann, 1997); Patricia Mohammed, "'But most of all mi love me browning': The emergence in Eighteenth and Nineteenth-Century Jamaica of the Mulatto Woman as the Desired," *Feminist Review* 65, (2000): 22-48.

27. Tony Ballantyne and Antoinette Burton, eds. *Bodies in Contact: Rethinking Colonial Encounters in World History* (Durham, N.C., and London: Duke University Press, 2005), 416.

28. Daniel Balderston and Donna Guy, eds., *Sex and Sexuality in Latin America* (New York: New York University Press, 1997); Laura Briggs, *Reproducing Empire: Race, Sex, Science and U.S. Imperialism in Puerto Rico* (Berkeley and London: University of California Press, 2002); Eileen Findlay, *Imposing Decency: The Politics of Sexuality and Race in Puerto Rico, 1870-1920* (Durham, N.C.: Duke University Press, 1999); Donna J. Guy, *Sex and Danger in Buenos Aires: Prostitution, Family and Nation in Argentina* (Lincoln: University of Nebraska Press, 1990); Sarah Radcliffe and Sallie Westwood, *Remaking the Nation: Place, Identity and Politics in Latin America* (London and New York: Routledge, 1996); Nancy Stepan, *The Hour of Eugenics: Race, Gender and Nation in Latin America* (Ithaca, N.Y.: Cornell University Press, 1991); Nancy Stepan, *Picturing Tropical Nature* (London: Reaktion Books, 2001).

29. Ballantyne and Burton, *Bodies in Contact*, 406; Pratt, *Imperial Eyes*.

30. Carolyn Cooper, *Noises in the Blood: Orality, Gender and the "Vulgar" Body of Jamaican Popular Culture* (Durham, N.C.: Duke University Press, 1993), x.

31. See Warner, "Publics and Counterpublics."

32. Janelle Hobson, *Venus in the Dark: Blackness and Beauty in Popular Culture* (New York and London: Routledge, 2005); Kempadoo, *Sexing the Caribbean*; bell hooks, "Feminism Inside: Toward a Black Body Politics," in Golden, *Black Male*, 127-140.

33. Hortense Spillers, "Mama's Baby, Papa's Maybe: An American Grammar Book," *Diacritics: A Review of Contemporary Criticism* 17, no. 2 (1987): 67, italics in original.

34. Spillers, "Mama's Baby," 67.
35. Spillers, "Mama's Baby," 67.
36. Spillers, "Mama's Baby," 77.
37. Sheller, "Sword-Bearing Citizens"; Sheller, "Quasheba, Mother Queen"; Sheller, "Acting as Free Men"; Sheller, "Her Majesty's Sable Subjects."
38. hooks, "Feminism Inside," 130-131.
39. Parker et al., *Nationalisms and Sexualities*, 7.
40. Alexander, *Pedagogies of Crossing*, 206.
41. Lauren Berlant, "National Brands/National Body: *Imitation of Life*," in Robbins, *Phantom Public Sphere*, 1993, 178.
42. Berlant, "National Brands," 176, 178.
43. Berlant, *Queen of America*, 244-246, 239.
44. Golden, *Black Male*; Collins, *Black Sexual Politics*.
45. Cooper, *Noises in the Blood*, xi; cf. Collins, *Black Sexual Politics*.
46. Cooper, *Noises in the Blood*, 11.
47. Belinda Edmondson, "Public Spectacles: Caribbean Women and the Politics of Public Performance," *Small Axe* 13 (March 2003): 5.
48. Edmondson, "Publics Spectacles," 5, 15.
49. hooks, "Feminism Inside," 127.
50. Collins, *Black Sexual Politics*, 35.
51. Kempadoo, *Sexing the Caribbean*, 15-25.
52. Kempadoo, *Sexing the Caribbean*, 11, 3-4.
53. Kempadoo, *Sexing the Caribbean*, 2.
54. Kempadoo defines transactional sex as "sexual-economic relationships and exchanges where gifts are given in exchange for sex, multiple partnerships may be maintained, and an up-front monetary transaction does not necessarily take place" (Kempadoo, *Sexing the Caribbean*, 42). This is characteristic of certain forms of sexual exchange

associated with tourism in the Caribbean, but also can be understood as deeply informing histories of sexual transactions in slavery and post-slavery societies, which involved many kinds of non-monetary exchanges for sex.

55. Carolle Charles, "Popular Imageries of Gender and Sexuality: Poor and Working-Class Haitian Women's Discourses on the Use of Their Bodies," in *The Culture of Gender and Sexuality in the Caribbean*, ed. Linden Lewis (Gainesville: University of Florida Press, 2003), 169-170.

56. Charles, "Popular Imageries," 170.

57. Gloria Wekker, "Mati-ism and Black Lesbianism: Two Idealtypical Expressions of Female Homosexuality in Black Communities of the Diaspora," in *The Greatest Taboo: homosexuality in Black communities*, ed. Delroy Constanine-Simms (Los Angeles: Alyson Books, 2000), 149.

58. Gloria Wekker, "One Finger Does Not Drink Okra Soup: Afro-Surinamese Women and Critical Agency," in *Feminist Genealogies, Colonial Legacies, Democratic Futures* (New York: Routledge, 1997), 331, 338.

59. Denise deCaires Narain, "Body Talk: Writing and Speaking the Body in the Texts of Caribbean Women Writiers," in *Caribbean Portraits: Essays on gender Ideologies and Identities*, ed. Christine Barrow (Kingston, Jamaica: Ian Randle Publishers, 1998), 256.

60. Barbara Bush, *Slave Women in Caribbean Society 1650-1838* (London, Kingston, Jamaica, and Bloomington: James Currey, Heinemann, and Indiana University Press, 1990), 110.

61. Charles, "Popular Imageries," 179.

62. Kempadoo, *Sexing the Caribbean*, 53-55.

63. Cooper, *Noises in the Blood*, 9.

64. Berlant, "National Brands/National Body," 177.

65. Robin D. G. Kelley, *Race Rebels: Culture, Politics, and the Black Working Class* (New York and London: The Free Press, 1996), 8-9.

66. Kelley, *Race Rebels*, 44-45.

67. Davis, *Blues Legacies*, 4.

68. Davis, *Blues Legacies*, 10.

69. Davis, *Blues Legacies*, 24.

70. Davis, *Blues Legacies*, 29-30.

71. Hazel Carby, "It Just Be's Dat Way Sometime: The Sexual Politics of Women's Blues," *Radical America* 20, no. 4 (June-July 1986): 12.

72. Carby, "It Just Be's Dat Way," 18; Davis, *Blues Legacies*, 40.

73. Collins, *Black Sexual Politics*, 72-73.

74. Paul Gilroy, *There Ain't No Black in the Union Jack: The cultural politics of race and nation* (Chicago: University of Chicago Press, 1991), 199.

75. Gilroy, *There Ain't No Black*, 214-215, 202.

76. Gilroy, *There Ain't No Black*, 203, 210.

77. Denise Noble, "Ragga Music: Dis/Respecting Black Women and Dis/Reputable Sexualities," in *Un/Settled Multiculturalisms; Diasporas, Entanglements, "Transruptions,"* ed. Barnor Hesse (London and New York: Zed, 2000), 157.

78. Patricia Saunders, "Is Not Everything Good to Eat, Good to Talk: Sexual Economy and Dancehall Music in the Global Marketplace," *Small Axe* 13 (March 2003): 105, 115.

79. Cooper, *Noises in the Blood*, 141.

80. See, for example, Tricia Rose, "Rap Music and the Demonization of Young Black Men," in *Black Male*, ed. Thelma Golden (New York: Whitney Museum of American Art), 149-57; Tracey Skelton, "Boom Bye Bye: Jamaican Ragga and Gay Resistance," in *Mapping Desire: Geography and Sexualities*, ed. David Bell and Gill Valentine (London: Routledge, 1995); and Mimi Sheller, "Queer Caribbean Sexual Citizenship and Erotic Agency," forthcoming in *Radical History Review* 100 (2008).

81. Deborah Thomas, *Modern Blackness: Nationalism, Globalization, and the Politics of Culture in Jamaica* (Durham, N.C., and London: Duke University Press, 2004), 114.

82. Thomas, *Modern Blackness*, 57.

83. Thomas, *Modern Blackness*, 252, 253, 256.

84. Noble, "Ragga Music," 149.

85. Noble, "Ragga Music," 154, 155, 157.

86. Noble, "Ragga Music," 159-160, 162.

87. Noble, "Ragga Music," 158.

88. Saunders, "Is Not Everything Good to Eat," 114-115.

89. Saunders, "Is Not Everything Good to Eat," 115, italics in original.

90. Saunders, "Is Not Everything Good to Eat," 114, 108.

91. Evelyn O'Callaghan, "'Compulsory Heterosexuality' and Textual/ Sexual Alternatives in Selected Texts by West Indian Women Writers," in *Caribbean Portraits: Essays on Gender Ideologies and Identities*, ed. Christine Barrow (Kingston, Jamaica: Ian Randle, 1998); Wekker, "Mati-ism and Black Lesbianism"; Wekker, "One Finger"; Lewis, *Culture of Gender and Sexuality*; Alexander, *Pedagogies of Crossing*.

92. Noble, "Ragga Music," 166-167.

93. Audre Lorde, "Uses of the Erotic: The Erotic as Power," in *Sister Outsider: Essays and Speeches by Audre Lorde* (Freedom, Ca.: The Crossing Press, 1984), 55, 58-59.

94. Alexander, *Pedagogies of Crossing*, 297.

95. Alexander, *Pedagogies of Crossing*, 320, 322.

Bibliography

Ahmed, Sara. *Strange Encounters: Embodied Others in Post-Coloniality*. London and New York: Routledge, 2000.

Alexander, M. Jacqui. "Not Just (Any) Body Can Be a Citizen: The Politics of Law, Sexuality and Postcoloniality in Trinidad and Tobago and the Bahamas." *Feminist Review* 48 (1994): 5-23.

———. "Erotic autonomy as a politics of decolonization: an anatomy of feminist and state practices in the Bahamas tourist economy." Pp. 63-100 in *Feminist Genealogies, Colonial Legacies, Democratic Futures*, edited by J. Alexander and C. Mohanty. New York and London: Routledge, 1997.

———. *Pedagogies of Crossing: Meditations on Feminism, Sexual Politics, Memory, and the Sacred*. Durham, N.C., and London: Duke University Press, 2005.

Austin-Broos, Diane J. *Jamaica Genesis: Religion and the Politics of Moral Orders*. Chicago and London: University of Chicago Press, 1997.

Balderston, Daniel, and Donna Guy, eds. *Sex and Sexuality in Latin America*. New York: New York University Press, 1997.

Ballantyne, Tony, and Antoinette Burton, eds. *Bodies in Contact: Rethinking Colonial Encounters in World History*. Durham, N.C., and London: Duke University Press, 2005.

Beckles, Hilary. *Centering Woman: Gender Discourses in Caribbean Slave Society*. Kingston, Jamaica, Princeton, N.J., and Oxford: Ian Randle, Markus Weiner, & James Currey, 1999.

Bell, David and Jon Binnie. *The Sexual Citizen: Queer Politics and Beyond*. Cambridge: Polity, 2000.

Berlant, Lauren. "National Brands/National Body: *Imitation of Life*." Pp. 173-228 in *The Phantom Public Sphere*, edited by Bruce Robbins. Minneapolis and London: University of Minnesota Press, 1993.

———. *The Queen of America Goes to Washington City*. Durham, N.C., and London: Duke University Press, 1997.

Binnie, Jon. *The Globalization of Sexuality*. London: Sage, 2004.

Bordo, Susan. *Unbearable Weight: Feminism, Western Culture and the Body*. Berkeley: University of California Press, 1993.

Briggs, Laura. *Reproducing Empire: Race, Sex, Science and U.S. Imperialism in Puerto Rico*. Berkeley and London: University of California Press, 2002.

Burton, Antoinette. *Burdens of History: British Feminists, Indian Women, and Imperial Culture, 1865-1915*. Chapel Hill: University of North Carolina Press, 1994.

———. *At the Heart of the Empire: Indians and the Colonial Encounter in Late-Victorian Britain*. Berkeley: University of California Press, 1997.

Bush, Barbara. *Slave Women in Caribbean Society 1650-1838*. London, Kingston, Jamaica, and Bloomington: James Currey, Heinemann, and Indiana University Press, 1990.

Butler, Judith. "Variations on Sex and Gender: Beauvoir, Wittig and Foucault." Pp. 44-58 in *Feminism as Critique: On the Politics of Gender*, edited by Seyla Benhabib and Drucilla Cornell. Minneapolis: University of Minnesota Press, 1987.

———. *Gender Trouble: Feminism and the Subversion of Identity*. New York: Routledge, 1990.

Carby, Hazel. "It Just Be's Dat Way Sometime: The Sexual Politics of Women's Blues." *Radical America* 20, no. 4 (June-July 1986): 9-22.

Charles, Carolle. "Sexual Politics and the mediation of class, gender and race in former slave plantation societies: the case of Haiti." Pp. 44-58 in *Social Construction of the Past*, edited by G. C. Bond and A. Gilliam. London and New York: CQ Publisher, 1994.

———. "Popular Imageries of Gender and Sexuality: Poor and Working-Class Haitian Women's Discourses on the Use of Their Bodies." Pp. 169-189 in *The Culture of Gender and Sexuality in the Caribbean*, edited by Linden Lewis. Gainesville: University Press of Florida, 2003.

Collins, Patricia Hill. "It's All in the Family: Intersections of Gender, Race and Nation." Pp. 156-176 in *Decentering the Center: Philosophy for a Multicultural World*, edited by Uma Narayan and Sandra Harding. Bloomington and Indianapolis: Indiana University Press, 2000.

———. *Black Sexual Politics: African-Americans, Gender and the New Racism*. London and New York: Routledge, 2004.

Cooper, Carolyn. *Noises in the Blood: Orality, Gender, and the "Vulgar" Body of Jamaican Popular Culture*. Durham, N.C.: Duke University Press, 1993.

Davis, Angela. *Blues Legacies and Black Feminism: Gertrude "Ma" Rainey, Bessie Smith and Billie Holiday.* New York: Pantheon Books, 1998.

Edmondson, Belinda. "Public Spectacles: Caribbean Women and the Politics of Public Performance." *Small Axe* 13 (March 2003): 1-16.

Evans, D. T. *Sexual Citizenship: The Material Construction of Sexualities.* London: Routledge, 1993.

Findlay, Eileen. *Imposing Decency: The Politics of Sexuality and Race in Puerto Rico, 1870-1920.* Durham, NC: Duke University Press, 1999.

Fischer, Sibylle. *Modernity Disavowed: Haiti and the Cultures of Slavery in the Age of Revolution.* Durham, N.C., and London: Duke University Press, 2004.

Fraser, Nancy. *Unruly Practices: Power, Discourse, and Gender in Contemporary Social Theory.* Minneapolis: University of Minnesota Press, 1989.

———. "Rethinking the Public Sphere." Pp. 109-142 in *Habermas and the Public Sphere,* edited by Craig Calhoun. Cambridge, Mass., London: MIT Press, 1992.

Gikandi, Simon. *Maps of Englishness: Writing Identity in the Culture of Colonialism.* New York: Columbia University Press, 1997.

Gilroy, Paul. *There Ain't No Black in the Union Jack: The Cultural Politics of Race and Nation.* Chicago: University of Chicago Press, 1991.

Glenn, Evelyn Nakano. *Unequal Freedom: How Race and Gender Shaped American Citizenship and Labor.* Cambridge, Mass., and London: Harvard University Press, 2002.

Golden, Thelma, ed. *Black Male: Representations of Masculinity in Contemporary American Art.* New York: Whitney Museum of American Art, 1994.

Gopinath, Gayatri. *Impossible Desires: Queer Diasporas and South Asian Public Cultures.* Durham, N.C.: Duke University Press, 2005.

Guy, Donna J. *Sex and Danger in Buenos Aires: Prostitution, Family and Nation in Argentina.* Lincoln: University of Nebraska Press, 1990.

Hall, Catherine. *White, Male, and Middle Class: Explorations in Feminism and History.* Cambridge: Polity Press, 1992.

———. *Civilising Subjects: Metropole and Colony in the English Imagination 1830-1867.* Cambridge: Polity, 2002.

Hall, Stuart, and David Held. "Citizens and Citizenship." Pp. 173-190 in *New Times: The Changing Face of Politics in the 1990s,* edited by Stuart Hall and Martin Jacques. London: Lawrence and Wishart, 1989.

Hobson, Janelle. *Venus in the Dark: Blackness and Beauty in Popular Culture.* New York and London: Routledge, 2005.

Holt, Thomas. *The Problem of Freedom: Race, Labor, and Politics in Jamaica and Britain, 1832-1938.* Baltimore and London: Johns Hopkins University Press, 1992.

hooks, bell. "Feminism Inside: Toward a Black Body Politics." Pp. 127-140 in *Black Male: Representations of Masculinity in Contemporary American Art,* edited by Thelma Golden. New York: Whitney Museum of American Art, 1994.

Kelley, Robin D. G. *Race Rebels: Culture, Politics, and the Black Working Class.* New York and London: The Free Press, 1996.

Kempadoo, Kamala. *Sexing the Caribbean: Gender, Race, and Sexual Labor.* New York and London: Routledge, 2004.

Knowles, Caroline. *Race and Social Analysis.* London and New Delhi: Sage, 2003.

Landes, Joan. *Women and the Public Sphere in the Age of the French Revolution.* Ithaca, N.Y., and London: Cornell University Press, 1988.

Lewis, Linden, ed. *The Culture of Gender and Sexuality in the Caribbean*. Gainesville: University Press of Florida, 2003.

Lloyd, Genevieve. *The Man of Reason: "Male" and "Female" in Western Philosophy*. Minneapolis: University of Minnesota Press, 1984.

Lorde, Audre. "Uses of the Erotic: The Erotic as Power." Pp. 53-59 in *Sister Outsider: Essays and Speeches by Audre Lorde*. Freedom, CA: The Crossing Press, 1984.

Luibhéid, Eithne, and Lionel Cantú Jr., eds. *Queer Migrations: Sexuality, U.S. Citizenship, and Border Crossings*. Minneapolis and London: University of Minnesota Press, 2005.

McClintock, Anne. *Imperial Leather: Race, Gender and Sexuality in the Colonial Context*. New York and London: Routledge, 1995.

Mohammed, Patricia. "'But most of all mi love me browning': The emergence in Eighteenth and Nineteenth-Century Jamaica of the Mulatto Woman as the Desired." *Feminist Review* 65, (2000): 22-48.

———, ed. *Gendered Realities: Essays in Caribbean Feminist Thought*. Cave Hill, Barbados, and Mona, Jamaica: University of the West Indies Press and Centre for Gender and Development Studies, 2002.

Mohanram, Radhika. *Black Body: Women, Colonialism and Space*. Minneapolis and London: University of Minnesota Press, 1999.

Narain, Denise deCaires. "Body Talk: Writing and Speaking the Body in the Texts of Caribbean Women Writers." Pp. 255-275 in *Caribbean Portraits: Essays on Gender Ideologies and Identities*, edited by Christine Barrow. Kingston, Jamaica: Ian Randle Publishers, 1998.

Noble, Denise. "Ragga Music: Dis/Respecting Black Women and Dis/Reputable Sexualities." Pp. 148-169 in *Un/Settled Multiculturalisms: Diasporas, Entanglements, "Transruptions,"* edited by Barnor Hesse. London and New York: Zed Books, 2000.

O'Callaghan, Evelyn. "'Compulsory Heterosexuality' and Textual/Sexual Alternatives in Selected Texts by West Indian Women Writers." Pp. 294-319 in *Caribbean Portraits: Essays on Gender Ideologies and Identities*, edited by Christine Barrow. Kingston, Jamaica: Ian Randle Publishers, 1998.

Parker, Andrew, Mary Russo, Doris Sommer, and Patricia Yaeger, eds. *Nationalisms and Sexualities*. New York and London: Routledge, 1992.

Pateman, Carole. *The Sexual Contract*. Cambridge: Polity Press, 1988.

Pratt, Mary L. *Imperial Eyes: Travel Writing and Transculturation*. London: Routledge, 1992.

Radcliffe, Sarah, and Sallie Westwood. *Remaking the Nation: Place, Identity and Politics in Latin America*. London and New York: Routledge, 1996.

Richardson, Diane. *Rethinking Sexuality*. London: Sage, 2000.

Riley, Denise. *"Am I That Name?" Feminism and the Category of "Women" in History*. Minneapolis: University of Minnesota Press, 1988.

Roberts, Dorothy E. *Killing the Black Body: Race, Reproduction and the Meaning of Liberty*. New York: Pantheon, 1997.

Rose, Tricia. "Rap Music and the Demonization of Young Black Men." Pp. 149-157 in *Black Male: Representations of Masculinity in Contemporary American Art*, edited by Thelma Golden. New York: Whitney Museum of American Art, 1994.

Ryan, Mary. *Women in Public*. Baltimore: Johns Hopkins University Press, 1990.

Saunders, Patricia. "Is Not Everything Good to Eat, Good to Talk: Sexual Economy and Dancehall Music in the Global Marketplace." *Small Axe* 13 (March 2003): 95-115.

Scully, Pamela. *Liberating the Family? Gender and British Slave Emancipation in the Rural Western Cape, South Africa, 1823-1853*. Portsmouth, NH: Heinemann, 1997.

Scully, Pamela and Diana Paton, eds. *Gender and Emancipation in the Atlantic World*. Durham, N.C.: Duke University Press, 2005.

Sheller, Mimi. "Sword-Bearing Citizens: Militarism and Manhood in Nineteenth-Century Haiti." *Plantation Society in the Americas* 4, no. 2/3 (1997): 233-278.

———. "'Quasheba, Mother, Queen': Black Women's Public Leadership and Political Protest in Post-emancipation Jamaica, 1834-1865." *Slavery and Abolition* 19, no. 3 (1998): 90-117.

———. *Democracy After Slavery: Black Publics and Peasant Radicalism in Haiti and Jamaica*. London and Oxford: Macmillan, 2000.

———. "Acting as Free Men: Subaltern Masculinities and Citizenship in Post-slavery Jamaica." Pp. 79-98 in *Gender and Emancipation in the Atlantic World*, edited by Pamela Scully and Diana Paton. Durham, N.C.: Duke University Press, 2005.

———. "Her Majesty's Sable Subjects: Subaltern Masculinities in Post-emancipation Jamaica." *Political Power and Social Theory* 17 (2005): 71-99.

———. "Queer Caribbean Sexual Citizenship and Erotic Agency." Forthcoming in *Radical History Review* 100 (2008).

Shepherd, Verene, Bridget Brereton, and Barbara Bailey, eds. *Engendering History: Caribbean Women in Historical Perspective*. Kingston, Jamaica: Ian Randle; London: James Currey, 1995.

Skelton, Tracey. "Boom Bye Bye: Jamaican Ragga and Gay Resistance." in *Mapping Desire: Geography of Sexualities*, edited by David Bell and Gill Valentine. London: Routledge, 1995.

Smith, Dorothy. *The Everyday World as Problematic: A Feminist Sociology*. London: Open University Press, 1987.

Smith, Sidonie. *Subjectivity, Identity, and the Body*. Bloomington and Indianapolis: Indiana University Press, 1993.

Somers, Margaret. "Citizenship and the Place of the Public Sphere: Law, Community, and Political Culture in the Transition to Democracy." *American Sociological Review* 58 (October 1993): 587-620.

Spelman, Elizabeth. *Inessential Woman: Problems of Exclusion in Feminist Thought*. Boston: Beacon Press, 1988.

Spillers, Hortense. "Mama's Baby, Papa's Maybe: An American Grammar Book." *Diacritics: A Review of Contemporary Criticism* 17, no. 2 (1987): 65-81.

Stepan, Nancy L. *The Hour of Eugenics: Race, Gender and Nation in Latin America*. Ithaca, N.Y.: Cornell University Press, 1991.

———. "Race, gender, science and citizenship." Pp. 61-86 in *Cultures of Empire: A Reader*, edited by Catherine Hall. Manchester: Manchester University Press, 2000.

———. *Picturing Tropical Nature*. London: Reaktion Books, 2001.

Stoler, Ann L. *Race and the Education of Desire: Foucault's "History of Sexuality" and the Colonial Order of Things*. Durham, N.C., and London: Duke University Press, 1995.

———. *Carnal Knowledge and Imperial Power*. Berkeley: University of California Press, 2002.

Stoler, Ann L., and Frederick Cooper, eds. *Tensions of Empire: Colonial Cultures in a Bourgeois World*. Berkeley: University of California Press, 1997.

Thomas, Deborah A. *Modern Blackness: Nationalism, Globalization, and the Politics of Culture in Jamaica*. Durham, N.C., and London: Duke University Press, 2004.

Ware, Vron. *Beyond the Pale: White Women, Racism and History*. London: Verso, 1992.
Warner, Michael "The Mass Public and the Mass Subject." Pp. 234-256 in *The Phantom Public Sphere*, edited by Bruce Robbins. Minneapolis and London: University of Minnesota Press, 1993.
———. "Publics and Counterpublics." *Public Culture* 14, no. 1 (2002): 49-90.
Weeks, Jeffrey. "The sexual citizen." Pp. 35-52 in *Love and Eroticism*, edited by M. Featherstone. London: Sage, 1999.
Wekker, Gloria. "One Finger Does Not Drink Okra Soup: Afro-Surinamese Women and Critical Agency." Pp. 330-352 in *Feminist Genealogies, Colonial Legacies, Democratic Futures*, edited by M. Jacqui Alexander and Chandra Talpade Mohanty. New York: Routledge, 1997.
———. "Mati-ism and Black Lesbianism: Two Idealtypical Expressions of Female Homosexuality in Black Communities of the Diaspora." Pp. 149-162 in *The Greatest Taboo: Homosexuality in Black Communities*, edited by Delroy Constanine-Simms. Los Angeles: Alyson Books, 2000.
Young, Iris M. "Impartiality and the Civil Public: Some Implications of Feminist Critiques of Moral and Political Theory." Pp. 56-76 in *Feminism as Critique: On the Politics of Gender*, edited by Seyla Benhabib and Drucilla Cornell. Minneapolis: University of Minnesota Press, 1987.

15

Curwen Best

Caribbean Cyberculture: Towards an Understanding of Gender, Sexuality, and Identity within the Digital Culture Matrix

In the first decade of the twenty-first century Caribbean society expanded within and extended beyond familiar geographical space. In the article "The Reach of Transnationalism" Riva Kastoryano makes the point that "transnationalism appears as a new type of nationalism [...] that differs [...] from diaspora nationalism. Contemporary diaspora nationalism may transform into movements for 'reterritorialization' and statehood. Transnational nationalism takes form after nationalism and nation-states have become realities; it may extend state nationalism in new ways."[1] In the article "Getting There, Despite the Odds: Caribbean Migration to the United States in the 1990s," Dennis Conway suggests that Caribbean mobility trends are substantial. In particular he makes the point that where there appears to have been a decline in annual volumes of permanent Resident Alien admissions among Caribbean countries, this has been countered by "substantial increases in non-immigrant flows, which might suggest a 'substitution effect' of circulation."[2] These observations if read together point to the expansive, fluid nature of trans-Caribbean society in the age of digital culture. The digital culture matrix is characterized by a complex set of issues and transactions surrounding location, distance, speed, communication, experience, reality and virtuality.

Much has been written on the issue of migration, the Caribbean diaspora, and the fashioning/formation of new identities inside and outside of the region. Much has also been made of the role of gender in the process of Caribbean cultural export. In spite of all that has been written about gender, sexuality and identity, relatively little has appeared in academic writing that directly engages the relationship between gender, identity, the Caribbean/trans-Caribbean and leading edge technology culture. Academic discourse is only now beginning to consider the role that technology (particularly new, emerging cutting-edge technology) plays in mediating the kinds of productions, expressions and relationship formations that preoccupy women especially, but also men.

If the phenomenon of global migration foregrounds questions to do with nationalism, trans-nationalism, and imagined communities, then the advent of even newer technological phenomena such as the World Wide Web, the Internet and robust digital media introduces an even more problematic set of contingencies. The rise of digital culture poses a number of challenges to more traditional ways of conceiving presence, identity, nationality, gender, sexuality and power. This chapter wants to begin to consider the impact of contemporary digital culture on our conceptualization of the above phenomena. This chapter is even more intent on beginning to map out some of the spaces/arenas in which leading-edge culture reconfigures aspects of Caribbean society and the means by which this reconfiguration is performed.

Feminist discourse, gender and digital culture

Feminist theory and discourse has evolved significantly over the past twenty years. Rejecting Eurocentric formulations of "womanhood," even of "feminism," some post-Third-Worldist feminisms have claimed a different "location," arguing for specific vernacular forms of resistance in response to diverse forms of oppression.[3]

In discussing socialization and gender-role learning in the Caribbean Olive Senior suggests how "values, attitudes, behavior, choices and performance of men and women owe a great deal to the manner in which we learn or absorb the specific role that society associates with the male or female sex."[4] She rightly locates culture (and the lived vernacular experience) as a major factor influencing Caribbean socialization. Referencing earlier work by Kamau Brathwaite and Madeline Kerr[5] among others, she suggests what challenges might be posed to an understanding of Caribbean socialization due to the region's complex culture. She says that "[t]hough these societies are held together by institutions that are shared by all, different sectors might adhere to different value systems. The socialization process in the multicultural Caribbean might be complicated by the fact that individuals are always teetering between two or more racial and cultural ideas."[6]

Senior did not deal with the impact of digital and cyber culture on Caribbean socialization, identity, gender and sexuality, for her work was conducted before the great digital wave of the late 1980s and 1990s. But if anything, current developments signify an even more complex state of flux. Writing a little later in the article "Jobs, Gender and Development Strategy in the Commonwealth Caribbean" Ralph Henry rightly intimates that Caribbean societies will increasingly rely on external markets and technologies in the late twentieth century.[7]

Over the past decade or so, feminist scholars worldwide have called attention to globalization and its gendered agendas. They have urged others to consider gender and sexuality in a more global arena. In the Caribbean context this has often meant that scholars have focused on issues to do with women and migration and gender and international conventions. Where there has been some important work done in relation to gender, sexuality, technology and the Caribbean, this has tended to take the shape of official UN documents or similar descriptive studies on women and technology use.[8] There are also works that discuss gender and the role of women in local and trans-national contexts.[9] Still these works (all valuable documents) do not center the technological as a major preoccupation. This is not a particular failing of these works listed here, for even an examination of the work of leading critics on Caribbean culture reveals similar proclivities. Caribbean cultural critique is still rooted in pre- and early-digital culture praxis. In the work *Culture @ the Cutting Edge* the author makes the observation:[10]

> The advent of the Internet and the popularization of the World Wide Web in the Caribbean raised fundamental questions relating to Caribbean culture. In recent history Caribbean society was preoccupied with working towards national and regional community. These concepts were at play among politicians and technocrats throughout the past two decades. The expansion of the Internet has brought into sharp focus the additional challenge of defining and harnessing the community of people who share in this regional identity and passion by way of real and virtual connection. In the post-2000 period many people not residing in the region took some active part in the experiences of Caribbean people. Those individuals were virtual participants in regional activity, those who read regional newspapers on line, who followed the fortunes of regional teams via streaming audio and video, and who supported the region's initiatives on several fronts. The Internet has therefore challenged physical temporal and spatial categories. Its presence and experience has opened up the domain of Caribbean experience to a potentially limitless number of participants.

Brief discourse on WWW (and digital culture)

Trans-Caribbean migrants have responded in various ways to the condition of being outside the physical geographical place of the nation. In the book *Georges Woke Up Laughing* the authors explore the ambiguities of "long distance nationalism," where immigrants simultaneously build new lives in adopted countries while they continue to participate in the activities of their homelands.[11] Some Caribbean people have sought fervently to maintain a sense of roots, others have sought ways of connecting while also relinquishing some of their ties to the geographical region and its defining practices. Still others have given little thought to belonging, but have gone about their lives in full knowledge that they might or might not be fixed to a location, or to specific ways of being. Stuart Hall might summarize this process as producing a future "without guarantees."

The evolution of the World Wide Web as a set of commercial, social, cultural, and military, practices has challenged peoples of differing cultures to rethink questions of identity, community and nation. The Internet has brought into focus both the proximity and distance that there is between human beings who were traditionally socialized to think of national and cultural identity as having its presence within an exclusive, fixed, dedicated place. The Internet, because of its make-up, conflates and compresses space, making it possible to also expand and conflate social relations.

Caribbean culture has come under tremendous pressure especially in the latter decades of the twentieth and first decade of the twenty-first century. The digital revolution of the late 1980s and beyond has served to help reconfigure sexual and gender relations in the Caribbean region and abroad. Media like film, videos, Web videos, mobile and emerging technologies have brought issues of gender increasingly to the fore. As digital culture expands so too should discourses about the roles assigned, reassigned and acted out in the age of the machines. While there is some discussion of gender and popular music, gender and film, gender and literature, gender and development (and other more traditional permutations of the gender debate) there is only now beginning to be a critical interest in the relationship between gender, sexuality and digital culture. If in the past, Caribbean critics were satisfied to talk of digital culture as an afterthought within gender debates current trends demand careful investigation of how technology might reshape notions of gender, as well as how gendered subjects might refashion the very technologies.

Gender, sexuality and cyberculture

Globally there is substantial work that seeks to understand issues of gender relations within the context of contemporary technology mediation, for example Jacqueline Archibald's *The Gender Politics of ICT* and Linda Leung's *Virtual Ethnicity*.[12] Discussions concerning gender, sexuality and cyberspace have thrown up some conflicting observations about gender relations, representation of women and sexual role-play via digital media. For instance Kearney in "Don't need you: Rethinking Identity Politics and Separatism from a Girrrl Perspective" provides a quite favorable reading of women, the Web and digital culture.[13] Readings of this kind highlight how the digital revolution provides women with avenues of self-expression not offered by more traditional closed media and facilities. According to writers like Sherry Turkle,[14] women are allowed freer sexual expression, and are unencumbered by more traditional censure, laws, and other patriarchal gate-keeping mechanisms.

On the other hand Chineze Onyejekwe and like critics perceive the impact of digital technology differently.[15] For them digital culture is an extension of more traditional patriarchal systems of political, social, economic and cultural control. This view therefore highlights the extent to which digital cultural processes and practices perpetuate exploitation of women, exacerbate their portrayal as sexual objects and privilege men in the real and virtual domains of social power. In the article "What About Gender Issue in the Information Society" Dafne Sabanes Plou makes the significant point that

> ICTs are one of the fields where gender relations take place, sometimes reinforcing old ones, sometimes changing them, but making us aware that the social and the cultural context has an impact on ICT development and use, and that it is not possible to think of new communication technologies as neutral.[16]

She argues that technologies have changed but fundamentals have remained the same. Others have also convincingly argued that policy making in technological fields ignores gender issues.[17] While this chapter does not set out to align itself neatly to any single perspective, its discussion of gender and Caribbean digital culture examines the truths in both sides of the above debate.

Vernacular cyberculture

Vernacular culture encapsulates the variety of regional responses to contemporary situations. The idea of vernacular culture calls into presence its other, the official culture. Vernacular expressions in the real world have a way of assigning to themselves a clear sense of referencing to some other standard expression against which they clearly are weighed. In cyberspace it is not as easy to demarcate boundaries in this manner. Given the Internet's marked instability, given its dynamic state and given the fact that discourses are not yet as well identified and labeled in this environment, it is perhaps more difficult to brand specific kinds of activities as one thing or the other with clear precision. But this is not to deny the existence of Caribbean vernacular expression in cyberspace. There are numerous Caribbean cyber projects that emanate from agencies other than formal official bodies, and which speak the "language" (as unstable as it is) of everyday usage. For instance, consider the website Afiwi.com which sets out to "provide content and community for anyone with a love of the Caribbean." This site is owned and run by four staff members who work primarily in the arena of communications and technology. The CEO is an on air personality at South Florida's WLRN 91.3 FM "Sounds of the Caribbean." Other associates share a relationship with several islands of the Caribbean. Such sites are signifiers of how the real and virtual domains interpenetrate in the interest of several objectives, for in addition to its stated reason for existing the site is used by different people for divergent reasons. Its varied content means that it appeals to many interests.

Caribbean cyber vernaculars are not only defined by cultural expressions disseminated through "underground" websites, but they also relate to similarly culturally charged expressions embedded within mainstream "official" websites.

Cyberculture, cybercritique, digital divide

While it is acceptable to extrapolate debates about gender in the real world on to discussions about the virtual world, there is also the sense in which to do so would be to oversimplify the relation between the real and the virtual world. The fact must be respected that cyberculture both shares and transgresses the practices, structures and constructions of its other. There cannot therefore be any simplistic process of superimposing older real-world critical practices and conclusions onto emerging digital experience. My argument here is not that there are few similarities across the real and virtual arenas of critical transaction, but rather, that because of the unstable and fast expanding arena that is cyberspace, there is need for simultaneous scrutiny of the cultural data itself and of the very media/practices that contain and relay that cultural data. I therefore suggest that Caribbean cultural criticism itself should undergo a process of closer scrutiny of the raw material of virtual digital culture and of the very medium that relays, simulates, stands in for and supplants the said raw material. This is not an unreasonable suggestion, especially given the potential built into leading-edge technology, where the medium and the raw material interpenetrate to produce never before conceived relations.

There has been much discussion of the digital divide as a concept that explains the disparity in access to technology use between peoples of the world especially based on national, regional location and access to economic wealth. This concept leads Shaggy's Girl to conclude that Jamaica (and most of the Caribbean as well) does not have a cyberculture, since Internet usage is not widespread enough.[18] There are still perceptions of this kind that fail to realize the latent power and undetectable reach of digital culture. Notions of trans-Caribbean digital and cyberculture extend beyond an examination of the dedicated space called the Internet and World Wide Web. It is vital to understand that the wider realm of communication, entertainment and the activities that circulate therein also help to define digital culture. The cyberculture of individual nation states also extends beyond an examination of what takes place within the individual geographical local territory. If the notion of trans-Caribbean does away with the defining marker of geographical and political place, then the cyber-Caribbean is even broader and less solid in terms of the audience which it captures, since trans-Caribbean cyberculture might also seize within its net a whole set of people, institutions and agents, who are barely in virtual proximity to Caribbean transactions in cyberspace.

The digital divide also draws out discussion about the disparity across other categories such as gender. Although it has been argued that men have assigned to themselves leading positions of control with respect to technological access and use, the digital revolution has made it potentially more possible for women to participate, and even control to greater degree their own levels of participation within digital culture. If anything, the Caribbean's expanded presence within global culture allows for minority groups and groupings to find enhanced presence and assert agency via means that transcend more traditional repressive systems of control. For instance, special groups, and individuals have greater uninhibited access to communications media and tools like mobile phones and computers, which are gateways to national and extra-national forums. Caribbean citizens and especially women have looked increasingly beyond traditional boundaries in their attempt to confront traditional prohibitions, to secure individual empowerment and to live fuller lives. Although it should be acknowledged (as already mentioned) that facilities like the Internet also provide for consolidation of more traditional relations and systems of control, this chapter is more concerned with examining aspects of women's responses to and involvement within the late twentieth century early twenty-first century digital matrix. Cyberspace offers the possibility of erasing and re-inscribing the characteristics that have come to squarely define "woman" in the face-to-face environment. What this chapter also goes on to foregrounds is the role played by technology itself in helping to shape, encode and digitize gendered responses to the state of flux within Caribbean and trans-Caribbean global culture.

Digital bodies

Many feminist and other critics have focused on the body as a contested site of meaning regarding gender, identity and sexuality. Writing on the entry of the artist's body into the artwork itself, Barber acknowledges how this signifies that the artist's body is centered, becoming the subject and object of the action.[19] Lucy Lippard's comments on this process introduce an important question with which this section of my discussion begins. Lippard comments that "when women use their own bodies in their artwork, they are using their selves; a significant psychological factor converts these bodies of faces from object to subject."[20] The anomaly here is that on the Net there is a range of uses of women's bodies by men, and even by women themselves.

Caribbean women have always explored and exploited the border sites within their countries. With the advent of the digital revolution of the late twentieth century these women as others, turned increasingly to newer emerging spaces in order to make sense of their experiences and also to enhance their standing in many regards. While not a discontinuous space of cultural transaction, cyberspace has come to represent a frontier site of social activity. Although the Caribbean and its subjects did not readily immerse themselves in cyberculture in the early years of the revolution, as in the dot.com years, by the mid-2000s cyberspace represented a major location for conducting all kinds of activities. Women, and men turned to the expanding realm of cyberculture in search of new avenues of expression and also to test older systems of self-definition. Women embraced the tools of the digital economy. Since the digital corporate world knew this, it also advertised some of its ware to Caribbean women whom it appealed to on the basis of individual self-empowerment. But these women would also share a new/renewed relationship with other users, becoming part of a community of digital associates.

Caribbean women are increasingly involved with extra-regional agencies, especially commercial interests. Some Caribbean women (and whether they like it or not) have come to share digital experience with major producers of hard and software. These women are discoursed upon repeatedly in cyberculture. Motorola for instance, on their website around February 2005 places a photo of a woman holding a small phone.[21] She has just come from the water, or is about to go there. She holds in both hands a small phone, as if bearing an offering. While making this gesture she also supports a delicately worn strapless top, so that, the gesture calls attention to the technology and to her body.

The drop-down box on the webpage allows the surfer to access Motorola's several global sites. A visit to the Jamaican/West Indian site finds the same woman standing before the backdrop of a tropical landscape holding a new phone.

As this Caribbean (yet, world)subject teases, you come to behold a new slender mobile phone called the MotoPebl. This is predictable marketing. The semiotics of this marketing strategy is carried through in the words that promote this gadgetry. Some of the promo phrases include: "all the features you desire," "experience more," "nature's smooth curves," "organic lines," "stylish simplicity," "hold it in your palm," "enjoy." Arguably there is some measure of female objectification at play here. A critical point which should not be overlooked is the increasing importance and power of women in the economy, and hence their becoming a more important target group for ads of this kind. But there is an even deeper process at work in this advertisement, as often obtains in cyber marketing hermeneutics. The freckled woman who holds the phone appears to have multi-racial identity. Her grasping of the phone is partly an act of intimacy as it is recognition that she and Caribbean women have the potential to nurture and give breadth to emerging digital culture. If this promotion seeks to convey that message, it also begins to encode a set of gendered codes whereby the technology might eventually stand in for male and female subjects.

Promotions and ads of this kind are not mere commercially devised abstractions. Indeed they are conscious reflections on the current and future state of regional identity, and its sexual and technology politics. This promotion recognizes that Caribbean women are historically objects of sexual desire. It also reveals that these women have guarded the treasures of Caribbean society, as mothers, storytellers, and entrepreneurs. They are preservers of vernacular traditions and customs. As central agents of societal and cultural preservation and change Caribbean women are therefore at the core of the digital revolution. If the mobile phone is read as a symbol of masculinity, or as a phallic symbol then this provides even greater support for the suggestion that such an advertisement gestures to the pivotal location of females in the digital matrix. Their place, while still regarded by some as not equal to that of men in the digital age, is nonetheless situated at the cusp of digital culture. This advertisement is aware that Caribbean women as other women are turning increasingly outward to the wider world. With backs to the island they peer increasingly out onto a world that has opened up to them the potential of navigating beyond what can often be the confining politics of island life.

Like the island nymph in the Motorola advertisement, Caribbean women (especially young women) have embraced the tools and facilities of the digital revolution in a way not before seen. In the book *Cinderella or Cyberella? Empowering Women in the Knowledge Society* the authors consider the liberating potential locked within digital culture and acknowledge a new wave of interest in digital ware and enhanced proficiency of use of technology among women in societies south of the equator.[22] It is not unreasonable to surmise that Caribbean women also embrace digital culture for quite similar reasons. For some young women this act of embracing new technologies signifies the asserting of their identities, for others it has simply to do with their sex appeal, for many more it has to do with global interface/engagement, for others it is a way of reaching outwards while also remaining at home, still for some, digital culture's branding as a masculine space provides the impetus for a counter movement that enters the gendered digital matrix and wrestles with the skewed programs that infect the machines. Caribbean women might therefore be seen as participating within digital culture for this range of purposes.

Cyber-girrrlz: Literary models and cyber-griots

Caribbean women have engaged in a process of encoding their own signatures onto digital culture. Their vernacular imprint is therefore located in a number of ways. Websites that feature Caribbean women as agents of power reflect a series of markers that help to identify not only women as powerful sexes, but also as Caribbean-interfacing agents. This Caribbean digital vernacular imprint is often conveyed through writing, language, tech savvy, performance and other across the bandwidth of digital media.

Caribbean vernacular writers are to be found at a range of locations on the Internet. Leading female vernacular authors appear on formal and less formal sites. Their message is not always in sync with the ideology of the host site, but this paradox defines the highly conflictual nature of cyberspace. The online literary magazine *The Caribbean Writer Online* represents an initiative by the University of the Virgin Islands to "develop Caribbean writers no matter where they live."[23] Another similar site is the University of Miami's Caribbean writers' Summer Institute Archives, which provides video excerpts of Caribbean writers discussing and reading their work. This has promoted the work of several female writers like Erna Brodber, Olive Senior, Maryse Conde, and Zee Edgell the latter, discussing culture and ethnicity in Belize. University of Maryland and North Carolina State University also feature Caribbean authors online.[24]

These sites represent an effort to harness a range of creative talents within and outside of the region. These sites might also be read as outpost colonial projects that buttress a process of institutional consolidation. Given the failure of Caribbean institutions to package and display their very artists, some extra-regional institutions have stepped in to record, digitize and transmit Caribbean female poets of the diaspora, poets like Merle Collins, Valerie Bloom, Dionne Brand and Lorna Goodison. This harnessing and transmission of Caribbean talents by some institutions could be misinterpreted as ownership. However, the employment of rhetorical strategies and devices such as satire, parody, irony, digital orality, and "nation language" in their work online betrays any notion that these female voices are fully re-colonized in the virtual domain. The presence of these vernacular tropes signifies the imbedded-ness of counter discursive traits within cultural texts even as they move from the real to the virtual domain. Given the relatively high costs associated with staging a self-contained Web presence, many Caribbean vernacular artists have strategically placed their work on digital servers of wealthier institutions. In doing so, they allow their creative work to speak on their behalf. Not all female authors engage in this method. There are others who overtly promote their ideology. Caribbean-Canadian poet Dionne Brand on her author page at the Northwest Passages site declares defiantly that she is not a writer at the margin: "I don't consider myself on any margin, on the margin of Canadian Literature. I'm sitting right in the middle of Black Literature, because that's who I read, that's who I respond to." Her issues in writing have to do with the Caribbean Diaspora, national identity and immigration.[25]

Less formal sites like 57Productions.com offer a mix of established and little known authors and performers. Arguably this site is more revolutionary in spirit than the ones mentioned above. It associates itself more closely with the kind of vernacular expression that it promotes. Its roster of artists extends beyond the canonical performers within Caribbean diaspora culture. Although it has built its vernacular status around radicals like Linton Kwesi Johnson and Jean "Binta" Breeze it also embraces lesser known underground artists like Zena Edwards. Its ongoing quarrel with the "status crow"[26] is exemplified in its publicizing of the attempted censorship of Breeze's intended performance of the piece "Isaiah" at the 13th of June 2005 Human Rights Watch fund-raising event called "Cries from the Heart—a celebration of voices for justice," at the Globe Theatre, London.

Binta Breeze was born in Jamaica but moved to London in 1985. The 2005 censorship of Binta Breeze in London is a reminder of her precarious place in that society. In spite of the adoption of other countries by Caribbean people they still find themselves marginalized citizens. In a 2001 interview she discourses on the dynamics of being at home and abroad:[27]

> I find it very confusing, practically schizophrenic. It's really, really hard to try to live in two places, and I think the main problem with living in London is one, the distance from the Caribbean and two, the weather. Apart from that, it might have been possible to live there because there's such a strong West Indian community. I mean, it's a metropolis, London, so you can actually feel pretty much at home, especially in Brixton where most of the West Indian people live. You can have a sense of community and a sense of belonging, if it weren't for the dastardly weather, you know.

Caribbean women poets, writers and cyber-griots continue to extend the boundaries and perpetuate some of the functions of the oral tradition via several sites either authored by them or put up by underground affiliate bodies. The cyber realm has therefore become a meeting place for diasporic trans-nationals.[28]

Caribbean cyber-girrrlz: From trans/"trans"-Caribbean virtual porn to newsgroup debates and blog identities

Like young women elsewhere trans-Caribbean women have already started to create new spaces for articulation of their lifestyle and ideology.[29] Feeling marginalized by academic and established feminist discourses, women have set about a process of living out the meanings of their own womanist project. Caribbean women in the diaspora have also formed allegiances with other women in exile and have united around the common goal of using frontier media to network and to tackle minority issues. A site like preciousonline.co.uk supports the creative and business initiatives of black women. Among contributors to this site are women of Caribbean lineage who grew up in England. The site's message boards and certainly its "five minute stories" are its defining attributes. These mainly introspective creations tend to focus on the themes of history, loneliness, exile and love.

The digital revolution has given rise to a set of new feminist Girrrlz communities on the Net, especially among some white, western, educated young women.[30] Caribbean women especially young women have used the cyber domain to carry out a range of projects which have some bearing on gender, sexuality, nationality, identity and power.

There is no better source to consult when beginning to consider the challenges posed to terms such as "Caribbean" and "West Indian" than websites at the cusp of popular expression. In an article by Taran submitted to KnowProse.com Jan 29, 2006, the author asks what constituters the "Caribbean" presence in cyberspace, especially in blog subculture. Bloggers have themselves discoursed on the meaning of "Caribbean" and its geographical and cultural identification.[31] The responses range from the description of "Caribbean" as an identifiable region, to the suggestion that it is a term whose meaning no one knows, or that it is a descriptive reference to a set of islands over there that tourist brochures refer to in their advertising. In particular, cyber sites that feature Caribbean models and fashion have contemplated this debate. They tend to handle the matter in a way that reveals these near-porn sites of popular expression as being more permissive and assured than more conservative associations and formal bodies. Islandflave.com is a formulaic website to the extent that is showcases female models in a range of seductive wear and poses. But its projection of women and their proclamation of their nationalities breaches the conventional border of what constitutes "Caribbean/West Indian." The site declares itself as "an online Caribbean Community that features West Indian entertainment, culture, events for people who live in and visit south Florida." On the site some women give their Caribbean identities as Haitian, Aruban, Jamaican, Guyanese and Dominican, but more complex identities feed into the site as other women label themselves as African-American, Puerto Rican, Argentinean and even Hawaiian. The flagrant disregard for identifying a single specific location within the sub-region or region reveals the extent to which the domain of Caribbean fashion, modeling and entertainment culture embraces the complex mix of race, color and nationalities that feed into trans-Caribbean culture.

In addition to wrestling with the problematic of nationality, many sites contend with debates about gender (whether directly or indirectly). Blog sites like jdidthoughts.blogspot.com "Doan Mind Me. I duz talk nuff foolishness" attract Caribbean females and males living abroad. It focuses on personal as well as social issues facing the Caribbean. Indeed I would suggest that a number of these newsgroups and blog sites represent the new frontier arena for the playing out of debates that concern women. In addition they provide a space for the reinscription of gender roles and the erosion of conventional hierarchical and lateral categorizations.

The recognition that such avenues as weblogs can operate beneath the radar of hard print and surface experience reinforces the point that cyberspace is a gateway to limitless exposure and also an arena of covert possibility. Because identities, nationalities, names and motives can be masked, blurred, concealed in cyberspace it is therefore the most dynamic yet deceptive sphere of cultural production, reproduction, representation and simulation.

Globalvoicesonline.org provides a gateway to weblogs across the globe. Here there are countless Caribbean blog sites, including reference to significant moments in Caribbean Blog history. It is here in cyberspace that we meet one of the first Caribbean bloggers to consistently use the vernacular throughout her blogs, her Web name is Guyana-Gyal sapodilla.blogspot.com/. Her first post January 14, 2005, is fittingly a "shout out" to Guyanese living abroad who are homesick:[32]

> You a Guyanese homesick in Canada? America? England?
>
> If you're homesick [and there's no one more homesick dan all you Goyanese living in Foreign] . . . here's what's been cooking up in our home by de sea:
>
> This week's menu:
> Kathar curry cooked in cokenut milk.
> Boiled and fried breadfruit wth mackerel.
> Dhal an' rice an fish choka.
> Bhagee and dhal and roti.
> And don't forget the bird peppa.
> Or marawiriwee peppa sauce. Wid de lime achar.

Like other cyber rebels Francomenz at her Blog location called "Frankly Speaking . . . on a variety of subjects" addresses a range of topical issues relating to Trinidadian and Caribbean society.[33] She gives her opinion on the role of DJ's and shows her breadth of knowledge by reading David Rudder as "the Naipaul of calypso" someone who exposes the region to itself. There are various newsgroups like TriniCallalou (sixty-nine members) which unite Trinis and Tobagonians at its "online liming spot" groups.msncom/TriniCallaloo. In their "vent here" segment women like Trinigal discuss the spate of violence and the seeming lack of political will to do anything about it. The overriding tone within many such free domains of expression is derisive, and at other times parodic. These attitudes are defining features of vernacular expression and of subversive writing. While various levels of censorship exist within the traditional boundaries of island states, the borderless cyber-state is harder to police.

SparklingWaters group (2084 members) boasts members from throughout the region living at home and abroad. As on other sites there is a venting board here. Women's discussions here vary from the evils associated with satellite and digital technology to the challenges of regional integration and the provocative discussion as to whether Caribbean societies are too "feminine," with women demonstrating increased levels of participation in formal agencies and institutions of learning. The issue of feminine-ization of Caribbean society brings to the fore the alternative meaning of "trans-Caribbean." In the world of contemporary pop culture the "trans-" prefix has come to signify cross-gender and cross-sexual activity, such as men donning women's apparel, roles and vice versa. While most Caribbean societies are traditionally very rigid concerning sex and gender identity, it is significant to note that gender and sexual identities are often blurred in cyberspace. Although cyber-sobriquets can provide a clue to one's gender, many Caribbean male and female subjects have names that are difficult to locate along a spectrum of gendered nomenclatures.

Other issues taken up on the SparklinWaters site relate to whether Caribbean "cussing" should be allowed on the site. This kind of debate calls attention to the ongoing struggle to map out a set of behaviors that have a place in traditional Caribbean lifestyle culture, as well as the new limitless space of trans-Carib-global cyberculture. The attention paid to such concerns at these sites driven primarily by women reflects a level of conscious awareness by women about the touchy issues that often divide Caribbean peoples. This level of self-conscious debate is also a careful reflection on the meaning of digital cyber expression, what is possible, permissible for free-minded Caribbean women and their men in the second half of the first decade of the twenty-first century.[34]

VincyLinkup is much raunchier. Its women especially TechnicsexyCleopatha engages other members in playful, transgressive activity, like the one called "I'm sexy what are you!!!!!!!!!!"[35] Young Jamaican is a group dedicated to "all young Jamaicans 18-26 wishing to meet each other and go back to their roots."[36] The language register in effect here reflects the use of digital vernacular jargon. This is a crucial point since Caribbean cyber vernacular speak is also an evolving variety. It is a mixture of Web jargon, tech-speak and Caribbean linguistic idiosyncrasies.

Because the Net allows for the partial revelation and concealment of identities, Caribbean women who use weblogs and who post their personalities and identities at chat sites exploit this fact about the Internet. Better-known sites like Hi 5 play out the permutations of Web identity and representation. Enigmatic Feline's blog site deeliz.blogspot.com/ is even more provocative and playful. Her "about me" page describes herself as "Enigmatic, complex, hard to pin down, smart, sexy, beautiful [. . .]." Her range of interests include "books, men, medicine and passionate love."

CG (computer generated) women

Caribbean women are actively engaged in a process of digitizing their very presence. They create of/to themselves computer-generated subjects. The blog site belonging to Baby Blue Lee is a hodgepodge of racial jokes, love poems/reflections all told with an ironic gesture to cyber chat.[37] There is a certain measure of casual indifference to social proprieties within her cyber discourses. On her *About Me* page she declares: "I'm a female Scorpio . . . that should say it all." Her references to "Jamaica—a home well missed" connects her to and draws out comments from people like Cooldestiny, another Caribbean in exile. Another blogger, Anna D describes herself as a "34 year old Caribbean girl with lots on her mind and not afraid to say it. Myriad interests from movies, technology and gaming to D/s. I am known to be a little on the 'unusual' side but that is only because I accept and embrace differences. Unless I don't like it . . . then it's bad. . . . HAHAHA!"[38]

She also provides other information such as: "Hobbies: Geeky stuff What I'm doing now: Playing *Second Life* and *Sims 2*, decorating my own place, chatting with submissive men, watching a lot of Chinese cinema, fanatically following *Smallville*." And her provocative, playful, but profound commentary on her digital presence and body is described as what she looks like "in her other existence." Commenting on the controversial cowboy movie *Brokeback Mountain* she declares that "Caribbean men have to be the most homophobic on the planet." Her chiding of Caribbean men and her embracing of a simulated world as expressed through role play games/programs like *Second Life* and *Sims2* reflects the extent to which people of the region are increasingly diffuse in terms of their ideological, gendered and spatial constitution.

Baby Blue Lee declares a passion for the Caribbean but paradoxically (like Anna D), her iconographic cyber trope is an anime figure, partially clothed, consciously showing the derriere. Baby Blue Lee's adoption of a Japanese computer generated anime/image to represent her self is not unheard of. This indeed is a feature of Web representation politics.

It could be argued that her reflection on her own self, appearance, presence, substance and being is an apolitical practice. However, a deeper examination of this choice of representation of self brings into focus two points. Firstly, the ease with which cybersociety locates computerized icons, and secondly the ease with which trans-Caribbean and other cyber nationals put on digital bodies. It is important to note that the label of "anime" is the Japanese contraction and pronunciation of the word "animation," and refers to animation created in part or in whole on computers. Anime genres of art and film and video often blend vibrant colors, heightened action and represent the intersection of the real and the fantastical. Caribbean subjects growing up in the last three decades of the twentieth century fantasized about toys and cartoon figures like Magical Little Girls and *Space Battleship Yamato* (started 1974, called *Starblazers* in the West), which captured the imagination of youthful Caribbean subjects who would later reconnect with these fantasies when the Internet became the free conduit for self and identity fulfilment.[39] The embracing of fully digitized bodies within this genre is not only a virtual reconnection with past/childhood fantasies, but it is also a radical political act of embracing a certain kind of womanliness.

Japanese and in turn western pop culture computer generated heroines are an integral part of the consciousness of Caribbean and other women throughout the world.[40] Radically powerful and influential computer generated female characters have influenced and inspired girls and women whether *they* are immersed in pop culture or not. The heroines of *Sailor Moon* (1995) spawned a body of diehard fans that banded together in body and spirit and demonstrated to have the series continued in the United States. The star of *Mononoke Hime*, Sana is boisterous and often challenges authority where others are silent. Younger generations have embraced these computer generated beings because the emerging genres in which they feature cater to children, teens, adults, and portray infantile stories, moral tales, complex and subtle subjects as well as graphically violent and even pornographic material. Decidedly Western Video CG women like Lara Croft of *Tomb Raiders* fame and Yuna, Rikku and Paine of *Final Fantasy* trade domesticated roles for much more robust, assertive and critical stances.[41] These women skirt the realm of reality. They are often entrusted with the responsibility of saving nations and the world.

Marina Gržinić does not concur with this reading of women like Lara Croft whom she reads as an upper class woman who has been transformed into a "little engine in the process of re-territorialization."[42] This in another way of coming to digitized female icons within western popular culture, but the deeper significance of virtual heroines within cyberculture and in video games is that many gamers often superimpose their own set of values, ideologies and motives when they play for these heroines. In any case, Lara Croft's racial and ideological complexion is not as clearly fixed as Gržinić assumes. And this is exactly the point, since characters of this kind are hard to fix, and pin down. Real life Lara Croft embodiments have been carefully chosen to reflect her complex racial identity, which is central to her reception among women, and men around the world. Angelina Jolie's casting in this role was carefully done, especially given her humanitarian interest in countries of Africa. There are countless other women in particular who have taken on digital bodies as part of a process of concealment, embracing of cyber identities, but also as an act of recognition that conventionally bordered representations of the self are fading. The taking on of technologized bodies is also a practice among some trans-Caribbean male subjects.

Where's the vernacular in video games and big budget film?

The reconfiguration of notions of Caribbean nationalities, identities and cultures derives much of its impetus from the overt and covert ideologies at work within popular entertainment and popular culture. Trans-Caribbean bodies are therefore discoursed upon in Western big budget films and video games in a way that has hardly been noticed by Caribbean cultural criticism. Some might argue that big budget film coming out of the heart of the entertainment industry in the west has no bearing on a discussion about Caribbean vernacular culture. Nothing could be further from the truth, since, Caribbean cultural identities are increasingly fashioned by the popular discourses propagated by route of western entertainment culture. A reality (if paradox) of Caribbean popular and vernacular expression is that it is increasingly being fashioned via entertainment companies and re-exported to the islands and to their citizens abroad.

While there has been some mention of Caribbean references in big budget tech-driven films, there is no consideration of how big budget tech culture discourses on trans-gender issues in the Caribbean. Jar Jar Binks, the clumsy, garrulous sidekick of the main actors of the blockbuster movie *Star Wars Episode 1: The Phantom Menace*, has been critiqued for his baby talk, and his ears have been referred to as Caribbean dreadlocks. But Jar Jar's (jah jah's) slightly effeminate disposition means that it is problematic to affix a single specific gender to the digitized character. This is perhaps part of the unease that some African-Caribbean people have had with the Spielberg concoction.

The predator most recently seen in the movie *Alien vs. Predator* (*AVP*) is often read as dread-locked reincarnate. It predictably therefore sides with the movie's black female heroine. This suggests a symbiotic relation and hints at the primal origin of species and races, perhaps. The dreadlocked predator first seen up against Schwarzenegger, and then battling Danny Glover, Colombians and the Caribbean Posse in *Predator 2*, is attracted by violence and uses the same to facilitate its own drive for survival. The Predator's masculine-feminine disposition, especially when in silhouette, anticipates the eventual putative union of man/beast and woman in *AVP*. The Rayment Twins of *Matrix Reloaded* also have dubious genders. These dreadlocked twins like the two Rasta tam-wearing squids in *Shark Tale* seem so closely twinned they share some intimate association beyond the mere superficial label of identical twins. The hanging locks are therefore on one level a signifier of (and referent to the attire of) Rasta, but in another reading, they can be said to resemble a woman's hairdo. The fixation of digital culture with Caribbean iconography has therefore reflected a whole series of gendered transformations, transgressions and aberrations. These are based partly on mis-readings of the Caribbean but also on less well known ideological and cultural motives that drive the creative and economic enterprise of Western popular digital culture.

If contemporary film contorts male and female gendered bodies by means of digital and post-digital simulation, then the computer gaming industry (especially in the sports genre) is less democratic in its treatment of gendered subjects. Video games like *Cricket 2004* (based on the highly popular Caribbean pastime) feature only males in action. If observers of the sport view this as a fair reflection of the game's image in the real world, there are still some grounds for questioning the absence of women at various levels of the video game's construction and performance. But perhaps critical investigation into macho gaming culture does not readily recognize the ways in which cutting-edge digital culture turns upon itself to interrogate its very inefficiencies and absences. In Electronic Arts' *Cricket 2004* and *Cricket 2005* as well as *Brian Lara Cricket 2005* the game's simulation and modeling integrity wobbles. Because of the quirks within gaming simulation, the male players on the field at times appear to be their opposite. This is not a mere facetious commentary on Electronic Arts and Codemaster's computer generated (CG) technological application. It is rather an observation about the politics at work within the machines that promise to simulate and produce all kinds of human behaviors. If computer generated actions and antics contain within them the nodes of gendering architecture, then this is a reminder that technology itself often takes on the complexion, agenda, gender and virtual human traits of those who are in control of the technology. But it is also possible to theorize that the inability of technological wizards to perfectly simulate the idiosyncrasies of human subjects across cultures, nationality, sex, gender and race, reveals the limitations of technology itself.

In the digital age it is becoming less and less easy to rigidly demarcate the boundaries between Caribbean citizens at home and those abroad, between Caribbean men and women, between vernacular and official culture. It is easier to define these lines in the real world of our conventional experience, but the world of the digital matrix sees technology intervening to blur traditional lines of experience. While some more conventional discourses point to purely social, economic and political facets as the core determinants of the region's experiential reality, it does seem that there is need to factor in other emerging phenomena. Technology and the technological might be products and creations of economic and political agencies, but it does seem that given technology's intuitiveness and interactivity within current human relations, where individual citizens are able to fashion and reshape their experience and reconfigure the technology, there is an emerging set of transactions that points to the Machine as the region's most feared medium, yet its most critical ally in harnessing the individual and collective loyalty of its citizens.

Notes

1. Riva Kastoryano, "The Reach of Transnationalism," The Center for International Studies and Research, Social Science and Research Council Paris. http://www.ssrc.org/sept11/essays/kastoryano.htm. (accessed February 10, 2006).
2. Dennis Conway, "Getting There, Despite the Odds: Caribbean Migration to the U.S. in the 1990s," *Journal of Eastern Caribbean Studies* 27, no. 4 (Dec 2002): 100-134.
3. For more on the concept of "location," see, for example, Chandra Talpade Mohanty, "Feminist Encounters: Locating the Politics of Experience," *Copyright 1* (Fall 1987) 30-44; Michele Wallace, "The Politics of Location: Cinema/TheoryLiterature/Ethnicity/Sexuality/Me," *Framework* 36 (1989), 42-55; Lata Mani, "Multiple Mediations: Feminist Scholarship in the Age of Multinational Reception," 1989, http://humwww.ucsc.edu/CultStudies/PUBS/Inscriptions/vol_5/LataMani.html (accessed April 2006); and Inderpal Grewal, "Autobiographical Subjects and Diasporic Locations: Meatless Days and Borderlands," 231-254. And Caren Kaplan, "The Politics of Location as Transnational Feminist Practice," 137-152 in *Scattered Hegemonies: Postmodernity and Transnational Feminist Practice*, ed. Inderpal Grewal and Caren Kaplan (Minneapolis: University of Minnesota Press, 1994).
4. Olive Senior, *Working Miracles: Women's Lives in the English Speaking Caribbean* (London: James Currey, 2001), 26.

5. Kamau Brathwaite, *Contradictory Omens* (Mona: Savacou, 1974); and Madeline Kerr, *Personality and Conflict in Jamaica* (London: Collins 1952).
6. Senior, *Working Miracles*, 26.
7. Ralph Henry, "Jobs, Gender and Development Strategy in the Commonwealth Caribbean," in *Gender in Caribbean Development*, ed. Patricia Mohammed and Catherine Shepherd (Kingston, Jamaica: Canoe Press, 1999), 176-196.
8. See UN, "Science for the 21st Century," UNESCO June 26-July 1, 1999, www.unesco.org/science/wcs/meetings/list.htm (accessed April 17, 2007), and also "UN Flagship Publications," Women Watch. http://www.un.org/womenwatch/daw/public/flagship.htm (accessed April 17, 2007).
9. See Donna Hope, *Inna di Dancehall* (Kingston, Jamaica: University of the West Indies Press, 2006); and Curdella Forbes, *From Nation to Diaspora* (Kingston, Jamaica: University of the West Indies Press, 2005).
10. Curwen Best, *Culture @ the Cutting Edge* (Kingston, Jamaica: University of the West Indies Press, 2005), 4.
11. Nina Glick Schiller and Georges Eugene Fouron, *Georges Woke Up Laughing* (Durham, N.C.: Duke University Press, 2001).
12. Jacqueline Archibald, ed., *The Gender Politics of ICT* (Middlesex: Middlesex University Press, 2005); Linda Leung, *Virtual Ethnicity* (London: Ashgate, 2005).
13. Mary Kearney, "'Don't need you': Rethinking Identity Politics and Separatism from a Girrrl Perspective," 148-188, in *Youth Culture: Identity in a Postmodern World*, ed. J. S. Epstein (Oxford: Blackwell, 1998).
14. Sherry Turkle, *Life on the Screen: Identity in the Age of the Internet* (New York: Touchstone, 1995).
15. Chineze Onyejekwe, "The Internet and the Commercialization of Sex," *Nebula* 2 no. 3 (September 2005). Also see a copy at http://www.nobleworld.biz/images/Onyejekwe.pdf (accessed February 5, 2006).
16. Dafne Sabanes Plou, "What About Gender Issue in the Information Society," in *Communicating in the Information Society*, ed. Bruce Girard and Seán Ó Siochrú (Geneva: United Nations Research Institute for Social Development, 2003), 11.
17. See Nancy Hafkin, "Gender Issues in ICT Policies in Developing Countries: An Overview" (paper presented at the Expert Group Meeting UN Division for the Advancement of Women, Seoul, November 2002), 11-14.
18. See Shaggy's Girl "The Former Jamaican." December 15 2005, http://shaggyla.blogspot.com/2005/12/cyberculture.html (accessed April 17, 2007).
19. Bruce Barber, "Indexing Conditionalism and its Heretical Equivalents," in *Performance by Artists*, ed. Aa and Peggy Gale Bronson, (New York: Art Metropole, 1979).
20. Lucy Lippard, *Get the Message? A Decade of Art for Social Change* (New York: E. P. Dutton, 1976).
21. See Motorolla's, "HelloMoto," http://direct.motorola.com/hellomoto/index.htm (accessed April 17, 2007).
22. Nancy Hufkin and Sophia Huyer, *Cinderella or Cyberella? Empowering Women in the Knowledge Society* (Bloomfield: Humarian Press, 2006).
23. See The Caribbean Writer's "Welcome to thecaribbenwriter.com," *Caribbean Writer*, http://www.thecaribbeanwriter.com/about.html (accessed February 5, 2006).
24. See the University of Miami's, "Caribbean writers' Summer Institute Archival Video Collection," http://scholar.library.miami.edu/cls/speakersDisplay.php (accessed February 5, 2006). University of Maryland, "University of Maryland College of arts/Merle Collins," http://www.inform.umd.edu/ARHU/Depts/CompLit/Bios/col-

http://www.inform.umd.edu/ARHU/Depts/CompLit/Bios/collins.html (accessed February 5, 2006); Merle Collins, "Because the Dawn Breaks," http://social.chass.ncsu.edu/wyrick/debclass/dawnbr~1.htm (accessed February 5, 2006).

25. Carmen Lassotta, "Northwest Passages Author Profiles: Dionne Brand," Northwest Passages, http://www.nwpassages.com/bios/brand.asp (accessed February 5, 2006).

26. Brathwaite uses the term "status crow" in place of "status quo."

27. Jenny Sharpe, "A Conversation with Jean "Binta" Breeze," 2001 Interview, http://www.57productions.com/article_reader.php?id=8 (accessed February 5, 2006).

28. See the authorless article "Race for Cyberspace: Blacks open digital battle for race equality," *Chronicle World*, Nov. 2004, www.black-history-month.co.uk/articles/cyberspace.html (accessed February 5, 2006).

29. See Jane Armstrong, "Web Grrrls, Guerrill Tactics: Young Feminisms on the Web," in *Web.Studies*, ed. David Gauntlett (London: Arnold, 2004), 92.

30. See Armstrong, "Web Grrrls," 102.

31. Knowprose, "Creating the Cyber Caribbean," Jan 29, 2006, http://www.knowprose.com/node/10710 (accessed April 17, 2007); and "XML Version," http://el-oso.net/blog/archives/2006/01/08/%c2%bfquien-quiere-a-belice/feed (accessed February 5, 2006).

32. Guyana-Gyal January 14, 2005: "You a Guyanese homesick in Canada? America? England?" http://sapodilla.blogspot.com/2005/01/you-guyanese-homesick-in-canada.html (accessed February 5, 2006).

33. Francomenz, "Carnival Bacchanal," *Francomenz*, Feb 6, 2006, http://www.newcheeze.com/blog/?p=42 (accessed February 5, 2006).

34. Msn, "Sparkling Waters," *Msn Groups*, http://groups.msn.com/SparklingWaters/hotttopics.msnw. (accessed February 5, 2006).

35. Msn, "Vincy Link Up," Msn Groups, http://groups.msn.com/VincyLinkUp/funhouse (accessed February 5, 2006).

36. Msn, "Caribbean Groups," Msn Groups, http://groups.msn.com/browse.msnw?catid=268. (accessed February 5, 2006).

37. BabyBlueLee, "BabyBlueLee," March 1, 2006 http://babybluelee.blogspot.com (accessed February 5, 2006).

38. Anna D "Blogger," Blogger Profile Oct. 2004, http://www.blogger.com/profile/5040863 (accessed February 5, 2006).

39. Fred Patten, "A Capsule History of Anime," *AWM* Aug. 1996, http://www.awn.com/mag/issue1.5/articles/patten1.5.html (accessed February 5, 2006).

40. Sean Boden, "Women and Anime: Popular Culture and its reflection of Japanese Society," Nausicaa 2001, http://www.nausicaa.net/miyazaki/essay/files/Sean Boden_WomenandAnime.pdf (accessed February 5, 2006).

41. See the Women Gamers website http://womengamers.com/ (accessed February 5, 2006).

42. Marina Gržinić, "Utopia With Lara Croft and Some Other Monsters and Aliens," in *WEB ART-E-FACT*: Strategies of Resistance Issue 2: Utopia http://artefact.mi2.hr/_a02/lang_en/theory_grzinic_en.htm (accessed February 5, 2006).

Bibliography

Archibald, Jacqueline, ed. *The Gender Politics of ICT.* Middlesex: Middlesex University Press, 2005.

Armstrong, Jane. "Web Grrrls, Guerrill Tactics: Young Feminisms on the Web." Pp.92-102 in *Web.Studies,* edited by David Gauntlett. London: Arnold, 2004.

Best, Curwen. *Culture @ the Cutting Edge.* Kingston: University of the West Indies Press, 2005.

Boden, Sean. "Women and Anime: Popular Culture and its reflection of Japanese Society." *Nausicaa 2001,* http://www.nausicaa.net/miyazaki/essay/files/SeanBoden_WomenandAnime.pdf (accessed February 5, 2006).

Brathwaite, Kamau. *Contradictory Omens.* Mona: Savacou, 1974.

Collins, Merle. "Because the Dawn Breaks." http://social.chass.ncsu.edu/wyrick/debclass/dawnbr~1.htm (accessed February 5, 2006).

Conway, Dennis. "Getting There, Despite the Odds: Caribbean Migration to the U.S. in the 1990s." *Journal of Eastern Caribbean Studies* 27, no.4 (December 2002): 100-134.

Forbes, Curdella. *From Nation to Diaspora.* Kingston: UWI Press, 2005.

Grewal, Inderpal. "Autobiographical Subjects and Diasporic Locations: Meatless Days and Borderlands." Pp. 231-254 in *Scattered Hegemonies: Postmodernity and Transnational Feminist Practice,* edited by Inderpal Grewal and Caren Kaplan. Minneapolis: University of Minnesota Press, 1994.

Gržinić, Marina. "Utopia With Lara Croft and Some Other Monsters and Aliens." *WEB ART-E-FACT*: Strategies of Resistance, Issue 2: Utopia 2002. http://artefact.mi2.hr/_a02/lang_en/theory_grzinic_en.htm (accessed February 5, 2006).

Henry, Ralph. "Jobs, Gender and Development Strategy in the Commonwealth Caribbean." Pp.176-196 in *Gender in Caribbean Development,* edited by Patricia Mohammed and Catherine Shepherd. Kingston: Canoe Press, 1999.

Hope, Donna. *Inna di Dancehall.* Kingston: University of the West Indies Press, 2006.

Hufkin, Nancy, and Sophia Huyer. *Cinderella or Cyberella? Empowering Women in the Knowledge Society.* Bloomfield: Humarian Press, 2006.

Kaplan, Caren. "The Politics of Location as Transnational Feminist Practice." Pp. 137-152, in *Scattered Hegemonies: Postmodernity and Transnational Feminist Practice,* edited by Inderpal Grewal and Caren Kaplan. Minneapolis: University of Minnesota Press, 1994.

Kastoryano, Riva. "The Reach of Transnationalism." The Center for International Studies and Research, Social Science and Research Council, Paris. http://www.ssrc.org/sept11/essays/kastoryano.htm (accessed February 10, 2006).

Kearney, Mary. "'Don't need you': Rethinking Identity Politics and Separatism from a Girrrl Perspective." Pp. 148 in *Youth Culture: Identity in a Postmodern World,* edited by J. S. Epstein. Oxford: Blackwell, 1998.

Kerr, Madeline. *Personality and Conflict in Jamaica.* London: Collins, 1952.

Lassotta, Carmen. "Northwest Passages Author Profiles: Dionne Brand," Northwest Passages. http://www.nwpassages.com/bios/brand.asp (accessed February 5, 2006).

Leung, Linda. *Virtual Ethnicity.* London: Ashgate, 2005.

Mani, Lata. "Multiple Mediations: Feminist Scholarship in the Age of Multinational Reception," *Inscriptions* (1989). http://humwww.ucsc.edu/CultStudies/PUBS/Inscriptions/vol_5/LataMani.html (accessed April 2006).

Mohanty, Chandra Talpade. "Feminist Encounters: Locating the Politics of Experience," *Copyright 1* (Fall 1987): 30-44.

Onyejekwe, Chineze "The Internet and the Commercialization of Sex." *Nebula* 2, no. 3 (September 2005). Also see a copy at http://www.nobleworld.biz/images/Onyejekwe.pdf (accessed February 5, 2006).

Patten, Fred. "A Capsule History of Anime." *AWN 1996*. http://www.awn.com/mag/issue1.5/articles/patten1.5.html (accessed February 5, 2006).

Plou, Dafne Sabanes. "What About Gender Issues in the Information Society." Pp. 5-15 in *Communicating in the Information Society*, edited by Bruce Girard and Seán Ó Siochrú. Geneva: United Nations Research Institute for Social Development, 2003.

"Race for Cyberspace: Blacks open digital battle for race equality," *Chronicle World*. November 2004. www.black-history-month.co.uk/articles/cyberspace.html (accessed February 5, 2006).

Schiller, Nina Glick, and Georges Eugene Fouron. *Georges Woke Up Laughing*. Durham, N.C.: Duke University Press, 2001.

Senior, Olive. *Working Miracles: Women's Lives in the English Speaking Caribbean*. London: James Currey, 2001.

Sharpe, Jenny. "A Conversation with Jean "Binta" Breeze." 2001 Interview. http://www.57productions.com/article_reader.php?id=8 (accessed February 5, 2006).

Turkle, Sherry. *Life on the Screen: Identity in the Age of the Internet*. New York: Touchstone, 1995.

Wallace, Michele. "The Politics of Location: Cinema/Theory Literature/Ethnicity/Sexuality/Me." *Framework* 36 (1989): 42-55.

Index

African: African-American, 83, 148, 149, 223, 256n39, 359, 388; African-American family reunions, 56; African-Americans in Haiti, 72; African-Caribbean family reunions, 43–55; Afro-American societies, 29; Afro-Surinam-ese, 3–15; community in New York, 208; lesbian writers, 363; music, 87, 234; vernacular speech, 359. *See also* transnationalism

anthropology, 63, 88, 179; anthropological fieldwork, 4; anthropomorphic, 111; tropes of, 39n31, 39n34

Caribbean: Caribbeanness, xvi–xvii, 32–33; diasporic popular culture, xx; feminist emancipation, xx; identity, 27, 31–37, 388; mediascape, 56, 157; orality, 123; "trans-Caribbean imaginary," xx; women writers, 134. *See also* New York City

creolization, 26–28, 37, 102, 113–14; concept of family, 54; Creole (Jamaican) society, 136n14, 193; and Creole religions, 103, 113; Creoles or Afro-Surinamese, 3, 8; critique of, 155, 166, 168–69; as Hispano-American *criollo, créolité, mestizaje,* and *cultura criolla,* 25, 26, 28; and hybridization, 24–28, 37; and "polyphonic bricolage," 28–31; as "syncretic process of transverse dynamics," 27. *See also* Afro-Surinamese; hybridization

cultural/culture: Afro-cultural world, 67; Afro-Trinidadian culture, 113; Barbadian culture, 47; Barbadian popular culture, 245; Black popular culture, 360, 362, 365n1; capitalist commodity culture, 362; and Caribbean identity in New York City, 31–36; cultures, race, and history, 125; deculturation, 27; folk (oral) culture, 135; Haitian culture, 66, 85; hip-hop culture, 139; hybridity, 169; identity in Barbados, 219; and language, ix, xi, 169; Latin American indigenous culture, 303; nationalism, 64, 80, 88; religious culture, 87–88, 346; space, 77; trans-Caribbean, 37, 47, 346, 351, 356, 362, 365; transculturation, 26–27, 115, 256n39, 368n25; travel as culture, 184–87; vernacular cultures, ix–xi; West Indian culture, 247, 250–51; of the working class (Bajan), 228, 236, 240, 245–47, 249, 252. *See also* popular culture

deterritorialization, 269–70, 278, 291n26; deterritorialized border and citizen, 273, 285; and marronage, maroons, 114–15, 273; reterritorialization, 392

ethnicity, 4, 36, 45, 115, 141, 143, 147, 149, 150, 179, 181, 184, 189, 270, 276–77, 345–47, 349, 355, 380; ethnic difference, 54, 178, 268, 288–89, 328; ethnic economy, 16n6; ethnic identity, 10, 14, 15, 36, 48, 90n12, 269–70; ethnic violence, 267; "ethnic" way of life, 15, 33; ethnography, 58n6, 63, 65,

88, 102, 208; ethnoscapes, 116, 156–57, 165; and race, 80, 88
exile, xix, 80, 159, 166, 177, 179–82, 202, 207, 313n16, 351, 387, 390; and migration, 219–20

feminism, 358, 360–63, 378; first wave, 327; second wave, 321, 327, 329; third wave, xx–xxi, 321–42; and trans-Caribbean Black queer/feminist theory, 346–56; fear of feminism, 331–32
fiction, xix, 156, 225, 270, 323, 325, 363; and history, 269; Latino-Caribbean fiction, xix; Rasta fiction, 188, 198; Vodou fiction, 132. *See also* Rastafarian

gender: and agency, 347–55, 360–61, 363–65; and blues, dancehall, and ragga music, 346, 356, 360–63; computer-generated women, 390–92; and female digital bodies, 383–85; and female embodiment and sexuality, 345–49; and female sexual citizenship, xx, 346–51, 356; gender consciousness versus feminist consciousness, 336–37; ; migrating sexualities, 204–7; and the rise of a new matriarchy, 337–39; and sexual oppression, 352, 355–56, 359; and "slackness," 353, 360; and virtual porn, 387–90
geographical: boundaries, xviii, 178; geographies, national, racial, sexual, 345, 349, 352; geography, ix, 225–26, 269, 281; geography and sexuality, 371n80; location, 14, 114, 203, 377–78, 380, 382, 388; markers, 303; mobility, 8, 115

hybridity/hybridization, 24–28, 279; as an agonistic process, 169; and Caribana, 141; and creolization, xvii, 37; as *culturas híbridas*, xv, 25; and Homi K. Bhabha, 38n8, 38n9. *See also* creolization

language, ix, xv, xix, xx, 11, 15, 31, 35, 37, 38n9, 72, 88, 111, 113, 126, 129, 157, 169, 196, 228, 231, 233, 289, 309, 314n22, 360, 364, 381, 385–86, 390; and class, 301; Creole language, 28, 58n8, 70, 162, 166, 225–27, 229, 252; and culture, xi, 5, 13, 15, 143, 219, 222, 235, 239, 251–52, 285, 308, 327; language barriers, 25, 34, 222; nation language, 219, 232, 386; and religion, 109; sexualized language, 206; of television, 307; of walking, 193;

migration, xv, 4, 6, 7, 10, 16n5, 16n6, 18n40, 44, 54, 56, 71–72, 84, 101–4, 143, 157, 158, 159, 161, 162, 166, 178–80, 184, 189, 220–21, 226, 228, 239, 244, 255–56n39, 347, 377, 379, 386; African-American migrants, 67; and exile, 177–87, 219; migrating sexualities, 204–7; Muslim immigrants, 4; and social mobility, 4–6, 8, 14; and traveling, 188–89, 267, 282; post-migratory narratives, 185, 199; premigration cultural legacies, xvii, 3–6, 16n4, 17n15; trans-Caribbean migration, 88, 111, 116, 185, 278; trans-migrant reunions, 45; trans-migration, 88, 184–85, 267, 282, 350
mobility: and displacement, 155; and migration, xv, xx, 178, 182, 185–88, 307, 350, 377; and modernity, 159; postcolonial mobility, 187; social mobility, 4–6, 10, 14, 16n9, 44, 127–31, 162, 205, 356. *See also* postcolonialism

narration, 143; dialogic narrative, 169; narrative, 113, 140, 165, 167–70, 268, 278, 283, 290, 303, 306, 337–38, 353, 355, 362, 363; narrative and cinematic documents, 199; narrative discourse, 177, 183, 188, 208; narrative strategy, 124–29, 143; post-migratory narrative, 185; Vodou fiction, 132 nation: and Caribana, 139–42; Caribbean nations, xi, xv, 55, 67, 72, 101, 288–90; Latin American nations, 305; nation, concept of, 157, 301; nation-building, 273, 289, 301, 361; national and cultural ideology, xx, 25, 88, 113, 301, 303; national identity, xx, 33, 47–48, 66, 78, 203–4, 210n25, 220–22, 245, 286, 304, 307, 380, 386–88; nationalism, 80, 88, 203, 220, 240, 325, 330, 377–78; national narrative, 113; nation-states, 79, 286; transnational nation, 58n6, 163, 377. *See also* narration

New York City, ix–xi, 37n2, 49, 81–82, 85, 156, 177–200, 227, 300, 303, 305, 307; Caribbean culture in, 23–37; "Caribbean New York," 199, 208; migrations to, 177–216; "the walking city," 195

nomadology/nomadic, xvi; citizenship, 186; deterritorialized nomads, 185, 186–87; postcolonial nomad, 180–81, 185; rhizome/rhizomatic, xvi–xviii, 164–68, 268

popular culture, xix, 14, 63–65, 233, 245, 346, 348, 351, 356, 392; Anansi stories, 77; Barbadian "tuk" band, xix; black hip hop disrupting hegemonic carnival, 139, 141–50; Caribana, 139; Caribbean culture in New York, 31–37; Carnival as an image of female submission, 206; dancehall, 65, 78, 79, 80, 89, 354; Haitian Vodou, 23, 36, 76; Indian movies and music, 13; konpa in Haiti, 78, 85–87; music, 64, 70–71, 78, 94n103; "polyphonic bricolage," 24, 28–36; ragga, blues, dancehall and sexuality, 79, 80, 346, 353, 358–63; reggae, 78, 157, 183, 184, 197, 198, 202, 206; Santería ceremonies in New York, 31; soundscape, 149; West-Indian American Day Carnival and Parade in Brooklyn, xvii, 32–34, 197. *See also* New York City

postcolonial: African Caribbean history, xviii; Afro-Caribbean writers, 181; Caribbean art, 311–12; Caribbean author, 188; Caribbean people, 270; Caribbean society, 123, 126, 164, 277; city, 201–2; concept of nation, 157, 219–20, 273, 277, 355, 360–61; condition, 229, 239–40, 278; critique, 165; discourse, 180, 207, 208; hierarchies, 240; Jamaica, 126, 131, 202; message of exile, 180; migrant, 4, 181, 186; nomad, 179, 180, 186; poetry, 232; postcoloniality, 299, 367n17; sexual politics, 345, 350, 352, 355; society, 121–24, 129, 164, 185, 222, 285, 311; studies, 345, 350; traveler, xviii, 178, 185; U.S.-dominated postcoloniality, 299; West Indian discourse, 207

postmodern: Amerindian postmodernism, 268–69, 278, 289; diaspora, 162, 208; discourse, 187, 191, 208; and feminist practice, 152, 394n3; location, 188, 190, 203; metropolis, 189, 200, 208; MTV- and MacDonald societies, 25

Rastafarian, 65–66; culture, 90n12, 91, 193, 198, 202; discourse, 188, 194, 198

religion: Afro-Caribbean deities, 23; Black Baptism, 68, 72; Creole, 101, 103, 115–16; Evangelical revival, 73–77; Haitian Vodou, 23; Orisha, 103; Pentecostal Christianity and African beliefs, xviii, 64, 68; Pentecostalism, xvii, 63–66, 76–77, 79, 81–89, 95; popular religions, 34; Santería, 23, 31–32, 34, 103; Shango, 23; Spiritual Baptists, 101–16; and spiritual cosmology, 101, 103, 110–16; Wesleyan Methodism in Jamaica, 67, 69, 70–72. *See also* Rastafarian

space: postcolonial urban spaces, 203; trans-Caribbean space, xvi

translation, 132, 143, 225, 259n87, 272; untranslatability, 247
transnational/transnationalism, xvii, 3, 4, 12, 13–15, 43–57, 265, 267–72, 274, 277–78, 282, 345–46, 349–50, 355, 362–63, 375, 377; Amerindian transnational citizenship, xvii, 161, 166, 267–68, 285–86, 288–89; Guyanese Amerindians (Wapisiana), 268–70, 273–82, 285, 289n11; high tech communication intensifying transnationalism, xv; kin-ties and family reunions, 43–60; as a new emergent nationalism, xv, 377; the trans-Caribbean (or global) imagery, xix, 153, 170, 301, 345, 352, 360, 365; transnational (Barbadian) immigrants, 219–52; "transnational nationalism" and transnationalization, xv, 377; transnational West Indianness, 200–204; West Indian religious transnationalism, xviii
traveling: male upper-class mobility, 105; postcolonial traveler, 179; Rastafarian (traveling) mobility, 193; tropes of journey and mobility transcending boundaries, 185

urban: cityscape, 179, 187–89, 192, 196, 200–201; counter-discourse of the urban, 191–92, 196; culture, 35–36, 40n39, 142; landscape, 202; life, 5, 8, 25; locations, 6, 83, 139, 178, 185, 188, 189, 200, 208, 212n80, 359; metropolitan discourse, 188; population, 7, 104, 145, 282, 354; and rural, 28, 222, 323, 359; spatial significations of the city, 188, 196; trans-Caribbean urban, xvii–xviii; urban streetscapes, 199; walking, 187–95. *See also* walking

vernacular: African-American vernacular speech, 359; Caribbean culture ix–xi, xv–xxi, 144, 159–61, 170, 188, 191–92, 378, 392, 394; cyber-culture, 381–82, 385, 390, 394; expressions, 139, 386, 389; forms of resistance, 378; modernity, 155, 157–58, 161–62, 165–66, 168–70, 193; rhetoric, 188, 192–93, 385–86, 390; tradition, 162, 385

walking: its enunciative function ("footnotes"), 196–99; as a "peripatetic mode of signification," 178, 187–95; postmodern walking, 208; Rasta walking, 194

Contributors

Carol Bailey is a graduate of the University of the West Indies, Mona, Clark University, and the University of Massachusetts, Amherst. Dr. Bailey's primary areas of teaching and research are postcolonial, performance and women's studies. A former Mendenhall Fellow at Smith College, she is currently completing a postdoctoral teaching fellowship at the University of Massachusetts, Amherst.

Curwen Best is senior lecturer in popular culture, literary and cultural studies at the University of the West Indies, Cave Hill, Barbados, where he pioneered the teaching of Popular Culture. He is a leading authority on Caribbean pop culture. His numerous articles have appeared in international journals and publications. His major books include: *Barbadian Popular Music (1999)*; *Roots to Popular Culture (2001)*; *Culture @ the Cutting Edge (2005)*. His newest book is forthcoming with Palgrave and is titled *The Politics of Caribbean Cyberculture*.

Melvin Butler is assistant professor of critical and comparative studies in music at the University of Virginia. Prior to joining UVA's faculty, he was a Thurgood Marshall Dissertation Fellow-in-Residence at Dartmouth College (2004-2005). His ethnomusicological interests center on musical experience, national identity, and religious practice within African-Caribbean and African-American communities, and he has presented his research at meetings of the Society for Ethnomusicology, the Inter-American Conference on Black Music Research (2001), and other venues. Dr. Butler's published articles and book reviews have appeared in *Black Music Research Journal*, *Ethnomusicology*, *Journal of the American Academy of Religion*, and *Current Musicology*. His first book will examine music and negotiations of identity among Haitian Pentecostal Christians. As a professional saxophonist, he has performed with jazz artists, such as Brian Blade, Betty Carter, Donald Byrd, and Jimmy McGriff. He has also toured internationally with renowned Haitian konpa group, Tabou Combo.

Raphael Dalleo is assistant professor in the Department of English at Florida Atlantic University, where he teaches U.S. Latino/a, Caribbean, and postcolonial literatures and cultural studies. He serves on the international advisory board of the journal *Latino Studies*. His articles on Caribbean and U.S. Latino/a literature have appeared in *ARIEL*, *Anthurium*, *South Asian Review*, the *Journal of West Indian Literature*, *Latino Studies* and *Small Axe*. He is co-author of *The Latino/a*

Canon and the Emergence of Post-Sixties Literature (2007), an analysis of the relationship of contemporary Latino/a literature to politics and the market.

Maarit Forde is a postdoctoral research fellow and lecturer in social and cultural anthropology at the University of Helsinki. Her work focuses on the Anglophone Caribbean, and she has conducted extensive ethnographic fieldwork in Trinidad and Tobago as well as in the West Indian neighborhoods of Brooklyn. Her main areas of interest are Caribbean religions, rituals and cosmologies, migrations and transnationalism, gender, and literature. She is currently writing a manuscript on Caribbean migrants' religious transnationalism and designing a new project on transnational kinship in the context of Caribbean migrations. Her publications include articles in scholarly journals and edited collections as well as a published Ph.D. dissertation.

Holger Henke is assistant professor of political science at Metropolitan College of New York. He is also a senior research fellow for the Washington-based think tank Council on Hemispheric Affairs and a senior fellow of the Caribbean Research Center (Medgar Evers College, CUNY). He serves as the editor of *Wadabagei. A Journal of the Caribbean and its Diasporas*. As author and editor, Dr. Henke has published five books on development in East Asia, political culture in the Caribbean, Jamaica's foreign relations, West Indian Americans, and comparative migration in Europe and the United States. He also published numerous articles in journals such as *Cultural Critique, Latin American Perspectives, Social Epistemology, Social and Economic Studies, Identities: Global Studies in Culture and Power* and others.

Wendy Knepper is an independent scholar and guest lecturer at the Humboldt University in Berlin, where she teaches courses on Caribbean literature and theory. She has held visiting fellowships at Harvard University and New York University. Her research interests include comparative approaches to contemporary literature, transnational approaches to cultural studies, genre theory, gender issues and film studies. She has published numerous articles in essay collections and journals such as *Small Axe, Dalhousie French Studies, Arthuriana* and *PMLA*. She is also co-founder and co-director of a strategic communications agency for the IT sector and has published more than forty articles on mobility, networking and digital topics.

Karl-Heinz Magister was a member of the research group on literature, urbanism, space and ethnicity in New York City at the Center for Literary and Cultural Studies (Zentrum für Literatur- und Kulturforschung), Berlin (until 2005). From 1971 until 1991 his research focused on Shakespeare and his contemporaries (annual Shakespeare bibliography in Yearbook of the German Shakespeare Society/East) and on contemporary British literatures. He has published articles on early modern writings of the English "discoveries" of the New World and on Anglophone Caribbean literature and culture in several volumes of the Center

ABOUT THE CONTRIBUTORS

(including *Kontaktzone Amerika*, 2000; *Postmodern New York City*, 2003; *Cinematographies. Fictional Strategies and Visual Discourses in 1990s New York City*, co-ed. 2006). His special interests are issues of West Indian culture (carnival) and migration, and of historical mapping within the context of urban geography, topography, and cartography of New York City.

Patricia Mohammed is full professor for gender and cultural studies at the Centre for Gender and Development Studies, University of the West Indies, St. Augustine. From 1994-2002 she was Head of the Mona Unit, Centre for Gender and Development Studies, University of the West Indies, Jamaica. She has been involved in both feminist activism and scholarship for over two decades and increasingly over the last decade in cultural studies. Her academic publications include, *Gender Negotiations among Indians in Trinidad, 1917-1947* (2001), and *Gendered Realities: Essays in Caribbean Feminist Thought* (ed., 2002), along with numerous essays in journals and books, magazines and newspapers. Her main areas of interest are gender studies, history, documentary film and art. A manuscript entitled *Imaging the Caribbean: Culture and Visual Translation* is now in press at Macmillan United Kingdom. Dr. Mohammed is also engaged in making a six part series documentary film entitled "A Different Imagination" and has completed a forty minutes documentary entitled *Engendering Change: Caribbean Configurations*.

Mies van Niekerk is a cultural anthropologist and senior researcher at the Institute for Migration and Ethnic Studies (IMES) at the University of Amsterdam. She has conducted research into ethnic identity and youth culture, interethnic relations, immigrant elderly, urban poverty and immigrant entrepreneurship. Her main areas of interest include the relation between the socioeconomic integration of immigrants, their premigration history and postmigratory processes. She has specialized in the Caribbean migration to the Netherlands, in particular the integration of immigrants from Surinam, the former Dutch Guiana. In 2002 Dr. van Niekerk published: *Premigration Legacies and Immigrant Social Mobility. The Afro-Surinamese and Indo-Surinamese in the Netherlands*. She is editor of the IMES Book Series *Migratie- en Etnische Studies*.

Lyndon Phillip is a doctoral student at the Ontario Institute for Studies in Education of the University of Toronto.

Elaine Savory is associate professor and chair of literature at Eugene Lang College, New School University. She has published widely on African and Caribbean literatures, especially on poetry, drama and women's writing. She co-edited *Out of the Kumbla: Caribbean Women and Literature* (with Carole Boyce Davies), wrote *Jean Rhys*, and also wrote a collection of poems, *flame tree time*. She is presently editing the works of Bruce St. John and working on a book on the elegy in the shadow of empire. She formerly taught at the University of the West Indies, Barbados.

ABOUT THE CONTRIBUTORS

Bettina E. Schmidt is lecturer in the study of religions at the University of Wales, Bangor. She has been lecturer at the University of Oxford, "Privatdozentin" for cultural anthropology at the University of Marburg, Germany, and Visiting Professor at the City University of New York and of the Universidad Nacional de San Antonio Abad in Cusco, Peru. She is also a member of the editor board of the journal *Indiana* (published in Berlin by the Ibero-American Institute). Dr. Schmidt has written extensively on Caribbean and Latin American religions, cultural theories and migration. Her research interests are diaspora, anthropology of religion, cultural theories, urban studies, medical anthropology and gender issues. Her main fieldworks are conducted in Mexico, Puerto Rico, Ecuador and New York City. She is, for example, the author of *Karibische Diaspora in New York: Vom "Wilden Denken" zur "Polyphonen Kultur"* (2002) and co-editor of *Anthropology of Violence and Conflict* (2001).

Mimi Sheller is visiting associate professor in the Department of Sociology and Anthropology at Swarthmore College, Senior Research Fellow in the Centre for Mobilities Research at Lancaster University in England, and former Chair and Vice-Chair of the Society for Caribbean Studies in the UK. She is co-editor of the journal *Mobilities*, is on the international editorial boards of *Cultural Sociology* and the new *Journal of African and Black Diaspora Studies*, and serves on the advisory board of the Encyclopedia of the Caribbean, and the Marcus Garvey UNIA Papers. She has published two monographs on Caribbean history and has co-edited three books on themes of mobility, tourism, and migration. Her numerous articles appear in journals in Caribbean Studies (e.g., *Slavery and Abolition, New West Indian Guide, Plantation Society in the Americas*, etc.); in Geography (e.g., *Environment and Planning A, Environment and Planning D: Society and Space, International Journal of Urban and Regional Research, Singapore Journal of Tropical Geography*); and in Social Theory (e.g., *Theory and Society, Political Power and Social Theory*, and *Theory, Culture and Society*).

Tanya Shields is an assistant professor in the Curriculum of Women Studies at the University of North Carolina, Chapel Hill. She received her Ph.D. in comparative literature (2005) from the University of Maryland, College Park. Her area of specialization is the Caribbean, specifically literature and its role in Caribbean nation building. Dr. Shields has been involved with the television show *CaribNation* and is currently working on the manuscript *Engaging El Dorado: Literature and Pan-Caribbean Citizenship*.

Constance R. Sutton is professor emerita of anthropology, New York University, and an associate of its Center for Latin American and Caribbean Studies. She has carried out research on Caribbean labor and post-1965 Caribbean transnational migrations, on gender and power in both the Caribbean and Nigeria, and recently on memory and historical consciousness. She edited two well-received Caribbean themed books, *Caribbean Life in New York City: Sociocul-*

tural Dimensions (1987), with Elsa Chaney, and *Caribbean Labour Revisited* (2005). In the area of feminist anthropology, she has edited two collections: *From Labrador to Samoa: the theory and practice of Eleanor Burke Leacock* (1993) and *Feminism, Nationalism, and Militarism* (1995). She is currently researching Barbadian/Cuban connections.